*A RADICALLY SIMPLIFIED
AND COMMON-SENSE APPROACH
TO THE ENGLISH LANGUAGE*

The Two Hands Approach To The English Language: A Symphonic Assemblage

Volume 1

A Thorough Foundation
And
An Innovative Method
For The Teaching and Learning of English

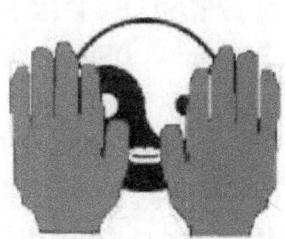

"Both warbling of one song, both in one key,
As if our hands, our sides, voices and minds
Had been incorporate."
  William Shakespeare *A Midsummer Night's Dream*

Richard Dowling   Stephen D. Watson

Printed by Createspace in Scotts Valley, CA USA.

Teachers and others are free to use all the charts and selections from the book for educational purposes, but not for commercial purposes or profit of any kind.
To contact us regarding future supplementary teaching material (classroom posters, card sets, etc) or if you have any questions or suggestions, please email us at 2ha_sa@excite.com
Visit us also at our website at
http://twohandsapproach.org

LIBRARY CLASSIFICATION CATEGORIES
Non-Fiction. Language. Grammar. Composition. Writing. Philosophy.

NOTE ON WEBSITE LINK FORMAT
we have included some website links, but in order to save space and to keep continuity of the text, we have shortened all URLs. For example, if a website link looks like this A9B5 , you put *http://tr.im/* in front of the short URL – like this http://tr.im/A9B5

Cover design, all interior layout, *tabla* lesson sketch, and hand graphics by **stedawa**.

ISBN 0973382236
EAN-13 9780973382235

© 2009 Richard Dowling and Stephen Watson
Two Hands Approach Publishing

yeah!... let it!...

by sallysense from her book of
collected poems *in a sallysense*

let it go to gather close...
let it flow to be...
let it ride to deep inside...
with life's infinity...
let it touch as in-so-much...
let it feel too...
let it make for its own sake...
what birth is born to do...
let it seed and let it feed...
let it have what is...
let it grow in souls to know...
the truth of all of this...
let it come to find a home...
let it dwell anew...
let it seep and let it keep...
the heart alive in you...
let it scatter over matter...
let it soak upon...
let it take by saving grace...
what's made to carry on...
let it dare to care'n'share...
let the spirit in...
let its love of depth above...
yeah! ...let it do its thing!...

Contents

Volume I

Preview

Preview, Meeting Together for Dialogue and Conversation, and Foretaste ... 1
The Spirit of Life and Death: Meso-American Ball Game and Petroglyphs ... 3
Opening Quotes ... 4
Acknowledgements ... 5
Quotations Foreshadowing the 7 Poetical Variations that Follow Them ... 9
Seven Poetic Variations ... 13
55 Innovations ... 17
Preamble ... 27
Prelude ... 28
Prologue ... 30

Part 1 – The Opening

Section Contents Listing ... 39
Opening-One ... 40
   3 Excerpts from Karen Armstrong
Opening-Two ... 49
   Only One, Two Twist, Three Thread, Four Foundation, Five Figure
Opening-Three ... 57
   First, Second, Third, Fourth, Fifth
Opening-Four ... 77
   Preface ... 104
   The 5 Main Polarities of Language ... 106
   The Approach and Metaphor of the Two Hands ... 124
   Maya Angelou from *A Brave and Startling Truth* ... 127
   Defining & Explaining The Symphonic Assemblage ... 128

  Into the Between 158
Opening-Five 163
  Proposal for an Innovative System of Writing 163
  A New Method of Reading 233
Three Charts and Quotes on the 3 Tongues 235
  Comparative Chart of the 3 Tongues 235
  Organic or Sequential Development Chart 240
  Ideal Interaction Chart 241
  Quotes on the 3 Tongues 242
Introduction to Mother Tongue 245

Part 2 – The First Movement: The Mother Tongue

Section Contents Listing 253
12 Turns of the English Language 254
Vocabulary Acquisition – **vovovovi** 269
Grammar 296
  The 12 Kinds of Words with Some New Names 301
  The 5 Jobs of they do in Sentences 308

The 12 Punctuation Marks – with New Names 328
Quotes on the Sentence and Thoughts on Form 338
Architecture of the Sentence 351
The 11 Forms of the Sentence with Excellent Examples 358
  1F Fundamental Forms 361
  2S Series Forms 368
  3V Verbals Forms 377
  4C Correlatives Forms 390
  5R Repetition Forms 398

Instructions for Teaching Sentence Forms in Class 404
Instructions & Student Models of 1-Paragraph 415
Sentence Forms 6 through 11 with Excellent Examples
  6CC Coordinating Conjunction Forms 436
  7AC Adverbial Clause Forms 441
  8RN Reference and Noun Clause Forms 456

Instructions, Student Models Comps. of Forms 6-8 466
The Hand by Janet Emig 489
Sentence Form 9PP with Excellent Examples 492
    The Colon 494
    The Semicolon 499
    The Dash 515
Instructions and Student Model Comps. for Form 9 543
Poet's Place of Residence 572
Workspaces for the sky blue trades of Writers 573
Sentence Forms 10 and 11 with Excellent Examples
    10TP   Three Places Forms 579
    11ADD   Additional Forms 631

Instructions and Student Model Comps for Forms 10-11 673
First Exam (Midterm) with Specified Forms 710

A. Debatable Use of *Mother, Father,* and *Tongue;* Quotes ... 774
B. Why Are There So Many Student Compositions? 780
C. General Instructions for Using Both Volumes to Maximum Advantage 784
D. Checklist of Required Written Assignments for Students Using Volumes I and II 788
E. Twofold Nature of the Human Being and Body 792
F. Summary Charts of all Essential Sentence Forms and Their Short Codes 799
G. Bio Notes on the Co-Assemblers 813

Volume II

Part 3 – The Second Movement: The Father Tongue

Part 4 – The Third Movement: The Imaginative Tongue

Part 5 – The Closing

> *Ultimate truth, if there is to be such a thing, demands the concert of many voices.*
> Carl Jung

Preview, Meeting Together for Dialogue and Conversation, and Foretaste

Throughout the book, we place quotations and passages which lead into, suggest, or foreshadow subsequent passages or quotations which more fully develop, explain, add to, and complement the earlier ones. Those subsequent quotations and passages in turn lead into, suggest, or foreshadow still more selections, passages, and quotes which eventually amplify and resound with greater range, diversity, and power – transforming, through organic growth, what began at first as only singular, solitary notes into a full-bodied symphony.

The succession of quotations, passages, and selections meet together in close collocation with one another on the page, where they were intended by the authors and may be perceived by the readers to enter into an extended dialogue and conversation with one another and with the reader about the ongoing personal discourse that involves, reflects, and expresses their personal lives, public concerns, and ultimate destiny as participating members of a common human community and destiny.

Every quotation or passage is a Foretaste or anticipation of the quotations and passages that follow and precede it, since the End is already in the Beginning, and the End itself brings to a culmination and Returns to the Beginning to complete the Circle of Life and Destiny. The Seed Emerges in the Beginning, Issues through its diverse Branches in the Middle, and Attains its final Fruit in the End, when it then in turn bears a new seed with a new beginning to bear in the fullness of time a new fruit – in the immemorial, perennial Way, Mode, and Process of continually ongoing Life and History.

So, we launch into this book following the immemorial, perennial Way, Mode, and Process of life. We commence with an anticipatory **Preview**. The Preview has several parts: (1) quotes foreshadowing the Whole Book and the *Acknowledgements*; (2) quotes foreshadowing 7 Poetical Variations followed by the 7 Poetical Variations themselves; and (3) the 55 Innovations of the book in chart form. We proceed next to **Meeting together For Dialogue and Conversation** (the *Preamble*), and go forward again to **Foretaste** (*The Prelude* setting forth the general thrust and character of the book and *The Prologue* with more extended quotes foreshowing the entire book).

Then the fivefold symphonic structure of the Book unfolds – with its **Opening**, **First Movement** or **Mother Tongue**, **Second Movement** or **Father Tongue**, **Third Movement** or **Imaginative Tongue**, and Culmination or **Closing**.

The Spirit of Life and Death: The Meso-American Ballgame

In the sweet sounding Nahuatl language of ancient central Mexico, the ballgame was called *tlaxli* or *tlachtle*. But it was more than a sport as we conceive it today. For over two millennia, the Mesoamerican game had profound symbolism and ritual. It was a cosmic ceremony; a true rite of life and death. Playing the ballgame symbolized duality – an encounter between opposites – night and day, masculine and feminine, and the sun against the stars and moon.

> Sari Bermvidez
> Presidenta
> Consejo Nacional Para La
> Cultura Y Las Artes

Amerindian Petroglyphs Depicting The 2 Hands as Polar Symbols of Life

Series of images, part of the Crow Canyon petroglyphs, depicting (1) symmetric and inverted images representing the 4 fingers and joined thumbs of the 2 hands; (2) 2 triangles; (3) a trio of flowing zigzag lines

"There is no consciousness without discrimination of opposites." Carl Jung

"The Dogon people may be wiser, since **they often feel the need to draw before they explain**, and they proclaim the primacy of drawing over speech in their myth of the creation:
> 'God, in creating, thought: before naming things, he drew them in his creative intention. . . . Creation, as it was offered to man, bore the mark of this divine intention, which he attempts to decipher and whose symbols he in turn reproduces. . . . It was by naming things that man affirmed his hold over them. If there had been no human consciousness to receive it and reproduce it, the divine word would have remained without response, hence without life.'"
>> Chapter 1: Writing Systems
>> *The History and Power of Writing*
>> by Henri-Jean Martin
>> trans. by Lydia G. Cochrane

"part mosaic, part vortex, **an elegant assembly of disparate pieces** into which all of the past, and all of geography, seems to have been sucked"
> Nomi Eve
> American novelist and reviewer
> from her review of the above book

Acknowledgements

The authors acknowledge the tremendous insight and wisdom developed and passed down for countless generations in many traditions.

The Native American and Meso-American traditions of the Maya, the Aztec, the Inca – and the too-many-to-list Amerindian tribes – impart a sense of balance and frugality, thankfulness and contentment that few other traditions can match. Furthermore, the precise precision at Tiahuanaco and the sophisticated Mayan calendar are superb human achievements that are not without their unanswered questions.

The Chinese insight first recorded by Lao-Tze and the ancients on the binary view of Reality and its constant and cyclic transformations between polar opposites guides us to keep a wider perspective and broader understanding on life.

India has given us the knowledge of the oneness of essence and form and teaches us that all matter is teeming with energy, a view that modern physics supports. Within the tradition of the latter, as well, we are told that matter has a dual nature – like waves and like particles, and that we cannot isolate it in one perspective alone without having to concede or explain the rest with the other perspective. We learn also that a piece of the whole still somehow contains the whole, somewhat like the piece of earthworm that grows back complete.

African and Polynesian traditions offer us strong oral and earth-centered traditions, in which symbols play a significant part, as we see in the Sphinx, the geometry of the Great Pyramid, and their pre-historic rock paintings.

Many other cultures have contributed to this work, and our gratitude can never be adequate.

Last, but not least, we honor and express our deep appreciation and lasting debt to those poets, novelists, writers of all genres, literary critics, scholars, and ordinary people of the English-speaking countries who have enriched and developed the English Language into the wonderfully precise, powerful, imaginative, and enthralling instrument of expression that it is.

> All the greatest achievements of mind have been beyond the power of unaided individuals.
> Charles Sanders Peirce
> American philosopher

Regarding the Formatting of the Book

Since we have published this book ourselves, you will doubtlessly notice that we have deliberately chosen not to follow the prescribed conventions concerning the formatting of the text itself. Thus, **we have frequently placed text in bold letters and freely italicized and underlined passages while placing excerpts often in larger than normal size**.

We realize that some readers may respond to this as an insult to their intelligence, and if that is the case, we apologize. However, the point is not to insult anyone; after all, this is not the age of the typewriter but the computer, and it makes no sense to avoid using all the formatting tools available to dramatize or highlight the relative importance of a sentence or paragraph because of undue deference to the stuffy and excessively rigid academic and printing conventions of the age.

Rather, authors should ensure the ease and convenience of the reader by making their intention and voice more clear as writers through the visual means of formatting. Besides, it seems to relieve the monotony of the reading text, and to make the reading experience more lively, unexpected, and interesting as well as clear and more meaningful.

Proponents and authorities on formatting like Beatrice Warde and Richard Lanham would likely agree with this.

Formal Acknowledgements

We are grateful to the following publishers who have granted us permission to reprint excerpts or full passages written by distinguished writers, plus the use of several black and white photos by a photographer.

VOLUME 1
The author of each passage is the copyright holder unless otherwise indicated. All passages **used with permission** of the copyright-holding author unless otherwise indicated and attributed.

Poems, passages, stories, and lyrics

Angelou, Maya (1995). Excerpt from *"A Brave And Startling Truth"*. ©1995. New York: Random House.

Armstrong, Karen. *The Great Transformation: the beginning of our religious traditions* (1st ed.) ©2006. New York: Alfred A. Knopf, a division of Random House, Inc.

Bolles, Richard N. and John E. Nelson. W*hat Color is Your Parachute? for Retirement?* ©2007. Berkeley: Ten Speed Press, a division of Random House.

DeLillo, Don *Underworld*. ©1997. New York: Scribner, a division of Simon & Schuster, Inc. All rights reserved.

Emig, Janet A. from the paper *Hand, Eye, Brain* originally presented at the Buffalo Conference on Researching Composing held at the State University of New York at Buffalo in 1975 and published in *Research on Composing: Points of Departure* edited by Charles R. Cooper and Lee Odell in 1978. Used with permission from publisher NCTE. ENdW

Gardner, Robert W. "*Thanksgiving's No Turkey*" from *Wall Street Journal* 11/20/95, copyright permission from Dow Jones & Company, Inc. (via Copyright Clearance Center).

Harjo, Joy. *"Remember"* from *She Had Some Horses*. ©2009, 2006, 1997, 1983. Thunder's Mouth Press, imprint of Avalon Publishing Group, W.W. Norton.

Kuralt, Charles. *"Places of Sorrows"* from *On the Road with Charles Kuralt*. ©1985 by CBS Inc. New York: G. P. Putnam's Sons (a division of Penguin Putnam).

Ludgate, John and Sheila. Song lyrics for *Steinbeck's Guitar* from their *Suburban Folk* CD. ©2009. Burlington, ON Canada. *http://suburbanfolk.ca.*

O'Reilly, Mary Rose. Excerpt from *The Peaceable Classroom.* ©1993. Published by Heinemann, Portsmouth, NH. All rights reserved.

Picard, Max. *The World of Silence.* ©2002 by Eighth Day Books. Wichita, Kansas: Eighth Day Books.

Ray, Paul H. and Sherry Ruth Anderson. *The Cultural Creatives: How 50 Million People are Changing the World.* 2000. New York: Crown Publishing Group, Three Rivers Press.

sallysense. *in a sallysense.* ©2009. Createspace. Used with permission from the author.

Sheehan, George. *Running & Being: The Total Experience.* New York: Warner Books. ©1978. Used with permission from the Estate of George Sheehan.

Steinbeck, John. *The Grapes of Wrath.* ©1939, renewed ©1967. Used by permission of Viking Penguin, a division of Penguin Group (USA) Inc.

Graphics

> - of sheet music covers and the Lynn Johnston book cover in the *Debatable Use of Mother and Father and Tongue in Reference to Different Modes of Discourse* section near the end of this volume are from http://coverbrowser.com.
> - *Bellebonnesage* musical heart image from wikimedia commons at yaOG.
> - Black and white photos of nature and human-made objects used gratefully courtesy of Steve Garrigues.
> - Medieval text and "Language is the amber" calligraphy (from color originals) used courtesy of Muriel Watson.
> - Photo of KyungJu teaching at a whiteboard and of her gesturing hands by stedawa.
> - Picture of the hand chair at the beginning of the Sentence Form section is from a color sales flyer put out by a furniture company in Guangzhou.

Quotations Foreshadowing the 7 Poetical Variations that Follow Them

In the ancient languages there was a silence in the interval between two words. The language breathed silence, spoke silence, into the great silence from which it came."

Max Picard

Language is more than silence because truth is manifested in language. There is truth in silence, too, but it is not so characteristic of silence as it is of language that truth is present in it... **In silence truth is passive and slumbering, but in language it is wide-awake; and in language active decisions are made concerning truth and falsehood**.

In itself, by its nature, language is only of short duration, like a break in the continuity of silence. **It is truth that gives it continuity, that enables it to become a world of its own; it is because it receives this continuity from truth that language does not pass away.** The silence out of which language came **is now transformed into the mystery surrounding truth.**

Without truth language would be a general fog of words above the silence; without truth it would collapse into an indistinct murmuring. It is truth that makes language clear and firm. The line separating the true from the false is the support that holds language back from falling. Truth is the scaffolding that gives language an independent foothold over against silence. Language becomes a world of its own...; *and language now has not only a world behind it – the world of silence, but a world near at hand – the world of truth.*

The word of truth must keep in *rapport* with silence, however, for without it truth would be too harsh and too hard. It would then seem as though there were only one *single* truth, since the austerity of the individual truth would suggest a denial of the self-relatedness of all truth. **The essential point about truth is that it all hangs together in an all-embracing context.**

> Max Picard
> Swiss philosopher
> from *The World of Silence*

EINSTEIN'S CREATIVITY AND MUSIC

"In his biography of Einstein, Walter Isaacson says, "As a young student, he never did well with rote learning. And later, as a theorist, **his success came not from the brute strength of his mental processing power but from this imagination and creativity.** He could construct complex equations, but more important, he knew that math is the language nature uses to describe her wonders.

"When confounded by a challenge in his work, Einstein often turned to the violin to help him. A friend of Einstein's told Isaacson, "He would often play his violin in his kitchen late at night, improvising melodies while he pondered complicated problems. Then, **suddenly, in the middle of playing he would announce excitedly, 'I've got it!' As if by inspiration, the answer to the problem would have come to him in the midst of the music.**"

Ken Robinson with Lou Aronica
from *The Element: How finding your passion changes everything*

"We should listen to the silence with the same attention that we give to the sounds."

John Cage
American music composer and theorist

Seven Poetic Variations on The Recurring Themes of Silence, Language, Music, and Sound

Words As Half Light Creatures

All Words are Poor Things
Creatures of the Half Light
Fleeting Shadows of the Bright Day
They Trail the Steps of our Way

If they Capture or Better the Path
Redeem or Relieve the Way
Some Use may Reside in them
Some Light may Abide in them

The Buddha Knew

The Buddha Knew
Words Would Not Do

So He trusted Deeds and Detachment
Would Carry us Through

And Silence
Renew

Words Resound With Another Ring

Words Resound with another Ring
Acquire Somehow a Distinctive Tinge
Announce that Things are not as Before
Imply the Future Reveals Still More

The Tenor of the Times Does Change

The Tenor of the Times does Change
A slight Shift in the Balance of Forces Comes
People notice and somehow Comprehend
The Past shattered to pieces Ends

The Present So Vivid and The Future Oncoming

The Trees Posted at the Corners
Seemed to Say that Here

There was a Circle
Where I could Stay

A Place to Stand and Contemplate
The Passage of Years and the Way

How Life Configures to Return and Renew
Resurrecting the Hours to a Brighter Day

The Light and Clearness of the Sky
The Blossoming and Fragrance of Flowers

Opening Over, Around, in Me
The Sacred Place and Vision

Of the Present So Vivid
And the Future Oncoming

Beneath the Wine Blue Skies of Spring

Beneath the Wine Blue Skies of Spring
And the Shining Round White Moon
Cool Breezes Ripple and Entrance Joyous Leaves
Whole Trees Sway and Dance New Melodies

Poems are Written in their Times

Poems are written in their Times
In Places and at Moments where they Rhyme

In Time Wound and to Circumstance Bound
Yet to the Soul and for Eternity they Resound

previous 7 poems
by Richard Dowling

The Many (55) Innovations, Breakthroughs, and Contributions of this book for Understanding the Speaking, Writing, and Reading of the English Language
In Chart and List Form

The next five pages provide you – in the Visual Form of Charts – multiple (26) Reasons and Incentives why you might desire to read this book with attention, active participation, and deep reflection and how you can specifically profit from doing so.

They are followed by a numbered listing of 29 further landmark contributions of this book.

Five Paramount Innovative Achievements of this Book

Unique Approach to English
→ Two Hands Approach & Metaphor

1. Person centered & Interpersonally realized
2. Holistic
3. Integral
4. Inclusive

Inventive Form or Genre
→ Symphonic Assemblage

1. Unified Theme
2. Guiding Metaphor
3. Clear Structure
4. Music and the Intervals of Silence
5. Harvest
6. Hologram

Novel Model for Thinking
→ 5 Numbered Forms of Thinking & Remembering

1. Only One
2. Two Twist
3. Three Thread
4. Four Foundation
5. Five Figure

Innovative System in Writing
→ Writing Breakthrough

11 Forms of the English Sentence

with model examples in student essays

New Method of Reading
→ Reading Breakthrough

Chunking of text into Meaning Units: Reading Moment + Meditation Moment; Return of Reading Out Loud & The Ear as Guide to The Music of Language; Storytelling and the Imaginative Tongue for Revealing Universal Meaning

5 Contributions to Vocabulary Acquisition, Grammar, and Punctuation

| Twelve Turns of the English Language | Effective Method for Vocabulary Acquisition | 12 Kinds of Words and their 5 Jobs in Sentences | 5 Architectural Levels of the Sentence | 12 Punctuation Marks with New Names |

5 Innovations in Pedagogy and Methodology

| Highlighting of Figurative Language | Vocalization | Imaging and Visualizing | Modeling | Body Movement and Interactive Participation |

11 Sets of Guidelines, Characteristics, and Instructions for Speaking, Writing, and Reading (Part 1)

① 5 Roles of the Reader

| ② 4 Interrelated and Indispensible Methods for Learning New Words | ③ 5 Methods for Chunking Reading Out Loud | ④ 5 Steps of the Writing Course 5 Parts of the Writing Puzzle | ⑤ Rubrics, Guidelines for Writing, Evaluating Essays | ⑥ 5 Hallmarks of Style |

11 Sets of Guidelines, Characteristics, and Instructions for Speaking, Writing, and Reading (Part 2)

#7	#8	#9	#10	#11
Alliterative Pairs of Nouns, Adjectives, and Attitudes Describing Style	3 Keys for the Balancing of the Sentence, Linking Sentences, and Bridging Paragraphs	8 Methods of Analyzing an Essay	4 Theories of Composition	Mottos and Tips for Good Style

Five Additional Sets of Consequences, Guidelines, Characteristics, Intelligences, and Principles

27. 5 Consequences of New Method of Reading
28. 5 Guidelines for Reading and Interpreting Literature
29. The Return and Revival of Poetry
30. 30 or more Intelligences of Human Beings
31. 25 Guiding Principles for the Design of a New Approach to English

Six Additional Innovations in Grammar

32. Invention of Sentence Word Analytics
33. Invention of Sentence Form Analytics for Writing of all kinds
34. Invention of *Descriptor* as one of Five Functions of the Sentence
35. Seven Conceptions and Definitions of Grammar
36. Discovery and Definition of *Noun of* Construction
37. Discovery and Definition of Noun Adjunct Construction

Fourteen Kinds of Assemblages

38. Extensive Assemblage of Charts and Mind Maps
39. Assemblage of excellent student and professional examples of 11 Forms of the Sentence

40. Assemblage of competent student examples of Paragraphs, notated and footnoted with all 11 Forms of Sentence
41. Assemblage of competent student examples of Expository, Narrative, Descriptive, Comparative, Cause and Effect, Classification, and Example Essays, notated and footnoted with all 11 Forms of the Sentence
42. Assemblage of competent student examples of Mid-term Exams, Final Exams, and student Autobiographies, Notated and footnoted with all 11 Forms of the Sentence.

    All of the above Assemblages from #39 to #42 are written by students of average to good intelligence and employ the vocabulary and language of Americans across gender, class, geographic regions, and a wide array of ethnocentric backgrounds, including Spanish-speaking, Korean, Japanese, Chinese, Nigerian, and Philippine speakers. They are thus an invaluable source for other students to learn the working vocabulary of native-speaking speakers of their own age group.

43. Assemblage of essays by Professional Writers of Expository, Narrative, Descriptive, and Comparative Essay Forms
44. Assemblage of Poetry by both well-known and lesser known Poets
45. Assemblage of Photos and Line Drawings
46. Comprehensive List and Definition of all Essay Forms
47. Assorted collection of 9 Short Stories, plus 2 longer Short Stories by a professional writer. The latter two stories are remarkable for their

especially effective use of Voice in Writing as well as the gift of superb storytelling
48. History and Brief Description of Precedents and Possible Prototypes of the Symphonic Assemblage
49. Initial Collective List of Literary Genres in need of further Definition and Classification
50. Comprehensive Bibliography – classified by categories – of Books relevant to instruction and reflection on the English Language
51. Essay Briefly Describing and Recommending Excellent Books about Writing.

Groundbreaking Innovations in Curriculum Instruction

52. With the 11 Forms of the Sentence, **for the first time a systematic method and program for teaching writing across the curriculum** is available, **from middle school to high school to university level**

53. With the 5 Forms of Thinking, **for the first time a sizable sample of a systematic method and program for teaching thinking across the curriculum** is available, **from middle school to high school to university level**

54. With the New Method of Reading, **for the first time a systematic method and program for teaching reading across the curriculum** is available, **from middle school to high school to university level**

55. With the Introduction of Types of Assemblage, especially the Symphonic Assemblage, and numerous alternate forms such as collage, multi-genre, fusion fiction, etc., **for the first time a systematic method and program for teaching across disciplines** is available, **from middle school to high school to university level.**

Preamble

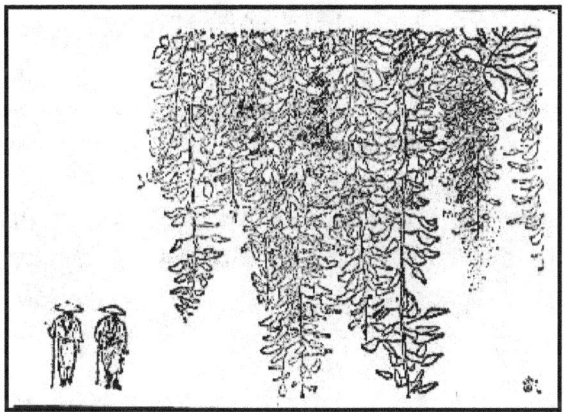

from a local newspaper in Shiga Prefecture, Japan (spring 1980)

"Max Picard... tells us that when two human beings converse together, there is always a third who listens, and this third is Silence."
    Gabriel Marcel
    quoted in Introduction to
    The World of Silence by Max Picard

"There is nothing so much like God in all the Universe as shared silence."
Oriah Mountain Dreamer
    New Dimensions Program 2899
    www.dimensions.org

"If there is anything worth calling theology, it is listening to people's stories, listening to them and cherishing them."
    Mary Pellauer in *The Riverside River* in an essay by
    Kathleen Norris called *The Holy Use of Gossip*

"It is sometimes easier to say thoughts than to write them because saying something is living it, feeling it, connecting with it again. No writing can capture that fully. In a way, speaking is alive, writing makes it become dead."
    Yvonne Johnson in *Stolen Life: The Journey of A Cree Woman* by
    Rudy Wiebe & Yvonne Johnson

A *preamble* suggests a walk together and a listening together – moving along the way together. It is human beings conversing and discussing together matters of mutual importance and shared concern. We invite you, readers, to join us in a walk through a somewhat familiar, but newly arranged, English language landscape.

Prelude

The secret of learning to write effective English paragraphs and essays now lies in your hands. Indeed, your own two hands are the primary instrument for teaching you this system. And it is a system.

Did you know that there are only eleven fundamental forms of the sentence in the English language, and all other sentences are just so many variations of these basic eleven forms?

Once you are able to identify and see these eleven forms in excellent sentence examples, and above all in operation in exemplary paragraphs and essays, you possess the primary secret and key to effective writing.

Using your two hands as a teaching and memory tool, metaphor, image, model, and tangible interactive instrument, you can then also easily learn and forever retain a clear, coherent knowledge and vision of the primary components of grammar and punctuation as well as of the stages of the composing process and of the skills necessary for becoming a master reader of literature.

The simplicity and elegance of this comprehensive presentation of the English language rests on its unified vision and integration of English – guided, informed, and embodied by the metaphor of the two hands, themselves the primary symbol of the initial polar character of all human thought and endeavor.

The simplicity, elegance, economy, and integral vision of this presentation flow from two additional sources of inspiration and guidance: (1) the principle of Ockham's Razor which asserts that the simplest, shortest, and most direct route to an answer is the best. The more uncluttered and plain, the more economical and elegant, the solution, the better it is; and (2) the certainty that integral vision is the imperative mandate of this time in history which is the Maturity of Humanity.

The Divided and Compartmentalized frame of mind and pattern of understanding – characteristic of the Modern Period of History from 1500-2000 – is now utterly outmoded and dysfunctional, even as it is out of tune with the vital, generative, and trans-formative novel forms of thought and understanding (integral vision systems) displayed by intuitive and comprehensive thinkers like Alfred North Whitehead, Ortega y Gasset, Sri Aurobindo, Pierre Teilhard de Chardin, Jean Gebser, Claire Graves, Richard Riso, Ken Wilbur, Steve McIntosh, Jamshid Gharajedaghi, and Daniel H. Pink.

Indeed, Pink's book *A Whole New Mind: Why Right Brainers will Rule the World*, discovered by us largely after this book was written though published earlier in 2005, is a perfect supplement and powerful argument for the central metaphor and theme of this book – that the two hands serve as the supreme explanatory model of English and language in general.

If you desire to escape the stuffy, outworn categories of your traditional instruction and cultures and to open your heart and eyes, all will become simple, clear, present, and accessible as your two hands.

Give it a try and see for yourself if what we assert is true, indeed self evident once you perceive it. You will lose nothing by venturing onto the paths of simplicity, economy, and elegance by mastering with ease this epitome of the English language which you hold in your hands.

Prologue

A Prologue is a first installment in seed form of the whole book. It provides a sometimes puzzling selection of excerpts which are yet also richly suggestive, arresting, and rewarding clues and guided instructions to the organization of the book, what the reader may expect from the text, and how to read it. The Prologue, while a constitutive part of the Book, also gives an **Entrance to it** and a **Foretaste of it**.

> "**Never interpret a work**
> **Until the work has a chance**
> **To interpret itself.**"
> Marion Woodman and Jill Mellick
> Canadians

"I wrote... that **teaching English is an intrinsically radical act. It talked about the teacher's role in changing the structure of consciousness, and hence, the way we do intellectual and emotional business in the Western world.** '*The Peaceable Classroom*' attempted to validate in the academy a place for *consensus, cooperation, interiority,* and *intuition.*

...Virginia Woolf calls this "developing in your presence a train of thought," as opposed to defending a rhetorical position.

The book, then, is not a how-to manual, still less an argument developed from premise to conclusion. **It's a collection of stories, tropes, and images that nudge up against each other and try to reproduce the "analysis" as an experience**, an experience I hope the reader will share the living-of. **Instead of constructing an argument in theoretical terms, I am trying to "make it happen."**

... In writing this book, you see, **I have had to ask myself how I might invite the reader into the fullest possible participation, because the book is about making connections.**

>Mary O'Reilly
>Irish-American teacher and essayist
>from *The Peaceable Classroom*

"The Beginning is difficult."
>Plato, Greek philosopher

"The Beginning is half the journey."
>Plato, Greek philosopher

"Readers without haste warned in advance that all just opinion is long in expression."
              Ortega y Gassett
              Spanish philosopher

"Simplicity Aims Circularly Directing Removing, Discreetly Returning Elusively Life's Mystery."
              Anna Waters
              Pawnee Native American

"And I say unto you, ask and you shall receive, seek and ye shall find, knock and the door will be opened to you."
              St. Luke 11: 9-13

"Questions seek, guide, and determine answers."
              Richard Dowling

"The human being is an intelligible mystery."
              Gabriel Marcel
              French Philosopher

"The Personal is the Philosophical Form of the 20th century."
              John McMurray
              Scottish philosopher

"The metaphor is an indispensable tool; it is a form of scientific thought... Poetry is metaphor; science uses nothing more than metaphor."
Ortega y Gasset, Spanish philosopher

"Man is the supreme talisman."
Bahá'u'lláh, Persian prophet

Activity, which is the expression of skill, is primary. Theory is for the sake of action. **Knowledge is a means to an end, not an end in itself.** ... Knowledge which is not learned in and through its application, knowledge which makes no immediate and recognized contact with action and life, is worse than useless....

The integration of theory and practice is impossible unless we recognize that the body and the life of the body are not subordinate.
John Macmurray, Scottish philosopher

"**To know**, **to will**, **to love**: this is man's whole nature and consequently it is his whole vocation and duty. **To know totally**, **to will freely**, **to love nobly**; or in other words: to know the Absolute, and *ipso facto* its relationships with the relative; to will what is demanded of us by virtue of this knowledge; and to love both **the true** and **the good**, and that which manifests them here below; thus to love **the beautiful** which leads to them. ***Knowledge* is total and integral to the extent that its object is the most essential and thus the most real**; the ***will* is free to the extent that its aim is that which, being the most real, frees us**; and ***love* is noble by the depth of the subject as much as by the loftiness of the object**; *nobleness depends on our sense of the sacred. Amore e'l cor gentil sono una cosa*: **the mystery of love and that of knowledge** [The Two] **coincide** [The One]."

      Frithjof Schuon, Swiss-French-Arabic scholar

The concise passage above – by the most eminent scholar, sage, and seer of religion and spirituality in the 20th century – identifies and defines **The Three (The Three Thread)**; **The Two (The Two Twist)**; and yes, **the One (the Only One)**.

But what and where is the Missing Fourth?

Is it this: **To get**, find, or discover **the Sense of something, anything, everything** – in other words, **to read the signs and symbols** of the text, the Time, nature, the other, self, universe, the Divine?

	To Know	
To Sense or Read (as understood figuratively)		*To Will*
	To Love	

What follows next is **The Opening** of the book which, as you will soon see, actually involves **Five Openings. The Opening as a Whole thus possesses a fivefold structure, with each of the five separate openings corresponding to one of the five fingers of the hand**.

Moreover, within the Five Openings you will initially encounter for the first time the **alliterative numerical names** or designations for **Five Forms of Thinking**: **The Only One**, **The Two Twist**, **The Three Thread**, **The Four Foundation**, and **The Five Figure**. And the five sections that follow thereafter – headed by the **Five Ordinal Numbers of First, Second, Third, Fourth, and Fifth** – will proceed to reflect and explain whatever has gone before at that point in the book as well as anticipate what will follow later in the text.

By this time, if not earlier, the reader will inevitably have realized that the book is not arranged and does not go forward in the conventional manner of most texts. Therefore, the reader will need and deserves now at this juncture some preliminary forewarning, advice, and instruction regarding the book's arrangement and what to expect when reading it.

The book is deliberately designed to require a **New Method of Reading** which places a premium on deep reflective thinking where the reader must stop often and engage the text actively, holistically, personally, and integrally. Thereby, the Act of Reading the text itself serves to instruct the reader regarding the **New Method of Reading** that we are proposing as one of the Five Paramount Achievements of the book.

This **New Method of Reading** the text actively, holistically, personally, and integrally is essential because the book introduces so many novel ideas and configurations of ideas that it is unproductive and confusing to read the text in the swift, hurried, logically sequential, horizontal mode and manner only of traditional reading. In this New Method of Reading **one does not read only horizontally from left to right but frequently vertically also from top to bottom**. Moreover, the **text itself does not go continuously forward only, but constantly returns and recurs to earlier passages and ideas in the book, so as to provide a fuller and more complete explanation than was previously provided, before proceeding forward again.**

Ideas and Configurations of ideas are thus encountered in multiple contexts rather than once only to demonstrate the value and extensive impact of the ideas and configurations of ideas on display. **The Act of Reading is less continuously forward only in a straight line, but circular and recursive, continuously going forward and then**

back, and then forward and back again, and so on.

Often, an arresting Allusion, a richly Suggestive or Imaginative Phrase or Clue is provided as the first presentation of an idea, configuration of ideas, or practice. Next, some brief but direct experience or encounter with the idea, configuration of ideas, theory, or practice is provided for the reader. And that in turn is followed almost immediately by deeper reflection and more extensive explanation and illustration of the idea, theory, or practice in question. Some of the many implications and consequences of the ideas, theories, and practices are then explored.

Finally, once again, the text moves forward anew, now using the mastered and explained ideas, theories, and practices to break still more new ground and illumine still deeper and broader reaches and vistas of the English language and human life experience – all this in the light of the emerging global future of the Maturity of Humanity on our fragile yet beloved common planet and home.

In other words, the book is organic: (1) it begins with pregnant, potent small seeds planted in the personal hearts and imaginative sensibilities of readers; (2) it develops – gradually but cumulatively – from within outwards through strong cultural common roots of vital and emotional resonance; (3) it achieves constructive and critical individual clarity, power, and public relevance through the branching forth of comprehensive philosophical conceptions, theories, and a systematic structural framework; and finally (4) it culminates and reaches fruition in the universal, imaginative, integral, personal and interpersonal authenticity and integrity of global communal awareness and the freedom and fraternity of noble human endeavor.

Go with us on this pilgrimage, quest, and journey toward a better tomorrow – with the English language as our foremost instrument of mutual dialogue, expression, and communication – that together we may leave an honorable contribution and enduring legacy to the posterity of Earth' s coming generations of children.

The Opening

THE OPENING

1. **Opening-One**
   3 Excerpts from Karen Armstrong
2. **Opening-Two**
   Only One, Two Twist, Three Thread, Four Foundation, Five Figure
3. **Opening-Three**
   First, Second, Third, Fourth, Fifth
4. **Opening-Four**
   Preface, The Polarities of Language, The Approach and Metaphor of the 2 Hands, Defining and Explaining the Symphonic Assemblage, Into the Between
5. **Opening-Five**
   Proposal for New Innovative System of Writing, A New Method for Reading
6. **2 Charts of the 3 Tongues**
   Organic and Sequential Development of the 3 Tongues, Ideal Interaction of the 3 Tongues
7. **Introduction to the Mother Tongue**

The Opening – One

> – in the four senses of (1) **Invitation,** (2) straightforward **Statement of Intention** and **Purpose**, (3) **Setting the Tone**, and (4) **Lead Into the book**

The Opening, like the book as a whole, can be read either **figuratively** or **literally**. According to the manner it is read, its various senses, understandings, and overall meaning will be disclosed, revealed, and appropriated by the reader. If it is read figuratively, **creative imagination** will draw upon all the resources of life experience and the collective experience of mankind to understand the text. If it is read literally, **logic and discursive reasoning** will be used to analyze and strictly define the meaning of the text, limiting the meaning to the immediately obvious, initial first appearance, surface, and denotative sense of words.

Unfortunately, all over the world today, millions of people adhere to fundamentalist, literal interpretations of their religious scriptures with consequences that breed destruction, hate, and war.

Though too many believe otherwise, it is not really an issue of absolutely and exclusively choosing one or the other manner of reading, because a figurative and literal reading can and should be reconciled, just as the left hand and the right hand are not totally opposed but potentially harmonious and complementary.

However, it remains a strange and sad commentary on our educational institutions and the common sense of our cultures that so many people remain profoundly ignorant that all language (especially as found in works of literary genius and all sacred scriptures) is inherently and pervasively figurative and metaphorical (in its deepest sense and bearing upon Life), even as it also carries a literal sense grounded in material and physical reality.

Thus, everyone knows literally what the word "Opening" means at first sight. However, we encourage you now to consider **its many possible figurative senses**, and the deep understanding and overall meaning we can derive by employing **Creative Imagination** to probe and explore the word in more depth.

Accordingly, we extend to you an **Invitation – to open up** your heart and creative imagination as well as your spirit to the meaning of what you read as well as your rational, logical mind and empirical senses. **We invite your whole Being and Life**

Experience as active partners and co-creators of the texts you read.

Moreover, we state straightforwardly that we pursue, advocate, and welcome only readings and interpretations that conduce to **creation**, **peace**, and **love** rather than to destruction, war, and hate. We welcome and embrace **Diversity**, but we seek also to discover, set forth, and explain **the Integral Unity** not only of the English language but of all Life and Reality.

The perfect historical, cultural, religious, sociological, philosophical, psychological, moral, and spiritual support and reinforcement of "Opening – One" above can be found in Karen Armstrong's magnificent and magisterial *The Great Transformation: the Beginning of our Religious Traditions*, a book which every educated person on the planet should have the blessing and benefit of reading.

Though only a full reading can do justice to the imaginative brilliance, comprehensively systematic grasp, formidably profound insight as well as lucid and compelling style of the author, the compressed gist and intended effect of Armstrong's book is captured in three excerpts below: the first, a short description of the four great civilization centers that between them wrought a radical transformation in our understanding of the nature and ideal purpose of life; the second, a longer insightful summary into the essence of the transformation that the four centers developed regarding our understanding of humanity; and the third, a telling short anecdote of the necessary unselfish yet truly natural way to bring **creation**, **peace**, and **love** to the planet.

FIRST EXCERPT OF KAREN ARMSTRONG

"From about 900 to 200 BCE, in four distinct regions, the great world traditions that have continued to nourish humanity came into being: *Confucianism and Daoism in China; Hinduism and Buddhism in India; monotheism in Israel; and philosophical rationalism in Greece*. This was the period of the Buddha, Socrates, Confucius, and Jeremiah, the mystics of the Upanishads, Mencius, and Euripides. *During this period of intense creativity, spiritual and philosophical geniuses pioneered an entirely new kind of human experience.* Many of them worked anonymously, but others became luminaries who can still fill us with emotion because they show us what a human being can be. **The Axial Age was one of the most seminal periods of intellectual, psychological, philosophical, and religious change in recorded history**; there would be nothing comparable until the Great Western Transformation, which created our own scientific and technological modernity."

SECOND EXCERPT OF KAREN ARMSTRONG

"All the traditions that were developed during the Axial Age pushed forward the frontiers of human consciousness and discovered a transcendent dimension in the core of their being, but they did not necessarily regard this as supernatural, and most of them refused to discuss it. **Precisely because the experience was ineffable, the only correct attitude was reverent silence**. The sages certainly did not seek to impose their own view of this ultimate reality on other people. Quite the contrary: **nobody, they believed, should ever take any religious teaching on faith or at second hand. It was essential to question everything and to test any teaching empirically, against your personal experience**. In fact, as we shall see, if a prophet or philosopher did start to insist on obligatory doctrines, it was usually a sign that the Axial Age had lost its momentum. If the Buddha or Confucius had been asked whether he believed in God, he would probably have winced slightly and explained – with great courtesy – that this was not an appropriate question. If anybody had asked Amos or Ezekiel if he was a "monotheist", who believed in only one God, he would have been equally perplexed. Monotheism was not the issue. We find very few unequivocal assertions of monotheism in the Bible, but – interestingly – the stridency of some of these doctrinal statements actually departs from the essential spirit of the Axial Age.

What mattered was not what you believed but how you behaved. Religion was about doing things that changed you at a profound level. Before the axial age, ritual and animal sacrifice had been central to the religious quest. You experienced the divine in sacred dramas that, like a great theatrical experience today, introduced you to another level of existence. **The Axial sages changed this; they still valued ritual, but gave it a new ethical significance and put morality at the heart of the spiritual life.** The only way you could encounter what they called "God," "Nirvana," "Brahman," or the "Way" was to live a compassionate life. **Indeed, religion *was* compassion.** Today, we often assume that before undertaking a religious lifestyle, we must prove to our satisfaction that "God" or the "Absolute" exists. This is a good scientific practice: first you establish a principle; only then can you apply it. But the Axial sages would say that this was to put the cart before the horse. **First you must commit yourself to the ethical life; then disciplined and habitual benevolence, not metaphysical conviction, would give intimations of the transcendence you sought.**

This meant that you had to be ready to change. The Axial sages were not interested in providing their disciples with a little edifying uplift, after which they could return with renewed vigor to their ordinary self-centered lives. Their objective

was to create a spirituality of empathy and compassion; they insisted that people must abandon their egotism and greed, their violence and unkindness. Not only was it wrong to kill another human being; you must not even speak a hostile word or make an irritable gesture. Further, **nearly all the Axial sages realized that you could not confine your benevolence to your own people: your concern must somehow extend to the entire world**. In fact, when people started to limit their horizon and sympathies, it was another sign that the Axial Age was coming to a close. **Each tradition developed its own formulation of the Golden Rule: do not do to others what you would not have done to you**. As far as the Axial sages were concerned, respect for the sacred rights of all beings – not orthodox belief – was religion. **If people behaved with kindness and generosity to their fellows, they could save the world**.

We need to rediscover this Axial ethos. In our global village, we can no longer afford a parochial or exclusive vision. **We must learn to live and behave as though people in countries remote from our own are as important as ourselves."**

THIRD EXCERPT OF KAREN ARMSTRONG

"**Egotism was the greatest obstacle to enlightenment. It was an inflated sense of self that made us identify with one opinion rather than another; ego made us quarrelsome and officious, because we wanted to change other people to suit ourselves**. Zhuangzi often mischievously used the figure of Confucius to express some of his own ideas. One day, he said, Yan Hui told Confucius that he was off to reform the king of Wei, a violent, reckless, and irresponsible young man. Marvelous, Confucius remarked wryly, but Yan Hui did not fully understand himself. How could he possibly change anybody else? All he could do was lay down the law and explain a few Confucian principles. How would these external directives affect the obscure subconscious impulses that were the source of the King's cruelty? There was only one thing that Yan Hui could do. He must empty his mind, **get rid of all this bustling self-importance, and find his inner core.**

> "**Centre your attention**," Confucius began. "Stop listening with your mind. Then stop listening with your mind and **listen with your primal spirit** [*qi*]. Hearing is limited to the ear. Mind is limited to tallying things up. But **the primal spirit's empty: it's simply that which awaits things**. Tao is emptiness merged and emptiness is the mind's fast."

Instead of using every opportunity to feed the ego, we had to starve it. Even our best intentions could be grist to the mill of our selfishness. But *qi* **had no agenda; it simply allowed itself to be shaped and transformed by the Way; and so everything turned out well.** If Yan Hui stopped blocking the *qi*, deflecting it from its natural course, the Way could act through him. Only then could he become a force for good in the world."

> "Our goal is to create a beloved community and this will require a qualitative change in our souls as well as a quantitative change in our lives."
> **Martin Luther King, Jr.**

Opening – Two

in six additional senses of (5) **The Inauguration Of**, (6) **The Encounter With**, and (7) **The Initiation Into** (8) the **First Presentation of Innovative Numerical Forms for Thinking and Remembering, Learning and Teaching** that serve as a (9) **Challenge to the Reader** and involve the (10) **Raising of Questions**.

Below we inaugurate a first Presentation of Five Numerical Forms of Thinking and Remembering, Learning and Teaching. We invite and encourage you to encounter these Forms. We initiate you into an understanding of them via one or more illuminating examples of each of them. **These singular examples will prove pivotal and structurally formative for the entire book.**

Together, they constitute a **friendly challenge** and incite you to **raise relevant questions** that we will answer, in due time, later.

The Only One
The Unified, Holistic, Integral Image

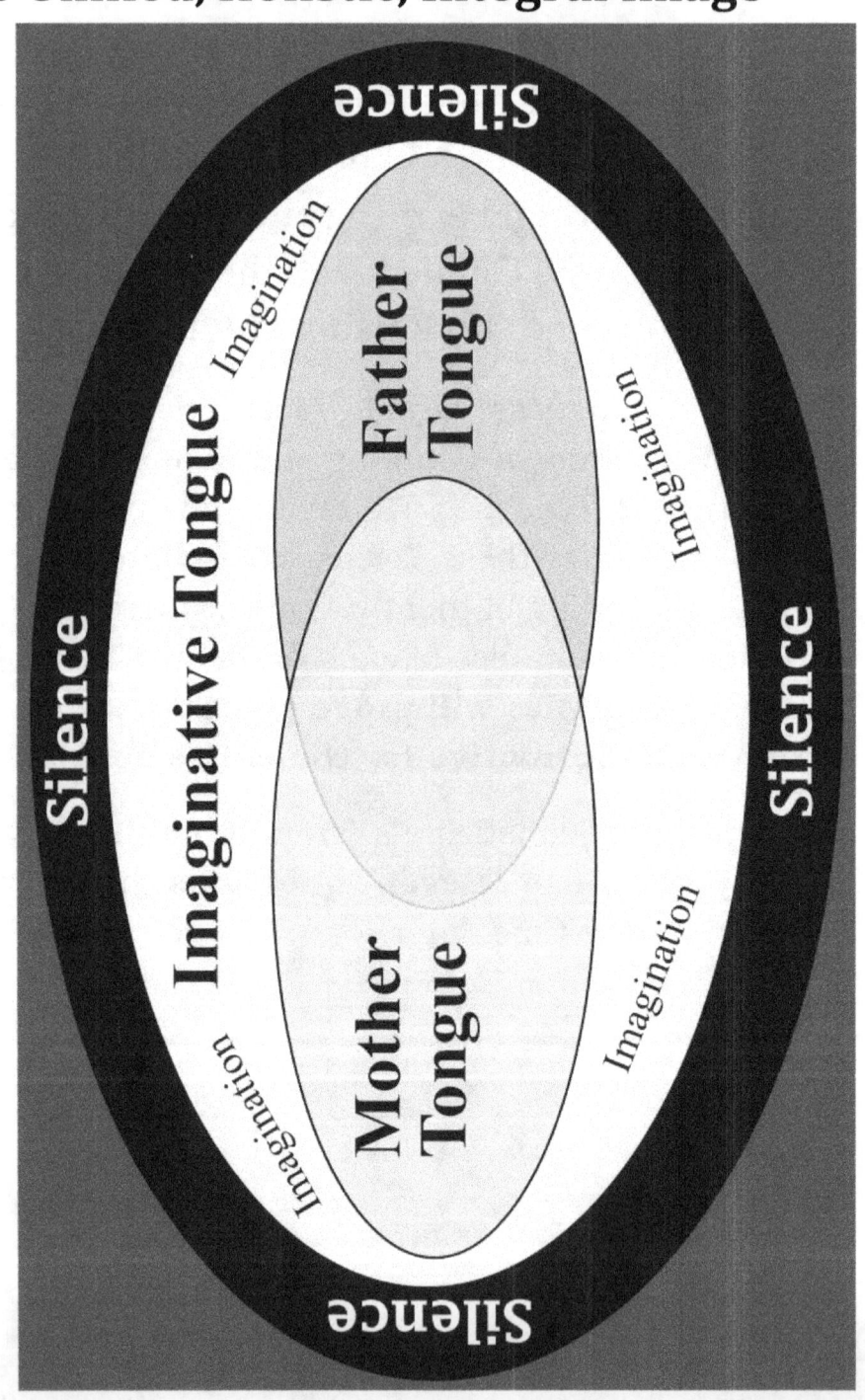

The Two Twist

Quotations on Silence and Language
by Swiss philosopher Max Picard

"Language and silence belong together: language has knowledge of silence as silence has knowledge of language."

"Still like some old, forgotten animal from the beginning of time, silence towers above all the puny world of noise; **but as a living animal, not an extinct species, it lies in wait**, and we can still see its broad back sinking ever deeper among the briers and bushes of the world of noise. It is as though this prehistoric creature were gradually sinking into the depths of its own silence. **And yet sometimes all the noise of the world today seems like the mere buzzing of insects on the broad back of silence.**"

"Silence is not simply what happens when we stop talking. It is more than the mere negative renunciation of language; it is more than simply a condition that we can produce at will.

When language ceases, silence begins. But it does not begin *because* language ceases. The absence of language simply makes the presence of Silence more apparent.

Silence is an autonomous phenomenon. It is therefore not identical with the suspension of language. It is not merely the negative condition that sets in when the positive is removed; **it is rather an independent whole subsisting in and through itself. It is creative, as language is creative; and it is formative of human beings as language is formative . . .** "

"**Silence belongs to the basic structure of man . . .** However . . . the reader should not be misled into despising language. **It is language and not silence that makes man truly human. The word has supremacy over silence**.

But language becomes emaciated if it loses its connection with silence. **Our task, therefore, is to uncover the world of silence so obscured today – not for the sake of silence but for the sake of language**."

from *The World of Silence*

The Three Thread

The Three Languages

"In my first talk I shipwrecked you on a South Sea island and tried to distinguish the attitudes of mind that might result. I suggested that there would be **three main attitudes**. First, **a state of consciousness or awareness that separates you as an individual from the rest of the world**. Second, **a practical attitude of creating a human way of life in that world**. Third, **an imaginative attitude, a vision or model of the world as you could imagine it and would like it to be**. I said that **there was a language for each attitude, and that these languages appear** in our society **as the language of ordinary conversation**, the **language of practical skills**, and the **language of literature**. We discovered that the language of literature was associative: it uses **figures of speech, like the simile and the metaphor**, to suggest an identity between the human mind and the world outside it."

Northrop Frye
The Educated Imagination
Canadian

The Four Foundation

The Four Great Directions

"The One gave birth to the Two;
the Two gave birth to the Three;
and the Three gave birth
to the 10,000 things."

Lao-Tzu in the *Tao-te-ching*

Subject

Language   *Four Aspects or Parts of all Writing Situations*   **Author**

Audience

adapted from *Little Brown Handbook*

The Five Figure

The Hand as Image, Figure, Number, Tool, Memory Device

Substantive Scheme and Structure of the Book with Five Key Components

1) The Opening
2) The First Movement – *The Mother Tongue*
3) The Second Movement – *The Father Tongue*
4) The Third Movement – *The Imaginative Tongue*
5) The Closing

Opening | Mother Tongue | Father Tongue | Imaginative Tongue | Closing

Opening – Three

> In one additional sense of (11) a **Preliminary Explanation** of unusual or unfamiliar features of the book in order to anticipate and forestall possible incipient reader confusion and disorientation.

Reader

Previously, we presented you with 5 numbered Forms of Thinking, along with some images and striking quotations by famous authors.

We present here in the beginning – and will continue to present throughout this book – powerful and pithy poetic and prose passages that we juxtapose to one another, because of the light and meaning they shed on one another.

In this book, we have assembled numerous such quotations which compose a quintessential summary of the whole history of reflection on the English Language.

And we have invented a **new expressive rhetorical Form or genre** to suitably express this representative summation of reflection on the English Language – the **Symphonic Assemblage.** Soon enough, at the proper time, we will identify and define the characteristic features of this new literary form. But permit us some additional **Preliminary Explanation** using the Ordinal Numbers.

First

Initially, we provided you (with the title on the book cover) the one unified theme of this book – **The Two Hands Approach to the English Language** with an image of the Two Hands.

Next, we presented you (on the cover of the book) with a quotation by the noted British author, Aldous Huxley. This wonderful quotation expresses how the wise old man of the village, representing the **ancient and traditional way of understanding (as opposed to the modern)**, expresses to the young people of the village – whenever they are finally able to stop talking to one another and to listen – the Great Truth that all of life is a long tension and interplay, an ongoing conversation, and (sometimes unfortunately too often) a long fight between the Left Hand and the Right Hand.

By implication, if the children listen to the wise old man, they will understand how to integrate the Left Hand and the Right Hand, the two polar sides of life, together in an imaginative understanding of their true integral unity.

Finally, we presented you with a unified holistic integral image – **The Only One** – which is a second *visualization* (in addition to the image of the Two Hands) of the title and Huxley quotation.

The quotation by Huxley and the unified, holistic, integral image of **The Only One** imaginatively together serve to highlight the five pairs of polarities of life below:

Left Hand	**Right Hand**
Right Brain	**Left Brain**
Silence	**Language**
Ancient	**Modern**
Image	**Word**

Second

At the very outset, we presented successive pages with no commentary in order **to involve and draw you as readers into the text, thereby encouraging an active reader response**.

Moreover, we have intentionally left larger spaces between the reading passages, where in the **Silence created** by the **Intervals** between passages, we provide you the space to stop, think, and reflect more deeply and interconnectedly about what you are reading.

Thereby, we **inaugurate and highlight a New Method of Reading** which we urge you to consider and adopt as may appear appropriate and advantageous in this book. .

This method of reading that highlights Silence and Language – **The Two Twist** – integrates imaginatively the following polarities:

Silence	Language
Deep Thinking & Reflecting	**Reading Passages**
Stopping	**Proceeding**
Left Hand	**Right Hand**
Right Brain	**Left Brain**
Holistic & Imaginative Integration	**Understanding Individual Parts of Text**

Third

The form of the book is a ***Symphonic Assemblage***, and it is constructed with a **First Movement**, a **Second Movement**, and a **Third Movement**. It also has an Opening which introduces the central themes and remarkable innovations of the book (as already presented earlier) and a Closing which brings the book to a fitting and conclusive end.

The three Movements present and explain the purpose and use of the three languages – the **Mother Tongue which discusses and teaches the language of ordinary conversation and the writing of self-expression;** the **Father Tongue which discusses and teaches the language of practical skills and the writing of thoughtful, discursive prose;** and the **Imaginative Tongue which discusses and teaches the language of literature with the reading and professional writing of poetry, stories, and imaginative literature of all kinds –** for learning and teaching **Speaking, Writing,** and **Reading**.

Below we provide a brief initial description and explanation of the three languages which we will develop at further length throughout the book.

MOTHER TONGUE

People absorb their Mother Tongue in Childhood **from the bottom up** -- steadily acquiring the basic words, skills, and fluency of language. **They speak and converse with one another in mutual conversation about ordinary life and experience. They develop fluency in the Mother Tongue,** learning subconsciously to trust and speak with their own **unique voice**, **feeling heart**, and **inner integrity**.

They identify emotionally and powerfully with the local cultural or social group which speaks their common Mother Tongue. Taken to extremes, if they identify too completely with their tribe or group, excessive loyalty and the fiery heat of emotional passion may limit and arrest their development within a rigid conformity and fanaticism that rejects all differences and is hostile to introspection, self-criticism, novel discoveries, and civil liberties.

FATHER TONGUE

The Father Tongue is **the more formal, disciplined, and abstract language first acquired in youth and in schools, and later expanded and employed pervasively in disciplines of knowledge and professional occupations.**

The Father Tongue detaches itself from the hearth and home, distancing and separating the individual from group conformity, custom, and dogmatism – **seeking the goals of independence, autonomy, and distinctive achievement**. **It privileges intellectual clarity** and distrusts feeling and messy emotions with their social and personal entanglements and obligations.

The Father Tongue in its positive mode focuses and concentrates thought, and provides clarity, structure, system, and direction. It empowers people to progressively set goals and accomplish them; it plans and foresees what has to be done in the public realm; and it discovers the conceptual knowledge and instrumental means to do what needs to be done.

For many, however, the Father Tongue unfortunately often has a negative side or feature – what we might call an unintended or subconsciously motivated patronizing tendency to interfere with the lives of others, insufficiently respecting them and failing to adequately respond and listen to them.

The Father Tongue, at times, in this negative mode, lectures, criticizes, corrects, and admonishes children, women, minorities, and non-native speaking peoples (especially when they can't write or read) to control their emotions, their disorderly ways and habits – in short, to discipline themselves, work harder, and get a better handle or grip on their lives.

If the Mother Tongue is the *thesis* (in the terminology of Hegel), then the Father Tongue is the *anti-thesis*. In ordinary language, this means the **First or Primary Experience of Life that is Childhood** comes into **opposition and conflict with the Secondary Experience of Life, which is Youth**.

The historical conflict and tension between these two experiences of life we might designate here **for dramatic effect "The Great Divorce"** – in other words, the split in consciousness, the divided loyalties, the forked tongue, and what the Biblical myth calls the Fall of Man. **The Fall of Man means that the inflated ego of the historical**

period of youth – mostly dominated by adventurous, competitive, and dominant men – **often suffocated and throttled the spontaneous natural self of the period of childhood.**

In other words, the Father Tongue has insisted that everyone talk and write in the formal language of discursive thought and the academic professions, and not much in the vital, informal, living and heartfelt voice of the Mother Tongue.

IMAGINATIVE TONGUE

The Imaginative Tongue is attained and realized in the adult stage or Maturity of Life, as the outcome and end-product of a long organic process in the course of which **a person learns to individually respect yet mutually marry the Mother Tongue with the Father Tongue**. The person who masters the Imaginative Tongue realizes that the Father Tongue and Mother Tongue are not, and should not, ideally be opposed to one another. Rather, both are indispensable and should be seen to have their own proper and particular function and role, yet to compensate and complement one another in harmony.

The Imaginative Tongue artfully uses the rich reservoirs of stories, metaphors, and figurative language in the achievement of imaginative literature – that treasure chest of fairy tales, fantastic stories, epic adventures, fables, novels, plays, poems, and stories of all stripes that are both the fountainhead and vital realization of cultural and social life, education, and reflection for human beings.

In its ripeness and fullness, the Imaginative Tongue blends the thought and structure, precision and breadth of the Father Tongue with the naturalness and fluency, heart and spirit of the Mother Tongue.

Employing the above three languages as the structural principle of the innovative expressive form of the **Symphonic Assemblage** constitutes **The** Major **Three Thread** of this book. ⌘

> **Cornel West** in *Hope on a Tightrope* writes with a friendly and familiar voice and points out both the potential and the plight of young people striving for social change:
>> "That's why I read all these hip-hop magazines. I read every page, because I'm concerned with how every young person is trying to escape misery, death, and pain. They throw themselves into it wholeheartedly. They spend 10 to 12 hours a day coming up with verses. It's unbelievable. Yet, too many young folk can't even play instruments. They don't understand how towering geniuses like Stevie Wonder or Prince – who played every instrument on all 30 albums – reached their heights. It took discipline, concentration, genius, sacrifice, deferred gratification, a deep sense of calling, and a love of music."

Fourth

The Daoist saying quoted earlier, when it speaks "of the ten thousand things", hints that there is – at a minimum – a missing fourth aspect or dimension of Life. Indeed, the great Swiss psychologist C. J. Jung said that in any sets of three, there was often a missing fourth needed to complete it.

Thus, the Little Brown Handbook of English, in its earlier editions, used to speak of the three aspects or parts of all writing situations: the **author**, the **subject**, and the **audience**. However, the latest edition identified the missing fourth, so now all writing situations involve four aspects or parts: the **author**, the **subject**, the **audience**, and **language**.

Subject

Language   **Author**

Audience

Native American religions, and sacred traditions from all parts of the earth and all epochs of world history, identify **Four Great Directions of Life – with their corresponding Powers and Gifts – as the Foundations for Reflection and Understanding of the World.**

```
                North
                White
                Buffalo
                Power
West                                East
Black                               Gold or Yellow
Bear                                Eagle
Introspection                       Illumination
                South
                Green
                Mouse
                Touching
```

*from the book Seven Arrows
by Hyemeyohsts Storm*

It is the purpose and mission of Philosophy to discover, among other things, the foundations of Knowledge; however, it has hitherto failed to develop a clear and comprehensive philosophical system that is adequately useful and serviceable for human beings across disciplines of learning and cultures. Our aim here is to lay out the initial framework and structure for such an adequate philosophy which we call **"The Four Foundation"**.

The **Numerical Forms of Thinking** designated here with their accompanying alliterative names – **The One (The Only One)**; **The Two (The Two**

Twist); **The Three (The Three Thread)**; and **The Four (The Four Foundation)** – refer to **analogous sets of words that resemble and correspond to one another** – according to whether they come in ones, twos, threes, or fours and according to patterns and hierarchies of relationship between the various words in each of the numbered groups or sets.

We began this book by presenting one or two supremely valuable and innovative examples of each of the first Four Numerical Forms of Thinking. Thus, we presented one novel integrated image of "The Only One"; highlighted "Silence and Language" as a salient and universal example of "The Two Twist"; stressed the Three languages that humans speak as a paradigm of "The Three Thread"; and noted above the four aspects of all writing situations as a telling introduction to and example of "The Four Foundation".

Throughout the book, we will deploy and use to explain the English Language innumerable examples – both traditional and well known examples and entirely novel and illuminating instances – of all Four Numerical Forms of Thinking. Deployed and used in this manner, they will shed light on one another, reinforce one another, and together provide a powerful visual and structural series of Forms for integrally and comprehensively conceiving and understanding all aspects of the English Language as well as all aspects of Human Life – individually, collectively, and historically.

On the next page, for instance, is *one contemporary illuminating example* of the Four Form of Thinking or The Four Foundation.

The Missing Fourth Movement of Life, with Life conceived metaphorically as the Music of a Symphony

"The *time* of Life that we are talking about here is traditionally called "Retirement." Some people love that word. I'm not one of them. For me, it implies "being put out to pasture" – to borrow an image from a cow. It implies a kind of parole from a thing called *work*, which is assumed to be onerous, and tedious. It implies "disengagement" from both *work* and *Life*, as one patiently – or impatiently – waits to die. It thinks of Life in terms of work.

I prefer instead to think of Life in terms of music. My favorite metaphor is that of a symphony. A symphony, traditionally, has four parts to it – four movements, as they're called. So does Life. There is **infancy**, then the time of **learning**, then the time of **working**, and finally this time that we are talking about, often called "**retirement**." But if we discourage the use of the word "retirement," then this might better be called the Fourth Movement."

Richard N. Bolles and John E. Nelson from
*What Color Is Your Parachute? For Retirement:
Planning Now For the Life You Want*

Working

Infancy   **Fourth Movement (retirement)**

Learning

> "The Fourth Movement, in the symphonic world, is a kind of blank slate. It was and is up to the composer to decide what to write upon it. Traditionally, the composer writes of triumph, victory, joy – as in Beethoven's Symphony #3. *the Eroica.* But it may, alternatively, be a kind of anticlimactic, meandering piece of music – as in Tchaikovsky's Symphony #6, *the Pathetique.* There the Third Movement ends with a bombastic, stirring march. The Fourth Movement, immediately following, is subdued, meditative, meandering, and sounds almost like an afterthought.
>
> Well, there are our choices about our own lives: shall the Fourth Movement, the final movement, of our lives be *pathetique* or *eroica* – pathetic or heroic? Your call!
>
> **I like this defining of our lives in terms of music, rather than in terms of work**."
>
> Bolles and Nelson as noted above

And then Bolles and Nelson go forward to still another Four Form of Thinking or Four Foundation as follows:

> "To carry the metaphor onward, in this Fourth Movement of our lives, **we have instruments, which we must treat with care.** They are: our **body,** our **mind,** our **spirit,** and what we poetically speak of as our **heart**, which Chinese medicine calls 'the Emperor.' Body, mind, spirit, heart. Some of these instruments are in shiny splendid condition. Others are slightly dented. Or greatly dented. But **these are the instruments that play the musical notes and themes of this time of our lives.**"
>
> Richard N. Bolles and John E. Nelson from *What Color Is Your Parachute? For Retirement: Planning Now For the Life You Want*

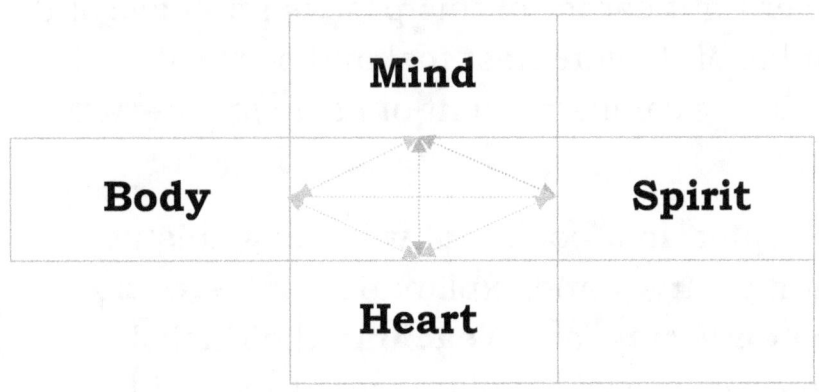

Fifth

The Five Figure can and has been used as a Numerical Form of Thinking like its Four Predecessors. For example, it is used as the primary system of explanation in Chinese medicine in the notable book *Between Heaven and Earth: A Guide to Chinese Medicine* by Harnset Beinfeld LAC and Efrom Korngod LAC, O.M.D.

Indeed, the Five Figure of the Pentagram in the upper left corner of this page is one of the ancient images and symbols of the Human Body as a whole while the figure of the hand in the upper right corner of this page is an image and symbol of the foremost tool and seminal technological instrument of *homo faber* – Man the Maker.

Later, in a book that will follow this two-volume survey and explanation of **Learning**, **Remembering**, and **Teaching** the English Language, we will explore more thoroughly additional ways in which the Five Figure can be employed with profit as a Numerical Form of

Thinking. However, the specific focus of this book and the constraints of time and space do not permit us to do that here.

For this book, we employ the Five Figure of the hand primarily as a vivid, visual image and tool for remembering what is learned and taught. It is thus used for perceiving and organizing together, as well as structurally beholding and thereby **comprehensively grasping and retaining in memory and consciousness, sets or groups of Five Components of varied content.**

More specifically and significantly, the Five Figure of the hand (or the chart and the list as its printed facsimiles) is used for **comprehensively grasping and retaining in memory and consciousness the two supremely important Charts** of all those presented earlier and now repeated below for paramount emphasis.

The 5 Paramount Innovations and Achievements of this Book

1. **The Interpersonal Approach and Metaphor of the Two Hands** with Responsible Vision for Integral Intuition;

2. **The Symphonic Form of the Assemblage**;

3. The Philosophical Systematic Conception of Thinking via **The Five Forms of Thinking**;

4. The **Innovative System in Writing** with its **Eleven Forms of the Sentence** and the Models of Student Sentences, Paragraphs, and Essays with notated and footnoted forms;

5. **The New Method of Reading** with the Body as Anchor, Root, and Reference for Learning, Remembering, and Teaching – embodying what is learned and mastering and retaining it through physical action and interaction with others.

The Overarching Scheme and Structure of this Book with its 5 Key Components:

1. **The Opening**
2. *The First Movement* – **The Mother Tongue**
3. *The Second Movement* – **The Father Tongue**
4. *The Third Movement* –**The Imaginative Tongue**
5. **The Closing**

Finally, if you look again at the charts in the front of the book, you will see how many are presented in sets or groups of Five, meaning all can be taught, learned, and remembered via the five fingers of the hand.

The Opening – Four

> – in five additional senses of (12) an **Introduction**; (13) a **Clear and Systematic Structure**; and (14) an **Initial and Concise Comprehensive Coverage as well as Exposition of, and Insight into, the Substantive Content of the Text** by explaining the Five Paramount Innovations of the book, including (15) **Preface;** and (16) **The Announcement.**

It is natural for an Opening to provide an Introduction. An Introduction tells the reader what makes the book unique, distinctive, and valuable – including the specific ways the book can benefit the reader. **Such information gives the reader the necessary motivation and incentive to engage the book and persist in reading it.** However, we have already accomplished this initial aim of an Introduction (at the very front of the text) by setting forth – in visual charts – the many innovations, breakthroughs, and contributions of this book for understanding the English Language.

An Introduction also informs the reader why and how the book was written – intimating or directly expressing not only the underlying intention and purpose of the authors but also indicating their tone and manner of presenting insights and ideas as well as their anticipated outcomes in impacting readers. This second aim of an Introduction we accomplished in our "Opening One" – stating our Intention, encouraging a figurative and metaphorical more than a literal writing and reading of the text, and seeking to awaken and foster creation, peace, and love in our readers as well as knowledge, for such are the qualities the world desperately needs today.

What then remains for this Introduction to do? Notably and specifically, it needs to accomplish five tasks, corresponding to the **Five Paramount Innovations of the book**:

(1) to declare and explain the unique approach, guiding metaphor, and integral theme of the book;

(2) to present, identify, and define the characteristic features of the Invention of the "Symphonic Assemblage" (first invented here), as a novel form or genre of literature in general and as the specific literary form or genre of this book;

(3) to set down a seminal and innovative Philosophical Conception of Thinking Via The Five Numerical Forms of Thinking (actually, we

already accomplished this third task in "Opening – Two" and "Opening – Three");

(4) to present, identify, and define the Innovative System in Writing with the Invention of the **"Eleven Forms of the Sentence"** and to establish and justify the pedagogical rationale for **Modeling competent, notated, and footnoted student examples** of Sentences, Paragraphs, and Essays for initial mastery of **self-expressive writing in the Mother Tongue** as well as **researched, discursively reasoned, and argued writing in the Father Tongue**.

Of course, this clearly requires that we first adequately define and explain the necessary distinctive – yet ultimately complementary and harmonious functions – of The Mother Tongue, The Father Tongue, and the Imaginative tongue, along with an accompanying statement of why we allocate three major parts of the Five Component Parts of the book to The Mother Tongue, The Father Tongue, and The Imaginative Tongue respectively (however, we have, in fact, already defined and explained the respective definitions and uses of the Mother Tongue, Father Tongue, and Imaginative Tongue previously);

(5) finally, we need to come full circle with the **New Method of Reading** – in the mode of integral

intuition and realization – by reuniting the human body with the whole human person. We must explain the necessity, naturalness, efficacy, and efficiency of ***anchoring, rooting, and referencing human learning, remembering, and teaching in the embodied movements, actions, interactions, and practices of the whole person*** – **soul** and **body** in the **Thinking Form of the Two Twist**; or **soul**, **mind** and **body** in the **Thinking Form of The Three Thread;** or **body**, **heart**, **mind**, and **soul** in the **Thinking Form of the Four Foundation;** or **body**, **heart**, **mind**, **soul**, and **spirit** in the **Thinking Form of the Five Figure**. Whatever the Thinking Form, the body must no longer be alienated, abandoned, and dismissed **but perceived, understood, and incorporated as an integral part of the Whole Person as well as into the holistic integrity of all Human Life and Learning.**

The above tasks appear quite demanding at first, yet they are doable. As always, initially at least, it pays to divide the respective tasks, dealing with them separately one at a time, for ease of management and greater clarity. Thus, in this "Opening – Four", **we will address ourselves to the first two Tasks only**.

Regarding the third task, we have already noted that we explained it at adequate length earlier. And we will leave the explication of the fourth and fifth tasks to "Opening – Five."

We proceed now to the **first task** which is to declare and explain the unique approach, guiding metaphor, and integral theme of the book:

The simplest and most dramatically obvious consequence and effect of the Two Hands Approach is to highlight that Language is inherently inseparable and inconceivable divorced from Silence. *Silence is the Left Hand* while **Language is the Right Hand**. If Language is the **Text or the Right Hand**, then Silence is the *Context or the Left Hand*. Moreover, this means, as highlighted at the outset in "Opening – One," that Language itself presents two sides or aspects to the reader, *a figurative side* (Left or L) *or aspect* which calls for a *metaphorical* reading and **a literal side** (Right or R) **or aspect** which calls for a reading or interpretation based on **discursive reasoning**. The *figurative, metaphorical* reading is (1L) *intuitive*, (2L) *imaginative*, and rests on a (3L) *deep* reading of (4L) *figures of speech* (à la metaphor, analogy, simile, images, symbols, hyperbole, synecdoche, etc) while the **literal, discursive** reading is (1R) **rational**, (2R) **logical**, and rests on a (3R) **surface** reading of (4R) **prose words** in the denotative sense only.

The Left Hand provides and affords a Poetic Approach and Response; **the Right Hand provides and affords a Prosaic Rendering and Reaction**. *The Left Hand and the Right Brain are Whole and Whole-Hearted, responding to the deeper tone, intention, ultimate purpose, resonance, and meaning of any passage*; **the Right Hand and Left Brain divide, analyze, and conceive the separate parts that compose the Whole with a detached systematic clarity that abstractly defines and coolly explains their theoretical place and importance in the worldly scheme of things**.

The Left Hand, in other words, is personal and expressively engaged – listening, speaking, thinking, writing, and reading with an *active, involved presence and living voice*; **The Right Hand is impersonal and publicly formal** – listening, speaking, thinking, writing, and reading with a **critical, detached mind and focused concentration**.

The Left Hand opens up our inner selves and expands the inclusive reach of our love for and concrete, involved, and concerned embrace of Reality;

the Right Hand confines and restrains our Focus and Knowledge into specific, detached, individualized fragments and segments of Reality held together by their systematic storage into properly designed formal structures of compartmentalized functions and locations.

A Chart, which visually maps The Two Twists in the paragraphs above, follows below:

Left Hand	**Right Hand**
Silence	**Language**
Context	**Text**
Figurative	**Literal**
Metaphorical	**Reasoning**
Intuitive	**Rational**
Imaginative	**Logical**
Deep	**Surface**
Figures of Speech	**Discursive Language**
Connotative	**Denotative**
Poetry or Poetic	**Prose or Prosaic**

Whole	**Parts**
Response	**Reaction**
Personal	**Impersonal**
Personally engaged	**Publicly formal**
Involved presence	**Detached mind**
Living voice	**Thoughtful focused concentration**
Open and Opening	**Confined and Confining**
Embracing and Inclusive	**Limiting and Restricting or Precluding**
Love	**Knowledge**
Expansive	**Restraining and Contracting**
Creative	**Critical**

Right Brain	**Left Brain**
Mother Tongue	**Father Tongue**

On the cover of the book and in the paragraphs above – including the chart which visually maps 22 instances of twosomes in the paragraphs – we highlight **The Two Hands** as the supreme and foremost example (along with **Silence** and **Language**) of the **Two Twist** or **Two Form of Thinking,** but we begin to show also how pervasive **The Two Twist** is in language.

Of course, the Chinese (from ancient times till now) provide the most famous example of a culture that has invented, developed, and extensively used **The Two Form of Thinking** by explaining all Reality and Life in the famous *yin* and *yang* system. This Chinese system remains the original, formative, and still valid premier model of The Two Form of Thinking; however, we have given it the name **The Two Twist** here for contemporary relevance, popular resonance, and ease of memory while we have also added and highlighted many new terms as instances of **The Two Twist**. These new terms are especially useful in illuminating language in general and the English language in particular.

Nevertheless, valuable though these expanded instances of **The Two Twist** are for explaining language, they are still insufficient to fully illuminate and explain by themselves **how central** the word *Approach* is to our way of addressing the English language.

Therefore, we place below an even more extensive chart of instances, but this time in the form of **The Three Thread,** which we ask you to consider and ponder with an open mind, because these instances suggest the varied depth, reach, and application of the word *Approach*. They also reveal why the **Approach** adopted here constitutes a Radical Return to the Root of Wisdom in the Ancient manner of being and thinking as opposed to the Modern Way:

Approach	**System**	Method
Feeling	**Thinking**	Doing
Heart	**Head**	Hand
Advancing	**Progressing**	Improving
With	**Through**	By
Soul	**Mind**	Body

Using	**Employing**	Applying
Artistic	**Scientific**	Technical
Arrangement	**Structure**	Organization
Tapping	**Transmitting**	Touching
Creative	**Generative**	Engendering
Inspiring	**Motivating**	Stimulating
Love	**Knowledge**	Skill
For	**In**	Of
Interpersonal	**Associative**	Collective
Relation	**Law**	Order
To	**From**	At
Whole	**Parts**	Pieces
Personal	**Individual**	Member
Beginning	**Middle**	End
Ancient	**Modern**	Contemporary
Radical	**Liberal**	Conservative
Root	**Branch**	Fruit
Return	**Recurrence**	Repetition
Choice	**Reflection**	Action

Good or Evil	**True or False**	Right or Wrong
Free	**Authoritative**	Responsible
Personal	**Theoretical**	Practical
Appropriation	**Comprehension**	Application
Spiritual	**Human**	Material
Transcendence	**Salvation**	Redemption
For	**In**	Of
Eternity	**Space**	Time
Loving	**Learning**	Doing
People	**Ideas**	Things
Questioning	**Answering**	Solving
Why	**What**	How
Future	**Past**	Present
Tomorrow	**Yesterday**	Today
Women	**Men**	Children
Historical	**Existential**	Temporal
Childhood	**Youth**	Maturity

Universe	**World**	Society
Origin	**Cause**	Effect
Going	**Stopping**	Pausing
Here	**There**	Now
Essential	**Fundamental**	Basic
Cardinal	**Fixed**	Mutable
Verb	**Noun**	Adjective
Essence	**Being**	Having
Always	**Ever**	Still
Accommodating	**Adapting**	Adjusting
Changing	**Stabilizing**	Converting
Renewal	**Restoration**	Revival
Ancient	**Modern**	Contemporary
Way	**Course**	Path

Background on Typographic Choices for the Words of a Three Thread

Some thought has gone into how to typographically represent each word (1-word, 2-word, 3-word) in a **Three Thread**.

personal *1-word*	**mental** **2-word**	factual 3-word
flowing interconnecting intuitive various artistic like handwriting	**clear assertive distinct pronounced rational and intellectual staked out ground the firm stance of the mind**	plain factual sensible verified for practical evidence and proof the body of facts
↳ *italicized*	↳ **bolded**	↳ underlined
If the interior pages were in color, we would put *Red for the 1-words to represent the heart, the blood, the birth passage, the spiritual requirement of sacrifice for any noble cause.*	If the interior pages were in color, we would put **Blue for the 2-words. Blue is the color of heaven and the realm of the mind. It expresses the calm composure of clear reflection and the disposition of cool detachment from excessive emotion.**	If the interior pages were in color, we would put Green for the 3-words. Green is the symbol of flourishing fullness, the full appearance and flowering and fruition in Nature of what was previously only latent in the mind and hidden in the spirit.
red	**blue**	green

You have seen just previously the chart of 52 instances of **The Three Thread** which are so many **variations** of **The Notable Three Thread** of *Approach*, **System**, Method that we place here at the forefront of consciousness and attention.

All these instances of The Three Thread are examples of the figure of speech called **analogy.** Thus, each **Three Thread** is an **implicit analogy** because it presents **a clear visible structure** of sets or groups of three words which **correspond** with one another; thus, all the first words in each set or group are somehow similar or resemble one another in the way they relate to the second words in their group. And in turn, of course, all the second words in every group are also curiously similar and suggestive of one another, as if they belonged to a **veritable family of words**, by the way they relate both to the first words that precede them and the third words that follow them in their respective sets or groups.

Normally, when people read the English language, they always read it **horizontally**, but try reading the sets of three above **vertically**, reading all the first words in succession, noticing all their suggestive and uncanny similarities and resonances with one another as if they had a **common family resemblance, function, and bearing**. Then read the second words all together the same way with the same methodical attention, and finally do the same with the third words in every group.

While this involves and demands initially an apparently radical new orientation to language, why should not words like people, while remaining uniquely and mysteriously their solitary selves, also belong and function as members of a family, in this case a **family of words.**

By referring to the Three Thread Chart above and noticing the **family resemblance** of the word *Approach* to the other first words in each group of threesomes, it will be easier for you to understand our choice of words, logic, and rationale in characterizing the **Two Hands Approach –** *in general in discursive prose* – in the following manner:

The approach here is interpersonal, artistic, imaginative, holistic, and inclusive; it is also, inevitably, spontaneous and experiential, culturally rooted, historically oriented, and practically motivated, referenced, and assessed. **It is interpersonal as opposed to impersonal, but it is also neither subjective nor objective but inter-subjective.** Learning, Remembering, and Teaching are all acquired and mastered in living community with others – in conversation and dialogue in the common Mother or cultural tongue initially and always, although the Father Tongue and the Imaginative Tongue also need to be fully developed.

The philosophical base and foundation of this approach, which is personal and interpersonal, rests on the magnificent, but unfortunately unduly neglected, philosophy of John Macmurray in his three volume trilogy *The Self in Relation*, *The Self as Agent*, and *Emotion As Reason*. The gist and essence of Macmurray's achievement resides in his simple statement that **"The Person is the philosophical form of the twentieth century**" to which we might add **"The Person is the philosophical metaphor of the twentieth century** (now 21st and subsequent centuries)."

What does this mean? As Macmurray and numerous other notable scholars have pointed out (including Lewis Mumford, E.A. Burtt, and Floyd Matson), the stupendous achievement of Newton in the 17th century influenced most thinkers in the 18th century to adopt a purely empirical and **Mechanical Form of Thought** based on physics and the mechanics of motion because Newton's system seemed the ultimate paradigm and model of success.

In the 19th century, the cultural imagination of the Romantic Movement, combined with the momentous publication of Darwin's *Origin of the Species* in 1857, insured that the supreme model and metaphor of human reflection would be an **Organic Form of Thought**.

| *Personal* | **Organic** | Mechanical |

These two forms of thought – the mechanical and the organic – while useful and valuable for some aspects and regions of reality and life were and are nonetheless essentially **reductive in nature**; they ignore the whole Reality and primary essence of human life which is expressed in the **Form of the Personal and Interpersonal**. The mechanical and organic forms of thought are inherently and fundamentally flawed (from the outset), because they rest on a false assumption – namely the assumption that human beings are primarily separated, autonomous individuals completely independent of the world who can conceive – **theoretically** – an absolutely true, objective idea or representation of the world that is not contaminated or influenced by their personal inclinations, dispositions, or emotions.

Of course, ***this assumption is the formative and pervasive pretence, conceit, and supremely (fruitful or tragic) illusion of Youth as a time of life and of all young people***. The young person, like the founding myth of the American Nation (and for that matter the whole Modern World), announces and declares that it has and is grounded by no Past in history and can, therefore, conceive and master the world by completely discovering and realizing a model and prototype – and a project for living according to – a conception and understanding of the world entirely of its own formulation. It conceives of the human being primarily as a Thinking entity that aims for a theoretical and comprehensive knowledge that enables it to master and control reality and life.

The Modern Period of the past five hundred years, and especially the Modern University, has thus esteemed and raised the **Rational Function** and **Theoretical Knowledge** to the exalted status of virtual idol worship – and this to the neglect (1) **of emotional and cultural understanding acquired in interaction and communion with others**, including the **understanding of the inherently and constitutively cultural and social character of human beings with concomitant moral responsibility for others**; (2) the **spiritual nature of the person** and with it the **role of creative imagination in learning and knowledge acquisition**; and (3) even the **neglect and disdain of the body as a vehicle and medium of self awareness and skill acquisition.**

This exaggerated emphasis on the **Rational Function** and **Theoretical Stance toward Reality and Life** was a necessary, indispensable, and inevitable development of important powers and capacities of human beings in the Modern Period. It represented and constituted a Progressive Achievement of substantial and enduring value, and it has brought a multitude of benefits and improvements to humanity. However, it has now gone to an excessive extreme, has become severely unbalanced, and threatens to endanger not only its own hard earned achievements but also the other notable powers, capacities, and accomplishments of human beings through the ages.

What does all this have to do with Learning, Remembering, and Teaching English? Everything.

When you misconceive human beings, more especially students, as mainly Thinking Machines or Organisms only, you require them to sit still in front of you as disembodied minds, without any trace of movement or vital energy, and proceed to lecture them about some remote and abstract subject stored in the separate and divided watertight compartments of that abstract program of instruction with the deadly and deadening name – curriculum.

And you are only concerned with What Students must know, not Why they should know it and what it might , could, or should mean for their personal and engaged lives here and now according to the formula, presumably, "Dwell in the Past, Forget the Future, and Ignore the Present," or otherwise phrased as "Live in your Mind; Forget your Soul and Spirit which anticipate, prophesy, and feel your future coming; and tightly repress, constrain, and dismiss your Body."

What kind of educational system is this and how can it possibly constitute an effective *approach*, **system**, and <u>method</u> for *teaching the future*, **instructing the past**, and <u>training the present</u> (note the **Three Threads** here)?

Moreover, the consequences and results of this Educational Model are clear: (1) Inspiration and Imagination, Intuition and creative depth of personal and interpersonal experience alienated and abandoned; (2) impersonal, cold, and aloof detachment (what Robert Frost designates *ice* in his poem *Fire and Ice*) promoted and praised everywhere in the guise of arrogant and powerful men, conceiving themselves thoroughly in control and so formidably and unquestionably important as to forestall conversation with ordinary mortals of limited intelligence, thus, the ubiquitous lecture and only the lecture; and (3) unused or underemployed hands for absent arts and crafts; animated and revealing gestures forbidden and demeaned; the grace of dance dismissed as idle entertainment and a diminished revelation of eternity, space, and time; and all joy and power of movement annulled, frozen, and blighted in conception and execution, because presumably the body is for lower and inferior laboring classes and beneath the superior, stuffy, rigid presumption and tired, boring conventions of schools.

Perhaps the above characterization is too severe an indictment of contemporary education, but at a minimum it points to a profound lack of balance in learning, remembering, and teaching so many subjects, especially English.

Our approach is based **on dialogue, not rigidly defined oppositions**. It is inclusive and thus does not reject the **two family of words – System**, the **Father Tongue**, the **Theoretical Stance**, **Critical Thought** and **Reflection**, the **Mind** and **Head** (the previous seven words are all instances of **2-words** or words in the second position of a triad). Nor does our approach devalue the three family of words – method, order, practical, technical, application, the body and hand (the previous seven words are all instances of 3-words, or words in the third position in a triad). Rather, our approach integrates and incorporates the **2-words** and the 3-words with *1-words* into a holistic unity of interacting, overlapping, mutually influencing, and reinforcing parts acting as a Whole. So, our approach is integral; **it accords with the Mature stage of human development in history which has dawned with the Global Age**. Such an Approach would have been neither conceivable nor possible prior to the Maturity of Humanity, but it is now an imperative and urgent requirement of this stage of history.

In this Age of the Maturity of Humanity and as an evident sign of that Maturity, the disciplines of linguistics, literary criticism, communications, and philosophy have all converged in the awareness and understanding of **Metaphor as the distinctively human and supreme mode of expression and condensed explanation of Reality and Life**.

The value of Metaphor for human understanding is brilliantly and succinctly expressed by the following five quotations:

"Metaphor is intelligibility's great imperative, its engine of radical amazement."

Cynthia Ozick
Renowned contemporary essayist

"Metaphors have a way of holding the most truth in the least space."

Orson Scott Card
Poet, Playwright, and only Science Fiction novelist to win both the Hugo Award and Nebula Award

"Metaphors aren't just ornaments, they're fundamental modes of knowledge – it's like – what's at a higher more difficult level appears to us first as a shadow, or an image – then we break through the image and move on."

> Iris Murdoch
> *Existentialists and Mystics*

"The metaphor is one of the most important means for the *creation of denominations* for complexes of representations, for those for which *adequate designations do not yet exist*. ... Even when an already existing denomination is available, *an internal impulse leads us to prefer a metaphorical expression*. The metaphor is precisely something which flows necessarily out of human nature and imposes itself, not only in poetic language, but also especially in colloquial, popular language, which always tends toward *graphic expression* and *picturesque characterization.* It is evident that for the creation of metaphor, in the measure in which it is natural and popular, there is generally recourse to those circles of representations which are most strongly present in the soul. What is most distant from comprehension and interest becomes more intuitive and familiar by means of something which is nearer. In the choice of the metaphorical expression, therefore, the individual diversity of interest is shown, and in the sum total of metaphors which have come to be usual in a language, one can recognize which interests have been

especially powerful among the people."

> Hermann Paul from *Prinzipien der Sprachgestchichte*on from *Jose Ortega y Gassett: Circumstance and Vocation* by Julian Marias

"For on the idea which we form of consciousness depends our whole concept of the world, on which, in their turn, depends our ethics, our politics, our art. I say that *the whole edifice of the universe and of life rests, in the end, on the tiny ethereal body of a metaphor.*"

> Jose Ortega y Gassett
> from *Circumstance and Vocation*,
> the biography of Ortega by Julien Marias

A deepened awareness of metaphor is necessary for tuning into and understanding the contents and arrangement of this book. The supreme metaphor of "The Two Hands of the Human Person" runs like a continuous and integrating thread and theme throughout the text.

For this reason, the **Metaphor of The Two Hands Approach** is centrally featured in the **Preface** to this book which appears on the next page.

Preface

The Two Hands Approach is the best short-term initial overview and introduction to language, and in particular the English language. Language is more than the simple and proper use of words; language possesses mysterious depth, and has a nature congenial to our persons and our world. Language is **bipolar;** its duality lies in the **Verb** and the **Noun**, and in the alternating rhythm of **Silence** and **Sound** in language.

After all, all sentences are built of parts that cluster around the **Verb** and the **Noun**. Language is essentially generative and transformative, but it always retains the essential inherent structure of movement (**change and the verb**) and stability (**continuity and the noun**).

The history of language teaching pedagogies reflect this awareness of fundamental and universal principles. Traditional grammar was derived from the Latin, and painted a worldview of a world permanent and unchanging, stable and eternal. Language was rooted in permanent structures, definable rules, and final definitions – **in the image of the Noun**. Finiteness and fitness-to-tradition were cherished. The modern Planck-Einstein view, however, is that the world – and thus also language – is creational, dynamic, and transformable – **in the image of the Verb**. Contemporary approaches should pick the best ideas from both camps: **a bipolar approach**.

The bipolar nature of language is reflected in the human form. We all recognize the bipolar feature of having two hands, right and left. They are with us at all times. We have them before we add watches or bangles to our wrists. We make, shake, create, mold, write, hold, pray with them. **The Two Hands Approach uses our hands and fingers as mnemonic tools** to help open the door of what is usually thought to be one of the most complex languages to learn, English. It instills in us a wider appreciation of the purposes and importance of language. **The 2HA gives us the essential blueprint of English in easy-to-remember handy formats and charts.**

Preface (cont'd)

Since The Two Hands Approach is the essential blueprint of the English Language, when we first introduce students to English, we should begin by giving them – **saying to them plainly** – the following concise statement:

"The English language is really very simple: it is just the left hand and the right hand, the Verb and the Noun, and all the rest is just Commentary."

For example, traditionally, people identified **Eight Parts of Speech** in English, but in this book, though eliminating the interjection as of minor significance, we have expanded the Parts of Speech to what we what we designate **The Twelve Kinds of Words** in English. Can we truthfully say then that the traditional Eight Parts of Speech, and especially our expanded list of Twelve Kinds of Words, can all be described accurately as **just Commentary**?

A moment's reflection will confirm that we can. Thus, the **Adjective** just describes or modifies, qualities or limits, specifies or restricts more exactly, nouns, and thus functions as a commentary on nouns. The **Adverb**, likewise, just describes or modifies, qualifies or limits, specifies or restricts more exactly, verbs and adjectives, and thus functions as a commentary on verbs and adjectives. The **Pronoun** just acts as a substitute for a noun, and thus is a commentary on it or reference to it.

The **Conjunction** and the **Preposition** just function to join the first five Parts of Speech or Kinds of Words – namely, the **Verb**, the **Noun**, the **Pronoun**, the **Adjective**, and the **Adverb** (what we call **The Big Five** for short hand) – and thus function as commentaries on how to join, bridge, or locate the **Big Five** in relation to one another.

The **Verbals** – the **Infinitive**, the **Gerund**, and the **Present and Past Participle** – which we incorporate into our expanded Twelve Kinds of Words are really just other forms of the Verb with different uses in the sentence. And the **Appositive** – likewise incorporated into our expanded list of Twelve Kinds of Works – is itself only another , more specified use of the Noun.

Moreover, with respect to the Sentence, which is the fundamental building block of all Writing, the **Essence of every Sentence** requires a **Verb as the Main Verb** and **a Noun or a Pronoun as the Subject** to constitute a Sentence. Everything else is built up or added to the Essence of Sentences.

Thus, we can repeat, with ample justification, **that the English language is simply the Verb and the Noun and the Rest is just Commentary.**

5 Primary Language Polarities

1 Silence encompasses language and the under-appreciated depths of the Invisible, emerging from the	**2 Language** first gives us Truth and expresses our prevailing rational worldviews emerging from our
3 Right Hemisphere which controls the	**4 Left Hemisphere** which controls the
5 Left Hand that generates the	**6 Right Hand** that consciously writes the
7 Image and invests it with color, animation, and movement, typified by the	**8 Word** which as text expresses and tells us about us and the world, discovers history, and is typified by the
9 Verb which represents going, change, movement	**10 Noun** which represents stopping, stability, permanence

1 3 5 7 **9**   **10** 8 6 4 2

THE FIVE PRIMARY POLARITIES RELATED TO LANGUAGE

Here is a memory-aid diagram to designate the five primary polarities from the total of ten polarities we will examine:

Five Primary Polarities	
Silence 1	2 **Language**
Right Hemisphere 3	4 **Left Hemisphere**
Left Hand 5	6 **Right Hand**
Image 7	8 **Word**
Verb 9	10 **Noun**

The first primary polarity is **Silence and Language**.

The nature and importance of the role of Silence in language has been lamentably underappreciated in modern times. Assuredly, for tens of thousands – if not millions – of years, early humans dwelled in and were fully aware of Silence. When silence is ignored or replaced by words that have little silence in them, history tells us that attempts are made to restore silence and reflection back into the language. This may be done by various means, including the use of rhyme, meter, and innovative typographical features. For example, the poets of the English industrial era – such as Blake and

Byron, Yeats and Shelley – popularized rhyming verse. This restored an element of **pause and silence** to the language which was found wanting amid the din and noise of the machines. E.E. Cummings – with his lower case blank verse – tried to restore significance to the power of the humble (even uncapitalized) word in his experimental blank verse. But these days like never before, we are inundated by a too rapidly spoken language, with mere noise following upon noise. There seems to be no let-up to this barrage.

Death

Despite all this, we still recall Silence during solemn moments. We publicly observe silence during times of profound importance such as at the end of a war or when we recall those who have joined the permanent silence beyond. Silence then has its place, and we value it. After World War I and after the attack on the New York World Trade Center, one or more minutes of silence typified our need for its indispensable healing power.

Holidays

Holidays are prescribed in every culture. Why is this necessary? It is a reflection of the rhythmical nature of all reality – rest and work, silence and language, sleep and activity. They are necessary **pauses** in the ongoing pulse of life.

Temple or Church Bells

Sound is best and deeply heard only when surrounded by silence. The great iron bell needs the silence of the surrounding monastic temple grounds and the silence of the forest to make its sounds resonate to our depths.

Love

Sometimes silence has a voice of its own. When we love strongly, we say, *"I love you more than words can say."* Great experiences are *indescribable* or *beyond words*. We can be *dumbfounded* when something traumatic or unusual and unexpected happens. During those moments, Silence again reigns, and we respect her. (Silence is feminine, while language is masculine).

Music

Why does music soothe us so? Music incorporates **pauses and rests** in a balanced and organized way; it repeats themes and sub-themes; it changes pace and timing; it rushes to crescendos and slips serenely into placid interludes. Without silence, we could not appreciate the unfolding of the melody.

Animals

When humans are paired for therapeutic or psychological reasons with animals, a bond of silence is shared between the human and the animal. The patient rediscovers the healing value of silence. The patient speaks; the animal offers an attentive but non-disruptive presence, a silent being there. But more than that, the animal offers a safe haven where the two can share quietude together, and find a bond in it. Pre-industrial society had a much closer relationship and kinship with the silent world of animals. Since the machine era, that silence – like so many other kinds of silence – has been driven from our urban lives.

Seasons

Max Picard, who wrote in the 1950s, talked of the necessary presence of silence amid our sound-filled world in his classic, **The World of Silence**.

He spoke of the seasons. The seasons fluctuate with silence and sound. Spring is like a babbling infant showing excitement for itself as it discovers the magic of sound and renewal and rebirth. Summer is talkative and teems with natural sounds. In fall, the sounds silently scurry away as days shorten and nights lengthen, and the warm becomes cool. Snow and winter are quiet and subdued. How silent are the mornings after a heavy snowfall, when the roads are not yet drivable before the snowplow cleans the streets!

Childhood and Old Age

Picard also talks of the silence of childhood and old age. He calls children *hills of silence.* Indeed, childhood is a verbally active time, but as we can all recall, it includes moments of reflection, moments that stretched on forever, when silence was our play partner and counselor.

Admirable Person

We also equate depth with a person's ability to be silent. Someone who talks all the time is considered to be unsettled, disturbed, and not within themselves. Someone who is taciturn and guarded in one's speech earns our respect more than a talkative person.

The Crippling Fear of Silence

Only in Silence are we with ourselves, comfortably with ourselves, and only in Silence do we come to know ourselves. Yet many people avoid its presence, as the following passage shows.

I didn't know any other person who paid as much attention to the symphony of the Garden Apartments as I did. They were too busy making their own noises to listen to anyone else's and rarely did an hour pass in their homes when silence wasn't broken. Silence, I learned early on, frightens people, or at least makes them feel very uncomfortable. The worst punishment imposed on my school friends seemed to be keeping them in detention, forcing them to be still and shutting them off from any communication. They squirmed, grimaced, put their heads down and waited as if spiders had been released inside them and were crawling up and down their stomachs and under their chests. When the bell that dismissed them finally rang, they would burst out like an explosion of confetti in every direction, each talking louder than the other, some even screaming so hard that veins strained and popped against their skin in their temples.

Mama wasn't any different. The moment she entered the apartment, she turned on the radio or clicked on the television set, crying, "Why is this place like a morgue?"

V.C. Andrews *Ice*

Silence is an indispensable aspect of language. We should appreciate this in our design of approaches and methods. Any method that circumvents or ignores this is incomplete. To use a set of analogies, Silence is the Background, while Language is the Foreground; Silence is the Context, while Language is the Text. Silence is the Whole, while Language is the Part, which always returns to the Whole from whence it emerged.

Language has stress, rhythm, juncture, intonation, pauses, volume, and voice quality settings, but all rise from, remain embedded in, and are surrounded by Silence.

A corollary of this is **Inhale/Exhale**. We must inhale air before we can speak. We derive our life-giving oxygen from the In-breath. We speak words and sentences in the Out-breath. We also expel waste gases, the result of metabolic processes in our body. We expel the carbon dioxide which is useful for the plants.

When we inhale, we receive the breath of life. We inspire; we take in new life which creatively activates. We process, digest, and distil the essence of what we have taken in. We then expire or expel, that is – give forth to the world – especially in our speech – the substance and product of our speech and assimilation and appropriation of life. We give form to life. **Inspiration is process; expiration is product.**

We continuously produce in speech more beautiful forms to capture and express the inner essence and feeling of our lives.

Furthermore, the value and uses of breathing and pausing in speaking, writing, and reading are matters of utmost importance – especially in the **oral tradition** - but they have been strangely neglected in contemporary times. Consider below Speech and Silence in the oral traditions in ancient and religious traditions.

Speech and Silence in the Ancient and Religious Oral Traditions

Oratory and public recitation of literature were once essential skills in the Greek, Roman, Medieval, Renaissance, African, and other traditions; **people spoke and heard words of power and meaning in their communal and public live**s. Entire communities were able to remember and recite long epic poems, relate innumerable stories, and share with one another public recitations of literature of all types. But the oral tradition has seriously been neglected since the days of Shakespeare.

Plato even said that writing would kill speech. Today that is happening. We have the written word, books, newspapers, but people withdraw into rooms and cubicles where they peruse the words undisturbed. **Speaking – both formal and informal – has become a lost art**. The power of the language has been diminished. Just as we have become numb to images (of violence, of questionable morality), **we have lost our sensitivity to words, their impact, and their importance in the scheme of things, because they are bereft and forlorn,** *divorced from silence, and exiled from public recitation*.

Ancient religious traditions have always cherished and nurtured both silence and chanting as inseparable practices for invoking the sacred. In the Christian and Hindu traditions, monks observed times of silence or went on silence fasts and frequently chanted their prayers. In Sanskrit the word for the practice of silence is called *mauna*. Wandering *guru*s and *sannyasin*s still practice this method as a means to view the world and to be able to absorb and be one with its true nature and essence. The *Rig Veda* consists of hymns that were meant to be chanted.

In Hawaii, hula dancing does not necessarily require instruments, but it does demand the chanting of the human voice in accompaniment with the dance. **The voice was considered the supreme instrument**. See f99n.

The second primary polarity is **Right Brain Hemisphere and Left Brain Hemisphere.**

Modern research on the twin hemispheres of the human brain has given rise to the mapping of the amazing uniqueness, the separateness of functions, yet the integral functioning, of the two hemispheres. Nature – in its uncanny and mysterious way – has shown us again the interdependence and converse aspect of reality: we know that the Right Brain controls the Left side of the body, while the Left Brain controls the Right side of the body. Language theorists know this, but have not incorporated it very well into their paradigms, models, or approaches. Howard Gardner's Multiple Intelligences Theory has, for instance, become well known to language educators and theorists, but such theorists do not seem to have incorporated his conclusions into the classroom in a substantial way. He explicitly tells teachers of the importance of the musical, artistic, and unconscious right brain, but **language is taught with little relevance to the musical and rhythmical character of speech, or with any visual supporting images or graphical aids**.

If it is true that in most people, two important areas of the brain that function in language ability (Broca's area and Warnicke's area) are found only in the left hemisphere of the brain, then is it not incumbent on us to devise teaching methods that appeal to the visual or right side of the brain, so as to ensure a greater amount of whole-brain activity as well as positive and more lasting reinforcement than with only single hemispheric usage?

In her book *My Stroke of Insight: A Brain Scientist's Personal Journey,* neuroanatomist Dr. Jill Bolte-Taylor, has fully documented the terrifying yet amazing experience of having a stroke to the left hemisphere of her brain, and of how she consciously followed the experience through, knowing full well the mechanics of the neural processes that were kicking in as the right hemisphere took over. Her book calls for a total re-evaluation of educational theories and practices.

For example, walk into any science classroom (biology, physics, chemistry, engineering) and you will be rewarded with an abundance of striking visual, color charts, posters, and schematics; walk into an English classroom and you will be hard-pressed to find any charts, posters, or schematics affording visual instruction and clarification of the structure, functions, and complex integral interrelatedness of language.

With such an absence, one would assume that structure and complexity are lacking in language, but is not language the primary medium and instrument by which we understand *all* disciplines of learning and communicate their meaning to one another?

Dr. Stanley I. Greenspan and Stewart G. Shanker, Ph.D. in *The First Idea* explain the brain responses and growth to each of the six essential developmental affective stages. They specify how certain activities for children activate either or both left-side and right-side neural branching and growth. Citing the work of Nobel Prize winning scientist Eric Kandel, they also say that emotionally meaningful experiences, even whole-brain activities, influence the structure of the brain and facilitate memory.

The third primary polarity is **Left Hand and Right Hand.**

Hands are used in language – for gesturing, for writing and typing, for clicking on the mouse, or for turning the page of a newspaper, magazine, or web page as we read. They are essential tools of our communication. We hold the paper with one hand, the pencil with the other. We use both hands to hold the text or book when we rehearse for a drama or play. It is such an obvious and easy polarity that it is impossible to forget.

We have a left hand and a right hand. Our fingers are different and we use them together in unconscious ways as we strum, pluck, push, pull, twist, write, erase, and do other actions with our hands. **Do human hands not lend themselves to being the metaphor or symbol for a learning system?** No batteries, no book required. All that is needed is two hands. The numbers {1, 2, 5, 10, 12} are numbers with which one can easily associate the hands, the fingers, or the hands and fingers together. **A system based on these numbers would seem to be a natural and common sense conclusion**.

The fourth primary polarity is **Image and Word.**

With our two hands and two cerebral hemispheres, we have created images and pictographs, symbols and words. Each of the two hemispheres performs special functions, and people in general tend to prefer and utilize one hemisphere over the other, such that it is for them the dominant hemisphere.

People who are *right-hemisphere dominant* are often artists; they generate pictures and *image*s. An image represents something that is not there, something that is not visible at that place. Thus <u>an image is a visible representation of the invisible</u>. <u>Images make the invisible (non-viewable) world visible</u>. A photo or painting shows you someone who lived a long time ago or in another place. Images as symbols stand for things. They make visible to us that which we can't immediately tangibly view. They make us think about something that isn't really there, but in our mind we imagine that it is. Flags are symbols for countries. When we see a flag, we think of the country. The country is not there – we can't see it in its entirety or even partially. It is not there tangibly or visibly, but we know what the symbol represents. Our modern world (especially the advertising and business world) is replete with symbols that are there to remind us of a distant yet obtainable company product or service. We call them *logos*.

Long ago in human history, someone carved an image, and it became a letter. <u>A letter is an image of a sound heard in its wholeness emerging from the silence that surrounds it and that invests it with beauty and depth</u>. All alphabets are scripts that we use to encode and to document the appearance and image of the world using collections of letters or symbols. We call those collections words. So even though a word is a piece of text, it is also an image or symbol for something. We say that word and image are different, but really word and image are both symbolic and interdependent.

People who are *left-hemisphere dominant* are the mathematicians and scientists, and generate *word*s (texts, reports). A word is an image before it's a sound for those who first encounter it as an image, though it was a sound in origin before it was an image. *A word is a sound captured in an image, but often people process the image and disregard and denigrate the sound.* One should never do this, never.

A word is both an *image* (you can see the printed letters) and *sound* (you can say it), and it stands for something else (the experience or reality behind it). But the word (as seen in print) is not the same as the object to which it refers. All words finally fail to capture the fullness of the reality to which they refer.

Words record what is Invisible in the Visible world. In science and religion, they reveal its structure, form, and inner truth. They distill outward reality to its structural and constitutional character. They are the scripture or plan of the world. They codify the Invisible. It's a code, but you have to interpret it, and interpret it correctly.

Words encode visible reality in a non-graphic format. We use words to describe things, and we mentally create pictures and images as we read. We visualize as we read. We respond to symbols and metaphors.

We use our blanket of words as our referential lens through which we gain and share our perspective on things. Words themselves do not display any material characteristic or image (other than that which they conjure). They are entirely intangible, immaterial, non-substantial, yet they evoke and call to our imagination, the name, form, and semblance of all things. We think they cover everything. We really think we've got reality covered. But, how far from the truth that is! To teach people that Language is the complete or adequate reflection of reality is a terrible misconception or deceit to practice on people. All language is but a footnote on the inexhaustible richness and mysteries of silence and manifest reality, which lie behind all words and from which all words emerge. Words are the map, not the territory.

The fifth primary polarity of **Verb and Noun.**

Written language is the beginning of modern history. It is the distinguishing hallmark of the beginning of civilization. As just speakers of languages, we were amateur humans. When we devised writing systems, we went professional.

Languages are comprised of *Vowels* and *Consonants*, which together give tens of thousands of combinations as syllables, yielding millions of words. In ancient Sumerian, single vowels were also words. Sound and breath had great significance. Vowels employ the breath freely and open-eddedly. They are the core of words. But consonants are formed by restricting or blocking the breath by constricting or channeling the air flow. Vowels symbolize the willingness to listen and speak freely, and move freely with the air and the universe around one, while consonants symbolize the need for containment, form, and pause in the onward movement of life. This is yet another polarity deeply embedded in the character of language, and the polarity is worth remembering.

In modern English, most sentences parse down to two main components: the **Verb** and the **Noun**.

The **Verb** represents change and malleability. The **Noun** represents stability, pause, and permanence. Language teaching has swung from a rigid grammar based approach (Latin has five noun declensions) that portrayed language as a system with a finite, measurable, and totally predictable aspect, *symbolized by the Noun*, to a non-grammar communicative based approach which emphasized talking, action, movement, innovation, which are *symbolized by the Verb*. Thus one can look at the history of modern language teaching theories as being a movement away from the Noun toward a more extensive embrace of the Verb.

The relevance of the Verb/Noun duality shows up, for instance, in the analysis of phrases in the English sentence. By highlighting the key importance of verbal and noun phrases, modern linguists acknowledge the importance of the Verb/Noun polarity.

Previously, there was little acknowledgement of the frequency and importance of phrases in all language usage. Linguists, however, have now identified the many forms of Noun phrases and Verbal phrases, and in addition, adverbial and adjectival phrases. They have not, however, developed a method of teaching students how to use verbal and noun phrases, adjective and adverbial phrases effectively. The important part, after all, is not the definition or the analysis of phrases in a sentence, but the actual use of them at the beginning, middle, and end of sentences. We will demonstrate thoroughly how this can be done later in the book.

We must remember that **not all parts of speech are equal.** Everything is clustered around the main verb and the main noun or its substitute, the pronoun. Thus, the verb and noun are paramount, with the <u>*verb* having a slight edge because of its frequently occurring related forms, the *verbals*, and because process and change (the verb) are more central to reality than product and stability (the noun)</u>. The TPR Approach starts with the simple and imperative form of the verb, thus also emphasizing its importance. English has four verbals which occur with a high frequency in journalistic and mainstream written English. The verb is the moving heart, but the noun is the stable head.

Just as *yin* carries the seed of *yang* in it, and vice versa, both Noun and Verb are often inter-transformable or interchangeable. The verb *create* can be written in the noun form as *creation*. *Die* changes to *death*, but *murder* doesn't need any changes – it already is both noun and verb. Korean has a formulaic way of making this conversion – as we are sure do most languages.

So, it appears as though linguists to some extent realize the importance of Verbs and Nouns, but *they do not see them as complementary pairs that reflect the bi-polar nature of language and how this verb-noun bipolarity constitutes the foundation for language instruction.*

They also do not seem to recognize that the Verb-Noun polarity is a fundamental expression of the character of the world, as seen respectively from an Eastern and Western viewpoint. Thus *the Orient* has stressed the outside world and the observation of nature as a continuous process of change and transformation, à la Hinduism and Buddhism, and therefore has stressed the *verb* as primary. The *western world*, on the other hand, has stressed the individual subject as the center of experience and therefore highlighted the *noun*.

So, in summary, we see that there is a linked and logical sequence to these primary five dualities. The chart can be read left to right, line by line, or it can be read top to bottom, down each column.

Five Primary Tonal Themes

↓ ↓	**Silence** encompasses language and symbolizes the hidden underappreciated underused, underdeveloped depths of the invisible, represented by the latency of the	**Language** (sound, utterance) represents the dominating rational worldview which is governed by our	↓ ↓
↓	**Right Hemisphere** which controls the	**Left Hemisphere** which controls the	↓
↓	**Left Hand** that generates an	**Right Hand,** the dominant controlling defining hand that holds pen in hand and writes the	↓
↓	**Image** and invests it then with color, animation, and movement, typified by the	**Word** which as text represents the world and stops history, is stable, and is typified by the	↓
↓	**Verb** which represents going, change, movement	**Noun** which represents stopping, stability, permanence	↓

Do you see now how clear it is and how easily it can be learned and taught when it is all summarized and condensed and holistically presented in charts and images and can be tangibly represented by a pair of hands? Who will not understand this? And who can ever forget it?

R. Buckminster Fuller – the famous American mathematician, post-industrialist, inventor, architect, and energy systems expert – entitled his book of photos of people, places, and machines, *I Seem to Be A Verb*. **Marshall McLuhan** and **Quentin Fiore**, the renowned Canadian media theorist, juxtaposed images and text in his book, *The Medium is The Massage*. **Paul D. Miller (D.J. Spooky)** in both his *Sinfonia Antarctica* as well as *Rhythm Science* attempts to code a *"generative syntax for the new languages of reality"* and fuses sound with words and images Still now, many people are struggling to understand the wherewithal of image and word and new media. Such thinkers force us to notice the different properties and converse roles that we accord to both a word-inspiring image (at least 1000 words according to the Chinese proverb) and a picture-conjuring and imagination-stimulating text passage.

First diagnosed as autistic and later with Aspergers Syndrome, **Dr. Temple Grandin** discovered an unusual kinship in her mode and animals' mode of experiencing the world: she realized that autistics and animals thought visually, not in words. Their experience is sensory-based. Her books, *Thinking in Pictures: My Life with Autism*, *Animals in Translation*, and *The Unwritten Rules of Social Relationships*, plus others, have certainly opened up for us new understandings of the world of autistics as well as a more humane treatment of animals. They bring us back to the role of the body, its signals, its sensory receptivity.

The insights from both Dr. Temple Grandin and previously mentioned Dr. Jill Bolte-Taylor should force us to re-think and alter how and what we teach, in addition to our attitude towards dyslexic and autistic children.

5 Solo Activities to Master English

The Left Hand

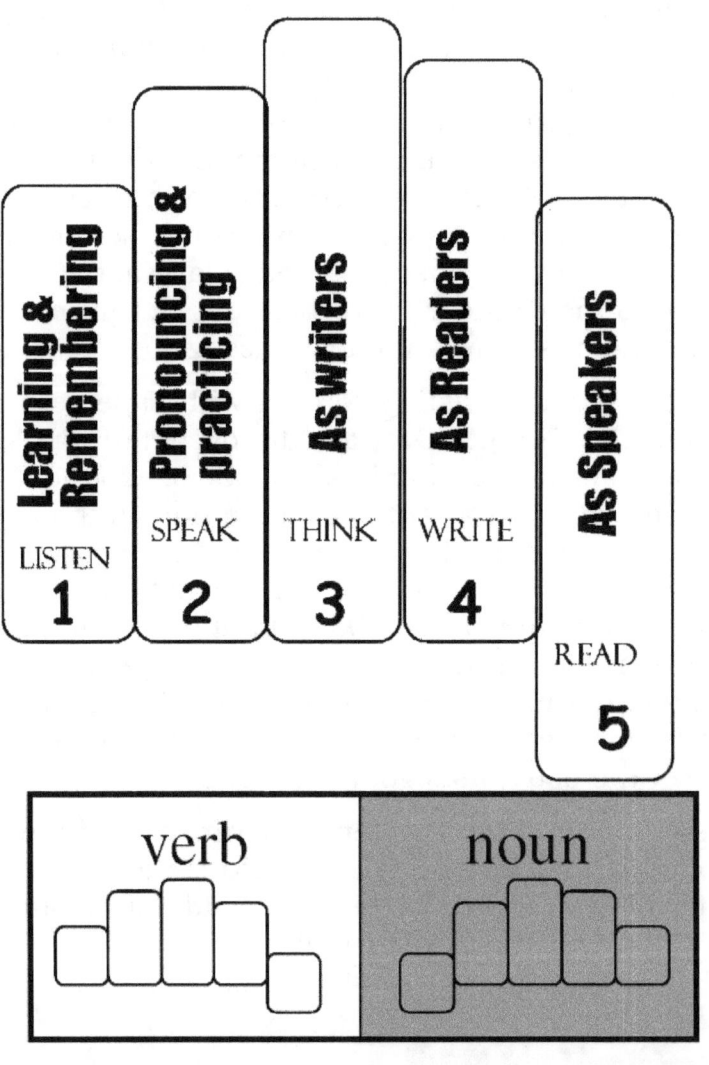

The Two Hands as the Supreme Instrument for Learning, Remembering, and Teaching English OR 5 Modes of Viewing the Suitability of the Hand as the Candidate of Choice for a New Learning Approach to English

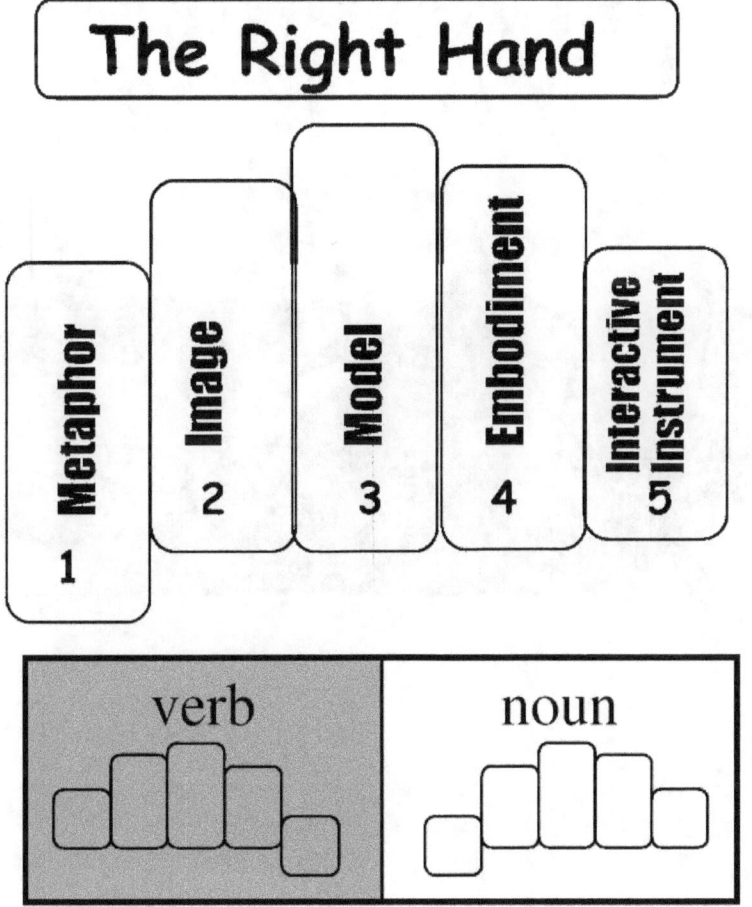

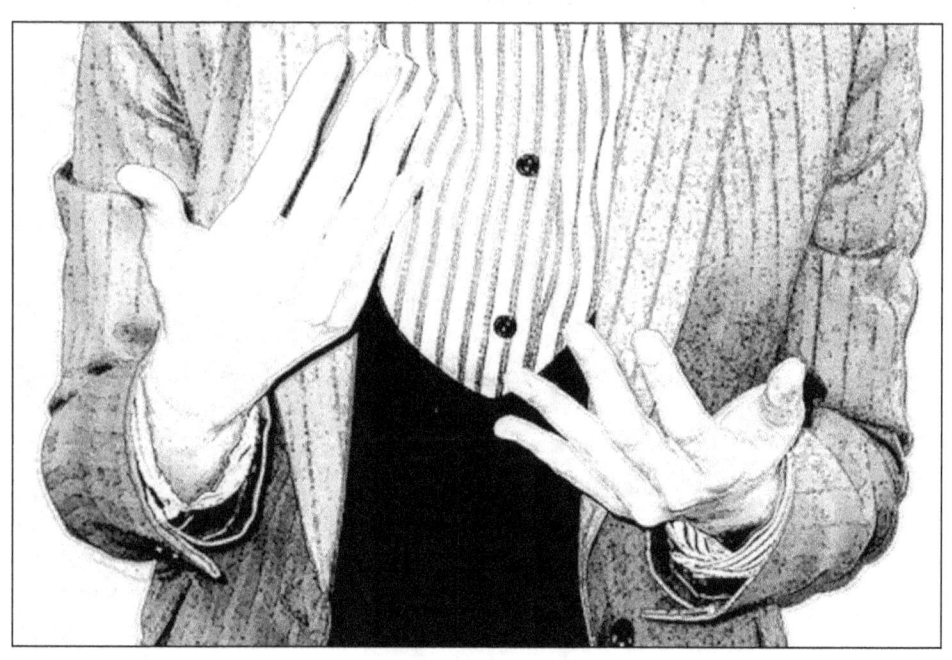

A Selection from

"A Brave and Startling Truth" by Maya Angelou

We, this people, on this small and drifting planet
Whose hands can strike with such abandon
That, in a twinkling, life is sapped from the living
Yet those same hands can touch with such healing,
    irresistible tenderness
That the haughty neck is happy to bow
And the proud back is glad to bend
Out of such chaos, of such a contradiction
We learn that we are neither devils nor divines

When we come to it...
Have the power to fashion for this earth
A climate where every man and every woman
Can live freely without sanctimonious piety
Without crippling fear...

We must confess that we are the possible
We are the miraculous, the true wonder of this
    world...

If the **Two Hands Approach** is the appropriate **Preface** to the Book in the Introduction, then the **Announcement** is the **Symphonic Assemblage** which it is our **Second Task** in this Introduction to explain in the pages that follow.

Preview of Symphonic Assemblage

"...**I have set myself the goal, at least, of leading you to feel my subject in bone as well as brain.**

Poems, of course, work this way at the cellular level of exchange; and perhaps it would help to say that **my method of arrangement here is more poetic than discursive**. As I said earlier, **the book evolves by repetition and the logic of images rather than by thesis and example**. It seems to me that there are bells that ring for each of us, sounding through the babble of daily life: **deep tones that call us at the most profound levels of our ability to hear.** I have tried to set some bells ringing in this text (it seems pretentious to say so, **though they are not *my* bells but imports**): an idea in chapter two that resonates in chapter six, a phrase here that calls to a phrase later. I have organized the book in this **poetic or symphonic way**; therefore you will not get a full discussion of something all at once: **you will hear a bell note, and when next you hear it, you will, I hope, bring forward not only a memory of its last sounding but also what you have made of it, you yourself, in the levels and layers of your own consciousness**. That is **the method I have devised** – however inadequately it may be realized – **of letting the reader engage with me in the writing of this book**. A better craftsman would do a better job, but that is at least the job I have tried to do. *Only in the reader's consciousness will the story be whole, and every reader will read a slightly different story.*"

Mary O'Reilly, Irish-American teacher and essayist

Symphonic Assemblage

We hereby set forth and exemplify a new form of literature – the **Symphonic Assemblage**. This form of literature is an instance of what we call the *Feminine conception of Form*, which is complementary to the *Masculine conception of Form*. Later in the book, we explain these two conceptions of Form. Briefly, the **Feminine understanding of Form is more relational, dynamic, elusive, and ever-changing, yet somehow perceptible and whole; the Masculine understanding of Form is more focused, stable, definitive, and structural**.

The book as a whole is an example and model of the Feminine understanding of Form. Our Assemblage gathers together varied ideas and passages of literature which cross the boundaries of disciplines, generations, genders, cultures, nationalities, religions, worldviews, and stages of life experience. The varied passages or notes provide a multitude of examples, illustrations, and verifications of a single, pervasive Theme, expressed in Symphonic Composition. As such, the Assemblage displays the wide, inclusive, integral, and relational perspective characteristic of women.

However, one of the central achievements of this book (though by no means the only one) consists also in the discovery and clear definition of **Eleven Forms of the English Sentence**. In the discovery and explanation of the **Eleven Forms of the English Sentence**, we are employing the Masculine sense of Form which is clearer, more focused, individual, and distinct.

Together, the Feminine and Masculine concepts or ideas of Form constitute the Left Hand and Right Hand of the greater structural framework of this book. Repeatedly throughout the book, we employ the unifying metaphor of Two Hands – in varied applications and configurations – to bring the English language home to all the people on Earth, as close and companionable as their own two hands.

Each soul must meet the morning sun, the new, sweet earth, and the Great Silence alone!
>Charles Alexander Eastman
>Santee Sioux

Just as notes of a melody are accentuated when sustained or surrounded by silence, so too spoken words and phrases gain distinction and greater palpable and penetrating power when surrounded by silence.
>Steve Watson

"In our hearts we know what actually surrounds the statue. The same surrounds every other work of art: empty space and silence."
>William H. Gass
>American literary critic

I found I had less and less to say, until finally, I became silent, and began to listen. I discovered in the silence, the voice of God.
>Soren Kierkegaard
>Danish philosopher

Beethoven Declaring That Silence Makes the Symphony

(from the movie *Copying Beethoven*)
Beethoven is talking with Anna Holz, his copyist.

Beethoven: The vibrations on the air are the breath of God, speaking to man's soul. Music is the Language of God. We musicians are as close to God as man can be.

We hear His voice. We read His lips. We give birth to the children of God who sing His praise.

That's what musicians are. And if we're not that, we're nothing.

Anna Holz: I just don't understand it, maestro. Where does the movement end?

Beethoven: **It doesn't end. It flows.** You have to stop thinking in terms of beginning and ending. This is not one of the bridges your iron man [boyfriend engineer] builds. This is a living thing, like clouds taking shape or tides shifting.

Anna Holz: Musically, how does it work?

Beethoven: It doesn't; it grows. You see, the first movement becomes the second. As each idea dies, a new one is born. In your work, you are obsessed with structure, with choosing the correct form. *You have to listen to the voice speaking inside of you.*

I didn't really hear it myself until I went deaf. Not that I want you to go deaf, my dear.

Anna Holz: You're telling me that I must find the silence in myself to hear the music.

Beethoven: Yes, **Silence is the Key, the Silence between the Notes. When that Silence envelopes you, then your soul can sing.**

The Innovative, Cumulative, and Culminating Form of the *Symphonic Assemblage*

The Key Note of This Form:

• • •

> Simplicity Aims Circularly
>
> Directly Removing; Discreetly Returning
>
> Elusively Life's Mystery

Anna Walters
Native American Pawnee

• • •

The **Form of this Book** is a **Symphonic Assemblage**, with a central, **unifying Theme** as its animating tone, keynote, and guiding metaphor, but with **varied notes** that evoke, signify, demonstrate, and validate the one Theme.

We often initiate or sound a new note, seeming to remove ourselves from the unifying central Theme, but directly, you will notice, we always Return to the center, to that Ever Present Origin that abides and continues to the End.

In the Intervals of the various notes or passages that the book provides (selected from the great traditions of humanity and from the contributions of genius of many nations on earth); in the Silence, Rest, and Creative Refreshment afforded by **these Intervals of Silence**, you, the reader, must listen for the inner meaning and discover the **multiple connections in the Symphonic Assemblage** that we have composed so that **the final Composition vibrates and sings in Performance**.

This is a text that invites and demands **Readers as Mutual Participants and Joint Performers of the work**. Readers as Audience must be active, involved, moved, and moving Participants in the Process.

Set Forth with us, then, on this **Radical Venture** (radical because returning to the Ancient roots of human nature and creation) where we **essay** an **ever elusive Exploration**, **Examination**, **Exemplification**, **Explanation**, and **Exposition** of the **English language** in a mode and manner that you may never have previously encountered but are unlikely ever to forget.

Footnote:

We feel it is best for you to first experience what we here designate a new form of literature – the *Symphonic Assemblage* – before we define and elaborate its main features. The Forerunners, Nature, Characteristics, and Effects of the Symphonic Assemblage as a literary form are set forth at length in The Closing in Volume 2. If you are curious about this literary form – its predecessors and multiple uses and virtues – go directly to The

Closing in Volume 2 before proceeding further. As you will discover in reading this book, The Closing contains much more valuable information than is usual in a book. We did not want to overburden this first volume with too much scholarly support and validation.

> # Construction of the Whole
> The need to create sound syntheses and systemizations of knowledge will call out a kind of scientific genius which hitherto has existed only as an aberration: the genius for integration. Of necessity, this means specialization, as all creative effort does, but this time the [person] will be specializing in the construction of the whole.
> José Ortega y Gasset
> *Mission of the University* 1930

Assemblage

"Philosophy can exclude nothing. Thus it should never start from systematization. Its primary stage can be termed *assemblage*. ...

Systematic philosophy is a subject of study for specialists. On the other hand, the philosophic process of assemblage should have received some attention from every educated mind, in its escape from its own specialism."

Alfred North Whitehead, British philosopher

"It seems, then that **the atmosphere of the new world has already affected philosophy in two ways**. In the first place, **it has accelerated and rendered fearless the disintegration of conventional categories; a disintegration on which modern philosophy has always been at work, and which has precipitated its successive phases**. *In the second place, the younger cosmopolitan America has favoured the impartial assemblage and mutual confrontation of all sorts of ideas. It has produced, in intellectual matters, a sort of happy watchfulness and insecurity.* **Never was the human mind master of so many facts and sure of so few principles. Will this suspense and fluidity of thought crystallise into some great new system?** Positive gifts of imagination and moral heroism are requisite to make a great philosopher, gifts which must come from the gods and not from circumstances. But if the genius should arise, **this vast collection of suggestions and this radical analysis of presumptions which he will find in America may keep him from going astray**. Nietzsche said that the earth has been a madhouse long enough. Without contradicting him **we might** perhaps soften the expression, and **say that philosophy has been long enough an asylum for enthusiasts. It is time for it to become less solemn and more serious.** <u>*We may be frightened at first to learn on what thin ice we have been skating, in speculation as in government; but we shall not be in a worse plight for knowing it, only wiser to-day and perhaps safer tomorrow.*</u> "

George Santayana from *Character & Opinion in the United States* (1920)

"All knowledge, all science, thus aims to grasp the meaning of objects and events, and **this process always consists in taking them out of their apparent brute isolation..., and finding them to be parts of some larger whole *suggested by them*, which, in turn, *accounts for, explains, interprets them*; ie. renders them significant.**"

John Dewey, American philosopher

"Ortega adds that 'each period brings with it a radical interpretation of man,' and amends his own expression by saying that 'it does not bring this interpretation with it, but rather each period is just that,' and this is the reason why **each period prefers a certain genre**. Each period is an interpretation of man, and one of the fundamental modes in which man *executes* and realizes himself is the most authentic genre, the one which the period creates or recreates."

Julian Marias, Spanish philosopher

Becoming Being

Form is a springboard, launching into air
a fact that wasn't, but that now is, there.
Bruce Bennett, American poet

Thoughts on Originality

"Originality may be characterized by entirely new thinking or by collating and making sense of and with old ideas. The practical utilization of existing knowledge, not original with you, may be in the realm of your own originality.

... So, we can be wonderfully original without ever first creating anything;... we can also be original even if someone else thought of our original idea first. ... The question offers the opportunity of putting originality into a perspective that best includes developing ideas in conjunction with others and allowing originality to be judged in retrospect."

> Bifford V. Debs, M.D., American doctor and novelist

Let no one say that I have said nothing new; the arrangement of the subject is new. When we play tennis, we both play with the same ball, but one of us places it better.

> Blaise Pascal, *Pensées*

Difference is the beginning of synergy.

> Stephen R. Covey, American author

Some aesthetic forms fix; others engender flux. Of course, this isn't a static opposite either. Most do both in different degrees.

> Joan Retallack, American literary critic

"When Keith Jarrett plays *Ol' Man River*, the delight and satisfaction is not so much in the melody itself but in recognizing it when it surfaces and when it is hidden, and when it goes away completely, what is put in its place. **Not so much in the original line as in all the echoes and shades and turns and pivots Jarrett plays around it.** I was trying to do something similar with the plot in *Jazz*. I wanted the story to be the vehicle that moved us from page one to the end, but **I wanted the delight to be found in moving away from the story and coming back to it, looking around it, and through it, as though it was a prism, constantly turning**.

This playful aspect of *Jazz* may well cause a great deal of dissatisfaction in readers who just want the melody, who want to know what happened, who did it and why. But the jazzlike structure wasn't a secondary thing for me – it was the *raison d'être* of the book. The process of trial and error by which the narrator revealed the plot was as important and exciting to me as telling the story."

Toni Morrison, Nobel Prize author, speaking about her novel *Jazz* in an interview printed in *The Paris Review Interviews Volume II*

Defining a Symphonic Assemblage

A *Symphonic Assemblage*, as a new literary genre, has the following characteristics:

1. It has a **single, central, main theme**.
2. It has a **guiding metaphor**.
3. It has a **single recurring image** representative of the central metaphor.
4. It has an **intuitively realized and laid out, discernable structure or framework** that yokes together the main parts, much like the separate movements of a symphony or the separate stones in a Fieldstone Wall.
5. It comprises **many independent autonomous units** whose range encompasses **more than one genre and more than one discipline or research area,** and that have been very **carefully culled from one's own sources, new authoritative sources, or sources from the past**. It incorporates valuable excerpts from famous as well as previously unrecognized authors.
6. The **many independent autonomous units** constitute – individually in themselves as units – brief, compressed, distilled nuggets of insight, wisdom, and knowledge notable for their precise, brilliant, and memorably illuminating, arresting, and artistic expression.
7. The **many independent autonomous units** (excerpts or selections of written text) are separated by a **wider physical space** on the page than usual. The physical, visible separation on the page represents and symbolizes an **interval of silence** that encloses and embraces the **many independent autonomous units.**

Defining a Symphonic Assemblage (pt.2)

before and after they are read. The experienced silence preceding and following the reading of the **many independent autonomous units** means that the reader should think and meditatively absorb the meaning of each unit before proceeding to another. Why? First, because *each unit is a compressed and felicitous expression of insight, wisdom, and knowledge* which calls for and requires deeper reflection and thought. Second, **each new unit resonates in the silence with many of the units before and after it in the total Symphonic Assemblage**.

8. The awareness that comes from this **way of proceeding, this method of reading**, provides what many have called the ***aha pause*** or ***eureka moment of realization***. *The onus is on the reader to discover, fathom, and appreciate the way in which the current unit connects to its predecessors and successors as well as to the Symphonic Assemblage as a whole,* since this connection is not always initially obvious and proceeds from a deeper level of understanding.

   Moreover, this **way of proceeding, this method of reading**, characterizes the Symphonic Assemblage as a literary form that demands and requires a more active and involved reader who participates with their entire being (soul, mind, and body) in the an imaginative re-creation and personal appropriation of the individual units and unfolding whole of the Assemblage. Thus,

Defining a Symphonic Assemblage (pt.3)

reading is more *a continuous process of ongoing integration and appropriation* (making the text one's own or taking ownership of it) *than a passive momentary encounter with an isolated written passage on the physical printed page.*

The pace, posture, and involvement of the reader is not like that of the ordinary passers-by on Main Street, or the reporters and readers of newspapers on Fleet Street, or the purely utilitarian focus of businessmen on Wall Street, but more like the leisurely and contemplative stroll in silence of the walker in New York Central Park or by the shores of Lake Louise in Canada.

9. Each of the **many independent autonomous units** stands on its own and speaks its own clear, distinct, individual truth in its own distinct, individual voice and manner, yet all of the **many independent autonomous units** *mutually expand and comment upon one another, mutually reinforce, illuminate, reflect and complement one another*, **in consonance or dissonance**, like the blended harmony and dissonance of the independent instruments of a symphonic orchestra – the woodwinds, the brass, the drums, the strings, the piano – mutually reinforce, mutually expand and advance the unified theme of a symphony with a new movement (or return recursively for a fuller re-integration or further development of an earlier movement with the new movement). The whole symphony, distinct in each of its notes and instruments, is yet **synergistic (in its essence)**, bringing the combined richness and diversity of its content into one artistic unity: **the whole greater with power and resonance, feeling (in its playing and reception) and beauty than the sum of its parts.**

Defining a Symphonic Assemblage (pt. 4)

10. The Symphonic Assemblage is the **representative, necessary, and indispensible art form expressive of the life experience and tasks of our time in history**. As a character in one of Shakespeare's plays observes, *"Our virtue lies in the interpretation of the time."*

    This time in history is the Age of Maturity for humanity on this planet. When an organism is mature, **all its powers and capacities reach the plenitude of their fulfillment**. This means the organism integrates all its previously separate component parts and aspects and experiences into the focused purpose and pursuit of its destiny. As humanity experiences its maturity in our time, the peoples, races, genders, and nationalities gather, come together, and come home to bring to fruition the grand, integrated Assemblage of Humanity as a whole. Human beings assemble and integrate the previously separated disciplines of learning, cultures, and divisions that have hitherto separated humanity by too frequent occasions of violence, aggression, and wasteful, unproductive conflicts. Mature people do not invoke aggression and violence to solve problems and disputes; they face, find, and forge answers to problems and open possibilities previously unimagined. The 21st and succeeding centuries will witness the Grand Assemblage of Humanity in peace and unity, and that Assemblage is heralded, prepared for, and catalyzed by **Symphonic Assemblages** of the thoughts and written expressions of human beings everywhere on the planet.

11. Is the Symphonic Assemblage an inventive and original work of creation? Should the compiler of the Assemblage be called the *author*, or the *assembler*, the *compiler*, or the *orchestrator*?

    Inasmuch as most of the content of a Symphonic Assemblage consists of a putting together of the writings of others, how can the compiler of the assemblage be called an *author*? Even if they may contribute some or a considerable portion of their own original writing to the content of the Assemblage, does that small contribution entitle them to the title of *author*? But, what if their inventiveness and originality

Defining a Symphonic Assemblage (pt. 5)

does not consist only or solely in their original writings as part of the Assemblage, but in the perception, insight, and imaginative constructive power that has enabled them to select only the most excellent and compressed brilliant writings of others, so that from those autonomous units of meaning that they first discovered, they were able to imagine and construct a greater whole to which the units belonged in a very particular and concrete sequence of mutual resonance and organization.

They did not create and write all or even most of the autonomous units of meaning in the Assemblage, but they did envision and construct the symphonic whole from the autonomous units that they first discovered in all their compressed excellence. And they embraced and surrounded and embedded those autonomous units in the silence that they require to be properly recognized and appreciated.

In short, the name doesn't matter here. Whether you call one who puts the Assemblage together the *author, compiler,* or *co-assembler* – whatever the name – he or she has demonstrated critical acumen, a refined taste and sensibility, and an imaginative power of conception and construction of a new literary form.

12. The Symphonic Assemblage is a product that evolves over time through widespread reading across disciplines and genres, by continuous reflection , and as a consequence of integral awareness, vision, and imagination.

    Often an Assemblage is so vast in scope that it requires and nurtures collaboration between several authors or assemblers. Thus, it heralds the advent of a time when mutual and cooperative projects may be brought to fruition by people working harmoniously together, rather than by isolated individuals pursuing fame and fortune.

The following passage is a dramatic narrative of the virtually shattering experience of a *sonic boom* by two travelling companions driving alone in a jeep in the desert.

The narrative captures the *aha pause* or *eureka moment of realization* that emerges from a **pregnant space of Silence** which enables one to step out of Time into a new dimension of experience beyond the ordinary.

Faster than the Speed of Sound, the Awesome Power of a Sonic Boom

from *Underworld* p.467-468 by Don DeLillo

Matt drove the jeep, Janet drowsed next to him, drowsed a while and got bounced awake and nodded off again.

He felt good, clear-minded, he drove and thought, he saw everything, he identified plants without the book.

The sun was still very low and the track would take them right into it for a time before veering gradually north.

He saw the rubble turn to sand.

He saw the silty limestone bottoms of dried-out creeks that paralleled the track.

He heard the wing-whir of mourning doves breaking out of the bush.

He saw a dust devil on a level stretch of desert doing slow-motion spirals.

There was an odd charged pause.

Then the roar descended on them, so close it stopped his blood, and Janet grabbed an arm. No, first she fell against him, knocked sideways by the force of the noise, a flat cracking boom, and then she snatched his arm and missed and grabbed again. He sat there with his head hammered into his shoulders. The jeep left the track but he freed his arm from Janet's clutch and steered it back. He realized his other arm was raised just over his head, curled above him in defense.

The noise broke over them and washed past, nearly taking them with it, and Janet was looking at him. Her mouth made a smooth lonesome oval.

Sonic Boom Ripple Effect (cont'd)

Matt was intently absorbing the news. He was sorting through. He was looking towards the mountains, ready to be happy. Then he saw the twin glint just before they disappeared, a pair of F-4 Phantoms in silver skin reaching the top of their arc before leveling off – just thought they'd skim the desert on a quiet morning.

He was happy, hearing the echo carom off the ranges now, a remnant thunder that cross-called from the Little Ajo Mountains to the Gnowler Mountains to the Granites and the Mohawks and out into the towns and truck stops. Yes, he loved the way power rises out into the towns and truck stops. Yes, he loved the way power rises out of the self-caressing secrecy to become a roar in the sky. He imagined the sound waves passing over the land and lapping forward in time, over weeks and months, cross-country, eventually becoming the gentlest sort of rockabye rhyme in a small safe room where a mother nurses a baby and a man stands with his arm over his head, a research fellow, not in fear of shattered plaster and flying glass but only to draw down the shade –the sky is going dark, and a tangy savor drifts from the kitchen, and there is music in the house.

But it was the steroid jolt he experienced now, the gooseflesh, the prickling thrill that traveled over the body as they sat trembling in the little jeep. They were not yet ready to talk to each other. They needed a moment to collect themselves, speechless in the wake of a power and thrust snatched from nature's own greatness, or how men bend heaven to their methods."

The narrative above is so brilliantly rendered that its impact is overwhelming in its power, intensity, and reach of imaginative embrace.

The passage produces an expansion of consciousness that amounts to what James Joyce called an *epiphany* or what others or ourselves refer to as an *aha pause* or *eureka moment of realization.*

Sonic Boom Ripple Effect
and the Aha Pause (cont'd)

A new clarity or depth of human experience is realized or encountered in the *aha pause* or *eureka moment of realization*. **Time seems to stop, and we sit or gaze in a stunned wonder which occasions a** *pregnant space of Silence* **where we step our of Time and into a reach or dimension of experience beyond or within the ordinary or everyday. Somehow, we are at once out of or completely removed from our ordinary life, yet more deeply rooted in it.** The ultimate effect on us is that we feel larger and more whole, more at one with ourselves as well as more related to the whole of Life.

The selection above produces a particularly powerful *aha* experience. However, **the *aha pause* or *eureka moment of realization* comes in degrees of power and impact: from a powerful, overwhelming, and almost shattering impact to a more muted, soft, and mellow awareness. Indeed, the narrative above is a kind of metaphor for the range of possible *eureka* experiences.** Thus, the two travelers are so close to the sonic boom that it has a *eureka* effect on them of shattering proportions, seeming at first to threaten their very survival. The sonic boom, however, as it moves across the country in the story has a continuing though ever lessening rippling effect on the entire continent. As the sonic boom goes from its first shattering, to a then more powerful, and finally ultimate effect of "becoming

Sonic Boom Ripple Effect and the Aha Pause (cont'd)

the gentlest sort of rockabye rhyme where a mother nurses a baby... and there is music in the house", so also the *aha pause* or *eureka moment of realization* can range from the shattering to the gentle, much as a Beethoven symphony at different times strikes notes or tones that are muted and soft and mellow, while other notes or tones are more distinct and pronounced and forceful, and still others rise to a culminating crescendo like the end of the Fifth and Ninth Symphonies.

The ultimate insight or realization of these two travelers is a profound new appreciation of the power of the human mind and imagination that can produce a technology that has this effect on the ground-bound consciousness of human beings and the continent they inhabit. After this experience, they are clearly no longer ground-bound in their consciousness; rather, their imagination soars like the two jets **they experienced and witnessed.**

Whitman's *Ensemble* as Suggestive Forerunner of Symphonic Assemblage

O such themes – equalities! O divine average!

Warblings under the sun, usher'd as now, or at noon, or setting,

Strains musical flowing through ages, now reaching hither,

I take to your reckless and composite chords, add to them, and cheerfully pass them forward.

. . .

I will not make poems with reference to parts,

But I will make poems, songs, thoughts, with reference to *ensemble*,

And I will not sing with reference to a day, but with reference to all days,

And I will not make a poem nor the least part of a poem but has reference to the soul,

Because having look'd at the objects of the universe, I find there is no one nor any particle of one but has reference to the soul.

Walt Whitman
Starting from Paumanok 1856

Are There Three or Four Movements in a Symphony and in the Symphonic Assemblage?

In our Contents, we have listed only 3 movements to our Symphonic Assemblage, and this may appear to be an oversight. Readers who have listened to classical symphonies (but not more modern ones) may want to inform us that a Symphony has four, not three, movements. Traditionally, that was so. However, Concertos had 3 movements. This may have been the norm for the 16th through to the 19th century, but the modern 20th century widened and loosened the definition. Some composers followed the traditional 4-movement form, while others took different approaches: Jean Sibelius' *Symphony No. 7*, his last, is in 1 movement, whereas Alan Hovhaness's Symphony No. 9, *Saint Vartan* (1949–50) is in 24.

The traditional 4th movement may appear to be missing from our Symphonic Assemblage. What has become of the quickening of the pulse in allegro time, the return of the ever-abiding theme leading to that triumphant crescendo, the peaking and culminating power of all the participating orchestral instruments, all participating and holding their place and pace – the drum roll, the piano keys and chords played by the hands' rapidly flying fingers, the cascading rush and majestic timbre of the violins moving and marching us on to the finish line – a full and royal escort to the court of ecstasy and affirmation? Even a raga builds up and gets the blood flowing, and the heart moving, and the mind touched by sounds that are heard and held for the shortest of moments, then fly skywards, out to the universe. Have we ignored this?

No, hopefully not. As we have hinted in The Opening-3 in the quotes by Richard N. Bolles, **each person's life can be considered a Symphony**. Bolles suggests 4 stages: Infancy, Learning, Working, Retirement. A young person can march forward and show much insight into things, but truly it is the cumulative wisdom of many years that gives the mature person the ability to be the conductor who knows the piece of music, and who leads the players with their instruments on towards that exuberant and audacious expression that represents the final closing designed by that mature person. And a mature person can design or conduct more than one symphony, indeed many symphonies. One can retire, but should never tire. 98-year-olds can run marathons, and 85-year-olds produce artwork or novels.

Perhaps we could playfully say that every person needs to construct their own *audiobiography* when the person's words and the voice that emerges from those words sound forth with the power and richness of a symphony.

Just as a person has phases of awareness and experience, so too does Humanity. We are now passing from an era of turbulent Youth to an unfolding new Age of Maturity and Fulfillment. In historical stages, we can trace 4 movements or historical periods: Infancy (prehistoric human); Childhood; Youth; and Maturity (21st century on onwards), which is collectively the 4th movement. So, our Symphonic Assemblage does have a 4th Movement, but it is a Movement that will emerge in the coming Future when the personal symphonies or audiobiographies of people everywhere can be collected as the written expression of the Final and Fourth Movement of the Maturity of Humanity on this planet.

Yet, one other aspect of our metaphor needs mentioning. As Wikipedia informs us, symphonies were "still, on the whole, orchestral works. Symphonies with vocal parts, or parts for solo instrumentalists, were the exception rather than the rule. Designating a work a "symphony" still implied a degree of sophistication, and seriousness of purpose. The word *sinfonietta* came into use to designate a work that was "lighter" than a symphony."

Although some symphonies have been written for high-school bands, symphonies usually require the inclusion of the full gamut of orchestral instruments: winds, brass, drums, strings. Likewise, in our grand analogy, a *Symphonic Assemblage* should reflect and include the best of the best from many eras and points of the compass. **It reflects the in-gathering of Humanity which now shine forth from the horizon of this Age of Maturity**. Our friends and associates and contacts and all the people we meet throughout our life are the instruments of *our* Symphony, just as *we* are the instruments of their Symphony.

Clearly, the future is rich with possibilities, not only of peace and prosperity, but of a time when *everyone*'s story can be told, documented, preserved. Let no citizen be without such a cultural artifact to share and pass on to tomorrow's children.

May those stories resound and ring out – as the no longer missing 4th movement of everyone's personal symphony and the collective symphony of a Mature Humanity.

Levels and Types of an Assemblage

Below are the definitions of five levels or types of an *Assemblage*.

1. Level 1 – **Culled** Assemblage

   A **Culled Assemblage** is a well-ordered selection of excellent excerpts – notable for their compressed and felicitous expression of insight, wisdom, and knowledge – from a single field of learning or expertise. A Culled Assemblage is not a mere listing or collection of selections, because a mere listing or collection includes poor and mediocre selections as well as excellent ones. Moreover, a mere collection is not informed by any artistic principle of organization.

2. Level 2 – **Re-Cast** Assemblage

   A **Re-Cast Assemblage** is a novel and creative arrangement of a previously Culled Assemblage (possibly with expansion with a limited amount of new material from new sources), giving new meaning and resonance to the Assemblage by virtue of the fresh placement of the parts and arrangement of the whole.

3. Level 3 – **Novel and Original** Assemblage

   A **Novel and Original Assemblage** consists of the sizable addition of important novel, original, enriching, augmenting, amplifying, and valuable material to a previous Assemblage. The additions may be created by the Assembler alone, or selected from unrecognized or under-appreciated sources or distant cultures.

4. Level 4 - **Symphonic** Assemblage

   The Symphonic Assemblage involves the interweaving of several lesser Assemblages into a unified whole with one central guiding theme, a guiding metaphor, and recurring image reflective of the guiding metaphor, along with the other seven characteristic features of the Symphonic Assemblage presented previously.

5. Level 5 - **Grand Symphonic** Assemblage

   The Grand Symphonic Assemblage, only at a conceptual stage now, would be an Assemblage of several Symphonic Assemblages. Cross-disciplinary, cross-cultural, across both genre and gender, it would be vast in scope, as high as a mountain in the range of its material, and insightful as an imaginative third eye could be in its comprehensive overview of the sweep and bearing of human history.

Lesser Assemblages Within this Symphonic Assemblage

What we conceptualize as a *Symphonic Assemblage*, this *oeuvre* or *magnum opus* in two volumes, involves the interweaving of several lesser assemblages as listed below:

1. Assemblage of the Five Forms of thinking
2. Assemblage of Sentence Forms as models for new students and others
3. A systematic Assemblage of newly invented, memorable names for Sentence Forms
4. Assemblage of Student Paragraphs as models for new students and others
5. Assemblage of Student Essays as models for new students and others
6. Assemblage of Student Biographies as cross-cultural peer experiences for new students and others
7. Assemblage of Quotations and shorter Excerpts from famous as well as unrecognized writers
8. Assemblage of Essays and Passages by professional writers
9. Assemblage of Poems by famous as well as unrecognized writers
10. Assemblage of Figures of speech (metaphor, analogy, irony) as models for new students
11. Assemblage of scholarly Sources (Research Round-up) in the form of an annotated, organized, and prioritized bibliography
12. Assemblage of visually appealing summary and explanatory charts
13. Assemblage of black and white photos of Forms of Nature and the human world

A Final Look at Symphonic Assemblage

The **Symphonic Assemblage** highlights the Vision, Intuition, and Thoughtfulness required to compose many diverse pieces and parts of different Disciplines of Learning, Cultures, Stages of Life Experience, Genders, Genres, and Nationalities into a Unified Whole by achieving a Centered Inwardness and Balance through the deep appreciation of Silence and Integral Reflection.

We come full circle and conclude this section which announces **The Symphonic Assemblage** as the Invention of a new Form or Genre of Literature, by citing six additional selections. The first selection is by the renowned German philosopher, Ernst Cassirer, who pioneered the study of Symbolic Forms in four groundbreaking volumes. In the selection below, Cassirer brilliantly describes the inseparable and mutually illuminating roles played by the constituent Parts and the Organic Whole which animates and integrates the Parts. The selection is a perfect description of the Symphonic Assemblage prior to our Invention of it.

> "Every part of a whole is the whole itself; every specimen is equivalent to the entire species. The part does not merely represent the whole, or the specimen its class; they are identical with the totality to which they belong; not merely as mediating aids to reflective thought, but **as genuine presences which actually contain the power, significance and efficacy of the whole**. Here one is reminded forcefully of the principle which might be called the basic principle of verbal as well as mythic "metaphor" – the principle of *pars pro toto*. It is a familiar fact that all mythic thinking is governed and permeated by this principle. **Whoever has brought any part of a whole into his power has thereby acquired power, in the magical sense, over**

the whole itself. What significance the part in question may have in the structure and coherence of the whole, what function it fulfills, is relatively unimportant – **the mere fact that it is or has been a part, that it has been connected with the whole, no matter how casually, is enough to lend it the full significance and power of that greater unity**."
    Ernst Cassirer, German Jewish philosopher

The second selection from *The Rainbow and the Worm* – a book about physics, bio-energetics, and Nature – by Mae-Wan Ho echoes Cassirer about the mutual and reciprocal influence of the Whole and its Parts in the compositions of Nature and Art.

> "A coherent state thus maximizes *both* global cohesion and also local freedom. Nature presents us a deep riddle that compels us to accommodate seemingly polar opposites. What she is telling us is that coherence does not mean uniformity: where everybody must be doing the same thing all the time. You can begin to understand it by thinking of an orchestra, or a grand ballet, or better yet a large jazz band, where everyone is doing his or her own thing, as yet keeping perfectly in tune or in step with the whole. But even that is a paltry representation.
>
>   Imagine an immensely huge superorchestra playing with instruments spanning an incredible spectrum of sizes from a piccolo of 10^{-9} metre up to a bassoon or a bass viol of 1 metre or more, and a musical range of *seventy-two octaves*. The amazing thing about this superorchestra is that **it never ceases to play out our individual songlines, with a certain recurring rhythm and beat, but in endless variations that never repeat exactly. Always, there is something new, something made up as it goes along.** It can change key, change tempo, change tune perfectly, as it feels like it, or as the situation demands, spontaneously and without

hesitation. Furthermore, each and every player, however small, can enjoy maximum freedom of expression, improvising from moment to moment, while maintaining in step and in tune with the whole."
Dr. Mae-Wan Ho, British geneticist

The third selection is a poem at the personal level describing the balance and calm evoked by the silence permeating and enveloping a natural Korean scene and landscape – that "Something in Between" that the poem tries to capture.

SOMETHING IN BETWEEN

Something In Between
The Presence of Extremes

Something neither Here nor There
Resting in the Silent Air

Something about the Full Moon
Over Tiled Korean Roofs

Stirs the Heart beyond Measure
Calms the Will Forever
    Richard Dowling

The fourth selection explores "Into the Between" at a more universal, powerful, and cosmic level through the life story and personal experience of an American Hindu woman.

INTO THE BETWEEN

If there is any wisdom running through my life now, in my walking on this earth, it came from listening in the Great Silence to the stones, trees, space, the wild animals, to the pulse of all life as my own heartbeat.

VIJALI HAMILTON, *In the Fields of Life 21*

"Listening in the Great Silence, as Vijali calls it, was a five-year period from 1982 to 1987 when she lived in virtual solitude on Boney Mountain, the highest ridge of the Santa Monica range running east from the Pacific Ocean. She had come there in something close to desperation, after an intense period of spiritual awakening and the emergence of the powerful *kundalini* energies that Indian mystics have described in detail.

From the time she was fourteen until she turned twenty-five, Vijali had lived in a Hindu convent in southern California. She was the youngest Vedanta nun in North America, and at the time she entered, it was the answer to her prayers for a place of peace and spiritual practice. But by the time she left, she was eager to be in the world. "I'm not allowed to make any mistakes here," she complained to her teacher, Swami Prabhavananda, "and I'm not growing." She wanted to go to college and study art. She headed for Montreal, where her talents won her full scholarships.

Three years later she returned to California, married, and became a stepmother and a full-time artist. And then, when she was in the midst of hosting art shows and poetry readings and keeping up with the life of a very popular artist, everything changed: "One quiet evening while I was visiting with friends and listening to music, a slow heat began rising from my heart. It burned its way up through my spine and on out of the top of my head, melting everything into a great ocean of light."

After that, change swept through Vijali's life. She could see that "there were no boundaries or borders. It was as if my mind had once long ago made up a story about separate objects with boundaries but the story wasn't true. **The true story is that there is a luminous, spacious energy that flows through everything all the time. It's within matter, within things as well as within space, and you can tune in to it at any time,** just like changing the frequency on the radio. **There is no distance between this essence and ourselves. It is not otherworldly. It is right here, closer than our own flesh."**

 It was utterly bewildering to have energy and consuming light blasting through her body at any time of the day or night. Although the traditional Indian teachings say that this energy release is aroused gradually through yoga or other spiritual practices, for Vijali it wasn't gradual at all. At last, in an effort to integrate and stabilize what she was experiencing and discovering, she sought refuge on Boney Mountain.

It was a time of deep learning, and her life took on a new simplicity. Synchronizing her days to the rhythms of the sunrise and sunset, she greeted the sun every morning from a high plateau near her trailer and returned every evening to bid it farewell. As every act became a ritual, hauling water and bathing outside, gathering wild greens for salad and sage for tea, she told us, **she learned that "a sacred space may be *any* place, not just the ones designated by our ancestors, not just some special power spot. We can create sacred spaces** as I did on the mountain, by entering into the spirit of a place through simple actions performed in a reverent way.

Her years on Boney Mountain were a period of almost continual bliss.

'Sometimes I would sit in the dark for hours and hours,' she said, 'and I feel a kind of current from my heart that goes out into the universe and then it pauses and comes back into me, and goes out again. There are streams, matrices, lattices of light that must be some universal pattern. Sometimes you see it and sometimes you don't. But when you relax, it's there like a great connecting with everything. It feels like it has always been there.'

Paul H. Ray and Sherry Ruth Anderson, American sociologists from *The Cultural Creatives*

Finally, the last three selections hint at the possible implications of the **Symphonic Assemblage** for our perception and interpretation of the Universe as a Whole.

"The day, with the noise of this little earth, drowns the silence of all worlds."
Rabrindrinath Tagore, poet, sage, singer of India

"All life on Earth is closely related. We have a common organic chemistry and a common evolutionary heritage. As a result, our biologists are profoundly limited. They study only a single kind of biology, one lonely theme in the music of life. Is this faint and reedy tune the only voice for thousands of light-years? Or is there a kind of cosmic fugue, with themes and counterpoints, dissonances and harmonies, a billion different voices playing the life music of the Galaxy?"
Carl Sagan, American astronomer

"A team of 70 astronomers from Europe, America and Japan used the Hubble space telescope to build up a picture of dark matter in a vast region of space where some of the galaxies date back to half the age of the universe – nearly 7 billion years.

They used a phenomenon known as gravitational lensing, first predicted by Albert Einstein, to investigate an area of the sky nine times the size of a full moon. Gravitational lensing occurs when light from distant galaxies is bent by the gravitational influence of any matter that it passes on its journey through space.

The scientists were able to exploit the technique by collecting the distorted light from half a million faraway galaxies to reconstruct some of the missing mass of the universe which is otherwise invisible to conventional telescopes.

'We have, for the first time, mapped the large-scale distribution of dark matter in the universe," said Richard Massey of the California Institute of Technology in Pasadena, one of the lead scientists in the team. "Dark matter is a mysterious and invisible form of matter, about which we know very little, yet it dominates the mass of the universe.'

One of the most important discoveries to emerge from the study is that dark matter appears to form an invisible scaffold or skeleton around which the visible universe has formed.

Although cosmologists have theorized that this would be the case, **the findings are dramatic proof that their calculations are correct and that, without dark matter, the known universe that we can see would not be able to exist.**

'A filamentary web of dark matter is threaded through the entire universe, and acts as scaffolding within which the ordinary matter - including stars, galaxies and planets - can later be built,' Dr Massey said. 'The most surprising aspect of our map is how unsurprising it is. Overall, we seem to understand really well what happens during the formation of structure and the evolution of the universe,' he said."

> Steve Connor
> The Independent newspaper, UK
> ga4w

Opening – Five

> In the two senses of (17) a **Proposal** of an *Innovative, Inclusive, Vital, adequately Modeled, Universally and Practically Doable,* and *Imaginative* **System of Writing**; and (18) the Recommended **Adoption** *of a New, Embodied, Deeply Reflective, Dramatically Vocal,* and *Communally Participatory* **Method of Reading**.

"Readers without haste warned in advance that all just opinion is long in expression." Ortega y Gasset

A **Proposa**l is a initial formal statement or recommendation that a plan or course of action be adopted, in this case that a **System of Writing** be instituted as a course of instruction to teach students Writing. As a necessary preliminary, we must explain each of the six adjectives or set of adjectives) that we use to characterize and qualify **System of Writing**: namely, the words *Innovative, Inclusive, Vital, adequately Modeled, Universally and Practically Doable, and Imaginative.*

To explain the adjective *Innovative* in a telling manner, there are four relevant distinctions that highlight the major differences between the *Innovative* **System in Writing** presented in this book versus the **Traditional** way in writing. The four relevant distinctions are the following ones:

Holistic and therefore Systematic and Comprehensive	vs	<u>Atomistic and therefore narrowly and intensively</u> **Focused and Concentrated**
Integral	vs	**Separated, Fragmented, and Compartmentalized**
Person Centered	vs	**Subject Centered**
Process Oriented	vs	**Product Focused**

Immediately, you will notice we have 4 instances of **The Two Twist**.

If we examine the first Two Twist, *Holistic* vs. **Atomistic**, it will provide the key not only for understanding the remaining three **Two Twists applicable here**, but also reveal the **Determining Characteristic of the Two Twist as a Form of Thinking.**

Let us proceed then to explain *Holistic* vs. **Atomistic**. To say that something is Holistic is to say that it composes a Whole which is more than the sum of its parts. It is also to say that as a Whole it belongs to an **Implicate Order of Reality.** This is a phrase coined by the contemporary physicist and philosopher David Bohm) where wholes unfold as **processes from within outwards** rather than coming into existence as simple aggregates or external collections of parts and pieces joined by mechanical association from the outside; thus, all the several parts of a whole are **implicated and intimately, inextricably involved with one another and ever influencing one another**.

Wholes are thus *unified processes* which unfold or develop over time from a *beginning seed of spirit*, through middle branches of thought, to a <u>final end fruit of matter</u>, all the while informed, animated, and *impelled by a inner spirit or principle of life that emerges gradually from within* <u>outwards by interaction with surrounding circumstances</u>. A striking and memorable instance of this principle for human beings was formulated by the great Spanish philosopher Ortega y Gasset with his coinage of the motto concerning personal life and destiny : **"I am I and my**

circumstance". Indeed, that phrase **"I am I and my circumstance"** was the vital core and hallmark signature of Ortega Gasset as a human being and as a philosopher. The contemporary world has yet to adequately appreciate, assimilate, and properly assess and esteem the lasting contributions of Ortega whose name will appear often in this book in key contexts and situations.

Be it noted that every *whole* **as an organic** *unity* **constitutes a system** of inseparable, necessary, and interrelated **parts** and pieces which mutually influence and require one another to function properly. **As Ortega notes, "Philosophical thinking is a system and in a system every concept includes all the others."** In fact, no single or **individual part** can be comprehended and properly **understood** in separation without reference to its **function** and interaction with all the other **parts** and the *whole*. All the **parts** and the pieces of the **system** are *integral* and *interdependent with one another* and not merely externally joined and associated by physical causation and linkage.

This brings us to the **Defining or Determining Chief Characteristic of The Two Twist**. The physicist and philosopher Michael Polanyi – in his book Personal Knowledge and other texts – has demonstrated that human beings perceive **Reality in two Modes,** as *Wholes* or **as Parts**. Of course, this corresponds exactly with contemporary research on the **Left Brain** which perceives **individual parts sequentially** while the *Right Brain* perceives the **Parts** of *Wholes simultaneously together as One*. So, Polanyi and countless others have demonstrated that some persons can recognize a human face as a whole without being able to specify the individual features or parts that enabled them to make the identification. On the other hand, other persons can identify individual features or parts of something without being able to identify it as a whole.

Indeed, the Swiss Psychologist C.G.Jung divided people into two types – *the intuitive type* and the sensation type. *Intuitive types of people* talk more about and direct their attention to ideas and possibilities, in other words to the always emerging *Whole of Reality* rather than on presently sensed and observed life. Sensation types, on the other hand, talk more about what they hear, see, touch, and taste with their senses and less about intangible ideas and possibilities likely to emerge in the future.

The **Two Twist** is rooted and based in these **Two Modes of Perception of the Human Being.** The **Defining and Determining Characteristic of The Two Twist** resides precisely then in the **Two Modes of Perception of the Human Being.**

Now the Traditional way of writing perceives reality with the Left Brain – with the **Parts or Partial Mode of Perception** in the manner of sensation types – and accordingly perceives writing as atomistic, and therefore intensely focused and concentrated, fragmented, subject centered, and as a product. Using the logical left brain, it examines **Writing** analytically as a subject compartmentalized and strongly focused on **Thinking** but not particularly integral with **Listening**, **Speaking**, and **Reading**. Students are taught by an analytical and exhaustive dissection of usage, grammar, and mechanics. Writing is taught as a discipline of theoretical understanding and imitation of finished products of composition without regard for the creative invention or process of production of the writer. The subject and the language of writing are emphasized with an analytical method and a rational, theoretical stance toward reality, largely to the exclusion and neglect of the writer or author as a person with a heart, soul, and individual tone and style of expression as well as with little attention to the reader, audience, or cultural sensibility that eventually read the writing.

Because the *Innovative* **System of Writing of this book is** *Holistic*, it displays global interests and concerns and reaches across the too tightly defined boundaries of class, race, gender, nationality, and disciplines of learning. It is receptively open to, receives, and accepts wisdom wherever it finds it, and it incorporates what it receives into a vision of emerging possibilities and expanding horizons – *the emerging Whole of the Future*. The Holistic perspective is as immense and rich as the universe and the cultural world at large. It does not confine itself to the artificially determined and imposed conventions, constraints, and restrictions of the academic stance and the classroom sense of space and stricture.

Because the *Innovative* **System of Writing of this book** is *Systematic* and *Comprehensive*, it identifies clearly the fundamental parts or stages of instruction for writing – namely, **The Mother Tongue, The Father Tongue,** and **The Imaginative Tongue** – and designs a content of instruction and a pedagogy appropriate for each stage, both conceived separately and together.

Because the *Innovative* **System of Writing of this book** is not only *Holistic, Systematic,* and *Comprehensive,* but also *Integral*, it does not conceive or present Writing as an entirely self-contained, autonomous subject that can possibly be adequately understood, learned, or taught without repeated reference to **Writing's integral relation** to **Listening, Speaking,** and **Reading**, not to mention **Thinking. The Five Skills are as integral and essential to one another as the five fingers of the Hand which perfectly symbolize them**. If the Writer **does not Listen** and remain **receptively open** to the **creative unconscious** of himself or herself and universal humanity, they **will create or invent nothing original, authentic, or deeply felt**; moreover, whatever they conceive **will not be figuratively or inspirationally rendered**. If the Writer fails to attend to the **Living Voice and vibrant rhythms of their own speech and that of their mother culture**, they will be forever condemned to sterile prose and a dull, boring, and lifeless style devoid of character or individuality. If the Writer **fails to think deeply and clearly**, he or she will have **little of substance to say and precious little form, structure, or grasp of strategy** to properly and cogently convey what they think. If the Writer **fails to read widely, deeply, and with careful attention and scrutiny**, they will never fully develop the **professional craft and integral imagination** to excel at writing.

Because the *Innovative* **System of Writing of this book** is *Person Centered* and not **Subject Centered** and also *Process*

Oriented and not **Product Focused**, the pedagogy employed in teaching Writing is "From the Bottom up" more than "From the Top Down" and more "From the Inside Out" than "From the Outside In". Let us place these four mottos in a visual graphic chart below and then explain their implications and consequences for writing instruction:

	From the Top Down	
From the Outside In		*From the Inside Out*
	From the Bottom Up	

These four mottos correspond **to the Four Great Directions of Life and the Earth** which is its physical embodiment and environment. Obviously, all four are necessary and indispensable to Life; they constitute a System of independent, yet integrally interdependent, Parts which comprise a Whole. Unless the function and importance of all Four Parts are **Recognized** and **Balanced** with each other and **with the Whole**, lack of harmony, distortion, and dysfunction will ensue with detrimental effects and consequences.

With the four mottos, we have a **stable comprehensive Model of the Four Principal Mottos of a Systematic Pedagogy**. However, this *Model needs to be Dynamic to be Adequate*, because it needs to account not only for how the subject is taught and the character of the final product that is desired, but also for the persons who are instructed and the process by which they grow and develop. To meet these requirements, we need to know (1) the hierarchal priority and value of the Four Mottos and (2) the chronological order and necessity of Implementation of each of the Mottos.

"From the Inside Out" has hierarchal priority and value over the other three mottos and constitutes the informing animating principle and motto which guides and integrates the system of pedagogy as a whole. However, as the highest goal and aim of instruction, it is **the last to be fully achieved in chronological order and the last to be fully implemented**. It symbolizes and *represents intuitively the Whole* – the Person Centered, integrally realized, actual fulfillment of the seed potentials originally deposited and enfolded in the seminal, beginning process.

By analogy with the Human person and his or her development in the process of growth, the Adult appears at the end of the Process of Growth as the Fulfillment of the Child. **The fully realized Adult has hierarchical priority and value over the Child, but the Child comes before the Adult in the chronological order of achievement**. The Motto which applies to the Child, therefore, is "From the Outside In" which is the direct opposite for the motto of the Adult "From the Inside Out". *"From the Inside Out" is a spiritual motto*; "From the Outside In'" is a physical motto; they are opposed to one another **as the sensory and** *intuitive* **modes of perception are opposed to another,** as the many parts of physical life are opposed to the integral fulfillment of unified spiritual realization and attunement.

The Child must first be developed physically, then emotionally, then intellectually, and finally spiritually in the chronological order of achievement and attainment. However, *the spiritual is superior to the intellectual, the intellectual is superior to the emotional, and the emotional is superior to the physical in terms of hierarchical priority and value*. **Thus, the hierarchical priority and value is the direct reverse of the chronological order and necessity of implementation.**

We make these distinctions for the sake of understanding and comprehension to discern and characterize the four component mottos and aspects of human nature and reality with which we must deal; **however, in life, in reality, in the happening of personal destiny and human history**, *these component parts are all there from the very beginning and at all times thereafter*, not neatly, logically, theoretically, and sequentially divided in left brain fashion, but rather constantly occurring simultaneously together, integrally influencing and responding to one another – unfortunately, too often and tragically conflicting and competing with one another, but at other times working in tandem, harmoniously and cooperatively, with the complementary and synergistic rhythm, power, and diverse richness and fullness of a symphony.

If *"From the Inside Out"* is the *spiritual one whole* and "From the Outside In" is the physical many pieces, then **"From the Top Down" and "From the Bottom Up" constitute the few mental or human parts in this Drama,** namely **the intellectual and emotional functions or aspects of life.** If we express these distinctions in **The Three Thread**, we get the visual configuration below:

one	**few**	many
spiritual	**intellectual or emotional**	physical
whole	**parts**	pieces
"From the Inside Out"	**"From the Top Down" and "From the Bottom Up"**	"From the Outside In"

If we express the same distinctions with **The Four Foundation** or **Four Form of Thinking**, we obtain the visual graphic chart below as an addition to the previous earlier graphic of the four mottos:

	Intellectual	
Physical		*Spiritual*
many pieces	**few parts**	*one whole*
	Emotional	

We now come to the necessity and pivotal importance for all we are saying here of explaining why the adjective *Inclusive* **sets our System of Writing entirely apart not only from the traditional way of writing but also from all previous and current innovations in teaching writing.**

Uniquely and Precisely because our *Innovative* **System of Writing** is *Holistic and therefore Systematic and Comprehensive, Integral, Person Centered, and Process Oriented,* it is *Inclusive,* unlike all previous innovations, and therefore does not reject, nullify, disparage, ignore, or fail to include either the traditional way of writing or recent innovations **into its own System of Writing**. Rather, **it incorporates and includes the best aspects and achievements of traditional and recent innovations, but integrates them with its own insight into and understanding of how they all work best together.** It is able to do this because its *Holistic* and *Person Centered Approach* to *Life Experience,* **Reflection**, and Action (note another **Three Thread**) has enabled it to conceive and articulate what the traditional and recent innovations never attained: namely, four necessary and indispensable comprehensive theories accessed through the **Four Foundation** or **Four Form of Thinking** (1) an adequate and comprehensive pedagogy of instruction; (2) an adequate and comprehensive theory of human nature; (3) an adequate and comprehensive theory of Composition or Way to Teach Writing;

and (4) an adequate and comprehensive theory of human history, development, and consciousness.

However, before we proceed to explain these four adequate and comprehensive theories essential to our *Inclusive* System **in Writing,** we need to explain why the Traditional way of writing and all recent innovations failed to be *Inclusive* and failed to develop these four requisite theories.

The short answer to this question is that the Modern World, and the Models of Education of the Modern World, had an ingrained preference, even prejudice, for Individuality rather than Unity and a corresponding tendency to disparage Philosophy whose principal proper office and function is to relate to Life holistically – to be *Inclusively just in its perspective* – and to conceive comprehensive and systematic conceptions of Knowledge.

The Modern World represented a decisive Break and Departure from the Ancient World – in fact, the decisive Break and Departure of the Youth of Humanity from the Childhood of Humanity. Young people don't look back, especially revolutionary young people, and they conceive life as a progressive linear improvement upon the past. They love new things and ideas and formulate their views of the world and their actions in the world as a competitive contest for how best to break away from the past and leave it behind. People are encouraged and incessantly exhorted and rewarded for being individual and unique, for what sets them apart and not for what they have in common with others.

And Modern Universities are structured to separate and distinctively develop independent, autonomous individual disciplines and bodies of knowledge with their own respective perspectives and methods of learning and instruction. All of these Universities have an ingrained preference, and prejudice, in favor of purely **Rational** and theoretical knowledge based on **Empirical** verification, so they deal superbly with the **Rational** and **Sensory Functions of the Human Being**, but they virtually ignore the **emotional, cultural and social Function and dimensions of**

human life as well as **the spiritual and volitional or Intuitive Function or dimension of human life**.

Like all intense, preoccupied, and rather frantically busy young people, the Modern World – and the Universities which reflect and embody the perspective, preferences, and blind spots of the Modern World – lives overwhelmingly in the present, disdains the past, and tends to trust the future will take of itself. What matters in the here and now is the bottom line – to move ahead and get ahead, making as much money as possible and utilizing, managing, and exploiting every resource and avenue to succeed as an individual in a contest where strength, power, and speed matter preeminently and emphatically – not insight, compassion, a social conscience, a sense of imagination and beauty, or a concern for unborn generations yet to inhabit our common, and rather increasingly fragile, planet.

The young demand freedom, and do indeed need freedom and room to grow and express themselves, but they are not equally enamored of responsibility and accountability for the eventual medium or long term consequences of their favorite and intense pastimes, preoccupations, and calculated compromises in pursuit of achievement, success, ambition, and the glory of pride, power, and profit. They take care of themselves and their own, but they don't lose too much sleep or concern over anyone not belonging to their special tribe or group. "Youth," as Ortega, once memorably noted, "is the formidably egoistical stage of life," for both much good and much ill, we might add.

Professors in modern universities, therefore, like everyone else in the Modern World, seek to distinguish themselves by conceiving an idea or theory that sets them apart as an Innovator or Inventor, as a sterling Individual, who demonstrates the useless inadequacy of the Past in favor of a new way to understand or do things. **The Critical Function is highly esteemed in the Modern, and perhaps even more the Contemporary and Postmodern, University**. Your job is not to say what is right or good about the world, not to praise or commend it, because that might sound like being, God forbid, too moral or religious, or what is equally bad, artistically motivated and conscious, and so not susceptible to rational or empirical verification and thus suspect.

Praise is not the order of the day or the game in play; no, criticism and competition is the order of the day and the game in play – namely, the approved conventional order and the rules for how one advances and gets promotions and a bigger salary. So professors and innovators are not inclined to praise or value any past idea or way of doing something, especially when they must demonstrate its inadequacy so their own improved idea or way of doing something will be adopted to replace it. Modern education is thus often a succession of fashionable ideas and inventions of real but only partial value that completely condemn and replace earlier ideas or ways of doing something, though the earlier idea or way also had its own definite but only partial value, or otherwise it would not have lasted as long as it did.

Ideas and Innovations, in other words, are all conceived and promoted **as preclusive or exclusive of earlier ideas and practices**. Innovators, and their followers, get all excited about one prevailing fashion or practice after another, because everyone lacks altogether sufficiently comprehensive theories (1) of educational pedagogy, (2) of human nature, (3) of the actual subjects in question, or (4) of how humanity and civilization have developed as a whole that would help them to see both the merits and limitations of whatever new innovation is trumpeted as the answer to the latest crisis.

The Modern World has been and remains essentially experimental, fragmentary and disjointed, careening from one enthusiasm to another with all the narrow experience and unseasoned judgment of a young person who will try anything but lacks the mature experience and comprehensive knowledge, above all wisdom, to decide correctly – with adequate integral vision and foresight – what to do in any particular case.

And so the long answer for why the traditional ways and recent innovations of educators **never became inclusive or developed the four requisite theories is because it was counter-intuitive to their entire cultural training and support system, not to**

mention the monetary incentives and rewards for their work. Moreover, the sheer difficulty of the task, the sheer volume and conflicting claims of the respective traditional ways and recent innovations as well as the breadth and depth of the scholarship required in many fields – especially in the despised field, mode, and manner of ancient philosophy and also in the equally suspect field of contemporary spiritual exploration – made it almost prohibitive that anyone could ever or easily become *Inclusive and therefore master the four requisite theories.*

However, we claim to have done so here and will proceed to lay out the four requisite theories in question. In due time we will also note why we were able to accomplish this difficult task so that our claim is more believable and understandable and thus lead to the more ready acceptance and application of the book's innovations.

It is also essential to point out, if there is a formidable and difficult task involved in conceiving these theories, there is perhaps an even more formidable and difficult task involved in persuading people to exert the necessary care and reflection they must display to master the innovative theories and practices presented here as well as the monumental patience they must show to wait long enough for us to demonstrate how these theories prove themselves in practice.

In short, we must present the theory first, before we can demonstrate how adequate, comprehensive, and effective it is in practice. So, we request a certain forbearance and patience on the part of the reader as we proceed now to lay out the four requisite theories that are necessary and indispensable at this point.

The Four Requisite Theories

The salient characteristic of all Four Requisite Theories, as already noted, is that they are *inclusive*: although they introduce and add innovative ideas and practices for consideration, they do not reject or exclude the value of previously stressed components of earlier theories. The Four Requisite Theories are **all inherently cooperative in orientation and outlook; they are not competitive**. They are **affirming and appreciative of all cultures and perspectives rather than unduly trumpeting one cultural perspective as superior to others**. They are **socially engaged as well as individually focused**, and they are **spiritually animated and artistically inspired as well as rigorously rational and empirically measured.**

It is **counter-intuitive to the Approach here**, which conceives and espouses these Four Requisite Theories, **to excessively criticize or radically condemn any aspect or development of human culture or history**. Our Approach is that anyone, or anything, must first be dispassionately witnessed and accepted before being judged, must first be appreciated and praised for whatever value or goodness it possesses before being analytically dissected and criticized. *The overriding imperative and guidance followed as a universal principle is, before all else, to seek and find whatever is good or valuable in a person or idea before proceeding to limit, qualify, criticize, or evaluate the person or idea in question.*

The restraint and removal of egotism and ethno-centrism in the formation of judgment is central to this Approach. Empathy with and sympathetic understanding of alternative perspectives and prescriptions is always an initial requirement and preliminary necessity before arriving at any just or balanced judgment or assessment.

Before all else, such an Approach is rooted in a reverence for all human beings and respect for their experience – culturally, historically, and as immediately situated in present surrounding circumstances.

Human experience always has its reason for existing and being, so any inclusive, comprehensive theory must account for, include, and incorporate all human experience – from the past till now and even anticipate the Future, which lies already waiting enfolded within the past and present so as to emerge and manifest itself in seed form. In short, all inclusive, comprehensive theories are **cumulative: they gather up and carry forward the best of all that has been achieved in the past as an inherent necessity of the constitutive continuity of all human life**. Thereby, they validate and justify whatever of the past deserves to be perpetuated, and they estimate the relative, but no longer absolute or exclusive worth, of all earlier ideas, practices, and material inventions and endowments.

To speak of the **inherent necessity of the constitutive continuity of all human life** is to say that human beings cannot leave their pasts behind them by simply forgetting about them, **because every major stage of human life and civilization creates and leaves as a legacy for the future certain key gifts, capacities, and achievements which serve as ongoing necessary foundations for all later achievements**. *The full understanding of this essential truth, however, is only a relatively recent realization of contemporary seminal thinkers and even they have not understood the cause of this circumstance.*

And here is why we come once again to why figurative language is preferable to literal language, though both are necessary, and to why storytelling remains so much more central for all human life than the relating of facts, though again both are necessary in the end. *Figurative language, storytelling, myth, metaphor, analogy, and rhythmic speech and repetition speak to the soul of experience and the center of self awareness; they go <u>from the inside out</u>, from the center of feeling and out of concern with what needs urgently to be done to serve, resurrect, and revitalize life in the present.*

On the contrary, literal language, deliberative thought, discursive logic, and empirical citation and factual verification go <u>from the outside in</u>; they demonstrate the general and public truth of something, but they do not address the need to personally appropriate and assume responsibility for what, when, and how to do something about what is discussed. **The sheer impersonality and abstract voice of the public address fails to capture, vivify, and hold the attention of the reader and thereby fails to enlarge the world of concern and comprehensive imagination of the one addressed**. The consequence too often is that many individuals, and entire professions and domains of culture, fall asleep at the helm of their lives and thereby abrogate their destinies as persons. Entire generations vacate their roles in history, being only passive spectators rather than formative participants and players in their moment and place in history. History is perceived and witnessed as something that is inflicted on human beings rather than as something persons create and bear responsibility for enacting.

We must now tell you a story for you to get inside what our discursive prose is trying rationally to convey in its long, laborious, sequential, often torturous language. What the dickens are we talking about here, what are we getting at?

Let us go to the story to tell you at last. Here is the story or anecdote about Mark Twain.

Twain reportedly made the following remarks: "When I was sixteen, I thought my father was a damn fool. When I was nineteen, I was amazed at how much he had learned in three years."

At sixteen, in the adolescence of early youth, Twain set himself in conscious opposition and competition against his father. He announced that his father was a fool; and thus by implication, he asserted he himself was no fool and thereby completely unlike his father.

This first judgment by Twain excluded his father from being anything like himself. However, within only three years, he acknowledges – with wry self-deprecating humor rather than direct admission of the error of his own earlier harsh judgment of his father – that he was surprised his father had learned so much in just three years.

This last comment of course is completely and humorously ironic: it is not the father who has learned so much in three years, but Twain's growth in maturity and perspective that has enabled him to perceive that he and his father are very much alike after all. Yes, he has realized that he is an individual and not like his father in one sense, but in another sense, he is still the child of his father, and he can now see and appreciate how his father is included in his own being.

Twain has gone from being a young, independent individual to being a mature, interdependent person. He has gone from perceiving himself and the world from an isolated, fragmented, and egotistical perspective to an awareness of himself and his relation to others in an appreciative and integral manner and mode of being. He is more disposed to laugh gently and obliquely at himself than to unduly blame or criticize others, especially when he no longer seems all that special and different from others. After all, in the end, we are all human no matter how we try to ignore or disguise that common bond. The older and wiser we are, the more we understand and the less we condemn. Differences remain, but they are less obsessive and deadly, more amenable to mutual tolerance and forbearance than occasions for intense conflict and rash, unforgiving violence. The way to peace opens, and perhaps even the healing touch of mutual recognition and love.

We move forward by accepting, including, and incorporating the redeemable past, and not by the denial of human experience and the rejection of others out of preference for overly rigid formulas and definitions of life.

Now this story of Mark Twain has a still larger and more comprehensive meaning than is apparent at first sight on the surface. **Yes, it is literally a story about Mark Twain,** *but figuratively it is a symbol, analogue, or analogy of the collective history of human civilization as a whole.* Indeed, *the story itself is a Hologram or representative image or replica of human history just as every individual is a hologram or representative image of humanity as a whole, as we know from the Hologram theory* *enunciated by the physicist David Bohm and the integral philosophy and psychology of Ken Wilbur.*

Specifically, just as Twain passed from his youth to his maturity as an individual, humanity as a whole is now passing from its collective Youth to its Maturity. And just as Twain experienced, expressed, and understood himself, others, and the world from a egotistical, fragmented, and compartmentalized perspective in his youth, so humanity in the Youth of its History – in the Modern World and in Modern Universities – has experienced, expressed, and understood itself, others, and the world from the egotistical, fragmented, and compartmentalized perspective of a young person. However, as and when humanity develops and graduates into its Maturity, it will realize a global, integral, and balanced perspective that will include and incorporate the best of earlier perspectives, ideas, and practices.

The key word is **balanced**. The Four Requisite Theories **achieve and maintain Balance between and among their respective constitutive components as well as between and among themselves**. They mutually inform, illumine, and reinforce one another. Let us examine the Four Requisite Theories Holistically, as they actually interact, support, complement, reinforce, and require one another to function – independently yet also interdependently – to achieve in the end an Adequate, Comprehensive, and Balanced Understanding of Education, Learning, and Teaching in General and The Proposal For an Innovative Writing Program in Particular.

We begin by constructing a **Pedagogy of Instruction** which requires understanding the Guiding Model, Paradigm, and Purpose of Education as well as a theory of both learning and teaching. Indeed, let us begin by listing briefly what such a Pedagogy requires to be complete:

1. The Guiding Model, Paradigm, and Purpose of Education;

2. The Historical basis and root of the Guiding Model, Paradigm, and Purpose of Education;

3. The Four Mottos of Instruction;

4. A Theory of Learning;

5. Prevailing View of Human Nature;

6. A Theory of Teaching;

7. Four Contemporary Breakthrough Disciplines of Learning;

8. Four Theories of Composition;

9. The Goals of Instruction;

10. The Methods of Instruction;

11. The Materials of Instruction;

12. The Questions of Instruction;

13. The Intelligences of Instruction;

14. The Modalities of Perception and Instruction;

15. The Conception of the Subjects of Instruction;

16. The Stages of Instruction;

17. The Course of Instruction;

18. The Understanding of History

If you examine the 18 items above, **you will see the Four Requisite Theories both directly stated and implied**. In general, we will now examine each of the 18 items in turn, in roughly sequential fashion, but with some overlap and jumping back and forth between the individual items, to present a **Balanced Pedagogy In General** and *more particularly for the Innovative Writing Program we propose.*

As Starting Points and Anchors for our Presentation of a Balanced Pedagogy, we commence by invoking again and reminding you of the two earlier Four Forms of Thinking which we introduced and which we will now further develop and apply. The

First Four Form of Thinking concerned the four aspects of all Writing Situations: namely, the Writer, the Subject, the Audience, and Language. The Second Four Form of Thinking involved the Four Mottos of Instruction: namely, From the Inside Out, the Top Down, the Bottom Up, and the Outside In. A visual graph of the Two Four Forms of Thinking together would look as below:

	The Subject **From the Top Down**	
The Language From the Outside In		*The Writer* *From the Inside Out*
	The Audience **From the Bottom Up**	

What do these two Four Forms of Thinking suggest, imply, or outright tell us about the Guiding Model, Paradigm, and Purpose of Education, respectively, in the Modern Period and in Recent Contemporary Times?

For starters, the Model, Paradigm, and Purpose of Education in Modern Times, more specifically from the late 19th century until the 1960s and 1970s, was **objective and impersonal**, From the Outside in and From the Top Down, driven by the immediate social needs and prerogatives of society, while the Model, Paradigm, and Purpose of Education in the recent Contemporary World, specifically from the 1960s until now, has been *more subjective and personal*, From the Inside Out and From the Bottom Up, *motivated by humanistic respect for persons in their uniqueness and a concern for integral and holistic approaches to life and learning.* In other words, the **Model of the Modern Period represented the Right Hand or Left Brained Rational and**

Logical Approach; the *Model of the Contemporary Period represented the Left Hand or Right Brained Intuitive and Imaginative Approach.* ***This book advocates including, integrating, and harmoniously blending or marrying the Two Approaches into a Holistic, Innovative, and fully mature, comprehensive Approach or Model.***

The Guiding Model, Paradigm, and Purpose of Education in the Modern Period was based on and driven by the overwhelming experience, formal model and image, as well as gigantic scale and organizational genius of the Industrial Revolution. The mental view and understanding of the world that underlay this model was grounded in the almost exclusively rational and empirical conception of life and the universe first expressed in the scientific formulation of Newton that the universe was composed of atomistic, self-enclosed, individual units of matter controlled by the unvarying laws of nature that the human mind could discover and follow, thereby controlling the course and operations of the material world, insuring steady material progress and improvement.

There was thus an inherent contradiction and inconsistency in the Modern Model of Education from the outset which we need to explain, and the outcome was that there both **an admirable** and **a deplorable aspect** to the Modern Model of Education. Ostensibly and sometimes Admirably, the Model posited, by analogy with Newton's individual units of matter in the universe, that the world was composed of isolated, self-enclosed individuals who should be instructed to become independent, autonomous, self-governing individuals – able to function as full rational and self-regulating members of civil society and government by virtue of their detached objectivity and critical reflection on the problems and ills of social, political, and economic life, gained by rational proficiency in thinking and empirical observation of facts methodically compiled and organized.

Human beings were freed **from the tribal blood ties and emotional bonds and strictures of the conformity-based customs and norms of traditional societies and social groups,**

freed in effect from thralldom to the Childhood Stage of Human Civilization and Prepared and Liberated for active involvement in the Youthful Stage of Human Civilization. And still more to the point, they were also as a more immediate and imperative necessity, *freed from Religion by Science, liberated from the excessive and mindless religious fanaticism that had devastated and almost destroyed Western Civilization in the 16th and 17th centuries*. Nobody wished to return to that lamentable state of affairs, so feeling and the heart were out or severely diminished and put in their "proper inferior places", and thinking and the head were in and on top of the prestige scale and hierarchy of values. And nobody should bother or talk about the transcendent or spiritual dimension of reality because reason and the empirical senses could not prove such a dimension existed, so it was not allowed to exist, or even mentioned in preference to the pervasive, here and now, awesome material world that was churning out in abundance unprecedented goods and making life richer and better for everyone.

And therein was the contradiction and inconsistency. Who was number One and had priority in this equation: Was it the independent, autonomous Individual or all pervading, all conquering Material Reality and Material Products? Could you process Individuals, and better yet Whole Human Beings, through a Educational Course or school in the virtually identical mode and manner that you processed or churned out Products in a Factory?

Can Individuals, and even more Whole Human Beings, be defined and reduced to Products or Commodities? Are human beings all the same, cut to one standard mold, like a Product? Can you always deal with individuals, human beings in the same way that you can with products? Are human beings predictable, and therefore conceivable or controllable by unvarying scientific laws? Don't real, actual, truly independent individuals change their minds, their behaviors, even – God forbid, their unmentionable feelings – sometimes, even frequently, occasionally dramatically, and in a transformative way, as when they pass from Infancy to Childhood, from Childhood to Youth, or from Youth to Maturity. What happens to Predictability then, and one's plans for uniformly, efficiently, and meticulously scheduling, according to a mechanical time clock, how students will exit schools like perfect products ready to market, with pre-ordained jobs waiting for them to fill to society's everlasting relief and assurance that nothing will change in any decisive or even catastrophic way?

But alas, society and the world not only do change (and all the people who compose society and inhabit the world), but they have in fact changed, drastically and in a transformative way, in our time – in the last thirty or so years. We no longer live in the Industrial Age , but in the electronic, computer, and digital Age; no longer in the primarily Product Producing Society but in the Knowledge Society; no longer in the Age of Primacy of the Nation State but the Global Society and Community; no longer in the Age of flagrant exploitation of natural environment and the earth's resources but in the Age of Global Warming and Environmental Awareness; no longer in the Age of the Dominance of Men but the Age of the Equality of Men and Women; no longer in the Age when Religion and Science are perpetually antagonistic and at war with one another but in an emerging Age of Holistic and Integral Intuition where Religion and Science harmonize and reinforce one another; no longer in the Age of National Corporations, Markets, and Financial Centers but the Age of Global and International Corporations, Markets, and Financial Centers; no longer the Age of the telephone, the radio, and the automobile but the Age of Skype, the cell phone, the computer, the DVD player, the supersonic jet, and expeditions to the Moon and beyond; no longer in the Age of Newton and a limited universe, but in the Age of Einstein, Max Planck and the Uncertainty Principle, and an infinitely expanding universe; no longer with people dying on the average in their early or late fifties, after one job or career in a lifetime, but to people living into their 80s and 90s and working four or five jobs, with more than one career in a lifetime; **in short, no longer in the Youth of Humanity but in the Maturity of Humanity.**

The powers and capacities of an individual human being are relative to the stage of their development in life. The powers and capacities of a youth vastly exceed the powers and capacities of a

Child, and by the same token the powers and capacities of a Mature Person vastly excel those of a young person. **In like manner, the powers and capacities of the Maturity of Humanity as a Whole vastly exceed the powers and capacities of the Youth of Humanity.**

Inevitably, therefore, the Guiding Model, Paradigm, and Purpose of Education in the Modern Period or Youth of Humanity, while suitable and serviceable for the Modern Period and Youth of Humanity, cannot possibly be adequate or relevant for the Dawning or Emerging Age of the Maturity of Humanity. Moreover, the Guiding Model, Paradigm, and Purpose of Education *invented and formulated in the* **Recent Contemporary Age of the past 30 or 40 years is a Transitional Model** – *reacting, sometimes properly but also too excessively, against the previous Model while heralding and anticipating the aspects, elements, ideas, and practices that must be added and made to complement and complete the previous Modern Model.*

Let us now demonstrate the fully Mature Model and how it will impact each of the 18 items that we designated above. In essence, we have already discussed at length the first three items with one exception, namely, **the Purpose of Education**. So, we will cover next **the Purpose of Education** and then proceed to examine the remaining items of a complete Pedagogy.

Generally speaking, alternately three or four purposes of Education have been advocated historically at different times and places. Thus education can be *Person Centered*, **Knowledge Centered**, or <u>Society and Practically Centered</u>. Thus, one may conceive the purpose of education – in the humanist tradition going back to the Renaissance, to the Jesuit tradition in education, and ever further to Greek and Roman ideals of education – to be the development of a whole human person, a well rounded human being in their *spiritual,* **mental,** and <u>physical</u> aspects, conversant with learning across many fields of knowledge and in command and at ease both in the wider world and with everyday reality.

Or, one may conceive the purpose of education as primarily the transmission of clearly defined, autonomous disciplines of knowledge taught by professionally trained scholars and proven teachers who systematically convey through lectures the structure and substance of their knowledge to studious and diligent students. The students master the subjects they are assigned to learn, and then employ what they learn in professional careers related to their fields of chosen expertise. **The university is the Royal Road to the prestige, status, and monetary rewards of a professional career in an ever expanding economy.**

Or again, one may see the purpose of education less for its intrinsic character, for the knowledge it conveys, than simply as the means to an end – <u>a ticket to a good job, a rite of passage or entry onto a launching pad that will enable one to pursue a life of action, achievement, and possibly immense monetary reward in the wider world and expanding economic markets</u>.

An amazing correlation as well as confirmation of these three purposes of education, both in their positive and negative effects, was discovered, documented, and clearly explained by the Yale psychologist Robert Sternberg in the late 1980s by his description of **Three different Kinds of Intelligence** typically displayed by students. Sternberg identified control groups of students with identical IQs and access to equally excellent colleges and graduate schools and tracked the progress of the students whom he divided into the three types or categories of Intelligence they displayed:
(1) those students with a *Personal Orientation or Approach to learning*, students who determined what to study, and how to understand what they studied, *motivated by the need to personally appropriate and integrate whatever they learned relevant to their personal desires, preferences, interests, and meanings in life*;
(2) **those students who were Analytical, rationally and studiously diligent in mastering systematically the disciplines of knowledge** they examined in college and graduate work; and finally (3) the <u>Society</u> or <u>Practically Oriented students</u> who excelled, not in feeling personally related to what they studied or in thinking comprehensively and systematically about what they

studied, but <u>in understanding how to apply what they learned to the real world around them in society</u>.

What is even more amazing is what he discovered where and how these three kinds of students, with their three kinds of intelligences, succeeded or failed. The second group of students, as one might expect, got the highest grades of the three types of students in college, with the first group getting the second highest grades, and the third group obtaining the lowest grades. However, when all three groups went onto graduate school, the first group excelled the most because they found it easier to be original, creative, and imaginative in conceiving and writing their Master's and Doctorate Final Papers while the other two groups came in second and third places with little difference between them. And then, when all three groups left school completely and had to find work in the actual world, it turned out that the third, or those with a Practically Oriented Intelligence, excelled with the other two groups lagging well behind.

Schools and the knowledge they convey, in other words, may be a necessary ticket to some kind of success in the wider world and economy, but they are clearly not the sole or primary indicator of success. And the definition of the Intelligence of a human being according to the sole criteria of rational, logical, and analytical objective comprehension is clearly partial (therefore only partly true), and in need of being supplemented with a more adequate understanding of the wider human intelligence of human beings.

In fact, Howard Gardner has become world famous for identifying eight separate Intelligences in human beings. Moreover, in The Closing part of this two volume survey of English, we list 30 kinds of intelligence discernible in human beings. Whether our vast expansion of the Kinds of Intelligence proves tenable and practical or not, it is obvious that our present understanding of the powers and capacities of the human being, in this case of students, has undergone a transformation, one appropriate to the stage of the Maturity of Humanity. Given what we now know, given these many different types of Intelligences, are the three Purposes for Education described above adequate and comprehensive to include and explain all we know? Clearly, they are not.

Of course, we already indicated that there was a Fourfold Model of the Purposes of Education. **So where, in this instance, is that Missing Fourth and What is it?** Perhaps, it will provide us with a truly adequate and comprehensive Model for the Purposes of Education, and we surely know by now that there is more than one Purpose, and only one exclusive Purpose, for Education.

There is always a method for finding that Missing Fourth. And we bring up the method now because it enables us to explain, at this point in our exposition, the **Defining Characteristics of both The Three Thread** and **The Four Foundation**, as we earlier explained the **Defining Characteristic of The Two Twist as residing in the Two Modes of Perception of the Human Being.**

The Defining Characteristic of the Three Thread is that it identifies and explains the Three Dimensions of Life and Reality – namely, the *Divine*, the **Human**, and the Natural dimensions *or The Spiritual, the* **Human***,* and the Material dimensions, respectively. Symbolically speaking, the *Divine* represents the *One Whole Reality*; the **Human**, the **Few Partial Aspects**; and the Natural, the Many Piecemeal Views. They stand, respectively, for the Principles of *Spiritual Identity*, **Human Similarity, Diversity, and Plurality**, and Material Difference. See the chart below for Visual Clarification of the Three Dimensions with 29 instances of **The Three Thread.** The 29 instances are listed below because we use and refer to parts or the whole of the 29 instances in the paragraphs that follow the chart. For now, glance at the chart for a first impression of the 29 instances, and then read the paragraphs that follow to see how we employ them.

Divine	**Human**	Natural
Spiritual	**Human**	Material

One	**Few**	Many
Universal	**General**	Particular
Whole	**Parts**	Pieces
Word	**Name**	Term
Sharing	**Belonging**	Participating
With	**Through**	By
Persons	**Ideas**	Things
Identity	**Similarity, Diversity**	Difference
Duality	**Plurality**	Multiplicity
Unity	**Individuality**	Conformity
Kingdom of God	**Realm of Humanity**	Domain of Nature
Perception	**Conception**	Observation
Insight	**Understanding**	Realization
Insistent	**Accommodating**	Persistent

Soul	**Mind**	Body
Attributes	**Characteristics**	Traits
Reality	**Aspects**	Views
Scheme	**Category**	Class
Notion	**Idea**	Opinion
Interpersonal	**Associational**	Collective
Personal	**Individual**	Member
For	**In**	Of
Band	**Group**	Mass
Simple	**Compound**	Complex
Self	**Other**	Thing
Awareness	**Enlightenment**	Presence
Person Centered	**Knowledge Centered**	Society or Practically Centered

We know from scientific investigation and evidence that every grain of sand in the world is different from every other grain of sand, just as we know the material fingerprints of any one person are completely different from the material fingerprints of any other person. Why then do we have one **name** only for two, or for that matter millions, of completely different grains of sand or even fingerprints? We have one name, or often as well a few – but never a real multitude – of names, because the **human mind** can perceive, **conceive**, and **comprehend** (through a **concept** with a **name**) that millions of grains of sand share certain common characteristics which makes them **Belong** to a **Group** or **Category**.

A Group or Category has two sides, or two hands if you like, corresponding to the fact that it is a product of a Human Being and a Human Mind. You see the **Human Being** and the **Human Mind** are in the **Middle** – the **Mean Point**, if you will, between the two extremes of *God* and the *Divine* or Nature and the Natural, between the *Universal Identity* we *perceive* with the *Spiritual Awareness* of *Divine Insight* or *Intuition* and the Particular Differences we find with the Material Presence of our Natural Senses. One side or Hand or Handle of any **Group** or **Category** enables us to see the **Similarity** in **Aspects** of Reality, as the Similarity between millions of grains of sand, and that side or Hand or Handle of a category draws it closer to the *Universal Identity* found in *Spiritual* or *Divine perception* and *Integral Unity*.

However, there is also the other Side or Hand or Handle of any Group or Category, the Side of Diversity that draws it closer to the Particular Differences found in the Material or Natural Observation of the Senses, and that is the Side or Hand Or Handle of Diversity that asserts that all Groups and Categories are clearly Distinct from one another, not at all alike and similar, not to be confused or joined or amalgamated with one another, but independent and autonomous, separate from one another by clear lines and boundaries of demarcation. Of course, the lines of demarcation exist in the mind only and not either in actual physical reality or spiritual perception and life where they merge and intermingle all the time.

Where the dickens is New York City in any way that anyone can infallibly define in a physical, material sense, or for that matter, where is the entire United States of America? Oh, we know they are clearly visible in **maps, but maps are visual categories; they are constructs of the human mind that conceives and defines the world into groups and categories that enlighten us about the Similarities and Diversities** of actual *People*, **Ideas,** and <u>Things</u> in the world, but boundaries are just lines drawn on paper to represent divisions of physical territory that human beings claim belong to them. They emphatically don't exist anywhere in physical fact, and Native American people never could, justifiably one might add, comprehend the nonsense and arrogance of Europeans who asserted that because they were the first ones to discover or settle territory (which they never in fact were the first to do since all kinds of people traversed the same earth for thousands of years before they ever arrived on the scene), that, therefore, they could divide it up, mark the divisions with lines on a map, and then claim it belonged to them and them only.

Native American peoples observed that they didn't see, nor had anyone else ever seen, actual lines or boundaries on the earth. On the contrary, the earth belonged to the Great Spirit and belonged to all the People as a Trust that they were obliged to reverence, preserve, and share for the common good of all.

 In stressing that the earth was shared by everyone and did not belong just to a special few, the Native Americans were reverencing the spiritual unity, integrity, and Identical Reality of the One Earth inhabited by all human beings, as taught by their native teachings or religions. They were emphasizing the Similarity Side or Handle of the Concept of Humanity, what human beings had in common, the attributes they shared, but Europeans chose the Diversity Side or Handle of the Concept of Humanity, what made groups of human beings not like each other, and therefore often prone to set themselves apart as special and entitled to their particular special territories and clear boundaries.

Of course, Native Americans also suffered from the same endemic problems as Europeans. They did not in fact even have a designation of Native Americans to indicate what they had in common, just individual names for tribes or nations with similar characteristics but diverse from other tribes or nations, with the diversity being the occasion for endless wars and conflicts, not over lines on a paper but over cultural antagonisms or emotional feuds and disagreements, hunting grounds, or water and pasturage rights.

So, the problem is universal, after all, with no segment of humanity exempt, only the degrees and intensity of blame and ignorance varying. **In all cases, it is just the human ego asserting itself disproportionately and excessively, disorienting and upsetting the harmony and equilibrium of reality and life**, by, as Robert Frost would say in a poem we will later examine at more length, **too much ice or too much fire – ice being too much mind and thinking and fire too much personal and cultural emotion and feeling.**

Thinking and Feeling are opposed to one another, like ice and fire, like the Individual and the Communal Group or Tribe or Nation, like the Europeans and the Native Americans, like the Youth and the Childhood of Humanity.

And something is gained and something lost in living every day, as the famous song by Judy Collins goes. We gain something by becoming young and leaving our childhood behind, by relying more on thinking and less on feeling, by asserting more our rights as individuals to be special and less our common bonds, obligations, and loyalty to others in the Group or Culture that nurtured and raised us. But we lose also an expansive openness, communion, and receptivity to the sky and earth, an innocence and lack of contrivance and pretentiousness and inflated self-importance that we seemed to have so effortlessly in Childhood, a trust and willingness and venturous reaching out to and embracing others with the surprises and new excitement of every dawning day.

We knew less in Childhood, but we were wiser and so often kinder and more generous, less greedy and hoarding of every possession, but then our possessions and achievements were not hard earned so perhaps we could afford to be more spontaneous and flowing, less cautious and careful and critical. They who roam the earth freely at will have less invested or accumulated in any particular section or plot of it, and so are not as attached to a particular plot but to the romance and joy of roaming at will, unconstrained as the wind, with every day a new adventure with nature, and no burdens of imposing monuments to the Past or Feverish Dreams of a Glorious Future to Motivate, Prod, Drive, or Distract them.

Is the Missing Fourth obvious and transparent now? We have divided the Middle designations **Human** or **Mind** or **Knowledge Centered** into two designations or categories instead of one only – into **Diversity** in the North, and *Similarity* in the South, into **Thinking** in the North and *Feeling* in the South, into the **Head** in the North and the *Heart* in the South, into **Analytical** in the North as a purpose of education and *Empathetic* in the South as a purpose of education. See the Visual Chart below for clarification of these and other designations of **The Four Foundation** preceded by a **Visual Chart of the Four Purposes of Education** followed by more extensive explanations of the meaning of these various **Foursomes** for our understanding of Pedagogy.

The Four Purposes of Education

	Analytically Thinking and Individually Centered	
Society or Practically Centered		*Person Centered*
	Empathically Feeling and Culturally Centered	

Visual Chart of Fourfold Designations Below

1. Individual
2. Mind
3. Reason and the Father Tongue
4. Cognitive Concepts
5. Knowing
6. Thinking
7. Diversity
8. Head
9. Detached
10. Through
11. Intellectual
12. Idea

1. Material
2. Body
3. Senses
4. Mass Instincts
5. Living
6. Sensing
7. Difference
8. Hand
9. Engaged
10. By
11. Physical
12. Thing

1. *Spiritual*
2. *Soul*
3. *Spirit and The Imaginative Tongue*
4. *Interpersonal Bonds*
5. *Choosing*
6. *Intuiting*
7. *Identity*
8. *Holistic Spirit*
9. *Involved*
10. *With*
11. *Spiritual*
12. *Self*

1. Cultural
2. Sensibility
3. Speech and the Mother Tongue
4. Group Ties
5. Loving
6. Feeling
7. Similarity
8. Heart
9. Attached
10. To
11. Emotional
12. Other

What, if anything, do all these **Foursomes**, these instances of **The Four Foundation**, do for our understanding of Pedagogy? Well, for one thing, they bring into prominent focus the outstanding and obvious candidate for **the Fourth Intelligence**, namely, **The Emotional Intelligence** which has been so brilliantly presented by Daniel Goleman and which has become an educational and social sensation, because Goleman marshaled such abundant and incontrovertible evidence to prove the overriding importance and pervasive influence of the Emotional Intelligence for success in all aspects of life. It is far more important for success in life to know how to emotionally interact, appreciate, understand, and work with other people that it is to be intellectually brilliant or analytically astute.

Of course, why this came as such a shock or revelation is itself rather humorous, and tells us a great deal about the excessive attention the Modern World and Model of Education has paid to Knowledge, Ideas, and the Mind. If you simply look carefully at **The Three Thread** of *People*, **Idea**, Thing, it will tell you instantly that People are more important and have priority over **Ideas**, and that **Ideas** are more important and have priority over Things. We *reverence* and *honor* People; we have **respect** and **esteem** for **Ideas**; we regard and admire Things.

In the United States, we don't kill people over ideas because the Declaration of Independence teaches us to reverence people too much to allow us to kill them over a mere disagreement about **ideas** or possessions. Simply because a person happens to be poor or uneducated or crippled or retarded, or God forbid, less intelligent in any way than the rest of us presume ourselves to be, does not give us the right to take their life under any circumstance. Human beings are more than their minds. For instance, if we reverence human beings, we will not, under any circumstances, torture them because such an action is repulsive to our understanding of the mystery and nobility of human life and our reverence for the freedom of moral choice and responsibility for the future with which Providence has endowed all human beings.

Let's face it: **The Modern World and the Modern University have a positive dread of Human Emotion and the Human Heart, and they are distinctly uncomfortable informing or telling Individuals of their obligation to others, to society, and the common good**. The Education is geared to telling students to develop the Individuality that will set them apart and make them distinct from others – enable them to compete in a harsh and unforgiving world of impersonal mechanical laws and forces where calculated thinking, more than compassionate empathy or feeling for others, will bring one power and prestige if not inner solace or the perception and enjoyment of beauty. After all, art is for dilettantes, decorative and subjective; science, for the Modern World, is serious, indispensable and objective, and so alone, truly real.

Well, we acknowledge, that perhaps we are overdoing things ourselves here, engaging in hyperbole if you will, drawing too harsh a portrait of the Modern World's preference for the Individual over the Cultural or Social; Thinking over Feeling; the Head over the Heart; Science over Art; the Impersonal Force, Law, or Part over the Personal Whole, but it is **in the interest of restoring Balance**, of melding the Detached Thinking Mind of Ice with the Attached Feeling Heart of Fire – in other words of blending and harmonizing The Father Tongue with the Mother Tongue into the Holistic Imaginative Tongue.

But what about those other Intelligences of human beings, if they exist? Where do they belong in this fourfold scheme of things? And why can we count on the fourfold model to address adequately and comprehensively all the other items of our list that we have yet to address in general, not to mention their application to the Innovative Proposal for Writing that we are putting forward in this book?

These questions bring us to the **Defining Characteristic of the Four Foundation**. We give it the name of Four Foundation for two enduring reasons: (1) **it rests on an adequate and comprehensive philosophic knowledge or Model of human nature**; and (1) **it rests on an adequate and comprehensive**

philosophic knowledge or Model of the World as the Dwelling Place of human Language and the Mind.

However, we need first to be clear and explicit about stating some fundamental truths here. Only **human beings** pursue **Knowledge** by constructing **Models** using their **minds.** God, if God exists, already possesses by definition all knowledge so does not need to go looking for it. <u>Other natural creatures in the animal kingdom live by instinct and are confined solely to the Present</u>. They do not possess minds that enable them to conceive languages and the knowledge that enables them to categorize Parts of Reality so that they can live not only in the Present but in the Past, and also conceive a possibly alternative Future which is progressively better than the Past.

God, if God exists, is happy and content to be God since God is Perfection and a Perfect being is not, by definition, lacking and therefore seeking or looking for anything. Perfect beings do not need to Progress since they are already completely fulfilled and complete and perfect. Animals are not lacking or looking for anything either because they are perfect in their restricted state or condition of living by instinct. <u>Animals live entirely in the Present</u>: **they do not regret or yearn for the Past** *or imagine or long for the Future*. Animals are what they are; they do not and cannot pretend to be something else or mess themselves up by imagining or trying to be what they can't possibly ever be. Only human beings can manage to do such things to themselves for **human beings are Problematic by definition**: they are never completely what they are but are in the **Process or Progress, or else in Retrogress, of becoming what they were meant to be in the fullness of time and eternity.**

And here **we must go a little deeper to the more essential root of the Defining Characteristic of the Two Twist before we can tackle and explain more fully the Defining Characteristic of the Four Foundation**. We said earlier that the Defining Characteristic of the Two Twist resided in the Polar Modes of human perception: namely, that human beings perceive reality either as Wholes or Parts and Pieces, using respectively either what Jung called the *Intuitive Function* or the Sensory Function. **However, the root of the Defining Characteristic of the Two Twist is ultimately metaphysical, not confined solely to the human dimension, and consists in Polarity being a constituent Principle of the structure of the universe.**

And if Polarity is a constituent Principle of the structure of the universe, if it is indeed the metaphysical ground and underpinning of Reality as we encounter it everywhere, every way, and every day, do we not need to know what it is, some insight or explanation for why it exists and functions as it does throughout all of existence, **why indeed it is mirrored so prominently, unmistakably, and conspicuously in the very structure and appearance of our human bodies?**

If we ask what is the one, or the several, root polarities, from which all the others are derived or the ones which make all the others clearer and more intelligible, which enable us to see all the others in a more holistic and Integral Way, perhaps we can find the answer that will give us the insight or explanation that we need.

We would like to suggest 19 Polarities might be very helpful in this endeavor, though others might serve equally well for other purposes and people: namely, *One*/Many; *Spirit*/Matter; *Self*/Thing; *Invisible*/Tangible; *Hidden*/Manifest; *Awareness***/**Object**;** *Subjective*/Objective; *Inner*/Outer ; *God*/Nature; *Abide*/Inhabit; *Universe*/Earth; *Eternity*/Time; *Unknown*/*Whole*/Pieces; *Perfection*/Restriction; *Absolute*/Contingent; *Omniscience*/Instincts; *Might*/Force; *Silence*/Gesture; *Mystery*/Fact

Now **if we expand these 19 Two Twists or Polarities** into **Three Threads**, what we see is quite curious and revealing as follows:

One	**Few**	Many
Spirit	**Mind**	Body

Self	Other	Thing
Invisible	Visible	Tangible
Hidden	Latent	Manifest
Awareness	Idea	Object
Subjective	Two Sides	Objective
Inner	Two Sides	Outer
God	Humanity	Nature
Abide	Dwell	Inhabit
Universe	World	Earth
Eternity	Space	Time
Unknown Whole	Known Part	Sensed Pieces
Perfection	Progress or Limitation	Restriction
Absolute	Relative	Contingent
Omniscience	Knowledge	Instincts
Might	Power	Force
Silence	Language	Gesture
Mystery	Problem	Fact

If one starts with the human body, it is clear that it has many pieces and parts, yet the body works together as a smooth, integrated unitary Whole. A spirit or self that is invisible and hidden, yet possessed of a subjective inner awareness, animates and moves the body to work together toward goals and ends determined by the inner self or spirit.

The outer or outside of the body of a self is tangible and visible from the outside by the inside awareness of the self, and is generally known and better understood by the self and others because it is so tangible and visible. However, the inner or inside of the self, though likewise available to the inner awareness of the self, is still largely unknown and inaccessible, because it is largely invisible and not available to the external senses of the self and others.

Moreover, the self has an inner or inside awareness or experience of things and Nature, but things and nature are outer or outside of the human being. Because things and nature are outer or outside of the human being, they are tangible and visible and so can be more clearly known by the self and others. However, this raises the question of whether there is an inner or inside of things and nature, accessible to an inner awareness, that similarly animates and moves things and nature to work together as the human self and spirit animates and moves things and nature to work together. Perhaps, there are many other, or one other greater spirit, than the human spirit or self that animates and moves all of nature to work together.

Nature certainly does not seem to be entirely, or even mainly, random in its working and operations. The more one observes it, the more recurrences and regularities it begins to exhibit, beginning with the invariable Night and Day - night seeming like a less accessible, tangible, and visible known reality but one of which everyone is vividly aware, while Day is a more accessible, tangible, and visible reality of which everyone is also aware, so Night is more subjective and inner (because less commonly accessible to self and others by the senses) while day is more objective and outer(because more accessible to self and others by the senses).

Why all these curiously suggestive similarities and correspondences between human experience and nature? In fact, the more human beings observe and think about the recurrences and patterns in both their inner or outer experience, the more they seem to find or discover a striking or corresponding similarity in nature, and the more human beings observe and think about Nature, the more they seem to find and discover a revealing corresponding regularity or pattern in human beings.

Something about the human mind enables it to know two aspects of Reality – an outer and objective aspect and an inner and subjective aspect of Reality or experience. Moreover, those two aspects or sides show up in two Distinct dimensions of Reality, the Dimension of Nature and the Dimension of Humanity. Humanity partakes of and participates in Nature by virtue of its outer or objective aspect of having a physical body, but its inner or subjective aspect or side puts it in a Dimension above and beyond Nature.

Everything merely natural is confined to the present only and to the perpetual repetition of a severely restricted range of behaviors determined by instinct. <u>Animals inhabit nature instinctively because they participate totally and only in the Dimension of Nature</u>, **but human beings construct and build a World where they dwell together through the instrument of the human mind, composed of the head and the heart, and through the medium of human language. The Instrument of the human mind and the medium of human language together enable human beings to have knowledge of the Future, Past, and Present and through that same knowledge to dwell in common worlds and communities of diverse, complementary, progressive, and ever advancing cultures and civilizations.**

Since the World and Knowledge are both human constructions, they must and can only reflect and express the powers and capacities of human beings. The World in which

we Dwell and the knowledge we discover are both derived from, founded upon, reflect, and express the powers and capacities of human nature. Human nature itself, however, is the mean between two extremes – partaking of, residing in, but not perpetually restricted to the instincts and present of Nature; belonging to, and dwelling in, the World and communities of progressing human cultures and civilizations; and anticipating, sharing, and experiencing emerging portions of a Divine Perfection it can only always Approach but never Become or Be.

> "Only Dwelling, however, is the *basic character* of Being in keeping with which mortals exist...building belongs to dwelling...and...receives its nature from dwelling. Building and thinking are, each in their own way, inescapable for dwelling."
>
> Martin Heidegger

> "What the word for space, *Raum, Rum,* designates is said by its ancient meaning. *Raum* means a place cleared or freed for settlement and lodging. A space is something that has been made room for, something that is cleared and free, namely within a boundary, Greek *peras*. A boundary is not that at which something stops but, as the Greeks recognized, the boundary is that from which something *begins its presencing.*"
>
> Martin Heidegger

As the Mean between two extremes, the Human Being has experience of the Divine and Eternal, of Perfection compared to its own more limited state, yet it also knows the severe restrictions, though also benefits, of the Natural State; however, it Dwells, mostly in between, as the Being who is always **in Progress** from imperfection to Perfection, from a more restricted State to a freer and more expansive Reality. ***The Human Being has always Two Sides but lives in Three Dimensions*** – the Short term, the Medium term, and the Long Term; in Childhood, Youth, and Maturity; with preponderant consciousness variously in the Present, the Past, and the Future; and so with three languages: the language of everyday life, the Mother Tongue, which is principally the language of self-expression and communication with others in a cultural community; the language of Rational Discourse and Focused systematic thought, the Father Tongue, aimed at constructing and building a common World of conceptual understanding and scientific power; and the language of the Imaginative Tongue, of the Integral Apprehension and unitary experience of the Divine Love and Beauty which rest at the center and heart of the Universe and confer peace and wholeness on those who encounter it.

Speaking in Figurative language with metaphor, we can say that Human Life is a Journey, a Quest, and a Pilgrimage. In Childhood, it is a journey through the fields of initial experience, a romantic and fantastic seeking of the expansive possibilities of life with the Cohort of one's companions by birth. In Youth, it is a still more extended Adventure but also now a Quest for Knowledge and for one's place, function, and proper power and role in Life with one's generation and the existential life span of one's culture and nationality. Finally, it is a Pilgrimage through the extension, depth, breadth, and heights of all human experience and History – through all the Ages of life and the cultures and civilizations of human experience and endeavor to uncover and lay bare the ultimate meaning, purpose, and splendor of nature, humanity, and the divine spirit which animates and inspires all creation. One cannot attain the End without going and progressing through the Middle, nor come to the Middle without first Advancing with the Beginning.

And the End, of course, in its fullness and ripeness – its maturity – must sacrifice itself, shed its attachment to its accomplishments and attainments, for the sake and seed of still another Advancing Process of a still greater Future Awaiting and already Emerging. For this, the Imaginative poets and the wisdom of the ages have told us repeatedly:

> "What we call the beginning of often the end
> And to make an end is to make a beginning.
> The end is where we start from."
> T. S. Eliot

> "Beginning and End shake hands with each other."
> German Proverb

> "Time present and time past
> Are both perhaps present in time future,
> And time future contained in time past."
> T. S. Eliot

By now, our choice of the Three Tongues or Languages as central to the structure of this book should be clear as also perhaps why we stipulate three stages of instruction for Learning and teaching Writing in the book as a whole.

We hope that we have also made it a little more clear why all knowledge and any Pedagogy that aims to transit Knowledge rests ultimately and inevitably on an adequate and comprehensive philosophic understanding of both human nature and human history. Since Knowledge and the Common World in which Humans Dwell are both Constructions of the Human Mind and Language, then understanding Knowledge and the Common Human World depend on the nature or character of human beings.

Because human nature exists in an eternal Dimension that restricts it neither completely to nature nor allows it ever to remotely adequately comprehend the Divine (though humans glimpse and experience the Divine in varying degrees of intensity, awareness, and self-realization), human beings share the same common capacities, powers, characteristics, and limitations that give them an essentially identical nature. We need, therefore, to discover, designate, and define the powers and capacities of that identical human nature. However, we must not assume, or make the mistake of asserting, that all human beings are, therefore, totally like one another in every key aspect of life – say in their Intelligences, Preferences, Perceptions, Decisions, Judgments, Wants, Values, Self Conceptions, or ways of speaking and acting as well as in a multitude of other instances.

Now this may be very disconcerting and initially disturbing and confusing to realize, but such is the case, as we will shortly demonstrate, based on a very ancient yet only notional understanding in the past, but now attaining a full mature awareness and clear definition in scores of brilliant books in several fields of learning, especially in contemporary psychology, education research, and business and organizational studies.

It turns out that, though human beings possess the same powers and capacities, they emphasize, deploy, and develop those diverse powers and capacities in a multitude of different ways. The Patterns, Dynamics, and Configurations of such diverse emphasis, deployment, and development of the diverse powers and capacities of human nature have now been clarified and explained; they are, consequently, available to be used by **a mature and comprehensive pedagogy in the Stage of Human History to which humanity has now advanced: namely, the Maturity of Humanity.**

And that is the reason one must possess an adequate and comprehensive understanding of the four stages of human history: namely, Infancy, Childhood, Youth, and Maturity. Not only does the emphasis and deployment of the powers and capacities of human nature result in human diversity, but that diversity is increased enormously, as and when the development and increase of the powers and capacities of human beings themselves develop and increase, both qualitatively and quantitatively, in the subsequent stages of human history. **The Model of Education and Pedagogical Theory depend on the understanding of the powers and capacities of human nature, and those very powers and capacities are qualitatively and quantifiably different in the four stages of Human history.**

What then, finally, are the powers and capacities of Human Nature which we must know to have an adequate and comprehensive Pedagogy? Well, by now, you will have guessed or assumed correctly that there are four such powers or capacities, and it should be clear as well what is the **Defining Characteristic of The Four Foundation. The Defining Characteristic of The Four Foundation is that it rests on the Fourfold Character, Directions, Parts, Powers and Capacities, or Functions of Human Nature.**

The Fourfold Character of Human Nature, however, is itself rooted in the Metaphysical Polarity of the Universe which is mirrored in the Human Body. *The human body mirrors the number 1 and the Divine Unity of the universe in the unity and mutually flowing and animated functioning of its many parts and pieces.* **It mirrors the number 2 and the Polarity of the universe in the 22 pairs of polar opposites discernible in the human body**. It mirrors the number 3 in the mouth as the common intermediary, reflection, and expression of the Heart and the Head – heart, mouth, head - even as the Mind is the common intermediary, reflection, and expression of the inner and outer and the subjective and the objective aspects of Reality.

And from now on, as you might expect, everything will come in Fours according to the Four Foundation, as we expound the remainder of our construction of a Mature Pedagogy, one that rests indeed on the Four Foundation.

We begin by designating, and graphing in succession the many Foursomes necessary and relevant for understanding human nature, including the Four Powers and Capacities of human nature, but present the Foursomes in a sequence, proceeding from the easiest to understand to the more difficult, in the hope that such a presentation will be largely self-explanatory and cumulatively revealing, illuminating, and convincing.

We will conclude with a summary statement that integrates the foursomes and discusses their relevance for education and pedagogy.

First, we designate and graph the **Four Abstract Perspectives of Human Nature**: namely, the outer, subjective, objective, and inner perspectives.

	Objective	
Outer		*Inner*
	Subjective	

Second, we designate and graph the **Four Referral Domains for the Four Perspectives of Human Nature**: namely, thing, other, idea, and self.

	Idea	
Thing		*Self*
	Other	

Third, we designate and graph the **Four Aspects of Human Nature**: namely, the physical, emotional, intellectual, and spiritual aspects.

	Intellectual	
Physical		*Spiritual*
	Emotional	

Fourth, we designate and graph the **Four Faculties of Human Nature**: namely, the Senses, the Heart, the Head, and the Will.

	Head	
Senses		Will
	Heart	

Fifth, we designate and graph the **Four Powers and Capacities of Human Nature:** namely, Sensing, Loving, Knowing, and Choosing.

	Knowing	
Senses		Choosing
	Loving	

Sixth, we designate and graph what Jung first identified as the **Four Functions of Human Nature.**

	Thinking	
Sensing		Intuiting
	Feeling	

Seventh, we designate and graph the **Four Factors of Human life**.

	Place	
Physical Condition		Person
	Moment	

Eighth we designate and graph the **Four Stages of Development of Human Nature**, both **for Individual human beings and for the Historical Development of Humanity as a Whole**.

	Youth	
Infancy		Maturity
	Childhood	

Ninth, we designate and graph **Four Salient Characterizations of Human Nature in the Four Stages of Historical Human Development.**

	Individual	
Instinctive		Integral
	Cultural	

Tenth, we designate and graph the **Four Stages of Consciousness of Human Nature in the Four Stages of Historical Human Development**.

	Consciousness	
Pre-Consciousness		Transcendent, Cosmic (Bucke), SuperConsciousness (Sorokin), Supramental (Aurobindo)
	Subconsciousness	

Eleventh, we designate and graph the **Four Attitude Priorities of Human Nature**.

	Recognizing	
Attending		*Witnessing*
	Appreciating	

Twelfth, we designate and graph the **Four Key Virtues of Human Nature in the Four Stages of Historical Human Development**.

	Faith	
Strength and Endurance		*Balance and Tolerance*
	Obedience	

Thirteenth, we designate and graph the **Four Primary Reliance Factors for Human Nature in the Four Stages of Historical Human Development**.

	Freedom	
Skill		*Responsibility*
	Authority	

Fourteenth, we designate and graph the **Four Primary Social Orientations of Human Nature in the Four Stages of Historical Human Development.**

	Independence	
Adaptability		*Interdependence*
	Dependence	

Fifteenth, we designate and graph the **Four Primary Social Tasks of Human Nature in the Four Stages of Historical Human Development**.

	Competition	
Coordination		*Cooperation*
	Organization	

Sixteenth, we designate and graph the **Four Primary Goals of Human Nature in the Four Stages of Historical Human** Development.

	Achievement	
Survival		*Personal Integration and Self-Realization*
	Security	

Seventeenth, we designate and graph the **Four Primary Economic Bases of Human Nature in the Four Stages of Historical Human Development**.

	Commercial and Industrial	
Hunting and Gathering		*Digital*
	Agricultural and Pastoral	

Eighteenth, we designate and graph the **Four Primary Methods of Solving Conflict for Human Nature in the Four Stages of Historical Human Development**.

	Political Compromise	
Physical Force		*Spiritual Awareness, Understanding, Love*
	Social Compulsion	

Nineteenth, we designate and graph the **Four Geographic Locations of Human Beings in the Four Stages of Historical Human Development**.

	National	
Local		*Global*
	Regional	

Twentieth, we designate and graph the **Four Ancient or Traditional Names for the Four Temperaments of Human Nature** by the ancient physician Galen around 190 B.C. and used and applied effectively in contemporary life in the books of the Christian writer Tim Lahaye such as *Transformed Temperaments* and *The Spirit Controlled Temperament.*

	Choleric	
Sanguine		Melancholic
	Phelgmatic	

Twenty-first, we designate and graph **The Four Ancient Temperaments with the more Memorable, Alliterative, Accessible, and Contemporary Names coined by Florence Littauer** in her book *Personality Plus* and expanded in the spiritual applications of the temperaments to Christianity and spirituality by her daughter Marita Littauer in her book *Your Spiritual Personality.*

	Powerful	
Popular		Perfect
	Peaceful	

Twenty-second, we designate and list 28 different sets of names coined by 23 different individuals in the Modern and Contemporary Periods to characterize the characteristics, values, needs, talents, behaviors, and social and interactional styles of **The Four Temperaments** which are themselves just different versions of **Jung's Four Functions of Human Nature**. Or, you could also say, Jung's Four Functions are just another modern version of the ancient Four Temperaments.

While there is some confusion (though very little considering their variety) surrounding the different names employed for the Four Temperaments, it would be a great mistake to assume that they don't all contribute in varying degrees of importance to an increased understanding of the Temperaments because they do. **Their sheer variety, illuminating capacity, and employment with millions of people around the world in repeated tests, studies, and innumerable personal applications and verifications attest to the universal validity and value of the Four Temperaments as an indispensable guide to understanding the diversity of human nature in a multitude of ways.**

Version	West	*South*	**North**	*East*
Ezekiel 590 BCE	Lion	*Ox*	**Eagle**	*Man*
	(Bold)	*(Sturdy)*	**(Far Seeing)**	*(Humane)*
Plato 340 BCE	Artistic	*Sensible*	**Reasoning**	*Intuitive*
Aristotle 325 BCE	Sensual	*Material*	**Logical**	*Ethical*
Irenaeus 185 CE	Spontaneous	*Historical*	**Scholarly**	*Spiritual*
Galen 190	Sanguine	*Phlegmatic*	**Choleric**	*Melancholic*
Paracelsus 1550	Salamander	*Gnome*	**Sylph**	*Nymphs*
	Impulsive & Changeable	*Industrious and Guarded*	**Curious and Calm**	*Inspired and Passionate*
Adickes 1905	Innovative	*Traditional*	**Skeptical**	*Doctrinaire*
Spranger 1914	Aesthetic	*Economic*	**Theoretical**	*Religious*

Kretschmer 1920	Manic	Depressive	**Insensitive**	Oversensitive
Myers 1958	Perceiving	Judging	**Thinking**	Feeling
Fromm	Exploitive	Hoarding	**Marketing**	Receptive
Keirsey 1978	Dionysian	Epimethean	**Promethean**	Apollonian
Keirsey	Artful	Dutiful	**Technological**	Soulful
Keirsey	Artisans	Guardians	**Rationalists**	Idealists
Don Lowry	Orange	Gold	**Green**	Blue
	Spontaneous	Responsible	**Conceptual**	Compassionate
Stephen Mongomery	Action	Cornerstone	**Technology**	Personal Growth
	Spontaneous And Playful	Sensible and Judicious	**Ingenious and theoretical**	Intuitive and Fervent
Carol Ritberger	Red	Orange	**Yellow**	Green
	Realistic	(Service Oriented)	**Clear Minded, Strong, Self Reliant**	(Sensitive and Kind)
Tom Maddron	Orange	Gold	**Green**	Blue
	Freedom)	(Order)	**(Rationality**	(Authenticity)
Taylor Hartman	Yellow	White	**Red**	Blue
	(Fun)	(Peace)	**(Power)**	(Love)
Linda Berens &	Improvisor	Stabilizer	**Theorist**	Catalyst

Dario Nardi				
DISC Model	Influencing	Compliance	**Dominance**	Steadiness

Tony Alessandra	Socializer	Relater	**Director**	Thinker
Merrill_Reid Social Styles	Expressive	Amiable	**Driving**	Analytical
Berens & Nardi	Get-things-Going	Behind-the Scenes	**In-Charge**	Chart-the-Course

Of the 30 or more **Foursomes above**, the last four designate the interaction or social or behavioral styles of the Four Temperaments. However, they correspond perfectly with the Four Temperaments, so they are conceptually a part of them. Moreover, the DISC, Alessandra, and Merrill Reid Social Styles Foursomes have been used between them by more than 50 million people in hundreds of countries and have been employed by thousands of businesses and hundreds of Fortune 500 Corporations with vast success and approval by their customers and consumers. The amazing thing is how little they are known and used in schools, though that is rapidly changing. The DISC model for one has been around since before World War II, is incredibly easy to use and accurate, and was essentially, along with the ancient Four Temperaments, the basis for the other ones though all are beneficial and useful.

Concerning the relative importance of these various designations and descriptions, there is no question that the Myers-Briggs description of 16 Personality types, with four sub-types for each of the major Four Temperaments, was the first major and decisive breakthrough. Kiersey then wrote several absolutely brilliant books, the last and most comprehensive being *Please Understand Me II*, which clarified the Four Temperaments as foundational for understanding human beings initially. He then also added four or more major conceptual distinctions, which time and space do not permit us to discuss here, that vastly improved understanding all 16 personality types, including excellent new descriptions of each type, and more than 20 sets of extremely revealing **Foursomes** about various features of the Four Temperaments.

The two Littauers have a list of 40 Foursomes describing the Four Temperaments, 20 describing the Strengths of the Temperaments and 20 their Weaknesses. Moreover, they are all **Alliterative Foursomes**, with each of the four terms in every **Foursome beginning with the same letter;** thus, one sample **Foursome of Strength** is Playful for Sanguine, *Peaceful for Phlegmatic*, **Persuasive for Choleric**, *and Persistent for Melancholic.*

In other words, if you add the 40 Foursomes of Littauer with the 26 or so of Kiersey plus the 30 above, you get over 90 or more Foursomes describing the Four Temperaments which can hardly be a coincidence. Together, they bring an amazing clarity to understanding the Four Temperaments. Moreover, the slightly different sets of names and descriptions of the 16 Personality Types provided by Myers Briggs, David Kiersey, the latest DISC model, Alessandra, and Berens all work to clarify and expand upon one another.

At this point, by far the best, easiest, most concise, most graphically well presented, and most insightful, comprehensive, and thoroughly accurate introduction to the Four Temperaments and 16 Personality Types is provided by Linda V. Berens and Dario Nardi in their 50 or so page book *The 16 Personality Types*. It is a masterpiece of compression, but needs to be balanced and explained by reading Kiersey's masterful *Please Understand Me II*.

For beginners, perhaps the most accessible and immediately engaging introduction to the 16 personality types is Renee Baron's *What Type Am I?*

Another approachable, enjoyable, comprehensive, as well as insightful and accurate portrayal of The Four Temperaments is Mary Miscisin's *Showing Our True Colors* which is based on the very accurate model of Don Lowry who based most of his work on Keirsey since he was Keirsey's student, but Lowry corrected the strangely wrong categories in which Keirsey, for all his brilliance, had placed the Ancient Four Temperaments. Frankly, we ourselves were quite certain Keirsey had misplaced the Four Ancient Temperaments, but it bothered us, considering the expertise of Keirsey, and we worried that perhaps we might be wrong until we encountered the correction that Lowry made which agreed with our view.

In any case, two other brilliant descriptions of the Four Temperaments are available. The first is by Carol Ritberger (*What Color Is Your Personality?*) who provides a short, accurate test which gauges the extent to which one uses each of the Four Functions of Jung though she does not call them The Four Functions or the Four Temperaments, but calls them by the Fours Colors of Red, Orange, Yellow, and Green. However, the accurate test and her brilliant descriptions proceed to prove that Jung's Functions are simply the Four Temperaments under another name and completely identical to her four colors. It is a wonderful little book. The same is true, but even more so, of *Understand Your Temperament: A Guide to the Four Temperaments – Choleric, Sanguine, Phlegmatic, and Melancholic* by Gilbert Childs who provides such stunning and insightful descriptions of the Four Temperaments that he leaves one laughing out loud at the typical characteristics, virtues, and shortcomings of all Four Temperaments. Laughter is the invariable measure of sanity and common sense in such matters, and you will not ever again find yourself questioning the validity of the Four Temperaments as a remarkable and important truth about human life.

One final important truth to know about the Four Temperaments is that not only does everyone have various degrees of all Four Temperaments, but also most people possess not just one dominant temperament but the very weak temperament directly opposite to their dominant temperament as well as at least one strong complementary temperament and sometimes two strong complementary temperaments. When one tries to compute the various possible temperaments, with the various combinations possible, it has been estimated that people have possibly thousands of individually unique personalities. In other words, human beings may be understood through a general understanding of temperaments, but every person remains unique and somewhat mysterious both to themselves and others. "A human being," as the French philosopher Gabriel Marcel once said so admirably, "is an intelligible Mystery."

Now, the point of our long discourse above on the various **Foursomes and the Four Temperaments,** which reflect and reveal human nature, is to demonstrate that a pedagogy suitable for this emerging Mature Age of Human History rests, like the Traditional and Modern Pedagogies, on the fact that human beings share a common human nature, but also to acknowledge, with Contemporary Pedagogies, that Human Nature is also characterized by considerable diversity, a diversity which must be addressed in the classroom, in the curriculum, in the stages of instruction, in the conception of subjects, and in the goals, methods, and materials of instruction. We will address each of these and other remaining items of pedagogical concern by directly examining how they will operate in the specific Proposal which we set forth here for a **Innovative System of Writing.**

Since we are proposing an Innovative System of Writing, it should reflect advance research and discovery on the Frontiers and Cutting Edge of scholarship. In fact, as you might expect by now, there has been breakthrough scholarship in four fields in the past 20 to 30 years respectively (1) in Linguistics and Language studies; (2) in Reader Response Theory and in Social and Cultural Interaction for Learning; (3) in Critical Thinking; and (4) in Competing Approaches to Writing and Composition.

Let us get directly to Writing itself by examining first the competing Approaches to Writing and Composition, and that will open up into a clear discussion of the character and relevance of the other three breakthrough areas of scholarship for Writing.

Again, as you would probably guess by now, there are Four Competing Approaches to Writing, the older <u>Traditional</u> and **Modern** Approaches and the newer, more recent <u>Rhetorica</u>l and *Process* theories.

    We will place the Four Competing Approaches to Writing at the top of several Charts below which will then list the varied content and implications of each of the Four Approaches in a series of **Foursomes**. We will designate an identifying name for the Foursomes or else list them as a **Clarifying Foursome** because they make clearer the Foursomes before and after them in the Charts. All of the Foursomes are more or less clarified or coined by us, though many are based on known standard fourfold distinctions. While and as we present the Charts, we will describe the Four Approaches to Composition at greater length at various points in our exposition. We will then **apply our Mature and Balanced Integration of all Four theories to the Innovative System of Writing that we propose**.

Name	<u>West</u>	*South*	**North**	*East*
Composition Theories	<u>Traditional</u>	*Rhetorical*	**Modern**	*Process*
Aspects of Writing Situation	<u>Language</u>	*Audience*	**Subject**	*Writer*
Domain Referrals	<u>Thing</u>	*Other*	**Idea**	*Self*

4 Purposes of Writing: <u>The Purpose of Writing in the Traditional Theory is Accuracy and correctness of Usage, Grammar, Syntax, and Punctuation</u>; *the Purpose of Writing in Rhetorical Theory is the effective deployment of invention, arrangement, and style to make a persuasive, powerful impact on the reader or audience for writing*; **the Purpose of Writing in the Modern Period is to represent, analyze, or synthesize part of reality and the world through focused thinking, logical and consistent reasoning, comprehensive conception, and clear expression**; *the Purpose of Writing in Process Theory is self-expression and growth as a person through trusting oneself and developing confidence in one's own authentic voice, authenticity, and integrity as a writer and human being.*

Teaching Situation	<u>Materials</u>	*Class*	**Teacher**	*Student*
Clarifying Foursome	<u>Environment</u>	*Effect*	**Cause**	*Origin*
Clarifying Foursome	<u>Order</u>	*Content*	**Form**	*Energy*
Clarifying Foursome	<u>Matter</u>	*Substance*	**Structure**	*Essence*
Aristotle's Causes	<u>Material</u>	*Final*	**Formal**	*Efficient*
Aims for Writing	<u>Efficient</u>	*Effective*	**Thoughtful**	*Authentic*
Qualities of Writing	<u>Cohesion</u>	*Texture*	**Coherence**	*Unity*

Questions of Writing	How	To Whom, Where, When	**What**	Who and Why
Criteria of Writing	Brevity	Style	**Clarity**	Integrity
Salient Features of Writing	Craft	Strategy	**System**	Intention
Aspects of Writing	Technical	Artistic	**Scientific**	Personal
Values of Writing	Useful	Beautiful	**True**	Good
Communication	Communication	Impact	**Message**	Meaning
Learning Modes	Movement	Speaking	**Writing**	Reading
Organ Preferences	Hand	Ear	**Eye**	Whole Body

Goals of Writing: <u>The Traditional Goal of Writing is to enable students to achieve Organization, Efficiency, and Mechanical Accuracy and Correctness in Usage, Grammar, Syntax, and Punctuation. Targeted and graduated exercises are employed to help students recognize and correct errors as well as to instill attention to detail, organization, and proper formatting and editing of written material.</u> *The Rhetorical Goal of Writing is to enable students to emotionally understand and relate to their fellow students as well as learn more effectively through social interaction, collaborative invention and writing, and various kinds of peer reviewing of writing. The aim is to empower students to imagine prospective readers of their papers and to appreciate and deploy strategies and stylistic devices to dramatically and powerfully impact those readers*. **The Modern Goal of Writing is to enable students to investigate and reflect about the objective world, to think and write clearly about its character, systematic laws, and problems, and then to convey in logical deductive reasoning, through structured and focused expositions, their conclusions and discoveries about that world and how to improve it.** *The Process Goal of Writing is to enable students to discover their true selves and Living Authentic Voices as writers so they can write with fluency, confidence, feeling, heart, soul, imagination, and spirit – unafraid of failure but instead able, through awareness of their own writing process, to reflect on their writing and regularly and consistently improve it, because they have come to love and esteem writing. They do not use writing only to express what they already know, but also as a generative instrument for discovering what they don't yet know or understand. They have come to realize that writing is not only **reflective**, but **<u>generative</u>**, that language is the very medium and means by which we create, discover, build, and dwell in a common cultural and social community and world.*

Ideal Writing Forms	Description	*Persuasion*	**Exposition & Argumentation**	*Narration*
Mental Processes	Analysis	*Evaluation*	**Synthesis & Comprehension**	*Integration*
Psychology Domains	Psycho-Motor	*Affective*	**Cognitive**	*Connative*
Social Domains	Private	*Social*	**Public**	*Communal*
Kolbe's Action Modes	Implementor	*Fact Finder*	**Quick Start**	*Follow Thru*
Language Referents	Term	*Idiom*	**Name**	*Word*
Language Domains	Fact	*Symbol*	**Concept**	*Allusion*
Figurative Language	Simile	*Personification*	**Analogy**	*Metaphor*

How To Master Writing: <u>The Traditional Approach believes that Writing is learned by mastering the mechanics, rules, and details of language with attention to external correct examples of writing.</u> *The Rhetorical Approach believes that Writing is mastered by observing the Consequences and Impact of Writing resulting from empathetic appreciation for diverse audiences of gender, race, ethnicity, nationality, class, and occupation, using alternative dramatic strategies and stylistic devices.* **The Modern Approach believes that Writing is mastered through studying writing and through critical reflection; rational, objective, detached thought; logical reasoning; clear conceptions; structured exposition; solid organization; and clear writing.** *The Process Approach believes that writing is mastered, well, by writing – often, regularly, and incessantly – and with deep awareness of one's own unique writing process, writing with personal purpose, intention, passion, and an enduring desire (1) to learn who one is by writing and (2) to share with others whatever one might have learned that could lead to a more universal and deeper communion and community with others, nature, and the Transcendent.*

Ideal Writing Forms	<u>Outside In</u>	*Bottom Up*	**Top Down**	*Inside Out*
Relating Modes	<u>Nurturing</u>	*Cultivating*	**Reflecting, Criticizing & Constructing**	*Communing*
Four Methods	<u>Body Movement</u>	*Peer Cooperation & Collaboration*	**Models & Forms**	*Choices*
Four Perspectives	<u>Outer</u>	*Subjective*	**Objective**	*Inner*

Writing Outcomes: Writing confers four kinds of benefits and blessings: namely, Practical Applications; *Emotional Balance and Equilibrium;* **Intellectual Comprehension**; *and Spiritual Vision and Integration.*

As the many foursomes above make clear, the Modern Approach to Writing centers around Writing as Clear and Critical Thinking. A great deal of research and innumerable college symposiums and workshops have addressed the field of Critical Thinking over the past 20 or so years, but without much notable success or clear consensus. We submit that the **Five Forms of Thinking** that we have begun to provide in this book will finally provide the workable framework for a truly useful course in critical thinking that cuts across the curriculum. We will bring forth at least a 1000 **Three Threads** and many additional Two Twists and Foursomes in a subsequent book that follows these two volumes. These abundant **Three Threads** and numerous **Foursomes** will provide a huge foundational fund of ordinary words whose philosophical meanings and systematic connections with one another will become transparent for the first time, thereby fulfilling the aspiration and convictions of ordinary language philosophers who tried but failed to accomplish that task.

The time has finally arrived to conclude this section by explaining the last three adjectives or sets of adjectives that describe our Proposal for an Innovative System of Writing: namely, the adjectives *Vital, Universally Modeled and Doable, and Imaginative.*

Our proposed System of Writing is *Vital* and not artificial because it addresses the Four aspects, functions, capacities and powers, and temperaments of human nature, because it roots and begins writing instruction in the natural Mother Tongue of everyday life and mutual conversation and not in the impersonal Father Tongue. It recognizes, while Writing inherently stops Speaking and requires structure and thought, it is always rooted, anchored, and thrives or dies by its umbilical cord to Speaking through the supreme necessity and virtue of Living Voice as the first requirement of all competent and great writing. Writing must begin with the student, their personal interests and concerns. They must be allowed to choose their own themes and topics for writing and to employ the language and idiom of their own cultures and peers to express their experiences.

The British philosopher Whitehead noted in his short book *The Aims of Education* that education had three aims corresponding to the three stages of elementary and middle school, high school, and university. Whitehead named the aims romantic, precise, and <u>general</u> which we would here rename universal. Those three aims correspond perfectly with The Mother Tongue, The Father Tongue, and The Imaginative Tongue. Whitehead insisted the first stage of all instruction was <u>romantic</u> because it should aim to inspire and encourage the student to explore in a free, spontaneous, and constantly encouraged way all the possibilities, opportunities, and joys of learning a subject – inciting creativity, discovery, and the tolerance of mistakes while avoiding all premature discouraging criticism or restriction and narrowing of focus and concern.

However, he insisted that by late high school the student had to advance, leaving what we would call using only the Mother Tongue in writing, so as to engage with more reflection and criticism, so as to focus thought and reasoning powers on one precise field or area and thereby to develop the discipline, concentration, and persistence necessary for any progress and worthwhile product to result.

Then, once the concentrated power of thought and reflection had been developed (or what we would call the Father Tongue in writing), the student, leaving high school or the early years of the University, should expand their horizons and fields of study and begin to see connections between and among subjects, using, in other words, their Imaginations or Imaginative Tongue to produce work of enduring value and benefit to themselves and others.

You could rename these three aims the open, expansive, and self-expressive stage; the disciplined, restrictive, and publicly addressed stage; and the imaginative, personally integrated, and universally accomplished stage: in short, the Mother Tongue, the

Father Tongue, and the Imaginative Tongue. Further ahead in the book, we have placed a Chart describing over thirty different ways to describe and characterize the differences between the Three Tongues. If you examine the chart at length, it will confirm the *vital* character of our **Proposed System of Writing**. It is *Vital* because it follows the natural course and stages of Progress in learning to write and does not impose undue burdens and requirements on students and gives them immediate feedback on the degree, extent, and fruit of their progress as writers.

What then makes our System *Universally Modeled and Doable?* **This is indeed the most important and transformative feature of our proposed system of writing.** While Writing is rooted in Speaking and The Mother Tongue, it is inherently about structuring and expressing thought or clear ideas as a first requirement of necessary coherence. And here again, we go to figurative language for some profound metaphors, insight, and personal experiential clarity.

Speaking is Music, flowing and involving the primacy of sound, the ear, and voice; Writing is Architecture, structured in form and function, involving the eye and the Recognition and Cognition of Form; Reading is Sculpture, involving touch and the whole body in movement and gesture, pulling and pushing and handling the text to analyze, take it apart, and appropriate it before putting it back together again imaginatively or holistically.

Since Form is so essential, the Greeks and Romans invented the standard Forms of Discourse – narration, exposition, description etc – that are still the macro-forms used in university English composition classes. Students are given anthologies of the Forms and then asked to read and imitate them in their own writing. This works reasonably well for students who can already write competently, but tends to befuddle and intimidate students who are just learning to write or who have little confidence or facility in writing.

At the micro level of learning to write, students are exposed to phrases, clauses, and sentences as formative features of language along with the form or look of some of the traditional parts of speech, such as the adverb; otherwise, **language instruction is impoverished by the lack of forms that can be used to provide models for students to learn to write**.

Our System of Writing provides the huge Missing link in composition instruction by its invention and classification of 11 Sentence Forms which provide the foundation for all sentences used in English. We provide excellent examples of all the sentences, so that students can use their own content and imagination to construct sentences that are similar in Form. Students are given a choice to use a variety of the Forms in paragraphs and longer essays, and they are initially required to identify and footnote the forms they use.

Students are allowed to choose their own themes and topics with their own content, but they must practice using the variety of forms in varied assignments. **This both encourages and disciplines them to employ a wide variety of sentences, ensuring that they will acquire over time a formidable repertoire of forms of sentences and with them options for expressing their thoughts, feelings, and experiences**. *It also overcomes quickly and thoroughly any initial lack of confidence or blocks to writing that students and others often experience. The requirement of concentrating initially on the Forms of Sentences focuses and directs attention to the accomplishment of small, incremental concrete tasks that require regular, systematic, yet manageable exertions of effort and accomplishment.* Moreover, others in any given class are doing the same tasks, though they must supply their own content reflecting their unique life experience and imagination. Students can read their paragraphs and essays aloud to the entire class or to one another, and they can cooperate and collaborate in reviewing, evaluating, and revising their assignments to improve their voice, thought, word and sentence choice, structure and organization, and mechanical correctness in usage, grammar, punctuation, spelling, and formatting.

In other words, the Proposed System of Writing employs all Four Approaches to Writing. However, **the 11 Sentence Forms**

provide, in addition and qualitatively, a **Precision,** as well as **a Systematic Conception and Implementation of Learning to Write**, unavailable in any other prevailing theory.

The **Proposed System of Writing employs clear models** (1) **with the 11 diverse sentence forms,** (2) **with excellent examples of all the sentences,** and (3) **with excellent student models of paragraphs and longer essays employing all the varied sentences.** Because it is so clearly modeled; because it is realized in gradual, clearly distinct, and manageable stages, reflecting Whitehead's three aims of education; and because it concentrates on teaching writing initially as primarily a process of self-expression and writing itself as a way not only of reflecting life but also of generating and discovering its purpose and meaning, this **Proposed System of Writing** is *Universally Modeled and Doable, but also inspiring, motivating, and empowering.*

Finally, it is *Imaginative* (1) by virtue of its calling on the students always to choose their own subjects, themes, and topics for writing, and (2) and always to supply their own content for papers from the substance of their own life experience. Moreover, this book highlights and promotes a **New Method of Reading** as the royal road to a renewed and revived awareness of the central importance and role of Imagination – as fostered and fashioned by the reading of poetry, stories, and literature of all kinds. For it is the Reading of Imaginative Literature that shapes, makes, and insures the accomplishments of great writers, the sanity and common sense of humanity, and in the end the preservation and transmission of the enduring contributions and legacies of advancing culture and civilization.

We proceed now, therefore, briefly to explain (18) of this "Opening Five" which is concerned with the Recommended **Adoption** *of a New, Embodied, Deeply Reflective, Dramatically Vocal,* and *Communally Participatory* **Method of Reading**.

A New Method of Reading

We will be brief here because the New Method of Reading will actually be presented and explained at length in the second volume and not in this first volume. However, we have already introduced some of the main features and characteristics of our way of understanding and creatively using reading.

As we mentioned earlier, we believe Reading is best understood through comparing it metaphorically with the art of Sculpture. A sculptor works with bodies of material to carve that material into a visible, beautiful, and intelligible Form of dense texture and substance. They must use their entire bodies, and especially their hands, to push, pull, and shape the material into the intelligible form they see with their inner eye and sensibility. They are intensely active and involved, not in the least passive, yet they must pause often and observe the work in progress to insure the integrity and wholeness with which the sculpture gradually takes shape.

In the same way, reading is intensely active and not at all passive, as many sometimes believe. The hands and eyes of the reader should carve the text into individual chunks of meaning which must be taken apart, analyzed, and deeply reflected upon. Reading should alternate between intense active reading of intelligible chunks of meaning and regular intervals of silence where deep reflection of the chunks is processed and integrated into a vividly realized appreciation and understanding of the reading passage or text.

To become fully alive and recreated with the same intensity with which it was written by a gifted writer, it is often essential and necessary to read aloud key sections or the whole of a text, with as much dramatic intensity and accompanying gestures and bodily responses as one sees in good, or even great, acting. When great writing is read aloud, the sound, tone, pitch, rise and fall, and varied intonations of the human voice (accompanied by animated movement and gestures) can create and foster a depth of community between diverse people very sorely needed in today's crowded contemporary cities and sometimes alienated circumstances.

The paradigm and pattern of all such community is found wherever one encounters the enraptured faces of enthralled children being read aloud to by loving parents or devoted teachers of all kinds and ages. All of us need to become like little children every now and again – alive and vital with awe, wonder, and the animating spell and moving power of imagination, as it plays its magical flute of possibility, nobler truth, and finer beauty to liberate life and the world from what they are to what they might and could be in a better and more splendid tomorrow.

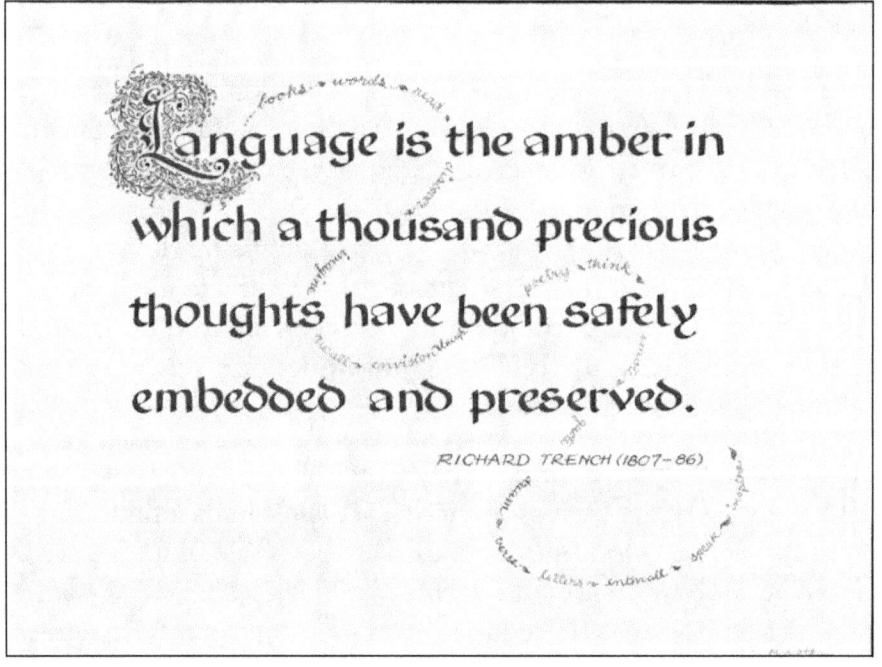

Calligraphy by Muriel Watson

Chart of the Distinctive Features and Characteristics of the Three Movements or Tongues

First Movement	Second Movement	Third Movement
Mother Tongue	**Father Tongue**	*Imaginative Tongue*
Speaking	**Writing**	*Reading*
Language of Everyday Life and Affairs	**Language of Constructing and Improving the World**	*Language of Realizing Unity and Communion with Reality*
Seed	**Branch**	*Fruit*
Beginning	**Middle**	*End*
Origin	**Cause**	*Effect*
Music	**Architecture**	*Sculpture*
Ear	**Eye**	*Body*
Hearing	**Seeing**	*Touching*
Speech	**Thought**	*Imagination*
With	**Through**	*By*

Heart Feeling	**Head** **Thinking**	*Hand* *Doing*
Living Authentic Voice	**Thoughtful** **Clear** **Structure**	*Skillful* *Practiced* *Craft*
Fluently Flowing Flows Easily	**Formally** **Focused** **Follows** **Logically**	*Finely Crafted* *Finishes* *Brilliantly*
Uses Ordinary, Everyday Language	**Employs Public, Disciplinary Discourse**	*Expresses with Figurative Language*
Trust and Confidence in Self and Voice	**Rational and Logical Focus & Self-Critical Reflection**	*Holistic Spirit and Inspiration and Deep Self-Realization and Awareness*
Personal Appropriation	**Theoretical Comprehension**	*Practical Application*

Self-Expressive	**Publicly Addressed and Relevant**	*Imaginatively Conceived and Universally Resonant*
Personally Engaged	**Socially Conscious**	*Universally Attuned*
Locally, Culturally, Extensively Rooted	**Regionally, Nationally, Broadly Cultivated**	*Globally, Universally, Deeply Nurturing*
Celebration of Difference	**Celebration of Similarity and Diversity**	*Celebration of Unity and Universal Humanity*
Celebration of Living Voices	**Celebration of Learning Disciplines and Discourse**	*Celebration of Loving, Inspirational, Imaginative, and Universal Language*
Life Speaking	**Thought Connecting**	*Reality Vibrating & Resonating*

Daily	**Publicly**	*Historically*
With Advancing Spirit	**Through Progressing Mind**	*By Attaining Body*
Personal Growth and Cultural Appreciation	**Social Consciousness and National Development**	*Universal Realization and Global Community*
Outside In and Bottom Up	**Top Down**	*Inside Out*
Sender	**Message**	*Receiver*
Dialogue Conversation	**Dialectic Lecture**	*Rhetoric Manuscript or Embodiment*
Venture	**Reflection**	*Accomplishment*

In the passage below, the Nobel Prize-winning novelist Toni Morrison presents her three names for the three discourses of language that we designate above as the Mother Tongue, the Father Tongue, and the Imaginative Tongue, with their almost 40 corresponding other names and characteristics. Morrison dubs the three discourses or languages the Colloquial, the **Standard**, and the *Lyrical*.

> "I don't trust my writing that is not written [ie. for instance, she does not begin by dictating to a tape recorder and then later transcribing it to paper; in fact, she drafts using a pencil and a yellow legal pad of paper], although I work very hard in subsequent revisions to remove the writerly-ness from it, to give it a combination of *lyrical*, **standard**, and colloquial language. **To pull all these things together into something that I think is much more alive and representative.**"
>
> Toni Morrison
> from the *Paris Review Interviews Volume II*, ed. by Philip Gourevitch

The Organic or Sequential Development of the 3 Tongues

Imaginative Tongue

The use of figurative language, images, and stories to realize universal harmony between inner self and universe; blends precision and breadth of the Father Tongue with the naturalness, fluency, heart, and spirit of the Mother Tongue

Father Tongue

The use of formal public language with reference to solving problems, investigating reality, and designing ways to improve public life; writing to discover and develop concentrated thought, focused planning and organization, and clear, logical expression

Mother Tongue

The use of native cultural or ordinary language with reference to persons, events, and circumstances of everyday life; writes from the heart and genuine feeling; discovers and develops own authentic individual Voice and increased Fluency and Confidence in writing

Order of Acuisition by Individual and Achievement in History — First → Last

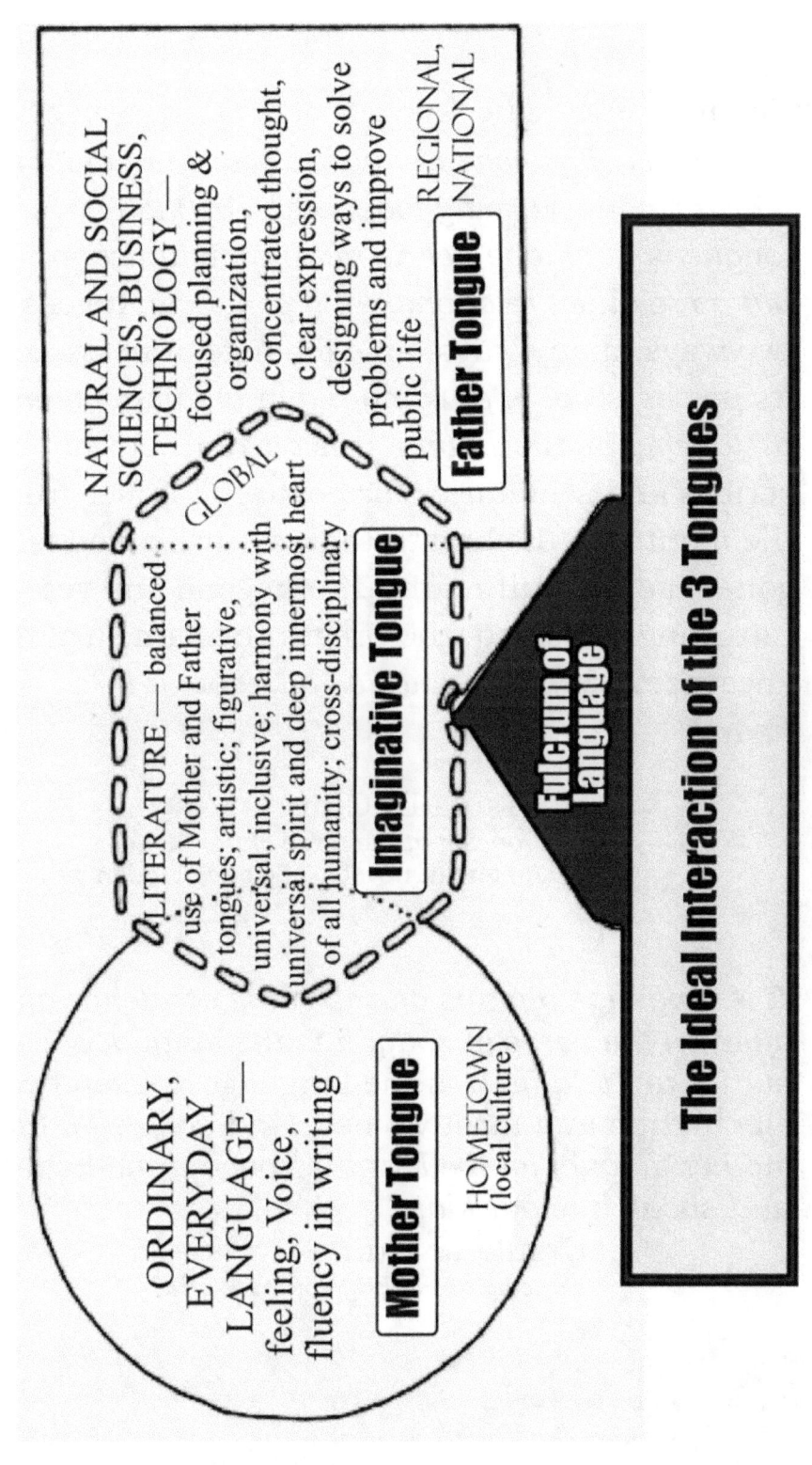

"The mother tongue, spoken or written, expects an answer. *It is conversation, a word the root of which means "turning together." The mother tongue is language not as mere communication but as relation, relationship. It connects.* It goes two ways, many ways, an exchange, a network. *Its power is not in dividing but in binding, not in distancing but in uniting.* It is written, but not by scribes and secretaries for posterity; it flies from the mouth on the breath that is our life and is gone, like the outbreath, utterly gone and yet returning, repeated, the breath the same again always, everywhere, *and we all know it by heart.*"

>Ursula Le Guin
>*Dancing at the Edge of the World*
>American novelist, Science Fiction writer

"*It is language always on the verge of silence and often on the verge of song. It is the language stories are told in.* It is the language spoken by all children and most women, and *so I call it the mother tongue, for we learn it from our mothers and speak it to our kids.*"
>Ursula Le Guin
>*Dancing at the Edge of the World*

"That man is a biological being equipped with many of the same genetically transmitted drives and mechanisms we find in lower orders of life permits no doubt whatever. Man is, after all, a product of the evolutionary process in the organic world. But out of this same evolution has come a set of capacities which man does not share with other animals – capacities which serve profoundly to modify the operation of instincts and drives. **I refer to man's capacities for speech, for abstract thought, for symbolic communication, and for interaction around values which are socially, not biologically, transmitted in time. To overlook this immensely important sphere of human personality, and of human association, is to overlook not merely what is distinctive in man but also what is generally decisive in his behavior.**"

Robert Nisbet
American sociologist

"**Consciousness of my environment began with the sound of talk.** It was not hysterical talk, not bravado, through it might well have been, for my father had bought in a neighborhood formerly forbidden, and we lived, I realize now, under an armistice. But in the early years, when we were a young family, **there was always talk at our house;**

a great deal of it mere talk, a kind of boundless and robustious overflow of family feeling. Our shouts roared through the house with the exuberant gush of flood waters through an open sluice, **for talk, generated by any trifle, was the power that turned the wheels of our inner family life**. It was the strength and that very quality of our living that made impregnable, it seemed, even to time itself, the walls of our home. *But it was in the beginning of the second decade of the century, when the family was an institution still as inviolate as the swing of the earth.*

There was talk of school, of food, of religion, of people. **There were the shouted recitations of poems and Biblical passages and orations from Bryan, Phillips, and John Brown**. My mother liked rolling apostrophes. **We children were all trained at home in the declining art of oratory and were regular contestants for prizes at school**. **My father could quote with appropriate gestures** bits from Beveridge, whom he had never heard, and Teddy Roosevelt and Fred Douglass, whom he had. "

    Dr. J. Saunders Redding *No Day of Triumph*

Introduction to The Mother Tongue

We all first learn language by listening and speaking the Mother Tongue, the language of our native culture. *All the later thought and expression of our lives remains rooted in the unfathomable richness of our native language and the sensibility and native soil of the culture that initially raised and nurtured us.* **We can only learn language as members of a human community incessantly engaged in social and mutual dialogue, discussion, and communication** (1) first, regarding the way we relate to, understand, and interact with one another; and (2) second, regarding the practical concerns and activities of daily life.

Indeed, if human beings had not in some way already learned to relate to, understand, and interact with one another, they could never have learned how to invent a human language and communicate with one another. ***The first necessity of human life in all cultures is to learn to speak with others in mutual dialogue.*** *Without such a capacity, the human being is forever confined to the animal world.*

The animal lives only in the present and remains always what it is. It is finished, complete. The animal senses and undergoes change of a limited character, but **the animal itself does not change in any fundamental way. Its behavior is predictable and unavoidable, following the prescribed path of instinct in unvarying**

repetition. In a way, the animal is whole and perfect: What you see is what you get which is one of the reasons for the perpetual appeal of animals for human beings. Animals are content to be themselves; they don't put on airs and pretend to be what they are not. They have a refreshing innocence and natural responsiveness to the world they inhabit.

Animals are whole and complete like God – but in the image and mode of severe limitation, confinement, weakness, and constrained imperfection whereas God is in the image and mode of unbounded possibility, freedom, strength, and the Splendor of Ultimate Perfection.

Now the animal lives in a Perpetual Present: it cannot imagine a Past other than the Present, or Project a Future other or better than its same endless Present. Animals don't tell stories about old times and cherished ancestors and memories. They don't commemorate or honor the dead, much less erect monuments to them; in fact, they don't even mention or remember them. And they don't mention them, because they don't even have a language that would empower them to mention their ancestors, or for that matter their posterity, and therefore they can't remember them. **Because you can only remember what you can speak about in words** and **because only language and words take you out of the Perpetual Present and enable you to also dwell in the Receding Past and the Emerging Future.**

And why do human beings, unlike animals, dwell also in the Receding, even Ancient, Past and the Emerging Future as well as the Perpetual Present?

They do so because they must inherently do so by their nature, whereas animals do not and inherently do not need to dwell anywhere but in the Perpetual Present due to their nature. As creatures of instinct, animals are automatically programmed to function the way they do: they do not learn what they do from their parents and their cultures. *They do not need to be educated: to be told what to do; to be told when, where, and how to do what they need or should do.* And what they do never undergoes any *profound transmutation*, any **important transformation**, or even any significant alternation or conversion to a different novel or innovative mode, practice, or procedure. The days, weeks, months, years, and centuries follow one after another, but they are all the same for the animal; indeed, because they are so much the same for the animal, why would the animal need different words and names to designate or express a diversity it never encounters or can even conceive?

In contrast, the human being does not function by instinct, evidently because it is not designed or programmed to do perpetually the same thing over and over again without the encounter with, and the introduction of, significant alternation, **transformation**, even (however uncomfortable and disconcerting) *profound transmutation*. Precisely because the human being seems designed and programmed for change and the encounter with the novel, instinct (however admirable) is inadequate and insufficient by itself; rather, the human being must be able to be taught and learn not only new experiences, ideas, and skills, but also how to appropriate and integrate whatever is new with the past and the present.

And the supreme and defining instrument that empowers and enables human beings to be taught, to learn, and to teach their children in turn is human language, The Mother Tongue. The possession of language empowers human beings to commune and communicate with others in a human community that dwells in three realms: *the Kingdom of the Future*, the **Realm of the Past**, and the <u>Domain of the Present</u>.

> "It is only through language that man becomes more than a mere physical phenomenon and breaks through the limitations of his own body. Through language he becomes firmly established: not a fleeting, transient animal, but a firm, enduring reality, held fast by language. **The word takes man out of the state of pure momentary actuality of the animal into the state of the moment that endures.** The word that is truth creates an enduring reality and an enduring support not only for what it holds fast itself but for things outside itself as well."
>
> —Max Picard

The tale here is clear: if we cannot relate to, understand, and interact with one another, we cannot survive as human beings who can provide joint defense, protection, and security to a sufficient degree to allow us to build, maintain, and transmit viable cultures and human communities. **And it is language that empowers us to engage in dialogue and discussion with one another, to learn from older generations and teach new generations, and thereby to navigate change and insure both continuity and progress.**

Other than Speech itself and Language, Writing was the supreme instrument by which human beings enabled and empowered themselves to hold in memory, store, and transmit to succeeding generations and Humanity as a Whole, the great and enduring achievements of past cultures and civilizations. It brought lasting stability, structure, and eventually and inevitably, the power and capacity for systematic thought, reflection, and construction.

If Writing is so great, the very foundation of stability and continuity in knowledge, why does learning to write need to begin with the Mother Tongue which seems so much closer to Speaking than Writing, to the music and flow and changing rhythms of sound whereas Writing belongs to the fixed symbols on the page seen by the eye and conceived by the Head and not the Heart?

Well, that is the way it first happened in time and history and that is the way it still is in human nature and metaphysical reality. Speech came first as the origin and seed ground of language; Writing came much later as a branch, a branching off from the seed but still rooted in it and thriving always only because of it. Most of us were first loved, spoken to with tender hearted words by a mother before anyone ever knew or understood us by name. Everybody speaks and talks, but only some people have written or write. First things, first; second things, second.

The Tongue Speaks, the Voice Sounds, We Hear and Respond, and it is We who hear, not just I or me. We begin in community, in mutual living and sharing, everyday exchanging and communicating. Only later do we go apart, some distance away where we wish to think and reflect, discover and discourse with our individual, separate, increasingly distinctive selves and similar others, in the Group to which we now belong, but no longer amid the Community that first loved us and shared everything with us.

However, no matter how special and independent we conceive and imagine ourselves to be, we cannot remove ourselves too far from the Root and Ground of our Being, our Mother Tongue and Culture, for the very language we employ to define our distinction is rooted and grows from the Mother Tongue.

Accordingly, the First Movement of this Book roots and grounds language, and even Writing , especially the All Important Voice of Writing, in the Mother Tongue.

It begins by Speaking out Loud about English as a Whole with **The Twelve Turns of the English Language**, using the Two Hands to talk about the **Twelve Turns of English** which provides us with a overview or overture to the Skills and Tasks that must be learned to master English.

We then employ ***Speaking Aloud – Sound – but interspersed with Silence***, and supported and **assisted by the sight of words**, **along with the recurrent stress placed upon the consonants of English**, to ease and speed considerably our learning and remembering of new vocabulary.

Next, we briefly but comprehensively cover the highlights of both grammar and punctuation, but with some new Kinds of Words (formerly 8 Parts of Speech but now **12 Kinds of Words**) and a new name for one of the **Five Jobs or Functions of the English Language**, not to mention new, arresting, even Jazzy, names for Punctuation Marks. We also describe and understand Punctuation by reference to sound as well as sight and by metaphorically comparing **The Twelve Punctuation Marks** to red and yellow traffic signals. ***And we Speak of all these things with the Two Hands, by referencing and locating them with the Two Hands, and by asking students to speak out loud, using their own Two Hands to learn and remember everything.***

And we do all this is in a short time, with plenty of opportunity for review and frequent reinforcement, by having students Speak Aloud again what they may have momentarily forgotten. Have you ever repeated out loud the phone number of a friend to others often enough, so that you suddenly, without intention or effort, remember it?

How do actors remember so many lines? Are they all geniuses or possess some extraordinary gift unlike the rest of us. No way. <u>They just repeat their</u>

<u>lines out loud, moving and employing their bodies and gestures.</u> <u>You see, the body remembers and retains so much that the brain won't learn and will forget.</u>

Finally, we get to the core and center of the Mother Tongue and tackle learning to write, by modeling the 11 Sentence Forms with excellent examples that students emulate – gradually, together in class at the board, **speaking their sentences out loud in frequent, but not too difficult or embarrassing, mini-performances.**

Then students – following model writing samples by other students – write, notate, and footnote four assignments of their own, using the required 11 sentence forms. They read and discuss their assignments in cooperation and collaboration with other students as well as in ongoing class consultations with the teacher.

The Mother Tongue then concludes with student model samples of a First Examination students should write, using the required 11 Sentence Forms with their own exams.

The numerous student models, for all four writing assignments as well as for the First Exam, are all notated and footnoted to show clearly which of the 11 Sentence Forms were used in various situations. The sheer number of these excellent examples in varied contexts, along with the assignments employing the language and engaging the concerns of fellow students, insures their dramatic impact and relevance for beginning writing students.

The First Movement – The Mother Tongue

MOTHER TONGUE

1. The 12 Turns of the English Language
2. Vocabulary Acquisition vovovovi
3. Grammar
4. a) 12 Kinds of Words
   b) 5 Jobs that they do
5. 12 Punctuation Marks with New Names
6. Definition and Description of *Form*
7. The 5-Level Architecture of the Sentence
8. The 11 Forms of the Sentence with Model Examples
9. Instructions and Guidance to Students for Writing 4 Model Compositions and First Examination
10. Student Examples of 4 Model Compositions
11. Student Examples of First Examination With Notated & Footnoted Sentence Forms

Twelve Turns of the English Language

5 **Skills** (proficient performance) (unconscious)	5 **Tasks** (attentive mastery) (conscious)
1 **Listening**	6 **Vocabulary**
2 **Speaking**	7 **Basic English**

a	Usage
b	Grammar
c	Syntax & Mechanics (i) Pronunciation (speaking) (ii) Spelling (writing) (iii) Punctuation (reading)

3 **Thinking**	8 **Sentences**
4 **Writing**	9 **Paragraphs**
5 **Reading**	10 **Essays**
Left Hand: 11 **Long Paper**	Right Hand: 12 **Book**

Clap!

| 11 | 2 3 4
1 5 | 9 8 7
10 6 | 12 |

The 12 Turns of the English Language:
an Overture, Overview, and Introductory Map of the Basics of the English Language

The Two Hands Approach begins with a presentation *called The Twelve Turns of the English Language*, which is called an *overture*. **As an *overture*, it suggests the importance of sound and the musical rhythms that underlie language.**

The overture also functions as an *introduction and an overview* of the English language. As an ***introduction***, the Twelve Turns of the English language provides an initial identification and acquaintance with the elements of English, and as an ***overview***, it affords an aerial survey of the English language as a whole.

The **Twelve Turns of the English Language** are not polarities, but consist of five interdependent skills and five tasks which must be successively, continuously, and interactively developed, plus two crowning achievements that signify the final goal and desired outcomes of all language instruction.

These *turns* can be looked at as sequential and proprietary (*it's your turn*), as in the fleeting ownership of someone engaged in a conversation, or it can be looked at as circular, rotational, winding, coiling, as in the subtle yet irrefutable connections that exist between successive phases of any process. These twelve turns involve a linear progression down each of the columns (see chart), yet have a returning arc back to the top, keeping one always in constant awareness of each of the parts separately and yet of the whole that informs the parts.

FIVE SKILLS

(1) **Listening** – From amid the tumult of sounds that fill our waking and sleeping ears, we pick out sets of significant sounds. The sounds are words, and they have significance. MacNeil (1988) points out that our human

aural conditioning goes back to the *"remotest origins of our species"*, and that the *"aural pathways to the brain – to say nothing of the heart – must be very sophisticated."* **He emphatically maintains that we need to restore the importance of listening in our society**. He says that *"even for the literate adult undervaluing the importance of the sound of the language shrivels the language sense....Words heard clearly form the earliest layers because children live in the oral tradition."* As children, we revel in the sound of words newly learned. As older learners of additional languages, we may *revel*, or we may occasionally *revile* – depending upon the degree of mastery of those sounds, the phonetic inventory, of the target language.

The word *revile* comes from the Old French word, *viler*, which meant *to humiliate*. As an intransitive verb, *revile* means *"to use abusive language"*. Certainly, a major reason for the use of abusive language by various sectors of society is because they feel humiliated, and they lack the resources to express this frustration or inadequacy, and therefore resort to the most expedient and least laborious of means, the limited use (sometimes unlimited use) of the widening set of coarse and vulgar language noticeably slowly percolating through all levels of the society and the media. A child who is surrounded by such language learns to relish and delight in a very limited set of words, words which do not uplift or *accentuate the positive* (as songwriter Johnny Mercer once wrote), but instead resonate, connote, and denote marginal words lacking beauty and depth, and respect for self and others.

You have to listen before you can speak.

(2) Speaking

– In speaking, we undertake the initial construction and expression of life in connected words, deployed first to hear ourselves think and hold our thoughts in mind, and second to communicate with others. Everyone observes that children talk out loud to themselves constantly, as if to ground and root themselves in the sounds and permanence of words from their own mute silence and lack of communicative ability. **We must talk to ourselves for a long time out loud before we can know and understand ourselves, and talk out loud to others much longer to communicate with them**. Speaking is a long process of trial and error where many failures precede success. <u>You have to speak a long time in a language before you can think in it</u>.

You have to speak frequently before you can stop speech by thought and reconfigure it to become structurally coherent and connected.

(3) Thinking

—We must learn to think in the target language. We begin to piece the words together. Thinking is perception of structure and order. **Thinking is visual and architectural, and can be powerfully represented by all kinds of maps, charts, and models worthy of imitation**. We sometimes create new words or phrases, jumping quickly, perhaps, to a conclusion on the structure of the language long before we are formally taught about the language. In our new language mindfulness, we start to relate to people and things and events. Word by word and phrase by phrase, the vernacular is heard, perceived, recognized, connected, and absorbed. Elated in the joy of recognition, we store, keep, and upon a not-too-distant occasion in the future, we usher the language out from its new habitat in our mind, duplicate it, and launch it with full confidence and optimism, pondering the success or failure of the operation, pending the sign or response that the intended connection was made with the receiver. Then, does our repertoire of reusable and recyclable resources develop, enlarge, and consolidate. Ideas are put into the most basic of sentences or fragments thereof, **and the mind becomes accustomed to the new, strange, and**

wonderful land where thoughts are clearly expressed in suitable forms in language. Thinking is structural and visual. You have to think in the language a long time before you can break speech apart, and then reconfigure it in the coherent, clear, and meaningful manner required by writing.

(4) Writing – Someone drew before someone wrote. Someone wrote before someone read. We had symbols before we had words and literature. Paleolithic art tells us we were artists before we were writers. But then <u>at about the time of the Sumerians, the symbols became the words</u>. Initial writing was used to record mercantile transactions, but later developed into a higher level of complexity and capability by means of which we could record and convey thoughts and information. Some people maintain that writing is more complex than speech, but as Brown (1994) says:

> ...that would be difficult to demonstrate. Writing and speech represent different modes of complexity, and the most salient difference is in the nature of clauses. Spoken language tends to have shorter clauses connected by more coordinate conjunctions while writing has longer clauses and more subordination.

Written language is rooted in and derived from spoken language, but is more structural and hierarchical in its determination of different levels of complexity and subordination. Writing also clarifies and reinforces the usage of many of the most common sentence forms. It permits the assurance that someone far away can understand our thoughts, feelings, and ideas. Family or social records, religious scripture written on papyrus or mulberry paper or directly on palm leaves, business receipts made with impressions on wet clay, memories scratched on bones or treated animal hides, typeset or diaries written with quill pens have been with us since the times of the **Mahabharata**, the **New Testament**, and Sumerian clay tablets.

Even in this age of keyboards, taking pencil or pen in hand is still an act of supreme importance, and one that should never be lost or eliminated from the curriculum. With the ever-threatening possibility of hard drive failure or operating system freeze, hand-written copies acquire an even greater strategic importance for the survival of the spoken and the scripted word. The paper mode, like one's hands, is independent of technology and is therefore more in a timeframe of its own. **This system needs no other basic hardware than pencil and paper**.

But not only is a piece of paper in a timeframe of its own, so is the writer. **Preferring solitude and places far from maddening crowds, the writer attunes her or his mind to silence**, resets the background music to something unobtrusive, picaresque, or pastoral. One draws away from the dimensioned world, the dymaxion grid, and prepares for comprehensible and comprehensive intake from the unconscious and the webs of conscious thought. One slips from the cocoon of ego and self and time, shedding it like someone gracefully disrobing, whereupon the self flies freely to another level of consciousness, somewhere at the interface of the unconscious and the conscious, of self and the Greater Self, being and the Greater Being.

This *ex-stasis* (ecstasy) is a wonderful moment, an irreproducible interval of pleasure, a moment of real bliss. It is love; the moment is full of great portent, great potential, great power. Words surface from the unconscious, display themselves in their conspicuous and awesome and rare beauty, and we – as writer and judge – surmise and select and use them one at a time, or in small groups. For those not selected, we let them of their own accord slip silently back from whence they came, drifting down from our stage of consciousness whilst yet others clamor for fame and publicity – to be the next one, to be the next one to be remembered forever. The bevy, the array, those waiting in the wings – such strikingly suitable and beautiful candidates they are – but if they cannot appear now, they know their time will come, at the right place and the right time with the writer who has the right poise and the right keenness of mind. Time wavers or flies by or is no longer there, as the student-writer's mind – somewhere in that unknown untapped dimension – draws from that Infinite source, catching all the fallen stars, meteoric and rising stars, and putting them on paper, or in a pocket, perhaps, maybe, for later use. It is a moment of forgetfulness of self, a remembrance of the true nature of being human. **It is with words that we are drawn out from the realms of ordinariness and dreariness. Writing is a setting down, for now and for posterity, the results of that momentary brush with the Infinite, with newly mined or minted words that are set down with multi-skill mastery.**

You must write frequently and in a variety of grammatical forms and styles to read effectively whatever a writer places on the page.

(5) Reading

– We decode the symbols. We grasp the word. We understand the meaning. Proper reading is as essential a skill as writing, and is inseparable from that skill. One must write before one can read well. Once you are aware of the structures of the language, you can perceive the form of the discourse, digest the meaning, and grasp the essence of what is written.

Reading aloud is essential for reading well, though the last 500 years of history has terribly neglected and maligned the oral tradition. Reading should not be a silent activity, devoid of the sound, color, and movement of speech. In the library, silent reading is suitable. But somewhere in the learning environs, there should be a space for students to read aloud. Actors learn by reading aloud. *When you say something out loud and combine it with action or movement or gesture, there is a higher probability that it will be retained, vividly experienced, and appreciated.* If we don't read aloud, we should at least *sub-vocalize*, and listen to our voice. This takes us back to the first skill.

You have to read frequently so that, only by internally detecting the clear forms, the layout, and the resting stops in the written landscape, will you almost imperceptibly be able to detect the writer's voice and the nuances of his or her language, and the underlying pulse and rhythm of the reading passage itself. Then does reading become the rich experience that it is, where one finds *"the most disinterested and deepest acceptance, the most memorable pathos, the most resilient and inexhaustible humor, joy, suffering, pleasure, and human laughter without letup or end."* (Dowling).

Integral Interdependence of the Five Skills

The skills are **independent, interdependent, and integral with one another**. Focusing on one skill entails aspects of some of the other skills. The skills may be learned individually one at a time, but they are cumulative and integral in their operation, constantly reinforcing and influencing one another. **To become fluent and literate in the target language, students must be made aware of the different factors involved in the skills and how they are interactive**.

Writing Before Reading

You will notice that we place writing before reading, a departure from the usual way in which the skills are listed. Usually, we read to increase our vocabulary, to understand ideas, to enjoy story narratives, and <u>it is assumed that the framework of the passage being read is self-evident to all readers</u>. To think this way, however, is wrong. We may have chapter titles for books, but **rarely do books display clearly for readers the paragraph formations and sentence forms that render the books clear and coherent**. It is automatically assumed that students will be able to recognize these noteworthy features (paragraph formation and sentence forms) in the books they read and be able to duplicate them in the essays they write. This is a false assumption, for unless they are taught to recognize and imitate these features themselves, they will fail to understand and appreciate them. *Having seen a building, are we to assume that a person can construct a building or appreciate in any way its structure and beauty, without any training in building techniques or experience in building? To think so is foolish.*

We insist that only by having the direct and personal experience of duplicating the numerous established sentence forms will students ever be able to better absorb and understand the written word. <u>Sentences have recognizable features</u>. Corpus research is trying to program computers to parse and dissect text to its meaningful constituents, and we have trillions of bytes of parsed and analyzed texts, all fully searchable. **Yet, lamentably, prior to the 2HA, no one has devised a system that will teach students to write and read with recognition the essential sentence forms in any type of text whatsoever**.

Another reason for the early emphasis on writing involves *focus*. Writing causes a person to concentrate. Focus is part of the Periphery/Focus polarity. **Michael Polyani** has emphasized this polarity. Pencil in hand or fingertips on the keyboard – with intensity – one drafts, edits, re-phrases, successively re-drafts until the intended meaning comes clear. **The students must be aware of the constant focus and concentrated attention that writing demands, if their writing is ever to be deeply felt and clearly articulated**.

FIVE TASKS

(6) Vocabulary

The Natural Approach maintains that vocabulary is the heart of language. As such, it is the first and foremost task. The 2HA believes that focused listening to bite-sized repeatedly spoken lexical items is still a useful way to learn a language, both in self-study and even more in social settings where one hears a native speaker.

Slowly, very slowly, a native speaker repeats the words syllable by syllable. At the same time that the native speaker pronounces the vocabulary word slowly, an image of what the word names should be presented to the learner as well as a very large printed rendering of the word in the native script.

Thus, if a foreign language student were to learn the English word "classroom", the native English speaker would pronounce each of the two syllables of "classroom" very slowly with a pause of 1-2 seconds between each syllable. At the same time, a picture of a "classroom" would be presented to the student. An enlarged printed version of the word should be placed on the screen or presented via a card to the student (type size should be at least 48pt).

The student should repeat the word aloud slowly, syllable by syllable, and 4 to 5 seconds of silence should elapse before the student hears the next word. Then the next word should be presented in a similar fashion. When 5 words have been presented, the student is asked to repeat them using the fingers of one hand, one word at a time, with proper pronunciation.

The next 5 are presented. Students are then asked to repeat the 10 words.

Vocabulary will not only include words, but commonly spoken collocations, idioms, and other phrases or expressions of popular usage. Words are magnets, and words have wings. With some we soar, and with some we sing. The 2HA realizes the importance of vocabulary as the foundation of the language. With the advent of the mp3 player that has the ability to store speech digitally in a very compact portable format, there is no doubt that such devices will become available to assist people to build up their foreign and native vocabularies. Such portability gives the learner the ability to experience and iterate words and phrases while moving or when in settings with varied backdrops.

(7) Basic English – Usage, Grammar, Syntax &Mechanics

Elements from each of these three must be taught, giving students adequate opportunity for practice and self-expression. Students must be taught that **_usage_** _governs what to write in terms of what is acceptable at that time_. The rules and terms of reference as governed by grammar can never pin or strap down language. Language will wriggle free; new structures and forms will emerge over time. *Usage must be taught – inclusive of idioms, collocations, colloquialisms, and all.*

Grammar *must be taught more as the need arises* in the stream of events as students unveil their novel creations. The basic foundation of grammar has been stripped down and simplified greatly. The working parts are ten plus two kinds of word that perform only five functions or jobs.

Syntax refers to the proper order, location, position, and sequence of words in a sentence.

The **mechanics** of **pronunciation** and **spelling** also receive attention in the 2HA. The sole exception to turning attention to this postponed area is that pronunciation of any new word, phrase or sentence must be heard clearly and precisely punctuated from the onset. The mechanics of **punctuation**, however, will be taught using a new descriptive nomenclature and analogies. Notice how the 3 skills given here proceed (in priority) from sound to sight.

(8) Sentences

As we see later in The Eleven Sentence Forms Chart (with an additional one added), **an appreciation of sentence forms is *the most important* part of this method. The Sentence has a new and different focus in the 2HA. The 2HA looks at the outward appearance of the sentence – the distinguishing traits, the visible markers, and the discernible patterns of it**.

> The **form** is a part of the world over which we have control, and which we decide to shape while leaving the rest of the world as it is. The **context** is that part of the world which puts demands on this form; anything in the world that makes demands on the form is context. **Fitness** is a relation of mutual acceptability between these two. . . . it is only through the form that we can create order in the ensemble.
>
> Christopher Alexander *Notes on the Synthesis of Form* 1964
> British urban planner and architect

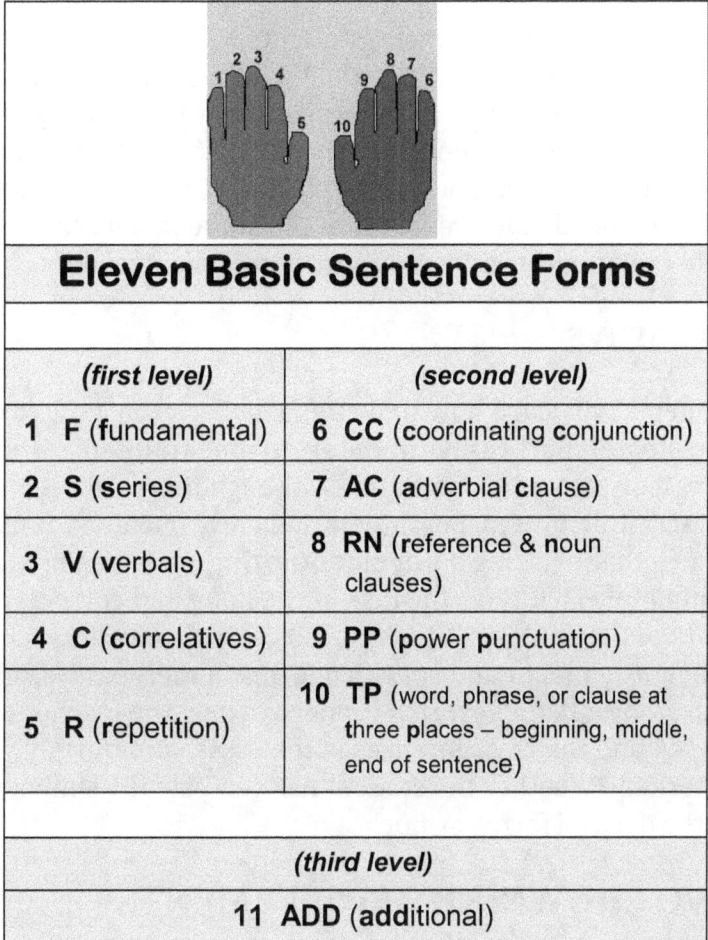

Eleven Basic Sentence Forms

(first level)	(second level)
1 F (fundamental)	6 CC (coordinating conjunction)
2 S (series)	7 AC (adverbial clause)
3 V (verbals)	8 RN (reference & noun clauses)
4 C (correlatives)	9 PP (power punctuation)
5 R (repetition)	10 TP (word, phrase, or clause at three places – beginning, middle, end of sentence)

(third level)
11 ADD (additional)

Students will acquire the ability to recognize and recreate a multitude of *more than 100 sentence forms* – using an easy-to-recall and logical classification system. The topics in the sentences will reflect the important experiences and events in the actual lives and times of the students and their contemporaries. The Two Hands Approach is a constantly renewing resource bank that will never fail to win and to keep the attention of the students.

(9) Paragraphs

Having mastered sentences, students will then be taught and learn the factors involved in the Writing Course, and especially how to develop paragraphs in a cohesive way. They will learn how to vary the sentence length and form to achieve balance, tone, effect, power, and subtlety. Rhetorical devices will be examined and mastered, so that the students will capture and hold the attention and concentration of their readers.

(10) Essays

Students will learn how to distinguish between, how to design and create, short essays in the six to nine traditional rhetorical forms, on freely chosen topics. Although this might seem a prescription for teacher fatigue and early burn-out, it will be shown that by using **a novel footnoting system**, the 2HA completely facilitates the task of checking and correcting the work of the students. Students must correctly use certain previously taught and specified forms in their essays, and they must footnote these forms properly. Then, the teacher can at a glance find the key sentences in the essay, and quickly determine whether the student has successfully shown mastery of the desired forms or not.

TWO CROWNING ACHIEVEMENTS

(11) Long Paper
(12) Book

These are what you hope your students will achieve at some point in the future, having been adequately and rigorously instructed by you in all the key aspects of the language.

The system is meant to encourage a deep and lasting love of language. Students, inspired by the awesome potential of language and of their own deeper selves and creativity, will continue to read, appreciate, and produce good writing.

Vocabulary Acquisition To Speak the English Language With Confidence and Assurance (as well as at a faster rate)

Vocabulary acquisition is crucial in the early stages of acquiring any language. Traditionally, students learn to do vocabulary by using wordlists with the words listed side-by-side. Often the students practice writing the words out and practice using them in various phrases and sentences in workbooks and worksheets.

Another conventional method has been to listen to language tapes and to try to retain and learn to speak in the same manner as native speakers. The conventional wisdom among language teachers everywhere in the world – which everyone takes as sacrosanct, absolute truth – is that students must learn to speak exactly like native speakers talk. This means listening to and speaking at the same rate and speed as native speakers.

If anyone bothered to reflect about this method of teaching a foreign language (which nobody apparently has), it should become immediately apparent that this method is grossly ineffective and completely contrary to the way everyone learns this own first language. It also ignores the fact that the acquisition of a second language is entirely different in difficulty and manner than learning one's native language. Linguists know very well now that children have an inborn capacity to acquire any language with relative ease.

However, the ability to learn a language with the ease is only available in one's early years. If one can learn two or three languages in the early years, one may acquire the additional languages to their native language, with much greater facility than would be the case in later life. Even then, the second and third languages learned are seldom learned with the same ease and proficiency as the native tongue. When people first learn their native language, they learn words first, then phrases, and then sentences. Moreover, the first thing they do is learn how to pronounce the words, phrases, sentences. When they have learned to thoroughly hear and pronounce the language confidently, they willingly and freely use the language often, and their memory of words and their proficiency in the language increases exponentially because their language use is related to their meaningful interaction with others and their environment in daily life. The memory of human beings retains things best when it is driven by meaningful associations with experience, and when language is used repeatedly in various instances and circumstances.

Now what happens when people try to learn a language using contemporary methods? If they use wordlists, they almost never pronounce the words out loud or use them in any meaningful interaction with others, so they have no confidence and assurance in speaking the language. They fear if they say something out loud, they will sound stupid, so they speak out as little as possible, and therefore their pronunciation remains terrible, and their knowledge of the language remains at a deficient level that never grows because they never or seldom use it.

If they listen to tapes of native speakers, the native speakers talk so fast that they cannot hear or distinguish what the speakers are saying. Most of the words are a blur. They have no confidence that they can recognize them, much less confidently pronounce them. They must rewind the tape anywhere from four to ten times, to even begin to recognize the individual words being uttered, must look the words up in a dictionary, and then try to make sense of the entire sentence. Inevitably, progress is slow; most people just give up.

What would one have to do to learn a foreign language in an obviously practical, efficient, and effective way? First and foremost, and of supreme importance, the native speakers must simply *slow down considerably the way they speak the language*, with pauses of silence between the phrases and groups of words into which normally all sentences are divided anyway when people read well.

We acknowledge that only in this book have we made explicitly clear that, if everyone is to read effectively, they must read words in groups or chunks of meaning. Though all good readers do this, it is utterly remarkable that most people have been unconscious of doing this until now. If native speakers of the language for hundreds of years have been largely unaware of the half pauses and divisions by which they separate the language into chunks of meaning, how much more difficult must it be for a foreign speaker to recognize such chunks of meaning. Clearly, they must hear the language more slowly, with more marked pauses of silence between what they distinctly hear so that they (1) distinctly hear the words; (2) effectively absorb and retain what they hear with the aid of the assistance of the intervals of silence; (3) confidently practice out loud, imitating what they have heard. Then when they have confidence pronouncing the words singly, in phrases and entire sentences, they can then confidently go out into the world speaking the language, and the more they speak the language in daily life, the more they will remember, master, and use it.

If they must start more slowly to hear the language, **_slower is better_**; faster leads nowhere. If they begin slowly, they will begin to gradually increase their confidence and competence with exponential progress.

Furthermore, there are two additional ways of learning vocabulary to master language, in addition to the confidence and assurance gained when native speakers speak more slowly to assist them.

First, in English pronunciation, the simplest way to teach people to speak the language well is to tell them to underline and bold all the consonants in a passage so that they stand out visually, and they pronounce the word with all the consonants stressed (even slightly exaggerated) and the word split into distinct syllables.

Then show the same words in a few phrases and finally in an entire sentence with all the consonants bolded in every word. Moreover, the sentence should be chunked with slashes or spaces between the chunks, and spoken with intervals of silence between the chunks, allowing the hearer to absorb what they are hearing.

Finally, a third method is to present the vocabulary words not only with sound, but with a picture accompanying the word. An effective vocabulary program would incorporate all the following features:

1. The words – even the syllables of the words – would be slowed down, far slower than a native speaker ever speaks;

2. The sentences read would be divided into divisions or chunks of meaning to permit their full absorption and retention;

3. The consonants of all English words in such a vocabulary program would be in **bold font**, possibly brightly colored, and those consonants would be stressed (even slightly exaggerated) so that the learner would absorb and retain them;

4. All vocabulary items should be shown with pictures to assist in their retention by virtue of association with the visual images. For instance, they could be shown a video animation, presenting manual sign language, or the use of logical or simple symbols such as those used in the Earth Language (*earthlanguage.org*). The use of such visual symbols would ignite or trigger more cerebral circuits in the brain of the student. In addition, various body movements could be used to dramatize or enact words, thereby awakening the right side of the brain and increasing retention;

5. Finally, it is also known from the research of Georgi Lozanov and many proponents of Accelerated Learning that if certain music is played, it will assist in the retention of words.

Such a program has three immeasurable and lasting consequences for the learning of a language: first, it increases immensely the speed and sheer volume of vocabulary words that can be effectively employed by a language learner; secondly, it increases the confidence and assurance of learners so that they actively employ the language more in daily life; and third, it unconsciously inculcates in hearers greater feeling for and recognition of the natural units of meaning in English.

The methods described above can be used effectively in direct personal instruction, and perhaps even more effectively by employing a database of sound and image files to replace direct instruction. In fact, because learners can repeat with ease the items they are learning, the databases are more user-friendly by virtue of their enabling ease of repetition anywhere and anytime of any linguistic item being learned. Moreover, the student can study at the time and place of their choosing, and they can repeat all lessons until they fully retain them.

The following pages summarize why such a vovovovi method would work and show how such vocabulary items might look on a computer or TV screen. The scenario portrayed is that of a Korean student learning English. Unfortunately, because the pages of this are black and white and shades of grey, the added appeal and benefits of color and sound cannot be fully conveyed.

It is important to emphasize that **if these methods are applied to a reasonably extensive degree, they will revolutionize the teaching of all languages around the world and save endless hours of frustration as well as change the conviction of many people that they cannot learn a foreign language**. Certainly, some can learn languages much faster than others, but everyone can learn a foreign language by these methods.

vovovovi

vocabulary

vocalization +

vocabulary

visualization

The Five Reasons Why *vovovovi* Works

1. **Silence**
2. **Slowness**
3. **Vocalization**
4. **Visualization**
5. **Chunking**

The Value and Necessity of Silence

1. First, **Silence** plays the vital role in framing words as a whole and in their individual syllables, enabling the receptive mind to retain new words. It is impossible to appreciate sufficiently the overwhelming value of Silence for enabling people to initially learn and retain words. Only the practice of preceding and succeeding vocabulary with Silence, when words are first learned, will convince people of the difference this makes in learning vocabulary for the first time. However, just a short period of trying this method will serve to convince people of the value of this practice. It has never been tried adequately before, and thus its value has gone unrecognized.

Four Interrelated and Indispensible Methods for Learning New Words

2. **Slowness** - Vocabulary must be spoken dramatically and slowly, initially with longer pauses and then at normal speed.
3. **Vocalization** - The accent on the strong syllable of a word must be clearly emphasized vocally. Then the consonants must also be spoken vocally out loud with slightly exaggerated emphasis and pitch.
4. **Visualization** - The accent on the strong syllable of a word must be clearly emphasized visually. Also, the consonants of words must also be visually identified with bold formatting. Blended consonants are underlined.
5. **Chunking** - A sentence with the target word is broken into chunks separated by intervals of silence designated visually by white underlined spaces.

Dramatic Innovative Advantages of **vovovovi** for learning vocabulary

- **Visual Aids to Pronunciation of English:**
    - Color or *italics* emphasizes the *ac*cented *syl*lable
    - **Bold** formatting emphasizes **cons**o**nants**
    - Underlining emphasizes blended consonants
- **Visual Aid to Retention**
    - Target language item is in large sized font so that the learner begins to recognize the word's visual profile
- **Audio clip**
    - Strong emphasis on pronunciation of accented syllable
    - Slow pace in initial pronunciation between the syllables of the word and adequate pauses for Silence between them
    - Louder pronunciation of consonants

Additional Advantages

❖ **Audio clip** (cont'd)
- Repetition of **word** with very slow pronunciation followed by pronunciation at normal speed
- **Phrases** with targeted word are spoken once with consonants spoken louder
- **Sentence** with targeted word is spoken once in distinct chunks with intervals of Silence

❖ **Method of Recitation and Retention:**
- Students are free to repeat items frequently if so desired
- Separate sound files for Word, Phrase, Sentence

Economic Incentive

- ❖ Prepare sorted word lists
    - Words are put into a relational database
    - Students choose items according to level, kind of word, flag (such as unlearned, learned, important)
    - Teachers *tag* items in the lists for their occurrence in a book or story, or their probable occurrence in a particular test (GED, SAT, GMAT, IELTS, TOEFL, etc)
    - Students make filtered selection at the start
- ❖ mp3 files and images and database front and back end can be put on a chip and embedded into a microphone, and used in vovovovi booths in classrooms, train stations, airports, travel agency offices, and living rooms at home:
    - Hand-held trackball mouse facilitates navigation or multi-touch resistive touchscreen allows for handy navigation
    - Students repeat loudly rather than softly, and enjoy themselves, thus leading to a relaxed state which is optimal for long-term retention
    - Students work in pairs or trios or quartets

Repetitions and Gap Interval

- For the **Word** slide, the word is repeated 3 times
  - The first repetition *is pro –nounced ve–ry slow–ly* yet clearly, with intervals of silence between the syllables and speaking all the consonants loudly
  - The second repetition is spoken in the identical manner of the first repetition, but slightly faster though still slower than normal
  - The third repetition is spoken at normal conversational speed, as spoken to a stranger asking for directions, or a teacher outlining a homework exercise, or someone discussing a motion in a staff meeting of a company or institution
- For the **Phrase** slide, the phrase is repeated once
  - There is a 1 second pause before the target word in the phrase
  - All the consonants in the entire phrase are visually bolded and are spoken loudly
  - The target word at normal speed without separating the syllables
- For the **Sentence** slide, the sentence is repeated once
  - The sentence is broken into chunks, visually separated from one another by a bold white underlined space
  - The sentence is spoken out loud with 2 second intervals of silence between the chunks where the bold underlined white spaces are

Sample Spacing of Repeated Items

- **Word**
  - "*moun*"- [3 sec.] – "**tain**"
  - [silence 1 sec.] "*moun*"- [1 sec.]   – "**tain**"
  - [silence 1 sec.] "*moun*tain"
- **Phrase**
  - "to <u>th</u>e " [1 sec.] – "*moun*tain"
- **Sentence**
  - "I <u>cl</u>imbed" [1 sec.] – "Mou<u>nt</u> Sorak."[

Coloring Coding & Markup

- Color
  - Strong syllable of word is put in RED *italics* or (for greyscale) *italics*
- Consonants
  - All consonants are put in **bold**
  - Silent consonants are crossed out (ie. **c̶limb̶**)
  - Blended and single-sounding double consonants are underlined (ie **<u>cl</u>imb̶**, **cro<u>ss</u>ed**)
- Vowels
  - Vowels are not marked up
- Phonetic representation
  - Each word is represented phonetically using a system that uses only regular US/UK keyboard characters, such as stedawa's *Letrason* or that of the WriteExpress Rhyming Dictionary http://tr.im/1z0q
- Reading chunk gap
  - This is shown with a ▢ bold white bar

Category: nature

moun
tain

m*a*o*n* *t*eu*n*

산

Photo by Jaroslaw Pocztarski at
http://tr.im/1yx5

Word
Phrases   Sentences

to the **moun** tain;
clim**b** **th**e
moun tain
산으로; 산악
등반

Photo by revolution cycle at
http://tr.im/1ywx

Word · Phrase · Sentences

o cean liner; the o cean floor

바다 라이너;는 바다의 바닥

Photo by Riverman72
http://tr.im/1zdu

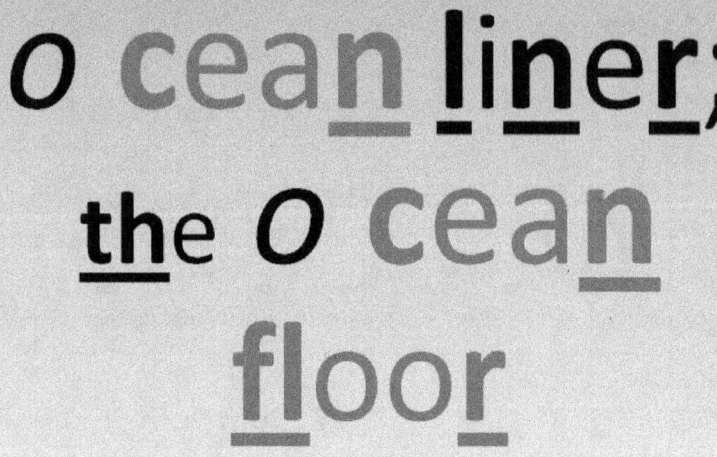
Photo by World Resources Institute Staff
http://tr.im/1zdz

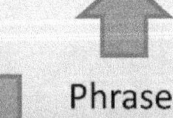 Phrase
Word Sentences

We **w**en**t** | **t**o **th**e **o** cea**n** | to **pl**ay | on **th**e **b**ea**ch**.

우리가 바다의 해변에서 놀이를 했다.

Photo by respres at
http://tr.im/1zee

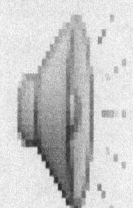

 Sentence

 Phrases

pl<u>a</u>nt t<u>he</u> **_tr_ee**;
<u>c</u>limb t<u>he</u> **_tr_ee**

공장 트리; 나무에 올라가서

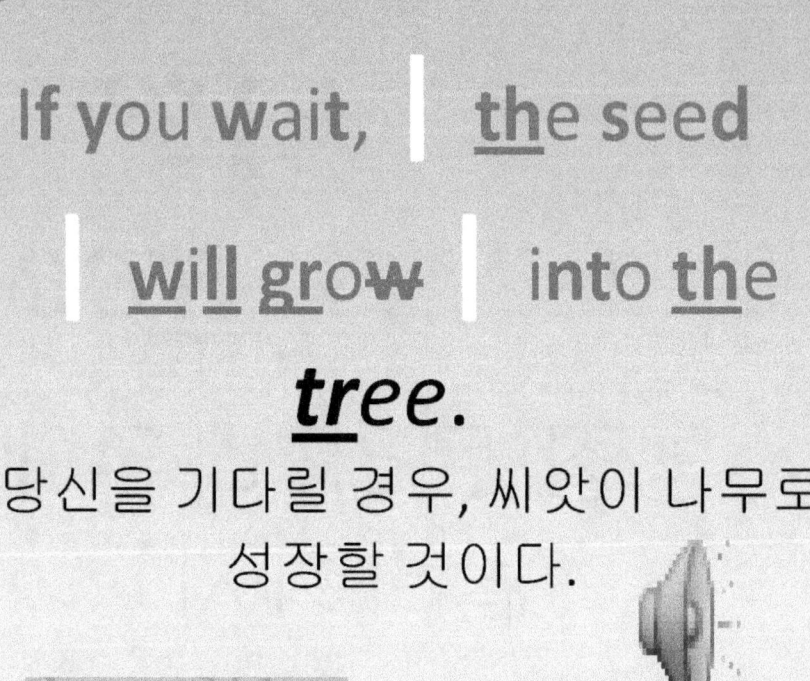

If you wait, | <u>th</u>e seed | <u>w</u>i<u>ll gr</u>ow | into <u>th</u>e <u>tr</u>ee.

당신을 기다릴 경우, 씨앗이 나무로 성장할 것이다.

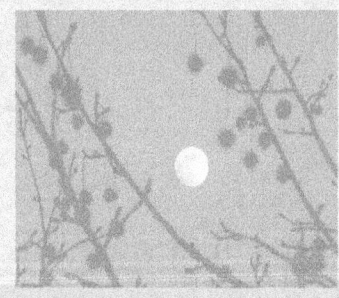

Photo by joiseyshowaa
at http://tr.im/1zgm

Phrases

Sentence

Category: nature

_r_i _v_e_r_

_r_i _v_eu_r_

강

Word
Phrases Sentences

Photo by Wolfgang Staudt
http://tr.im/1zhc

cross the _ri_ ver;
the longest _ri_ ver
in China

빛이 비취보기 교차;
중국에서 가장 긴 진량읍보기

Photo by PhillipC   See also
http://tr.im/1zhv   http://tr.im/1zi8

Phrase

Word   Sentences

The children | jumped | into the ri ver.

아이들은 강물에 뛰어들었다.

Photo by Fabio Pinheiro Staudt
http://tr.im/1zif

Sentence

Phrases

GRAMMAR

The crucial thing, in seeking out a congenial grammar book, is to find one whose authors have an ear for the way language evolves and changes, and show good judgment about the point at which we might want to adopt or surrender to neologisms and new usages.
>> Francine Prose

To understand grammar is to understand sentence structure – and vice versa. To understand sentence structure is to understand grammar.
>> Martha Kolln and Robert Funk

But the truth is that grammar is always interesting, always useful. Mastering the logic of grammar contributes, in a mysterious way that again evokes some process of osmosis, to the logic of thought.
>> Francine Prose

When a thought takes one's breath away, a grammar lesson seems an impertinence.
>> Thomas W. Higginson

Language is the anvil of life, and poems, proverbs, novels, and such are the finely tempered artifacts produced on it. But how and where is the anvil made? It must be in the hallowed halls of silence.
>> Octavio Paz

Like everything metaphysical, the harmony between thought and reality is to be found in the grammar of the language.
>> Ludwig Wittgenstein

Among the questions that writers need to ask themselves in the process of revision – is this the best word I can find? Is my meaning clear? Can a word or phrase be cut from this without sacrificing anything essential? – perhaps the most important question is : Is this grammatical?
>> Francine Prose

GRAMMAR

John W. DuBois in *Discourse and Grammar* from Michael Tomasello's *The New Psychology of Language* Volume 2

"Differences that separate grammar from discourse are not hard to find. Grammar describes sentences; discourse goes beyond the sentence. Grammar limits options by rules; discourse is what the speakers do with the freedom that is left. Grammar is general; discourse varies at the will of its speakers and whim of their topics. Grammar is meaningless, proudly so; meaning and pragmatic force lie at the heart of discourse. Grammar is pointless in a sense, possibly a good sense; discourse realizes the ends, whether communicative, cognitive, interactional, ideological, aesthetic or otherwise, that its producers seek to attain. It is no surprise that the study of grammar and the study of discourse are so often seen as worlds apart, pursued with different goals and different methodologies by different people. And yet language itself, in its actual occurrences, would seem to display at once the characteristics that attract both the grammarian and the discourse specialist. If language responds to either approach taken, can the distance between grammar and discourse be so great as the dichotomies imply?

Perhaps this perceived gulf makes it needlessly difficult to reach a full understanding of language. If we hope to learn how language works we will need to pursue multiple vantage points, while encompassing grammar and discourse within a single field of view. We need to exploit a stereoptical vision to integrate the two into one unified domain of phenomenal inquiry, even as our theoretical constructs retain the character distinctive of their separate origins."

GRAMMAR

Carolyn Ericksen Hill in *Writing from the Margins*

"We begin ...with the idea that every structure is frozen force ... I use two motivating ideas. One is from Eugene Hammond's *Informative Writing*, the idea that the basic noun/verb relation of a sentence is "a relation between matter and energy" with both subjects and objects supplying "'matter' we can get hold of," and verbs carrying either kinetic energy (verbs of action) or potential energy (verbs of being). The other motivating idea comes from Ernest Fenollosa and is also related to "transferences of force from agent to object" (*The Chinese Written Character as a Medium for Poetry* in *Prose Keys to Modern Poetry*, ed. by Karl Shapiro, p139), a movement he claims constitutes natural phenomena and can be duplicated in imagination for linguistic phenomena as well. The "rapid continuity of this action" is never broken up in nature, claims Fenollosa, and should not be broken up in imagining grammatical movement either. A sentence should be simply a redistribution of force:

> *A true noun, an isolated thing, does not exist in nature. Things are only terminal points, or rather the meeting of points of actions, cross-sections cut through actions, snapshots. Neither can a pure verb, an abstract motion, be possible in nature. The eye sees noun and verb as one: things in motion, motion in things, and so the Chinese conception tends to represent them.*

...As Thomas Wheeler says, "grammar books ignore the tactile and sensory aspect of writing.... But grammar is not separate from the senses, but a form through which the senses find clarity". And it is by analogy, as he claims, that they understand grammar, "not by rote."
(Thomas Wheeler 1979 *The Great American Writing Block: Causes and Cures of the New Illiteracy*)

"**Verbs** are the heart because they supply a sentence with energy and allow it to move. A good sentence is balanced, as the body is balanced , with equal weight on either side. The whole weight does not go into a main clause, but into its limbs, allowing the sentence to stretch. Style is like the grace of an athlete or dancer. As the dancer rises, so a sentence ascends toward its importance. It does not come down at the end with a thud, but climbs – as feeling climbs – to a peak. The end of one sentence is a springboard to another. Paragraphs fit together into closely related parts.

Overviews of Grammar

Just as there are rules of protocol related to various literary genres, so too the English sentence has its rules and traditions. There is no single lens, however, on how to look at the sentence and English grammar. Most people manage quite well in figuring things out without much formal training. Powers of observation serve the individual well in this regard. As with a coach's strategy to win a game, there are many ways to pick apart and piece together the language.

Function or Performance-based Grammar: Words have to be doing something, and sometimes groups of words (kinds of words) do the same kind of thing. What they have to do is called their job or function. Remember the kinds of words and what jobs or functions each perform. Take apart the sentence that way, and figure out how words function and do their jobs in the sentence.

Context-based Grammar: This grammar holds that the context of a text or passage is all important (either the context of the text as a whole, or more likely, the implied situation or setting where a given passage or utterance occurs). In short, words acquire their meaning from the context in which they appear. If someone says, *Time to crash*, literally they might mean they are about to commit suicide, or else they may just be indicating that they are tired and that it is time to go to bed. So the meanings of the words change with the contexts in which they appear. *The stock market crashed* uses the word *crash* just as the expression above has the word *crash* in it; however, it does not mean in this instance that anyone will either commit suicide or go to bed very suddenly because they are feeling extremely tired. Context determines so much in language.

Syntax or Position-based Grammar: This grammar locates the meaning of a text in the position or location of words in the sentence. Syntax just means the order and succession of the words as they appear in the sentence. Words placed at the beginning and end of sentences have more power and influence than those generally placed in the middle of the sentence. In English, the subject, which is usually a noun, normally comes first, while the verb customarily comes second while objects and sentence complements come third.

Class or Kind-based Grammar: In this grammar, words are categorized by their Class or Category to which they are assigned by virtue of both their meaning and function in the sentence. In our usage in this book, Class or Kind-based grammar simply corresponds to what we call the 12 kinds of words along with their 5 jobs in the sentence. Such a grammar provides a coherent structure and mental map of the few component parts which compose the totality of a language – in our case, the 12 kinds of words, or in traditional grammar the 8 parts of speech.

Form-based Grammar: In this grammar, language is understood and mastered by means of perceiving standard, recognizable, and frequently repeated **Forms** or **a Recognizable Look or Appearance** that words assume in a text. Thus, for example, prefixes and suffixes give a distinct look or form or appearance to classes, types, or kinds of words. Adverbs frequently have *–ly* at the end of them; words that end with *-ness* and *-ation* usually indicate nouns. Gerunds and present participles end in *–ing*, but also this can be confusing because some adjectives and many main verbs end in *–ing*. At the level of analyzing the classes and kinds of words that compose a sentence, Form-based grammar is rarely adequate, comprehensive, or immensely helpful, but it can be a useful, complementary, and at times helpful supplement and support for other grammars.

Meaning-based Grammar: Words have meanings. As long as they are assembled logically and with the aim of clear communication, although they may be grammatically incorrect, they can still be understood and convey a clear message. A toddler says *I hungry* or an ESL student writes *We went to store buy apple*. Though many rules or conventions may have been ignored in the previous sentence, we understand what the student is saying. The elegance of correctness is missing; however, but there is still an elegance of simplicity.

Utilitarian-based Grammar: Rules are generalizations that cover most of the instances. Exceptions do exist, and should be remembered. However, rules are not hard and fast and inflexible, or etched in stone. Language is mutable and flexible, so one has to find what works and go with go with the common usage and idioms of the language.

Twelve Kinds of Words

Little Five	Big Five
6 **Conjunction**	1 **Verb**
7 **Preposition**	2 **Noun**
8 **Verbal: infinitive**	3 **Pronoun**
9 **Verbal: gerund**	4 **Adjective**
10 **Verbal: participle** (a) *present participle* (b) *past participle*	5 **Adverb**
Two More	
12 **Other**	11 **Appositive**
Clap!	

| 12 | 10 9 8 7 **6** | **1** 2 3 4 5 | 11 |

The Two Exceptions in The Twelve Kinds of Words

The **Ten Kinds of Words** have **two** exceptions that are so designated that way because of their great importance and frequent usage in the language as fundamental building blocks.

The **Appositive** is the first of the two Exceptions because it is not really a separate kind of word, but actually a sub-category of a Noun, just as the articles (*the*, *a*, and *and*) are sub-categories of the Adjective, or personal, definite, and indefinite Pronouns are sub-categories of the Pronoun. However, *we single out the Appositive because of its importance and frequency of use in language* which is undoubtedly why *traditional grammar gave it a special name without adequately highlighting its importance and frequency of usage.*

Finally, we mention the second Exception as an open Exception to include kinds of words like interjections which have little importance or frequency of usage in written language. We call them the **Other** kind of word. They are used in every language, and serve various functions such as conveying very emotion (*gosh, crikey*) or getting someone's attention (*hey, yo!*). See *The Closing* (in Volume 2) for a more detailed explanation.

People should begin the study of grammar by concentrating on the Ten Main and The Eleventh Exception, and noticing the second Exception with limited attention or scrutiny.

The 12 Kinds of Words

The Two Hands Approach designates twelve **kinds of words** in the English language. The term **part of speech** is confusing and imprecise, since the entities to which it refers are used not only in speech, but also in writing. The constituents used in *both* speech and writing deserve a more exact and correct term for their collective reference, and a word that is less mechanical and more organic in its connotation. As replacement, we suggest the phrase **Kinds of Words**.

Traditional grammar designates the eight *parts of speech (Kinds of Words),* including the insignificant and seldom used *interjection*. The 2HA removes the interjection from its place of primary importance, but retains the remaining seven. To the status of Kinds of Words, it nominates five additional kinds of words: the three **Verbals**, the **Appositive**, and a final kind called the **Other**. It is to the latter group that the lowly interjection is re-located.

It is not crucial to spend a lot of time trying to explain the abstruse differences between some of these older terms and their corollaries - such as *specifier, determiner, article* (which previous grammarians have kept in separate categories or classes). **They should not be part of a course outlining the foundation of language. These words can be explained when the occasion arises; they are of only marginal importance for this foundational approach to language.**

Five Primary Kinds of Words

The Two Hands Approach calls the **first five kinds of words** *primary* or *dominant*. They are used most of the time, and the right hand is used to remember them. With the fingers of **our right hand**, we can form a triangle with our fingertips. In the following diagram, the parentheses represent the fingertips of the right hand, **with the fingertips facing** toward you, with the thumb to the far right and the little finger to the far left (palm inward)

(**P**) right middle finger

right ring finger (**Adj**) ⟶ (**N**) right forefinger

right little finger (**Adv**) ⟶ (**V**) right thumb

The right thumb is the (1) **Verb**. The right pointer finger is the (2) **Noun**. The right index finger represents the (3) **Pronoun**. The index or middle finger often has a kind of axial or pivotal property. The Pronoun at the top stands for "I", **the first person singular, pivot and rivet of attention in everyone's mind's eye**. The right ring finger is the (4) **Adjective**. The Adjective is horizontally across from the Kind of Word it describes, the Noun. *Articles*[1], *determiners*[2], and *enumeratives*[3] are put in this group. The fifth right finger is the (5) **Adverb**. It is horizontally across from the Verb, which is one of the Kinds of words that the Adverb modifies or describes. *Intensifiers*[4] are put under adverbs.

This finger formation is an easy way to remember the relationship between the Kinds of words. Thus, Adjectives describe Nouns. Adverbs describe Verbs, but they also modify themselves (curl up the little finger), as well as Adjectives (the right ring finger).

You can also pinch the right thumb and forefinger together. **Placing these two fingers together designates that these two kinds of words, the Verb and the Noun, are the two most important of all kinds of words.**[5]

---

[1] *the, an, a*
[2] *Determiner* is a general word that refers to articles, possessive pronouns, possessive nouns, demonstrative pronouns, and numbers.
[3] *first* customer, *second* day, *third*, …
[4] *very, more, less, somewhat, a bit,…*
[5] It is interesting to note that in some cultures, rubbing the thumb and first finger together is sign language for *money*. In the Information Age, it is the skilled

The other three right hand digits designate the other three kinds of words, and complete the set of the **5 dominant kinds of words** that have the most meaning in English, and which are **the most important, the most meaningful, and the most frequently used**.

Five Secondary or Sub-Dominant Kinds of Words

The **second set of five**, called *secondary* or *subdominant* ones, are significant, but not as critical. (6) **Conjunctions** and (7) **Prepositions** (left thumb and forefinger) are both connectors and do not contribute as much to the meaning of a sentence as the five dominant Kinds of Words.

The remaining left hand fingers represent the three Verbals. The left index finger is the (8) **Infinitive**. This, in the *to-* form or stem form, represents the essence or basic form of the verb. The left ring finger is the (9) **Gerund**, and the last finger represents two types of (10) **Participles**, the Present Participle and the Past Participle.

Looking at the ends of our left fingers (palm inward), we have the following memory-aid diagram:

　　　　　　　　　　left middle **(V-inf)**

　　　　　left forefinger **(Prep.)**　　　**(V-ger)** left ring finger

　　left thumb **(Conj.)**　　　　　　　　**(V-part)** left little finger

The **Verbals are multi-functional Kinds of words**, performing the roles simultaneously in specific double combinations of verb, noun, adjective, and/or adverb (for example, verb + noun, verb +adjective, verb + adverb).

The Verbal Kinds of Words, together with the Verb, convey *the energy, the movement, and the dynamism* of the language. The inclusion of these three Verbals together with the Verb in our

---

use of Verbs (thumb) and Nouns (1st finger) in well-constructed sentences that will gain advantage and promotion in most work settings!

master list of Kinds of Words establishes the supremacy of the Verb over the Noun in all language.

Traditional grammar failed altogether in this respect, and violated both common sense and ignored the everyday usage of language, where verbals occur with great frequency. Words that recur with such frequency cannot be consigned to the margins of language instruction. They are indeed in practice, with respect to their meaning and power, more important as Kinds of Words than Connectors and Prepositions (which follow). Traditional grammar undoubtedly viewed the Verbals as subcategories of the Verb, but thereby, unfortunately, minimalized and marginalized their pivotal role in language. This system now elevates Verbals to equal rank with the other seven primary and secondary Kinds of Words.

The Two Additional Kinds of Words

The eleventh category is the (11) **Appositive**. **An *appositive* is an additional name for another noun that usually precedes it in the sentence.** For example, in the sentence *Jenny, my best friend, lives down the street,* in our system, the appositive part is *friend.* Since it is the more important of the two additional Kinds of Words, we associate it with the *right hand* when teaching students to remember it.[6]

The (12) **Other** category is for the ever-present, non-conforming, idiosyncratic cases. You always have to expect the unexpected in English grammar; thus, the need for this coverall designation of "**Other**". We allocate to this category the short words previously called *expletives, interjections, fillers, invocative words, topic shifters, salutations, summons,* and (from discourse analysis) *pause and boundary markers*. Any additional items of this kind may simply be appropriately named and

---

[6] The Appositive is a Noun that immediately follows another Noun or Pronoun and explains them further. The Appositive makes the antecedent Noun or Pronoun more definite or clear and is separated by a comma.

included in this category of *the **Other**[7]*. Since the *Other* is the less important of the two additional Kinds of Words (it is used primarily in speech and not in written text), we associate it with the **left hand** when teaching students to remember it.

See *The Closing* in Volume II for a full description of the *Other*.

The list of the twelve Kinds of Words is concise and gives priority to the kinds of words in the sequence of their importance. Inspect any passage from a novel or mainstream media, and it will be seen that no important kind of word has been left out.

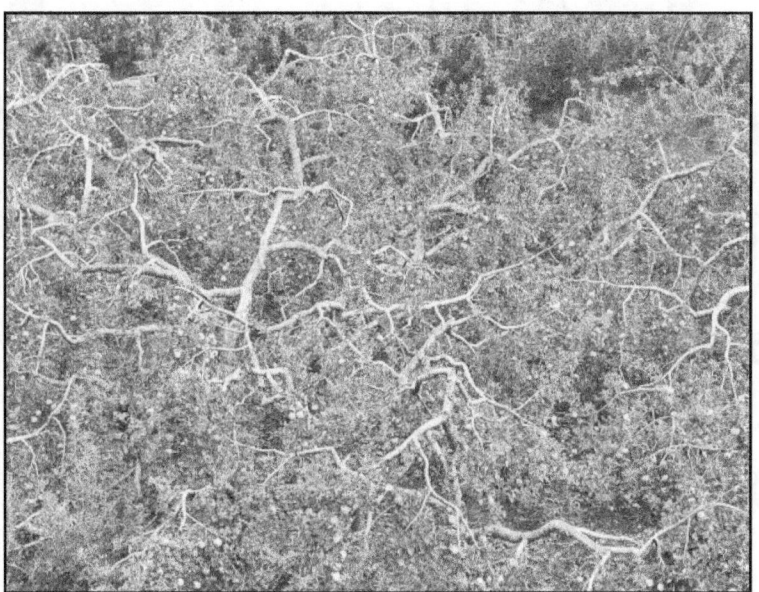

---

[7] Take an in-depth look our very comprehensive description and list of examples of *the Other* in The Closing in Volume 2.

Five Jobs or Functions of the Twelve Kinds of Words

Right Hand – Jobs that Words Do

1 Main Verb	MV
2 Subject	S
3 Descriptor	D
4 Object [*left hand*] 　1) *direct* 　2) *indirect* 　3) *object descriptor* 　4) *object of preposition* 　5) *object of verbal*	O
5 Connector	C

Job or Function of the Twelfth Kind of Word, the Other
The twelfth Kind of Word performs the job of expressing a variety of emotions and speech expressions.
We call this job the **Emotive and Speech Modes.**

6 Emotive and Speech Modes	SM

　　　5 4 3 2 1　　　1 2 3 4 5

　　5 Kinds of Objects　　5 Jobs of 12 Kinds of Words

The 5 Jobs of the 12 Kinds of Words

The functions that the 12 kinds of words play are 5 in number. The first three functions are placed in the above order to establish the primacy of the Verb over the Noun in learning and using language. It also emphasizes again the dual primacy of the Verb and the Noun. Finally, this order corresponds typically to the way people learn the various kinds of words, and employ them.

The word *Predicate* is not used at the outset, since it is not essential for understanding the foundations of the language, and since it is confusing. **Discussions about the Predicate should come much later in language instruction *after* the foundations have been laid with this approach.**[8]

The order has a simple logic:

- **Main Verb** (*we first learn a language listening to our mother's verbal commands*);

- **Subject** (*we then learn the word "I", since a baby's first emerging awareness is in response to the question "Who am I?" - probably as yet not existent in words, but perhaps there in spirit or another form in its memory*);

- **Descriptor** (*we certainly know what happiness [smile], sadness, anxiety, and fear are right from the start of life (nice baby, good girl)*);

- **Object** (*we learn that as agents we act upon, shape, and manipulate entities as objects (persons, things, ideas)*; and then we learn something about

- **Connectors**, the putting together and joining of persons, ideas, and things, and the words which join, unite, and establish relationships between the persons, ideas, and things.
    ie.   Bill *and* Jane, the boy *in* the home

---

[8]   To say it another way, familiar to us all: *Keep It Simple, Stupid.*

Conjunctions and prepositions, as in the examples above, are working as Connectors.

We learn that all reality is a connection and interplay of objects and motion, and words are the glue or links that we use to reference all accountable and visible entities, and all the mental and invisible reality around us. (For those with an interest in physics, they should tackle reading Brian R. Greene's *The Elegant Universe* or his 2004 book *The Fabric of the Cosmos* whose culminating vision is of "a vibrant eleven-dimensional 'multiverse', pulsating with ever-changing textures, where space and time themselves may dissolve into subtler, more fundamental entities.")

Let's have a closer look at each of the 5 functions we listed above.

(1) <u>Main Verb</u>

We learn first about the **Main Verb.** Every human starts by responding to a simple imperative verb: *look, see, (don't) cry, smile.* It is accompanied with actions simultaneously. The whole body is involved; therefore, the mind easily remembers and uses verbal commands. **The learning of language begins with the Verb**[9].

The Verb is the only Kind of word that can legitimately stand on its own, and be considered a sentence.

There are 3 kinds of **Main Verbs** as are shown in the following 2 charts. In each case, the Constituent Verb is the part of the verb that indicates the action or process, and is not indicative of time (*I <u>have</u> **seen** the movie twice*) or volitional (*I <u>might</u> **go** there later*).

Phrasal verbs abound in spoken English and thus are a bugbear and burden for EFL and ESL students to learn. A phrasal verb can have a helping verb component as well as the basic verb and basic postposition components. For example, in *The child **is putting away** her toys*, we see all three possible components of the Main Verb (Helping Verb, Basic Verb, Preposition in post-position).

For native English speakers, the main verbs are read and can be identified with not much confusion; for EFL students, however, main verbs are not always easily noticed at first glance.

---

[9] This is why the learning of all vocabulary begins with verbal commands involving action. This is the merit of the TPR method, which works best and usually only effectively at the beginning of language instruction.

Five Kinds of Main Verbs I

Five Kinds of Main Verbs

1	**Linking Verb** **MV = LV** Main Verb = Linking Verb *is, was, were, are, look, seem, feel, taste, sound, get, become, remain*	She **is** smart. He **was** rich. There **are** students. They **became** weary. The food **tastes** good. You **look** great! That **sounds** good.
2	**Basic Verb (alone)** **MV = BV** Main Verb = Basic Verb	Jan **sings** very well. I **stand** alone. Betty **typed**. John **ran**. They **relaxed**. The news **spread**. Infants **cry**.
3	**Basic Verb (with Helping Verb)** **MV = HV + BV** Main Verb = Helping Verb + Basic Verb *be, do, have*	Dad **is watching** TV. I **have been waiting** for 20 minutes. He **didn't notice** the time. We**'ve been studying** this for two weeks. **Did** you **see** the movie? The clerk **had** already **left** by then.

Five Kinds of Main Verbs II

4	**Basic Verb (with Special Helping Verb)** **MV = SHV + BV** Main Verb = Basic Verb preceded by Special Helping Verb that: 1. that is Future-related; or 2. that indicates condition or limitation on action	**Future-Related** 1. Potentiality (or Ability) You **can** do it. (ability) [past form: *could* as in Last year I *couldn't* drive at all.] 2. Possibility I **might** go. I **may** be a bit late. 3. Suggestion You **should** get here on time. You**'d better** call first. We **should** renovate the house. 4. Preference I **would** stay here if I were you. 5. Proposition or Proposal We **should** raise the drinking age. We **should** update the highway system. You **could** look in the yellow pages. 6. Prediction I **will** be there soon. I think she **will** win the prize. **Condition or Limitation on Action** 7. Obligation You **must** see the film. They **have to** make monthly mortgage payments. You**'ve got to** try. 8. Permission You **may** leave now. You **can** go if you want. Last time, we **couldn't** reach the top because of rain. 9. Prohibition You **can't** do that.
5	**Phrasal Verb** **MV = (HV) + BV + PiP** Main Verb = (Helping Verb) + Basic Verb + Preposition-or-Adverb-in-Postposition	**Transitive: separable** **Turn on** the radio. **Turn** the radio **on**. **Hand in** your homework. **Hand** it **in**. **Turn down** the music. **Turn** it **down**. They all **put on** their boots. They all **put** their boots **on**. **Transitive: inseparable** She can't **get over** the breakup. **Get off** the bus at the third stop. You're **taking on** too much work. **Transitive: separated** You're **putting** me **on** (but not: You're putting on me.) That really **ticks** me **off**. **Intransitive** Many people **showed up** at the meeting. They are just **getting by** these days. I **woke up** at 6:00 am.

(2) **Subject**

The second, most important function is the **Subject**. For the most part, every sentence must have, as its heart or center, words doing the jobs of subject and main verb.

The Verb often finds its partner in meaning in the **Noun** or **Pronoun** used as the subject. The sentence organically branches from the words functioning as subject and main verb, in accordance with the rules of structure, and from then on the sentence accrues layer by layer, organically branching from wherever it will, always in accordance with the rules of structure, always in accordance with the care and vision that only an experienced writer or conversationalist can bring.

All writing and all conversation is organic. Within both, patterns can be discerned if one is looking for form, but the variety of combinations of those forms can in no ways be computed. Even revisiting a text will offer new meaning. As Harold Bloom notes, "We cannot step even once in the same river. We cannot step even once in the same text." This organic process is comparable to the process of *scaffolding* or *co-construction* that goes on during a conversation.

A Noun, Pronoun, Infinitive, or Gerund may perform the function of the subject of the sentence. The Subject represents the main animate or inanimate entity, or abstract quality of reality, which assumes the agent or main actor role in the sentence. The Subject (agent or main actor) along with the Main Verb forms the **essence** of the sentence (or what some linguists have called the *kernel sentence*[10]) on which everything else builds.

---

[10] The concept of the **kernel sentence** along with its multiple transformations is the key concept of the process of teaching writing by Sentence Combining. This is a premier, innovative, and empirically proven method of teaching composition, which we recommend in addition to our own Approach.

(3) Descriptors

Descriptors come in 4 varieties:

Descriptor Functions		
Distant Descriptors		
1	Those that describe Nouns or Pronouns at a distance: (a) **Nouns** (b) **Adjectives**	Examples: [subject] [main verb] [distant descriptor] | Subject	Main verb	**Distant descriptor**
noun or pronoun	verb	noun or adjective
I	am	a cyclist.
Jane	is	studious. | The main verb (2nd sentence) is a linking verb, such as *become, appear, look, feel, grow*.
Descriptors		

2	Those that describe Nouns:
	
	(a) **Adjectives**
	(b) **Participles**
	(c) **Infinitives**
	(d) **other Nouns**[11]
		Examples:
		Adjectives can describe Nouns
		  (a) *hollow* feeling; *full* stomach; *green* eyes
		Participles can describe Nouns
		  (b) *rhyming* verse; *spreading* virus; *paved* street; *powdered* milk
		Infinitives can describe Nouns
		  (c) The need *to make peace* is very important. The will *to survive* is the law of the jungle.
		Other Nouns can "describe" Nouns
		  (d) *brain* surgery, *news* stand, *corner* store.

---

[11] See discussion in Vol. 2 in The Closing on the property of Nouns performing the role or function as Descriptors. (ex. *roller suitcase, wheelchair access,* etc)

3	Those that describe Verbs
	(a) **Adverbs**
	(b) **Infinitives**
		<u>Adverbs can describe Verbs</u>
		(a) She left *quickly*.
		    She dove *gracefully* from the diving board.
		<u>Infinitives can describe Verbs</u>
		(b) I went to the library *to study*.
		    I bought a book *to help* me learn Korean.

4	Those that describe other descriptors (a) **Adverbs** (b) **Adjectives**	<u>Adverbs can describe Adverbs</u> (a) The cars moved *very* slowly. <u>Adverbs can describe Adjectives</u> (b) This one is *more* expensive. That was *very* painful decision.

Located after the Main Verb, but referring always to the serving as the Subject of the Main Verb, is what was previously called the **Subjective Complement**. This will now be designated a **Distant Descriptor**, regardless of whether it was previously called a *predicate nominative* (a noun) or a *predicate adjective* (an adjective). The advantage of this new terminology is that is allows us to identify only five functions that can be remembered with only one hand as an image and apt memory device. It also does not require us to distinguish between the *predicate nominative* and the *predicate adjective*, a distinction which has little practical relevance for learning how to write.

For clarification, let us consider these two sentences:
> *Tom is a diver.*
> *Tom is tired.*

In both cases, we learn something more about Tom. In the first case (the former *predicate nominative*), we learn about his profession. In the second case (the former *predicate adjective*), we learn about Tom's physical condition. This is an example of what we think of as words that describe Tom from a distance, or on the other side of the main verb. Hence, we feel that the designation of **Distant Descriptor** is an easy and comprehensible term, and we can then dispense with the term *predicate adjective, predicate nominative,* and *subjective complement*.

The fact that we call Nouns "Descriptors", as when we call predicate nominatives Distant Descriptors, moreover, is not without precedent. Nouns have often been used as Descriptors, as when we say, *The car hit the brick wall. Brick* is a noun, and in our terminology, it remains a Noun as a Kind of Word, but functions as a Descriptor. Furthermore, there are what we call *Adjuncts*, which are pairs of Nouns: the first in the pair functions as a descriptor for the second Noun of the Pair.

The role of the **Appositive**, the eleventh kind of word, poses a challenge to our classification scheme. It presents a substitutable noun referring to another noun. For example, in *"Mrs. Lucas, our next door neighbor, loves gardening."*, the Appositive is *neighbor*. For the sake of simplification, we must think of an Appositive as a *noun working as a Descriptor*. The Appositive is placed not before the word it describes (the usual location), but soon after it.

An Appositive carries inherent attributes, and, as such, adds more to the attribute list of the Noun to which it refers. This is slightly different from the Adjective, which adds an attribute or attributes themselves to Nouns – without reference to another self-contained nominative entity.

Infinitives are also Descriptors, as are present and past participles. In fact, present and past Participles have assumed overwhelming significance in the English language, and their importance needs to be highlighted and underscored in all English instruction, contrary to contemporary practice in this regard. This is why we have promoted the present and past participle to the rank and status of Kinds of Words.

Any possessive (ie. Bill's, Jane's, his, her, their) will be thought of as doing a Descriptor function.

(4) Object

The **Object** comes in 5 varieties: ***direct object, indirect object, object complement, object of a preposition, object of a verbal***. Once again, they can be displayed and remembered in the image of a single hand. The underlying theme of using the hands returns and recurs, as you see.

The **Direct Object** usually answers the question "[*main verb (ate, took, gave)*] **what?**". The Direct Object can be the same kinds of word as the Subject: *a Noun, Pronoun, Infinitive, or Gerund*.

The **Indirect Object** usually answers the question "[*main verb bought, gave*] **to/for whom?**" The **Indirect Object** is usually a word referring to a person: a name, a relationship word (*Mom, my friend, grandmother, her*). It is usually a noun or pronoun. The indirect object can be placed before the direct object without using the preposition *to*; if it follows the direct object, *to* must be used.

    Examples: *Mom gave me*$_{\text{indirect object}}$ *a dress*$_{\text{direct object}}$.
                        Mom gave a dress$_{\text{direct object}}$ *to me*$_{\text{object of preposition}}$.

The **Object Complement** is not really functioning as an Object; it is functioning like what we called the Descriptor earlier. One might protest that this is improper. However, it *is* a word that comes immediately after an object and, in fact, traditional grammar has given it a name, *object complement*. So, you may call it an *Object Complement* or *Object Descriptor*. We place it here for the convenience of the reader who may wish to retain the traditional designation – **a word that is in close proximity to an Object and that contributes extra features to that Object**. For example, *"They painted the house grey."* What did they paint? *The house* is the Direct Object. *What color* did they paint their house? *Grey* is in our terminology functioning as a Descriptor since it describes the Noun. Traditional grammar, however, possesses this category of Object Complement, and we retain it since **it permits us to designate 5 kinds of objects for ease of memory on one hand**. But if you prefer, you can call the Object Complement a Descriptor in using our terminology; either way is satisfactory.

There are **3 kinds of Object Complements**:

    (a) <u>Noun Object Complement</u> (or <u>Noun After Descriptor</u>)
        They called Michael Jackson the *king* of pop.
        Many Americans consider Cubans communist *enemies*.
        The company named Jane Smith *C.E.O.*
        (Note: This really is a double object or a noun with an appositive.)

    (b) <u>Adjective Object Complement</u> (or <u>Adjective Near Descriptor</u>)
        You made her *sad*.
        I painted the walls *brown*.
        She found the test *easy*.

    (c) <u>Infinitive Object Complement</u> (or <u>Infinitive After Descriptor</u>) (or arguably Adverb Verbal Infinitive Phrase as Adverb Descriptor)
        Teachers should prepare students *to be critical thinkers*.
        NASA trains astronauts *to fly into space*.
        The UN sends its ambassadors and workers *to give help to disaster area*s.

We will discuss the **Object of a Preposition** shortly, but suffice it to say, a word that is doing this job must be a Noun, Pronoun, Infinitive, or Gerund.

The **Object of a Verbal** can be the same kinds of words as the **Direct Object**. For example,

    Reading the **newspaper**_{direct object of present participle}, the commuter missed his stop.

    To overcome **poverty**_{direct object of infinitive} was the group's main objective.

    After *watching* the **video**_{direct object of gerund}, I wrote a review.

    After *calling* **her**_{direct object of gerund}, I felt much better.

    Before *trying* **trike gliding**, you have to complete a training course.

(5) Connectors
A word functions as a **Connector** when it links two or more words together. There are 2 kinds of words that do this job: *conjunctions* and *prepositions*.

(1) Conjunctions
There are 4 main types:

	Types of Conjunctions						
1	**COORDINATE CONJUNCTIONS** join equal words, phrases, independent clauses. There are 7 coordinate conjunctions.						
	and	for	or	yet	but	nor	so
2	**CORRELATIVE CONJUNCTIONS** consists of two or more words that work in tandem, relating two ideas or events together in a variety of ways. An exhaustive list is not needed here now, as these conjunctions comprise the fourth form, **4C The Correlatives.**						
3	**ADVERBIAL CONJUNCTIONS** function only as connectors of dependent clauses with other clauses that can be either dependent or independent. There are 18 adverbial conjunctions. The use of these comprises Form 7. Traditionally, they are called *subordinate conjunctions*.						

	Cause	Condition	Qualification	Time
	because	if	though	when
3	since	whether	although	as
	so that	once	even though	while
		whenever		since
		unless		befor
		until		after
		in case		once
				as

4	**REFERENCE[12] CONJUNCTIONS** function always as connectors, and sometimes as subjects or objects. There are 10 main RN conjunctions. This is **Form 8**.		
	who	where	when
	why	what	how
	that	which	whose
		whom	

> There is a satisfactory boniness about grammar which the flesh of sheer vocabulary requires before it can become vertebrate and walk the earth. But to study it for its own sake, without relating it to function, is utter madness.
>
> - Anthony Burgess

---

[12] What we here call *Reference Conjunctions* have traditionally been called *Relative Conjunctions*. We feel that this designation is confusing and should be replaced with *Reference Conjunction*. We explain this fully in Form 8RN.

(2) Prepositions

Prepositions are words that must be followed by an object. The preposition and its object together form a phrase. Usually the phrase describes a noun (then it is called an *adjective phrase*), or else it describes a verb (then it's called an *adverb phrase*).

Prepositions in Alphabetical Order

about	above	according to	across	after	against
along, alongside	amid	among	around	as	aside from
at	because of	before	behind	below	beneath
beside	between	beyond	by	down	during
except	for	from	in	inside	in the midst of
into	near	of	off	on	on account of
outside	owing to	over	past	pertaining to	previous to
since	through	throughout	to	toward	under
underneath	until	up	up against	upon	while
with	within	without	with regard to	in addition to	

Prepositions in Groups
Sorted by Thought Categories

Space	Time	Logic
about	about	.cause or reason
after	above	according to
ahead of	across	against
along, alongside	against	as
around	ahead of	because of
at	along	on account of
before	amid	owing to
between	among	pertaining to
by	around	.concession
during	at	aside from
for	below	as well as
from	beneath	notwithstanding

321

Space	Time	Logic
in	beside	**.exception**
in the midst of	between	despite
on	beyond	except
over	down	**.addition**
past	in	in addition to
previous to	inside	**.specific instance**
since	into	in case of
throughout	near	**.comparison**
under	off	like
until	on	**.possession**
while	onto	of
within	out of	**.co-distinction**
	outside	apart from
	past	**.co-placement**
	previous to	up against
	through	with
	to	without
	toward	with regard to
	underneath	
	up	
	up against	
	upon	

(6) Speech Modes

Words such as *Hi, on the other hand, Lord, I'm sure, yes, no, sure, wow!, that's great, for example, no doubt, of course, thanks, etc* we named earlier as belonging to the category of Other[13] as one of the Kinds of Words. <u>The function which this Kind of Word (the *Other*) performs in the sentence we designate as **Emotive and Speech Modes**</u>. As Speech Modes, they perform the duties of expressing politeness, complying, topic shifting, answering, requesting, complimenting, expressing surprise or anger, endorsing, etc.

---

[13] These include: emotives (swearing, cursing, invoking), pause fillers, markers, salutations/summons lexical phrases, lexical phrase markers of spoken discourse, topic shifters, discourse devices, etc. They are significant but not core constituent elements of a sentence.

The words whose job is Speech Modes have been grammatically orphaned before our system, because until now, no names for them or designations that describe their function were forthcoming. We have named them and specified their function as Speech Modes.

Most people learn these words through repeated conversation. Admittedly, they were and are important in conversation. Their meaning often depends on the *context* of the conversation. They make ideas and information exchange flow more smoothly in the spoken medium. They are rarely found in journalistic, scientific, or prose writing, except within embedded direct quoted speech.

Now they have been clearly identified, and their function and usefulness in spoken and written language described.

The chart on the following page summarizes the Kinds of Words and their respective Jobs or Functions. We must include, however, a category for a group of words that perform odd jobs usually in spoken English. We call this sixth type of job, the Speech Modes.

No grammatical rules have sufficient authority to control the firm and established usage of language. Established custom, in speaking and writing, is the standard to which we must at last resort for determining every controverted point in language and style."
— Hugh Blair

"The fashion of the world is to avoid cost."
- Shakespeare
Much Ado About Nothing

Summary Chart of the 12 Kinds of Words and their 5 Jobs

12 Kinds of Word	5 Jobs				
	subject	main verb	descriptor	object	connector	emotive & speech modes
verb		●				
noun	●		●	●		
pronoun	●		●	●		
adjective			●			
adverb			●			
conjunction					●	
preposition					●	
verbal: infinitive	●		●	●		
verbal: gerund	●			●		
verbal: present participle past participle			●			
appositive			●			
other						●

Traditional Grammar in a Nougat Without the Interjection

A ***verb* identifies**. It is the action, observed. Life happens, and the verb reflects that. If there ever was a candidate for a symbol for the verb, it would have to be rock'n'roll, or a lion waiting, heart pounding and eyes alert, scanning the teeming herd on the savannah, those shapely split-hoofed prancing masters of lightness and speed, the Thompson's gazelle.

A ***noun* defines**. It tackles motion and ideas, and wrestles them down into notions and nation-states, pearls and rubles. The circle of life of which we are part encompasses myriad forms of being and forms of becoming; their label instances their becoming. Even stones metamorphose, or get eroded away by water. But, nouns help us believe that life has solidity, and permanence, and that we can stop and look, as at a gallery, and observe differences and similarities, contrast and compare, annotate and collate. That's what nouns are. They give form and seeming substance to the flights of fancy that we call thought and the kinetoscope of our daily spread of images.

That's the big duality – **Verb-Noun**. They are in a perpetual tango. In sentences, we see them, and tap our mental fingers to their rhythm as they emerge on the page.

Nouns are the dance hall; verbs are the dance. Nouns are the stadium and the benches; verbs are the game. Nouns are the coffee shop; verbs are the motions of minds visible and visible in the laughter on the faces, the gestures of the hands, the tones of the voices.

A *pronoun* **replaces a noun**. Since time is of the essence, and thought has continuity, they are timesavers, and help convey meaning with greater clarity and considerable saving of space and vocal effort.

Adjectives and *adverbs* **describe**. Our powers of observation, with the help of adjectives and adverbs, enable us to distinguish and equate differences, sizes, shapes, colors – qualifiers and quantifiers of all kinds.

So there we have the **big five** – as close to you as your right hand.

Prepositions and *conjunctions* **connect** the above big five. They serve as bridges and connectors that indicate temporal, spatial, and logical relationships. Reality is meant to be interpreted in its broader context, not piecemeal. Positioning in space and time allows one to pinpoint one's circumstances more precisely.

PUNCTUATION

Since the late 16th century the theory and practice of punctuation have varied between two main schools of thought: the elocutionary school, following late medieval practice, treated points or stops as indications of the pauses of various lengths that might be observed by a reader, particularly when he was reading aloud to an audience; the syntactic school, which had won the argument by the end of the 17th century, saw them as something less arbitrary, namely, as guides to the grammatical construction of sentences. Pauses in speech and breaks in syntax tend in any case to coincide; and although writers are now agreed that the main purpose of punctuation is to clarify the grammar of a text, they also require it to take account of the speed and rhythm of actual speech.

Encyclopedia Britannica

Punctuation in skilled hands is a remarkably subtle system of signals, signs, symbols and winks that keep readers on the smoothest road. Too subtle, perhaps: Has any critic or reviewer ever praised an author for being a master of punctuation, a virtuoso of commas? Has anyone ever won a Pulitzer, much less a Nobel, for elegant distinctions between dash and colon, semicolon and comma?   —Rene J. Cappon

The Associated Press Guide To Punctuation

12 Punctuation Marks Ⅰ

Punctuation sets the pace for the reader, and assists the reader to determine the importance, association, and relationship of elements within the sentence.

Right Hand – The Big Five Punctuation Marks

	Traditional Name	Symbol	Nickname	Traffic Signal	Rhythm & Pace
1	Period	.	The Terminator	Red	Stop
2	Colon	:	Dramatic Pointer	Red	Stop
3	Semi-Colon	;	The Balancer / The Equalizer	Red	Stop
4	Dash	—	The Highlighter / The Commentator / The Amplifier	Yellow	Pause
5	Comma	,	The Flow Manager	Yellow	Pause

1 2 3 4 5

12 Punctuation Marks II

Left Hand – The Little Five
Punctuation Marks

	Name	Symbol	Use & Effect
6	Question Mark	?	inquiry
7	Parenthesis	( )	addition of minor importance
8	Exclamation Mark	!	excitement, surprise, emphatic statement
9	Apostrophe	'	shows possession or contraction of two words
10	Hyphen	-	word joiner

Two Talkative Punctuation Marks
used to indicate direct speech or omitted speech

	Name	Symbol	Use & Effect
11	Quotation Marks	" "	marks off dialogue; citation of words of others; technical term; foreign word or phrase; notation of jargon; notation of ironic use of a word;
12	Ellipses Dots	...	indicates omitted words

12   10 9 8 7 6   11

Margaret Atwood on Punctuation

How important do you think it is for us to teach the conventions of good writing to our students? I'm thinking especially about punctuation.

I think you *should* teach the conventions. Punctuation was invented in the 19th century, as far as I can tell. That is, *regularized* punctuation which – like regularized all kinds of things! – came in during the age when Scrooges multiplied, and Cratchits were required. Many people were sent to school and they were trained to [...] sit at a desk, be underpaid, add up figures, and punctuate. So there had to be a system that everybody agreed upon. You see the same kind of systematization going on now in the wonderful world of computerland. You start off with all kinds of different systems, and then you realize that these things are not going to be able to communicate with each other unless you have one system that everybody agrees on – that *this* means *that*.

Originally however punctuation was more like musical notation. If you look at Roman texts, at the way they're actually written, there isn't any punctuation at all. There's the occasional period once in a while, but no commas or semicolons or anything like that. The meaning is contained in the inflections of the language itself. So, it's a lately-come system [...].

Before the 19th century, I think that punctuation was geared to the ear. The sermons of John Donne, for instance, were orations and meant to be spoken out loud. The 19th century was the age when silent reading really took over, although it didn't take over completely. If you read histories or novels of the time, or even Isabella Beaton's *Book of Household Management*, you will hear that in the evening the ladies should be doing needlework while somebody else reads an instructive book out loud to them, explaining the difficult parts. A friend of mine has just finished a history of reading, and it turns out that in the days of monasteries and illuminated manuscripts, reading was done out loud and in groups. If you were found reading silently it was assumed that the devil had your ear. You were making your own interpretation. Very bad idea.

Excerpted from a transcript of the talk given by Margaret Atwood at the May, 1995 gathering of the Toronto Council of Teachers of English, held at the University of Toronto Women's Club. At Ms. Atwood's request, questions were submitted by TCTE members and placed into a hat beforehand.

This excerpt is reprinted with the permission of the author.

3. Punctuation

Traditional instruction in punctuation has suffered from several shortcomings:

1. *Traditional instruction provides no clear distinction between the more important and the less important punctuation marks, but instead they are all treated more or less equally.* **The 2HA distinguishes between the five punctuation marks that are primary, and the five punctuation marks that are secondary, plus two additional ones, for a total of twelve.**
2. *The names of traditional punctuation marks are not suggestive of what they do or how they function in the sentence.* The purpose of punctuation marks is to control the flow of movement within the sentence; they need names that clearly describe their function. **The 2HA gives new names for the punctuation marks, words that are more indicative of the functions they that they do in the sentence.**
3. *The traditional names for punctuation marks carry no powerful images descriptive of their functions* as traffic policeman and pace-setters, controlling the flow of movement, the pauses, and stops within and between sentences. **The 2HA provides analogies and images of punctuation marks as traffic signals, with pauses representing yellow lights and stops designated as red lights.**
4. *Traditional names fail miserably to capture and convey the inherent musical character of language with its qualities of rhythm and pacing, beat and measure, pitch and tonality.* It is the pauses and stops in language that enable the reader to invest the words with the tone, melody, and mood which together convey the full range of human feeling. **The 2HA teaches the timing and pacing involved with each of the punctuation marks, and fully elucidates the proper and judicious use of the full use of such in one of the Sentence Forms as a means to establishing mood, and emphasis.**

Students, indeed, are seldom told the purpose or meaning of punctuation, so they never really understand, but simply memorize rules, which they soon forget. Having forgotten the rules, they then cannot reconstruct them by simply thinking about them, which they could do if they understood their meaning and purpose and had an image to guide their reconstruction of the rules. The 2HA provides a simple memory-aid diagram for that purpose.

Five Primary Punctuation Marks

There are *five primary punctuation marks*, symbolized by the **right hand**. The 2HA uses new names and traffic signals to help students remember and differentiate between the diverse functions of punctuation marks. Below are the primary punctuation marks, so designated because of their primary importance over the other punctuation marks.

FIVE PRIMARY PUNCTUATION MARKS

	#	TRADITIONAL NAME	DESCRIPTOR	TRAFFIC SIGNAL	RHYTHM AND PACE
	1	**Period** .	the Terminator	red	Stop
	2	**Colon** :	the Dramatic Pointer	red	
	3	**Semi-Colon** ;	the Equalizer, the Balancer	red	
	4	**Dash** —	the Afterthought, the Commentator, the Amplifier	yellow	Pause
	5	**Comma** ,	the Flow Manager	yellow	

In this instance, we use the right hand and fingers to identify the most common and significant punctuation marks. The right hand is thus both a visual image and a tactile device for remembering the punctuation marks and their functions. **When the right thumb and the small finger (#1 and #5) are put together** (they represent the most common punctuation marks), **the middle three fingers** form a **side-by-side triple alliance. This is**

important, as these three punctuation marks will occupy an important rank in the formation of the Power Punctuation Sentence Forms, which will be discussed later. The three middle fingers symbolize respectively the **power punctuation** marks: the forefinger stands for the **colon**, the middle finger stands for the **semi-colon**, and the fourth finger, the **dash**.

The use of the traffic signals emphasizes the functions of the punctuation marks as speed control managers in the sentence. **The function of the comma and the dash is to make the reader _slow down_, and so commas and dashes are represented by the traffic signals of _yellow_ lights. The function of the period, semi-colon, and the colon is to make the reader _stop and reflect_ at greater length; therefore, the period, the semi-colon, and the colon are designated as the traffic signals of _red_ lights.**

> In the eye method, you're told to put a period at the end of the sentence. In order to do this, you have to know what a sentence is. But no one knows. In the ear method I tell you put a period whenever your voice makes the sound of the period. That is, the voice slows down, the _tone_ falls, and the voice comes to a full, complete, solid stop. Like that. Did you hear the period? Read it aloud, and then you will.
>
> Robert C. Pinckert
> _The Truth about English_

Seven Secondary Punctuation Marks

There are *five secondary punctuation marks*, symbolized by the **left hand**. These are also significant, but do not rank in importance with the first five. **We indicate their secondary importance by not assigning them new names or traffic signals.**

SEVEN SECONDARY PUNCTUATION MARKS

		TRADITIONAL NAME	
	6	Question Mark	?
	7	Parentheses	( )
	8	Exclamation Point	!
	9	Apostrophe	' or '
	10	Hyphen	-
	11	Quotation Marks	" " ' '
	12	Ellipsis	...

The **Question Mark** goes at the end of question sentences.

Parentheses include all the four pairs of bracket symbols found on most computer keyboards ({ }, [ ], < >). The curved Parenthesis symbol will be discussed in Form 10.13 and 10.14 as parenthetical asides or elucidators.

The **Exclamation Point** goes at the end of sentences to indicate a stronger voice, an urgent intention or warning, or a surprising fact.

The **Apostrophe** indicates possession, and is also used to indicate that some letters are missing from a contracted word or phrase, as in *I'm, we're, etc.*

The **Hyphen** is used in many compound words, as in *vice-president, mother-in-law, X-ray*, and is also used to split up words that can't fit on a single line in a typeset setting such as a newspaper column.

Finally, there are ***two additional punctuation marks*** that are used in communicating directly the spoken or written words of others: **Quotation Marks** and **Ellipsis.**

Quotation Marks include both paired *single* and *double* quotation marks (' ' and " "), or less stylish hash marks (' ' and " "). They indicate the direct and exact words spoken or written by another person. They were used to quote special expressions, titles of books or magazines, and foreign words when typewriters were used (italics is often used to do that now).

Ellipsis (three dots ...) indicate that some part of someone's dialogue or written passage (beginning or end of a sentence, or paragraph) has been omitted or left out. There should be a single space before and after the ellipsis, but the spaces at both ends are omitted if the ellipsis is followed by a period, comma, question mark, or exclamation mark . Also, if you quote the latter part of a sentence, do not place an ellipsis at the beginning of a quotation to indicate the omission of material. Some typographic style guides advocate spaces between the dots (. . .). Typographer Robert Bringhurst has written a respected reference and style guide, *The Elements of Typographic Style*. The book "teaches the history of and the artistic and practical perspectives on a variety of type families that are available in Europe and America today."

For the **hand sign for Quotation Marks**, the student can slightly move the curved forefinger and middle fingers up and down to represent the hash mark style Quotation Marks. For the **hand sign for Ellipses**, the student can move the right or left hand in a slight chopping action three times from left to right. Or students can invent their own hand sign for the hand gestures for #11 and #12.

Quiz on Grammar Charts

Based on Grammar Charts contained in Volume I

1) What are the Twelve Turns of the English Language> Specifically, (1) what are *The Five Skills* that an English student must constantly master; (2) what are *The Five Tasks* that an English student must successively accomplish; and (3) what are *The Two Crowning Achievements* of English study? Value: 24 pts.

2) What are The Ten Plus Two Kinds of Words in the English language (otherwise called The Twelve Kinds of Words or The Twelve Parts of Speech of the English language)? Specifically, (1) What are The Big Five Kinds of Words; (2) What are The Little Five Kinds of Words; and (3) What are The Other Two Kinds of Words? Value: 24 pts.

3) What are The Five Functions that the Twelve Kinds of Words Perform in the English Sentence or What are The Five Uses of the Twelve Kinds of Words (or the Twelve Parts of Speech) in the English sentence? Value: 20 pts.

4) What are The Twelve Punctuation Marks in the English Language? Specifically, (1) What are The Big Five Punctuation Marks; (2) What are The Little Five Punctuation Marks; and (2) What are The Other Two Punctuation Marks of English? Value: 24 pts.

SENTENCE FORMS

> "The sentence has changed. Once I could not remember. Now I cannot forget."
>
> Elly Danica
>
> from *Don't: A Woman's Word* in *Stolen Life: The Journey of a Cree Woman* by Rudy Wiebe and Yvonne Johnston

Quotes on the Sentence

Sentences, the most important building blocks of prose, the foundation of written communication, and always the essential units of prose style."
Brooks Landon

"This is what I mean when I call myself a writer . . . I construct sentences." **Don DeLillo**

"...only the sentences ...can be proved to exist. Even at the stage of the paragraph things are becoming theoretical and arbitrary. A 'novel' is an utter hallucination: no definition of it, for example, can really distinguish it from a laundry list. But a sentence – there you have something essential, to which nothing can be added and from which nothing can be taken." **Thomas Berger**

"The sentence is where we must start if we hope to understand why some sentences captivate us and other writing leaves us unmoved and uninterested."
Brooks Landon

"To be better writers, we must first and foremost write better sentences. **Brooks Landon**

"Longer sentences, when carefully crafted and tightly controlled, are essential keys to elegant and effective writing." **Brooks Landon**

"Prose proceeds forward in time by steps less closely measured, but not less propelling, than the steps of verse. While every few feet, verse reverses, repeats, and reassures the pattern of its progression, prose picks up momentum toward its forward goal in strides variably adapted to its burdens and purposes. Both use steps; neither merely flows, each may be perceived by its own stages of articulation [the sentence in prose, verse in poetry]."
      Josephine Miles (1911-1985)
      Style and Proportion: The Language of Prose and Poetry (1967)

"This is the nature, the great beauty of approaching the art of the sentence through ...categories along with prolific displays of the splendid sentences good writers achieve. *Artful Sentences* show... specific skills widely applicable, that a writer can learn. ... [They] offer... models that can be imitated, organizing them in a way that makes them accessible and comprehensive. Forms that seem limited, and even limiting, in fact offer a range of opportunities to a writer in command of them – and one who knows how to transgress against them – to achieve undreamed of effectiveness, grace, and versatility.
    Virginia Tufte *Artful Sentences: Syntax as Style*

Understanding Form in General and The Forms of the English Sentence

We best see, understand, and master sentence construction when we notice that **sentences possess visually distinct and recognizable forms**.

What follows is a preliminary discussion on the idea, uses, and value of form (1) in daily life and experience and (2) in sentence construction.

Our discussion of form in daily life and experience covers three topics: first, form from the male and female viewpoints; second, form as requiring discipline for mastery; and third, form as necessary for skilled performance in writing.

After **the discussion on form in general**, we proceed to specifically define **the Twelve Forms of the English Sentence**.

Preliminary Thoughts on Form in Daily Life and Experience from Male and Female Perspectives

Definition of Form: Male View

Form as the Look or Visible Appearance of Something

"By 'form', philosophers mean the look of the sock, by which you recognize it as a sock. ...Form is thus visible shape, and the shaping force of the visible. ...*form individualizes. What causes each person and each ... to be different from other persons and things is the active force of form.*" James Hillman, *The Force of Character*

Definition of Form: Female View

The short passage next is an example of an expanded meaning of "form" to designate any distinct entity, period, quality, movement, artistic, or in this case, architectural style. It represents the more diffuse and intuitive awareness of women in general, and their tendency to interrelate and fuse concepts and ideas rather than the tendency of men (as seen above) to more clearly dramatize and focus on the separation and distinction between concepts and forms.

Preliminary Thoughts on Form In Daily Life and Experience

> The two sisters went on, up the road. They were passing between the trees just below Shortlands. They looked up at the long, low house, dim and glamorous in the wet morning, its cedar trees slanting before the windows. Gudrun seemed to be studying it closely.
> "Don't you think it's attractive, Ursula?' asked Gudrun.
> "Very,' said Ursula. 'Very peaceful and charming."
> "It has form, too—it has a period."
> "What period?"
> "Oh, eighteenth century, for certain; Dorothy Wordsworth and Jane Austen, don't you think?"
> Ursula laughed.

D.H. Lawrence, *Women in Love*, Chapter 4 *Diver*

Women are not necessarily more knowledgeable about architectural or literary forms than men, but in many ways and in many matters women's thinking is more holistic than men's.[1]

[1] The work of leading scholars of women such as Deborah Tannen and Carol Gilligan have shed light on the tendency of men to separate, distinguish, and partition aspects of reality, whereas women tend towards a more relational emphasis which tends to merge, meld, and less clearly focus and differentiate the diverse aspects of reality.
With men, concepts and forms are always clearly defined and focused; with women they are more diffuse and vague, but still there, and perhaps more subtle and profound.
A summary of some of the more notable differences between men and women that has emerged from recent research has been summarized aptly by Ken Wilbur as follows:
"...feminists now champion the notion that there are generally speaking, very strong differences between the male and female value spheres – that is, in both sex and gender. Men tend toward hyperindividuality, stressing autonomy, rights, justice, and agency, and women tend toward a more relational awareness, with emphasis on communion, care, responsibility, and relationship. Men tend to stress autonomy and fear relationship; women tend to stress relationship and fear autonomy." Ken Wilbur in *A Brief History of Everything* (2000, Boston: Shambala, p.2)

Preliminary Thoughts on Form In Daily Life and Experience II

Definition of Form as Discipline

Form as Something That In Its Execution and Mastery Requires Discipline By Both Males and Females

" I will tell you what I am talking about,' he said. 'Most kinds of power require a substantial sacrifice by whoever wants the power. There is an apprenticeship, a discipline lasting many years. Whatever kind of power you want. President of the company. Black belt in karate. Spiritual guru. Whatever it is you seek, you have to put in the time, the practice, the effort. You must give up a lot to get it. It has to be very important to you. **And once you have attained it, it is your power. It can't be given away: it resides in you. It is literally the result of your discipline.**'" M. Crichton, *Jurassic Park*.

To be disciplined is *to have or be in good form.*

Discipline is the use and realization of form. To be "disciplined" is to be "in good form." Interestingly, the Sanskrit word *dharma* means *discipline*, and the word is used to refer to what is otherwise known as *religion*. Attention to form in writing, and inner and outer discipline, together can bring awesome results.

Preliminary Thoughts on Form in Sentence Construction I

Form in Look of the Sentence

The "*sentence forms*" refers not only to the forms of entire sentences, but also to key or recognizable marks or features displayed within the sentence itself. Form, in its most basic manner of designation or appellation, simply means the overt, distinguishable, and noticeable look or appearance of something – in this case, a section of a sentence or even the entire sentence. As we read, we scan ahead quickly with our eyes to look for the forms; we recognize certain words and assign them primary or secondary roles; we notice punctuation marks and mentally make chunks of related meaningful content, and try to sense the intended pace and tone and emphasis that should be assigned to each of the chunks. As we proceed, we gather the intimations of meaning until we pass the point where the full meaning of the sentence becomes clear. Gopen calls this the *stress position* or *moment of full syntactic disclosure*; it could alternatively be called the *Completed Meaning Disclosure Moment*.

And then we may say: *Ah, that's how the puzzle fits together! That's what the writer wants to say! Those are the forms, and there is the meaning!*

Preliminary Thoughts on Form in Sentence Construction II

We call them *Sentence Forms* for a number of important reasons. In the idiom of Plato, they constitute eleven fundamental *ideas or concepts* of sentences, under which all other sentences may be classified. Plato used the word *form* to indicate that something has a visible look or appearance that made it distinguishable and set it apart. The *form,* with its visible aspect, made the entity stand out, and the Greeks always relied on the sense of sight as the primary metaphor for their vision of the world and their understanding of the mind. The **ear** is *aural*, but the **reading eye** is *visual,* as the **hand** is *tangible*.

Sound can be heard from any direction without turning the head, but *sight* must look in a single direction at the object of focus. Vision is directed. So, we use the word *form* to help make us notice the visual aspect of the sentence.

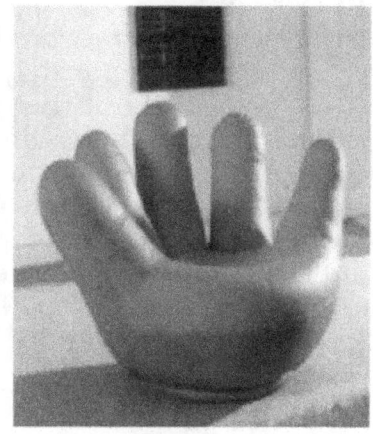

Preliminary Thoughts on Form as Acquired Skills III

Form in Action: Skill Acquisition & Practice

Form is indispensable for another key reason. All those who practice skills or the performing arts rely on the repeated performance of orchestrated **forms of action**. Thus, an **ice skater** performs first a set of established forms or shapes on the ice. These forms are identifiable by their look, their geometric appearance, their kinetic shape, their bodily motion. Each part of his or her routine is a part or component of the whole performance.

A **basketball player** does a jump shot; a **dancer** moves effortlessly and gracefully in a ballet or folk dance; a **pianist**'s fingers dance so wondrously fast over the piano keys; a **rock guitarist** wakes his gently sleeping guitar up in a fast-fingered riff that resounds through the concert hall – all these are examples of **great form achieved through hard work and practice**.

Performers must *repeatedly practice* each of the parts or components separately, with painstaking attention to detail at first, but then meld them into a sweep of action and movement that looks as though it is done with considerable ease and with almost minimal concentration. In the crux and crunch at game time or in the dazzle of the spotlight, the unconscious Mind and the stored skills come to the surface and almost automatically take over. The person and the Mind and the action are one; and we applaud.

Preliminary Thoughts on Form as Action Performance IV

Recognition and mastery of form is the crucial key to effective performance. Shakespeare, in **Midsummer's Night Dream**, wrote "**Take pains; be perfect**.", which we may paraphrase as "**Take pains with the forms; and eventually you will hold the key to effective writing competence**."

Recognizing form when reading is a visual experience, but it can be an auditory one if we vocalize or sub-vocalize when we read. In music and poetry, the form is given in the rhythm and beat; in India, there are very complex *tabla* rhythms. If tablas are in short supply, the teacher will play the rhythms on a wooden table, and students listen with their ears against the table. Students are then called on to duplicate the rhythm.

The absence of a comprehensive, but economically limited set of sentence forms, has been and remains the crucial <u>missing link</u> in methods aimed at teaching English composition.

Human Pleasure and Enjoyment of All Formed Things Harmonious and Beautiful

It is natural for the heart and spirit to take pleasure and enjoyment in **all the things** that show forth symmetry, harmony and perfection. For instance: a beautiful house, a well-designed garden, a symmetrical line, a graceful action, a well-written book, pleasing garments – in fact, all things that have in themselves grace or beauty are pleasing to the heart and spirit.

'Abdu'l-Bahá

The Strata of the English Language

	Construction Unit	Has Sound	Expresses Meaning	Expresses One Idea	Expresses Several Ideas
1	Letter	●			
2	Syllable	●			
3	Word	●	●		
4	Phrase	●	●		
5	Clause — Dependent	●	●		
5	Clause — Independent	●	●	●	
6	Sentence	●	●	●	●
7	Paragraph	●	●	●	●
8	Essay, Story, Blog Entry	●	●	●	●
9	Talk, Short Story, Essay, Long Paper, Series of Podcasts	●	●	●	●
10	Book	●	●	●	●

1 2 3 4 5   6 7 8 9 10

5-Level Architecture of the English Sentence

1 2 3 4 5

Five Architectural Levels or Analytical Stages of the Sentence	Subject	Main Verb	Direct Object or Distant Descriptor	Attachments to subject, verb, object	Additions
1 **Heart** = main verb		●			
2 **Essence** = heart + subject	●	●			
3 **Core** = essence + object or distant descriptor	●	●	●		
4 **Base** = core + attachments	●	●	●	●	
5 **Total** = essence + additions = core + additions = base + additions	●	●	(●)	(●)	●

<u>Base Level</u>: includes **attachments** which are words or phrases *attached* to one or more words in the Core (that is, the subject, main verb, and direct object or distant descriptor if there is one).

<u>Total Level</u>: includes **additions** which are words, phrases, or clauses placed in the beginning, middle, or end of the sentence as openers, interruptions, or closers of the sentence. They can be added to the Essence, Core or Base. They are separated by one or more punctuation marks.

> The **Main Verb** earns the title for **Heart** of the sentence, because when we read we should initially locate the Main Verb and then find the other parts assembled around it. It is relevant to note here that the Main Verb is primary in Japanese, Korean, German, and several Amerindian languages, and it is placed at the end of the sentence to highlight its importance. Lastly, Verbs in general (especially the Main Verb) allow us to place ourselves and events in the perspective of time.

Samples That Illustrate the 5-Level Architecture of the English Sentence

Sentence →	1 My mother, who made real corn bread almost every day of my growing up life, has a great pan, a square cast-iron skillet given by my great aunt. Ronni Lundy **Corn Bread with Character** in Sarah Skwire *Writing with a Thesis* 10th ed.	2 With the help of a basketball scholarship, Cassidy had attended junior college in his small hometown in Kentucky before laying out a year to work and raise enough money to attend a university. Sandra Brown **French Silk**
1 heart verb	has	had attended
2 essence + subject	<u>mother</u> has	<u>Cassidy</u> had attended
3 core + d. object or obj. desc.	mother has <u>pan</u>	Cassidy had attended <u>college</u>
4 base + attachments to core words	my mother has <u>a great</u> pan	Cassidy had attended <u>junior college in his small hometown in Kentucky before laying out a year to work and raise enough money to attend a university</u>.
5 total +other **additions** (side branching)	My mother, <u>who made real corn bread almost every day of my growing up life</u>, has a great pan, <u>a square cast-iron skillet given by my great aunt</u>.	<u>With the help of a basketball scholarship</u>, Cassidy had attended junior college in his small hometown in Kentucky before laying out a year to work and raise enough money to attend a university.

Another Graphic Representation of the 5-Level Architecture of the English Sentence

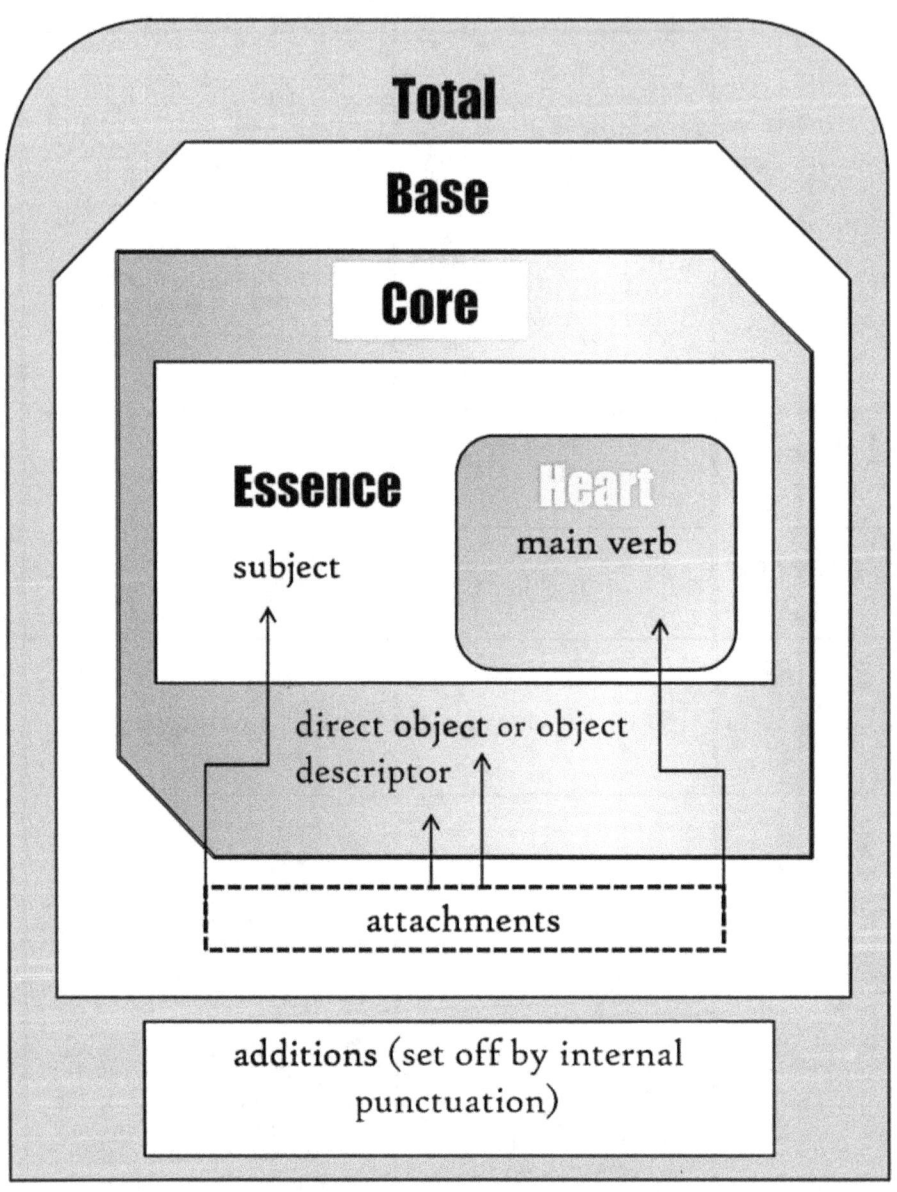

> "**The sentence is not simply a subject and verb but rather a base containing a subject and verb to which all other information can be attached**, either directly to the base itself or indirectly to words that are attached to that base. **The perception of the sentence as a structure rather than a string of words is probably the most important insight a student can gain from the study of grammar**, an insight that is likely to influence him not only as a proofreader but as a writer."
>
> – Mina Shaughnessy *Errors & Expectations*

> For him [Hermann Broch], what is essential about language is that it syntactically indicates an abrogation of time "within the sentence" because it necessarily "places subject and object in a relationship of simultaneity." The "assignment" which is imposed on the speaker is "to make cognitive units audible and visible," and this is "the sole task of language." **Whatever is frozen into the simultaneity of the sentence -- to wit, thought, which "in a single moment can comprehend wholes of extraordinary extent" -- is wrenched out of the passages of time.**
>
> – Hannah Arendt *Men in Dark Times*

> *The transposition of time into a relation with space, as alive and alert as earth and sky, has been a long effort in modern poetry.*
>
> – Robin Blaser *The Fire*

Traditional Names of Types of Sentences with a New Classification

A. Expressive Types of Sentences
1. Declarative
2. Interrogative
3. Imperative
4. Exclamatory

B. Grammatical Types of Sentences
1. Simple
2. Compound
3. Complex
4. Compound Complex

C. Stylistic Types of Sentences
1. Loose
2. Balanced
3. Periodic

D. Improper Types of Sentences
1. Run On
2. Fragment

"Traditional Types of Sentences"
in Tabular Format

Below is a table that summarizes the various combinations that the traditional ten types of sentences give rise to:

	Simple	Compound	Complex	Compound Complex
Declarative	✓	✓	✓	✓
Exclamatory	✓	✓	✓	✓
Imperative	✓	✓	✓	✓
Interrogative	✓	✓	✓	✓
Run-On	These types of sentences – for the most part – are not acceptable where good writing is valued. Unless your name is Gertrude Stein or James Joyce.			
Fragment				

We see that our "traditional ten types of sentences" (when presented in table form) can actually give rise to 18 types of sentences, of which 16 are considered acceptable. Examples of such **traditionally acceptable** sentences would be: *Sit up and shut up. We won, so we celebrated! After winning, we went drinking and got tanked. After winning, we went drinking and got tanked! Are you happy, or are you sad? The email that I received had taken 0.534 seconds to arrive at my computer. After studying, do you want to shoot some hoops? The farmer committed suicide. Life happens. Does life happen? Life happens!* Examples of **traditionally unacceptable** sentences would be: *No way! A bit later. Some sentences have the peculiar characteristic of going somewhere, but the reader is never quite sure, as it just kind of wends and winds its way to who knows where, and stops who knows when; such a sentence sentences the reader to continual torment and the added pressure of tracing the thrown line of thought throughout, with absolutely no guarantee of getting to the writer's main idea or purport.*

Occam's Razor, Life and Language

Area	Constituent Forms	Use, Range, Variation
1) Alphabet	26 letters	all words of the English dictionary
2) Genetics	4 nitrogen bases	DNA coding for all animal, plant, bacterial, viral, and fungal species
3) Proteins	20 amino acids	essential and active in all life forms (actually not 20, but 5 are enough to make a protein)
4) Music	8 tones	all melodies, tunes, symphonies, etc
5) Screen color	red-green-blue	16.8 million RGB colors
6) Digital Information	0 and 1 (*bits = binary digits*)	all digitized texts, websites, files, digital media, CDs
7) Sentences	11 basic forms	127 forms – infinite in variation and recombination, and found across the curriculum

Occam's Razor: the more elegant, economical, and simple the solution, the better it is.

The 11 Forms of Sentences

(simple level)	(compound & complex level)
1 Fundamental	6 Coordinating Conjunction
2 Series	7 Adverbial Clause
3 Verbals	8 Reference & Noun Clause
4 Correlatives	9 Power Punctuation
5 Repetition	10 Three Places
(third level - additional + new forms not in the above 10 groups)	
	11 ADDitional

1 2 3 4 5   10 9 8 7 6   11

from right fist, flick forefinger upwards twice

Sentence Forms Count

Left Hand	31	Right Hand	97
1F Fundamental	6	6CC Coordinating Conjunction	7
2S Series	7	7AC Adverbial Clause	16
3V Verbals	5	8RN Reference & Noun Clause	11
4C Correlatives	10	9PP Power Punctuation	27
5R Repetition	3	10TP Three Places	25
		11ADD Additional	11
Grand Total			127

Sentence Forms Mastery Checklist

1F Fundamental 1 2 3 4 5 6 **6**	**6CC Coordinating Conjunction** 1 2 3 4 5 6 7 **7**
2S Series 1 2 3 4 5 6 7 **7**	**7AC Adverbial Clause** 1 2 3 4 5 6 7 8 9 10 11 12 13 14 15 16 **16**
3V Verbals 1 2 3 4 5 **5**	**8RN Reference & Noun Clause** 1 2 3 4 5 6 7 8 9 10 11 **11**
4C Correlatives 1 2 3 4 5 6 7 8 9 10 **10**	**9PP Power Punctuation** colon 1 2 3 semicolon 1 2 3 4 5 6 7 8 9 dash 1 2 3 4 5 6 7 8 9 10 11 12 13 14 15 **27**
5R Repetition 1 2 3 **3**	**10TP Three Places** Beginning 1 2 3 4 5 6 7 Middle 8 9 10 11 12 13 14 15 16 End 17 18 19 20 21 22 23 24 25 **25**
	11ADD Additional 1 2 3 4 5 6 7 8 9 10 **10**
Grand Total	**127**

1 (F) Fundamental Forms

1.1	**F main verb**		**F**mv
	Think. Smile. Write. Remember.		

1.2	**F subject**		**F**s
	We went. **They** are eating. **Friends** are talking. The **rabbit** hopped. **Dad** is cooking. **Mom** is reading.		

	F descriptor		**F**d
1.3	(distant noun) I am a **student**. Mom is an **engineer**. Jake is a **cook**.		
	(distant adjective) The ball is **round**. This course is **tough**. Jake is **studious**.		
	(adjective) **Red** leaves are falling. They built a **small** hut. **Tall** trees grow.		
	(adverb) You sang **beautifully**. The couple danced **effortlessly**.		
	(noun) The ball hit the **brick** wall. Let's go to the **bus** station.		

	F object		**F**o
	Direct	Dad cooked **spaghetti**. Juliet plays **harp**. Jan designs **pictures**.	
	Indirect	Ted made **her** a tea tray. She gave **him** the tickets.	
1.4	After Object Descriptors (noun and adjective)	Noun: The company named Jane Smith **president**. The students elected Tom **treasurer**.	
		Adjective: I pushed the window **open**. He painted the car **silver**. This is driving me **crazy**.	
	Object of Prep.	She sat in the **boat**. They played until **lunch**.	
	Object of Verbal	I really want to visit **you**. My sister likes baking **cookies**. I want to learn **physics**.	

	F connector		**F**c
1.5	Conjunction	They are poor **but** optimistic. The food was good **but** salty. Can you sketch **or** paint?	
	Preposition	She grew up **in** the 70s. He dove **into** the water. The rocket went **into** space.	

1.6 s	**F there and it construction**	There are four people in the car. It was a cold day.	**F**there or it

1 F Fundamental Forms

These simple forms are effective when used among longer sentences. They slow down the pace. They make us notice the simple beauty of words in a well-written short sentence.

1.1 F main verb
●Look! ●Hurry up! ●Don't go! ●Write! ●Speak! ⌘

1.2 F subject
●**We** went. ●**They** are eating. ●**Friends** are talking.

●The **rabbit** hopped. ●**People** gathered. ●**Politicians** promised. ●**People** believed. ●The **snow** came down.

●**They** whispered. ●**Hearts** pounded. ●**Birds** chirped.

●The **crowd** laughed. ⌘

1.3 F descriptor (4)
①distant noun ●I am a **student**. ●Mom is an **engineer**.

●Dad was a **fireman**. ●Tara is a **gardener**. ●She became a **dentist**. ●Our boss is not a **tyrant**. ⌘

②distant adjective ■Jake is **serious**. ■The ball is round. ■Sushi is **delicious**. ■The course is not **easy**.

■Jade is **witty**. ■Their company is **innovative**. ■Your idea is **creative**. ⌘

③ adjective ●**Plum** trees blossomed. ●The **strong** wrestler will fight. ●**All** workers showed up. ●The **fluffy** clouds drifted. ●**Tall** trees grow. ●The **grumpy** man sat down. ⌘

④ adverb ■The eagle soared **gracefully**. ■The couple danced **effortlessly**. ■The toddler walked **carefully**. ■They ate **quickly**. ■She sings **well**. ■The baby wailed **loudly**. ■The siren blared **noisily**. ■The team played **expertly**. ■The climbers continued **bravely**. ■The business failed **miserably**. ■They prospered **moderately**. ⌘

⑤ noun ■ I have **motion** sickness. ■ You need a **bread** knife. ■ They went to a **rock** concert. ●He made a **jump** shot. ■ They said goodbye at the **train** station. ■ I'll have a **cheese** sandwich. ■ I'm going to the **language** center. ⌘

1.4 F object (5 types)

① direct object

• Dad cooked **spaghetti**. • Juliet plays **harp**. • Jan designs **pictures**. • Singleton cooks **breakfast**. • Let's shoot some **hoops**. • They built a **bridge**. • I like **piano**. • The clerk counted the **money**. ⌘

② indirect object

• Ted made **her** a bookcase. ■ She gave **him** the concert tickets. ■ I'll send **you** a postcard. ■ Give **me** your homework. • She lent **Julie** her book. ⌘

③ object descriptor (adjective)

• I made Mom **angry**. • They painted their house **gray**. • I found Canada **interesting**. • Computers make life **easy**. • She made the food **spicy**. ⌘

③ object descriptor (noun)

• Call it **fear**. • We elected Sam **captain**. • They selected Betty **Chief Executive Officer**. ⌘

④ object of preposition

■ Put the book on the **table**. ■ He sat on the **floor**. ■ She drove her car through the small **village**. ■ The task was beyond his **ability**. ■ She lives in the next **town**. ■ It rained until **noon**. ⌘

⑤ object of verbal

To make five types of objects, we include this object here, but it should not be taught until after Forms 1 and 2 are finished. A few examples are given for brief illustration.

object of gerund: ●My brother likes fixing **bikes**. ●I went outside after doing my **homework**. ●Learning **English** takes time. ●After polishing my **shoes**, I put them on. ●Before submitting your **paper**, make sure your name and number are on it. ●The teacher praised the student for noticing the Form 1 **sentence** in the novel.

object of infinitive: ●I really want to visit **you**. ●I asked him to fill in the **form**. ●I want to learn oil **painting**. ●You went out to get a **newspaper**. ●I worked hard to pass the **test**.

object of present participle: ●The teacher caught the student copying the **answers** from his neighbor. ●The police saw the man opening the **door**. ● She saw him calling **someone** on his cell phone. ●I imagined myself giving a **speech** to a big group. ⌘

1.5 F connector (2 types)
Conjunction [*but, or, nor, yet, and*]
• A good hammer is cheap **but** durable. • The food was good **but** too salty. • Do you like vanilla **or** chocolate.

• Walk **or** take a cab. • I won't buy you lasers **nor** trinkets for Christmas. • I was curious **yet** cautious. ⌘

Preposition
■ Think **about** it. ■ Put the book **on** the table.

■ They drove on **through** the sunny morning fields. (John Steinbeck *The Grapes of Wrath*)

■ She rollerbladed **along** the park path.

■ I grew up **in** the '50s. ■ I can park **between** those two cars **across** the street. ■ They looked **for** bodies **under** the rubble. ■ He froze **in** his tracks.

■ There's a bug **in** the program. ■ You're on **after** her.

■ They sang **until** dawn. ■ The thief ran **between** the cars. ■ The news was **on** the radio. ■ A bridge will be constructed **across** the Bering Strait.

■ The woman wore a shawl **over** her hair. ⌘

1.6 F Starting there or it
• **There is** a reason for this. • **There are** 60 or so people here on a good day. • **It is** foolish to think that.

Short Code Chart for Fundamental Forms

		1 F Fundamental	
NUMBER	SENTENCE FORM LETTER CODE	DESCRIPTION OR FORMULA	SUBFORM NOTATION (NAME OR SHORT CODE)
1.1	F	Main verb	1F Main Verb
1.2		Subject	1F Subject
1.3		Distant and Regular Descriptor	1F Descriptor (distant, regular)
1.4		Five kinds of objects	1F Object
1.5		Conjunctions and prepositions as connectors	1F Connector
1.6s		There is (there are, it is) construction	1F Starting There or It

 2 (S) Series Forms

2.1	**A and B The Pair** • **Barney and Wilma** live down the street. • The bag was **heavy and full**. • I like **apples and bananas**.
2.2	**A, B Compact Duo** • The soup was **creamy, chunky**. • Korean trains are always **punctual, reliable**. • The motorcycle ride was **fast, risky**.
2.3	**A, B, and C Standard Series** • Chocolate is **sweet, yummy, and divine**. • Fall is **cool, mellow, and colorful**. • The triathlon consists of **running, swimming, and cycling**.
2.4	**A, B, C Triple Force** • The apple was **red, crisp, delicious**. • Chantel is **smart, talented, humble**. • Mount Kilauea is a **majestic, powerful, active** volcano.
2.5	**A and B and C Lyrical Series** • **Green and blue and gold** were the colors of the peacock's proud tail. • The forest is **dark and deep and mysterious**.
2.6	**A and B, C and D Rhythmical Pairs** • We need better **schools and hospitals, streets and playgrounds**. • The new generation is **bold and inventive, idealistic and hopeful**.
2.7	**A, B, or C Choices Series** • Rehema will move to **Turkey, India, or Chile**. • Water can be a **solid or a liquid or a gas**.

2 S Series Forms

A *series* is two or more items (adjectives, nouns, adverbs, verbs, phrases) put together in a list. Commas or *and*s are used to separate the elements of the list. Omitting the *and* before the last item in the series (as in Forms 2.2 and 2.4) makes the sentence more forceful, punchy, and direct – an almost staccato effect that conveys thriftiness and seriousness in which every impressionable word counts. To a small extent, especially in The Triple Force, it slightly highlights the last item in the series.

2.1 The Pair Series A and B

●**Stop and think.** ●**Barney and Wilma** live down the street. ●The food was **delicious and cheap.** ●Keep it **short and sweet.** ●She likes **diamonds and pearls.** ●He likes **jazz and soft rock.** ●My favorite colors are **red and green.** ⌘

2.2 Compact Duo Series A, B

●The new house was **spacious, luxurious.** ■The drummer was **young, talented.** ■I put cream on my **dry, sunburned** hands. ■The **confused, lost** traveler asked the policewoman for help. ■The **black, striped** sweater belongs to Jill. ■Olympians are always **fit, confident.** ⌘

2.3 Standard Series Series A, B, and C
● The triathlon consists of **running, swimming, and cycling.** ● In Canada fall is **cool, mellow, and colorful.** ● She is a **bright, educated, and wise** woman. ● Three forms of water are **solid, liquid, and gas.** ● That band can play **reggae, waltz, and calypso** dance styles. ● Korean food is always **nutritious, colorful, and delicious.** ⌘

2.4 Triple Force Series A, B, C
● That mountain is a **majestic, powerful, active** volcano. ■ She bought a **cute, little, red** sports car. ■ The apple was **red, crisp, delicious.** ■ The actor's performance **impressed, dazzled, electrified** the audience. ■ The children played with **blocks, sand, a beachball.** ■ The troops won the war with **courage, determination, faith.** ■ The new father was **laughing, crying, whooping** with happiness. ■ She described **the time, the place, the moment** that the murder occurred. ■ A responsibility

of literature is to make people **awake, present, alive**.

(Natalie Goldberg *Writing Down Bones*) ⌘

2.5 Lyrical Series   Series A and B and C

- The forest was **dark and deep and mysterious**.
- Friendship is wrapped in **loyalty and trust and love**.
- Amidst the smoldering **heat and** the unquenchable **thirst and** the terrible **hunger**, the people of Ethiopia continued to search for a new home.
- She is **tall and beautiful and athletic**.
- "He runs up a shadowed ramp and into a crossweave of **girders and pillars and spilling light**." (Don DeLillo *Underworld* describing someone in a baseball stadium)
- Derek's talk was **informative and timely and uplifting**. ⌘

2.6 Rhythmical Pairs   Series A and B, C and D

- The new generation is **bold and beautiful, young and restless**.
- Winter in Korea is **cold and frigid, dreary and lonely**.
- **Lennon and McCartney, Jagger and Richards** were popular singer-songwriter duos in the sixties.
- **Pam and Sam, Jill and Bill** were the best-dressed couples at the dance.
- **Bananas and cream,**

milk and cookies are good late night snacks. ■**Books and notebooks, pens and pencils, cups and glasses** cluttered up the desk. ■**Blue and orange, red and green** are two pairs of complementary colors.
■**Scott and Kathy, Tim and Beth, John and Louise** all rode to the dance in Scott's old but faithful DeSoto. [old car from the 1950s] ⌘

2.7 Choices
  (a) Choices A or B
  (b) Choices A or B or C
  (c) Choices A, B, or C

●The boy always had **rice, toast, or porridge** for breakfast. ●I'll have some **juice or green tea**, thanks. ●They could **flee, surrender, or continue to fight.** ●A popular game in Asia that uses black and white saucer-shaped pieces on a 19x19 grid is called *igo* or *go* in Japanese, *weiqi or wei ch'i* in Mandarin, or *baduk* in Korean. ●We will take a vacation in Florida or California or Mazatlan. ●The answer is A, or B, or C. ⌘

Short Code Chart for Series Forms

2S Series			
NUMBER	SENTENCE FORM LETTER CODE	DESCRIPTION OR FORMULA	SUBFORM NOTATION (NAME OR SHORT CODE)
2.1	S	A and B	2S The Pair
2.2		A, B	2S Compact Duo
2.3		A, B, and C	2S Standard Series
2.4		A, B, C	2S Triple Force
2.5		A and B and C	2S Lyrical Series
2.6		A and B, C and D	2S Rhythmical Pairs
2.7		A or B; A, B, or C	2S Choice(s) Series

from Running & Being: The Total Experience

by Dr. George Sheehan (1978)

[This chapter has many of the Two Hands Approach sentence forms; in particular, the **Lyrical Series A and B and C** is an overwhelming favorite of Dr. Sheehan.]

I reached my peak in creativity when I was five. I could **draw and paint and sculpt**. I could **sing and dance and act**. I possessed my body completely. And with it became completely absorbed in a life that was **good and beautiful and joyful**.

I examined and tested and explored. I could not bear to watch. My every day was filled with the creativity that Rollo May defined: "the encounter of an intensely conscious human being with his world."

I do not confuse creativity with talent. I never had talent. Few do. But I was aware and responded and I responded totally. And I had what in older people is called purpose or dedication. At five, I was **creative and authentic**. At five, I did it my way. At five, I was like most five-year-olds, a genius without talent.

That genius came from **energy and effort and taking risks**. I would not know for years that Thoreau had commended arduous work for the artist. "Hard, steady and engrossing labor," he said, "is invaluable to the literary man."

And I would not read until even later that the Greeks had no word for "art" or "artist". That they never separated, any more than I did, the useful from the beautiful. For them, either a thing was useful and therefore beautiful or it was sacred and therefore beautiful.

The five-year-old does not yet know sin, but he may well know what is sacred. **Poetry and painting and music** are, according to Blake, "three powers in man of conversing with Paradise." The five-year-old sees that Paradise correctly, not in technology but in the fairy story, in the great myths that control and guide our lives. And myth is meaning divined rather than defined, implicit rather than explicit.

At five, I had that intuitive, instinctive faith that my cosmos, my family and the world were **good and true and beautiful**. That somehow I had always been and always would be. And I knew in a way of a five-year-old that I had worth and dignity and individuality. Later, when I read Nietzsche's statement that these are not given to us by nature but are tasks which we must somehow solve, I knew him to be wrong. We all had them once.

We lost them when we substituted watching for doing. When we saw the lack of perfection as a reason not to participate. When we became specialists and learned to ignore what was the province of other people.

For me, this meant no further interest in how things worked, in construction and making things, in crafts of any kind. I lost control of my life and in time became helpless in front of any malfunctioning machine. Now, if left to my own devices, I could not **house or feed or clothe** myself. Were I a castaway on a desert island, I would not know how to apply the efforts of all the scientists since the time of Archimedes. I would have to live as if they never existed. As if their talent and the products of their intense encounter with the world had never occurred.

And this all because **my encounter, my absorption, my purpose and my interest and intensity** had never occurred. I had changed from a genius without talent into the worst of all possible beings, a consumer.

The consumer is passivity objectified. Where the five-year-old finds the day too short, the consumer finds the day too long. I had lost the absorption of the five-year-old and gained boredom. I had lost my self-respect and gained self-doubt. Being middle-class, I had neither the need to use myself physically to survive, which poverty imposes, nor the absolute freedom to complete myself physically that wealth allows the aristocrat.

The five-year-old is just such an aristocrat. He seeks his own truth, his own perfection, his own excellence without care for the expense. He could well be a millionaire in his lack of concern for money and the family bank account.

But the five-year-old is more than the aristocrat; he is the worker Thoreau commended. He is the artist the Greeks saw no need to define. He is the athlete we all wish to be. And the saint we will never be. Every five-year-old is a success, just as every consumer is a failure.

The road back for a fifty-nine-year-old consumer is a long one. But there must be untapped resources of **enthusiasm and energy and purpose** deep in me somewhere. Somewhere I have the same creativity I had when I was five. I suspect that it is hidden under my clean, neatly folded and seldom-used soul.

3 (V) Verbal Forms

Verbals — function like a verb (but never as Main Verb) plus →		Other duties
3.1	**Verbal Infinitive** **Vinf** • She wants **to travel**. • Remember **to call** me later. • **To learn** another language is not easy. • The plan **to restore** peace will cost millions. • She went to the store **to buy** bread. • Let me **help** you. Watch me **flip**. Help me **move**. [infinitive missing *to*]	Noun Adjective Adverb
3.2	**Verbal Gerund** **Vger** • I sometimes like **baking** bread. • I did my homework after **watching** TV. • Turn on the alarm before **sleeping**.	Noun
3.3	**Verbal Present Participle** **Vprp** • The **passing** ship blasted its horn. • The skater gave a **dazzling** show. • A **growing** toddler needs proper food. • Catch a **falling** star.	Adjective
3.4	**Verbal Past Participle** **Vpap** • I bought some **bottled** water. • See the **attached** file. • I drank some **chilled** juice. • The **damaged** goods were returned. • Shoppers enjoyed the **reduced** prices.	Adjective
3.5	**Verbal Headlines** **Vhl** • Green belt **to encircle** desert. • Pilots **to have** stun guns. • **Dying** words reveal secret. • **Kidnapped** girl found.	The above four forms help enliven headlines.

3 V Verbal Forms

For far too long, the importance of these forms has been overlooked and undervalued. They occur with high frequency in all good writing, and deserve and accordingly receive a higher recognition in our scheme of sentence forms.
Word of Caution: Do not confuse the Participle Verbals and Gerund Verbals with look-alike (*-ing, -ed*) Basic Verbs contained in the Main Verb of a sentence.

Verbals add action, life, and movement to sentences.

3.1 Verbal infinitive   Vinf

●Remember *to call* me later. ●The family wants *to travel* to the east coast. ●It's hard *to forget*. ●She went out *to play*. ●She is determined *to succeed*. ●He wants *to learn to fly*. ●The children started *to giggle*. ●She went to the store *to buy* some moon cakes and yogurt. ●They wanted *to try* sailing a catamaran. ●I plan *to visit* Vietnam next year. ●He bought a tool *to simplify* trimming the lawn.

<u>Omitted *to*</u>: ●Could you help me [*to*] *push* my car? Just let him [*to*] *be*. The teacher made the students [*to*] *stay* after school.⌘

3.2 Verbal gerund   Vger

■I sometimes like *baking* bread. ■They fell asleep while *watching* the movie. ■Turn on the alarm before *sleeping*. ■*Writing* sentences demands full attention. ■After *swimming* I took the bus home. ■He started this business by *borrowing* money from his aunt. ■*Working* in the sun takes *getting* used to. ⌘

3.3 Verbal present participle   Vprp

●I saw her *standing* there. ●I saw the man *giving* her a brown envelope. ●A *rolling* stone gathers no moss. ●She likes to wear *twinkling* jewelry. ●He bought a new *carving* knife. ●Karl and I went through the children's room [at the local library] like word-*seeking* missiles. (Ursula LeGuin *The Wave in the Mind*) ●The *singing* waiter sang as he brought the food. ●*Beginning* to consider the rhythms of writing, my mind wandered about among the world's beats: the clock, the heart, the interval between the last meal and the next meal, the alternation of day and night. (LeGuin *ibid*) ●They bought some *folding* chairs. ●The baby's *smiling* face made everyone happy. ●His life was but a *fleeting* shadow in his family's history. ●The *gathering* clouds indicated imminent rain. ●They went to the *skating* rink. ●The *parking* lot was full. ■I bought a new *jogging* suit. ●She takes *dancing* lessons.⌘

3.4 V past participle   Vpap

■The *overjoyed* crowd clapped and yelled for more. ■The *smuggled* owls were put in apple boxes. ■The *broken* toy could not be fixed. ■*Loaded* weapons were gathered and exchanged for agricultural machinery after the truce. ■"We slept in a *bookwalled* room with creamy shelves and deep carpets and lighting that had a halftone density..." (Don DeLillo *Underworld*) ■He drove the *broken-down* car to the repair shop. ■The *cured* patient left the hospital. ■The *buried* landmine blew the child's foot off. ■A *caged* bird never sings. ■The *endangered* pandas moved to a smaller patch of bamboo. ■The *abandoned* mine became the home for a new year-round, thermally-**heated** greenhouse experiment. ■Two *lost* children emerged from the jungle mist. ■The post office will compensate for these *damaged* goods. ■The *flooded* plain looked like a huge lake. ⌘

3.5 Verbal headlines or titles   Vhl

Note: Actually, this is not a separate or novel sub-form, but rather is included so as to draw attention to the enlivening use of Verbals in headlines, as well as book titles, song titles, album titles, and movie titles.

• Seven *lost* in avalanche. • Green belt *to encircle* desert. • Pilots *to have* stun guns. • Tax system *to get tough* on drinkers. • New funds *to protect* against bio-terrorism. • *Eradicating* poverty a **shared** duty. • New laws *to protect* old-growth forests. • History plentiful below *frozen* tundra. • *Buried* treasure found in **sunken** wreck. • Newly-*minted* Chinese coin features Zheng He. • *Regulating* tourism in the Three Gorges. • Traffic signals *to include* audible countdown timer. • International trade fair *to benefit* Pacific Rim islands. • Gumi bus routes *reassigned*. • Young people gather *to cherish* peace. • *Tapping* offshore oil to new depths. • Under Rug **Swept**. *Jagged* Little Pill. *Tainted* Love.

(album and song titles by Alanis Morissette) ⌘

Short Code Chart for Verbals Forms

		3 V Verbals	
NUMBER	SENTENCE FORM LETTER CODE	DESCRIPTION OR FORMULA	SUBFORM NOTATION (NAME OR SHORT CODE)
3.1	V	Infinitive	3V Infinitive
3.2		Gerund	3V Gerund
3.3		Present Participle	3V Present Participle
3.4		Past Participle	3V Past Participle
3.5		Headlines or Titles	3V Headline or 3V Title

SENTENCE WORD ANALYTICS, PART 1

Word analytics is a new term that is equivalent to the old term, ***parsing***. Sentences are written in charts. The student analyzes each word individually, writing the word, its kind, and its function in the appropriate box. Sentences are written downwards on the left side, one word at a time. This is best done at the board.

There is a definite procedural order when doing word analytics. The student should follow this order exactly and not deviate from it in order to become efficient at taking a sentence apart and thereby discerning its architectural structure.

SEQUENCE FOR DOING WORD ANALYTICS	
1	Locate the **main verb** (with its auxiliary if present) and underline it twice.
2	By asking who performed the action of the verb, locate the **subject**, and underline it once.
3	Look to see if the main verb is a linking verb, and, if it is, look for a **distant descriptor.** (see Grammar section on the 5 Jobs)
4	Look for the **direct object**, and if there is one, underline it three times.
5	Ask if there is an **indirect object**, by asking, To whom? or For whom? something was done.
6	Identify all **adverbs** and **adjectives** attached respectively to the previous five elements
7	Identify all **prepositions**, their **objects**, and their **attachments**
8	Identify all **verbal elements** (infinitives, present and past participles, gerunds)
9	Identify all **noun, adjective, adverb phrases**

For some sentences, the process of classification may tend to bog down and seem hazy or too difficult. In such instances, considerable time should not be spent wrangling over the correct analysis.

The practice of Analytics is intended to make students able to **confidently grasp at a glance the construction of the sentence**, and **to know which parts of the sentence are more important to understand** (the main verb and subject), and which parts may be less important. Analytics shows familiarity with the building materials of the sentence; it enables a student to deconstruct a sentence to its word level components.

SENTENCE WORD ANALYTICS OF SOME FIRST LEVEL SIMPLE SENTENCES		
Sentence 1: *Tina went to the store and bought some gouda cheese.*		
Word	Kind	Job
Tina	noun	subject
went	verb	main verb
to	preposition	connector
the	adjective	descriptor
store	noun	object of preposition
and	conjunction	connector
bought	verb	2nd main verb
some	adjective	descriptor
gouda	adjective	descriptor
cheese.	noun	object of preposition
Sentence 2: *Tired from her trip to Europe, Tammy rested all afternoon.*		
Word	Kind	Job
Tired	verbal past participle	descriptor [Tammy]
from	preposition	connector
her	adjective	descriptor
trip	noun	object of preposition
to	preposition	connector
Europe,	noun	object of preposition
Tammy	noun	subject
rested	verb	main verb
all	adjective	descriptor
afternoon.	noun	descriptor

...MORE SENTENCE WORD ANALYTICS ON FIRST LEVEL SIMPLE SENTENCES

Sentence 3:
Flashing her new engagement ring, Tina strolled triumphantly down the sunny street.

Word	Kind	Job
Flashing	verbal present participle	descriptor [*Tina*]
her	adjective	descriptor
new	adjective	descriptor
engagement	noun	descriptor
ring,	noun	object of verbal
Tina	noun	subject
strolled	verb	main verb
triumphantly	adverb	descriptor
down	preposition	connector
the	adjective	descriptor
sunny	adjective	descriptor
street.	noun	object of preposition

Sentence 4:
After eating breakfast, the children went to school.

Word	Kind	Job
After	preposition	connector
eating	verbal gerund	object of preposition
breakfast,	noun	object of verbal
the	adjective	descriptor
children	noun	subject
went	verb	main verb
to	preposition	connector
school.	noun	object of preposition

Sentence Word Analytics, Part 2

The purpose of analytics is not to enable one to exhaustively and perfectly analyze every word in every sentence. Such an aim is a recipe for frustration, as there are many exceptions that will always elude the most brilliant teachers of grammar, not to mention the students.

When one encounters – as one often does – words or combinations of words that are difficult to analyze, one should simply guess at the best possible answer, and laugh at the difficulty of grammar. Students can be reminded about how difficult grammar is, but that it is not essential to know grammar perfectly when learning to write.

What they must understand is that they can analyze effectively 80% to 90% of what they read and write. That *does* matter a great deal. *Students must feel competent and confident that they can grammatically understand the overwhelming majority of the words of the sentences that they write and read.* Once they know that they can do this, they are not intimidated or frightened by the language, nor do they worry too much or take too seriously minor failures to understand difficult points of grammar that would challenge or even defeat a very gifted student or teacher of grammar.

It is a notorious commonplace that excessive attention on the fine points of grammar serves only to depress and frustrate students and afflict them with the conviction that they can never master the simplest forms of expression. At the outset, students need only to understand the basic fundamentals of grammar as we have set them forth in this book, and then practice some Sentence Word Analytics. This skill can be used sporadically as a change of pace without undue stress and emphasis, or it can become an in-depth lesson on how grammar can nail down functional labels most of the time, but not all, as some exceptions and puzzling phrases may stump even the teacher in trying to provide an explanation.

For the real understanding of sentences comes not with Sentence Word Analytics but with the mastery of the Eleven Sentence Forms. Only after they have seen and used all the Forms and gained a sense that they have a fluid mastery of multiple options in self-expression should further attention be paid to more complex exercises in Word Analytics or Analysis.

Even then, only some attention (and never excessive attention) should be given to Sentence Word Analytics. Sentence Word Analytics will help some students, especially beginning linguists, and give some confidence to others. Some people, however, may always find word analytics unduly frustrating. In such cases, forget it, and concentrate on improving the student's mastery of the sentence forms.

In the following sentences, students have analyzed sentences taken from the National Geographic website. The article was about an old growth forest in Alaska. The last example is taken from a children's storybook.

Sentence Word Analytics

from the Tongass National Park (Alaska) interview with a concerned forester at the National Geographic website at *nationalgeographic.com*.

STUDENT 1

And you look up and you see the ragged canopy of this forest.

Word	Kind	Job
And	conjunction	connector
you	pronoun	subject
look	verb	main verb
up	pre/postposition	(part of) main verb (a phrasal verb)
and	conjunction	connector
you	pronoun	subject of second clause
see	verb	main verb of second clause
the	adjective	descriptor
ragged	verbal - past participle	descriptor
canopy	noun	direct object

of	preposition	connector
this	adjective	descriptor
forest.	noun	object of preposition

Student 2

This is the forest duff, the organic soil in the forest, and it is very thin.

Word	Kind	Job
This	pronoun	subject
is	verb	main verb
the	adj.	descriptor
forest	noun	descriptor
duff,	noun	distant descriptor
the	adj.	descriptor
organic	adjective	descriptor
soil	appositive	descriptor
in	preposition	connector
the	adj.	descriptor
forest,	noun	object of preposition
and	conjunction	connector
it	pronoun	subject
is	verb	second main verb
very	adverb	descriptor
thin.	adjective	descriptor

Student 3

Though maps of the Tongass show mostly green, less than half is forested.

Word	Kind	Job
Though	conjunction	connector
maps	noun	subject

of	preposition	connector
the	adjective	descriptor
Tongass	noun	object of preposition
show	verb	secondary main verb
mostly	adverb	descriptor
green,	adjective	descriptor
less	adverb	descriptor
than	conjunction	connector
half	noun	subject
is	verb	helping verb for main verb
forested.	verbal - past participle	main verb

Student 4

Jenny calmly ate her breakfast and got ready for school.

Word	Kind	Job
Jenny	noun	subject
calmly	adverb	descriptor
ate	verb	descriptor
her	adjective	descriptor
breakfast	noun	direct object
and	conjunction	connector
got	verb	(second) main verb
ready	adjective	descriptor
for	preposition	connector
school.	noun	object of preposition
[from the children's book *I Am Not Jenny*]		

4 (C) Correlatives

		Opposition or Contrast	
4.1	**C** A, not B	• The car was <u>black, **not** red</u>. • It's the <u>job experience</u> that counts, <u>**not** the money</u>.	

		Addition or Putting Together	
4.2	**C** not only A, but (also) B	• My new bag is ***not only*** colorful, ***but also*** large. • We ***not only*** laughed, ***but also*** cried.	
4.3	**C** as well as	• Sam <u>**as well as**</u> Sally wanted to be a dentist. • She can swim <u>**as well as**</u> ski.	

		Choice or Preference	
4.4	**C** either A or B	• I'll get ***either*** the green ***or*** the blue one. • ***Either*** you ***or*** I have to go.	
4.5	**C** neither A nor B	• ***Neither*** Bob ***nor*** Sol enjoyed the movie. • I can neither *dance* nor *sing*..	
4.6	**C** A rather than B, rather A than B	• I'll have mineral water ***rather than*** lemonade. • I'd ***rather*** jog ***than*** walk.	

		Pre-Condition, Consequence, or Result	
4.7	**C** more, more less, less -er -er	• The ***more*** you try, the ***more*** you'll learn. • The ***faster*** you go, the ***greater*** the chance for error. • The **less** time you have, the **greater** the need for time management.	
4.8	**C** no A, no B	• ***No*** trade, ***no*** wealth. • ***No*** music, ***no*** life. Tower Records	

		Parallel Context, Analogy, or Comparison	
4.9	**C** just as A, so (too) B	• ***Just as*** many Koreans enjoy eating pizza, ***so too*** Italians are discovering the taste of *kimchi*. • ***Just as*** winter gives way to spring, ***so too*** will your problems soon be solved.	

		Range	
4.10	**C** from A to B	• I like all music ***from*** classical ***to*** jazz. • ***From*** Algeria ***to*** Zanzibar, the news spread worldwide.	

4 C Correlative Forms

When writing or speaking, we often need to compare things, or say how things are similar, or add more information, or indicate a range or choice when describing events, things, people, or ideas. We use _paired connectors_ called _correlatives_ to do this. **They allow us to put the items together in a way that shows a certain logical relationship between those events, things, people, or ideas.**

OPPOSITION
4.1 C A, not B; not A, but B

- The car was _black_, **not** _red_. ●Go _left_, **not** _right_. ●We should _walk_, **not** _take_ a taxi. ●The child was _calm_, **not** _excited_. ●These days we don't need more _money_, **but** more _honesty_. ● "The Christian God revealed himself as a man, **not** _as a coyote or a raven._" (Robert V. Hine & John Mack Faragher _The American West_) ● "The salt was another matter, **not** _cheap_ like today." (Amy Tan _The Hundred Secret Senses_) ⌘

ADDITION OR PUTTING TOGETHER
4.2 C not only A, but B
   Note: Joseph M. Williams in his lucid and insightful book _Style: Ten Lessons in Grace and Clarity_ (1997) posits that in the paired connectors we call _correlatives_, there is a slight emphasize that goes to the "last element of the pair". He recommends that one should end the pair with the "positive half of the construction." So, instead of "_We_

must clarify these issues and develop trust." can be rendered as *"We must not only clarify these issues, but also develop trust (as well)."*

- The trip was **not only** *relaxing*, **but also** *educational*.
- The new governor is **not only** *bi-racial*, **but also** *tri-lingual*.
- **Not only** *did* I *fall*, **but** I **also** *hurt* my knee.
- **Not only** *did* the trip *give* me a chance to relax, **but** it **also** *gave* me a chance to see the Rockies around Banff.
- The broadcast *was* **not only** *televised*, **but** *was* **also** *streamed* on the Internet. ⌘

4.3 C A as well as B

■ She took her sunglasses **as well as** her purse. ■ We will serve sushi **as well as** deep-fried shrimp. ■ Tom **as well as** Ursula went to the mountaintop. ■ He gave her a ring **as well as** a necklace. ■ Tutorials, seminars, and group teaching are used **as well as** lecture methods. ⌘

CHOICE
4.4 C either A or B   A or else B

■ I'll have **either** a *Coke* **or** a *Pepsi*. ■ **Either** *you sink* **or** *you swim*. ■ We can play **either** *long ball* **or** *frisbee*. ■ We could go to **either** *Cyprus* **or** *Malta*. ■ I'd like to

either *go* for a walk **or** *watch* a video. ■(variant) We have to *increase* sales **or else** we will *go* bankrupt. ⌘

4.5 C neither A nor B
●**Neither** the little *boy* **nor** the little *girl* wanted to play outside in the rain. ●**Neither** *Bob* **nor** *Sandy* enjoyed the new movie. ●**Neither** *North* **nor** *South* Korea wants any more armed conflict. ●**Neither** *oxygen* **nor** *heart massage* could revive the flood victim. ⌘

4.6 C rather A than B
■I'd **rather** catch an overnight bus **than** stay in that cheap hotel. ■Would you **rather** be there **than** here? ■She'd **rather** have water **than** milk. ■Would you **rather** have a veggie burger **than** a Caesar salad? ⌘

Pre-Condition, Consequence, or Result
4.7 C more -er
●The **more** you read, the **more** you will learn. ●The **more** I live here, the **less** I want to leave. ●The **further** you run, the **faster** your shoes will wear out. ●The **faster** we drive, the **sooner** we'll get there. ●The **sooner** I do

my homework, the **quicker** I can go outside. ●The **richer** you get, the **more possessive** you become. ●The **longer** I wait for her, the **more upset** I become. ⌘

4.8 no A, no B
Note: This form usually implies a precondition that implies a certain consequence: that is, A is necessary before B can happen.

●**No** pain, **no** gain. ■**No** trade, **no** wealth. ■**No** music, **no** life. (Tower Records, Japan) ■**No** exercise, **no** fitness. ■**No** tries, **no** prize. ■**No** love, **no** laughter. ■**No** language, no country. (motto of Manx Language Society, Isle of Man) ■**No** music, **no** passengers. (local daladala buses, Tanzania) ■**No** scenery, **no** visitors. ■**No** money, **no** food. ■**No** rain, **no** grain. ⌘

COMPARISON OR ANALOGY
4.9 C just as A, so too B
Note: This correlative should not be confused with the preposition *just as* which has the meaning of *at the same time as*.

●**Just as** your parents were once young and met life's challenges, **so too** will you survive your youthful years.
●**Just as** East and West Germany took two political systems and made them one, **so too** North and South Korea may merge their differences and re-unite. ●**Just as** the sun shines for all that live on the earth, **so too**

should a good leader listen to and give attention to each and every person in their region. ●**Just as** many are convinced that there is only one way to properly pronounce their language, **so** others are sure that it is wrong for their language to change over time. (Joel Davis *Mother Tongue*) ●(variation) One word may lead to another, **just as** one topic of conversation may lead to another. ⌘

Range
4.10 C from A to B

■It's a 30-hour bus ride **from** Winnipeg **to** Toronto.
■You should learn these forms **from** Form 1 **to** Form 11.
■**From** rock climbing **to** paragliding, extreme sports offer you many exciting challenges. ■**From** armadillos **to** zebras, humans enjoy confining animals in cages in unnatural man-made environments. ■She can count **from** 1 **to** 100 in six languages. ■The show will be on **from** 7:00 **to** 9:00 pm. ■**From** dawn **to** dusk the farmer worked outside. ■The city will stage 106 performances ranging **from** singing, dancing, drama, symphonies, traditional Chinese operas, and acrobatics **to** puppet plays. ■**From** baking cakes **to** grilling chicken, my mother

has a recipe for every dish. ⌘

Short Code Chart for Correlative Forms

NUMBER	SENTENCE FORM LETTER CODE	DESCRIPTION OR FORMULA	SUBFORM NOTATION (NAME OR SHORT CODE)
		4 C Correlatives	
4.1	C	A, not B	4C A, not B
4.2		not only A, but B	4C not only, but
4.3		A as well as B	4C as well as
4.4		either A or B	4C either or
4.5		neither A nor B	4C neither nor
4.6		A rather than B	4C rather than
4.7		more (less) -er	4C more -er
4.8		no A, no B	4C no no
4.9		just as A, so (too) B	4C just as
4.10		from A to B	4C from to

E.L. Doctorow: The Far Reaches of Life

from *City of God* by E.L. Doctorow

In the selection below, E.L. Doctorow makes excellent use of the Correlative 4C *just as* A, *so too* B in three instances as well as a variant correlative *As, So Does*.

"So be thankful to God that this system of cosmic checks and balances, as eccentric as it is, seems to be working. And **just as** there are the Alps and the Himalayas and the Andes and the Rockies, **so** there are undersea mountain ranges even more vast. And **just as** we have our sunlit river-running canyons, **so** does the sea bottom have its deep trenches. And **as** we have our flatlands and deserts, **so does** the seabed stretch for endless miles of abyssal plain. And **just as** we have our mountain goats standing transfixedly faced into the wind on the unequal crags of our highest mountains, **so does** the lightless, airless ocean bottom, with its tons of pressure per square inch, have its living tube worms and anglerfish, sea spiders, whipnoses, and sea lilies undulating slimed in the soundless blackness, their mouths agape and tentacles upheld to catch the flocculent dead matter drifting like snow from the blue and green ocean above."

 5 (R) Repetition Forms

5.1	**Repetition** of Key Word — • Tammy dreamed of living a glamorous **life**, a comfortable **life**, a **life** full of luxury. • If you want to be happy, then live in love – **love** for yourself, **love** for others, **love** for life. • Your victory makes this a **time** for celebration, a **time** for elation, a **time** for action.	**R**ᴋᴡ
5.2	**Repetition** of Word — • He had **no** fears, **no** questions, **no** worries. • Graduation is a grand conclusion to **all** the hard work, **all** the sleepless nights, **all** the headaches. • The school is **so** clean, **so** beautiful, **so** quiet. • There was **no** pause, **no** pity, **no** peace, **no** interval of relenting rest, **no** measurement of time. Charles Dickens • "…**no** limits, **no** frames, **no** boundaries" Rusty Schweickart (Apollo 9 space walker)	**RW**
5.3	**Repetition** of Adverbial Conjunction at Beginning of Sentence — **Note**: Though this form technically should be classified as Form 7 because it is a complex sentence, we place it here because it is a stunning example of the valuable use of repetition. • **If** it snows, **if** it hails, **if** it sleets, then you're definitely not on Guam. • **Because** I thought it was difficult, **because** I was tired, **because** it baffled me, I almost gave up on Form 5.3.	**RAC**

5 R REPETITION FORMS

The echoing of a word or phrase deeply emphasizes it, and lets us take momentary delight in its sound and meaning. Repetition also is a form of parallelism between the parts of the sentence that share the repeated common word. It is a common thread as well as reinforcement.

In ancient Greek drama, the mix of dancing, poetry, and singing by the *chorus* included repetition. Pop songs have their verses, but more importantly, their memorable and repeated choruses that again and again strengthen the sentiment being conveyed.

Repetition also has its place in ritual and ceremony, where the evocative power and pace, timing and volume of the spoken and repeated word are all brought into play (or are all finely tuned to create the intended effect).

5.1 Repetition of key word or phrase

● This is a **moment** like no other, a **moment** to etch in our hearts, a **moment** to cherish forever. ● She wanted a comfortable **life**, a happy **life**, a **life** with him. ● There is **pollution** in the air, **pollution** in the water, **pollution** in ground, and **pollution** in the heart. ● There was **light** all around, **light** above, **light** below, and **light** on all sides. ● She is **in a hurry** to get ready, **in a hurry** to get there, and **in a hurry** to get down to work. ⌘

5.2 Repetition of word

●The feather is **very** small, **very** soft, **very** white. ●This school is **so** clean, **so** beautiful, **so** quiet. ●She was **tired** of his lies, **tired** of his laziness, **tired** of the struggle. ■They had **no** fears, **no** worries, **no** questions. ■The students were **against** large classes, **against** expensive fees, and **against** homework. ■**All** muffins, **all** loaves of bread, and **all** bagels taste delicious if they were made at the Millstone Bakery. ⌘

5.3 Repetition of adverbial or reference conjunction in several clauses

> **Note:** This form can be saved until Form 7 and 8 have been completed, or practiced in advance here if the teacher and students wish to do so. It's worth the try.

●**If** he studies hard, **if** he practices daily, **if** he checks previous tests, he will surely do well on this math exam.

●**After** she had come back from her trip, **after** she had recovered from jet lag, **after** she had all her film developed, she couldn't stop telling everyone about all the places she had visited in Switzerland and Scotland.

●What occurs when something goes wrong is that

someone reaches out, **someone** soothes, **someone** protects. (Sidney Poitier *The Measure of a Man*) ●**If** it snows, **if** it hails, **if** it sleets, then you're definitely not on Guam. ⌘

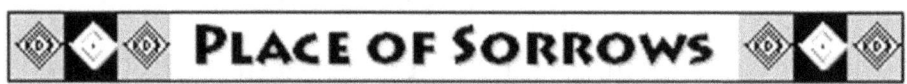 PLACE OF SORROWS

(Little Big Horn, Montana)
from *On the Road* with Charles Kuralt

In the essay below, Kuralt makes wonderful use of all the first 5 Sentence Forms from 1F to 5R.

This is about a place where the wind blows and the grass grows and a river flows below a hill.**1** Nothing is here but the wind and the grass and the river.**2** But of all the places in America, this is the saddest place I know.

The Indians called the river the Greasy Grass.**3** White men called it the Little Big Horn.**4** From a gap in the mountains to the east, Brevet Major General A. Custer's proud Seventh Cavalry came riding, early in the morning of June 25th, 1876, riding toward the Little Big Horn.**5**

Custer sent one battalion, under Major Marcus Reno, across the river to attack what he thought might be a small village of hostile Sioux.**6** His own battalion he galloped behind the ridges to ride down on the village from the rear.**7** When at last Custer brought his two hundred and thirty-one troops to the top of a hill and looked down toward the river, what he saw was an encampment of fifteen thousand Indians stretching for two and a half miles, the largest assembly of Indians the plains had ever known – and a thousand mounted warriors coming straight at him.**8**

Reno's men, meantime, had been turned, routed, chased across the river, joined by the rest of the regiment, surrounded, and now were dying, defending a nameless brown hill.**9**

In a low, protected swale in the middle of their narrowing circle, the one surviving doctor improvised a field hospital and did what he could for the wounded.**10** The grass covers the place now and grows in the shallow rifle trenches above, which were dug that day by knives and tin cups and fingernails.**11**

Two friends in H Company, Private Charles Windolph and Private Julian Jones, fought up here, side by side, all that day, and stayed awake all that night, talking both of them scared.**12** Charles Windolph said: "The next morning when the firing commenced, I said to Julian, 'We'd better get our coats off.'**13** He didn't move.**14** I looked at him.**15** He was shot through the heart.**16**" Charles Windolph won the Congressional Medal of Honor up here, survived, lived to be ninety-eight.**17** He didn't die until 1950.**18** And never a day passed in all those years that he didn't think of Julian Jones.

And Custer's men, four miles away? There are stones in the grass that tell the story of Custer's men. The stones all say the same things: "U.S. soldier, Seventh Cavalry, fell here, June 25, 1876."

The warriors of Sitting Bull, under the great Chief Gall, struck Custer first and divided his troops. Two

Moon and the northern Cheyenne struck him next.**19** And when he tried to gain a hilltop with the last remnants of his command, Crazy Horse rode over that hill with hundreds of warriors and right through his battalion.

The Indians who were there later agreed on two things: that Custer and his men fought with exceeding bravery; and that after half an hour, not one of them was alive.

The Army came back that winter – of course, the Army came back – and broke the Sioux and the Cheyenne and forced them back to the starvation of the reservations and, in time, murdered more old warriors and women and children on the Pine Ridge Reservation that Custer lost young men in battle there.**20**

That's why this is the saddest place. For Custer and the Seventh Cavalry, courage only led to defeat.**21** For Crazy Horse and the Sioux, victory only led to Wounded Knee.**22**

Come here sometime, and you'll see. There is melancholy in the wind and sorrow in the grass, and the river weeps.**23**

We list below the short codes that are used to footnote instances of the first 5 forms in the essay. We will use this system throughout the remainder of the book.

<u>Without viewing the next page</u>, how many of the Forms 1 to 5 Sentence Forms can you find?

Sentence Forms:

1) 2S Lyrical Series
2) 2S Lyrical Series
3) 1F
4) 1F
5) 3V Present Participle (or 3V Gerund)
6) 3V Infinitive
7) 3V Infinitive
8) 3V Present Participle (2); 3V Past Participle
9) 2S Triple Force; 3V Past Participle (2); 3V Present Participle
10) 3V Past Participle; 3V Present Participle
11) 2S Lyrical Series
12) 3V Present Participle; 3V Past Participle
13) 3V Gerund
14) 1F
15) 1F
16) 1F
17) 2S Triple Force
18) 1F
19) 2S The Pair
20) 5R Key Word; 2S Lyrical Series (2); 2S The Pair
21) 2S The Pair
22) 2S The Pair
23) 2S Lyrical Series

Instruction for the Teaching of Sentence Forms in the Classroom

At this point, we will outline a typical day during the Sentence Forms part of the course.

On the first day a sentence form is taught, the teacher should give the name of the new form and explain how it is used. Several easy as well as a few literary examples should be given for the student to scrutinize and discern the exact features of each sentence form. The students are then given some time to write a few samples of their own, and then told to put them on the board. These examples are then reviewed by the teacher and students, with the teacher making comments on and checking the accuracy of each example as is appropriate.

By this method, right away the students are involved personally in the creative process in the classroom. Students are next told to write several examples for homework, which will be put on the board and looked at by the whole class the next day. Students may talk over questions they may have or discuss their concerns about their sentences with some fellow students while other classmates write their sentence on the board. The atmosphere should be relaxed, and the students should feel comfortable comparing notes and observing what others are doing.

The teacher can move around the classroom talking to students at their seats, helping the students at the board, or commenting about the final sentences placed on the board. The teacher is a combination coach, facilitator, encourager, and monitor of the ongoing efforts at sentence construction.

Although the atmosphere is relaxed, students realize that they must eventually put their sentences on the board. No one likes to appear foolish and incompetent in public, so students will naturally want to perfect the sentences that they want to display to others on the board.

Furthermore, we see that the content of this system is not confined to a single printed book, but instead will grow each time the course is given. From new additions by new classes of students, better samples of writing can be saved by the teacher and shared with subsequent classes. Posting better sentences on the internet also provides a unique enriching resource for teachers and students practicing this method.

Grammar is explained "on the go". Praise is given more often than criticism. Corrections are made with little or no fanfare or derogatory comments. **More attention is paid when the sentence forms are rendered correctly, rather than incorrectly.**

Students will, of course, make mistakes on the board, but that is also one of the purposes of the exercise. The primary purpose is to furnish the students with excellent examples of sentence forms and to inspire students with confidence so that they can write such excellent sentences.

A secondary purpose of the exercise, however, is for students to discover by themselves, with some correction and assistance from the teacher, the typical kinds of errors and mistakes that everyone makes when they first try to develop their skill at writing these sentence forms.

"The mistakes of others are good teachers." says an Estonian proverb. Letting students experience in public their mistakes and errors in writing these sentence forms will enable them to acquire mastery over those mistakes and take full control of the form. Students learn best by sharing their own writing publicly before others. They automatically pay greater attention to corrections of their errors when their classmates are watching them. Public sharing of sentences is a form of real-world accountability where one shines or realizes painfully but constructively that one needs to improve.

Wilga M. Rivers in *Interactive Language Teaching* talks about students keeping **dialogue journals** and recommends that teachers *"rephrase awkward expressions while commenting on the content."* She also notes:

> *Learning grammar, however, is not listening to exposition of rules but rather inductively developing rules from **living language material** and then [the] **performing** [of the] **rules**.* [bold emphasis added]

Teachers should correct students, and students should correct one another in these exercises, in a kind way. The first half of a Scottish proverb rings true for this situation: **"Wink at small faults…"**. Students, however, should be tolerant and supportive when others make mistakes, and should not deride their classmates. The real focus of every student should be on themselves, their own here-and-now, their own sentences. Students should pay close attention, understand the form, and then emulate them many times to master them – not once, not twice, but maybe a dozen times. ***Students should not let up until they understand the forms and can replicate them in their writing***.

Sources of Examples for Students to Emulate

This is not an exhaustive chart, but it might help acquaint the students with various styles of English by exhibiting to them examples taken not from a single book, but from the following five sources:

	FIVE RELIABLE SOURCES FOR GOOD EXAMPLES FOR STUDENTS
1	Examples of sentences **by students themselves** (most important by far);
2	Examples of sentences **by the teacher**;
3	Examples of sentences **by published writers whose first language was/is only English** i.e. Emerson, Twain; Stowe; Austen; Shakespeare; Margaret Atwood; Maya Angelou; Lisa See; John Grisham; Susan Sontag; and many more
4	Examples of sentences **by published writers whose first language was/is not English** i.e. Chinua Achebe, Joseph Conrad, ChangRae Lee, Phillis Wheatley, Rabindranath Tagore, Lin Yutang, Amos Tutuola, Paolo Soleri, Amy Lee, Ayi Kwei Armah, Sri Aurobindo, Nam Le, and many more
5	Examples of translated sentences **from non-English literary traditions** such as *proverbs*, folk tales, wisdom stories from non-English-speaking nations and peoples (see Bhcw for proverbs about language and http://www.worldofquotes.com/)

Once the students latch on to the system, they too may become sources of excellent examples of the Eleven Sentence Forms. They too will want to show off their latest flashy or witty, insightful or scholarly efforts that beat new paths and remove the flotsam and washed-up debris where only sand and water should meet.

The teacher functions as a *coach*, insisting on *moderate discipline, conscientious effort, and diligent practice* — coordinating, delegating, reviewing completed work, and giving students new relevant assignments.

The Two Hands Approach Charts should be displayed around the room, helping to inspire and reinforce in the minds of the students the key components of the language. The various components of all the charts can be repeated, memorized, and recited individually or together at various times when called upon by the teacher. In this way, the teacher has available a repertoire of both written work and oral recitation that can be used in an interactive and integral function according to the needs of the students and the disposition of the teacher on any given day. The teacher can vary at will the content of the classroom in an interesting, varied, and non-repetitive manner.

Learning to write by imitation and emulation is not a new concept. When we are young readers, we always are attracted to certain writers or genres, because of the special style that we find featured in such books. We should extend and refine this natural practice by asking students to find examples of the sentence forms in their favorite books. **We should teach our children to read and to look for the recognizable features buried in the sentence. Those features are there, students should become aware of them, and recognize their force, function, and nuance.**

The Centrality and Importance of Oral Recitation in the Method of Instruction

There is another practice that is important in the instruction of this approach. **Students must read their sentences when their turn comes**. Only by doing so will they have sufficient practice in oral recitation to understand how to take apart and properly read what we will later describe as the moments of meaning and meditation in a sentence. Only by reciting out loud will they learn to emphasize by sound the adverbs and to emphasize the adjectives by driving them into the nouns.

Effective punctuation is as much a matter of sound as of sight; they are referees of time. Only oral recitation will enable students to really understand the power and potency of the three power punctuation marks: the colon, the semi-colon, and the dash (which we will come to soon). It is hardly any accident that most students after sometimes 16 years in public schools and colleges seem unacquainted with any punctuation marks except the comma and the period. Extensive oral recitation will remedy this lapse forever.

The Two Hands Approach thus incorporates public performance in front of the class, and enables the teacher to quickly publicly grade them based on their language as well as participation or leadership in the class and in their group activities and recitals.

> "The imitation of other artists is one of the means by which a person enriches and finally establishes his own individuality." Lewis Mumford

Students Learn to Write During Class Time Even Without Doing Homework

The students are required to participate by writing fresh, original examples of every new form. They must then place their sentences on the board in class as already discussed. Social peer pressure induces them to participate. Students must learn in class, and will learn the forms even if they don't do the homework. Inevitably, they will practice the forms so frequently in the classroom that they will master the forms even if they don't do all the homework. This fact is of major importance, because it is common knowledge that in innumerable American high schools, students do little or no homework. They must be taught to write during class time, but few present methods succeed in doing that.

Method of Assigning Compositions

Once several forms have been studied, the teacher should then assign a composition that must include a specified set of sentence forms, anywhere from 3 to 15 sentence forms, in whatever combination or frequency the teacher specifies. Obviously, the teacher should begin by assigning 1 or 2 paragraphs with 2 to 5 specified forms, then, gradually, increasing the number of paragraphs until they become essays, then varying the types of essays assigned. The students can mix in their own sentences written without attention to or without following the specified forms of the current assignment, but they must include at least those specified forms.

Whenever the student uses one of the assigned forms in their composition, that student **must specify by a footnote or endnote which sentence forms they used. In the footnote or endnote, they should designate the**

sentence form that was used by giving the form's short code. Thus, by just glancing at the footnotes or endnotes, the teacher can tell which forms were used and which ones were not used, and it is an easy task to see whether or not the student has done the assignment correctly. **The forms are a control on the student to pay attention to what they write, and the teacher can look below at the footnote or endnote to see the various forms used in the composition**. The teacher has manageable control over the output.

There are many advantages of this system. First, the student is given clear and concrete directions on how to vary their sentences; for another reason, the teacher has a running record of the sentence forms that a student has mastered or not mastered, and can make assignments to correct any shortcomings. Still another advantage of this system is that it eliminates the increasing problem of plagiarism.

We may echo the sentiments of Barry M. Maid when he wrote his book review of Barbara Danish's *Writing as a Second Language* in 1981, and hope that even young learners will write suitably sterling examples of these sentence forms:

> What's most impressive about most of the student responses, which are written by primary to junior high students, is that while some of the student pieces are better than others, all of them are real. All of them say something. It is clear the students are not merely giving the teacher pieces of writing intended to impress the teacher, but are writing about things which they consider important. There is no appropriation of the writing by the teacher. It clearly belongs to the students, and it is writing the student writers want to share with their readers. If only all student writers were that honest. Though the student examples

come from the lower grades, the assignments are workable at any level.

Sentence Combining As an Aid to Writing and Especially a Great Aid to Teaching Students Re-writing

Students can then go on to practice sentence combining. After they have learned the eleven basic forms, the **practice of sentence combining is especially effective in teaching the importance of re-writing the original drafts. They learn that re-writing involves selection of not just the first and only thing they think of writing, but that they must choose the best among many options**.

Students can be provided with kernels of sentences written by someone else, and then must combine these using various stylistic options. Students are less embarrassed when they have to manipulate and rewrite other people's initial thoughts and words, rather than their own. They are forced to think about how to combine kernel sentences and re-write their compositions effectively.

Inevitably, there is a huge variety of narrative possibilities, and a wide variety of other sentence combining techniques and materials. By sharing their work with the class and publicly seeing the possible changes that can be made once something is on the paper, students will learn to write with economy, vision, and clarity.

Students do not have to spend undue time creating initial drafts, but can spend time on rewriting itself and working at a higher level of complexity, sentence structure, and style.

Two books by William Strong (1973, 1981) provide plenty of examples and exercises. Students will learn to write sentences with greater variety. Within the class, sentence kernels will be transformed into a wide array of interesting sentences – all done by the students.

Critics may argue that the content in sentence-combining textbooks is contrived or unimaginative, the drab and dull product of an author who may be much older than the students who are now in the driver's seat. But, heat hones metal, and practice brings perfection. Not all coaches use the same method. But the victory will certainly go to the practitioner has practiced sufficiently, reviewed the game plans, and excelled in the performance when called upon to do so.

Clustering

Clustering is an outlining technique that uses a graphic method of arranging ideas, also called a *mind map, topic tree, bubble diagram, branching diagram,* or *idea map.* It is a diagram in which the writer writes down a main idea in a bubble or oval located in the center of the page, and then adds spokes with words at the end of the spokes, and continues adding new spokes and words at the end, breaking down a topic into its related sub-topics as one brainstorms to think of themThe writer then organizes and clusters them, perhaps shifting or re-grouping some words to new locations, and then puts the main central spokes into an executable sequence. Having spent a few valuable minutes planning, the student will be able to proceed with confidence, using the diagram as a skeletal outline and a keyword reminder when beginning to write the initial draft.

Here is a sample start for a topic tree for the topic of the power of the symbol of the hand.

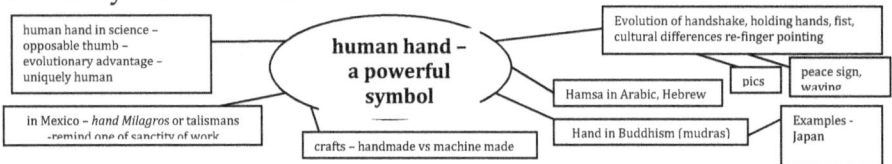

The student then begins to write, constructing simple kernel sentences. After that, the student is challenged to combine the kernel sentences into longer and more varied sentences. Finally, the student should link the sentences into paragraphs and the paragraphs into an essay or composition that is within the required word limit (if there is one).

photo S.Guarrigues

General Instructions to Students and Teachers regarding the Character and Sequence of Written Assignments

After students have identified, studied, and written practice examples of several Sentence Forms and shared those forms with their fellow classmates, they will be assigned the task of incorporating a number of the practiced forms into written assignments. The written assignments at first will be very simple, requiring students to incorporate some of the learned Sentence Forms into one, then two, and then three or more paragraphs.

Students will always be given the choice of incorporating about half of the sentence forms they examine, but the ones they do incorporate in their paragraphs and essays must be footnoted in the paper itself and then identified by number and name at the bottom or side of the page. If students feel some choice and latitude concerning which sentence forms they use (rather than be required to do every one), they will invest more actively in the writing process and feel less resistance to using specified Sentence Forms. Moreover, as students read and share their respective writing assignments with one another, they will eventually see the full display of all the Sentence Forms they studied and practiced, both the ones they employed in class practice and in their papers as well as the ones they chose not to use but others did. They will also see how well or how poorly other students employed the identical Sentence Forms that they used.

Reading the various student papers in class thus becomes a telling exercise in perceiving and realizing how and when certain Sentence Forms are graceful or awkward, obscure or clarifying, trite or compelling, commonplace or memorable. While the written assignments are precise and exacting, they are doable and not overwhelming. Moreover, whatever any student writes contributes to the learning of all the other students in the class. The Sentence Forms will be familiar from previous study and practice, yet novel and interesting in the variety of their usages in the context of similar writing assignments by diverse students. The class review of papers thus becomes an apt exercise in the familiar and novel – in stability and change, in the variety of language usage but also in the constancy and power of Sentence Forms as a structuring force of language.

Later, the written assignments will become more difficult, requiring students to write full length essays and incorporating 15 to 20 Sentence Forms in them. In general, the written assignments will be divided into two parts: in the first part, consisting of **six or more assignments**, students will be required to *use and document specified Sentence Forms* in their compositions; in the second part, also consisting of **six or more assignments**, students will be able to *write freely* without the requirement of employing specified Sentence Forms.

Students should thus be notified at the outset that they will not always be required to use specified Sentence Forms for the whole class and that greater freedom and options to write will be given to them as the class progresses. Hopefully, they will then view the first six assignments as useful experiments, rehearsals, and preparation for the later part of the class when they can write freely. They will be expected at that point, however, by the end of the class to display the mastery of a varied repertoire of Sentence Forms and constructions.

The purpose of requiring students to use specified Sentence Forms in the first six written assignments is to familiarize students with the variety of Sentence Forms available to them and to concentrate and focus their attention on the active employment of such forms in their writing. Students should be told that the instructor realizes that writing assignments which require the use of specified Sentence Forms might make writing papers more difficult at first and result in a prose that is more artificial and less natural than would normally be the case. **The aim of such assignments, however, is less a polished, finished product than a rehearsal or practice session in the use of varied Sentence Forms in writing.** The fact that one does not at first aim for a polished, finished sample of writing should encourage students to experiment and make mistakes, learning from their failures as well as successes. Perfection, or a more finished and refined writing product, is not expected all at once, but it is to be achieved gradually and progressively in a continuous Process of steady development and improvement in the fluency and grace of one's writing style.

A mid-term and final examination, however, will be administered in which students will be required to complete a composition in class based on a choice of five topics. In the mid-term exam, they will be required to employ a number of specified Sentence Forms, but in the final exam they will be able to write freely without any stipulated forms. In both exams, students will be graded on the accuracy, fitness, and grace of the Sentence Forms they employ as well as on their grammar, spelling, organization, imagination, and thinking.

Regarding the method of notating and footnoting the various Sentence Forms employed by the students, a simplified *short code* is provided for each sub-Form. The *short code* is the Form Number and the Form Letter Code plus its short nickname or descriptive phrase; for example, *2S Compact Duo*, or *4C rather than*, or *5R word*. We do not feel that the names of the forms should be reduced further to formulaic codes or technical abbreviations. Instead, the notations of the forms should be presented in clear, plain English that accurately and vividly describes the function and use of the form in the text, but in a shorthand that is memorable and easy to recognize.

While it is commendable if a student can remember the exact form number (such as *9.sc7*) for many forms, we feel it is **better to remember the name or nickname**. Although it may seem laborious at first, by writing this name (the one in the short code) out repeatedly in the footnote to identify a form, the student ineradicably fixes that form's name in the their long-term memory, thereby making it easier for them to recall and use the various forms – rather like memorizing the multiplication tables for mathematical proficiency.

By checking the short codes at the bottom of each page for this or any given composition assignment, all will easily see how the system works with little effort and confusion. Minimally, the teacher just needs to find the footnoted sentences, check them for accuracy, and then make sure the student has written the required number of assigned forms.

You will also note that when there are two or more Sentence Forms displayed in one sentence, we separate the individual short codes with a semicolon.

Twelve Written Assignments
Assignment One: One Paragraph

Students should be told to write one paragraph of five to seven sentences in which they incorporate, notate, and footnote at least 3 or 4 of the various subforms of the Forms 2, 3, 4, and 5. Since the Fundamental Form is so basic, there is no need for them to write, notate, and footnote any of its sub-Forms, though they will often employ simple Fundamental sub-Forms in their prose. However, they should write at least one Series, one Correlative, and one additional Form of the other first Five Forms.

Students should provide a title for their paragraph which identifies or suggests the main idea of the paragraph, and the paragraph should thereby be unified with all the sentences developing or revolving around the one main idea.

Students may be told to write either a paragraph based on a topic or theme of their own choice, or the teacher may ask them to write a paragraph about one of the four seasons of the year: spring, summer, fall, and winter. Those in the tropics can write about monsoon and dry season.

Below are some examples of one paragraph assignments written by students which show the required notations and footnotes that should accompany this assignment. Students can survey these examples as models to emulate and adapt in a way that will give them guidance in writing their own assignments.

However, before doing so, we first offer a superb example of a few paragraphs by a student that is a wonderful introduction of the value of writing as self-expression using the Mother Tongue.

ON BED TALKS

by Cecilia, Jinan University, Guangzhou

This excellent example of student writing vividly describes the value and virtue of mutual dialogue and conversation in the common Mother Tongue (or one's native cultural language).

Such mutual dialogue and exchange is the seed and fountainhead of personal formation and integration, of social fellowship, and in time of that intellectual development and imaginative craft that can blossom into professional and enduring writing.

As such, the selection is a superb initial example of **Writing As Self-Expression.**

When talking about our dormitory life, and probably all students' dormitory life, we should never leave out one thing: bed talks. Nothing will stop us from deliberately starting a heated (or lively) discussion right after lights are out. It was our favorite and only way to end each day, and we were as punctual for it as our parents are for work.

Psychiatrists say that to lie comfortable in bed is the only way to make someone open his mind. Therefore, during bed talks, we were able to touch the most intrinsic part of others. What were the topics? Almost everything – making nicknames for ourselves, school life, classmates, tutors, boys (of course), and even politics, policies, communication theories, and more.

I assume that this is how those bed talks changed us. I was amazed at realizing the great difference among people in terms of their ways of thinking, and the diversity of personalities. This may change our attitudes towards others, because it is also a process of sharing.

One Paragraph no.1   Bungee Jumping
Aram Messina

One of the things I have always wanted to do in my life before I die is to go bungee jumping.**1** The thought of free falling down from a thousand feet up gives you this thrilling, exhilarating, and invigorating feeling that sends shivers down your spine.**2** Once I do go bungee jumping, I know that feeling will hit unexpectedly and unknowingly and surprisingly.**3** Hopefully, I can go bungee jumping in the near future.

Sentence Forms:

1) 3V infinitive
2) 2S Standard Series; 3V Present Participle
3) 3V Gerund (2); 2S Lyrical Series

One Paragraph no.2   Italy   Daniel Bregaglio

The blue beaches, the beautiful Alps, the wild cities, the wonderful culture, and the outstanding art make Italy one of the greatest countries to visit and live in.**1** You can hike up the Italian Alps after swimming in the Mediterranean Sea.**2** In addition to these wonderful attractions, you can also tour the renowned historical monuments.**3** If you love culture, if you love excitement, if you love travel, then Italy is the place for you.**4** Start planning today.**5**

Sentence Forms:

1) 2S Standard Series (extended)
2) 3V Gerund
3) 4C Supplemental (in addition, also)
4) 5R Adverbial Conjunction If
5) 3V Gerund

One Paragraph no.3   My Favorite Animals
Brandie Stevens

Cats are my favorite animals; I have three of them. Their names are Shadow, Marmalade, and Tinker.**1** They love to run and play and sleep.**2** The only bad thing about them is that they play – run, chase, fight – all night long.**3** Even though they are hell makers, still I love, adore, and worship them.**4**

Sentence Forms:

1) 2S Standard Series
2) 2S Lyrical Series
3) 2S Triple Force
4) 2S Standard Series

One Paragraph no.4 Longing For Orange Sherbet April Turner

I love ice cream. It is, by far, one of the best foods ever invented.**1** Ice cream is a dessert, though I will eat it any time of the day. My favorite is sherbet. I used to eat it all the time when I was younger.**2** I hate strawberry ice cream, and this used to be a problem since my mother loved strawberry.**3** She would always remind me that I had to eat whatever ice cream she bought, for she was paying for it – not me.**4** I thought that was so cruel and unjust of her.**5** Oh, how I longed for a bowl of fruity, orange sherbet.**6** I have since forgiven my mother for her misdeeds of the past, but I will never forget watching her eating that bowl of strawberry ice cream in front of me – knowing all I wanted was sherbet.**7**

Sentence Forms:

1) 3V Past Participle
2) 3V Infinitive
3) 3V Infinitive
4) 3V Infinitive; 4C A, not B
5) 2SThe Pair
6) 2S Compact Duo
7) 3V Gerund; 3V Present Participle

One Paragraph no. 5   The Benefits of Exercise
Allen Terrance

Exercise is therapeutic – therapeutic for the mind, therapeutic for the body, and therapeutic for overall health.**1** When you exercise, a study shows that your brain releases endorphins. Endorphins create a feeling of well-being, thus relieving stress.**2** It has been proven that relieving stress takes pressure off the body and the mind.**3** Just as exercise strengthens the body, so also it clears the mind from stress, giving way to a sense of well being.**4** Swimming, boxing, and running are all exercises that make you look and feel great as well as relieve stress.**5** Not only will you look your best with daily exercise, you will feel your best.**6** With the new energy you experience from exercise, you will feel empowered – with renewed mental and physical health.**7** So, exercise today and every day, experiencing the benefits that follow.**8**

Sentence Forms:

1) 5R keyword
2) 3V present participle
3) 3V present participle; 2S the pair
4) 4C just as
5) 2S standard series
6) 4C not only, but
7) 3V past participle
8) 3V present participle

One Paragraph no. 6   Shocking News
Anthony Tremblay

The night was dark and foggy, cool and damp.**1** The young man thought it was unusual and knew that something was not right. After the noon hour passed, he had a vision of tragedy in his mind. It brought him great fear, sorrow, and disbelief; yet he could not figure out why.**2**

Suddenly, the phone rang. It was his mother. She had not called since he left town several months earlier. He felt sudden incredulity. His father had died that morning.

Sentence Forms:

1) 2S Rhythmical Pairs
2) 2S Standard Series

One Paragraph no. 7   Change of Attitude
Anthony Tremblay

It was a sorrowing feeling when I found out that my assignment was for Korea.**1** I sat in complete dismay. My roommate was reassuring, consoling, and supportive, but I still didn't handle it well.**2** I was extremely unhappy with the situation. I wanted to run and hide and disappear from sight.**3** However, after conferring with a few friends, I decided that I couldn't wait to go.**4**

Sentence Forms:

1) 3V Present Participle
2) 2S Standard Series
3) 2S Lyrical Series
4) 3V Gerund; 3V Infinitive

One Paragraph no. 8   Superstitious
Rosemarie Ciccariello

Pete always took superstitions for granted. His friends as well as his family used to warn him that spilling salt, walking under a ladder, and getting out of the wrong side of the bed would cause bad luck or severe misfortunes.**1** He always laughed at them, but one day changed everything. Walking to work one morning, Pete stared long and hard at a black cat and walked into his office with an umbrella opened.**2** That afternoon the phone rang; it was the police. They called to tell him that his mother and father, sister and brother were all instantly killed in a car crash that morning on Friday, June 13.**3** He was shocked and grief-stricken and devastated.**4** Not only did he realize at that moment that his friends were right all along, but he also resolved never to take superstitions for granted again.**5**

Sentence Forms:

24) 4C as well as; 3V Gerund; 2S Standard Series; 2S The Pair
25) 3V Present Participle; 2S The Pair
26) 3V Infinitive; 2S Rhythmical Pairs
27) 2S Lyrical Series
28) 4C not only, but; 3V Infinitive

One Paragraph no. 8   Christmas
Ronald Wright

When Christmas comes around, people seem more gentle and cheerful and happy.**1** It seems like people remember to forget about being hateful or degrading of each other.**2** I see people at the airports and train stations getting frustrated, people in the streets trying to get a taxi and not being able to get one, and people at the local malls trying to buy their last minute gifts, but the air of the people is one hundred times more lenient, more bright, and more placid than if it were an ordinary day.**3** I seldom see people frowning or moody at Christmas.**4** Christmas is the most beautiful holiday of the year because it brings out the best in people.

Sentence Forms:

1) 2S Lyrical Series
2) 3V Infinitive; 2S The Pair
3) 2S The Pair; 3V Present Participle; 3V Past Participle; 3V Infinitive; 5R Word; 2S Standard Series

4) 2S The Pair

One Paragraph no. 10   Coping with Humidity
Jill Friend

The weather is humid outside. It makes me feel miserable, hot, and crabby.**1** I have to make sure to drink a lot of water.**2** If I don't, then I will start to feel weak as well as sluggish.**3** In weather like this, it is important to stay alert, stay hydrated, stay in the shade, and stay alive.**4** If I don't plan on becoming a hot weather casualty, I need to attend to my health and above all stay hydrated.**5**

Sentence Forms:

1) 2S Standard Series
2) 3V Infinitive
3) 4C as well as
4) 5R word; 2S Standard Series
5) 3V Infinitive

One Paragraph no. 11   Spring   Joshua Delange

The spring leaves beautify the streets. The flowers are colorful and beautiful, full and vibrant.**1** Just as the flowers are beautiful, so too are the fields, the mountains, and the lakes.**2** Spring is the best season for it shows us the beauty of nature.

Sentence Forms:

1) 2S Rhythmical Pairs
2) 4C just as A

One Paragraph no. 12   Spring   Truequynh Hua

Spring is the prettiest and most exhilarating time of the year.**1** People spend more time outdoors to enjoy the beauty of the blooming flowers, the fresh air under the warming sun, and the longer day time.**2** They also get together to participate in many outdoor activities such as hiking, biking, and picnicking.**3** Spring brings liveliness and togetherness, cheerfulness and happiness to people's daily activities.**4**

Sentence Forms:

1) 2S the pair
2) 3V Infinitive; 3V Present Participle; 2S Standard Series
3) 3V Infinitive; 2S Standard Series
4) 2S Rhythmical Pairs

One Paragraph no. 13   Spring
Aaron Marshall

The season of love, warmth, and beauty, spring in one of the best seasons.**1** Not too hot, not too cold, not too bright, not too dark, it marks the balance of the extreme seasons, summer and winter.**2** No heavy coats, no bathing suits, only light clothing is needed.**3** Picnicking in the park, people find many different ways to enjoy the weather and beauty of a spring afternoon.**4** Many sports are played outdoors such as baseball and soccer and football.**5** The more free time that we spend outdoors, the more we can enjoy the season of spring.**6**

Sentence Forms:

1) 2S Standard Series
2) 5R word
3) 4C supplement
4) 3V Present Participle; 3V Infinitive; 2S The Pair
5) 2S Lyrical Series
6) 4C more (less) -er

One Paragraph no. 14   Spring
Yoko Kitagawa

When Spring comes, it gets warmer and warmer every day.**1** The nicer it gets, the more colorful flowers are seen in the parks, all over the mountains, and even on the streets.**2** They are so beautiful, lovely, and cute.**3** Many Japanese people get together to picnic under the cherry blossoms.**4** On the one hand, some people enjoy the beauty of the spring; on the other hand, others enjoy drinking and being merry.**5** The spring makes people happy, cheerful, and refreshed with its colorfulness and liveliness.**6**

Sentence Forms:

1) 4C more -er
2) 4C more -er; 2S Standard Series
3) 2S Standard Series
4) 3V Infinitive
5) 4C supplemental; 3V Gerund; 2S The Pair
6) 2S Standard Series; 3V Past Participle; 2S The Pair

One Paragraph no. 15   Summer   John Contreras

There are many things that can be said about all seasons, but summer is the season that sticks out most in my mind. When most people think of the summer months, they think of the hot weather, outdoor activities, and enjoyable times with friends and family.**1** Most of the time during the summer, I spend surfing with friends.**2** Many things can be said about summer: it's fun, it's hot, and it's a time for forming close and lasting relationships with others.**3** In addition to all that, it is the season to sit back and enjoy life.**4**

Sentence Forms:

1) 2S Standard Series; 2S The Pair
2) 3V Gerund
3) 5R word; 2S Standard Series; 3V Gerund; 2S The Pair
4) 4C supplemental In addition to*; 3V infinitive

*see end of Vol.II

One Paragraph no. 16   Summer   Ben Lukes

Summer is the time for family and friends, swimming and cookouts.**1** The summertime brings relaxation, not work.**2** I always love to catch up with old friends with no sense of urgency, no time restraints, no distractions.**3** On the one hand, I enjoy making the most of my summer; on the other hand, I also enjoy catching up on sleep.**4** Though I enjoy sleeping, I also like staying up late.**5** However, just as you start getting used to the freedoms of summer, so too you have to start preparing for the year to come.**6** In the end, summer is the season that gets you through the year.

Sentence Forms:

1) 2S Rhythmical Pairs
2) 4C A, not B
3) 3V Infinitive; 2S Triple Force; 5R word
4) 4C supplemental On the one hand; 3V Gerund
5) 3V Gerund (2)

6) 3V Gerund; 3V Infinitive; 4C just as

One Paragraph no.17   Summer

Thomas Dockery

Summer is the season one loves most. I wish the weather would stay hot all year around, but that would be too good to be true.**1** There are many great sports played outdoors in the summer season: basketball, baseball, soccer, and football to name a few.**2** I love running outside in the warm, inviting, beautiful weather.**3** And don't forget swimming!**4** I always jump in some sparkling water at a park or beach.**5** The outdoor picnics and cookouts are also fabulous.**6** I eat all the barbecued hotdogs, the corn, the hamburgers, and the grilled chicken and ribs.**7** Summer wouldn't be the season one desires without the warm weather, without swimming at the beach, without the outdoor sports, without the picnics and the cookouts.**8** Summer is the best season of all.

Sentence Forms:

1) 3V Infinitive
2) 2S Standard Series
3) 3V Gerund; 2S Triple Force
4) 3V Gerund
5) 3V Present Participle
6) 2S The Pair
7) 2S Standard Series
8) 5R Word

One Paragraph no. 18   Summer

Anjeannette Hammett

I love summer. It's the season to be free, free from school and homework, sweaters and jackets.**1** Summer is a time when you can just let yourself go. Every year at the beginning of spring, I wish and wait and long for the summer weather to begin even sooner than the year before.**2** I am so partial to the heat that summer brings, yet enjoy a refreshing dip in a nice cool swimming pool.**3** In addition to the heat, I enjoy the sunshine and longer days.**4** When I was younger, I loathed the moments when my mother would call for me to come into the house.**5** I would think to myself "doesn't she know the sun is still out, and I'm right in the middle of some really great game." Of course as I got older and older, I realized the reasoning of my mother for calling me in early: she was protecting me from unwarranted danger, and I appreciate that to this day.**6** I just wanted the long summer days to last forever.**7**

Sentence Forms:

1) 5R Key Word; 2S Rhythmical Pairs
2) 2S Lyrical Series; 3V Infinitive
3) 3V Present Participle
4) 4C supplemental
5) 3V Infinitive
6) 3V Gerund
7) 3V Infinitive

One Paragraph no. 19   Fall
Rita Chung, Ronald Wright

It is the season when the rain pours, the warmth of the summer fades, baseball ends, and football begins.**1** Crisp, fallen leaves and cool, fresh breezes bring this season forgotten by those who delight only in spring and summer.**2** It is the season of Fall – by far my favorite season. With Fall come the holidays of Halloween and Thanksgiving, two holidays notable for their fun, relaxed times, and variety of tasty foods.**3** Fall has also the ideal temperature for outdoor fun with a next door neighbor, bike riding with a close friend, and soothing walks around the park with a loved one.**4** Fall strikes the perfect balance in temperature with mild mornings and invigorating nights.**5** The trees turn into a brilliant variety of colors, and crumbling leaves underfoot yield their familiar sound.**6** Fall lasts only a short time, but it is intense and invigorating, vivid and unforgettable.**7**

Sentence Forms:
1) 2S Standard Series
2) 2S Compact Duo; 3V Past Participle
3) 2S The Pair; 5R Key Word; 2S Standard Series
4) 2S Standard Series; 3V Present Participle; 3V Past Participle
5) 2S The Pair
6) 3V Present Participle
7) 2S Rhythmical Pairs

One Paragraph no. 20   Winter   James White

Winter is not only the most beautiful but also my favorite time of the year.**1** The trees lose their leaves, a blanket of snow covers the ground, and icicles hanging from the houses seem to make everyone happy.**2** Some of the most popular pastimes during the winter are Skiing, sled riding, and ice skating.**3** Even though you have to get bundled up for the cold, it is all worth the trouble once you are out enjoying the snow.**4** After you've skated on the lake, after you've ridden a sled down a hill, and after you've made a snow angel, you'll come to appreciate and love the winter as I do.**5**

Sentence Forms:

1) 4C Not Only, But
2) 2S Standard Series; 3V Present Participle
3) 2S Standard Series
4) 3V Infinitive
5) 5R Word; 2S Standard Series

One Paragraph no. 21   Winter   Melissa Hatfield

The season of winter brings many wonderful gifts. Winter is the season that includes the holidays of both Christmas and New Years.**1** I love the sounds of laughter that come from the children, the warmth of a cozy fire, and the sweet aroma of pine cone trees in the winter.**2** Winter is the only season that you can look out your window and watch as it is snowing. During the winter season, the world seems to be so calm, so peaceful, so quiet.**3** Winter is the only season that forces us inside to spend quality time with our friends and family, making sure that we share our stories of happy times and our fondest memories.**4** One the one hand, it seems as though winter brings us much happiness when it come; on the other hand, it brings us sadness when it leaves.**5**

Sentence Forms:
1) 2S The Pair
2) 2S Standard Series)
3) 2S Triple Force; 5R Key Word
4) 3V Infinitive; 3V Present Participle; 2S The Pair
5) 4C supplemental

Well-written language is like a snow plough at the front of a great locomotive, a *logo*motive, clearing the tracks of loose speech, fuzzy thought, and approximation, exposing the usable rails of understanding and mutuality.

6 (CC) Coordinating Conjunction Forms

This conjunction joins **two equal and independent clauses**. Either clause could be a sentence by itself.
A **comma** is placed before the coordinating conjunction.

6.1	**and**	• Jane will do the report, **and** Sally will present it. • I'll find the firewood, **and** you get the matches.
6.2	**but**	• She was in a hurry, **but** the bus didn't come. • Kurt was ready to go to the airport, **but** Coco couldn't find her ticket.
6.3	**or**	• Job conditions must get better, **or** I'll quit. • We have to buy a new car, **or** we will be walking.
6.4	**nor**	• I was not hungry, **nor** was I thirsty. (Note: S-HV switch) • The dog would not sit, **nor** would he roll over.
6.5	**for**	second part explains reason for first part • I went for a walk in the evening, **for** I had been inside all day. • We stayed in a hostel, **for** we were low on funds.
6.6	**so**	first event leads to occurrence of second event • My class is starting just now, **so** I have to run. • My neighbor dropped by, **so** we decided to order Chinese food.
6.7	**yet**	like *but*, but not as strong • The leader had died two weeks ago, **yet** the public still piled flowers on her grave. • I had finished my English homework, **yet** I still had lots more to do before going to bed.

6 CC Coordinating Conjunction Forms

A coordinating conjunction joins two equal and independent clauses. Either clause could be a sentence by itself. Always, unless the clauses are both very short, a comma is placed before the coordinating conjunction.

6.1 CC and

●I'll find the rake, **and** you get the mower. ●She was late for class, **and** her research paper was due. ●Josh will clean his room, **and** Jeremy will water the garden. ●Forgive us our trespasses, **and** deliver us from email. ●Tom washed the car, **and** Brenda cleaned out the garage. ●She sorted the mail, **and** I sorted the trash. ⌘

6.2 CC but

■John went to school, **but** he did not feel well. ■Nobody lives in the Empire State Building, **but** it has many floors of offices and shops. ■Her mother was a Phys. Ed. teacher, **but** she wanted to be an astronaut. ■In North America there is the shopping mall, **but** in South Korea there is the shopping building. ⌘

6.3 CC or

●I'll contact you by email, **or** you can call me in a few days. ●We will have to raise the workers' wages, **or** they will quit. ●You can catch a flight at 9:00pm, **or** there is a train leaving this afternoon at 2:35pm. ●We'll visit the Parthenon and Acropolis, **or** we'll travel to a nearby Greek island by boat. ⌘

6.4 CC nor

Note: The second independent clause has an inverted subject/auxiliary verb word order.

■None of the students aced the exam, **nor** did any of them do well in the community service category. ■She won't listen to the advice of her parents, **nor** will she seek the guidance of any of her friends. ■The business was not doing well, **nor** were its owners keeping healthy lifestyles. ■I don't approve of that expenditure, **nor** will I assign any funds for such related matters. ■He will not be allowed to go out to play, **nor** will he be allowed to watch television. ⌘

6.5 CC for

Note: The second part explains the reason for or justifies the first part

●I came inside, **for** it had started to snow. ●I went for a walk in the evening, **for** I had been inside all day. ●She wanted to go, **for** skating was one of the joys of her life. ●James read the book, **for** he was interested in computers. ●He was thinking of changing his minor, **for** Psychology doesn't quite interest him enough. ●The people returned to the store, **for** the service was outstanding. ●The meeting went late, **for** many people stayed back and asked the speaker questions. ⌘

6.6 CC so
Note: The first event leads to the occurrence of the second event.

■My class starts in a few minutes, **so** I have to run. ■My neighbor dropped by, **so** we decided to order rotis. ■My class finished early, **so** I went for a walk to see the cherry blossoms. ■It was a beautiful morning, **so** he decided to walk to work. ■The bus hadn't arrived, **so** I took a taxi. ■When she saw the ice cream vendor Mary realized she was short of money, **so** she ran all the way back home to get more. ■I have a lot to do right now, **so** I won't be able to meet you today. ⌘

6.7 CC yet
Note: The second part is a strange or surprising event that almost contradicts the first part

●He wanted to move to Mongolia, **yet** he hesitated because he knew the salary would be quite lower. ●I hate being busy, **yet** I hate being bored even more. ●He went to his school guidance counselor for assistance, **yet** the counselor offered little help. ●Many people chose to handwrite their essay, **yet** the easiest way is to type it on a computer. ●Nate "Kryptonate" Robinson is short by NBA standards, **yet** he still gets by the tall players and scores baskets. ●Sidney Poitier grew up in a little house on Cat Island in the Bahamas, **yet** he went on to prove himself an excellent actor in Hollywood cinema. ⌘

Short Code Chart for Coordinating Conjunction Forms

NUMBER	SENTENCE FORM LETTER CODE	DESCRIPTION OR FORMULA	SUBFORM NOTATION (NAME OR SHORT CODE)
	6 CC Coordinating Conjunctions		
6.1	CC	and	6CC and
6.2		but	6CC but
6.3		or	6CC or
6.4		nor	6CC nor
6.5		for	6CC for
6.6		so	6CC so
6.7		yet	6CC yet

7 (AC) Adverbial Clause Forms

Cause	7.1	• Because the snow had melted, the river ran high.
	7.2	• Since we were away on vacation, the plant died of thirst.
Condition	7.3	• If anyone calls for me, please take a message.
	7.4	• Whether we win or lose, we know we tried our best.
	7.5	• Unless you save for your retirement now, you could end up living on a prayer and a shoestring.
	7.6	• Until you master these forms, you may get lost reading English sentences.
	7.7	• Once he saw the pattern, he could compose many variations using it.
Concession	7.8	more frequent and casual • Though she isn't tall, she can still play basketball well. • Though the police surrounded the bank, the thieves still got away.
	7.9	more formal • Although she was lacking experience, her enthusiasm and cheerfulness got her the job.
	7.10	more emphatic • Even though it's 2:30am, I am not really tired.
Time	7.11	• I'll call you from the airport when I reach Cebu.
	7.12	• As the parents slept, the teen chatted online.
	7.13	• Before you apply for a passport, you need photos. • I always write in my diary before I sleep.
	7.14	• After they broke up, they still were good friends.
	7.15	• While the babies slept, the mothers chatted.
	7.16	• Since moving to Toronto, she has opened a hair salon that specializes in dreadlock, French, cornrow, and interlock braid styles.

7 AC Adverbial Clause Forms

Subordinate adverbial clauses start with easily identifiable subordinate adverbial conjunctions. They are called **subordinate** because they are *dependent* clauses, not *independent*. They are *dependent* because they cannot stand on their own and make sense alone. We change the name to ***adverbial*** because they explain *why, when,* or *how* the action of the main verb was or is or will be done.

These adverbial conjunctions fall into four categories: **Cause, Condition, Concession**, and **Time** (C-C-C-T). **Students should memorize these conjunctions as signifying markers or red flags: they are not the main part of the sentence, but introduce a clause with a subject and verb, and this clause explains the event of the main verb in the main clause**.

A **comma** is used <u>after the adverbial clause</u> when it begins the sentence. *Usually*, the adverbial clause at the end of a sentence *is <u>not</u>* preceded by a comma.

CAUSE

The adverbial clause gives a reason for the event or action or occurrence in the main clause.

7.1 AC Ca because

- **Because she had an appointment**, she left work right at 5:00.
- **Because I had a flat tire on the way**, I arrived late for the job interview.
- **Because the snow has melted**, the rivers run high.
- **Because the cheese has melted**, I have to wait a bit for the burger to cool

off. ●**Because he was broke**, he could not sign up for the class. ●**Because there were many tribal languages**, Native Americans developed a sign language in order to communicate together. ●**Because they wanted to save money**, the family decided to plant their own vegetables and bake their own bread. ●She ran **because the bus was starting to pull away from the curb**. ●I love snakes **because they are smooth, sleek, and powerful**. ●He started to run **because bees were chasing him**. ⌘

7.2 AC Ca since, now that

■**Since I have little money**, I'll have to eat instant noodles for dinner. ■**Since it is late**, I'd better go home. ■**Since it snowed**, all traffic slowed down to a crawl. ■**Since you insist**, I had better write a sentence with *since* in it. ■**Since I have moved to New Delhi**, I've had several intense, enlightening experiences. ■**Since we did not want to live in an apartment**, we decided to rent a house. ■**Since the plant died while we were away**, my mother decided to buy a new one. ■My legs really hurt **since I climbed Mount Sorak last** weekend. ∎I'm really tired **since I stayed up until 2:30 last night.** ∎**Now that he has become a parent**, he has gotten much closer and friendlier to his own parents and parents-in-law. ∎**Now that the monsoons are over**, I can work on replacing the palmyra leaves of my roof. ∎**Now that you have learned a few more of these forms**, you should have no problem in composing interesting sentences of your own. ⌘

Condition

A condition is described in the adverbial clause, and the main part of the sentence gives the consequence if the condition is true or is met. However, information in an *as if* clause is assumed to be true when in fact it is not.

7.3 AC Co if, as if, (should)

∎**If anyone calls for me**, please take a message. ∎**If you're healthy**, you're wealthy. ∎**If the waves don't get smaller**, we'll have to cancel the surfing contest. ∎**If you buy it on the installment plan**, you'll end up paying a bit more. ∎**If you continue with your heavy drinking habit**, you'll have to be admitted to the AA. ∎Stay away from the water **if you can't swim.** ∎Don't give the child any dessert **if she refuses to eat** dinner. ■Should any of you have any questions, our trained staff are ready and willing to talk to you. ■She looked at me **as if she knew me**. ■You treat me **as if I am a juvenile**. ■The woman drove wildly, **as if she was in a hurry**. ■You look at me **as if you think I know nothing at all about teaching children**. ⌘

7.4 AC Co whether

This conjunction offers a kind of yes-no or diametrically opposite situation in the adverbial clause, but then presents a third situation that must be done or met regardless of the first two.

■**Whether all workers are there or not**, the meeting will begin at 4:30. ■**Whether you win or lose**, it's more important how you play the game. ■**Whether you like it or not**, you will still have to correct your mistakes in your sentence forms homework. ■It's not important **whether you were born in the countryside or the city**. ■**Whether it snows or not**, we will still try to enjoy our year-end holidays. ■**Whether the economy is good or bad**, I will still try to give the best service I can to each and every customer. ■**Whether the food tastes good or strange**, it is still good manners to compliment the chef at a formal summit dinner. ■We will continue construction of the complex **whether the weather is warm or freezing.** ⌘

7.5 AC Co unless

■**Unless I really pour it on now**, I won't be able to win this race. ■**Unless the weather clears up**, the game will be cancelled. ■**Unless you join the club**, you won't receive any of the benefits. ■**Unless we get more sales**, we may slide into bankruptcy. ■I won't be able to go **unless I can get some more money together.** ■**Unless more students show up**, we'll have to postpone today's lecture. ■**Unless there is greater equality**, there will never be any peace. ■**Unless you think now about your old age and retirement**, you could end up in the poor house. ■**Unless it rains**, we will lose this summer's wheat crop. ⌘

7.6 AC Co until

●**Until both groups agree to put down their guns**, there can be no hope of peace. ●**Until you master these forms**, you may get lost reading English sentences. ●Until I get in contact with the bank, I will not be able to take out any money. ●I can't wait until I see you. ●I'll wait at the track until you come. ●He will continue at the same job until he retires. ●Hold her head back until her nosebleed stops. ●I can't get my allowance until my parents come home. ●They stayed in the shelter until the hurricane was over.

7.7 AC Co once

■Once you've seen how the system works, you can never forget it. ■Once Melinda ate, she felt better. ■Once she got off work, she called her boyfriend. ■Once you've finished sweeping the dance floor, mop and wax it. ■Once you drink the herbal medicine, you'll feel better. ■Once the lake freezes over, trucks will drive over the ice as a shortcut route to the towns in northern Manitoba. ■Once she arrives, we can start the meeting. ■Once the stain has dried on the wooden sofa, you can apply the first topcoat of lacquer on it.

QUALIFICATION/CONCESSION

The adverbial clause describes a concession, qualification or circumstance that gives rise to an unexpected or surprise result in the main clause.

7.8 AC Q though (more frequent and casual)

●**Though she was not tall**, she could still play basketball well. ●**Though my legs felt like rubber**, I knew I had to continue my mountain trek. ●**Though you might not believe it**, women have a larger connection between the two sides of their brain than men have. ●**Though I had been there before**, I found my second visit to China much more interesting than the first. ●**Though some people think that a university degree is necessary to become financially stable**, there are still many people who have proven that the converse is true. ●**Though he plays cards well**, he can't play dominoes. ●She completed her homework assignment **though she was extremely tired**.

7.9 AC Q although (more formal)

■**Although they lost the game**, they were not too disappointed. ■**Although Ron and Chrissy broke up as a campus couple**, they still remain friends and meet every once in a while. ■**Although his work was not** *finished*, he went home early. ■**Although the experience was not good**, the job did not pay enough. ■**Although the man works as a carpenter**, he is also an electrician. ■Everybody sat on the edge of the stage **although we could have sat at the tables**.

7.10 AC Q even though (more emphatic)

●**Even though it's raining**, I'll go jogging. ●**Even though it looks easy**, snowboarding takes a while to master. ●**Even though the skater tilted off balance after one jump**, she still won top marks at the figure skating competition. ●**Even though he couldn't swim**, he still managed to get to shore after the raft topped over. ●**Even though she grew up in a wealthy neighborhood**, she still did not care much about getting a good-paying job. ●They kept the cow **even though they had no meat to eat**. ●I went to work **even though I had a splitting headache**.

<u>Variation</u>: *even though* with a comma in front

●Jim went to the club, **even though he had parental duties at home**. ●They say there will be a clear sky to see the full moon tonight, **even though it's pouring rain right now**.

Time

The action in the adverbial clause precedes, is simultaneous, or follows the action of the main clause.

7.11 AC T when

- **When I leave class today**, I have to get a shot.
- **When she goes home**, she will stop by the daycare center to pick up her kids.
- **When you join our academy**, you will be expected to do some homework almost every day.
- **When you finish the repair work**, please call me.
- Who was at the wheel **when the crash took place**?
- We will start the party **when Dana arrives**.
- Call me **when you're finished**.
- The debriefing of the astronauts will take place on Tuesday **when their spaceship returns to Earth**.

7.12 AC T as

- **As I was leaving**, I remembered to bring the letter.
- **As it was getting late**, I decided to head home and zonk out.
- **As she stood in front of the cheering crowd of fans**, she realized that her dream had come true.
- **As the family slept**, the burglar picked the lock

and stealthily entered the house. ■**As you slowly inhale and exhale**, be sure to focus also on your spine. ■The results of the survey are disappointing **as you predicted they would be**.

Variation: *like* instead of *as*

■**Like you said**, some sentences are hard to understand. ■I don't know if I will ever feel **like I did then**. ■Life is just **like Grandma said it would be**.

7.13 AC T before

●**Before you lock the door**, don't forget to turn on the security alarm. ●**Before you jump to any conclusions**, I'd like to give you the full scoop on what happened - and that may take a while. ●**Before you do your piano practice**, could you please feed the fish? ●**Before the guest arrived**, we thoroughly cleaned the house. ●**Before we went to class**, we had to memorize the Two Hands chart. ●**Before you marry**, you should take a course together to make sure you understand the many aspects of your commitment. ●You should make a bag lunch **before you go**. ●Wash your hands **before you**

eat. ●You have to learn to walk **before you can run.**
●Remove your shoes **before you enter the living room.**

7.14 AC T after

■**After she went home**, she cooked some spicy tuna and fermented cabbage soup. ■**After I thought about it**, I knew that what she said was true: it weren't meant to be together. ■**After we broke up**, I had a near-death experience. ■**After families celebrate Christmas and New Year**, the parents are usually in debt. ■**After the decision had been made**, Jim wished he had voiced his opinion. ■**After we saw *Lord of the Rings***, we went for a pizza. ■**After it got mild**, the snowman melted. ■**After you take a bath**, make sure to moisturize your skin to prevent dryness. ■You can play computer games **after you finish your lunch.** ■Refreshments will be served **after the ceremony is over.** ■Construction will begin on the Tata Nano Housing Project **after the Mumbai city central committee approves the urban design and financial plans.**

7.15 AC T while

●**While you are waiting for the bus**, you can also review some vocabulary. ●**While the sun shone**, the birds sang and chirped. ●You shouldn't talk on your cell phone **while** you are driving. ●**While their parents were gone**, Jill and Jen had a party. ●Students are not allowed to talk **while the teacher is lecturing**. ●The dog waited in the car **while I went to the video store**. ●The chicken was being baked in the oven **while the rice was boiling in the pressure cooker**. ●**While the baby was asleep**, the mother studied over the internet. ●Make hay **while the sun shines**.

7.16 AC T since, ever since, now that

■**Since I moved to Guam**, my life has been exciting and interesting. ■**Since you started pestering me**, I can't get my work done. ■**Since she has begun her studies abroad**, she has become responsible and mature. ■I've been working part-time or full-time **since I was 14 years old**. ■I feel better **since I quit smoking**. ■They had to use public transportation **since their car broke** down. ■They've been at war ever **since the Xanadulians invaded in 2183**. ■My Mom has had short hair ever **since I can remember**. ■She's been feeling uneasy ever **since the family dog died**. ■**Now that you mentioned it**, I think that security control is of vital importance. ■**Now that spring is here**, we can all go for beautiful walks.

S. Garrigues

Short Code Chart for 7 AC Adverbial Conjunction Forms

NUMBER	SENTENCE FORM LETTER CODE	DESCRIPTION OR FORMULA	SUBFORM NOTATION (NAME OR SHORT CODE)
		Cause	
7.1		because	7AC Though
7.2		since	7AC Since
		Condition	
7.3		if	7AC If
7.4		whether	7AC Whether
7.5		unless	7AC Unless
7.6		until	7AC Until
7.7	A C	once	7AC Once
		Qualification or Concession	
7.8		though	7AC Though
7.9		although	7AC Although
7.10		even though	7AC Even though
		Time	
7.11		when	7AC When
7.12		as	7AC As
7.13		before	7AC Before
7.14		after	7AC After
7.15		while	7AC While
7.16		since	7AC since

8 (RN) Reference and Noun Clause Forms

		Reference Clause	Noun Clause
8.1	who	Sam, **who is our coach**, runs every morning.	I don't know **who used the bicycle last**.
8.2	where	Toronto is the city **where I was born**.	I know exactly **where I will go on my trip**.
8.3	when	This is a time **when everyone should be glad**.	She doesn't know **when she will be finished**.
8.4	why	~	I wonder **why she hasn't called yet**.
8.5	what, whatever	That feeling, **what the French call** *ennui*, sets in sometimes, and life seems boring.	Did you hear **what I said**? **Whatever you do** is fine by me.
8.6	how	~	It depends on **how you do in the qualifying matches**.
8.7	that	The house **that Jack built** is beside his beanstalk.	I understand **that you spent three years on a tropical island**.
8.8	which	The hat **which you bought** is very becoming.	You'll have to decide **which is best**.
8.9	whose	I rented a car **whose radio was broken**.	I'll try to find out **whose book it is**.
8.10	whom	The person **whom you met yesterday** is from Alpha Centauri.	I don't know **whom you're talking about**.
Reference and Noun Clause Forms — the odd one			
8.11	Missing **[that]**	The comic books **[that] I bought** are funny.	I think **[that] it's time to go**.

8 RN Reference and Noun Clause Forms

A **subordinate reference clause** starts with a *wh-* word[1] or *that,* and the clause *refers back* to the preceding noun or pronoun. The clause adds to it like an adjective does.

A **subordinate noun clause** starts with a *wh-* word, *how* or *that,* and the clause functions as the subject or an object in the sentence.

Both forms are called *subordinate* because they are dependent, can't stand by themselves, and are subservient to the main clause of the sentence in which they occur.

8.1 RN who, whoever

REFERENCE CLAUSE

●She **who studies hard** will get some respect in the working world. ●Bill Gates, **who is the owner of Microsoft**, retired early to do philanthropy in the area of world health. ●Ming, **who is a co-worker of mine**, will be teaching the calligraphy class. ●The president, **who met with CIA and FBI officials yesterday**, has scheduled a press conference for 2:00pm.

NOUN CLAUSE

●I do not know **who my soul mate is**. ●She wanted to know **who stole her money**. ●We still don't know **who sent the flowers**. ●**Whoever did the gag** meant no harm.

---

[1] *who, whoever, where, when, whenever, why, which, whose, whom*

8.2 RN where

REFERENCE CLAUSE

■The house **where he lived** is for sale. ■South Korea is the country **where the 1988 Summer Olympics were held**. ■I plan to vacation in Bali, **where the weather is always warm**. ■I will go to Christchurch, **where my parents live**. ■"I want to live in a world **where I belong**." [UK pop group Travis in *Turn*] ■We will go **where we are wanted**. ■I looked **where you said**, but couldn't find it.

NOUN CLAUSE

■Australia is **where you can find the kookaburra bird**. ■I know exactly **where I want to live** – Santiago. ■On the rack is **where you should place your hat**. ■Let's decide **where we should put the sofa**.

8.3 RN when

REFERENCE CLAUSE

<u>Note</u>: This signifying marker may cause some confusion, since it is also an adverbial conjunction of time used in the subordinate adverbial clauses in Form 7AC. To spend large amounts of time debating whether a clause that starts with *when* is a reference or adverbial clause would seem to us to be waste of time. It is more important that you learn to recognize and compose such sentences.

●Spring is the season **when we all rejoice with nature**.
●It is a time **when all people like to walk outdoors**.
●This is the time **when you can speak your mind**

freely.

NOUN CLAUSE

- **When I sleep** is when I'm happiest. •I don't know **when I will be going there**. •How will I know **when you arrive**? •We need to decide **when we'll meet next**. •**When I was in my twenties** was the most exciting time of my life.

8.4 RN why

NOUN CLAUSE

■I don't know **why I didn't do my homework.** ■Hinduism's versatility is **why I find it interesting.** ■I don't know **why I can't stop thinking about her.** ■Her sparkling eyes are **why I find her so attractive.** ■I wonder **why he left in a hurry.** ■He wants to know **why you are late.** ■**Why I didn't think of that sooner** really eludes me. ■Although someone tried to explain it to me, I still don't get **why water expands when it turns to ice.** ■The ultimate philosophical question is **why is there something and not nothing?**

8.5 RN what, whatever

REFERENCE CLAUSE

•A strong feeling of boredom, **what French people call** *ennui*, slowly crept into their relationship. •That feeling – **what sociologists call** *sibling rivalry* – is a factor that is present in families with more than one child.

NOUN CLAUSE

●**What I like most** is the small town atmosphere. ●No one understood **what the new policy stated**. ●Did you hear **what I said**? ●She always knows **what he is thinking**. ●I will do **whatever it takes to complete this project**. ●I don't know **what I was thinking when I joined the military**. ●He accomplished **what every human dreams of doing** - walking on the moon. ●I will make do with **what I have**. ●I'm okay with **whatever you decide to do**.

8.6 RN how

NOUN CLAUSE

■Do you know **how to make *kimchi*?** ■Tracy was contemplating **how to get rich**. ■**How they survived two weeks adrift at sea** is a real miracle. ■She doesn't know **how she got there**. ■Show me **how to cook *tortillas*.** ■She wondered **how she would ever get all the work done in time**. ■Do you think I will ever learn **how to speak Mandarin**? ■They teach you **how to set up a solar charging unit**.

8.7 RN that

REFERENCE CLAUSE

●The houses **that the three pigs built** would not pass modern construction standards. ●The report **that you** sent me last week was impressive. ●The possibility that there was something wrong with the rocket engine started to bother the astronauts. ●A hammer is a tool that you usually use when making a house out of wooden planks and beams.

NOUN CLAUSE

●I can't assume that you understand all of this. ●I realize that you will be busy next week. ●It was obvious that he was the better player. ●The big news is that the company president has resigned.

8.8 RN which

REFERENCE CLAUSE

■The hat which I bought is very warm. ■The argument which you put forth is a good one. ■The song which you wrote sounds beautiful. ■That which is done is not always that which is intended. ■The store which is on the corner gives the best deals on books.

REFERENCE CLAUSE WHICH REFERS TO THE BASE SENTENCE

Here, *which* refers back to the base sentence preceding part of the sentence, not just to the word before it.

■They argued continuously which later resulted in a fight. ■I fell down the stairs which caused me to break my leg. ■My husband always came with me to every one of my prenatal checkups, which meant that he also got to hear the baby's heartbeat at ten weeks.

Noun Clause

■You'll have to decide **which is best**. ■It's not important **which one you do first**. ■I can't figure out **which piece is connected to the wingnut**. ■Have you decided **which college you want to attend**?

8.9 RN whose

Reference Clause

●The man, **whose lawyers were very good**, was acquitted. ●Teddy, **whose house is made from home-made bricks and a palm leaf roof**, recently bought a Rajdoot motorcycle. ●I met my neighbor **whose dog had just died**. ●I rented a car **whose heater was broken**. ●Bill Clinton will always be remembered as the president **whose marital infidelity almost caused his impeachment**.

Noun Clause

●I don't know **whose boy that is**. ●They couldn't figure out **whose DNA it was**. ●There was nothing left at the scene of the attack that could further lead investigators to determine **whose prayer shawl it was**.

8.10 RN whom

Reference Clause

■The lady **whom you met yesterday** is related to Ann Landers. ■The officer **whom I talked with last week** is not here today. ■The student **whom I gave the prize to** later went on to become a lawyer.

NOUN CLAUSE

■I don't know **whom you're referring to**. ■The architect for **whom I worked last year** has moved her offices to Mumbai. ■The woman on **whom the greatest responsibility rests** is now the president of the country.

8.11 RN missing *that*

In the following sentences, the *that* is left out. To show that you understand this form, find the place where *[that]* should go, and write it in.

REFERENCE CLAUSE

●Some of the people [that] you meet in life make it all worthwhile. ●The next slide [that] I want to show you illustrates the IIO philosophy for language learning. ●The comic books [that] I bought are funny. ●The suitcase [that] Dad gave me is old but useful. ●The CD [that] I bought is exceptionally good. ●"It destroys all evidence [that] it was ever there." [Crichton *Jurassic Park*]

NOUN CLAUSE

●I think [that] she'll be happy if you get her some flowers. ●I know [that] you did your best. ●The computer [that] I bought is really great. ●I think [that] it's time to go. ●I think [that] we need more practice. ●We know [that] you tried your best.

Short Code Chart for Reference & Noun Forms

8 RN Reference and Noun Conjunctions

NUMBER	SENTENCE FORM LETTER CODE	DESCRIPTION OR FORMULA	SUBFORM NOTATION (NAME OR SHORT CODE)
8.1	R N	who	8RN who
8.2		where	8RN where
8.3		when	8RN when
8.4		why	8RN why
8.5		what	8RN what
8.6		how	8RN how
8.7		that	8RN that
8.8		which	8RN which
8.9		whose	8RN whose
8.10		whom	8RN whom
8.11		missing *that*	8RN missing *that*

The *Yin* and *Yang* of Black and White Photography

The *Symphonic Assemblage* of this book involves the thoughtful placement of lesser assemblages of photos of both natural and human forms.

Like the *yin/yang*, every photo contains many in-between gradations of gray – just as the yin and yang are constantly flowing into each other. Shadows and surfaces are more easily perceived when put in greyscale. As Jun'ichiro Tanizaki notes in his naturally flowing essay *In Praise of Shadows*, the beauty of a Japanese room depends on "a variation of shadows – heavy shadows against light shadows." and the "soft, fragile beauty of the feeble light."

BLACK | WHITE

INVISIBLE | VISIBLE

NEGATIVE | POSITIVE SPACE

Black and white photography corresponds to *yin* and *yang* in more than just the opposite word meanings of black and white. Unlike in color photography, black and white photography highlights two other examples of *yin/yang* oppositions: namely, negative space | positive space, and the invisible world | the visible world.

Instructions for Second Assignment

In the previous assignment, students were asked to incorporate several different examples of the First Five Simple Sentence Forms into their paragraphs. In this second assignment, students should continue to incorporate 2 or 3 examples of the First Five Simple Sentence Forms; however, in addition, they should also now incorporate 2 to 4 examples of the Compound and Complex Sentence Forms 6, 7, and 8 into a theme with a length of two or three paragraphs. Once again, they should have a focused title, and they should notate and footnote the Sentence Forms that they choose to employ.

Below are some examples of how earlier students completed this assignment to serve as models for students to follow who are doing this assignment for the first time.

In the model paragraphs below, we have notated and footnoted most, but not all of the Sentence Forms, used. The aim is simply to highlight a representative sample of the Sentence Forms employed, not necessarily to designate every single form used. Occasionally, we also notate and footnote, by way of foreshadowing, some of the upcoming Form 9 Sentence Forms. By foreshadowing and notating certain select instances of the upcoming, all important Form 9, we hope to gradually introduce students to the pivotal and central importance of Form 9 for the full mastery of effective prose.

The third assignment will deal exclusively with learning and incorporating various examples of Sentence Form 9.

Student Compositions Forms 6, 7, 8
Lending a Helping Hand by Hee Gon Yang

I think that I have accomplished plenty of things in my short life.**1** Of all the accomplishments, the one that I recall most vividly is volunteering to refurbish the worn-down library of an elementary school in a small village in Romania.**2** Volunteering just meant a little time out of my day, yet it meant the world to the children who attended that school.**3** The building required new walls, new roof, and repainting.**4** The work was strenuous, but it was very rewarding and satisfying.**5**

The image that will permanently be burned in my memory of that day will be the gratitude and joy, playfulness and friendship on the faces of the children.**6** Though most of the children barely spoke English, we could sense a special bond building between us.**7** We definitely had an eventful day. Although volunteering took most of our free time that day, I believe it was time very well spent.**8** Because on that day, we fostered friendship that will last a lifetime.**9**

Sentence Forms
1) 8RN That
2) 8RN That; 3V Gerund; 3V Infinitive
3) 3V Gerund; 6CC Yet; 8RN Who
4) 2S Standard Series
5) 6CC But; 2S The Pair
6) 8RN That; 2S Rhythmical Pairs

7) 7AC Though; 3V Present Participle
8) 3V Gerund; 7AC Although; 8RN Missing that
9) 8RN That

Mom's Applesauce by Caroline Daniels

When it comes to food, I have never been very picky.**1** For me a child, however, the taste of store bought applesauce wasn't appealing to me. The consistency of the sauce slid across my tongue like slime. Even though I knew the slimy sauce was made from apples, I couldn't understand why it didn't taste like apples.**2** It almost reminded me of rotten pears.**3** My mother, after an exhausting battle, finally stopped serving it to me.**4** She had another plan. She was going to prove to me that I would like applesauce.**5**

I came home from school one day and walked into the kitchen. My mother was cutting the most gorgeous Granny Smith apples. I just assumed she was cutting slices for us to eat, but when I picked up a slice, she slapped my hand gently and told me they weren't ready yet.**6** I didn't understand why they wouldn't be ready.**7** They were already cut into slices. I wondered what else she was planning on doing with them.**8** I proceeded to go into my room and put my school bag down. I knew I wouldn't be able to help my mother without washing my hands, so I went straight to the restroom and scrubbed them clean.**9** My next step was to find out what she had planned for those absolutely beautiful apples.**10**

I walked back into the kitchen, and I noticed that my mother had cut the apples into much smaller pieces than before.**11** She motioned for me to come closer and handed me a knife.**12** I smiled. I always liked helping in the kitchen.**13** I began to cut the apples into small pieces. When all the apples were cut, I helped her put the pieces into a pot on the stove.**14** I kept asking her what we were making, but she refused to tell me.**15** "You'll see, you'll see," she kept saying. She poured water, sugar, and cinnamon into the pot and began stirring.**16** After about 20 minutes, the smell of the sauce caressed my senses and made my stomach rumble with anticipation. It was almost ready and I was excited.

Finally, the applesauce was done. By then, I knew it was applesauce, but I didn't care.**17** My mom made it, so I figured it had to taste good.**18** She served me only one spoonful, and I gave her a look that could kill. "Well, you don't like applesauce," my mother sarcastically stated. I just politely asked for more and she served me a bowl's worth. The apple chunks were sweet and soft.**19** I chewed the delectable sauce slowly to enjoy every bite. I absolutely loved it. It was sweet and sugary; it did not feel slimy.**20** It wasn't boring or unpleasing.**21** It was perfect. My mother laughed as I sighed with pleasure after every bite.**22** My mother had proved me wrong: I loved applesauce.**23**

Sentence Forms:

1) 7AC When
2) 7AC Even Though; 8RN Why
3) 3V Past Participle
4) 3V Present Participle; 3V Gerund
5) 8RN That

6) 8RN Missing *that* (2); 6CC But; 7AC When

7) 8RN Why
8) 8RN What
9) 8RN Missing *that*; 3V Infinitive; 3V Gerund; 6CC So;
10) 3V Infinitive; 8RN What

11) 8RN That;6CC And
12) 3V Infinitive
13) 3V Gerund
14) 7AC When
15) 8RN What; 6CC But
16) 2S Standard Series; 3V Gerund

17) 6CC But
18) 6CC So; 8RN Missing *that*
19) 6CC And
20) 2S The Pair
21) 2S Choices
22) 7AC As
23) 9PP Explanation Colon

The Day I Left Home by Joseph M. Auzenne

The day finally came for me to transition from a civilian to a soldier.**1** I can remember that day all too well; I was excited and scared, nervous and anxious.**2** To leave my family would be devastating.**3** On the one hand, I was ready to explore a new life; on the other hand, I did not want to leave my comfort zone.**4** My family and friends, with whom I had grown up, were at the bus station to see me off.**5** While I was saying my final goodbyes, I watched my dad wipe the tears from my mother's eyes.**6** I told myself that I would be strong, that I would be a man, that I would not cry, even though I knew it was just a matter of time, before I would have to wipe my eyes.**7**

The bus driver opened the door to the bus, for the time had come for me to depart.**8** My mother, with tears in her face, hugged me one last time, and my dad promised me she would be fine.**9** My heart started beating faster and faster. Thoughts of changing my mind went through my head, yet I knew it was too late, according to what my recruiter had said.**10** As I entered the bus, I looked back in tears, knowing this would be the day I left home.**11**

Sentence Forms

1) 3V Infinitive; 4C From To
2) 2S Rhythmical Pairs
3) 3V Infinitive
4) 4C On the One Hand; 3V Infinitive (2)
5) 8RN Whom; 3V Infinitive
6) 7AC While
7) 5R Adverbial Conjunction; 8RN Missing *that*; 7AC Before; 3V Infinitive
8) 6CC For; 3V Infinitive
9) 6CC And; 8RN Missing *that*
10) 3V Gerund; 6CC Yet; 8RN What
11) 7AC As; 8RN Missing *that*

Combat Medic by Jill Friend

Combat medics have one of the most exciting and interesting, mentally and physically challenging jobs in today's army.**1** We are the ones that see all of the guts and gore.**2** We are expected to help the bleeding soldiers, with amputated limbs and spurting blood.**3** Neither books nor pictures can prepare you for what types of injuries you encounter.**4** You have to keep your head, and work quickly to get casualties to safety.**5**

Not only do we save lives on the battlefield, but also in the TMCs [Troop Medical Clinics], clinics, and hospitals.**6** We take care of all soldiers as well as their families.**7** Since we work long hours and holidays, we have little time off.**8** Until you stand in our shoes, you don't know all the things that we go through and all the graphic and painful things we have to see.**9** I love my job, and I love what I do: Medical Aid and Support!**10**

Sentence Forms

1) 2S Rhythmical Pairs
2) 8RN That; 2S The Pair
3) 3V Infinitive; 3VPresent Participle; 3V Past Participle; 3V Present Participle
4) 4C Neither Nor; 8RN What
5) 3V Infinitive (2)

6) 4C Not Only, But; 2S Standard Series
7) 4C As Well As
8) 7AC Since; 2S The Pair
9) 7AC Until; 8RN That; 2S The Pair
10) 8RN What; 9PP Explanation Colon

Me and My iPod by Lafayette G. Dennis

All I need in this life of sin is my iPod.**1** Apple was really thinking of me when they invented this costly, worthwhile piece of hardware.**2** Who could ever imagine storing an entire music library in the palm of your hand?**3** With my iPod, I am freed from my collection of CDs and cassettes which often are damaged.**4** I am sad to report, however, that I only recently jumped on the bandwagon.**5** At first, I was reluctant about purchasing one, but once I did, I saw what all the hoopla was about.**6**

The iPod is convenient, produces crisp sounding music, and has multiple capabilities.**7** What more could you ask for in an entertainment device? You have not lived until you have held one in your hands and have felt the power of this device.**8** No one can do it for you nor can they explain the feeling; it has to be experienced first hand.**9** What are you waiting on? You heard me, so get out there and buy yourself an iPod!**10** Whether you buy it with cash or a credit card, it will be one of the most rewarding purchases of your life.**11**

Sentence Forms

1) 8RN Missing that
2) 7AC When; 2S Compact Duo
3) 3V Gerund
4) 8RN Which
5) 8RN That
6) 3V Gerund; 6CC But; 7AC Once; 8RN What
7) 2S Standard Series; 3V Present Participle
8) 7AC Until; 2S The Pair
9) 6CC Nor
10) 6CC So;
11) 7AC Whether

Mio Padre by Daniel Bregaglio

From the time I was born till today, he has always been there for me.**1** He has always treated me as if I was a king.**2** He works hard so that I may have anything I want.**3** Neither rain nor snow can keep him from making sure I'm happy.**4** He is kind, and he is loving.

When I grow up, I hope to be like him.**5** I am stronger and smarter from the things he has taught me.**6** I wish I could repay him for everything he has done for me, but I'll never be able to.**7** All I have to offer him is my love, so for now that will have to do.**8** He is my best friend, but most of all he is my father.**9**

Sentence Forms

1) 4C From Till
2) 7AC As If
3) 7AC So That (supplemental)
4) 4C Neither Nor; 3V Gerund
5) 7AC When
6) 2S The Pair; 8RN Missing that
7) 8RN Missing that; 6CC but
8) 6CC So 8RN That
9) 6CC But

Words of Wisdom by Kareem Byam

Words of wisdom have an important and powerful influence on the human body.**1** My grandmother always provided words of wisdom to me. She always said "Wisdom will make you very strong and knowledgeable in life". The first time I rode a bike, I couldn't stay on it for a long time, and I kept falling and falling – until one day when my grandmother saw me trying and trying to stay on the bike.**2** She then told me, "Kareem, you have to be like a lion chasing after a zebra".**3** I thought about her words of wisdom for many days. But finally one day, it hit me – like a baseball thrown to you at 100mph.**4** I understood what my grandmother was telling me that time: have bravery, courage, and determination, and toughness, too.**5** I learned how to ride and stay on a bike for a long period of time, day or night.**6**

My grandmother's words of wisdom were spiritually moving and physically touching.**7** I still can't express how I feel about her words of wisdom.**8** They fostered my evolution – like a new creation being touched by God.**9** No other woman's words could ever replace my grandmother's words of wisdom.

However, it was my mother, and not my grandmother, who told me, when my uncle had passed away a few days earlier, "Your favorite uncle is looking down at you every day, and he wants the best for you".**10** When my mother told me that, I got a Spiderman sense, as if he was right there in the room with me.**11** That touched me, and from then on, I have always been strong in heeding words of wisdom. My mom's and grandmother's words and wisdom will always flow through my veins and blood, and be passed to my son.**12**

Sentence Forms

1) 2S The Pair
2) 6CC And; 9PP Dash E Adverb Phrase; 7AC When; 3V Present Participle (2) ??
3) 3V Present Participle
4) 3V Past Participle
5) 8RN What; 9PP Explanation Colon; 2S Standard Series
6) 8RN How
7) 2S The Pair
8) 8RN How
9) 6CC And
10) 7AC When; 7AC As If (supplemental)
11) 2S The Pair (3)

Purpose by Mark Strickland

What is our purpose in this lifetime? Is it to go to school, get a job, work for a while, and then just die?**1** I think about this a lot – maybe too much. What I have realized is that there are no clear answers.**2** We are all left to make the trying, hard, and sometimes very inevitable decisions on our own.**3** Yet, I still want to know. And, I see that I am learning by living, which is the only way.**4**

My purpose is to not only to live a full life, but also a happy one.**5** A happy life for me would include lots of knowledge, lots of adventures, and lots of experiences.**6** But what I do now as an adult will make major paragraphs in the book of my personal story; this I know.**7** And, when my life is over and I look back, I want to know that my life had a purpose and resulted in many achievements.**8**

Sentence Forms

1) 3V Infinitive; 2S Standard Series (Extended)
2) 8RN What; 8RN That
3) 3V Present Participle; 2S Standard Series
4) 8RN That; 3V Gerund; 8RN Which
5) 4C Not Only, But; 3V Infinitive (2)
6) 5R Word
7) 8RN What; 9PP Association Semicolon
8) 7AC When; 6CC And; 3V Infinitive; 8RN That

Long Awaited Trip by Addonis Hawkins

"Good morning," I said to my wife as I rolled out of bed.**1** She replied the same to me as she peeped through the covers.**2** This is the morning we waited so long for: we were going on our honeymoon cruise to the Bahamas!**3** I grabbed my list to ensure that I didn't forget anything: luggage packed, tickets in hand, kids at grandparents, check, check and check!**4** Now we were off to the docks to board the ship and hit the casino. As the ship pulled away from the dock, my wife and I waited at the stern waving good-bye as if we would never return.**5** As I stood in amazement at the glory of this huge city on water, I noticed the shoreline getting further and further away.**6**

Not only did the shoreline disappear, but the ship began to sway back and forth and up and down.**7** I began feeling dizzy which I thought was caused by the four Martini's that I drank earlier, but then I realized that it was my first drink.**8** I couldn't believe what was happening to me.**9** I was getting seasick, and we had just got underway, yet still my wife was unaffected from what was happening around us.**10** Since this was our honeymoon, I didn't want to ruin it for my wife, so I hurried to the ship doctor to retrieve some motion sickness pills.**11** About an hour after I took the pills, I started feeling a whole lot better.**12** When I finally found my wife, she said to me, "I didn't even know that you were gone!" – as she pulled the handle on the slot machine, shouting "BIG MONEY!"**13**

Sentence Forms:

1) 7AC As

2) 7AC As
   3) 8RN Missing that; 9PP Explanation Colon
   4) 3V Infinitive; 8RN That; 9PP List Colon; 3V Past Participle
   5) 7AC As; 3V Present Participle; 7AC As (supplemental)
   6) 7AC As
   7) 4C Not Only, But
   8) 8RN Which; 8RN That (2); 6CC But
   9) 8RN What
   10) 6CC And; 6CC Yet; 8RN What
   11) 7AC Since; 6CC So; 3V Infinitive (2)
   12) 7AC After
   13) 7AC When; 8RN That; 7AC That; 3V Present Participle

Cookies and Rain by Caroline Daniels

Although the rain had almost stopped, Jackie's mother insisted that Jackie play inside today.**1** Jackie looked from the kitchen to her room at the scattered toys.**2** She did not want to play dress-up nor tea-time.**3** She studied the rooms again and again, but she didn't want to play with any of the toys.**4** Jackie's mother watched and giggled as if she knew exactly what her daughter needed.**5**

She took Jackie's hand and led her into the kitchen. "Because there is a bake sale tomorrow, we have to make cookies," her mother said.**6** Jackie's smile stretched from ear to ear. She loved helping out when it was bake sale time.**7** She enjoyed the sweet, delicious, delectable scent of cookies baking.**8** Since Jackie was too short to reach, her mother would allow her to stand up on a chair and stir the cookie dough with her hands.**9** After about an hour, Jackie had forgotten all about playing outside.**10**

Who cared whether it was raining or not?**11** Baking with her mom was much more fun.**12**

Sentence Forms

1) 7AC Although; 8RN That
2) 3V Past Participle
3) 3V Infinitive; 2S Choice
4) 6CC But; 3V Infinitive
5) 2S The Pair; 7AC As If (supplemental); 8RN What
6) 7AC Because
7) 7AC When
8) 2S Triple Force; 3V Present Participle
9) 7AC Since; 3V Infinitive
10) 3V Gerund
11) 8RN Whether (supplemental)
12) 3V Gerund

The Bald-Headed Truth by Charlie Sanders Jr.

A lot of people ask bald-headed people why they shave their head, as if they have to have a reason why they do it.**1** There are a lot of reasons why people shave their heads. Here are just a few of the reasons: some do it because they are starting to go bald; some do it for fashion; some do it for medical reasons; and some do it because it's quick and easy.**2** There are additional reasons why people shave their heads, but these are just some of the main reasons.**3**

Personally, I just like to shave my head. I remember the first time I did so.**4** I was cutting my head with my clippers, and my son, who was five at the time, hit me between the legs.**5** Needless to say, I then had a large section on my head without hair. Since I had messed up my hair, I just cut it all off.**6** That was the start of my shaving my head.**7** I guess I just got used to having my head bald, as well as paying less to having it cut professionally.**8** To be truthful, the only time I miss my hair is during the winter months.

Sentence Forms

1) 8RN Why (2); 7AC As If (supplemental)
2) 9PP Explanation Colon; 9PP Trio Semicolon
3) 6CC But; 8RN Why
4) 8RN Missing that
5) 6CC And; 8RN Who
6) 7AC Since
7) 3V Gerund
8) 8RN Missing that; 3V Gerund (2); 4C As Well As

Favorite Foods by Rita Chung

As I awake from my slumber every morning, the first thing that comes to mind is what I should have for breakfast as well as lunch and dinner.**1** When it comes to food, I tend to think ahead and plan my meals according to my current mood.**2** There are certain scrumptious edibles that I usually choose to delight in: lasagna, fried chicken, and peanut butter and jelly sandwiches.**3** For the most part, I take the time to cook almost any type of food I desire, which gives me self-satisfaction and pride in what I have prepared: delicious, fine cuisine.**4** Both family and friends will agree that I can cook quite a meal.**5** But my major talent when it comes to food is devouring it all with little time to spare.**6**

Indeed, I do have a rather large appetite that can surprise those who don't know me or aren't familiar with my eating habits.**7** One day, I crave a small salad; the next, a 16-ounce rib eye steak.**8** To be honest, I'm not extremely particular in what I eat, because I basically consume anything that is placed on my plate.**9** Most friends would say I eat meals as if inhaling them unconsciously, and I can neither confirm nor deny that specific statement.**10** However, I will admit that my hunger can strike at any moment, thus leaving me yearning for snacks frequently before attempting to feast upon a full course meal.**11** There are distinctive snacks that earn my attention on a daily basis: candy, chocolate chip cookies, and a bowl of cereal.**12**

You would think that after having about three meals a day with snacks in between, I would consequently blow up like a balloon; by that I mean, I would gain excessive weight.**13** And without hesitation or resistance, I can concur with that assumption. So in order to maintain that toned, sexy body of mine, I squeeze in a few workouts a week to lose those unsightly pounds that insist on growing all over my body.**14** It is not easy, and I do not enjoy cardio exercises, but to indulge in my favorite foods, I must sacrifice at least three nights a week or more at the gym.**15** Overall, I would do anything possible to be able to eat whatever I choose to eat without going overboard or endangering my health.**16** Therefore, all food, which can come in numerous different shapes and sizes, is welcome on my silver platter.**17** From meats to vegetables, appetizers to desserts, I have no problem showing my excitement and eagerness to gobble all edibles that make their way to my mouth.**18**

Sentence Forms

1) 7AC As; 8RN That; 8RN What; 4C As Well As

2) 7AC When
   3) 8RN That; 9PP Explanation Colon
   4) 3V Infinitive; 8RN Missing that; 8RN Which; 2S The Pair; 8RN What; 2S Compact Duo
   5) 4C Both And; 8RN That
   6) 7AC When; 3V Gerund; 3V Infinitive
   7) 8RN That; 8RN Who; 3V Present Participle
   8) 9PP Stylish Semicolon
   9) 8RN What; 7AC Because; 8RN That
   10) 8RN Missing that; 6CC And
   11) 8RN That; 3V Present Participle (2); 3V Gerund
   12) 1F There Are; 8RN That
   13) 8RN That; 3V Gerund
   14) 2S Compact Duo; 3V Infinitive; 8RN That
   15) 3V Infinitive; 6CC But; 6CC And
   16) 3V Infinitive (2); 3V Gerund (2); 8RN Which
   17) 8RN Which
   18) 4C From To; 3V Infinitive; 8RN That; 2S The Pair

The Day of Promise by Carlos Jones

The day started out bright and full of promise.**1** The sun beamed high, lively, refreshing.**2** The wind carried whispers of no pain, only happiness.**3** The man knew it was time to get dressed, time to work.**4**

He would follow the will of the wind, and providence would follow in his wake.**5** He excitedly got prepared, but he was not in a rush.**6** Because he was happy, he did not allow himself to be concerned with time.**7** Until she came for him, he would be patiently waiting for her.**8**

Sentence Forms

   1) 2S The Pair
   2) 2S Triple Force
   3) 4C No, Only (supplemental)
   4) 8RN Missing that; 5R Key Word; 3V Infinitive (2)

5) 6CC And
6) 6CC But
7) 7AC Because; 3V Infinitive
8) 7AC Until

Running on Faith by Alphonse Arlene

One summer night at sunset, while I was visiting in a quaint little town in Georgia, I took a long leisurely walk down a back road to enjoy one of my favorite views of the countryside.**1** While walking, I heard the sound of thunder rolling, and it seemed as if it was headed in my direction.**2**

It was so majestic and magical, magnificent and grand.**3** I turned to see ten wild horses running freely.**4** The night revealed these most beautiful creatures in their natural habitat, moving together as if they were going somewhere, anywhere, nowhere.**5** They appeared to be running on faith, naturally following God's lead, just knowing that they were heading in the right direction.**6** At that moment, I also understood and knew what it feels like to be heading in the right direction.**7**

Sentence Forms

1) 7AC While; 3V Infinitive
2) 3V Gerund; 3V Present Participle; 6CC And
3) 2S Rhythmical Pairs
4) 3V Infinitive; 3V Present Participle
5) 3V Present Participle; 7AC As If (supplemental); 2S Triple Force
6) 3V Present Participle (2); 8RN That
7) 2S The Pair; 8RN What

Benevolent Mountains by Littlejohn

Mountains are something mysterious. I used to wonder about their source of strength, their height, and their unshakable essence.**1** They are not easily understood.

Well, I've given much thought and attention to the quality and characteristics of mountains, and I have walked them many times.**2** Hence, I have come to respect and feel a connection to mountains in a personal way.

Mountains are strong and serene, making their presence known out of utter silence.**3** I find that kind of cool and breath-taking. Not many things I know possess those qualities. Mountains don't bend for nature or man. Whether or not animals inhabit them, and man exploits them, they still remain standing.**4** They stand on their own, and are independent.

Mountains provide shelter from the elements to all creatures that run to them; therefore, I believe that they are defenders of the helpless.**5**

Mountains are unshakable. Whether or not a disaster comes so that mountains are stripped and bare, still they stand there, as stubborn as a mule, as if to say, "You have to do better than that."**6**

I respect mountains for all these qualities that seem so benevolent.**7** Mountains don't change their design with time. They are rough and jagged, full of justice and provision for weary creatures.**8** For all these reasons, mountains constitute an imposing, enduring, and under-appreciated feature of nature.**9**

Sentence Forms

1) 2S Standard Series
2) 2S The Pair (2); 6CC And
3) 2S The Pair; 3V Present Participle
4) 7AC Whether
5) 9PP Expansive Semicolon
6) 6CC So; 2S The Pair; 7AC As If (supplemental)
7) 8RN That
8) 2S The Pair (2)
9) 2S Standard Series

Christmas by Joshua D. DeLange

It was a cool winter morning. The crispness of the air let you know change was present.**1** The fall temperatures had dropped, and snow had begun to fall.**2** Because of the temperature drop, lakes and streams had begun to freeze; the streets became icy; driving was difficult.**3** All of these signs left us expectant and excited, for Christmas was upon us.**4**

It is the time for friends and family, food and presents.**5** On the eve of Christmas, the women prepare the meal; the men watch football; the children play and hope for that special gift.**6** Darkness arrives; the children sleep.**7** Dad, who is downstairs, puts out the remaining gifts.**8** He then goes up to bed where he gives mom a goodnight kiss.**9** Every year it comes and goes, but there are never two alike.**10** It is Christmas, the season for family, celebration.**11**

Sentence Forms

1) 8RN Missing that
2) 6CC And

3) 9PP Trio Semicolon
4) 6CC For
5) 2S Rhythmical Pairs
6) 9PP Trio Semicolon
7) 9PP Stylish Semicolon
8) 8RN Who
9) 8RN Where
10) 6CC But
11) 2S Compact Duo

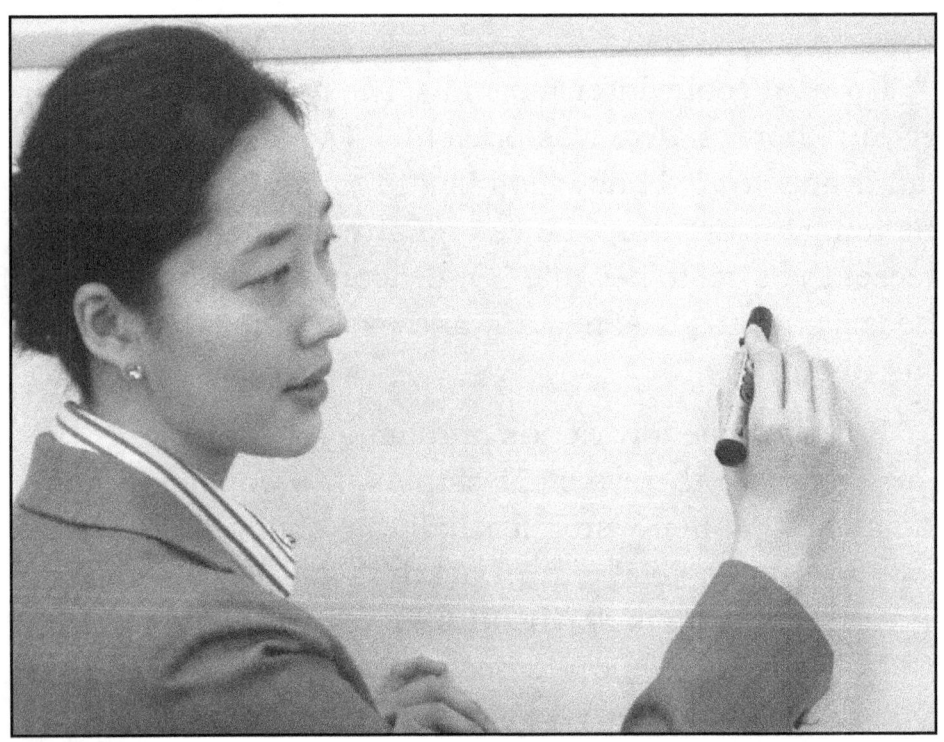

Life and the Modes of Writing Then and Now

by Kevin, Jinan University, Guangzhou

The following longer piece of writing was the result of a journal-writing assignment with no specific instructions on using any particular Forms. It is placed here because it includes a high number of Form 8RN Forms and because it compares aspects of writing with a pen with Life in general.

We have <u>underlined</u> the 8RN Forms. Can you guess their Short Codes? Can you guess what the symbol △ represents?

The computer has eased every respect of our lives. People seldom use pens now. They type on the computer with the help of some office application software.

Take Microsoft Word as an example. It is user-friendly. More importantly, it is easy to change <u>what you have typed</u>. When you find something wrong or something △ you want to change, you only need to move the mouse and delete it, without any trace.

Now suppose someone gave you a pen – a sealed and solid-colored pen.

You couldn't see <u>how much ink it had</u>. It might run dry after the first few tentative words or last just long enough to create a masterpiece <u>that would last forever and make a difference in the scheme of things</u>. But you don't know either way before you begin.

Under the rules of the game, you really never know. You have to think seriously about your choice of words. You have to be careful about <u>what you write</u>. And you have to bear the frustration of having to rewrite the whole page when you realize <u>that you have left something out or could say it better</u>.

Someone <u>who is used to writing on the computer</u> might find <u>that writing with a pen is a dreadful experience</u>. They might just write some words or sentences down until the ink ran out, with lots of strikethroughs to cancel parts of <u>what they have written</u>. They would find <u>that they could not compose in such a carefree way as they did on the computer</u>.

Children initially use a pencil to write with and use an eraser to correct wrong words. People start using pens when they or their teachers think they have become mature enough to write down something with few or no mistakes. But now, with the computer, some people may develop the disposition to act like a child without thinking carefully and seriously before writing because it is so easy to type words on a computer and then easily erase them like a child does with a pencil. Unlike a pen, a computer does not encourage thoughtful reflection and planning before writing and may lead too easily to carelessness.

Are people losing their responsibility to face the consequences of their actions nowadays because of too much time with computers and the careless disposition △ they may promote? We may think △ everything, including our actions and their consequences, are correctable after the events are completed. But that is not so.

We may become too dependent on the computer and feel frustrated when writing with a pen and having to pick the best words just as in Life in general we could fail to make important decisions because they are too difficult and not easy. We may then have problems making choices – just like the beginning writer starting to write with a pen who can't adjust to the difficulty of thoughtful writing when they have gotten used to careless composition on the computer. We may even childishly wish <u>that we could easily erase or correct our mistakes in important Life choices △ we have made and things we have done</u> the same way △ we can erase our mistakes on a computer.

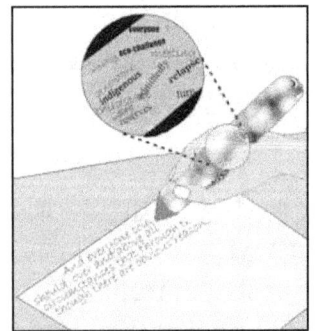

But Life is rarely like that. Designing one's Life is like writing with a pen <u>whose ink supply we can't see and requires us to be careful with our resources and time.</u> Life is like the pen <u>whose ink level you never know</u> and <u>whose words cannot be changed</u> once the ink has dried on the page.

Learning to write with a pen is better preparation for both good writing and sound life choices than learning to write with a computer.

The Hand

from **Hand, Eye, Brain: Some "Basics" in the Writing Process** by **Janet Emig** in her excellent book *The Web of Meaning* 1978

"In his introduction to *Writers at Work,* Malcolm Cowley recounts a statement Hemingway made after an automobile accident when he feared he had lost the use of his right arm: Hemingway commented simply that he thought he would probably have to give up writing. For how many others of us is the action of the hand, the literal act of writing, the motoric component, equally crucial? If we check sources of data from introspection to interviews with professional writers, we find there are many among us who, like Hemingway, must write at least first drafts by hand. I am one of this group. (Others like Henry James, Paul Gallico, and Donald Murray can dictate even novels, that mode of perhaps greatest intricacy, to a secretary.) We cannot compose initially with any ease or skill at a typewriter or into a tape recorder. Why? The speculations that follow come from introspection and from conversations with "like-handed" friends.

There seem to be at least four possible reasons for the cruciality of literal writing in the composing process. First, the literal act of writing is activating, mobilizing. It physically thrusts the writer from a state of inaction into engagement with the process and with the task. We have actually, physically begun to do something. In a very interesting paper, Linda Bannister of the University of Southern California suggests that the state of inaction is more properly thought of as resistance—"anti-writing" she calls it.

Second, the literal act of writing may be for some of us an aesthetically necessary part of the process. We may be able to make personal statements initially or steadily only in our own personalized script, with all of its individualities, even idiosyncrasies. To employ the impersonal and uniform font of the typewriter may for some of us belie the personal nature of our first formulations. Our own language must first appear in our own script. In any case, the aesthetic pleasure of their own script has been important to well-known writers. Arnold Bennett, for example, taught himself a special script of great beauty in which to write his works of fiction (Drabble, 1974). And to examine authors' manuscripts is to be struck by the lucidity of many scripts, from Gerard Manley Hopkins's and Thomas Hardy's to John Berryman's and May Swenson's. In writing, our sense of physically creating an artifact is less than in any other mode except perhaps composing music; thus, the literal act of writing may provide some sense of carving or sculpting our statements, as in wood or stone.

Third, and correlated with the first, the literal act of writing, with its linear organization in most Western systems, may reinforce in some way the work of the left hemisphere of the brain, also linear in nature. The matter could just as well be formulated, however, in an inverse way, since we don't know which is the antecedent and which the consequent variable: because of the innate predisposition of the left hemisphere to proceed linearly, most written language is inevitably linear in form as visible analogue of the brain's workings.

A fourth reason is that writing by hand keeps the process slowed down. In an interview (Literary Guild News, 1977), Paul Theroux put one value on this slower pace: It allows for surprise, time for the unexpected to intrude and even take over.

> It's fatal to get ahead of yourself. Typing, you can take a wrong turning. But if you do it slowly, writing a foolscap page or two a day, in a year you are all done. That may sound like a long time, but it's not. It's like carving a statue. You can't rush it. (p. ii)

Writing by hand of course has disadvantages as well. Observing a slow pace, one can lose as well as find material since such a pace obviously puts a greater strain on the memory. For the child learning, perhaps at almost the same time, both to handwrite and to compose, the act of literally forming the words may well be, or become, the dominant and absorbing activity (those of us who have observed seven and eight year olds writing can attest to the accuracy of this statement). Such simultaneity of learnings may cause the later (lifelong?) confusion many of us have observed in older writers, the reversal of what Michael Polanyi (1967) calls "from-to attending." The writer attends from the message *to* the graphic formulation, rather than the other way around.

In all these speculations there are obviously research questions about the role or roles of the hand in the writing process. Here are a few:

Theoretical
For what kind of writer engaging in what mode or modes of writing is writing initially or steadily by hand a crucial component in the writing process? For what kind of writer does initial or later dictation or use of the typewriter serve?

Applied
Should children be presented with composing and handwriting at the same time, age, or grade level?
How can teachers and administrators be made sophisticated enough not to use writing as a term that can mean equally penmanship and composing?"

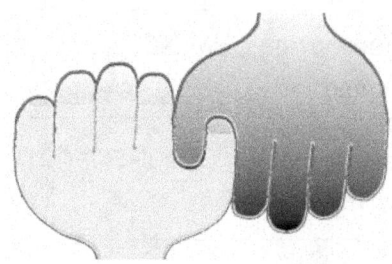

9 PP Power Punctuation Forms

There are three power punctuation marks used in English: the **colon**, the **semi-colon**, and the **dash**. They are each used for different purposes. The chart below list the sub-Forms.

9 PP	Power Punctuation Forms	
COLON: Dramatic Pointer		*(a STOP-sign)*
9.c1	Numeric Precursor COLON	
9.c2	List COLON	
9.c3	Explanation COLON	
SEMI-COLON: The Balancer		*(a STOP-sign)*
Two Supremely Important SEMI-COLONS		
9.sc1	Association SEMI-COLON	
9.sc2	Opposition SEMI-COLON	
Five Useful SEMI-COLONS		
9.sc3	Expansive SEMI-COLON	
9.sc4	Consequence SEMI-COLON	
9.sc5	Trio SEMI-COLON	
9.sc6	Stylish SEMI-COLON	
9.sc7	Complicated SEMI-COLON	
Two Difficult SEMI-COLONS Separating Items in a Series		
9.sc8	First Separating SEMI-COLON – series items with commas	
9.sc9	Second Separating SEMI-COLON – long series items without commas	

DASH: The Highlighter, The Commentator, The Amplifier (a YELLOW light)

Beginning List Wrap-Up – dash followed by a summary word			
Dash Beginning	9.d1	DASH Beginning List Wrap-Up	
Amplify, Clarify, Comment on, or Add an Afterthought			
Dash Middle	9.d2	DASH Middle Word	
	9.d3	DASH Middle Prepositional Phrase	
	9.d4	DASH Middle Verbal Phrase	
	9.d5	DASH Middle Noun Phrase	
	9.d6	DASH Middle Adjective Phrase	
	9.d7	DASH Middle Adverb Phrase	
	9.d8	DASH Middle Appositive, or Series of Appositives	
Dash End	9.d9	DASH End Word	
	9.d10	DASH End Prepositional Phrase	
	9.d11	DASH End Verbal Phrase	
	9.d12	DASH End Noun Phrase	
	9.d13	DASH End Adverb Phrase	
Dash End List	9.d14	DASH End Informal List	
Dash shift or change in direction	9.d15	DASH END Shift or departure in the Content, Thought, or Direction of the Sentence	

9 (PP) Power Punctuation Forms I

Three COLONS (a STOP sign)

9.c 1	**NUMERIC PRECURSOR Colon** — marks off a set of items or instances that refer to a preceding numbered quantity	• Three things keep me here: **good food, good people, clean air.** • One thing that matters on this team: **how fairly you play.** • I had **two** things to do after class: **post a letter and workout at the gym.**
9.c 2	**LIST Colon** — specifies items or instances of a general word that precedes the colon	• Our design has <u>advantages</u>: portability, simplicity, and low cost. • The following <u>athletes</u> will compete: Abe, Vanna, Brown. • The recipe has just a few <u>ingredients</u>: eggs, milk, sugar, flour.
9.c 3	**EXPLANATION Colon** — explanation of a significant word or whole clause preceding the colon	• Today is **unforgettable**: *I got my driver's license.* • The bread was **flat**: *the yeast was too old.* • I love my **job**: *it is always interesting and challenging.*

Two Supremely Important SEMI-COLONS (a STOP Sign)

9.sc 1	**ASSOCIATION Semi-Colon**	• It was early evening; the reds of the sunset gave way to the hood of night.. • The wind is picking up; a storm is brewing.
9.sc 2	**OPPOSITION Semi-Colon**	• Some people dream of being something; others stay awake and are. Robert Kennedy • Min Joo is vegetarian; Bill eats all kinds of food.

Power Punctuation - The Colon

The first power punctuation mark is the *colon*. It indicates an abrupt stop in the flow of the sentence.

9.c1 PP Numeric Precursor COLON

Note: The colon – which we call one of the **STOP** signs punctuation marks – draws attention to the list that follows it. This means that it requires a **full stop or pause** when reading. *Comparatively, the colon is more formal than the dash when used to start a list.*

- We draw your attention to **three** advantages: portability, simplicity, and low cost.
- The Galapagos Islands are the home of **two** very interesting lizards: the marine iguana and the land iguana.
- The small town now had to deal with **three** problems: flood damage to roads and bridges, contaminated drinking water, and temporary housing.
- **Four** advantages stand out why you should do business here: low license fee, dedicated economic zone, legal assistance, and available workforce.
- **One** thing I saw plainly: I was no longer able to leap up the stair two at a time and not feel tired.
- I went to Seoul for **one** reason: to buy a computer.
- My wife had **two** things to accomplish: one was shopping, and the other was

mailing a letter. • "**One** thing's for sure: If we keep doing what we're doing, we're going to keep getting what we're getting." [Stephen Covey *First Things First Every Day*] • **One** thing was clear: she no longer wanted to live at home with her parents.

9.c2 PP List COLON

• This is what we need for our camping trip: **a tent, the sleeping bags, the cooler full of food, canned soft drinks, mosquito repellant, and the fishing gear.** • "We must counter the horrors of a world that doesn't care: **a system that spews darkness, media that spew violence, governments that spew apathy, and industries that spew poison.**" (Marianne Williamson *A Woman's Worth*) • I greatly enjoy the following activities: **sleeping, watching movies, listening to music, and bouldering.** • You should always go to morning formations with these three things: **shaved face, pressed uniform, and shined boots.** • In some places, the following foods are considered delicacies: **snake (any part), pig (intestines),** monkey (brains), chicken (gizzard or feet), fish (head).   • The newspaper has many sections: **world news, editorial, lifestyle, sports, the classifieds, and the arts**.   • The baby's toys were scattered on the floor: **a robot, a spaceship, a LEGO tower, and a yellow ball**.

9.c3 PP Colon: Explanation

Note: There are three examples of this colon. The first two are easy to use, because it simply requires one to explain a preceding word which we have put in bold-face below. They are similar to the Form 9.c1 where we explain the Numeric Precursor. The third example is more difficult but important to learn to use effectively. If you practice the first two kinds of colons, you will naturally get a sense for the third kind. Basically, when you see a colon, you stop and say *Why? How? What? Where? When?* Answer the question in the given context, after the colon, and you probably got it right.

explanation of adjective or participle before a noun

• It was **early** morning: only the crickets, the cicadas, and a few birds were awake.   • Spring on the east coast is for me a **miserable** season: the pollen count is far too high.   • It was a **foggy** day: the mountains, the houses, the fields were all shrouded in mist.   • It was a **smoggy** day: the city was wrapped in a dense cloud of dirty air and polluted fog.   • September 11,

2001 was a **devastating** day of terror in American history: thousands of lives were lost, and symbolic landmarks desecrated.

<u>explanation of distant descriptor</u>

- The laundry was still **wet**: it had rained all day.
- The cake is **flat**: I forgot to add baking powder.
- The movie was **boring**: all they did was hit and shoot each other.

<u>explanation of whole statement</u>

- **Everybody knew why he was smiling**: he had won the national lottery.
- **I like to wear sandals**: they keep my feet nice and cool.
- **The Empire State Building is a popular spot for proposals and weddings**: there is a wedding ceremony there each year on St. Valentine's Day.
- **The end of the summer came quickly**: they had been so busy camping and hosting barbeques that they had hardly noticed how quickly the days went by.

Power Punctuation - The Semi-colon

The second power punctuation mark is the **semi-colon**. Like the colon, it indicates a full stop in the flow of the sentence. It is an equalizer or a balancer. It divides equal independent clauses or equal long items in a series, and then places the equal independent clauses or equal long items in a series in a **balanced relationship of close association or opposition**.

9.sc1 PP Association SEMI-COLON

Note: The first form using the semi-colon joins two independent clauses in close association:

association: the two clauses are closely connected or associated in meaning or in content to one another

- I just bought a car today; it has a standard gearshift.
- Writing is a skill; it has to be learned.
- I like to wear the color orange; it's very bright and beautiful.
- The wind is really getting stronger now; a hurricane must be approaching.
- Aroma filled the air; dinner must be ready soon.
- The computer processor is slow; I guess it's time to upgrade.
- My ball pen was a gift; it was given to me when I retired.
- Just be yourself; no one can tell you that you are doing it wrong.
- A person isn't born with wisdom; he acquires it.
- The birds are singing; spring is here at last.
- The lightning streaked across the sky; thunder quickly followed.

9.sc2 PP Opposition SEMI-COLON

Note: This form joins two independent clauses to show contrast.

contrast: _the two clauses are directly opposed or contrasted in their meaning_

- Min Joo is a vegetarian; Bill eats all kinds of food.
- "We're not in control; principles are." [S.Covey _First Things_]
- In Canada, a newlywed couple may look forward to owning a detached home or a townhouse; in South Korea, many newlyweds look forward to having a condo in a high-rise building.
- In daytime, the Beijing Financial Street beats with the pulse of a vibrant financial economy; at night, it dances with the breath of fashionable life.
- "When structures and systems are aligned, they facilitate empowerment; when they aren't, they work against it." [Covey _ibid_]
- Some walked right by; others stopped and looked on.
- "The ultimate purpose of ancient knowledge was the contemplation of reality, either sensible presence or ideal form; technological knowledge aspires to substitute a universe of machinery for the real reality." (Octavio Paz _The Bow and the Lyre_ quoted in Blaser _The Fire_)
- In many Western duets, singers perform at the same time; in the typical Indian duet called "_Kahbi, Kahbie_," the singers almost always alternate singing.

9 (PP) Semi-Colon Forms II

Five Useful SEMI-COLONS

9.sc 3	**CONSEQUENCE** Semi-Colon	• It stopped raining; I went outside. • The weather is too dry: my cello cracked. • The cat was too loud; I put it out..
9.sc 4	**EXPANSIVE** Semi-Colon	• The traffic was heavy; *however*, we weren't late. • The class is small; *nonetheless*, the group interacts well. • The results are negative; *consequently*, you have no polyps.

Common Conjunctive Adverbs

A **conjunctive adverb** is a word or phrase that qualifies or extends the clause preceding it and transitions to the clause following it. These adverbs generally convey an attitude or feeling of the writer or speaker. Like train track switch signals, they show where one's train of thought is going.

Consequence	consequently	therefore	as a result
	then	hence	
Adding Information	furthermore	moreover	in addition
Emphasis	in fact	indeed	then
Overcoming Obstacle; Indicating Exception or Unusual Alternative	nevertheless	however	rather
	nonetheless		
Specifying or Exemplifying	namely	specifically	in particular

9.sc 5	**TRIO** Semi-Colon	•Nam plays guitar; Eddy plays bass; Snow sings. • The food was delicious; the music was great; the talk was inspiring.
9.sc 6	**STYLISH** Semi-Colon	• One day there's rain; the next, fog. [note omitted verb] • I ordered salad; Lisa, shrimp.
9.sc 7	**COMPLICATED** Semi-Colon	• The phone rang, and he was quick to answer it; he was waiting for her call.

9 (PP) Semi-Colon Forms III

Two Difficult SEMI-COLONS
Separating Items in a Series

FIRST Separating Semi-Colon
clearly divides **items in a series in which one or more items has a comma in it**

9.sc8

- This Korean New Year I gave gifts to each member in my family: to my brother, an organizer; to my mother, a book she really wanted to read; to my father, a handkerchief.
- "Second, we have all the problems of a major zoo – care of the animals; health and welfare; feeding and cleanliness; protection from insects, pests, allergies, and illnesses; maintenance of barriers; and all the rest." Michael Crichton *Jurassic Park*
- "Our collection... includes directions in assorted shapes and sizes; handwritten or typed narratives; free-form, all-to-creative maps with little stick figures, cars and houses; on colored paper and white; some photocopied, others dictated casually over the phone..." Anne Bernays *Take a Left Turn Onto Nowhere Street* from Skwire *Writing* 233

SECOND Separating Semi-Colon
clearly divides **items in a series in which the items lack commas, but are long**

9.sc9

- The team's success comes from training that pushes one's limits; a coach who inspires confidence and knows all the strategies; team members who pour on the heat every minute of every game and workout.
- This exercise encapsulates my philosophy of education, which is based on the word *respect:* respect between student and teacher; respect for our cultural heritage; and respect for our natural neighbors. Robert Bateman *Thinking Like a Mountain*

9.sc3 PP Consequence SEMI-COLON

Note: Here the event in the second independent clause is an obvious consequence or follow-up to what happened in the first clause.

<u>consequence: the event(s) in the second clause is (are) an understandably immediate consequence of the events in the first one</u>

- It stopped raining: I went outside. •The weather is too dry; my cello cracked. •It snowed today; I went outside to make a snowman. •There was an accident on the highway; we got there late. •The shirt was very pretty; I decided to buy it for Mother's Day. •Meowing loudly, the cat kept scratching at the pantry door; I eventually put him outside for the rest of the night.

9.sc4 PP Expansive SEMI-COLON

Note: This semi-colon form places a **signal marker** - a **conjunctive adverb** - after the semi-colon. There are eighteen conjunctive adverbs. They were first listed for you in the Connectors section of grammar. They facilitate flow and transition in thought. These adverbs can be put into five groups according to the kind of change they indicate in the thought flow.

<u>**consequence:** consequently, therefore, then, hence, as a result</u>

Note: In the previous form, Form 9.sc3, there is no bridge word that helps the reader understand that what follows is a direct consequence of the event or action in the first clause. The connection by consequence is implied rather than stated. Here, however, we assist the reader with the use of the above five conjunctive adverbs. They help lay out the logic better.

- I can still see some streaks under the fresh black paint; **consequently**, we will have to give the car another coat of paint.
- Sam never took time to study; **consequently**, he failed the course.
- The Communications Exposition will take place in four weeks; **therefore**, preparations for it are being made now.
- Chinese New Year is in three weeks; **therefore**, I must finish my shopping soon.
- The turkey will be frozen;
- we must thaw it out the night before.
- Get settled first; **then**, we will assess your schedule.
- His grandmother died; **as a result**, he didn't attend Wednesday's class.
- The flowers are hand-pruned, hand-watered, hand-picked, and hand-delivered; **hence**, the price is a bit more than the floral chain shops.

adding information: furthermore, moreover, in addition

- Gino loves gospel music; **furthermore**, he sings with a choir in Daegu.
- They have not seen that film; **moreover**, they have not gone to the cinema for almost a year.
- She's a vegetarian; **in addition**, she is a running enthusiast and an advocate of all aspects of fitness and hygiene.

emphasis: _in fact, indeed, then_

• Sruti is hilarious; **in fact**, he could be professional comedian.   • An arthroscope helps a doctor examine the inside of an injured knee; **in fact**, the use of this instrument can prevent unnecessary surgery.   • He was happy to get the call for the job as the replacement drummer; **indeed**, it looks like Willy might now have a permanent job.

overcoming obstacles: _however, nevertheless, nonetheless_

• The traffic was very heavy; **however**, we did make it to the party on time.   • The car was low on fuel; **however**, I made it to work.   • My mom was really tired from work; **nevertheless**, she helped me with my homework.   • The team suffered a great defeat; **nevertheless**, they showed great sportsmanship.   • The troops were called in to sandbag against the rising river were tired; **nonetheless**, they toiled late into the evening stacking the bags to make a dike to prevent the farmhouse from being flooded.

exception or unusual alternative: _however, rather, nonetheless_

- The seniors group is quite small; **however**, we are a close-knit group.
- I could use this free time to study; **however**, my favorite show *Farscape* is on.
- The little girl loved to play in the grass; **however**, she had severe allergies, and was forced to play inside.
- Susan argued with her husband; **however**, she still loved him.
- The old bike was ten years old; **nevertheless**, it worked well and hardly ever broke down.
- After his release from prison he no longer wasted time playing cards; **rather**, he devoted all his spare time and energy into mastering the fundamentals of computer networking.

specifying or exemplifying: *namely, specifically, in particular*

- A foreigner should always try to learn the customs of the host nation; **in particular**, the visitor should become familiar with the greeting and eating protocol, acceptable discussion topics, and family and interpersonal customs.
- After joining the club, you will have more choices; **specifically**, you will have a say in determining the format, the frequency, and the content of our free monthly news digest.

9.sc5 PP Trio SEMI-COLON

Note: This form is an extension of Form 9.sc1 Association SEMI-COLON. Three or more short clauses are put together in a sentence, separated by semi-colons.
Examples:

●The song was touching; it brought back memories; I had to cry.   ●Debbie is good at spiking; Sung Min is good at setting; Gyeong Ae is good at serving the ball over the net.   ●Paula is unique; Kissa is exciting; Vanta is dull.   ●Keiko wants to go to California; Bahiyyih wants to go to Geneva; I just want to go to Rota.   ●Nam plays guitar; Snow sings; Eddy plays bass; Suji plays drums.   ●Bees eat nectar; birds eat seeds; fish eat plankton and worms.   ●Molly grew up to be a singer; Desmond plays in a band; Derrick sings in a blues group. ●He fought against himself; he forced himself to excel; he looked within on a regular basis.   ●"Some speculated that he [David Livingston] really was dead; others that he was in hiding; still others that he had discovered the fabled ancient cities of Christian Ethiopia and their mythical king, Prester John." (Arthur Herman *How the Scots Invented the Modern World*) ●In Canada, you get gasoline at a gas station; in Britain, they call it a petrol station; in Korea, they call it an oil

bank. ●Jenny rides a recumbent bike; Sarah powers a racing bike; Ian commutes on an electric scooter.
●"All was dark; all was doubt; all was confusion." [Virginia Woolf *Orlando*] ●"What they know very well, however, is that their lives are stretched to the breaking point; their children suffer from asthma, obesity, and a continuous bombardment of sex and violence on TV and of ads promoting junk food; and they are unable both to keep bread on the table and to supervise their children." [David Korten *The Great Turning*]

9.sc6 PP Stylish SEMI-COLON

Note: The main verb of the second independent clause is omitted. A comma is placed after the subject in the second independent clause. It is parallelism with a minimalist twist.

●I like potatoes; MaryAnn, beans. ●Robert ordered melted tuna for lunch; Lee, shrimp and salad. ■My dog is a sweetheart; my cat, a pest. ●One of Joanne's gifts was a watch; the other, a ring. ●The Chinese government is communist; the Canadian government, democratic. ●One day there's rain; the next, fog. ●My shirt is too small; my shoes, too big. ●Many of the families were wealthy; the others, poor. ●Johnny plays slide guitar; Frank, blues harmonica. ●Betty makes clothes; Barb, pottery. ●Some plants like a lot of sunshine; others, shade.

9.sc7 PP Complicated SEMI-COLON

Note: In this form, three clauses are joined. Two of them contain a coordinate conjunction preceded by a comma to form the longer part of the sentence. The third clause is separated from the other two by a semi-colon.

complicated semi-colon – first half has coordinating conjunction in it

●You can sing, and I can dance; Tom plays flamenco guitar. ●Sam pushed the car, and Sally steered it; they were out of gas and in the middle of nowhere. ●We boarded the plane at 6 pm, but our flight was delayed; we didn't take off for another hour.

complicated semi-colon – second half has coordinating conjunction in it

●Tomorrow is Saturday night; I would like to go out with my friends, but I should stay home with my family. ● He was gorgeous; he had a beautiful car, but his personality was the pits. ●I baked a cake; I followed all the directions, yet it tasted awful. ●"Some of these [icebergs] were as broad as a bowling green and as high as a house; others no bigger than a man's hat, but most fantastically twisted." [Virginia Woolf *Orlando*] ●"The name of the coachman was John Manley; he had a wife and one little child, and they lived in the coachman's cottage, very near the stables." [Anna Sewell *Black Beauty*]

<u>optional omitted comma (if the pair of clauses having the coordinating conjunction are short)</u>

●The wind blew[,] and the rain poured; an ominous funnel-shaped cloud loomed at the horizon. ●Students laughed[,] and parents smiled; the principal was an excellent speaker with a good sense of humor.

TWO DIFFICULT SEMI-COLONS SEPARATING ITEMS IN A SERIES

First Separating Semi-colon

9.sc8 PP Series items with commas SEMI-COLON

Note: This is the **first instance in which the semi-colon is not used to separate independent clauses**. Its main use in this form is to separate **items in a series in which one or more items has at least one comma in it**.

- This Christmas I bought gifts for the men and women in my family: for the men, I bought ties and socks; for the women I bought scarves and purses.
- We installed a new, synchromesh, autonomous clutch; repaired the dent on the left side; and painted the whole car a bright, glossy red.
- "This is why we tend to focus on such things as processes for community dialogue; quality of life indicators such as the ones introduced in Chapter 2; multiple viewpoint drama such as Anna Deavere Smith's work in Chapter 8; systems thinking; and the creative use of media as an ongoing, perceptive 'mirror' for the community." Tom Atlee *The Tao of Democracy*
- On December 2, 2004, the 20th anniversary of the Bhopal tragedy, a

major conference called "Detoxification" drew connections between the leak at the Union Carbide pesticide plant in 1984; the continued spread of toxins in agriculture through pesticides, herbicides, and GMOs; and the toxins in soft drinks sold by Coca-Cola and Pepsi, which farmers have shown to be effective as pesticides. Vandana Shiva *Earth Democracy* ●My job at the zoo involves all aspects of animal care: health, treatment, and welfare; feeding, exercise, and cleanliness; protection from insects, pests, allergies, other predators, and illnesses; maintenance of enclosures and their barriers; and all the international paperwork related to the capture and transfer of old, newly born, and released animals.

Second Separating Semi-colon
9.sc9 PP Series long items with no commas SEMI-COLON

<u>Note</u>: This is the **second instance in which the semi-colon is not used to separate independent clauses**. Its main use in this form is to **separate items in a series in which the items contain no commas, but are long**.

● "Most campuses have more serious and ancient problems: faculties still top-heavy with white males of

the monocultural persuasion; fraternities that harass minorities and women; date rape; alcohol abuse; and tuition that excludes all but the upper fringe of the middle class." (Barbara Ehrenreich *The Snarling Citizen* 1995) ●Peace involves the greater involvement of women in all levels of decision-making; a massive campaign to eradicate illiteracy and to improve education for all; a systematic and methodical sharing and distribution of all the planet's fossil and renewable resources; the adoption of a universal script and language that will become the global secondary language spoken and understood by all.
● I have to launder my stuff and pack them; clean up the place so it looks presentable when we come back; notify our neighbors to keep watch and to collect the mail and newspaper; and set the automatic lighting to go on at sunset.

Paying Attention to Form

There is a tale told in the fabled East about a learned and wise monk. Whenever he instructed his young pupils, he initially gave them a gem of advice: *Pay Attention*.

His most dedicated and diligent student did everything he was asked to do. The young man studied earnestly and practiced his lessons with zeal and persistence. However, he felt that he must be missing something, so (after a proper period of time) he respectfully requested that his teacher give him some additional counsel to ease the obstructions blocking his path and speed his progress to enlightenment. However, the wise monk simply said to him again in a slightly louder voice: *Pay Attention*.

Well, the young man now committed himself to learn everything, and he resolved to accomplish – with the utmost discipline – every task assigned him. He did all he was asked to do and more, and he did so with fidelity, care, and much questioning and reflection.

Finally, after long years and steadfast compliance with many and varied instructions, he returned once more to the wise monk and implored him to bestow the ultimate advice and secret for attaining mastery and enlightenment. In the loudest voice he could muster (or was it in the quietest and softest of tones, for this the young man could never remember), the wise monk repeated again: *Pay Attention*.

9(PP) Power Punctuation – Dash Forms I

The DASH – The Highlighter, The Commentator, The Amplifier As a speed controller, the **dash** is like a **Yellow Light**.

		A **dash** followed by a summary word can be used to **wrap up an introductory series**.	
DASH BEGINNING LIST WRAP-UP	9.d1		● Jordan, Pippen, and Rodman — **all** were part of the Bull's last three championships. ● San Diego, San Francisco, Lost Angeles — **these** are cities in California that have friends who are dear to me.
		A **pair of dashes** is used to **highlight** material inserted in the middle of the sentence. The inserted material amplifies, comments on, or clarifies *a word or idea in* the main part of the sentence.	
DASH MIDDLE	9.d2	Word	● The singer waited her turn — **nervously** — in the wings. [highlights]
	9.d3	Prepositional phrase	● The hockey player — **of Russian origin** — dazzled the crowd. [amplifies]
	9.d4	Verbal phrase	● Her goal - **to master databases** — was reached in less than 14 months. [clarifies] ● The music star — **forgotten by almost everyone** - released a new hit that shot straight to #1 on Billboard. [amplifies & clarifies]
	9.d5	Noun phrase	● The injured youth — **hours from death** — was taken by police to the hospital. [highlights] ● The price — **100,000 won** — reflects the rarity of the bowl. [clarifies]
	9.d6	Adjective phrase	● The soup — **thick and chunky** — tasted delicious. [amplifies] ● Her skirt — **short and tight** — brought many comments at the party. [amplifies & comment on]
	9.d7	Adverb phrase	● Tom — **rarely late** — had not arrive yet at the office. [highlights]
	9.d8	Appositive, Series of Appositives	● A big surprise — **a banner** — greeted him as he stepped down from the train. [clarifies] ● Of all the four seasons — **Spring, Summer, Fall, Winter** — I like Spring the best. [amplifies]

*

9(PP) Power Punctuation
– Dash Forms II

			A dash can be used **at the end** to highlight or emphasize a concluding **word** or **phrase**.
DASH END	9.d9	Word	● Psychologists say that one time of your life influences you later more than any other — **childhood**. ● One side dish was now noticeably missing from my meals — **kimchi**.
	9.d10	Prepositional phrase	● I finally found my keys — **under the car seat**. ● Isabel is engaged — **to the man** *she saw in her vision*.
	9.d11	Verbal phrase	● The gazelle paced back and forth — **cornered** *now by the newly-erected wire fences*.
	9.d12	Noun phrase	● The robotic rover clocked more than 1000 kilometers roaming on the Martian surface — **a new distance record** *for a remote-controlled vehicle on the planet*.
	9.d13	Adverb phrase	● I will have some copies made soon — **hopefully** *by early next week*. ● She doubts if she will stay long at her new job — **precisely** *because of having to work split shifts*.
DASH LIST	9.d14		● The product was tested under a **variety** of condition — **illumination, irradiation, immersion**. [amplifies]
			On occasion, the dash can be used to indicate a **Sudden Break** or **Shift in Direction** or **Departure** from the starting idea.
DASH SUDDEN SHIFT	9.d15		● The movie was memorable — but for all the wrong reasons. ● They were in love — and geographically only 3233 kilometers apart!

Power Punctuation – The Dash

The dash is used to highlight one or several of the following: (1) an elaboration and amplification; (2) an afterthought; (3) a short explanation; (4) a commentary; (5) a break in time; (6) a break in the continuity of expression; (7) a summary sentence that follows a list; (8) a sudden break, departure, or shift in the direction of the sentence.

Dashes are longer than a hyphen. Also, according to typographic tradition, there are **2 types of dashes** that are used – the shorter *en dash* (–) and the longer *em dash* (—). Although style preferences vary, the more popular style (perhaps) is the one we have used here – an **en dash** with a single space on both sides. See http://en.wikipedia.org/wiki/Dash for further information on the uses of each.

9.d1 PP Dash Beginning list wrap-up

Note: In this form, a dash is used after a short or medium-sized list or series. What follows the dash is *one or more summarizing words which sum up the list* and usually function as the subject of the sentence. Examples of summary words are *all, these, many, each, some, such.*

- Ginous, Larry, Aldo – **all three** were on last year's slow pitch team.
- Dispatches, load plans, and licenses - **all** are needed to drive a humvee.
- Research papers, vocabulary, sentence structure – **these** are the things I

despise most in Composition class. ●Parent-teacher conferences, my children's performances, charity fundraisers – **these** are things that I always try to attend at my children's school. ●San Diego, San Francisco, Oceanside, Oakland – **these** are cities in California that contain friends who are dear to me. ●Claudius, Polonius, Gertrude, Ophelia – **all** are characters in Shakespeare's tragedy *Hamlet*. ●Jordan, Pippen, and Rodman – **all** were part of the Bull's last three championship. ●Respectability, neatness, accuracy – **all** are required to be a good secretary.

Comment on PP Dash Middle Sentence Forms

Note: Each of these numbered forms for the Middle of the sentence using the Dash has many sub-forms. Indeed, so many are the sub-forms that they can overwhelm the students. Therefore, it is only necessary that the student write several examples of *any of the sub-forms*. We simply provide a wealth of examples to be comprehensive. Slowly, skill and understanding of the use of the Dash will improve.

9.d2 PP Dash Middle Word

●The football club needed one thing above all else – **teamwork** – to win the final championship. ●One ingredient – **friendship** – was missing in their relationship. ●"Wisdom is a marriage – a **synergy** – of heart and mind." [S. Covey *First Things First Every Day*] ● A big blessing – **rain** – finally came to the village. ●One word – **carelessness** – accounts for the tragic accident. ●Their viewpoint – **ultra-orthodox** – met with frequent resistance. ●The dog – **a collie** – pleased the buyer at the pet store. ●The new style of the furniture – **contemporary** – suited the décor of the hotel. ● One factor – **money** – seems to always enter the equation, but never leaves it. ●You should be responsible – **response-able** – in all that you do. ●His thoughts – **scattered** – resulted in his making many wrong decisions when he was young. ●The rat – **terrified** – fled from the cat. ●The victims of the robbery called – **frantically** – for help. ●The student – **submissively** – pleaded for an extension of the deadline. ●"While you can be efficient with things, you can't be efficient – **effectively** – with people." [S.Covey *First Things First*]

In this sub-form, we may occasionally have a word set off between dashes that we can see is in direct apposition or side-by-side replacement position, since that word (which we call an **appositive**) could very well be substituted for the noun to which it refers without little or no loss in meaning.

So we would include this sentence here:
- Our basketball coach – **Tina** – is great.

We could add more to the appositive to get an **appositive phrase**
- Our basketball coach – **Tina** *from Tijuana* – is great.

This would belong further down the list.

But what if we put together more than one appositive, making a **series of appositives**? Is it an Appositive phrase, or a multi-word unit, and include it as an extension of the Dash M Word sub-form?

Because the series of words is more "loosely" arranged without the binding that a phrase has, we chose the latter.

So, here are some examples of Appositive (Multi-)Word in Mid-Sentence.

multi-word appositive unit = series of appositives

- Three ingredients – **bacon, lettuce, and tomato** – are the main ingredients in the toasted BLT sandwich.
- He then decided he needed to go to Italy . . . in order to build up a visual data bank of classical designs and motifs – cornices, friezes, figures, bas-reliefs, vases, altars, columsn, windows, and doorways – which he could use for his own designs. (A.Herman *How the Scots Invented the Modern World*)
- My favorite food – **pizza, lasagna, and spaghetti** – are all Italian foods.
- "And our world starts to seem polluted in

fundamental ways – **air, and water, and land** – because of ungovernable science." [Michael Crichton *Jurassic Park*]

We likewise can consider several "unbound" adjectives strung together in a multi-word unit as being an extension of the Word sub-form, rather than in the Adjective Phrase sub-form.

<u>**multi-word adjective unit**</u> = adjective + [conjunction or comma] + adjective

Note: This sub-form is quite effective and easy to use. It is a The Pair Series made using two adjectives.

Examples: ● CJ's truck – ***rusty*** *and old* – had been in the auto shop for weeks. ● Kim's dress – ***short*** *and tight* – made everyone stare at her. ● His behavior – ***rude*** *and uncalled for* – was embarrassing to everyone. ● The teacher's lecture – ***long*** *and boring* – made everybody sleepy. ● The new car – ***lightweight*** *and battery-powered* – was the envy of all car enthusiasts at the auto show. ● The lost hikers – ***weary*** *and starving and distraught* – straggled out miraculously from the forest after nine days. ● "Jonesy looked up and saw a dozen glaring lights – ***some*** *red, some blue-white* – dancing around up there." (Stephen King *Dreamcatcher*) ● "Within months, plans to incarcerate us – ***alien*** *and citizen,* *rich and poor, sick and well –* were implemented."

(Wakako Yamaguchi *Otoko* in *The Riverside Reader* ed by J.Trimmer)

9.d3 PP Dash Middle Prepositional Phrase

●Her wandering was – **at best** – episodic yet it enables her to learn many things about the world.   ●"The early Sixties' vision of peace, nonviolent reform – **of ending poverty** *and racism* – evaporated." [B. Shulman *The Seventies*]
●"Iris patterns fulfill these requirements, as do – **to varying degrees** – fingerprints, face shapes, hand geometries, voices, and signatures." [Corrina Wu *Science News*]
●"So I applaud – **with one hand, anyway** – the multiculturalist goal of preparing us all for a wider world." (Barbara Ehrenreich *The Snarling Citizen*)   ●The face of fortune smiled on her – **during her youthful years** – as she began a life of unimaginable wealth, luxury, and freedom.   ●"But the market – **in particular**, *starting new businesses* – became the favored means for personal liberation and cultural revolution." [B. Shulman *The Seventies*]   ●The youth – **on a raft** *made of bamboo and balsa wood* – sailed up the west coast of Chile.   ●"For

all across the region – **in Japan** *and South Korea as much as in China and North Korea* – one finds the same remarkable gift for regimentation and self-surrender, for hard work and discipline." [P.Iyer *Falling Off the World*]

9.d4 PP Dash Middle Verbal Phrase

<u>verbal (infinitive) + its object</u>

●Her ambition – **to complete her bachelor degree** – came true after seven years of hard work.   ●Her idea – **to rid the neighborhood** *of drug-dealing, drug-taking, and prostitution* – required some convincing, but she and her noble assistants finally purged the hood of such hindrances to community well-being. ●Her action group with its one goal – **to help the needy** *and homeless in the city core* – eventually evolved into NPO agency that organized rural/urban youth exchange visits, homeless soccer competitions, a cadet corps, and drop-in learning centers for adults and students in need.

<u>verbal (present participle) + its object</u>

●Most of the townsfolk – **including those** *who have*

just recently moved to the neighborhood – feel the same way about keeping the young mayor. ●A package – **containing candy**, *flowers, and a teddy bear* – arrived at my doorstep on Valentine's Day.

<u>verbal (past participle) + prepositional phrase</u>

●The country's first multi-party democratic election – **supervised by UN observers** – ran smoothly with a large turnout. ●The orphaned youth – **raised by his aunt and uncle** – managed to get a good education and became an active advocate for poor children both at home and around the world. ●The poacher – **waiting in camouflage gear** *with a high-powered repeater rifle* – targeted the endangered panda. ●The students – **stunned by the madman's rampage** *and murder of seven of their teachers and classmates* – could not understand the motives that might have led to such a horrendous act.

9.d5 PP Dash Middle Noun Phrase

A **noun phrase** is defined as *a noun* (called **header** or first word) *plus its attendant and attached elements*. A **header** is the central word around which a phrase or multi-word unit revolves, and it often is the first word in the phrase. Exceptions will be explained later.

For example, it can be a noun that is followed by: a prepositional or verbal phrase; a lone participle; a reference clause; more nouns (in series)

Students need only give *a couple of examples* of any of these, but should *not have to practice all the sub-forms in this form*. We simply provide a wealth of examples for their review and understanding, and to be comprehensive.

noun phrase = noun + prepositional phrase

●It is life's noise – the **noise of the news** – that sings 'It's a Small World After All' again and again to lull you and cover the silence while your love boat slips off into the dark." (A. Dillard *For the Time Being*) ●At the meeting, there were women – **women of all hues** – and their excited chatter proved how quickly women can establish rapport with their own gender. ●The perspective of the week prompts us to plan for renewal – **a time for recreation and reflection** – weekly and daily. (S. Covey *First Things First Every*

Day) ● She had endured enough now – **nights of loneliness**, arguments of rage, episodes of deceit – and she knew it was curtains for their relationship.

noun phrase = noun + verbal phrase

● The new school had many restrictions – **rules to cover** all types of activities – that were hard for many students to accept. ● The huge Eden Project biome domes near Cornwall have plant species – exotic **ferns** and palms and fruit trees **obtained** from countries such as Malaysia, Cameroon, and the Seychelles – that have never before rooted in English soil. ● Someone has taped his blue umbilical cord – the **inch** or so **left** of it – upward on his belly." (Annie Dillard *For the Time Being*)

noun phrase = noun + lone participle (absolute construction)

● The Malaysian triathlon team – the **clock ticking** – scaled the steep Moroccan cliff, and passed the New Zealand team to take over the lead in the 1998 480 km Eco-Challenge expedition race. ● The amateur singer advanced to the stage – **heart pounding** – and then took the mike and started to sing.

Four exceptions to our header rule for noun phrases

We refer the reader to **4 supplemental sub-forms** for **PP dash M noun phrase** found in Volume 2 in the **Supplemental** section:
- the adjective-fronted noun phrase;
- the conjunction-fronted noun phrase;
- nouns-in-a-correlative noun phrase; and
- a combination noun phrase.

These phrases are **controlled more by the noun** than the adjective or conjunction, so we pick the **noun** as the **header** (dominant word on which the others depend) even though it is not the first word.

9.d6 PP Dash Middle Adjective Phrase

The **adjective phrase** will be defined as *an adjective* followed by:
- ☐ *a prepositional phrase;*
- ☐ *[conjunction or comma] + adjective;*
- ☐ *[+adjective]+ noun (noun preceded by many adjectives);*
- ☐ any of the above plus any extending attachments

adjective phrase = adjective + prepositional phrase

● The girl – *happy at the prospect of graduation* – began to consider various universities and their special programs.   ● The father – *elated by the safe birth of his first daughter* – could not stop bragging about it to his co-workers.   ● Robert – *furious at not making the final cut* – decided to confront the coach for an explanation.   ● The parents – *blind to what hidden changes were happening in their daughter's life and thoughts* – failed to intercept the thundercloud of depression that hit her and drove her to commit suicide.

- Jensen – ***impervious** to the advice and counsel of his friends* – started to bury himself in the dissipating world of excessive alcohol.

9.d7 PP Dash Middle Adverb Phrase

An adverb string will be defined as a **single-word adverb** followed by:
- one or more nouns with or without attachments;
- one or more adjectives;
- a prepositional phrase;
- a verbal phrase

In other words, it is a combination of words and/or phrases that fit together and follow a single-word adverb.

adverb phrase = adverb + noun with its associated attachments

In the following example, we have an adverb header followed by a noun and its front or back descriptors. These back attachments of the noun usually refer to a prepositional phrase. The prepositional phrase is often not autonomous, but is integrally involved with the earlier words and is read as a unit with the earlier words.

- Mosquitoes – ***frequently** unwelcome visitors in the summer* – bother me less than they do most people.

Dinner – **once**² *a common thing in our house* – has become a special event. • Sgt. Mark A. Linnell – **previously** *a police officer in the Royal Canadian Mounted Police* – has volunteered more than 8000 hours setting up Cadet programs for Métis youth in Alberta.

adverb phrase = adverb + adjective(s)

• The dragon boat paddling crew – **always** *keen and feisty* – plied the waters with their wide paddles in the powerful strokes; they brought the WanChu dragon boat first across the finish line. • Tom – **rarely** *late* – didn't show up for work the next day. • The hotel – **although** *old and obviously showing a past not present grandeur* – still offered excellent service at an affordable price.
•The man's salary – **although** *rather large* – was not enough for him to reduce his debts.

adverb phrase = adverb + prepositional phrase or extended phrase

• "In 139 of these visits – **ostensibly** *for a flare-up of chronic hip pain* – the correct treatment would have been acetaminophen but no anti-inflammatory drugs." (N.S. in Science

---

² *once* is an adverb here that means *at some time in the past, but not now.*

News vol. 152 1997.10.4) • The young salesman – *rarely at home because of his job* – racked up huge monthly phone bills calling his wife and daughter every evening.

adverb phrase = adverb + participle with its associated attachments

• Thawed-out rat skin cells – *earlier frozen* for 25 years – exhibit daily rhythms of gene activity that suggest that cells maintain their own biological clocks.   • The election – *strictly supervised* by UN observers – ran smoothly without any problems.   • The couple – *forever gazing* into each other's eyes – enjoyed their honeymoon at Montezuma Bay.

PP – Dash - End

9.d9   PP Dash End word or multi-word units

Footnote Code: 9PP DASH E Word or Multi-Word
Note: In fact, what follows the dash can be one or more words that explain, amplify, or add a telling comment, an observation, or an afterthought about the first part of the sentence. ***Stock phrases or collocations will be kept intact and considered as a one-word unit.***

Examples:

- I have only one favorite color – **blue**.   • The librarian stressed one thing with the students – **quietness**.   • After the battle the soldiers wanted one thing – **rest**.   • China's ancient capital is gearing up for the year's most important traditional celebration – the **Spring Festival**.

multi-word units at the end of the sentence

- "Ecologists use a computer model to explore how the different types of patches shift around in space and in time – **and why**." (Mari N. Jensen *Ecologists Go To Town* Science News Vol 153 1998.4.4)   • She was tall – **even statuesque**.
- Their decision was a recipe for one thing – **mutual happiness**.

9.d10 PP Dash End prepositional phrase

Note: We can place a prepositional phrase at the end of a sentence after a dash plus any elements extending or following from it.

Examples:

- The former high school grads decided to meet after the alumni reunion at their favorite meeting spot – **at Marla's Diner**.   • I finally found my keys in the one place I hadn't checked – **under the car seat.** ● The nightclub was strict in its refusal to admit young people based on two criteria – **under age,** *and inappropriately attired.* ● The picture would look good anywhere – **on that wall** *over there, on the big wall in the kitchen, or above the media console in the living room.* ● Each person in the group felt better able to cope with Life's stresses and challenges – **after undergoing a period** *of spiritual purfication.* ● *"'It's a very flimsy craft –* **like a tissue-paper spacecraft.'"** (Jim McDivitt quoted in Moon Shot by Alan Shepard and Deke Slayton) ● *"'You'll sauté my delicious dollops of doctored data into a confection that everyone will swallow –* **per my instructions,** *of course.'"* (Bruce Bower in The Deep Blue Sleep in Science News Vol .152 1997.12.20&27) ● *"Their family is performing a* **yajna,** *Vedic fire ceremony –* **at 4am** *in the morning!"* (Linda Forman in Hinduism Today Feb. 1998)

● *"The power to create quality of life is within us –* **in our ability** *to develop and use our own inner compass so that we can act with integrity in the moment of choice."* (Stephen Covey First Things First Every Day)

9.d11 PP Dash End verbal phrase

This includes the **initial verbal phrase** complete with any **objects** if they are required, plus any other **extended attachments** to the verbal or its objects.

infinitive

- "Only the president, Carter insisted, could be counted on to make a policy for the nation as a whole – **to consider freezing tenants** *in Boston as well as oil barons in Austin.*" (Bruce Shulman *The Seventies*)
- "For my part, whatever anguish of spirit it may cost, I am willing to know the whole truth – **to know the worst** *and provide for it.*" (Patrick Henry in M.Scott Peck *Abounding Grace*)
- "Yet I still have faith in this country's unique destiny – **to create generation** *after generation of hyphenates like me, to channel this new blood, this resilience and energy into an ever more vibrant future for all Americans.*" (Eric Liu in *A Chinaman's Dream* in *The Riverside Reader*)

gerund

- The entire season is a rehearsal for one goal – **reaching the playoffs.**
- His hobbies were all active ones – **climbing mountains**, *playing squash, photographing wildlife.*

present participle

- "Nearby, other people were doing as I was – **squinting** east into the wind." (Annie Dillard *For the Time Being*)
- "The hope and energy of the 1960s – **fueled** not only by a growing economy but by all the passions of a great national quest – is long gone." (Rosemary Bray in *So How Did I Get Here?* in *The Riverside Reader*)
- "For some unknown length of time (probably no more than five minutes, although it felt like longer) they watched those brilliant lights run across the sky – **circling**, skidding, hanging lefts and rights, appearing to leapfrog each other. (S.King *Dreamcatcher*)
- "The man loves trains – **riding** them, photographing them, even listening to them." (Rebecca Barry *Chicken Soup for the Teenage Soul*)
- "However, since World War II, agriculture has been undergoing a transformation – **moving** from a family enterprise to big business." (Janet Raloff *Dying Breeds* in Science News 1997.10.4 vol. 152 p. 217)

9.d12 PP Dash End noun phrase

noun phrase = noun + prepositional phrase

- Today was a good day – *a **day** of rest, a day of relaxation.*
- She was the perfect match – *a **paragon** of virtue, a a **maven** of fashion, a **personification** of finesse.*

- The child became a major concern – *a two-legged **dynamo** with endless energy and curiosity requiring constant supervision.*
- "Sly and the Family's music evinced an incredible freedom – ***freedom** of form, with band members trading lead vocals and instrumental solos..*" (Bruce Shulman *The Seventies*)
- "The two astronauts swooped toward the lunar landscape in their landing craft – *the **first** of their kind to descend on the moon.*" (Alan Shepard and Deke Slayton *Moon Shot*)
- "Instead of having a separate message photon as well as an entangled pair, De Martini and his coworkers used two aspects of each particle of the entangled pair – *the **polarization** and direction of motion.*" (Ivars Peterseon in *Instant Transport* in Science News Vol 153 1998.1.17)

noun phrase = noun + reference clause

- "So we have come to cash this check – *a **check** that will give us upon demand the riches of freedom and the security of justice.*" (Martin Luther King, Jr.in *I Have A Dream*)
- "To hear conscience clearly often requires us to be 'still' or 'reflective' or 'meditative' – *a **condition** [that] we rarely choose or find.*" (S.Covey in *First Things First Every Day*)
- Thornton's doubt was strong in his face, but his fighting spirit was aroused – *the fighting **spirit** that*

soars above the odds, fails to recognize the impossible, and is deaf to all save the clamor for battle. (Jack London) ● "As recently as 1894, bubonic plague killed 13 million people in Asia – *the same* **plague** *that killed twenty-five million Europeans five and a half centuries earlier.*" (Dillard For the Time Being) ●"The Department of Defense launched the MSX satellite in part to study what natural patterns exist in the atmosphere – *a* **prerequisite** *for being able to distinguish the signature of a warm trail left by a ballistic missile.*" (R. Monsastersk in Storms paint bull's-eyes in stratosphere in Science News Vol 153 1998.4.4) ● "He didn't want to trouble my mother – *a* **course** *that backfired, because the imagined is always worse than the reality.*" (Rose del Castillo Guilbault in Americanization is Tough on "Macho" in The Riverside Reader) ● Most people were against the proposed clear-cut logging except a few – *the* **loggers** *who worked for Fergus Paper Mill.* ● "Feminists campaigned for subsidized child care for working mothers and stricter sanctions against deadbeat dads – *those* who did not meet their financial obligations to their children." (Shulman The Seventies)

noun phrase = nouns in a correlative at end
● "My discovery of America was also a discovery of feminism – **not only** *Ms. magazine and The Feminine Mystique* **but also** *the open and straightforward manner of young American women I met.*" (Cathy Young in *Keeping Women Weak* in The Riverside Reader) ● "We choose – **either** *to live our lives* **or** *to let others live them for us.*" (Covey *First*)

noun phrase = noun + adverb + (adjective)
● The Mobile WiFi technology is made for villagers worldwide – **people moderately** *poor but who enjoy some of the new communications technology.* ● "British paper currency, which his team examined this summer, has more rounded fibers and far smaller holes – **none apparently** *large enough for the cocaine crystals to enter.* (from Why greenbacks make good 'drug money' *Science News* 1997.10.4 vol. 152 p 213)

noun phrase = noun + verbal phrase
● The hurricane swept across the prairie – a **vacuum cleaner** *ripping up trees and houses and buses high into the sky, and then letting them all smash mercilessly to the ground.* ● "When glaciers melt, they leave in outwash plains boulders, rocks, gravels, sand, and clays

— the **sand** *ground to floury powder."* (Annie Dillard *For the Time Being*)

● "Rather, they realized that the first step in building SDI would be the development of ground-based missile defenses — **weapons** *designed to protect U.S. missiles from attack."* (Shulman *The Seventies*) ● "In the United States, it took shape as the nuclear freeze — a massive social **movement** *encompassing a wide spectrum of social activists across America."* (Shulman *ibid*)

9.d13 PP Dash End adverb phrase

Note: The **header** is usually a **single-word adverb**.

● She doubts if she will stay long at her new job — **precisely** *because of having to work split shifts.* ● She finally got her degree — **nearly** *seven years after she started to take evening classes at U.S.Q. in Australia.*
● "They made grants that reinforced their notions of what was best and most deserving — **overwhelmingly** *New York-based abstract art."* (Shulman *The Seventies*) ● Maybe it wouldn't be such a bad idea to talk to Sylvia's parents — **better still**, *her sister.*

9.d14 PP Dash End less formal list

Footnote Code: 9PP Dash E List
Note: A dash can follow a list (as seen in Form 9.d1), or the dash can introduce a list, as we have here. As such, it highlights or draws attention to the list, though in a ***more casual and flowing manner than the more formal colon.***
Examples:

- "Segregation disappeared in arenas of casual contact between Americans – **restaurants, airports and train stations, hotel lobbies.** (Bruce Shulman)
- "The reason that Li finally gave for his appreciation of crab was that it was perfect in the three requisites of food – **color, fragrance, and flavor.**" (Lin Yutang *The Importance of Living*)
- "They constructed alternative institutions – **food co-ops, underground newspapers, free medical clinics.**" (B. Shulman)
- I need to buy some more stuff for the camping trip – **waterproof matches, a pack of cards, batteries for the flashlights, one new paddle, and the mosquito repellant.**
- There are many biometric approaches – **fingerprinting, face recognition, hand geometry, voice printing, and signature verification.**
- "Bjornstam could do anything with his hands – **solder a pan, weld an automobile spring,**

soothe a frightened filly, tinker a clock, carve a Gloucester schooner which magically went into a bottle." (Sinclair Lewis *Main Street*) ● "... a number of experts pointed to the national audience for the Nashville sound, the entry of non-southerners into the business, and the appeal of the country lifestyle across rural America – in the mountain West, the inland valleys of the Pacific Coast states, the desert Southwest, the Great Plains." (B. Shulman)
● "Dumpster things are often sad – abandoned teddy bears, shredded wedding albums, despaired-of sales kits." (Lars Eighner *My Daily Dives in the Dumpster* in *The Riverside Reader*) ● "Imagine a B & B[3] run by the Phantom of the Opera – huge chandeliers, voluminous drapes, richly patterned carpets, 14-foot high ceilings, dramatic shadows." (Kerry McPhedran Feb/Mar. 2000 issue *Elm Street*)

---

[3] bed and breakfast – a type of hotel accommodation where people rent rooms in a large family house and get a breakfast included

9.d15 PP Dash End Departure DASH

Footnote Code: 9PP Dash E Departure
Note: A dash can be used to indicate a sudden break or shift in direction of thought or departure from the starting idea.
Examples: ●She was charming and agreeable – *but only when she wanted to be.* ● He was an eloquent speaker – *when he wasn't drunk.* ● It's a nice house – *only it's on the wrong side of the river.*

ca.1400

(artistic musical notation from France)

Eight Ways to Express Association and Opposition

Eight Ways or Options to Express Association or Combination in Prose

1. by the singular conjunction "and";
2. by the singular correlative "also"
3. by the correlative expression "not only , but also";
4. by the correlative expressions "as well as":
5. by the correlative expression "in addition to";
6. by the Sixth Sentence Form 6.1 : "CC and";
7. by the Ninth Sentence Form 9.1: "The Associative Semicolon";
8. by the Ninth Sentence Form 9.4: "The Clause Adverb Semicolon (moreover, furthermore, etc.)"

Eight Ways or Options to express in Opposition in Prose

1. by the singular conjunction "but" ;
2. by the singular conjunction "yet";
3. by the correlative expression "this, not that";
4. by the Sixth Sentence Form 6.2: "CC but";
5. by the Sixth Sentence Form 6.7: "CC yet";
6. by the Seventh Sentence Form 7.19: "AC while";
7. by the Ninth Sentence Form 9.2: "The Oppositional Semicolon";
8. by the Ninth Sentence Form 9.4 : The Clause Adverb Semicolon (however)";

INSTRUCTIONS FOR ASSIGNMENT THREE

For this third assignment, students will concentrate on incorporating the all-important Form 9 Sentence Forms, using the punctuation marks of the colon, semicolon, and the dash in their sentences. What distinguishes excellent from only average writers is often the precise and effective use of the colon, semicolon, and dash, so the practice of writing and incorporating the various sub-forms of Form 9 into essays is critical to success in writing.

Students should write on a theme of two or three paragraphs with a focused title, and as before, should incorporate 3 or more different examples of Forms 2 to 8 in their paragraphs; however, they should now also incorporate 2 or 3 examples of Form 9 in their paragraphs, employing the colon, semicolon, and dash. As always, they should notate and footnote all the various sentences that they choose to highlight.

Below are examples by earlier students to serve as models for this assignment.

Compositions using Form 9

FROM UKELELE TO GUITAR BY MATTHEW ORMITA

There is only one thing that I want to do with my life.**1** I want to play music.**2** My musical career began in Hawaii three years ago, and since then, it is all that I think about.**3**

In Hawaii, there are two instruments of choice: the guitar and the ukulele.**4** Many of my family members can play the ukulele. They motivated me to learn also.**5** I have always loved attention, and in Hawaiian music, the ukulele player is the star; the guitar player, the supporter.**6** Troy Fernandez and Ernie Cruz Jr., Jake Shimabukuro and Jon Yamasato, Israel Kamakawiwo'ole and Louis Kauakahi are all perfect examples of star ukulele players and their supporting guitarists.**7** Because the ukulele gets all the attention, that is what I wanted to play.**8** So in 1997, I began taking ukulele lessons. Just as I expected, when my skills began to develop, so too did the attention on me.**9** I enjoyed playing the ukulele; however, all the music to which I listened did not use ukuleles.**10** Within a year's time, I had grown tired of playing the ukulele; I now started to play the guitar.**11**

The guitar, like the ukulele, took a while to feel comfortable playing.**12** Anger, frustration, despair – these were all emotions I felt throughout the learning process for both instruments.**13** The guitar, however, was not as difficult since I had been playing the uke for a year straight.**14** I have continued playing and learning the guitar for over two years now, and I am sure that the hunger and desire will never stop.**15** I will never be able to master an instrument, but I will be able to play it well enough to satisfy my soul.**16**

Sentence Forms:
1) 1F There is; 8RN That; 3V Infinitive
2) 3V Infinitive
3) 6CC And; 8RN That
4) 9PP Numeric Precursor Colon
5) 3V Infinitive
6) 9PP Stylish Semicolon; 6CC And
7) 2S Rhythmical Pairs (extended)
8) 7AC Because; 8RN What
9) 4C Just As; 7AC When
10) 3V Gerund; 9PP Expansive SemiColon
11) 9PP Association SemiColon
12) 3V Infinitive; 3V Gerund
13) 9PP Dash B Wrap-up; 8RN Missing that; 3V Present Participle
14) 7AC Since
15) 3V Gerund (2); 6CC And; 8RN That; 2S The Pair
16) 3V Infinitive (3); 6CC But

THE POWER OF MUSIC BY MELISSA HATFIELD

Music is not something you can touch and see; however, it is something you can feel and hear.**1** Just as the sweet taste of lemonade can bring back memories of a hot summer day, the sound of music can bring back memories of one's life.**2** For instance, a couple turns the radio up – remembering their first kiss – when the song that played that day comes on.**3** Or the sound of church bells helps a couple remember – walking down the aisle – the day of their wedding.**4** Whether the memories are good or bad, music is a constant reminder.**5**

You don't have to be able to read notes or play an instrument to appreciate the art of music; you just have to listen.**6** Love, heartbreak, and happiness – all are feelings we experience at different times, and expressing how we feel through music can be uplifting, consoling, and even therapeutic.**7**

No matter what your taste in music, the tone and point of the music is never difficult to understand.**8** The different notes played on an instrument can be powerful and expressive.**9** The lyrics of a song are often inspirational, and most of all music is always compelling and meaningful in ways hard to describe.**10**

Not all music is written down with lyrics and musical notes.**11** Music surrounds us every day, and sometimes we don't even bother to notice.**12** The chirping of birds up in the trees, the laughing of children outside as they play, the whistling of the wind on a breezy day – all are sounds, that either separately or together in chorus, contribute to the music of daily life.**13**

Sentence Forms

1) 9PP Expansive Semicolon; 2S The Pair (2)
2) 4C Just As
3) 9PP Dash M Verbal Phrase; 7AC When; 8RN That
4) 9PP Dash M Verbal Phrase; 3V Infinitive Missing *to*;
5) 7AC Whether; 2S Choice
6) 9PP Opposition Semicolon; 3V Infinitive (4); 2S Choice
7) 2S Standard Series (2); 9PP Dash B Wrap Up; 8RN Missing *that*; 3V Gerund; 8RN How
8) 2S The Pair; 3V Infinitive
9) 3V Past Participle; 2S The Pair
10) 6CC And; 2S The Pair; 3V Infinitive
11) 2S The Pair

12) 6CC And; 3V Infinitive
13) 2S Triple Force; 3V Gerund (3); 7AC As; 9PP B List Wrap Up; 8RN That; 2S Choice

A HEALTHY FRUIT BY TRUCQUYNH HUA

As indicated by the proverb "an apple a day will keep the doctor away," apples are undoubtedly one of humanity's healthier and more popular fruits.**1** Apples come in thousands of varieties and tastes, textures and colors; however, they are mostly found in three colors: red, green, or yellow.**2** Each variety of apples has slightly different flavors, from crisp to sweet, and from tart to bitter.**3** The textures vary amongst apple varieties, from soft and mushy to firm and crunchy.**4** Each variety of apples is grown for special food uses. Some types of apples are used to produce cider or juice; other kinds are used for cooking, baking, and fresh eating.**5** Eating them fresh is the healthiest way to eat apples, the only way to obtain all their natural nutrition.**6**

Fresh apples are low in calories, yet they are an excellent source of fiber and vitamin C.**7** Fiber helps reduce cholesterol; furthermore, it may help prevent certain types of cancer such as colon cancer.**8** There is no fat as well as no saturated fat in apples, so they help reduce the risk of cancer.**9** Apples help with heart disease, weight loss, and controlling cholesterol because they have no cholesterol, no sodium.**10** Like many fruits, apples contain vitamin C and other antioxidant compounds, which explains the reduced risk of cancer.**11** Almost half of the vitamin C content is just underneath the skin, so it is a good idea to eat apples with their skin.**12** Eating skin also increases the fiber content.**13**

Apples are delicious and healthy, easy to find and a natural mouth freshener.**14** If you want a tasty and healthy snack, just grab an apple.**15**

Sentence Forms:

1) 2S The Pair
2) 2S Rhythmical Pairs; 9PP Expansive Semicolon; 9PP Numeric Precursor Colon; 2S Choices
3) 4C From To (2)
4) 2S The Pair (2); 4C From To
5) 9PP Opposition Semicolon; 3V Infinitive; 2S Choice; 2S Standard Series; 3V Gerund (3)
6) 3V Gerund; 3V Infinitive (2)
7) 6CC Yet; 2S The Pair
8) 9PP Expansive Semicolon; 3V Infinitive Missing *to* (2);
9) 4C As Well As; 6CC So; 3V Infinitive Missing *to*
10) 2S Standard Series; 3V Gerund; 7AC Because; 5R Word
11) 2S The Pair; 8RN Which
12) 6CC So; 3V Infinitive
13) 3V Gerund
14) 2S Rhythmical Pair
15) 7AC If; 2S The Pair

SEARCHING FOR A TOPIC BY RICHARD PEACE

Today's writing assignment is to write two paragraphs; however, I do not have anything on my mind to write about.**1** I gave some thought to writing about penguins, or ostriches, or other birds that can't fly.**2** Writing about these birds would be silly, for I know little about them.**3** I have knowledge of the outdoors, so I should save that topic for a more important assignment.**4** The random thoughts bouncing in my head all lead to one conclusion: I must start writing soon, or I will never finish.**5**

After my break, I continue my search for just one thing – a topic.**6** My situation is turning desperate; head scratching, brainstorming, random doodling – nothing seems to help.**7** I am going to need a good excuse: I was sick; I had to work; the dog ate it.**8**

Sentence Forms:
1) 9PP Expansive Semicolon; 3V Present Participle; 3V Infinitive (2)
2) 2S Choices; 3VGerund; 8RN That
3) 3V Gerund; 6CC For
4) 6CC So
5) 3V Present Participle; 9PP Explanation Colon; 3V Gerund; 6CC Or
6) 9PP Dash E Word
7) 9PP Association Semicolon; 9PP Dash B Wrap-up (variation); 3V Gerund (3); 3V Infinitive
8) 3V Infinitive; 9PP Explanation Colon; 9PP Trio Semicolon

HIGHER EDUCATION BY MATTHEW J. GARVIN

Higher education is a necessity in today's world to get a job.**1** It is almost impossible for one to simply graduate from high school and be successful, thanks to technology and modernization.**2** They have made college degrees prized possessions, possessions everyone must have in order to survive.**3** There was a time in history when becoming a high school graduate was a significant achievement. Today, if you don't graduate from high school, if you don't have at least a bachelor's degree, if you don't have any prior experience, then your chances of getting a high paying job are slim.**4** Even in the military, an education is necessary in order to achieve higher ranks. Earning a two-year Associate's degree is an educational start; however, a four-year Bachelor's degree is even better.**5** Many people continue longer to obtain their Master's, and an even smaller group works toward the highest degree, a doctorate.**6**

This brings up the question, "How does one pay for education and better opportunities, and how much does it cost?" Most colleges and universities range from fifteen thousand to thirty thousand dollars a year. After four years, that is quite a hefty bill. Many apply for scholarships; many get loans; many have rich relatives that cover the cost.**7**

You can attend college for almost any subject. Some areas of study are common, and others are rare.**8** Science and history, math and English, psychology and anthropology – students must have some knowledge in all these areas, whether they have anything to do with their major or not.**9** Students even switch majors two or three times before graduating from college; hence, the birth of the term "life-time students".**10** Yet, in such a highly competitive world, there remains a high percentage of young individuals who do not make it past their freshman year.**11** Higher education in today's world has become high priority: if you don't have a degree already, then start working to get one.**12**

Sentence Forms:

1) 3V Infinitive
2) 2S The Pair (2); 3V Infinitive
3) 3V Past Participle; 5R Key Word; 8RN Missing *that*; 3V Infinitive
4) 5R Adverbial Conjunction *If*; 3V Gerund; 3V Present Participle

5) 3V Gerund; 9PP Expansive Semicolon
6) 6CC And; 3V Infinitive;
7) 5R Word; 9PP Trio Semicolon; 8RN That
8) 6CC And
9) 2S Rhythmical Pairs (extended); 9PP Dash B Wrap-up; 7AC Whether; 3V Infinitive
10) 3V Gerund; 9PP Expansive SemiColon
11) 8RN Who
12) 9PP Explanation Colon; 7AC If; 3V Gerund; 3V Infinitive

HORROR MOVIES BY BRANDIE STEVENS

Horror movies have been around since I can remember.**1** Also, they were here before my mother. Most people say that children should not watch horror movies because they will give the children nightmares; they will teach children bad things; they will damage children's minds.**2** Well, I grew up watching horror movies, and I turned out just fine.**3**

I asked my mother why – as a child – she let me watch horror movies, when most of my friends could not even watch "Pretty Woman".**4** She said, "Why should I shield you from what happens in a horror movie, only so you can be surprised by what happens in the real world?**5** It's better to learn now, and not be disappointed when you grow up."**6** She also pointed out that much worse stuff goes on in the news sometimes.**7**

In the news, they show terrorists blowing up buildings, gang wars going on in the streets, murderers and rapists getting away with crimes.**8** All these are much scarier than your average horror movie ("Nightmare On Elm Street" or "Puppet Master"), because they happen in real life.**9** But you don't really expect a puppet to come after you. **10** Bloody bodies, screaming girls, huge monsters – all are things in horror movies. **11** Most seem just ridiculous, unbelievable. **12** Does anyone really believe that" The Blob" is really going to come after him or her?**13**

Another thing that children are allowed to watch are the cartoons. **14** Almost every kid out there watches cartoons. The cartoon, however, is no better than the horror movie. In cartoons – *Transformer, X-men,* and even *Pokemon* – the figures show children it is okay to fight, shoot, and hurt one another. **15** At least in a horror movie, the actors show that you want to stay away from the bad guy. **16** The good guys don't go looking for a fight. In cartoons, the good guys and bad guys are always fighting; the good guys, of course, never get hurt. **17**

So, if parents want to keep their children innocent and good, they are going to have a hard time. **18** Unless they take away cartoons and the real world, unless they keep them locked up in a dream world of toy cars and fluffy clouds, children are bound to see what happens – whether it be in a horror movie or on TV or outside the house. **19** The real world is a lot scarier than any horror movie.

Sentence Forms:

1) 7AC since
2) 8RN That; 7AC Because; 9PP Trio Semicolon
3) 3V Gerund; 6CC And
4) 8RN Why; 9PP Dash M Prepositional Phrase; 7AC When
5) 8RN Why; 8RN What (2); 6CC So
6) 3V Infinitive; 7AC When
7) 8RN That

8) 3V Present Participle (3); 2S Standard Series; 2S The Pair
9) 2S Choice; 7AC Because
10) 3V Infinitive
11) 2S Triple Force; 3V Present Participle; 9PP Dash B Wrap-up
12) 2S Compact Duo
13) 8RN That; 3V Infinitive; 2S Choice
14) 8RN That; 3V Infinitive
15) 2S Standard Series (2); 3V Infinitive (3); 9PP Dash M Appositives
16) 8RN That; 3V Infinitive
17) 9PP Association Semicolon; 2S The Pair
18) 7AC If; 3V Infinitive; 2S The Pair; 3V Infinitive
19) 5R Adverbial Conjunction unless; 2S The Pair (2); 3V Gerund; 3V Infinitive; 8RN What; 9PP Dash E Clause; 2S Choices

FAVORITE HARD-HITTING SPORTS BY A STUDENT

For me, the most exciting thing to watch is sports. While some sports are on the rise and some are on a downward spiral, three sports remain my favorite to watch, no matter what people say: football, boxing, and mixed martial arts (UFC or Ultimate Fighting Championship).**1** These sports are the hardest hitting, the most exciting, and the most action-packed.**2** A lot of people would argue that baseball or basketball are just as exciting; however, those two sports just don't have the tempo on a constant basis as the other three.**3** As soon as the first bells rings or first whistle blows, there is an action-packed battle from beginning to end in all three sports.**4** This is why football, boxing, and the UFC stand out above all.**5**

Football is my overall favorite sport to watch.**6** The competition is always great, and the teamwork in this sport is like no other.**7** Football is a four quarter, high octane, fast paced slugfest.**8** This sport touches something deep inside me since I did play football in high school, and in that respect I am biased.**9** Most of the country also feels this way since the Super Bowl is the highest rated telecast every single year in the United States.**10** The football season is always the best time of the year— on every Sunday; there I am sitting in front of the TV screaming for my team to win.**11** Football is the best of the three sports for several reasons: it has the hardest hitters, the hardest runners, and the most dedicated team players.**12** Many think that baseball is the national pastime, but, sorry, football has now taken that title over.**13**

Boxing is also one of the bloodiest sports to watch nowadays. Frankly, this is the reason I love watching it, because it is fun to watch two guys beating each other up for a couple hours.**14** Currently, my favorite boxers are the Klitzchko brothers, Vladimir and Vitali. They are the premier heavyweights in today's boxing. Though the popularity of boxing over the years has dwindled in prize fights, due to the fall from greatness in the heavyweight division, I am an avid boxing fan.**15** There aren't many sports nowadays that resemble the gladiator days in Rome.**16** Two warriors duking it out in the center of the ring in front of millions—that would be the ultimate adrenaline rush.**17** One of the best parts of the fight is the commentary. They have old greats of the game going round by round, making it very interesting.**18** The best part for me, though, is the trash talking. "Bring it!" is the most common phrase you hear from a lot of fighters.**19** But no fight is complete without a knockout. When fighters say at the end of the fight, "But I really had no choice – knock him out or lose the flight," that is the case with a lot of fights since a lucky punch wins a lot of bouts.**20**

The UFC is the fastest rising sport right now, and rightfully so. The UFC features mixed martial art bouts – a mixture of boxing, jujitsu, boxing and kickboxing together .**21** These are the most brutal and greatest fights to watch. The training these men go through, and the punishment they put themselves through every fight is just amazing.**22** Most fights consist of three five-minute rounds of pure brutality. Title fights are five, five-minute rounds. Most sports writers are saying the UFC is the way of the future and boxing is a dying sport.**23** This of course is preposterous since they are two totally different disciplines and different tempos.**24** Most UFC fighters wouldn't last two rounds in the ring with a good boxer, whereas no boxer would last two minutes in the ring with a UFC fighter in the octagon.**25** My favorite fighter is Chuck Liddell; he is the fiercest and hardest hitting fighter in the UFC.**26** He has beaten everyone that they have put in front of him, except one fighter whom he faces this weekend.**27**

As you can see, I love to watch and participate in hard-hitting contact sports.**28** They are the most thrilling and fun to play and watch.**29** I encourage you to get into these sports as you will find them equally satisfying to watch.**30**

Sentence Forms:

1) 7AC While; 5R Word; 3V Infinitive; 9PP List Colon; 8RN What; 2S Standard Series; 3V Past Participle
2) 2S Standard Series; 3V Present Participle (2); 3V Past Participle
3) 8RN That; 2S Choice; 9PP Expansive Semicolon
4) 7AC As Soon As (supplemental); 2S Choice; 3V Past Participle;4C From To
5) 8RN Why; 2S Standard Series
6) 3V Infinitive
7) 8RN How; 8RN Why
8) 2S Triple Force
9) 6CC And; 7AC Since
10) 7AC Since; 6CC So
11) 9PP Dash E Prepositional Phrase; 9PP Association Semicolon; 3V Present Participle; 3V Infinitive
12) 9PP Explanation Colon; 2S Standard Series; 3V Past Participle
13) 8RN That; 6CC But
14) 3B Gerund; 7AC Because; 3V Infinitive; 3V Present Participle
15) 7AC Though;
16) 8RN That; 1F There Are
17) 3V Present Participle; 9PP Dash B Wrap-up
18) 2S Compact Duo; 3V Present Participle (2)
19) 8RN Missing *that*
20) 7AC When; 9PP Dash Break; 2S Choice
21) 9PP Dash E Appositive; 2S Standard Series; 3V Gerund; 2S The Pair
22) 8RN Missing *that* (2)
23) 8RN Missing *that* (2)
24) 7AV Since; 2S The Pair
25) 7AC Whereas (supplemental)
26) 9PP Association Semicolon; 2S The Pair
27) 8RN That; 8RN Whom
28) 7AC As; 3V Infinitive (2); 3V Present Participle
29) 2S The Pair (2); 3V Infinitive (2)
30) 3V Infinitive (2); 7AC As

Banyan tree in front of the Old Lee County Courthouse in Fort Myers, Florida.

THE TREE OF LIFE BY CHRIS LAPID

Coconut trees are useful in a lot of ways. People worldwide have benefited from several parts of the coconut: the roots, the trunk, the leaves, and the fruit.**1** Coconuts have supplied some families with food and drinks, shelter and many of their other needs.**2** Dye is extracted from the roots while the trunks are used to stabilize buildings.**3** Mats, baskets, and hats are all made out of the leaves and the fiber from the husk.**4**

The coconut fruit has a hard outside and white meat beneath with a hollow center in which there is coconut milk.**5** The white meat of the fruit is eaten, and the coconut milk is served as refreshment.**6** They get coconut cream by sifting the white meat until it turns soft and creamy; furthermore, they use this liquid for a nice refreshing drink.**7** Coconut oil can be pressed from the dried meat of the coconut. After pressing the edible oil, the leftover meat makes good food for animals: it contains proteins, sugar, and vitamins.**8** The dried meat is used in cakes and candies; the oil is primarily used in soap and margarine.**9**

From top to bottom, the coconut tree has unlimited applications.**10** This is why some people call it "the tree of life".**11**

Sentence Forms:
1) 9PP List Colon
2) 2S Rhythmical Pairs
3) 7AC While; 3V Infinitive
4) 2S Standard Series; 2S The Pair
5) 2S The Pair; 8RN Which; 1F There is
6) 6CC And

7) 9PP Expansive Semicolon; 3V Gerund; 7AC Until; 2S The Pair; 3V Present Participle
8) 3V Gerund; 9PP Explanation Colon; 2S Standard Series
9) 2S The Pair (2); 9PP Association Semicolon
10) 4C From To
11) 8RN Why

LOSING WEIGHT BY BRANDIE STEVENS

Many people these days say they need to lose weight.**1** They try to lose it in many different ways: dieting, not eating at all, exercising.**2** I have found that cutting back on certain types of food (pizza and potato chips) and exercising more helps me lose weight.**3**

The first thing I did when I got pregnant was eat anything; I did not care what it was, or if it was healthy.**4** Now that I look back, I realize that I should not have done that - eating and eating and eating – because I gained 50 pounds by the time I had my son.**5** I started out at 170 pounds and went up to 220 pounds.

I tried many different programs to lose weight. Workout videos, metabolism increasing pills, Atkin's diet – all are things that I tried and failed as methods for losing weight.**6** After losing only eight pounds, I decided to try something new, something miraculous, something doable.**7** I needed something that would work for me.**8**

I started eating less food that had sugar and carbohydrates.**9** I did not eliminate them completely because then I would have broken down and pigged out on all of the food I missed.**10** I ate more chicken, steak, fruit, vegetables.**11** But I steered clear of fried, greasy foods, like fried chicken, pizza, and french-fries.**12** I also stopped watching TV while I ate.**13** I still had a brownie or a popsicle every once in a while, though.

The other exercise I did to start losing more weight was walking and running and step aerobics/*tae bo*.**14** I first started jogging and walking until I could handle running a full four miles.**15** And I also started aerobics/*Tae Bo* class two to three nights a week. The way I kept motivated was to have someone – my 1st Sargent – working with me.**16**

Slowly but surely, I started running faster and farther, and started losing body weight and body fat. By the end of 6 months – from January to June – I had lost 30 pounds, going from 214 pounds to 184 pounds, and also losing 5% of my body fat in the process.**17** The best way for me to lose weight was to eat more conscientiously and to exercise more.**18**

And I am still trying!

Sentence Forms:

1) 8RN Missing that; 3V Infinitive
2) 3V Infinitive; 9PP List Colon; 2S Triple Force; 3V Gerund (3)
3) 8RN That; 3V Gerund (2); 2S The Pair; 9PP M (appositives); 3V Infinitive Missing *to*
4) 8RN Missing *that;* 7AC When; 9PP Association Semicolon; 8RN What; 2S Choice; 7AC If (or 8RN If/Whether supplemental)
5) 7AC Now That supplemental; 8RN That; 9PP Dash M Appositives; 2S Lyrical Series; 5R Key Word; 7AC Because; 8RN Missing *That*
6) 2S The Pair; 2S Triple Force; 9PP Dash B Wrap-up; 8RN That; 2S The Pair; 3V Gerund;
7) 3V Gerund; 3V Infinitive; 5R Word; 2S Triple Force

8) 8RN That
9) 3V Gerund; 8RN That; 2S The Pair
10) 7AC Because; 2S The Pair; 8RN Missing *that*
11) 2S Triple Force (extended)
12) 2S Compact Duo; 2S Standard Series
13) 3V Gerund; 7AC While
14) 8RN Missing that; 3V Gerund (3); 2S Lyrical Series
15) 2S The Pair; 3V Gerund (3); 7AC Until
16) 8RN Missing that; 3V Infinitive; 9PP Dash M Appositive; 3V Present Participle
17) 4C From To (2); 9PP Dash M Prepositional Phrase; 3V Present Participle (2)
18) 3V Infinitive (3)

SUMMERTIME IN THE SOUTH BY JOEL JONES

Hot, humid, sweaty – that is the kind of weather that reminds me of summer time in the South.**1** Summer camp, band camp, and the occasional family vacation – all take place during this season.**2** Late evening barbecues and gatherings under the shade tree to avoid the hot sun only lead to another friendly game of spades and gin, tonk and bid wiz, poker and dominoes.**3** It is what summer is all about: tops and daisy dukes, flip flop open toe sandals and painted toenails, while playing a little game of football or shooting some hoops.**4**

Yes, in the summer, the Ladies are the reason for the long hours in the gym: lifting the weights, running on the treadmill, and doing those extra laps in the pool.**5** The summer – the hot, humid, and beautiful Southern summer – is what I love.**6**

Sentence Forms:
1) 2S Triple Force; 9PP Dash B WrapUp; 8RN That
2) 2S Standard Series; 9PP Dash B WrapUp

3) 2S The Pair; 3V Infinitive; 2S Rhythmical Pairs (extended);
4) 9PP Explanation Colon; 2S Rhythmical Pairs; 3V Gerund (2); 2S Choice
5) 9PP Explanation Colon; 2S Standard Series; 3V Gerund (3)
6) 9PP Dash M Adjective Phrase; 2S Standard Series; 5R Key Word; 8RN What

WHAT I DO BY BETTY WARREN

I cannot count the times that I have been asked the same question "What do you do?"**1** Hmm, let me think about that for a moment. Even though I know exactly what they are referring to, I still feel compelled to answer with a question of my own: "What do I do, when?"**2** Since they have obviously never seen me in an office, never seen me behind a desk, and never seen me anywhere, that would imply that I am unemployed.**3** Why then, do they ask what I do?**4**

I am not trying to be rude: I am simply being defensive.**5** Because I am a housewife, I do not want people to assume that I do nothing.**6** I do a number of things: I care for my family; pay the bills; do the taxes; coordinate moves; plan vacations; and generally keep our lives in order.**7** The list is endless, for I am a housewife.**8**

And that is what I do.**9**

Sentence Forms

1) 8RN That
2) 7AC Even Though; 8RN What; 3V Infinitive
3) 7AC Since; 5R Key Word; 2S Standard Series; 8RN That
4) 8RN What

5) 3V Infinitive; 9PP Explanation Colon
6) 7AC Because; 3V Infinitive; 8RN That
7) 9PP Long Items in a List
8) 6CC For
9) 8RN What

CHRISTMAS IN CLEVELAND BY GENE A. WILLIAMS

There are three things I really love about Christmas in Cleveland: the snow, the beautiful decorations and lights downtown, and the special atmosphere I share with my family.**1** My mother enjoys having all her children home; I enjoy sampling all the cakes and pies.**2** My brothers and I get along so well at Christmas time; this is why I think the atmosphere is so special.**3**

With all the food that sits on the table, one dish always stands out to me – candy yams.**4** My daughter's face lights up, full of excitement – all of the lights and decorations catch her attention.**5** This is why I love Christmas time in Cleveland.**6**

Sentence Forms

1) 9PP Numeric Precursor Colon; 8RN Missing *that* (2); 2S Standard Series
2) 3V Gerund (2); 9PP Association Semicolon; 2S The Pair
3) 2S The Pair; 9PP Association Semicolon; 8RN Why; 8RN Missing *that*
4) 9PP Dash E Word; 8RN That
5) 9PP Dash Break; 2S The Pair
6) 8RN Why

FOOTBALL 101 BY CARLOS JONES

America is in need of its own Shakespearean type amphitheater to play out the modern day dramas of life; consequently, football was created.**1** Since I am from the city of Houston, football dictates that I should be a Houston Texan fan; however, I am actually a Dallas Cowboys fan.**2** There are so many virtues which football brings to our world: teamwork, competition, a healthy life, dedication.**3** Ming, Roman, British – all three were great empires that were arguably built around the central virtue that football is built around.**4** Those empires, like every football fan, knows that only one factor – loyalty – can bring about the fruits of victory.**5**

Such are my reflections when I am silent, serene, and secluded with my thoughts.**6** Football surely has to be God's gift to mankind! Where else can you see a spectacle so simple in its rhythm, so complex in its intricacies, so brutal in its passion?**7** The stories of everyday life are played out in each new game: See the team go from rags to riches; Delight in the pain and punishment of the sport; Bear witness to the world of football in all of its glory.**8** There are no cowards here, only warriors.**9**

And on the eighth day, God created FOOTBALL . . . and He said, IT IS GOOD!

Sentence Forms:

1) 9PP Expansive Semicolon; 3V Infinitive
2) 7AC Since; 8RN That; 9PP Expansive Semicolon
3) 1f There Are; 8RN Which; 9PP Colon List
4) 2S Triple Force; 9PP Dash B Wrap-up; 8RN That (2)
5) 9PP Explanation Semicolon; 9PP Trio Semicolon; 4C From To; 2S The Pair

6) 4C No, Only supplemental
7) 7AC When; 2S Standard Series
8) 2S Triple Force; 5R Word
9) 9PP Explanation Colon
10) 4C No, Only (supplemental)

NAVAL CAREER BY MR. SONNIER

After almost 18 years in the Navy, I occasionally now reflect on my naval career: the things I've seen, the places I've been, the people I've met.**1** I have seen landmarks that most people will never see in their lifetime: The Eiffel Tower, The Leaning Tower of Pisa, The Roman Coliseum, The Temple of Hercules, and many others.**2** I spent most of my Naval Career overseas, so I took full advantage of the chance to do some sightseeing.**3**

While in Israel, I stood in the very waters where John the Baptist baptized the followers of Jesus; I walked on the same beaches George S. Patton did during his invasion of Sicily; I strolled the same brick path that Zeus, the god of gods, supposedly walked.**4** My fondest memories, however, are the people I've encountered: George Bush Sr., Bill Clinton, and George Bush Jr.**5**

One could say I've experienced more in my 18 years than one could in a lifetime.**6** I owe this all to my Naval Career.

Sentence Forms:
1) 9PP List Colon; 2S Triple Force
2) 9PP List Colon; 8RN That; 3V Present Participle; 2S Standard (extended)
3) 6CC So; 3V Infinitive; 3V Gerund

4) 9PP Trio Semicolon; 8RN Where; 8RN Missing *that*; 8RN That
   5) 9PP List Colon; 2S Standard Series
   6) 8RN Missing *that*

PHYSICAL TRAINING BY JIMMY CURRIE

Physical training is a good thing for you; it builds the body's endurance.**1** I work out hard daily to stay physically fit.**2** I have three favorite activities: pushups, sit ups, and running; all three are part of the army physical fitness test.**3** Sometimes it makes your body really sore; however, the exercise is good for the body.**4** My muscles scream, ache, tremble while I lift the heavy weights, but I feel better afterwards.**5**

Racquetball, football, basketball – all are sports that give a person a good cardiovascular workout.**6** Before working out, I like to stretch my muscles, do warm up exercises, and mentally prepare myself.**7** The stretch and warm-up is good for sports or weight training as well as for aerobics workouts.**8** If one works really hard, if one sticks to a workout program, if one doesn't quit, he will be on his way to becoming physically fit.**9** Once you are physically fit, you are primed to succeed and win in all aspects of your life.**10**

Sentence Forms
   1) 9PP Association Semicolon
   2) 3V Infinitive
   3) 9PP Numeric Colon; 2S Standard Series; 9PP Association Semicolon
   4) 9PP Expansive Semicolon;
   5) 2S Triple Force; 7AC While; 6CC But
   6) 2S Triple Force; 9PP Dash B WrapUp
   7) 3V Gerund; 3V Infinitive; 2S Standard Series

8) 2S The Pair; 2S Choice; 4C As Well As
9) 5R Adverbial Conjunction *If*; 3V Gerund
10) 7AC Once; 2S The Pair

BEING ALONE BY GEORGE C. PINEDA

Today was unforgettable: I chatted with my kids.**1** It's been a long time since I talked to them, and I really miss them very much.**2** I had several things to do after I chatted with them: I sent a package by mail and started taking pictures for them to see what I do here in Korea.**3**

Some people cannot cope with being alone and far away from their family; I, on other hand, try to occupy myself with work and liberty.**4** That way I won't get depressed when I miss my children.**5** I try to be strong for them, so that I can live through being stationed here for another two years without them with me.**6** So, I try to keep very busy; with my hectic schedule and overloaded work, I never even thought of myself being alone until now.**7**

Sentence Forms:
1) 9PP Explanation Colon
2) 7AC Since; 6CC And
3) 9PP List Colon; 2S The Pair; 3V Gerund; 3V Infinitive; 8RN What
4) 9PP Opposition Semicolon; 2S The Pair (2); 3V Infinitive
5) 7AC When; 3V Gerund
6) 3V Infinitive; 6CC So That supplemental; 3V Gerund; 3V Past Participle
7) 9PP Association Semicolon; 3V Past Participle; 3V Gerund

TIPS ON WORKING RETAIL BY CAROLINE DANIELS

Working retail can be described as challenging and mildly interesting.**1** It is not exactly a bad experience, but it's not exactly a good one either.**2** There are two qualities you must possess to make it through the day: patience and understanding.**3** Some people who work retail leave work drained and angry; others can leave the building and still be calm and collected.**4** The difference is how much you let the customers upset you.**5** Long days of dealing with disgruntled customers can be stressful; however, if you know to contend with their problems, you can lower your stress level significantly.**6**

Anytime you're serving others, there will always be people who are not exactly the kindest or most appreciative.**7** Days like this are almost inevitable: it's karma.**8** If customers complain about something, the first rule is to try to understand their point of view.**9** The policy of most companies is that the customer is always right.**10** Usually this isn't true, but you have to pretend it is if you wish to keep your job.**11** So smile; you know they're wrong.**12** Smiling then looks good on the outside and feels good on the inside.**13** No matter what happens, just remember three things: smile, be patient, and understand their point of view.**14** With these three rules, you should be able to get through your day with no problems.**15**

Sentence Forms:

1) 3V Gerund; 2S The Pair
2) 6CC But
3) 8RN Missing That; 3V Infinitive; 9PP Numeric Colon; 2S The Pair

4) 9PP Opposition Semicolon; 2S The Pair (2)
5) 8RN How
6) 3V Gerund; 9PP Expansive Semicolon; 7AC If; 3V Infinitive
7) 8RN Missing That; 8RN Who; 2S The Pair
8) 9PP Explanation Colon
9) 7AC If; 3V Infinitives (2)
10) 8RN That
11) 6CC But; 8RN Missing *that*; 7AC If; 3V Infinitive
12) 9PP Association Semicolon
13) 3V Gerund; 5R Key Word
14) 9PP Numeric Colon; 2S Standard Series
15) 3V Infinitive

MY SECOND DRIVING SKILL BY TRUCQUYNH HUA

Learning is a process.**1** Learning is an occupation you never retire from.**2** You learn something new every day, at any age throughout your life.**3** For example, I learned how to ride a bicycle when I was at the age of seven. Then, when I was seventeen, my father taught me how to drive an automatic transmission car; however, I didn't learn how to drive a manual transmission car until two years ago.**4** In my opinion, driving a manual transmission car – better known as driving a stick shift – requires lots of time, lots of patience, and lots of practice.**5** Learning the skill to operate a manual vehicle is not easy, yet it can be done.**6**

While I was stationed in Sigonella, Italy, I decided to learn how to operate a manual car.**7** My friend Mitchell taught me how. It was a unique and wicked experience.**8** I was a little bit nervous during my first driving lesson, but Mitchell said I would be fine.**9** We got into the car, and I started it. He told me to adjust the seat and mirrors so that it would be comfortable for me.**10** Then he said,

"Put on your seat-belt and let's go!" Mitchell gave me simple instructions on what to do: he pointed out what each of the foot pedals were; he explained in words how to start a manual transmission, and at what speeds to move into the next shift and how to downshift; he also reminded me to always use the emergency brake when I parked.**11**

The instructions seemed pretty easy, and I was ready to go.**12** I began practicing the maneuvers in my head: left foot on clutch, right on brake, put it into first gear, gently press the gas and lift off the clutch.**13** I thought I could do it, but I was wrong.**14** It stalled. I started it again, yet it stalled again.**15** The third time, I failed; then, the fourth time, too.**16** I was very upset, and I wanted to give up; but Mitchell looked at me and said, "You are doing just fine. Just keep practicing, and soon enough you will get it."**17** I could not believe how hard it was.**18** It looked so easy and fun when he drove.**19** I took a deep breath and sighed and decided to give it another try.**20** Concentrating on releasing the clutch and pressing the gas pedal down at the same time, I finally shifted into first gear.**21** I drove for approximately 100 meters, and before I shifted into second gear, the car stalled again; however, I was happy because I felt like I accomplished the first step of my goal – to drive the manual car.**22** I kept practicing (releasing the clutch and pressing the gas pedal) and concentrating (feet, hand, and eyes in coordination) for several hours.**23** Finally, I was able to drive out of the parking lot and onto the road without a stall.**24**

Learning to drive stick shift was not easy for me, but I did it because I didn't give up.**25** I devoted my heart, my time, and my patience to it.**26** Once I learned the driving skill, it will never be forgotten; it will stay with me for the rest of my life.**27**

Sentence Forms:
1) 3V Gerund
2) 3V Gerund; 8RN Missing *that*
3) 10TP E Prepositional Phrase
4) 7AC When; 3V Infinitive (2); 9PP Expansion Semicolon
5) 3V Gerund; 9PP Dash M Verbal Phrase; 5R Word; 2S Standard Series
6) 3V Gerund; 3V Infinitive; 6CC Yet
7) 7AC While; 3V Infinitive (2)
8) 2S The Pair
9) 6CC But; 8RN Missing *that*
10) 2S The Pair; 7AC So that supplemental
11) 9PP Explanation Colon; 9PP Difficult Semicolon / List Items With Commas; 8RN What; 3V Infinitive (4); 7AC When
12) 7AC And; 3V Infinitive
13) 3V Gerund; 9PP List Colon
14) 6AC But; 8RN Missing *that*
15) 6AC Yet
16) 9PP Stylish Semicolon
17) 6CC But; 9PP Complicated Semicolon; 3V Gerund; 6CC And
18) 8RN How
19) 2S The Pair; 7AC When
20) 2S Lyrical Series
21) 3V Present Participle (2); 3V Gerund
22) 6CC And; 7AC Before; 9PP Expansion Semicolon; 7AC Because; 9PP Dash E Verbal Phrase
23) 9PP M Verbal Phrases; 3V Gerund (4); 9PP E Words
24) 3V Infinitive
25) 3V Gerund; 3V Infinitive; 6CC But; 7AC Because
26) 2S Standard Series; 5R Word
27) 7AC Once; 9PP Association Semicolon

Poets' Places of Sanctuary

> The tea ceremonies of Japan are conceived in the spirit of the Taoist earthly paradise. The tearoom, called "the abode of fancy," is an ephemeral structure built to enclose a moment of poetic intuition. Called too "the abode of vacancy," it is devoid of ornamentation. Temporarily it contains a single picture or flower-arrangement. The teahouse is called "the abode of the unsymmetrical": the unsymmetrical suggests movement; the purposely unfinished leaves a vacuum into which the imagination of the beholder can pour."
>
> Joseph Campbell *The Hero with a Thousand Faces*

Every morning, in the isolation of his seaside, "wordsplashed" writing shed at Langharne, Dylan Thomas worked at his poems, striving for an elusive perfection. He would make as many as 500 alterations in a single poem, copying out the entire poem after each alteration, so that he could see his 'word sculpture' taking shape before his eyes. **He was a craftsman extraordinaire.** As the Dylan Thomas Boathouse website xMix elaborates:

"Alone, in his 'water and tree room', above the tidal muds or estuary waters, changing weathers and skies, sheltered by the fig tree and willowy birches, **he could sometimes be heard reciting a work, over and over, rescuing the words, counting the syllables, sounding rhymes.** As Caitlin recalled: *'When I think of that concentrated muttering and mumbling and intoning, the realms of discarded lists of rhyming words, the innumerable repetitions and revisions and how at the end of an intensive five hour stretch* [from 2-7] *prompt as clockwork, Dylan would come out very pleased with himself saying,* **he had done a good days work, and present me proudly with one or two or three perhaps fiercely belaboured lines***'."

Workspaces for the sky blue trades of Writers

The photo on the previous page of Dylan Thomas' writing cottage shows the basic furnishings required for one very creative mind to operate within: a setting close to or overlooking nature, abundant light, solid work table, some shelves, some photos, writing gear (pencils, pens, erasers), and a supply of paper. His memorable phrase of *sky blue trades* from *Fern Hill* refers to the spaces the imagination needs to work effectively so that the writer can develop their trade or skill.

Every writer's room or space will be designed or chosen according to personal preferences and other intervening factors. As a single mom, **J.K. Rowling** drafted the first Harry Potter book in many cafés in Edinburgh. **Leonard Cohen** wrote in a three-story old whitewashed building he bought on the small Greek island of Hydra. Nature buff **Annie Dillard** admits to the problem of space: *How appalled I was to discover that, in order to write so much as a sonnet, you need a warehouse.* Even so, her warehouse was more like a log cabin or toolshed. What she really wanted was a place big enough to put a 20-foot conference table in it so that she could lay out the pages of her working draft.

She whimsically describes her mundane paper-moving and need to shuffle around the table to organize her material:

> I have often "written" with the mechanical aid of a twenty-foot conference table. You lay your pages along the table's edge and pace out the work. You walk along the rows; you weed bits, move bits, and dig out bits, bent over the rows with full hands like a gardener. After a couple of hours, you have taken an exceedingly dull nine-mile hike. You go home and soak your feet.

Come to think of it – a long utility table would be of great assistance to any writer, especially when compiling an assemblage as we have.

Beryl Singleton Bissell, writer of an initial and well-received memoir *The Scent of God*, also writes in a shed, a red one. Eaz2

All of the above writers found and shaped their personal writing spaces. Many of the noted writers of process theory and basic writing pedagogy, such as **Janet Emig, Peter Elbow, Linda Miller, Donald Murray**, and **Deborah Mutnick**, have highlighted and written extensively on the importance of not only one's private writing space, but also one's participation in the local and wider discourse community.

Ray Oldenburg (*Celebrating The Third Place* 1989 and *The Great Good Place* 1991) has coined the phrase ***third place*** to refer to an informal public gathering place, a place for dialogue, a place where ideas are shared, projects hatched, insights gained, futures traded. The *first space* is one's home, and the *second* is the classroom or work place.

It is true that a person finds her or himself only in relation to others, whether that dialogue is between a writer and a reader via a book, two writers over coffee, or a doctor and a computer programmer via a skylink. But as we will see in a minute, the actual ***public third space*** becomes the most meaningful and productive compared to the virtual or textual encounters.

For example, when the pioneers of early flight, the **Wright brothers** (who had dropped out of high school), set up a print shop and started to do independent research on aeronautics, they found they could use some of their bicycle design research for their glider. As well, they kept in touch with their former classmate, the poet and writer **Paul Laurence Dunbar**. In fact, Dunbar's newspaper for the African American community *Dayton Tattler* was printed at his classmates' print shop. They (the scientists) conquered the sky and Dunbar (the poet) in his superb poetry conquered the sky blue trades. Their story is an example of cooperation across the disciplines.

One can only conjecture as to what extent the print shop provided a rich context for discussions across several trades and disciplines – shop talk, visions, plans, theories, design principles. But obviously openness led to collaboration, genuine human concern led to encouragement and drive, sharing of ideas and resources led to materialization of a vision and their mutual successes.

The work of **Robert Putnam** (*Bowling Alone: America's Declining Social Capital* 1995, *Bowling Alone: The Collapse and Revival of American Community* 2000, *Better Together* 2003) thinks such civic engagement is on the decline. His recent work EhAk focuses on ethnic diversity, trust, and the harm indifference and conflict can sometimes do to voluntary civic organizations and public space. Where there is difference or conflict, though, he sees a form of social capital, something of substance and worth. In his research, he identifies 2 kinds of social capital: ***bonding*** *capital* and ***bridging*** *capital* – the former from within a group with similar interests, and the other from within a group with individuals of different interests. Perhaps the Wright-Dunbar connection is a glowing example of the second type and shows the benefits of bridging. Where *rebuff and aloofness* are to be expected, one replaces it with *trust and candor* (Ursula LeGuin). Once true dialogue has begun, the bridging begins, and the future can be full of amazing projects and accomplishments.

George Santayana once observed in 1920 this phenomenon in *Character & Opinion in the United States*: "A neighbour, even a competitor, where the field is so large and so little pre-empted, has more often proved a resource than a danger." And "Where individuality is so free, co-operation, when it is justified, can be all the more quick and hearty. Everywhere co-operation is taken for granted, as something that no one would be so mean or so short-sighted as to refuse." **Edgar F. Beckham** in his paper *Working through Intermediaries: The New Jersey Campus Diversity Initiative* reminds us that when we use diversity as a resource, "**diverse people...**" become "**active crafters of their own learning experience. And as we know, active learners learn more.**" "**When diversity is the strategy that informs curricular change, the texture of change is rich and complex. It will not settle for mere representation of multiple cultures, each cloaked in its own terms of reference, but rather insists on critical interrogation, on intercultural interaction, on cross-cultural communication.**"(Bachetti *Reconnecting* 293)

Julie Jung mentions that one of her students called the classroom a *fake space*, a place where the teacher is in control and is always right. Such a student may dis-identify with the school and never become enamoured or enchanted with words or stories. **Erin Gruwell**'s **Freedom Writers** story clearly shows the personally transformative effect that a bit of encouragement and a bit of insight can have on lives fraught with family and parental problems that adversely affect students and how they regard school and the unreal and simplified outlook on life that is portrayed and discussed within its walls.

So the classroom *can* become a place where good writing is done. But would a dedicated space for writers be any better? **Kenneth Bruffee** in 1972 wrote a handbook to help train writing tutors and got the wheel rolling to set up Writing Resource Centers or Labs at colleges and universities. There is even now an **International Writing Centers Association** (http://writingcenters.org/).

Rhonda C. Grego and **Nancy S. Thompson** (*Teaching/Writing in Thirdspaces: The Studio Approach* 2007) prefer to call these writing centers *studios*. They maintain that the *institutional geographies and material conditions*, the classroom itself, is sometimes seen as *monolithic and beyond an individual's power for change*. For some students, small group format and change of scenery is all that is needed to bring a change of attitude. But students must learn that dependency on one's environment is one thing that good writers learn to transcend or extract themselves from, in the process of identifying with the setting or place they are creating in their writing. Writing is about being there and being who you are, but also about not being there, and finding out who you are in the process of writing.

One example of a **writing resource center** where writers' paths can cross and where writing excellence is encouraged, cultivated, and pursued is the **Hopwood Room** located at the University of Michigan. **Avery Hopwood** was a playwright who enjoyed some commercial success. Upon his passing in 1921, he left part of his estate to the University for the purpose of establishing a Writing Room. The program started in 1933. Among the facilities, one finds a main writing specialist library, some oil paintings of the founders, and an alcove library. The Program gives a full range of writing awards annually to grad and undergrad students and hosts annual lectures by notable writers on the craft of writing. Many framed photos of the speakers grace the walls.

The **Avron Foundation** in Scotland goes one courageous step further: they have not writing rooms, but *writing houses* – big stately estate mansions in the countryside – all dedicated to the mission of inspiring and equipping young minds with the tools and training necessary to create enduring works of literature. Notable writers such as Seamus Heaney, Salman Rushdie FRSL, Wole Soyinka FRSL, musician Pete Townshend, among others, support the project.

We are *creatures of discourse* (**Owen Barfield**), word wielders and welders, language labourers and linguistic engineers, surveyors and excavators of the imagination. The base and crust of the pizza of life is language; it is also the sauce of life. **Janet Emig** (*Non-Magical Thinking*) calls for "enabling environments", that are "safe, structured, private, unobstrusive, and literate," and she refers to students as "practitioners, and "providers of possible content, experiences, and feedback."

When society recognizes this most fundamental and most important role that language plays in our lives, we could see entire classrooms of students and entire populations on new planes of thought with new frames of reference, moving along ever-generative pathways of expression, navigating varied textual territories with ease.

Such initiatives to set up writing spaces have not only come from universities and foundations. I saw an example of a study center or *thirdspace* that showed a **Japanese couple's renovations** done to their house to transform the main floor into a kind of **neighbourhood learning center**. The Sunday evening TV program is called *Before After* HLgd. Although the project may have been more for quiet reading and studying, the design innovations are worth noting as they optimized the use of their limited space with some ingenious space-saving ideas.

Japan is famous for their use of sliding doors; they also have roll-away bookcases. In this particular house, along one wall, they had at least 6 or so bookcases that went from floor to ceiling. They were on heavy-duty caster wheels and thus could be rolled out and there was a handle on the outward facing side. A student tugs and rolls out the long tall bookcase to make accessible both sides of the bookcase, each side with shelves full of books. Having located the book of one's choice, the bookcase back is then pushed back into its parking slot against the wall alongside the others. They also made some large rectangular storage boxes with removable padded top lids. The dual-function boxes are used to store other reading materials and usually serve as sectional sofas and tea tables in a lounge area. Occasionally, they are rolled over to the dining area to serve as benches on which to sit when the long, nested dining table is pulled out. All the neighbourhood teen visitors can take a break when the signal is given and sit down to a communal meal or snack at the extended dining table.

With the addition of a few surfaces for writers or groups of writers to work on, such a space could easily pass for a neighbourhood or community writing center. The above sketch imaginatively captures some of the innovations featured in the show, but with the sphere and hexagonal writing stations as added features.

Would that such enclaves of creativity and invention could flourish nation-wide and planet-wide! *Word-child* is a term coined by Negev desert and kibbutz writer **Amos Oz** to describe himself as a child in a house full of books - someone ravenous to read (and now to write). Should not every child on the planet be given the best possible access so that they too can thrive in writing spaces?

10 TP Three Places Forms

This tenth form involves an understanding of **more complicated sentences**. It involves making simple or more complex additions to a sentence in one of **Three** possible **Places**. Depending on the location of the addition, these types of sentences can be grouped and labeled as:
      (1) TP - B (beginning of sentence)
      (2) TP - M (middle of sentence)
      (3) TP - E (end of sentence)

ADDITIONS AT THE BEGINNING, MIDDLE, AND END OF A SENTENCE SET OFF WITH COMMAS OR PARENTHESES

A **sentence addition** refers to something that is placed at the *beginning, middle, or end of a sentence*, and is usually separated from the rest of the sentence by a punctuation mark. The punctuation mark for the beginning and end of sentence additions is a *comma*. The punctuation mark before and after the mid-sentence addition or interruption can be a *dash* (discussed in Form 9), *comma*, or *parenthesis*. The interruption itself can be a series of appositives, an explanation, a comment, or an afterthought. The interrupting portion can be removed, and the remaining sentence makes complete sense and is grammatically correct. The information contained in the interruption is useful, therefore, but is not essential for the meaning of the sentence.

Basically, there are **25 possible kinds of additions** that can be added to the three places (locations) mentioned above.

The *beginning of the sentence* and the *end of the sentence* refer to elements placed at either or both of those two locations.

By the *middle of the sentence* is meant such possible locations as
    1) anywhere between a subject and main verb;
    2) anywhere between a main verb and its object;
    3) before a coordinating conjunction in a sentence with compound main verbs; or
    4) after another introductory interrupting element.

A chart for determining which punctuation marks are most appropriate for enclosing the interrupting mid-sentence element follows later.

10 (TP) Three Places Sentence Forms – Introduction

Additions to a sentence build it up, giving it a unique topography, adding density and greater texture. Francis Christensen explains: *If a writer adds to few of his nouns or verbs or main clauses and adds little, the texture may be said to be thin. The style will be plain or bare. The writing of most of our students is thin – even threadbare. But if he adds frequently or much or both, then the texture may be said to be dense or rich. One of the marks of an effective style, especially in narrative, is variety in the texture, the texture varying with the change in pace, the variation in texture producing the change in pace.*

He later adds: *The real problem in writing is to reconcile these two seeming opposites – to pack much into little, but to pack it so that it can be readily unpacked.*

We divide the Forms (1) according to whether additions are placed at the beginning, middle, or end of the sentence; and (2) within each of these 3 groups, **we further divide the Forms – into Primary, Secondary, or Tertiary – according to their stylistic value, their frequency of use, and ease of learning**.

Initially, instructors may choose to have students learn and practice only the Primary Sentence Forms (since they are the really essential ones) in each of the 3 groups, and later have them return to practice the Secondary and Tertiary Sentence Forms.

10 (TP) Primary Three Places Sentence Forms – Beginning

10.1	Word or multiple words	• **Loudly**, Beth spoke over the megaphone. • **Desperately**, the mouse tried to outrun the cat. • **Weary and worn-out**, the traveller looked for a cheap hotel.
10.2	Prepositional phrase	• **On my way home**, I got hit by a drunk driver. • **Across the open fields**, you could see the next village. • **After lunch**, many Chinese people take a nap.
10.3	Verbal phrase	• **Waiting for the bus**, I listened to a podcast. • **Running behind the pack**, the small wolf struggled to keep up. • **Seated on the bench**, the old man read a book.

10 (TP) Secondary Three Places Sentence Forms – Beginning

10.4	Noun phrase	•**Hat in hand**, the beggar went from door to door. •**Mind in a daze**, the student struggled to remember. •**Pen in hand**, the student sat ready to begin the examination. • **Bottle in hand**, the alcoholic voiced his discontent loudly to fellow winos in the downtown park.
10.5	Absolute construction (noun + verbal participle)	•**Heart pounding** *in anticipation*, he knocked on her front door. •**Legs pumping** *furiously*, the cyclist stormed to the finish line. • **Purse missing**, she started to panic. •**Hair flying** *in the breeze*, Nick rode his motorcycle across the outback towards Killarney. • **Homework done**, Jenny flopped onto her bed.

10 (TP) Tertiary Three Places Sentence Forms – Beginning

Three Places – beginning of sentence - tertiary

10.6	Adjective phrase adjective is header	●Familiar *with all the topics*, the student found the exam a push-over. ●Upset *after the loss,* the youth decided to seek help.
10.7	Adverb phrase or string of related words reading as a unit	●Sometimes *after rain,* I go out for a walk. ●Early *next week*, I will finish this manuscript. ●Largely *through science*, billions of us live on one small world, densely packed and intercommunicating. M.Chrichton *Jurassic Park* ●Up ahead, there was a flashing red light. ●More often than not, Carol was an open book where her thoughts and feelings were concerned. Fern Michaels *The Guest List*

BEGINNING OF SENTENCE

Beginning Sentence Primary Form 10.1:
Word at beginning of Sentence before subject and main verb

Code: 10TP B Word

Note: The word is set off by a comma. The word is usually an adverb, but it sometimes is an adjective.

Intent: The pausing gives attention to the isolated word.

Examples:

10TP B Word

adverb

- **Frantically**, Elaine searched for her I.D. card.
- **Reluctantly**, Bert obeyed his wife and went in for therapy.
- **Calmly**, the doctor explained the fatal disease to the patient.
- **Angrily**, the father beat his fist upon the wall.
- **Happily**, the little girl went outside to play.
- **Cautiously**, they looked both ways before crossing the street.
- **Carefully**, they picked up the broken glass.
- **Excitedly**, Karen opened her present.
- **Alone**, the weary traveler pedaled his bike down the long, hot, coastal roadway.
- **Finally**, I finished writing my book.
- **Remarkably**, I won a lottery. (Ha Eun-hoon, Korea)
- **Suddenly**, the building was broken down. (Eddie, Gumi, Korea, 2HA class 2001.11)
- **Recently**, many people have lost their jobs. (Eddie, Gumi, Korea, 2HA class 2001.11)

- **Blindly**, the criminal fired his gun. (Seol-Mee-ryeon of Gumi, Korea, 2HA class 2001.11)
- **Carefully**, you take care of your baby. (Song Jun Woo of Korea, 2HA class 2001.11)
- **"Previously**, humanity had to rely on solar flow and on wind, water, and animal power for its sources of energy, ..." (Jeremy Rifkin *The Biotech Century*)
- **"Year-round**, the wail and hum of traffic comes with the urban territory." (Kerry McPhedran in *The Rescuers* in Feb/Mar. 2000 issue *Elm Street*)

adjective or participle

- **Exhausted**, the soldier continued to fight.
- **"Aching**, I gave up on sleep and ventured out with my tin cup in search of coffee." (R.Solnit *Sierra* 1991 Sept/Oct.)
- **Frustrated**, she continued to stare at the blank sheet of paper, unable to compose a single sentence.
- **'United**, there is little we cannot do in a host of cooperative ventures." (John F. Kennedy in his *Inaugural Address*)
- **"Dazed**, I pulled up to my feet." (Richard Wright *The Ethics of Living Jim Crow: An Autobiographical Sketch*)

Beginning Sentence Primary Form 10.2:
Prepositional phrase at beginning of Sentence before subject and main verb (usually an adverb phrase)

Code: 10TP B Prepositional Phrase
Note: This form also includes sentence that have extended phrases at the beginning of the sentence.
Examples:

10TP B Prepositional Phrase

- **Against the odds**, I learned to write. • **In the house**, we played games. • **Above the trees**, there flew a flock of birds. • **In the distance**, we could see gazelles, zebras. • **With style and grace**, the models strolled down the runway. • **Of all the students**, Mi Gyeong is the tallest. • **On the first day of school**, I had to fill out many forms. • **On Friday**, the convention will officially open. • **During the closing decades** of the *nineteenth century*, a number of people tried to photograph motion. • **In Korean culture**, the family is the most important aspect of life. • **Along every road in the valley**, festive lanterns could be seen. • **Without the support of my husband**, my success would not have been possible. • **On a beautiful day like today**, I enjoy an outdoor barbeque. • **In response to your recent inquiry**, we hereby enclose several maps and pamphlets of Kilwa Kisiwani, and hope that you will one day be able to visit this scenic and historic spot off the coast of Tanzania. • **After the rain**, I went outside. • **Before dawn**, the fishermen set out. • **Between the two of us**, I have to admit that I find you irresistible. • "**Among living animals**, erect posture occurred only in warm-blooded mammals and birds." (Crichton *Jurassic Park*)

- "**Without this**, they will forever play catch-up, both in school and in the job market." (Carol Jago in *English Only – For the Kid's Sake*)

extended phrases

- "**At the feet of the adults**, baby velociraptors skittered and chirped." (M. Crichton *Jurassic Park*)

- **With an explanation** *in English,* the performances are from the Beijing Peking Opera Theatre.

- "**By the light** *of a melon slice of moon*, Yiban told us the news." (Amy Tan *The Hundred Secret Senses*)

- "**In sunny Singapore where the heat never lets up**, it's no surprise that fruit juice bars and takeaway counters have sprouted up along Orchard Road and the business district like oases in a desert." (from *Straits Times* -web page removed - accessed 2002.03.05)

- "**Among some species** *of stalk-eyed flies*, the guy with the longer eye stems gets the girl." (from *Female flies pick mates with sexy eyes* in *Science News* 1998.01.17)

- **According to bylaw 230(a)** *in the jurisdiction of Hastings County*, we hereby give you notice that the icicles hanging dangerously from your eaves must be removed before they break off and hurt someone.   **Beside this man** *in blue flannel shirt, baggy khaki trousers, uneven suspenders, and vile felt hat*, she was small and exquisite.
(Sinclair Lewis *Main Street*)

prepositional phrase with verbal object

- **After cleaning my teeth**, I combed my hair and put on my makeup.   **After seeing the doctor**, the patient had her prescription filled at the pharmacy.   **After brushing my teeth**, I flossed and rinsed with mouthwash.   **After passing the security check**, the traveler went to the immigration desk to get clearance to exit the country.

- **On learning that Sung Min had got a higher mark than me on the last test**, I resolved to study non-stop in preparation for the next test.   **In order to understand the case**, the lawyer hired a detective to get more information.   **In order to do these sentences right**, I need to use the correct subordinate adverbial conjunction.   **Before dating Julie**, Tom had never had a girlfriend for more than three months.   **While riding on the

commuter train, you can also read a book or newspaper. • (extended) **Wanting to eat better,** *have more energy, and of course lose weight*, the participants each made some adjustments in their already demanding lives.

Beginning Sentence Primary Form 10.3:
Verbal Phrase at the Beginning of a Sentence
Code: 10TP B Verbal Phrase Present/Past Participle or Infinitive
Notes: Verbals (present or past participles) and their attendant words or phrases start off this type of addition.
Examples:

> **10TP B Verbal Phrase** Present / Past Participle or Infinitve

• **Outlining her stand on taxes**, the politician received a standing ovation. • **Leaning on the fence**, the cowboy surveyed the herd of cattle. • **Looking into each other's eyes**, the young couple saw the most beautiful sight that was better than any website or historical site that a packaged tour could offer to any place in the world. • **Leaving a tip** *on the table*, I put my coat on, paid the bill, and slipped out into the inky night. • **Reaching the summit** *of Mt. Gumoh*, the hikers had a magnificent view of the city of Gumi. • **Waiting for the bus**, I studied Hausa [language of Nigeria]. • **Having been neglected as a child**, the young man did not know how to be compassionate.

- **Writing all night**, the student finished the essay.
- **Thrashing back and forth in the swimming pool**, the boy shouted for help.
- **Meowing loudly**, the cat kept scratching at the pantry door.
- **Jolted by the shock of the electric fence,** the wandering elephant walked away quickly from the village compound.
- **Born of a movie projectionist father and an amateur actress mother**, Qin learned to dance at the Local Children's Palace not long after she was able to walk.
- **Founded in 1909**, the Beijing Library has remained open 365 days a year since 1998.
- **To dry the** clothes, she hung them on the balcony in the sun.
- **To repel the mosquitoes**, she soaked her mosquito netting in the special pesticide.

Beginning Sentence Secondary Form 10.4:
Noun Phrase at the Beginning of a Sentence

Code: 10TP B Noun Phrase

Note: We will introduce two types of **noun phrases** and one type of **appositive phrase** that can be placed at the beginning of sentences:

Examples:

10TP B Noun Phrase

- **Umbrella in hand**, I headed out into the misty morning rain.
- **Hat in hand**, the beggar went from door to door.
- **Diploma in hand**, the graduate stepped down from the stage and smiled for the photographers.
- **Arm in arm**, the newlyweds walked triumphantly down the busy Vancouver street.
- **Money in short supply**, the family had to economize on everything.
- **Hand in hand,** the couple walked dreamily through the park.
- **Wildflowers everywhere**, the children reveled and played on the Alpine mountain slope.
- **Arms akimbo**, my mother waited at the top of the stairs with a very serious expression on her face.
- Brightly colored tissue **caps on each head**, the children celebrated their friend's birthday in a fun and festive style.

Beginning Sentence Secondary Form 10.5: Absolute Construction at the Beginning of a Sentence

Code: 10TP B Absolute Construction
Examples:

10TP B Absolute Construction (noun + participle)

- **Cap switched** *backwards*, the youth spent some time skateboarding in the mall parking lot.
- **Poncho slung** *over his shoulders*, Pedro climbed over the Mexican hills in the cool morning mist.
- *Her* **adornments twinkling** *in the bright lights*, the model flashed a serious smile for the photographers.
- *His* **blanket torn**, Linus cried on Charlie Brown's shoulder.
- **Pistols drawn**, the cops were going to shoot the suspect.
- **Teeth clenched**, she held on as the roller coaster ride began.
- *His* **legs aching**, the soldier finished the fifteen kilometer cross-country march.
- "*Its electric* **motor whirring**, the cart raced forward down the dark underground tunnel." (M.Crichton *Jurassic Park*)
- **Feet shod** *in a new pair of high-tech runners*, I ran outside to catch the school bus.
- **Face beaming and arms waving**, the child ran to greet her father, clutching her new report card in her hand.
- **Plasma adscreens buzzing and chirping** *all along the metro platform*, the commuters waited.

Beginning Sentence Tertiary Form 10.6:
Adjective String at the Beginning of a Sentence
Code: 10TP B Adjective Phrase
Examples:

10TP B Adjective Phrase

- *Late for class*, the student went to the principal's office to get a note.
- *Limp and paralyzed in one leg at the age of two,* Wilma Rudolph conquered polio and the taunts and jibes of her high school classmates, and went on to become the first women ever to win three gold medals in one Olympiad.
- "*Pale, shivering, with rigid features and compressed lips,* she looked an entirely altered being from the soft and timid creature she had been hitherto." (H. Beecher Stowe *Uncle Tom's Cabin*)

Beginning Sentence Form 10.7:
Adverb Phrase at the Beginning of a Sentence
Code: 10TP B Adverb Phrase
Examples:

10TP B Adverb Phrase

- *Early yesterday morning,* the scout group packed up and slipped away in their canoes to a new frontier.
- *Sometime next week,* I have to finish typing my report and hand it in.

- ***Perhaps**, as a result of all her training,* Li is now a strong-minded and independent woman. - "***Largely** through science,* billions of us live on one small world, densely packed and intercommunicating." (Crichton *Jurassic Park*) - "***Up** ahead,* the rectangular maintenance shed emerged from the fog." (Crichton *Jurassic Park*) - "***More** often than not,* Carol was an open book where her thoughts and feelings were concerned." (Fern Michaels *The Guest List*) - "***Properly** executed,* any of these methods can work." (Carol Jago *English Only – For the Kid's Sake* in *The Contemporary Reader* 6/e) - ***Overly** excited on her birthday,* the child ran constantly to look out the front bay window to see who was arriving next for her party.

<u>variation</u>

- "***Moments later**,* Donovan came in from the garage." (Fern Michaels *The Guest List*) - *Last **Friday** while leaving,* I noticed a yellow envelope on the defendant's desk.

10(TP) Mid-Sentence Interruptions
Set Off with Paired Punctuation Marks

A chart for determining which punctuation marks are most appropriate for enclosing an interruption in the middle of sentences is given below:

Three Punctuation Marks to Set Off Interruptions			
Covered In ...	Punctuation Mark	Property or Nickname	Intended Literary Effect
Form 9	**dash** (non-list)	the *emphasized, outstanding or highlighted* comment	used to highlight, emphasize, or make conspicuous the addition
Form 10	**comma**	the *simply expressed, usual or normal* comment	used for regular, ordinary, or mild emphasis
Form 10	**parenthesis**	the *whispered, very slightly emphasized* comment	whispers or very slightly emphasizes the addition, almost as an afterthought or an aside

Mid-Sentence Interruptions in Form 10 Set Off with Paired Commas and Parentheses

In the previous section of the forms of Dashes in the Middle of the sentence (Form 9.d), we looked at the use of the dash to punctuate mid-sentence interruptions. In this form, we look at the use of the second and third punctuation marks (commas and parentheses) used as pairs to separate the interruption from the main part of the sentence.

A **pair of commas** or a **pair of parentheses** is used to set off a word, phrase, or clause placed in the middle of a sentence. This addition could be called an *interruption*. This means that the flow of the kernel or core part of the sentence has been deliberately interrupted somewhere about midway with the intention of adding some information that supplements in a major or minor way the information in the core part of the sentence.

In both cases, one should make sure that the inserted interruption **adds to the main idea**. Occasionally, the interruption is a kind *of candid remark from the writer*, generously offering us a tidbit of helpful or even surprising optional background information.

Primary 10 (TP) Three Places Sentence Forms – Middle

10.8	Word	● I regret to say, **however**, that I will be going away soon. ● It is, **undoubtedly**, the best example yet.
10.9	Noun phrase	● They lay in the shade, **their coats** *as pillows*, and talked of when they were young and carefree. ● She walked on, **the heavy pot** *of water on her head*, for still another hour before she reached home.
10.10	Appositive Phrase	● Zuda (**a herb** *from the Amazon jungle*) can cure cancer. ● Eva, **an undergrad** *at Jinan*, is in fine arts. ● Tom and Jerry (**enemies** *since their creation*) are still cartoon favorites.
10.11	Adjective phrase	● The parents, **certain that their son was lost**, looked for the nearest police station. ● Sobs, **heavy and loud**, shook the chair. [Harriet Beecher Stowe in *Uncle Tom's Cabin*]

Secondary 10 (TP) Three Places Sentence Forms – Middle

10.12	Prepositional phrase	• Juanita, **in her first film**, is simply astonishing. • The new student, **from South America**, was warmly welcomed by the class.
10.13	Verbal Phrase	• The girl scouts, **preparing for their trip**, talked excitedly. • A mother, **loving and caring** *for her children*, cannot be replaced.
10.14	Absolute construction	• They travelled at night, **the moonlight shining down**, on foot, by horse, by train. • She danced, **her mind fixed** *on every aspect of her routine*, and went on to win.

Tertiary 10 (TP) Three Places Sentence Forms – Middle

10.15	Adverb phrase	• Delaney's Delight (**always a good bet**) won the race with ease. • The police car, **like a cheetah running after its prey**, chased the speeding truck.
10.16	Insertion	• "All car owners," **he said**, "should have their car checked." [identifying speaker signal, dialogue in quotation marks] • She's better off now (**isn't she?**) than she was before. [anecdotal remark] • Ronald Reagan was an effective communicator (**some would say just a good storyteller**) when he served as president. [anecdotal remark]

Punctuation Marks for Middle of Sentence

Recall our chart of the punctuation marks that are used to demarcate additions:

Three Punctuation Marks to Set Off Additions		
Punctuation Mark	**Property or Nickname**	**Intended Literary Effect**
dash (non-list)	the *comment with flair*	used to highlight, emphasize, or make conspicuous the addition
comma	the *comment that clarifies*	used for regular, ordinary, or mild emphasis
parenthesis	the *comment that whispers*	whispers or very slightly emphasizes the addition, almost as an afterthought or an aside

One may ask how to know which punctuation should be used to set off or enclose an addition. A student must choose whether to use **dashes** or **commas** or **parentheses** for each mid-sentence addition. In each case, the student should **read the sentence aloud**, and try to note the degree of emphasis that is placed on the addition. As you go down the above chart, the degree of emphasis on the addition decreases; the presence of the addition is more subdued.

Some of the punctuation marks, along with the sentence length and the amount of branching, collectively act in a way as an **emotional barometer**. Through them, the intensity and tone of the writer's spoken voice and mood comes through together with the message of the words. For example, abrupt, short sentences ending in periods may indicate tension or anxiety or panic, or in the case of a beginning learner of English — shyness; an exclamation mark shows excitement or surprise; question marks reflect the speaker's curiosity; a dash or pair of dashes could show pride or congeniality on the part of the writer for including something just thought of that suddenly seems special and relevant; a semi-colon can show a logical or rational approach to the topic at hand; a long, branching or complex sentence can indicate that one is almost wallowing in delight in talking about the subject matter at hand, and has no problem in stitching together the component pieces that are intelligible and interesting into lengthy sentences.

Middle Sentence Primary Form 10.8:
Interrupting Word at middle of Sentence
Code: 10TP M Word
Note: A word set off by a pair of commas.
Examples:

10TP M Word

- The lioness, **surreptiously**, paused by the thicket and watched the gazelle in the distance.
- I understood, **clearly**, what you meant.
- Yee Yeong, **carefully**, jumped over the vase.
- "He could hear them, **faintly**, on the other side of the door." (Crichton)
- I regret to say, **unfortunately**, that your job performance is far below par.
- Between them sat three half-buried bluish spheres-the eggs , **presumably** , of some desert monstrosity. (David W. Goldman *Reunion*)
- Tawantinsuyu , **evidently**, consisted of an empire center at Cuzco with the four *suyus* (regions) placed to the north, south, east, and west.

Middle Sentence Form Primary 10.9:
Noun Phrase at Middle of Sentence
Footnote Code: TP M Noun Phrase
Examples:

10TP M Noun Phrase

- Jim and Jane lay in the shade, *their **coats** under their heads*, talking very little. • Jane walked slowly, *a **grocery bag** under each arm*, thankful that there was enough food for the next week. • Bill, *his **wallet** now gone*, stood at the corner wondering what to do next.

Middle Sentence Primary Form 10.10:
Appositive Phrase at Middle of Sentence
Code: 10TP M Appositive Phrase
Note: In most cases, the header or controlling word is usually the first word in the phrase, but for the appositive, there are often one or more adjectives in front of it.
Examples:

10TP M Appositive Phrase

- The Cowboys, *America's favorite football **team***, are riddled with criminal problems. • Tracy, *both a masculine and feminine **name***, was the name they chose for their son. • We, *the **staff** of Earlybird English magazine*, are starting a new column next month especially for you. • They took a pedicab, *a **tricycle** with a wide enclosed back seat and a driver who has to peddle very hard*, back to the hotel.

parentheses

- Sarah (*once a brilliant **writer***) is now a housewife.
- Tom and Jerry (***enemies** since their creation*) are still cartoon favorites.
- My class project (*A **Model** of the Solar System*) won the Science and Math competition.
- A herbal drink (*a **mixture** of honey, boiled onion roots, and ginger*) helped clear up his cold and sore throat quickly.
- The Worldmapper website ₍EyJF₎ produces density-equalizing maps (**equal area cartograms**) that re-size each territory according to the data values for the variable (**literacy, longevity**, etc) being mapped.

Middle Sentence Primary Form 10.11:
Adjective Phrase at middle of Sentence
Code: 10TP M Adjective Phrase
Examples:

10TP M Adjective Phrase

- The traveler, **certain that she was lost**, looked for the nearest police station.
- The young man, **happy at the thought of seeing her again**, counted away the days and hours remaining until they would meet.
- The Christmas tree, **tall and glowing with strings of lights**, gave the living room a wonderful pine scent.
- "The animal's huge leathery wings, **translucent in the sunlight**, flapped broadly on both

sides of her." (M. Crichton)   • The marathoner, **fit and long-winded from hours of pounding the pavement**, moved into the lead in the last kilometer, and never looked back.

• Tom, **resolute and firm**, told the workers that they would have to improve production or else face layoffs.

Middle Sentence Secondary Form 10.12:
Prepositional phrase at middle of Sentence
(usually an adverb phrase or extended phrase)
Code: TP 10M Prepositional Phrase
Examples:

10TP M Prepositional Phrase

• They heard the news, **over the loudspeaker**, at noon the next day. • Her eyes, **like two luminous stars**, can pull you with the gravity of black holes. • I went to my hometown last weekend, **by bus**, and had a great time with all my middle school buddies.   • I wrote my answers recklessly, **in a hurry and without thinking**, and immediately regretted that I hadn't studied more.   • Tyrone, **because of his past criminal record**, was prevented from entering the civil service. • The horses, **in the solitude** *of their stalls in the barn*, pricked up their ears when they heard the sound of footsteps. • The porcelain doll, **of unknown origin**, fascinated archeologists far and wide. • When I was a freshman, **in 1994**, I drank and played pool a lot. (Ha Eun Hoon, Korea) • Martha, **because of her weight**, was unable to join the military. "They are, **according to the tags clipped to their pockets**, obstetricians, gynecologists, pediatricians, pediatric nurse practitioners, and pediatric RNs." (Dillard *For the Time Being*) • "And sure enough, our mouths, **like those fireflies**, bobbed and weaved toward each other." (Amy Tan *The Hundred Secret Senses*) • The baby, **after gurgling and cooing like a little doll**, slept peacefully through the night.

use of parentheses

• The music **(like a choir of angels)** brings tears to my eyes. • Enthusiasts **(of all shapes and sizes)** crowded together at the starting line of the Boston Marathon.
• Many of the 49 percent **(of women earning $100,000 or more who are childless)** don't want children now and probably not in the future.

Middle Sentence Secondary Form 10.13:
Verbal phrase at middle of Sentence
Code: 10TP M Verbal Phrase
Examples:

10TP M Verbal Phrase

- The team coach, **wearing a new black sweatsuit**, called the players into the change room for an important discussion.
- There he sat, **rocking back and forth** *in the hammock*, in the cool shade of the porch at the front of the big old house built by his grandfather.
- The wind, **giving us now a favor**, changed direction, and we were able to sail home.
- The H_2 comes from a chemical reaction, **called dissociation**, that splits the hydrogen from water.
- A mother, **loving and caring** *toward her children*, cannot be replaced.
- A picture, **taken professionally**, can be beautiful.
- The boy scouts, **preparing themselves** *for their camping trip*, could not wait until the following day.
- Magnolias and cherry blossoms, **blooming beautifully** *at the start of spring*, gracefully enhanced the campus garden.
- A single open staircase, **lit by clerestory windows above**, joins the two floors mid-building." (Kerry McPhedran in Feb/Mar. 2000 issue *Elm Street*)

- "International Women's Day, **first held in 1911**, is celebrated on March 8." _(Judy Rebick *Radical Chic* Feb/Mar. 2000 issue *Elm Street*)

parentheses

- The thief **(thinking he could scale the fence)** ran to the brick wall at the end of the alleyway.
- The mouse **(shaking like a leaf)** cowered in the corner.
- NewTurf's excellent investment profits **(made mostly from real estate)** have doubled in the last five years.

Middle Sentence Secondary Form 10.14:
Absolute Construction at Middle of Sentence

Code: 10TP M Absolute Construction
Note: Absolute construction consists of noun followed by a participle and its attendant words.
Examples:

10TP M Absolute Construction

- The trekkers, **backpacks bulging** *with tents and supplies*, pressed on to the second base camp.
- Tony and Suzy, **arms** *clasped like ivy tendrils around each other*, danced and slinked slowly and dreamily around the dimly lit cafetorium dance floor, while up front the saxophone wailed and moaned like a lonely nightingale.
- "Abby stood, **her foot rooted** to the concrete, until the yellow cab was swallowed up in traffic." _(Fern Michaels *The Guest List*)
- "After they left the hotel, **fingers interlocked,** they entered dirt roads to walk slowly

past yellow bungalows and shafts of deep green Nipa palm."

(Peter Bollington *Salvos*)

Middle Sentence Tertiary Form 10.15:
Adverb String at middle of Sentence
Code: 10TP M Adverb Phrase
Examples:

10TP M Adverb Phrase

- "The Inka homeland, **uniquely high**, was also uniquely steep, with slopes of more than sixty-five degrees from the horizontal." (Charles C. Mann *1491: New Revelations of the Americas Before Columbus*)
- The newborn giraffe, **awkwardly adjusting to the world outside the womb**, stood momentarily on all fours, but then fell down when he tried to prance.
- She moved, **gracefully and without exception**, and showered each and every party guest with the warmth of her radiance and samples of her ample wit and latest cooking.
- The shuttle, **like a needle pointing to the stars**, blasted off at daybreak.
- "He would stand with his arms straight out, **like a ghost** *walking in the night*, claiming that the spirit of nature now flowed from the tree's limbs into his." (Amy Tan *The Hundred Secret Senses*)

parentheses

- Jane (**once thought to be very beautiful**) is now old.

- A handful of terrorists (**obviously with fewer options available day by day**) started to talk with one another about surrendering.
- She has been relishing an amazing week after inking a deal for her memoirs (**reportedly seven figures**) with PushPull Press.

Middle Sentence Tertiary Form 10.16:
Middle Sentence – Anecdotal Insertion
Code: 10TP M Insertion
Note: This consists of indirect personal quotations, or narrator or writer or discourse comments.

Anecdotal refers not to a whole story but *to the narrator of a story or writer of an essay who interrupts their narrative or essay with either a personal observation or amplification, or a personal comment, aside, or addition.* Such comments serve to involve the reader more intimately with the author and lend a nuance, tonality, and effective flow to the writing.

An anecdotal insertion also lends itself to designating and referring to third-party comments and observations relevant to the text itself. This second type of anecdotal interrupter records or reports indirectly and not verbatim someone's spoken or written words or idea(s).

Quoting someone's exact words as is often done in a story or news article is another type of anecdotal insertion. If the quoted part is split or is put at the beginning of the sentence, often the interrupting part or the part at the end identifies the speaker and can even indicate something of their manner of speaking.

Such constructs are indicative of the presence of the author's unique voice, tone, and style of writing, and serve to engage the reader with the author and keep the reader's attention and focus.

Examples:

10.16 10TP M Insertion

commas

- Someone, **she was sure**, would notice. • There is no way, **you see**, that he could have done it. • The Friday night games, **mark me well**, are always exciting. [anecdotal statement] • Korean spicy soup, **I'll have you know**, is one of my favorite dishes. [writer comment]

quotation marks and comma

- "All car owners," **he said**, "should have their car checked." [identifying speaker signal, dialogue in quotation marks] • "Get a move on," **Mom shouted**, "or you'll be late!" [speaker identification and tone, dialogue in quotation marks]

parenthesis

- Through an oversight **(or else probably, if you think about it, just plain politeness)**, they don't weigh the passengers. (Barbara Kingsolver *The Poisonwood Bible*) [writer comment] • She's better off now **(isn't she?)** than she was before. [anecdotal remark] • Ronald Reagan was an effective communicator **(some would say just a good storyteller)** as president. [anecdotal remark]

dashes – (another use of the mid-sentence dash –this could have been introduced as a supplemental Form 9.8).

In each of the following, the phrase or clause appearing between the dashes is **an additional and suddenly occuring thought that may have initially been thought irrelevant but suddenly is considered important,** or **a missing fact that just surfaced and is considered essential.** The new thought is considered to be important for purposes of relevancy or clarity or detail, so the thought is immediately spliced into the sentence at the next most suitable pause point. So, we can call this the *suddenly relevant and appearing afterthought insertion*.

Another possibility is that the speaker needs a moment to gather his or her thoughts together, and such a clause as *let me see* or *wait a minute* would be inserted after the beginning of the sentence.

The last possibility is a kind of aside or tipoff or comment by the writer on a more direct level to the reader than the normal narrative writer's point of view (narrative position).

- It was – **let me see** – around the middle of February when I was there. [thinking pause clause]
- Our debt – **let me see** if I can get this right – is ballooning at the rate of $300 billion dollars per year. [thinking pause clause]
- We had set up the string to catch the traffickers and – **as I found out later that day** – they caught Johnny Jingo at the airport trying to board a private jet. [future event tipoff, writer comment]
- Lincoln was shot in the back of the head on a

Friday – **in fact, it was Good Friday** – while he was sitting next to his wife. *(The Wit and Wisdom of Abraham Lincoln edited by Alex Ayres)* `[vital information insertion]`

third party speech (reporter) – in this case we learn who has said something, what exactly was said, and perhaps something of the manner in which it was said.

● In our time, **says a twentieth-century Hasidic rabbi**, we are in a coma. *(Annie Dillard)* ● The attempt to reestablish tuatara may provide insights into restocking other reptile populations on islands or in other ecosystems where they've been eliminated, **says Daugherty**, who described the project at last summer's meeting of the Society for Conservation Biology in Victoria, British Columbia. *(Christine Mlot Return of the Tuatara in Science News Vol. 152 1997.11.8)* ● This small house of Pascal's, **I realized**, was identical in material and design to the house in which he lived. *(Barbara Kingsolver The Poisonwood Bible)* ● The economy had gone into a slump, **they said**, and there was little hope of a short-term recovery."

Primary 10 (TP) Three Places Sentence Forms – End

10.17	Word	• The refugee lay on the deck, **unconscious**. • I stood there, **stunned**.

Secondary 10 (TP) Three Places Sentence Forms – End

10.18	Noun phrase	• He ate his dinner, **broccoli and all**. • He faced towards Mecca, **mind and soul as one**.
10.19	Prepositional phrase	• The Iraqi family departed in the night, **with only a few possessions**. • I finally finished my work, **despite the many tasks**.
10.20	Appositive phrase	• I'd like you to meet Mr. Pak, **my manager**. • You should climb Mt. Kilimanjaro, **the tallest mountain in Africa**.
10.21	Verbal phrase	• They decorated the Christmas tree, **adding lights, baubles, and tinsel**. • I could feel the rain, **falling gently on me**. • It was a rough trip (**to say the least**).
10.22	Absolute construction noun + participle	• They walked slowly, **minds filled** *with dreams of a life together*. • "It snarled, **the sound echoing** *in the darkness*." Crichton Jurassic Park 314

Tertiary 10 (TP) Three Places Sentence Forms – End

10.23	Adjective phrase	● May shrugged, **indifferent to Al's angry words.** ● She smiled, **happy to see her.**
10.24	Adverb phrase	● I can finish it, **probably by Thursday.** ● He moved along the path, **completely hidden from view.**
10.25	Insertion	● "Everyone will be affected." [quotation] ● They want to celebrate in a big way, **I think.** [writer comment] ● This will protect the city from future flooding, **she emphasized.** [identifying speaker signal]

END OF SENTENCE

End Sentence Primary Form 10.17:
Word at End of Sentence
Code: 10TP E Word
Examples:

10TP E Word

● The boxer laid on the mat, **unconscious**. ● The Korean middle school student put his head on his desk, **overwhelmed**. ● "Ellie held the radio in her hands, **listening**." (Crichton *Jurassic Park*) ● "Hermione remained with her face lifted up, **abstracted**." (D.H. Lawrence *Women in Love*) ● "He looked at her with a long, slow look, **malevolent, supercilious**." (D.H. Lawrence) ● "The foreigners liked to eat hot and cold things together, very **unhealthy**." (Amy Tan *The Hundred Secret Senses*) ● "She started out and stopped in the doorway, **smiling**." (V.C. Andrews *Ice*)

End Sentence Secondary Form 10.18:
Noun Phase at End of Sentence
Code: 10TP E Noun Phrase
Examples:

10TP E Noun Phrase

- She stood there, **arms** *akimbo*.
- Grant drove, *his* **foot** *to the floor*. (Crichton *Jurassic Park*)
- The racing car went by, *a deafening* **blur**.
- "On the Saturday it rained, *a soft drizzling* **rain** *that held off at times.*" (D.H. Lawrence)
- The student struggled to finish the exam, **head** *in a daze*.
- The baby tested her new mobility, *pudgy* **feet** and *tiny* **hands** *all here and there in the air*.
- The afternoon ride home was tortuous, **pollution** *and traffic jams and bumper to bumper creeping*.
- The blues signer's fingers flew and danced over the strings and fret board, **testimony** *to the hours of practice done by her*.

End Sentence Secondary Form 10.19:
Prepositional Phrase at End of Sentence
Code: 10TP E Prepositional Phrase
Examples:

> **10TP E Prepositional Phrase**

- He fought it, **like a lion.**
- The student waited for the late bus, **for about 40 minutes.**
- "One reached up and scratched his head, **with a five-fingered hand.**" (M. Crichton)
- "Pete was calling his name again and again, **with increasing panic.**" (S. King *Dreamcatcher*)
- "All her suppressed, subconscious fear sprang into being, **with anguish.**" (D.H. Lawrence *Women in Love*)
- "Soon they were chittering all around him, **like excited birds.**" (Crichton *Jurassic Park*)
- Sheena was going to perform a five-minute solo act using a silk red handkerchief and an umbrella as props, **while dancing to specific Ilokano folk dance routines.**
- I used to change my hairstyle, but now I hardly ever change it, **aside from hair color.**

extended phrase

- She spent most of her childhood taking music and dancing lessons, **at a time** when most children her age were having fun.
- "And the guy just stood there in his underwear, **like**

an android *whose memory circuits have been about three-quarters erased."* (King *Dreamcatcher*)

● "The Indians were descendents of ancient hunters who migrated from Asia to America across the Bering land bridge some thirty to forty thousand years ago, **about the time** *migrants elsewhere were settling the British Isles."* (Robert V. Hine and John Mack Faragher *The American West*)   ● "One reason is that black women are starved to see themselves portrayed in motion pictures as real people, **with the whole range** *of human emotions."* (Dorothy Gilliam in *Breathing Easier with a Rare Film* in *The Contemporary Reader* ed. by G.Goshgarian)   ● "In this movie food is on her mind and she forgets all about work, **except for an occasional phone call** *to see how everything is going."* (bell hooks in *Mock Feminism* in *The Contemporary Reader* ed. by G.Goshgarian)   ● "'I'm every woman, it's all in me,' Chaka Khan sings, and the chords in the bass modulate optimistically upward, **in a surge of possibility.**" (Holly Brubach *Heroine Worship: the Age of the Female Icon* in *The Contemporary Reader*)   ●"Scientists have since unearthed Clovis points and choppers at diggings **from** Montana **to** Mexico, Nova Scotia to Arizona." (Robert V. Hine and John Mack Faragher *The American West*)

variation This form has a clause as the object of a preposition.

● He had to do plenty of physical training, some **of which was martial arts**.   ● "Our elderly bellhops push us aside and with mighty huffs finish dragging in our suitcases and duffel bags, the bottoms **of which are spattered with mud**." (=*of which the bottoms are spattered with mud*) (Amy Tan *The Hundred Secret Senses*)   ● "In one L.A. school district alone, teachers have to gather and instruct students from 80 different nationalities, just 13% **of whom speak English as their first language**." (Rolando Flores Acosta in *Seeking Unity in Diversity* in *The Contemporary Reader* 6/e)

End Sentence Form 10.20:
Appositive Phrase at End of Sentence
Code: 10TP E Appositive Phrase
Examples:

10TP E Appositive Phrase

● They hired Belinda, *a top honors cum laude* **graduate** *from Buffalo University who was also valedictorian for her class*.   ● I met Jake, *the local fire* **chief**.   ● I'd like you to meet Mr. Pak, **one** *of my supervisors*.   ● You should climb Mt. Kilimanjaro, *the tallest* **mountain** *in Africa*.   ● Our new neighbour is really interesting, *a* **gal** *from Minnesota*.   ● The arcology in Arizona was designed by Paolo Soleri, *an Italian-born* **architect** *who came to America* *in the 1950s to apprentice under Frank Lloyd Wright.*

● *On these meridians there are 365 acupuncture points,* **one** *for each day of the year.*   ● *I'm pleased to introduce to you the well-known author of more than three dozen science fiction stories,* **Adrian Bruzinski**.   ● *She played the role of "daoma dau", the* **role** *of a female who has martial arts skills in a Peking Opera.*   ●*The concerts will star Li Yundi, a young but talented Chinese* **pianist** *who won first prize at the 14th International Chopin Competition in Warsaw in 2000.*

● *New York State became formally known as the "Empire State", hence the* **name** *for the Empire State Building.*   ●*The people might be frightening, but their world would surely be a paradise, a golden* **land** *somewhere beyond the setting sun.* (Robert V. Hine and John Mack Faragher *The American West*)   ● *"These times of ours are ordinary times, a* **slice** *of life like any other."* (Annie Dillard *For the Time Being*)   ●*"At noon I stopped for the day and took my recreation by flitting all about with the bees and the butterflies and reveling in the flowers, those beautiful* **creatures** *that catch the smile of God out of the sky and preserve it!"* (Mark Twain *Eve's Diary*)

End Sentence Secondary Form 10.21:
Verbal Phrase at End of Sentence
Code: 10TP E Verbal Phrase
Examples:

10TP E Verbal Phrase

- Daisies and tulips are so beautiful, **growing** *gracefully in the country fields.*
- "It looked like an ice cream vendor's push-cart, **parked** *incongruously on the badlands."* (Crichton *ibid*)
- "Columbus called the people of the Caribbean *los Indios,* mistakenly **thinking** *he had arrived in the East Indies."* (Robert V. Hine & John Mack Faragher *ibid*)
- "Within half a century "Indian" had passed into English, used to refer to all Native Americans, *ridiculously* **lumping** *together Aztec militarists, Hopi communalists, and Pequot horticulturalists."* (*ibid*)
- "But beyond the misty horizons of dreams was a real world, **throbbing** *with human possibility."* (*ibid*)
- "Previously, humanity had to rely on solar flow and on wind, water, and animal power for its sources of energy, **setting upper** *limits to the amount of economic activity that could be generated."* (Jeremy Rifkin *The Biotech Century*)
- Tom finally reached the base camp, *completely* **exhausted** *by the descent down the rugged mountain.*
- "An ice cream tuck overtook them **dinging** *a melody and children rushed to it."* (Peter Bollington *Salvos*)
- "Trawlers, the mega-bulldozers of the sea, drag giant,

weighted nets along the ocean floor, **destroying** everything in their path. (Robert Bateman) • "The DNA acts as a scaffold for the silver, **enabling** the scientists to make thinner wires than they can with conventional techniques." (C.W. in Grainy wire self-assembles along DNA in Science News Vol. 153 1998.4.4)

• The car moved swiftly down the country road, **kicking dust** in every direction and causing many of the hikers to cough and gag. • All of the rehabilitation and flight training rooms are constructed with the raptors' welfare in mind, each **equipped** with adjustable lighting, heating, ventilation, and easy cleaning features. • "The hypsy was small dryosaur, seven feet long, **weighing** about five hundred pounds." (Crichton Jurassic Park) • "Later I lay in my room, still not thinking about Miss Banner, **refusing** to give her one piece of my worry or anger or sadness." (Amy Tan The Hundred Secret Senses) • Thirty-six of the generals were women, **including the Trung sisters' mother.** • "It loomed in the shadows and corners of our Philadelphia apartment like bats sleeping, **waiting** to be nudged, disturbed." (V.C. Andrews Ice) • The huge crowd marched towards the palace, **tired of all the corruption** and empty promises. • "Instead he attacks with a pump fake, **turning a defender's legs** into jelly and then burying a jump shot." (Nelson George in *Rare Jordan* in *The Contemporary Reader* 6/e by Gary Goshgarian) • "Winter just seemed to be stubborn, **refusing** *to be driven off*." (V.C. Andrews *Ice*)

End Sentence Secondary Form 10.22:
Absolute Construction at End of Sentence
Code: 10TP E Absolute Construction
Examples:

10TP E Absolute Construction

- The dog stood, **tail** *wagging*. • "The crowd is up, **heads** *weaving* *for better views*." (Don DeLillo *Underworld*) • "At the door Dante turned round violently and shouted down the room, *her* **cheeks** *flushed and* ***quivering*** *with rage*." (James Joyce *Portrait of the Artist as a Young Man*) •"The banks of the river closed in on both sides, *the* **trees** *meeting* *overhead once more*. (Crichton *Jurassic Park*)
- "...he rolled away in flight, *his* **flashlight** ***swinging*** *wildly*." (Crichton *Jurassic Park*) •"It snarled, *the* **sound** ***echoing*** *in the darkness*." (Crichton in *Jurassic Park*) •"The lobby was quiet, *chilly* **fog** ***drifting*** *past them.* (Crichton in *Jurassic Park*)
- "Some of the hypsilophodonts were chewing, *the* **jaws** ***working***." (Crichton *Jurassic Park*) •"They looked up at the long, low house, dim and glamorous in the wet morning, *its cedar* **trees** ***slanting*** *before the windows*." (DH Lawrence *Women in Love*) • The

student dormitory room looked a mess, **books** *and* **papers** ***strewn*** *everywhere.* ●"He froze in place, most of his weight thrown forward on his good left leg, **rifle *raised*, barrel *angled*** *down that interlacing tunnel of light at a cool thirty-five degrees."* (Stephen King *Dreamcatcher*) ● "Two flickering bugs were zigzagging their way toward each other, *their* **attraction *looking*** *haphazard yet predestined."* (Amy Tan *The Hundred Secret Senses*) ●"'What do you mean, a date?' I asked, *my* **heart *thudding*** *like a fist on stone."* (V.C. Andrews *Ice*) ● "She glared at me a moment and then she stepped farther into my room, *her* **eyes *heating*** *over, her* **jaw *tightening****, her* **hands *folding*** *into small fists pressed firmly into her thighs as she hovered over me."* (V.C. Andrews *Ice*) ● "Dad sat back, *his* **smile *warming*** *again."* (V.C. Andrews *Ice*)

End Sentence Tertiary Form 10.23:
Adjective Phrase at End of Sentence
Code: 10TP E Adjective Phrase
Examples:

10TP E Adjective Phrase

- The place is a Shangri-la, *idyllic and tranquil.*
- "He listened on the phone and looked at his boss, Daniel Ross, *cold* as an undertaker in his dark pinstripe suit." (Crichton *Jurassic Park*)
- "He crouched down between the sheets, *glad* of their tepid glow." (DH Lawrence *Women in Love*)
- "In the classroom the last lesson was in progress, *peaceful* and still." (D.H. Lawrence *Women in Love*)
- Maggie shrugged, *indifferent* to Tom's outburst.
- "The foreigners stood like statues, *unable* to speak or move." (Amy Tan *The Hundred Secret Senses*)
- "That would have been shameful – showing you care more for your sweetheart than for all your family, *living* and dead." (Amy Tan *The Hundred Secret Senses*)
- "They were showing him respect because he was a good student, *polite* and very ambitious." (V.C. Andrews *Ice*)

End Sentence Form 10.24:
Adverbial Phrase at End of Sentence
Code: 10TP E Adverb Phrase
Examples:

10TP E Adverb Phrase

- He had to prepare for the opening, *only* a month away.
- It poured, *all day long*.
- The commander was certain that the rebels would surrender, sooner or later, *probably* within the next few days.

- "Presently she adds that it was an easy labor, *only twelve hours*." (Annie Dillard *For the Time Being*)
- "She couldn't wait to tell my daddy when he came home from work that evening, *a little* after ten." (V.C. Andrews *Ice*)
- I don't visit the doctor often, *only when I'm really sick*.
- The anxious wife waited for the results of her husband's brain tumor operation, *all night long*.
- She was hurt, *irrevocably* damaged beyond words.

End Sentence Tertiary Form 10.25:
Anecdotal Interrupter/Recorder at End of Sentence

Code: 10TP E insertion

Note: This form is used when interspersing a writer's comment directly into a passage or narration. It would be a departure from a more objective viewpoint, and perhaps shows a more personal side of the writer. As well, it is used to report third-party speech – that is, to report a person's exact words to someone else.

Examples:

| 10TP E Insertion |

writer/narrator comment

- "Fire is beautiful; some day it will be useful, **I think**." (Mark Twain *Eve's Diary*) [writer comment]
- The idea was a kind of time travel, and to bring them back alive, **so to speak**. [writer comment]
- The United Nations, using its power, must go in and basically, **if you will**, create a receivership – take over those systems and provide a consortium of organizations and non-government organizations to basically supply those functions until a viable, responsible government is in place (NPR_TalkNat 2009 01 15 *Investigating Zimbabwe^s Cholera Epidemic*) [speaker comment seeking consensus and listener agreement]

third party speech (recorder)

- The man was detained by police, and then the investigation started, **Han said.** [identifying speaker]
- Its upgrade is long overdue, **officials said.** [identifying speaker]
- "The economy's in a turmoil," **the financial advisor concluded.** [quotation, identifying speaker]
- They want to celebrate in a big way, **I think**. [writer comment]
- This will protect the city from future flooding, **she emphasized.** [identifying speaker signal]

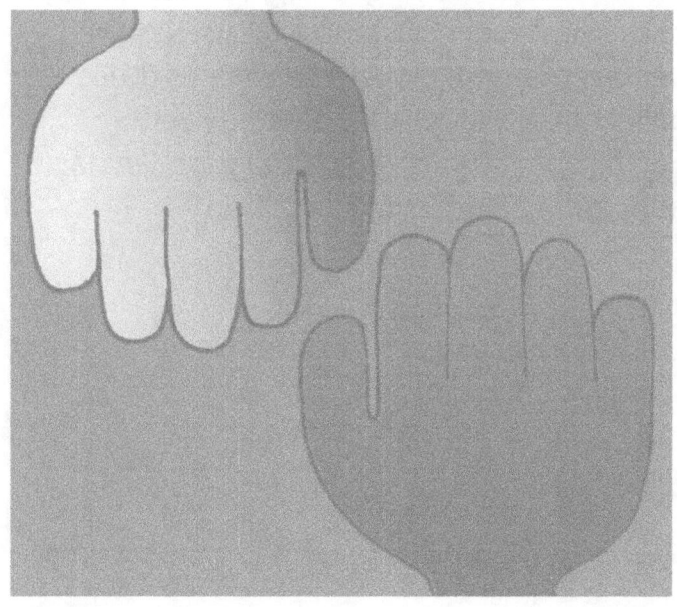

Short Codes for 10TP Three Places Sentence Forms

The charts on the next two pages presents the 10TP Sentence Forms and their short codes all together according to their placement at the Beginning, Middle, or End of the sentence. Students can use colored pencils to highlight within each of those 3 parts of the charts to indicate whether a Form is of Primary, Secondary, or Tertiary importance and usage.

10 TP Three Places

NUMBER	SENTENCE FORM LETTER CODE	DESCRIPTION OR FORMULA	SUBFORM NOTATION (NAME OR SHORT CODE)
		Beginning of Sentence	
10.1	TP	Word	10TP B word
10.2	TP	Prepositional phrase	10TP B prepositional phrase
10.3	TP	Verbal phrase	10TP B verbal phrase
10.4	TP	Noun phrase	10TP B noun phrase
10.5	TP	Absolute construction	10TP B absolute construction
10.6	TP	Adjective phrase	10TP B adjective phrase
10.7	TP	Adverb phrase	10TP B adverb phrase
		Middle of Sentence	
10.8	TP	Word(s)	10TP M word
10.9	TP	Noun phrase	10TP M noun phrase
10.10	TP	Appositive phrase	10TP M appositive phrase
10.11	TP	Absolute construction	10TP M absolute construction
10.12	TP	Adjective phrase	10TP M adjective phrase
10.13	TP	Adverb phrase	10TP M adverb phrase
10.14	TP	Prepositional phrase	10TP M prepositional phrase
10.15	TP	Verbal phrase	10TP M verbal phrase
10.16		Insertion	10TP Insertion

		End of Sentence	
10.17	T P	Word	10TP E word
10.18		Verbal phrase	10TP E verbal phrase
10.19		Appositive phrase	10TP E appositive phrase
10.20		Absolute construction	10TP E absolute
10.21		Adjective phrase	10TP E adjective phrase
10.22		Adverb phrase	10TP E adverb phrase
10.23		Prepositional phrase	10TP E prepositional phrase
10.24		Noun phrase	10TP E noun phrase
10.25		Insertion	10TP E Insertion

Short Code Procedure When Indicating Use of Parentheses:

If parentheses are used rather than commas to frame the interruption in the middle or end of the sentence, then add parentheses around the short code for the form inside the parentheses.

For example, in

*Cindy **(the youngest of three daughters)** works in a café.*

the interruption is coded – 10TP M (Appositive Phrase).

11 (ADD) Additional Forms
from right fist, flick forefinger upwards twice

11.1	**ADD** QUESTION	• What should we do? • What is our purpose? • Could your assumption be wrong? • What time are you going?
11.2	**ADD** BEGINNING VERB	• **Add** 270 ml of warm water. • **Remove** your shoes before entering. • **Bring** your compass.
11.3	**ADD** BEGINNING CO-ORDINATE CONJUNCTION	• **But** I really had no choice. • **And** that's that's where I stayed. • **So** that's it in a nutshell.
11.4	**ADD** INVERSION	• Happy was I. • Blithe was the singing of the young girls over their test tubes. Aldous Huxley • In the town where I was born lived a man who sailed the seas. The Beatles • Only once has the Empire State Building sustained damaged from an aircraft.
11.5	**ADD** AFTER DESCRIPTOR (not separated by a comma)	• The evening **warm and clear**, we went for a walk. • The new challenge was for minds **open**, spirits **willing**.

11 ADD Additional Forms

Any attempt to organize language (or any aspect of Life or Reality) must allow for the **exceptional**, the **different**, the **unexpected**, the **marginal** that do not fit conveniently into prevailing categories.

Thus, in the previous 10 Sentence Forms, we have tried our best to reduce *all sentence forms* to the **handy total of "10" main Forms**. But such is not the case, for our collection needs still one mixed bag of Forms before it can call itself complete.

We use the 3-letter abbreviation **ADD** for this assorted collection of forms. It deserves as much attention by the student as each of the previous 10 forms, as the Forms lend themselves to a wide range of creative possibilities when used by the aspiring writer.

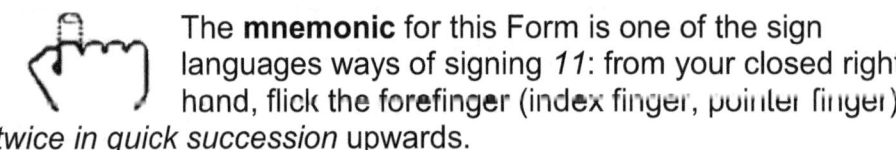

The **mnemonic** for this Form is one of the sign languages ways of signing *11*: from your closed right hand, flick the forefinger (index finger, pointer finger) *twice in quick succession* upwards.

11.1: Additional Form– Question

Code: 11ADD Question

Notes: One of the easiest forms of all. It is the root of all learning and knowledge – providing our initial greeting, and opening window to other cultures. It is our spirit of inquiry and curiosity that will never kill any cat, but might open doors, abolish wars, make new friends.

Examples:

- Who is going to the fair? ● What should we do? ● How will we get there? ● What's on TV? ● Is he really to blame? ● What time should we leave? ● Where is my wallet? ● "What could be more important for the future of our world than that we raise happy and well-adjusted, empowered and empowering children?" (Marianne Williamson *A Woman's Worth*) ● How was your trip? ● Where did we leave off last time? "What else makes sense when all is reduced to what matters?." (Marianne Williamson *A Woman's Worth*)

11.2: Additional Form - Beginning Verb

Code: 11ADD Beginning Verb

Note: This form is used constantly in self-help books. By including more of the verb forms, the pace and movement of the writing is increased, and the tone is more personal, more direct, and more dynamic.

Examples:

●*Look* at this! ●*Take* care! ●*Don't be* late! ●*Put* the dishes in the cabinet when you are finished. ●*Leave* the money with the teacher. ●*Think* before you speak. ●*Wait* a minute! ●*Stop* the ruckus, or everyone will have to go home! ●*Put on* your sweater, or you'll catch a cold! ●*Try* looking in your jacket pocket for your lost keys. ●*Turn* the left knob twice, and then push the green button. ●*Remind* yourself that you are essentially a unique being, amongst billions of unique beings. ● "*Keep* a vigil. *Stay* awake in the garden. *Hold* to the light. *Revere* goodness and integrity and truth." (Marianne Williamson *A Woman's Worth*)

●*Imagine* my surprise when I came home and saw the doorway decorated with balloons! ●*Let's collaborate* and *usher in* a glorious future. ●*Look* before you leap.

11.3: Additional Form - Beginning Coordinate Conjunction

Code: 11ADD Beginning Coordinate Conjunction

Note: Grammarians and purists may shudder at the thought of allowing students to use this form, but professional writers use it all the time, with incredible frequency once you start to observe it. This form also permits a longer moment of reflection following upon the period at the end of the preceding sentence.

The beginning conjunction connects the next sentence to the one before, and sometimes has a tone of surprise or finality.

Examples:

<u>and</u>

1) *And* he never thought about giving her another chance.
2) *And* they applauded with enthusiasm, for the home team had won.
3) *And* there you have it, a complete sentence beginning with "And".

4) ***And*** sure enough, at the end of the year, he packed up and went to China.

5) "***And*** let every other power know that this hemisphere intends to remain master of its own house." (J.F. Kennedy in *Inaugural Address*)

6) "***And*** the train raced on over the flat lands and past the Hill of Allen." (James Joyce *Portrait*)

7) ***And***, as he was so determined, he hit the ball with all his might.

8) ***And*** he never thought about giving her another chance.

9) "***And*** in any case, he finds he has less interest these days in such things as papers and journals and conventions and colloquia." (Stephen King *ibid*)

10) ***And*** that's all there is to it!

but

1) ***But*** you can always choose to go to the canteen instead.

2) ***But*** what about Melissa, she wanted to go too.

3) ***But*** this is not the end of the story.

4) ***But*** if I do not read the magazine review, I will have no idea what the play is about.

5) "***But*** you could not have a green rose." (James Joyce *Portrait*)

6) "**But** was there anything around the universe to show where it stopped before the nothing place began?" (*ibid*)

7) "**But** this peaceful revolution of hope cannot become the prey of hostile powers." (J.F. Kennedy *Inaugural Address*)

or

1) **Or** you might try on the red one – I think you'd look good in red, and, besides, you don't have any red clothing at all.

2) **Or** they cut holes in the fences.

3) **Or**, at least when you are going to start talking, get it all out on the table.

4) "**Or** bring me something of alien manufacture next time you're abducted." Neil deGrasse Tyson on NPR Science talking about *The Pluto Files*

for

1) **For** as soon as you start this system, you will find it getting easier each time.

2) **For**, in view of how little time there is, we must pack our bags and leave quickly and quietly.

3) "**For** man holds in his mortal hands the power to abolish all forms of human poverty and all forms of human life." (J.F. Kennedy *Inaugural Address*)

4) "**For** when the high priest recites the holy name and the blessing, the divine bends down and smites him." (Annie Dillard *ibid*)

so

1) **So** she buried her head in her hands, and wept profusely.
2) **So** that was all we could do.

yet

(1) **Yet** I felt sure that I could trust the newcomers on all accounts.
(2) **Yet** that wasn't the last they would hear of him.

11.4: Additional Form – Inversion of regular order

Code: 11ADD Inversion

Note: Inversion of subject and verb is usually kept for questions and poetry, but certain instances of it are found in modern prose.

Examples:

inversion (distant descriptor-S-MV)

In the following examples, the underlined part is the *inverted and relocated part*, and the ↑ is the part of the sentence from where the inverted part was taken.

a. <u>Sleek and silver-haired</u> the managers may be ↑, but by and large they tend to be men whose principal concerns involve money.
(Waddell)

b. <u>Young and svelte</u> she was ↑, a mystical presence as fresh as morning dew.

c. <u>Tired</u> I was ↑ – tired of the pain, tired of the lies, tired of the struggle.

inversion (distant descriptor-MV-S)

In the following examples, the <u>underlined parts</u> are the parts that have traded places.

d. "<u>Sublime</u> is <u>the dominion of the mind over the body</u>, that can make flesh and nerve impregnable, and string the sinews like steel, so that the weak become so mighty." (H. Beecher Stowe *Uncle Tom's Cabin*)

inversion (dir.object-MV-S)

In the following example, the <u>underlined part</u> is the *inverted and relocated part*, and the ↑ is the part of the sentence from where the inverted part was taken.

e. "<u>The whole other world, wet and remote</u>, he had to himself ↑." (DH Lawrence *ibid*)

inversion (MV-S)

In the following examples, the underlined parts are the parts that have traded places.

f. <u>Through the blue</u> sky soared <u>the young eagle</u>.
g. <u>In the cold blue depths</u> moved <u>the whale</u>.
h. <u>Over the hills and valleys</u> flies <u>a lonely bird</u>.
i. "<u>There</u> fell from the sky <u>a very bright and beautiful star</u>." (Oscar Wilde *The Star-Child*)
j. "<u>In front of them, at the corner of the lake, near the road</u>, was <u>a mossy boat-house under a walnut tree</u>." (D.H. Lawrence *ibid*)
k. <u>Here's the idea</u>.

split MV with inversion

In these examples, the subject is at the middle or end of the sentence, and the <u>main verb</u> is split.

l. "*<u>Standing</u>* on the riverbank <u>were</u> two dilophosaurs." (= Two dilophosaurs were standing on the river bank.) (Crichton *ibid*)
m. <u>Hovering</u> above my enclave of bedsheets <u>were</u> at least two mosquitoes whose buzzing woke me up.
n. Only once <u>has</u> the Empire State Building <u>sustained</u> damage from an aircraft.

11.5: Additional Form – The After Descriptor

Code: 11ADD After Descriptor
Note: This is an unusual and infrequently encountered construction, but for that reason is all the more noteworthy when used effectively. In this form, a noun is followed by an adjective or multiple-words-adjective. Usually, one or a series of adjectives follows a noun, with no punctuation in between.

noun after-descriptor

1. His wallet **empty**, he was reduced to begging.
2. She rated the movie **suitable**.
3. The evening **warm and clear**, the neighborhood kids played baseball on the corner lot.
4. They are hooked on keeping their bodies **thin** and weight **down**.
5. My mind a total **blank**, I stood there **motionless**. [occasionally the after-descriptor can be a noun]

11 (ADD) Additional Forms II

	Additional Forms	Examples
11.6	**ADD** NOUN OF noun + of + noun	Some types of *Noun-of* constructions are commonplace and matter-of-fact: **possession** (*conquest of Peru, voice of Whitney Houston*); **thing container** (*basket of apples, jar of jam*); **animal quantifier** (*herd of cattle, pride of lions*); **human quantifier** (*group of people, a few of us, majority of workers*); **qualitative specifier** (*sign of progress, speed of construction, tone of voice, guarantee of quality*); **material specifier** (*sheet of paper, heart of stone, nerves of steel*). The examples below, however, are what we term *impact duo Noun of*s. They connect words of power, creating an unlikely but powerful juxtaposition. Often metaphors, *impact duos* appeal to our visual sense.

- **Oceans of sadness**... Richard Marx
- ...the **chimes of freedom** flashing... Bob Dylan
- The baseball game was a **comedy of errors**.
- ...this **hive of activity**... Aldous Huxley
- I was afraid to utter one negative comment or **iota of hesitation**. V.C. Andrews
- I'm dizzy with joy, crying with relief, because I feel the **clarity of peace, the simplicity of trust, the purity of love.** Amy Tan *The Hundred Secret Senses*
- He strives vainly for **crumbs of dignity** as he watches everything he holds dear swept into the **dustbin of history**. Robert J Connors

11ADD Additional Forms (continued)

11.6: **Additional – Noun Of**
Code: 11ADD Noun of
Notes: We see *Noun Of* constructions in quite a few commonplace areas in English: **possession** (*conquest of Peru, voice of Whitney Houston*); **thing quantifier or container** (*basket of apples, piece of paper*); **animal quantifier** (*herd of cattle, pride of lions*); **human quantifier** (*group of people, a few of us, majority of workers*). For the most part, these types of *Noun Ofs* work limited word magic.

However, the most important *Noun Of* construction is the ***impact duo Noun Of***. It brings together two words in a rare, often figurative, association; as a result, our imagination is challenged to discover and savor the beauty and power of this new momentary kinship.

We provide examples of each below.

noun-of (possession)

The *noun-of* phrase has a much wider application and usage than to **indicate possession**, though it does that also, with elegance, formality, and dignity. When describing the writings of Charles Dickens or William Shakespeare, we would much rather refer to the *novels of Dickens* or the *sonnets of Shakespeare* than say *Dicken's novels* or *Shakespeare's sonnets*. Likewise, if a person (such as Whitney Houston) has a wonderful voice, we might prefer to say *the amazing voice of Whitney Houston* rather than *Whitney Houston's amazing voice*.

These examples show a kind of possession of one thing by or over another: *span of time, loss of soul, hand of treason, ground of dreams, change of mind.*

noun-of container (1) thing container, (2) thing quantifier, (3) thing composition)

Sometimes we use this form when referring to **numeric, quantitative or container terms that refer to things**: *sheet (pane) of glass, ream of paper, stack of books, kilo of sugar, basket of apples, jar of honey, bowl of soup, strand of hair, cube of sugar, slab of concrete, slice of bread, brick of cheese, drop of water, bar of soap, bottle of wine, fleet of boats, pile of paper, pair of tweezers, blob of paint, wad of banknotes, block of ice, piece of paper, round of applause, pinch of salt, speck of dirt, piece of advice, breath of fresh air, shot of liquor, coat of leather, dress of silk, wall of concrete, vial of pills, pocketful of dreams, cloud of dust, etc.*

noun-of (animal quantifier)

Included in this form are all of the unique quantitative nouns that English uses for **collections of animals** (*flock of sheep, a herd of cattle, herd of elephants, litter of pups, pack of wolves, swarm of bees, school of fish, gaggle of geese, colony of ants, etc.*)

noun-of (human quantifier)

Also included are **numeric or quantitative terms that refer to groups of humans**: *lots of people, a few of us, many of the group, some of them, group of students, a handful of people, the people of Guangzhou, school of thought, defenders of wildlife, Council of Europe, President of France, Inns of Court, etc.*

noun-of (place or institution indicator)

Here we include legal titles for institutions and places: *University of Pittsburg, Republic of Ireland, County of York, Bank of China, House of Representatives, Institute of Advanced Physics, Bureau of Investigation, Department of Immigration, Museum of Art, School of Esthetics, Institute of Technology, Province of Ontario, ...*

noun-of (impact duo)

*Noun Of*s can deal, however, with much more important things than counting and possessing. They bring together two words in a rare, often figurative, association.

Consider: *"A **wave of terror** swept across the city."* The Noun Of phrase is conjures up a more powerful image than if we had said *"They hit the city for a third time."*

A **wave** might be associated with the endlessly repeating, arching, and breaking walls of water rolling in to the shore, or it can be associated with something like a tsunami, while **terror** is a negative, deeply felt emotion that we usually associate with disruption, death, and disorder. As a result, our imagination is challenged to discover and appreciate the connection and symbolic meaning in this fused image.

Upon close observation of text material from both non-fiction and fiction sources, it appears as though we could expand our definition to include gerunds, perhaps more in the second position than the first, and create again a phrase that is memorable.

For example, we could include:

- **noun + of + gerund**
    - (emotional gerund **noun of**): *joy of having fun, joy of making money, fret of having kids, joy of cooking, trauma*

of losing a parent, fear of losing your investment, pain of breaking up, fear of flying, ...
- (technical gerund **noun of**) *art of making pickle, the process of gathering votes, the method of baking bread, repercussions of changing your mind, outcome of wanting to quit your job,...*
- **gerund + of + noun**:
  - outpouring of music, slackening of pace, numbing of feeling, ...

One could also argue that a **noun + of + the + noun** should qualify, as in:

- **noun + of + the + noun**
  - shore of the lake, beginning of the week, cusp of the curve, powers of the proletariat, wisdom of the saints, melting pot of the best of all cultures, hands of the sky-god, soup of the day, bulk of the stock market correlation matrix, ...

The later grouping could also be expanded to included **Noun + of + a + Noun**, or **Noun + of + some + Noun** (*mind of a child, image of a dying soldier, scent of a woman, enactment of a law, diary of a nobody, torture of some protesters, arrival of some assistance, control of some media, price of some commodities, ...*), and so on, and we would have hundreds or even millions of such phrases, many of which have to do with the idea of *possession* or *attachment*, or of the immediate proximity of something, or the nature of something in a certain context.

Since we identify our forms as *basic* ones, and since we do not want to come to a full and final conclusion that the above examples should or should not be included, we leave to the reader to decide the suitability of such phrases in their own writing. It's a **matter of choice**, and the **sense of style** preferred by the writer, and the **richness and degree of imagination** that they wish to employ, or they may even wish to create an **illusion of coolness** or a certain **amount of variety** so that – without any **fear of failure** whatsoever – the writer will feel a **sense of freedom, a taste of delight** about experimenting with these forms, and even experience a **burst of insight** or a **splurge of *creativity*** when pondering what to write next.

So, le*t* there be *porous boundaries* in our **classification of Forms**. The **art of styling sentences** is **the art also of buying time** and of waiting for the **crucible of imagination** to heat up and then for her liquid contents to come pouring forth.

<u>The short voiced word **of** is a thin partition, a paper wall, put between two connected giants.</u>[1] Somehow, though, shorn and shrift of non-essential *the* or *a* or other specifiers, the words in the paired phrase resound with all their in its simplicity.

Thus, it is the hunch of the co-authors that the more poetic ***impact duo* noun of** will probably be the one that gives the most satisfaction and inspiration to both writers and readers, but that the other "sub-types" of *Noun Of*s should be noticed and used on demand at the appropriate occasion.

Examples: No attempt has been made to sort or rank the Impact Duos in the following chart.

We follow the *Impact Duo Noun Of* Chart with sample student and professional model sentences exemplifying all of the types of *Noun Of*s. We then include some calligraphy rendering a Noun Of passage from the 8th century and follow that with a look at two famous literary critics who use *Impact Duo Noun Of*s often and well.

---

[1] Man y young people use an inappropriate phrase that resembles the noun-of, *kind of*. This popular phrase is used (with almost as much frequency as the ubiquitous *like*) in the utterances of some of today's youth, as in:
I'm feeling *kind of* tired.   You look *kind of* lonely.
The intended meaning here is *rather* or *a bit* or *somewhat*. **This is <u>not</u> a noun-of impact duo**.

11 (ADD) Additional III
Some *Noun Of*s including *impact duo*s

power of words	beacon of hope	sounds of silence
chimes of freedom	pulse of life	ounce of prevention
wail of sorrow	sigh of relief	rule of thumb
brink of extinction	heart of darkness	fit of laughter
tingle of positivism Cintra Wilson	scarcity of food	change of heart
purity of motive	joy of reunion	catalog of misery Ursula LeGuin
voice of authority	pain of separation	bundle of nerves
sorrows of empire Chalmers Johnson	power of attorney	trail of tears
simplicity of design	admission of guilt	tokens of peace Maya Angelou
glory of love	nudge of curiosity	invasion of privacy
ribbon of darkness Marty Robbins	surge of power	veil of silence
breastplate of justice	poison of hate	verge of extinction
mountain range of emotions [solbeam]	jungle of possibilities Thomas Knierim	pangs of consciousness
brink of war	maps of meaning Jordan Peters	flash of inspiration
blanket of fear	fists of hostilities Maya Angelou	expression of gratitude
mote of matter Maya Angelou	nightmares of abuse Maya Angelou	majesty of religion Cintra Wilson
spark of truth	tone of voice	trail of blood
society of equals	ease of access	sprig of hope
shred of evidence	break of dawn	beehive of activity
models of thought	prospects of success	likelihood of defeat
announcement of victory	delusion of grandeur	vote of confidence

11.6 ADD-noun of-thing container or quantifier

- My new **pack of cards** is on the table. • Last winter, the Winnipeg family ordered two **truckloads of firewood** from Botany 9 to use in their woodstove. • Jessie ordered a **round of beer** to share with his friends and associates. • For Valentine's Day, Charlie had a large **bouquet of flowers** sent to his girlfriend's workplace. • I bought some **cloves of garlic** to use in the ragout. • Where did that **jar of pickles** go that I just bought? • The law student found that there was a **plethora of cases** that had to be reviewed by the end of the week.

- "**Handful of dust, handful of dust**
  Sums up the richest and poorest of us
  True love makes priceless the worthless
  Whenever it's added to a **handful of dust**"
  (lyrics to *Handful of Dust* by Patty Loveless)

11.6   ADD-noun of-animal quantifier

●The **herd of buffalo** grazed peacefully in the lush green meadow. ●Someone spied a **pod of whales** in the distance and the B.C. tourists got their cameras out ready for action. ●The **clutch of chicks** ran around like balls of yellow fluff.

11.6   ADD-noun of-human quantifier

●A large **group of people** assembled in front of the main building. ●A **bevy of beauties** surrounded the Canadian popstar, clamoring for his autograph. ●**Lots of people** came to the wedding. ●A **gaggle of reporters** gathered around the sole survivor. ●A **crowd of civilians** inspected the damage at the police station. ●**Some of you** may remember that I talked about the threats to ancient forests last year. ●The **majority of_workers** are in favor of the

4-day work week. ●A **truckload of workers** arrived at the sugarcane field.

11.6   ADD Impact Duo Noun Of

●China is often considered the **kingdom of bikes**. ●We need new **models of thought**. ●The expression on the face of the accused showed no **admission of guilt**. ●The new software has a definite **ease of operation**. ● "...they tumbled, in a **pile of** immeasurable **giggle**, on the withered turf under the verandah ..." (H.B. Stowe *Uncle Tom's Cabin*) ●The **speed of construction** with which the new apartment went up was remarkable. ● "But, in general, behavioral effects were simply beyond the **reach of understanding**." (Crichton *Jurassic Park*) ●With the **approach of spring**, the pod of blue whales moved up the British Columbian coast. ●"...his comrade marveling much at his foolishness and **softness of heart**." (Oscar Wilde *The Star-Child*) ● "In this fatal **moment of choice** in which we might begin the patient **architecture of**

peace we may also take the last step across the **rim of chaos.**" (Thomas Merton) ● "Now I'm drowning in a **river of tears.**" (Eric Clapton) ● "And leaders meeting in London must supply **the oxygen of confidence** to today's global economy, to give people in all our countries renewed hope for the future." (UK PM Gordon Brown) ● <u>Book titles</u>: *Empire of Illusion: The End of Literacy* and *the Triumph of Spectacle* (Chris Hedges), *Frames Of Mind*: The Theory Of Multiple Intelligences (Howard E. Gardner) ● <u>Song, group, album, book titles</u>: *Masters of War* (Bob Dylan), *Eve of Destruction* (Barry McGuire), *Sound of Silence* (Paul Simon), *Mothers of Invention* (Frank Zappa), *Flavors of Entanglement* (Alanis Morissette), *Sultans of Swing* (M. Knopfler, Dire Straits) ● "I'm dizzy with joy, crying with relief, because I feel the **clarity of peace**, the **simplicity of trust**, the **purity of love**." (Amy Tan) ● "**cloak of fiction**" (Peter Carey *The Paris Review Interviews*) ● "A **crest of intention**, a **roar of purpose**, a sluice of slick, purpled body that Lacy quickly lifted into the mother's arms, . . ." (Jodi Picoult *Nineteen Minutes*)

7th Century Use of the *Noun Of* Form

Calligraphy by Muriel Watson

Northrop Frye Notices the *Noun of* Form

We first discovered and elaborated on the *Noun Of* Form and then later found that the Canadian literary critic Northrop Frye had noticed and described one particular variation of the *Noun Of* Form – the *adjective noun of noun*. Below are his observations on this specific instance of a *Noun Of* Form:

> In the twentieth century it was succeeded in favor by another phrase of "the **adjective noun of noun**" type, in which the first noun is usually concrete and the second abstract. Thus: *the pale dawn of longing, the broken collar-bone of silence, the massive eyelids of time, the crimson tree of love*. I have made these up myself, and they are free to any poet who wants them, but on examining a volume of twentieth-century lyrics I find, counting all the variants, thirty-eight phrases of this type in the first five poems.
>
> The fusion of the concrete and abstract is a special case, though a very important one, of a general principle that the technical development of the last century has exposed to critical view. All poetic imagery seems to be founded on metaphor, but in the lyric, where the associative process is strongest and the ready-made descriptive phrases of ordinary prose furthest away, **the unexpected or violent metaphor** that is called *catachresis* **has a peculiar importance. Much more frequently than any other genre does the lyric depend for its main effect on the fresh or surprising image**, a fact which often gives rise to the illusion that such imagery is radically new or unconventional. From Nashe's *Brightness falls from the air* to Dylan Thomas's *A grief ago*, the emotional crux of the lyric has over and over again tended to be this **"sudden glory" of fused metaphor**.
>
> *Anatomy of Criticism* Princeton University Press 1957 15th ed. [emphasis added]

Frye's observation is an astute and fair, yet inadequate tribute to the powerful, prevalent, and yet larger category of the *Noun of* Form. We have outlined, explained, and exemplified all the sub-types of *noun ofs* with much greater detail. Poets and playwrights have long used this form, and now this **dash of poetry**, this **allusion of inclusion** has crossed over into mainstream non-fiction, and is now a hallmark of good, imaginative writing, as if from a **mill of metaphor**.

Roland Barthes' Frequent Use of *Noun of*s

In his collection of essays and talks entitled *The Rustle of Language*, French post-structuralist, linguist, philosopher, and literary critic **Roland Barthes** shows that he has an affinity, knack, and zest for what we call the *Noun Of sentence* form. The title itself is a direct give-away.

Below we list *some* of the *noun of*s (of both the prosaic and poetic or *impact duo* type) with which he has peppered many of his 45 passages.

burst of ideas, … fears, delights, desires, oppressions	realm of structure	fragment of desire
delight of reading	society of consumption	lovers of writing
laws of argument	discourse of desire	wellspring of literature
flow of ideas	dawn of linguistics	disorganization of biography
garland of years	rustle of language	indecision of genres
snare of contradictions	retinue of friends	destruction of stereotypes
chain of discourses	power of language	shocks of fashion
offset of circularity	immobility of prattle	progress of discursivity
vanity of meta-language	voices of plurality	odor of language
pith of puns	odor of seriousness	violence of language
division of meanings	rigging of interpretation	space of speech
distribution of genres	experience of limits	energy of exclusion
prestige of method	shudder of meaning	floodgates of time
explosion of tendency	transcendence of egotism	strategies of writing
feats of discourse	scraps of identity	polyphony of pleasures
artifices of writing	man of statements	apocalypse of culture
Figures of system	violence of effacement	combat of languages

A page ago, we mentioned that **Northrop Frye** noted this construction, but did not highlight its significance and power; likewise, above, we see that **M. Roland Barthes** uses these forms but has not noticed himself the uniqueness of this form. For the first time in this book, this form is brought to the public eye for its *doors of understanding* it might open, the *curtains of fantasy* it might lift, and the *reservoirs of meaning* that it might open.

11 (ADD) Additional Forms IV

	Additional Forms	Examples
11.7	**ADD** ESPECIALLY	• I like fruit, **especially** mangoes. • I love all reptiles, **especially** Australian Bearded Dragons. • You should read this story, **especially the last part**.
11.8	**ADD** FRAGMENT	• Another great week. • Surely not. • Extraordinary. • The years of giving. • Too hard even to try! • Never! • Quite the opposite! • Too much! • Splendid! • Awesome! • A must-see site! http://tr.im/okfrag http://tr.im/crot2
11.9	**ADD** EXCLAMATION	• It rained all the time we were there! • We won! • I can hardly believe it! • Let's hit the road! • What a voice!
11.10	**ADD** COMPOUND	This involves the use of *compounds* (**more than one**) of **subjects, objects, main verbs, descriptors, and/or prepositions**. Often, the items are put *in parallel constructions*, effectively giving the text and ideas discernible structure and unity.
		• Compound (main) verbs The policeman **listened** and **wrote**. **Log on**, **open** heart, **blog out**. China Daily ezine.chinadaily.com.cn
		•Compound subjects •**Canadians**, **Koreans**, and **Japanese** participated in the research.
		• Compound subjects and and compound (main) verbs **Bruce** and **Bjorn played** hard and then **rested**.
		• Compound direct objects Ben sent **postcards** and **letters**. Jen sent **postcards**, **email**, and **letters**.
		• Compound (main) verbs, one of which has compound direct objects We **went** to the store, **bought** some **groceries** and a **newspaper**, and **ambled** home.

11 (ADD) Additional Forms v

Additional Forms	Examples
ADD COMPOUND continued	Pay close attention when using compounds. Make sure that parts are treated equally and are arranged properly as to avoid confusion.

- <u>Compound distant descriptor</u>
  He was **young** and **naive**.
  The plan was **incomplete** and **flawed**.
  So you **become** 21, **turn** 30, **push** 40, **reach** 50, and **make it** to 60.
  George Carlin on Aging

- <u>Compound (main) verbs with direct objects</u>
  Tracy **wrote** a poem and **read** it to her granny.

- <u>Compound (main) verbs with one direct object</u>
  Stella **buys** and **re-sells** clay tiles.

- <u>Compound indirect objects</u>
  The teacher told **Jon** and **Jen** their quiz results.

- <u>Compound objects of a preposition</u>
  He spoke in clear **tones** and memorable **phrases**.

- <u>Compound relative clause</u>
  It is clear **that** your writing **has improved** and **that** you still **aspire** to your dream of writing a book.

- <u>Compound adjectives</u>
  The **frisky** and **young** puppy played in front of the house.

- <u>Compound adverbs</u>
  The teacher waited **patiently** and **quietly** for the answer.

11.10

11.7: Additional - especially

Code: 11ADD especially
Note: This form is a very simple form to master. Keep in mind that it is somewhat informal, so be sure not to overuse it (, *especially* by beginning writers!). It must have a comma or dash in front of it. **Do not confuse it with the adverb *especially*,** as in *I was especially tired after the hike.*
Examples:

- Tina likes sweaters – *especially* **cashmere ones.**

- I love everything about Sumi, *especially* **the way she makes me laugh.**
- I love the musical style of The Slugs, *especially* **how they switch genres several time in a song.**

- We are impressed with all that you have done, *especially* **your work with the immigrant workers and the poor families in the outlying areas.**

- Cautious on account of the dark, the bus driver drove very slowly, *especially* **around hairpin curves.**

- There are many mosquitoes, *especially* at night.

- "In her collaborations with scientists, Frankel has learned a great deal about science and about the special needs and constraints of scientific photography, *especially* **the necessity for technical**

accuracy." (Ivars Peterson in *The Art of Scientific Photography* in Science News Vol 152)

● "His struggle to find the right words, or any words, was clearly visible on his face, **especially in his eyes.**" (V.C. Andrews *Ice*) ● "But having been raised in a Korean immigrant family, I saw every day the exacting price and power of language, **especially with my mother**, who was an outsider in an English-only world." (Chang-rae Lee in *Mute in an English-Only World* in The Contemporary Reader 6/e)

11.8: Additional – fragment
Code: **11ADD Fragment**
Notes: There will be an outcry against the admissibility of this form to our inventory of forms. We include it because professional writers use it sparingly but effectively in fiction and general documentary works.

Examples:

(1) You may think that he decided to study in the big city. **Not so.**

(2) You may think she has given up. **Never!**

(3) "And there it was on the navicomp screen. **The planet Earth.** They were home." (Grant Naylor *Red Dwarf*)
"Lister rang up 'no sale' on the old-fashioned wrought-iron till, and counted the week's takings.

Fourteen dollars and twenty-five cents. Another great week." _(Grant Naylor *Red Dwarf*)

(4) "The swirling interactions of humanity's three brains, like the shuttling of cups in a shell game, deftly disguise the rules of emotional life and the nature of love. Because people are most aware of the verbal, rational part of their brains, they assume that every part of their mind should be amenable to the pressure of argument and will. **Not so.** Words, good ideas, and logic mean nothing to at least two brains out of three [referring to the reptilian, limbic and cortical brains]. **Much of one's mind does not take orders.**" _(Thomas Lewis MD, Fari Amini MD, Richard Lannon MD *A General Theory of Love*)

(5) **Not this day or any day.**

(6) **Not with his family's consent.**

(7) **And no sight of relief anytime soon.**

(8) **Memorable and magical.**

(9) **Extraordinary.**

(10) **Too challenging even to attempt.**

11.9: Additional – Exclamation

Code: 11ADD Exclamation

Notes: *To exclaim means to cry out or speak suddenly and loudly*, as in a moment of surprise, strong emotion, or protest. An occasional exclamation can elevate a text or passage by bringing near life-like sound to it.

Examples:

- My G-d, we did it!

- "Our substitute for electricity!" (Barbara Kingsolver: *The Poisonwood Bible* 114)

- "Well, that did it!" (*ibid* 129)

- We won the tournament!

- We've almost reached the end of all the Sentence Forms!

11.10: ADDITIONAL – COMPOUND

Code: **11ADD Compound**

Notes: This form could be considered a repeat of $S_{A \text{ and } B}$ or any other of the Series forms – the **careful and balanced use of more than one subject, object, main verb, descriptor, or prepositional phrase**. Strict parallelism says that the look of each element running parallel should be the same; in most cases, this means the elements must be the same Kind of Word. Thus, *"She likes basketball, tennis, and squash."* might be acceptable, whereas **"***She likes basketball, swimming, and to chat online with* *her classmates."* is slightly askew. Depending on your tone, this lack of uniformity might have a certain desired effect, and you can let it stand. For ease of clarity and to bring cohesiveness, continuity, and unity to your sentences, however, standard practice normally requires the consistent use of similar Kinds of Words in both parallel constructions and in series.

EXAMPLES:

- After dinner, I will **finish** the homework *and* **do** some reading.

- He **went** outside *and* **looked** at the sky.

- The car went **down** the street *and* **around** the corner.

- The young bears **wrestled** with each other, **rolled** down the hill, **chased** each through the clearing.

- **Through** the window *and* **on top of** the swinging chandelier, the bird **had** somehow **gotten** in *and* **was perched** staring down at us.

- The gypsy rover **rode** over the hill, *and* **down** through the valley so shady...

- **In** your heart and **in** your mind is where I want to be.

- She earned a college **degree** in electrical engineering *and* a master's **degree** in computer science in Canada.

- In this interview, Vanna Karina talks about her **career moves** *and* her **struggles** as a mother.

- "The mnemonic **redundancy** of oral communication *and* the subjective **eccentricities** of medieval script were replaced by a more rational, calculating, analytical approach to knowledge." (J.Rifkin *The Biotech Century*)

- "**Phenomena** *could be* rigorously examined, observed, and described *and* **experiments** *could be* made repeatable with exacting **standards** *and* **protocols**, something that was far more difficult to achieve in a **manuscript** *or* **oral** culture." (*ibid*)

● "Finally he **squatted** back on his heels *and* **looked** over his work with an earnest, furrowed forehead."

(Barbara Kingsolver: *The Poisonwood Bible* 114)

S. Guarrigues

11ADD Additional Forms Short Codes

11 ADD Additional Forms			
NUMBER	**SENTENCE FORM LETTER CODE**	**DESCRIPTION OR FORMULA**	**SUBFORM NOTATION (NAME OR SHORT CODE)**
11.1	ADD	Question	11ADD Question
11.2		Beginning verb	11ADD Beginning Verb
11.3		Beginning coordinate conjunction	11ADD Beginning Coordinate Conjunction
11.4		Inversion	11ADD Inversion
11.5		Near descriptor Adjective or adverb near descriptor	11ADD Near Descriptor
11.6		Noun of	11ADD Noun of
11.7		Especially	11ADD Especially
11.8		Fragment	11ADD Fragment
11.9		Exclamation	11ADD Exclamation
11.10		Compound	11ADD Compound

Thanksgiving's No Turkey
Robert W Gardner

This passage uses a different way to summarize the sentence forms. The forms are listed below using letters *a, b, c,* d, e, and f, and these letters are put at the end of the sentence that represents an instance of that form.

Normally, when students notate specified forms and footnote them, they should use the short codes listed at the beginning of this section.

However, we present this alternative as just one instance that there is more than one way to notate and footnote the sentence forms. Teachers can use whatever system works best for them.

Only forms from 11ADD have been identified.

Sentence Forms:

- a. 11ADD Question
- b. 11ADD Beginning Verb
- c. 11ADD Fragment
- d. 11ADD Beginning Coordinate Conjunction
- e. 11ADD Exclamation
- f. 11ADD Noun of

    I have never had to return a Thanksgiving gift. Of course not, you say, there are no Thanksgiving gifts. Exactly.**c** That's just one reason I vastly prefer the coming celebration of turkey to its neighbor just down the calendar, Christmas.

Don't get me wrong. I love Christmas. The joy of anticipation in little children. The warmth of gathered families. The promise of redemption and salvation embodied in the religious celebration. I just can't stand what we've done to Christmas. The traffic at the malls. The chaos. The pressure. The endless advertising urging us to give, to spend, to buy happiness. The bills.

Thanksgiving is so easy. When was the last time you saw a neighbor standing in the snow trying to string Thanksgiving lights around his house? Do people shell out sixty-five bucks for a dead Thanksgiving tree for their family room? Do they sit hour after hour, addressing Thanksgiving cards they bought on sale back in May? Who, late on Thanksgiving Eve, will be driven to thoughts of suicide, murder or at least divorce upon reading the words "some assembly required"?

Thanksgiving is more like an old friend come to visit. There's a knock on the door, you greet each other warmly, and soon it seems you've never been apart. Here are the complete instructions for a Happy Thanksgiving: Roast a turkey, make way too much other food, and top it off with one of three or four approved desserts. You can watch a little football, or not. Take a walk.

Loaf.**b** Whatever.**c** No one expects you to decorate the house, make a killer table centerpiece, invite the president's entire cabinet to your cocktail party, or stroll the neighborhood singing Thanksgiving carols.

At work, no one gets looped at the office Thanksgiving party or chases the secretaries into the storage rooms. Working couples don't have to wrestle with which party to attend (and which boss to offend) if their office wingdings are on the same day.

Christmas can come any day of the week, and does. Thanksgiving is always on Thursday. Most folks get Friday off. A four-day weekend every year!**e** No other holiday can make this offer.

Thanksgiving is budget-friendly. If you are invited out, bring the hosts a bottle of wine or a nice dessert. That's it. No gifts you can't afford.**c** No endless worrying about what so-and-so got you last year or whether Grandma really wants another a) robe, b) toaster, or c) bottle of cologne.**c**

There's the story one son told of giving his dad a bottle of Old Spice aftershave every year for 30-plus years, only to find half of them, unused, in a dresser drawer after his dad passed away. True story.**c**

Why do you think retail chains have fiscal years that end Jan. 31?**a** Because they do half or more of their annual sales in the days before Christmas. And who do you think buys all that stuff?**a,d** You and me.**c** Know anyone who went into debt counseling after a pre-Thanksgiving buying binge?**a** Me neither.**c**

Despite these clear advantages, Thanksgiving gets no respect. Oh sure, the kids bring home a picture they drew of the pilgrims or a one-eyed turkey. But everyone understands these are just warm-ups for the major Christmas art push about to follow.**d** Thanksgiving was once the kick-off for the Christmas buying season, but even that distinction has decamped for a spot nearer to Halloween. The Thanksgiving parades can't hold a candle to the ones on Jan. 1. It's tough going for Turkey Day. So what should we do with Thanksgiving?**a**

I think we should celebrate Thanksgiving as the last holiday that hasn't been taken away from us. No cute bunny.**c** No speeches celebrating democracy.**c** No collection of seven nearby presidential birthdays. No pressure to make this a "Thanksgiving to remember."**c** Just four days off and one really good meal.**c** And no kids waking you at 5 A.M. to see if some turkey's come down the chimney.**d**

Steinbeck Exemplifies Form 11ADD

John Steinbeck
from Chapter 23 of *The Grapes of Wrath*

We include this excerpt for several reasons: (1) it is an excellent example of good writing done in the Mother Tongue or natural conversational voice; (2) it captures the Saturday Night Live excitement as it was during the opening of the West in the last half of the 19th century; (3) it shows an effective use of many of the Form 11 ADD forms previously introduced in this book.

The notation system is done differently, however, as we wish to highlight just the Form 11ADD forms and not the others (although they are present). Thus, we use the following alphabetic labeling system to identify those forms.

Sentence Forms:

a. 11ADD Question
b. 11ADD Beginning Verb
c. 11ADD Fragment
d. 11ADD Beginning Coordinate Conjunction
e. 11ADD Exclamation
f. 11ADD Noun of

A harmonica is easy to carry. Take it out of your hip pocket, knock it against your palm to shake out the dirt and pocket fuzz and bits of tobacco.**b** Now it's ready. You can do anything with a harmonica: thin reedy single note, or chords, or melody with rhythmic chords. You can mold the music with curved hands, making it wail and cry like bagpipes, make it full and round like an organ, making it as sharp and bitter as the reed pipes of the hills. And you can play and put it back in your pocket.**d** It is always with you, always in your pocket. And as you play, you learn new tricks, new ways to mold the tone with your hands, to pinch the tone with your lips, and no one teaches you.**d** You feel around — sometimes alone in the shade at noon, sometimes in the tent door after supper when the women are washing up. Your foot taps gently on the ground. Your eyebrows rise and fall in rhythm. And if you lose it or break it, why, it's no great loss.**d** You can buy another for a quarter.

A guitar is more precious. Must learn this thing.**b** Fingers of the left hand must have callus caps. Thumb of the right hand a horn of callus.**c** Stretch the left-hand fingers, stretch them like a spider's legs to get the hard pads on the frets.**b**

This was my father's box. Wasn't no bigger'n a bug first time he give me a C chord.**c** An' when I learned as good as him, he hardly never played no more.**d** Used to set it in the door, an' listen an' tap his foot.**c** I'm tryin' for a break, an' he'd scowl mean till I get her, an' then he'd settle back easy an' he'd nod. "Play," he'd say, "Play nice." It's a good box. See how the head is wore.**b** They's many a million songs wore down that wood an' scooped her out. Some day she'll cave in like an egg. But you can't patch her nor worry her no way or she'll lose tone.**d** Play her in the evening, an' they's a harmonica player in the nex' tent.**b** Makes it pretty nice together.**c**

The fiddle is rare, hard to learn. No frets, no teacher.**c**

Jes' listen to a ol' man an' try to pick it up. Won't tell how to double. Says it's a secret. But I watched. Here's how he done it.

Shrill as a wind, the fiddle, quick and nervous and shrill.**c**

She ain't much of a fiddle. Give two dollars for her.**b** Fella says they's fiddles four hundred years old, and they git mellow like whisky. Says they'll cost fifty-sixty thousan' dollars.**b** I don't know. Soun's like a lie.**b** Harsh ol' bastard, ain't she?**a** Wanta dance?**a** I'll rub up the bow with plenty rosin. Man!**e** Then she'll squawk. Hear her a mile.**b**

These three in the morning, harmonica and fiddle and guitar.**c** Playing a reel and tapping out the tune, and the big deep strings of the guitar beating like a heart, and the harmonica's sharp chords and the skirl and squeal of the fiddle.**c** People have to move close. They can't help it. "Chicken Reel" now, and the feet tap and a young lean buck takes three quick steps, and his arms hang limp. The square closes up and the dancing starts, feet on the bare ground, beating dull, strike with your heels. Hands 'round and swing.**c** Hair falls down, and panting breaths. Lean to the side now.**b**

Look at that Texas boy, long legs loose, taps four times for ever' damn step.**b** Never seen a boy swing aroun' like that.**c** Look at him swing that Cherokee girl, red in her cheeks an' her toe points out.**b** Look at her pant, look at her heave.**b** Think she's tired?**a** Think she's winded?**a** Well, she ain't. Texas boy got his hair in his eyes, mouth's wide open, can't get air, but he pats four times for ever' darn step, an' he'll keep a-goin' with the Cherokee girl.

The fiddle squeaks and the guitar bongs. Mouth-organ man is red in the face. Texas boy and the Cherokee girl, pantin' like dogs an' a-beatin' the groun'. Ol' folks stan' a-pattin' their han's. Smilin' a little, tappin' their feet.**c**

We include the following song written by John and Sheila Ludgate as a response to Steinbeck's excellent depiction of a Saturday night jam session in the '30s in California.

Assemblers should be on the lookout for such original responses in which an excellent passage lives on now in another medium or form of expression.

The song as an inspired response to excellent writing echoes again our *circle* theme – this time around a campfire, with singing and guitar playing and stories.

Steinbeck's Guitar

The man brings his guitar out as the twilight turns to night;
He sits down by the fire and starts to play.
His listeners draw in slowly to a circle 'round the light,
And each one feels some sadness slip away.

The melody runs along like little footsteps on the strings,
While heavy fingers march along the frets.
The bass notes beat the rhythm while a deep voice softly sings
Another lonesome ballad of regrets.

Chorus Steinbeck's guitar
*tells a thousand stories from afar
of weary souls out on a dusty road,
wondering do they really walk alone.*

The night is getting older and the man stands with a yawn;
His fingers stop and silence every string.
And as they bid goodnight each wish they too could pick guitar
Because it is a gracious thing.

repeat Chorus
The weary souls out on a dusty road
Wonder if they really walk alone.

Music and lyrics by John & Sheila Ludgate from their CD *Suburban Folk* and based on an excerpt from Steinbeck's *Grapes of Wrath*

The Fourth Assignment for Forms 10 and 11

When students have written and shared several individual examples of Forms 10TP and 11ADD, they should incorporate three to four instances of these forms in a 2 to 4 paragraph essay. They should also incorporate a varied selection of earlier sentence forms in the essay, especially one or more examples of form 9PP. Once again as in the previous three assignments, they should have a title that suggests, focuses, and unifies the main theme of their essay, and they should notate and footnote the sentence forms that they employ.

Below are some essays by earlier students to serve as models for this assignment.

INDOOR ROCK CLIMBING GYMS by Destiny Larberg

Rock climbing has become an increasingly popular sport, but for beginners the great outdoors is not the best place to start.**1** To rock climb outdoors is expensive and not always safe; therefore, more and more people are choosing indoor rock climbing gyms as a starting point.**2**

Indoor rock climbing gyms are now fairly common in large cities around the world.**3** Membership fees are at an affordable price and can be purchased for 1 year, 1 month, or even 1 day at a time.**4** The expensive outdoor anchoring gear is not needed in a gym, and the personal gear (shoes, harness, chalk bag) can be rented on a daily basis for a very low price.**5**

Choosing an indoor rock climbing gym is not only cheaper, but is also far safer than climbing outdoors.**6** There are no rock slides, no inclement weather, no bad anchoring for climbs to worry about.**7** Everything in the gym is safely constructed with varying routes for all skill levels.**8** Moreover, staff members are always available to give help and answer questions.**9**

For just 20 bucks, you can try out the wonderful sport of rock climbing for a whole day at an indoor rock climbing gym.**10** And don't worry about the weather forecast – an indoor gym is ready for climbing, rain or shine.**11**

Sentence Forms:
1) 6CC But
2) 3V Infinitive; 9PP Expansive Semi-colon; 2S The Pair; 3V Present Participle (2)
3) 3V Present Participle
4) 2S Choice Series
5) 3V Present Participle; 6CC and; 10TP M (Noun Phrase); 2S Triple Force
6) 3V Gerund (2); 3V Present Participle; 6CC But; 4C Not only, but
7) 5R Word; 2S Triple Force; 3V Gerund; 3V Infinitive
8) 3V Present Participle
9) 10TP B Word; 3V Infinitive
10) 10TP B Prepositional Phrase; 3V Gerund; 3V Present Participle
11) 11ADD Beginning Conjunction; 9PP Dash Break; 3V Gerund; 10TP E Adjective Phrase; 2S Choice Series

MY FUTURE OF POSSIBLE POVERTY by Joshua Gatcomb

It was a hot sunny afternoon when I discovered my future – poverty.**1** My latest venture as an entrepreneur was to sell lemonade during the hottest summer on record.**2** Lemon World, the produce giant, had exponentially raised the price of lemons due to the drought.**3** I made the mistake of selling below my cost, losing money on every sale.**4** I would have lost my entire life savings if it had not been for Sarah, my sister.**5**

Once I discovered my *faux pas*, I worked two extra hours a day; Sarah, four extra hours a day.**6** Sarah had three rules (patience, practice, persistence) that kept the business from filing chapter 13 (for bankruptcy).**7**

I think back on those playground days while I am flipping burgers.**8** Money, greed, power – all of these things blinded me.**9** Yes, it was a hot sunny afternoon when I discovered my future: poverty comes to those who fail to count their costs, husband their resources, and work hard and earnestly to progress.**10**

Sentence Forms:
1) 8RN When; 9PP Dash E Word
2) 3V Infinitive
3) 10TP M Appositive
4) 3V Gerund; 3V Present Participle
5) 7AC If; 10 TP E Appositive
6) 7AC Once; 9PP Stylish Semicolon
7) 10 TP M (Appositives); 2S Triple Force; 8RN That; 3V Gerund; 10TP E (Prepositional Phrase)
8) 7AC While
9) 2S Triple Force; 9PP Dash B Wrap-up
10) 10TP B Word; 7AC When; 9PP Explanation Colon; 8RN Who; 3V Infinitive (2); 2S Standard Series; 2S The Pair

A City of Dreams by Trucquynh Hua

Everyone has at least one dream, one goal, and one hobby.**1** I always dream of visiting new places and trying new things, so travel is one of my hobbies.**2** In my opinion, traveling should be fun and relaxing, as well as provide new learning opportunities.**3** I discovered three amazing vacation destinations – Paris, Berlin, and Amsterdam – during my European tours.**4**

Paris is my favorite city: it has many interesting and historical sites; there are many wonderful restaurants with amazing and delicious food; it is also a fashion capital of the world.**5** Paris is the largest city in France as well as its capital; furthermore, it is considered to be one of the greatest cities in the world.**6** The Eiffel Tower, the Cathedral of Notre Dame, the Louvre, and the Arc de Triumph – all are famous Paris landmarks.**7** The most distinctive symbol of Paris is the Eiffel Tower. From the third-level of this magnificent structure, it is possible to see all across the lovely city.**8** After witnessing the ironwork of the tower, one may then wish to visit the famous Gothic Cathedral of Paris, Notre Dame.**9** This gorgeous cathedral is a repository of French art and history; moreover, it represents the geographical and spiritual heart of France.**10** Another must-see attraction in Paris is the Louvre – the world's most impressive and largest art museum.**11** Most of the Louvre's collections come from six countries: French paintings and sculptures; Egyptian antiquities; Greek antiquities; Italian paintings and sculptures; Dutch paintings; and Islamic arts.**12** This famous museum contains more than 350,000 priceless objects, including the Mona Lisa and the Venus de Milo.**13** Moving from indoors to outdoors, one can enjoy the beautiful glass pyramids (Pei's Pyramids) outside of the Louvre.**14**

From the Louvre, one can stroll down the Champs-Elysées – one of the world's most famous avenues – to see the Arc de Triomphe.**15** It is Napoleon's triumphal arch; in addition, in the center of the arch flickers the eternal flame on the Tomb of the Unknown Soldier, a victim of War World I buried on 11 November 1920.**16**

After pleasing the eyes with Paris's famous landmarks, one needs to please the stomach with some delicious Parisian food.**17** Good food and restaurants are easy to find in Paris.**18** A very popular appetizer and French delicacy is *escargot* which is merely just snails.**19** There is a popular chicken entrée called *coq au vin*.**20** One of the delicious desserts found in Paris is *crème brulée*; it is like chocolate pudding and brown sugar, and it is very rich and creamy.**21** France is also renowned for its pastries. They have the best in the world!**22** Paris also has many elegant and formal restaurants if that is what one prefers.**23** In addition, there are many casual sidewalk cafés and restaurants with food that is both fast and cheap.**24**

Besides distinguished as well as delicious food, Paris is no doubt the fashion capital of the world.**25** The city has many famous designer clothing stores: Gucci, Versace, Valentino, Louis Vuitton, Prada, Chanel, and Christian Dior.**26** Beautiful supermodels come to Paris to do fashion shows and photo shoots.**27** Fashion shows mainly consist of models walking down a runway while showing off high fashion clothing.**28** Most people who attend fashion shows are people of high society.**29** An average Parisian will not wear designer clothing. Only the rich and the famous can afford designer clothing; furthermore, they always want to be wearing the latest fashions.**30** Fashion is a big part of French culture.

Overall, Paris is certainly one of the most beautiful and exciting cities in the world.**31** There are many interesting and historical sites in this fabulous city.**32** It has great food and restaurants.**33** And it is the place to go for the best names in the fashion industry.**34** I hope to come back to Paris – a city of dreams – in the near future.**35**

Sentence Forms:

1) 5R Word; 2S Standard Series
2) 3V Gerund (2); 2S The Pair; 6CC So
3) 10TP B Prepositional Phrase; 2S The Pair; 4C As Well As; 3V Present Participle
4) 9PP Dash M Appositives; 2S Standard Series
5) 9PP Explanation Colon; 9PP Trio Semicolon; 2S The Pair (2)
6) 4C As well as; 9PP Expansive Semicolon
7) 9PP Dash B Wrap-up; 2S Standard Series extended

8) 10TP B Prepositional Phrase; 3V Infinitive
9) 10TP B Prepositional Phrase; 3V Gerund; 3V Infinitive; 10TP E Appositive
10) 9PP Expansive Semicolon; 2S The Pair (2)
11) 9PP Dash E Appositive; 2S The Pair
12) 9PP Numeric Precursor Colon; 9PP Difficult Semicolon Long Items In List; 2S The Pair (2)
13) 10TP E Verbal Phrase; 2S The Pair
14) 10TP B Verbal Phrase; 4C From To; 10TP M (Appositive)
15) 10TP B Prepositional Phrase; 9PP Dash M Appositive; 3V Infinitive
16) 9PP Expansive Semicolon; 10 TP E Appositive Phrase; 3V Past Participle
17) 10TP B Prepositional Phrase; 3V Gerund; 3V Infinitive
18) 2S The Pair; 3V Infinitive
19) 2S The Pair; 8RN Which
20) 3V Past Participle
21) 9PP Complicated Semicolon; 2S The Pair (2)
22) 11ADD Exclamation
23) 2S The Pair; 7AC If; 8RN What
24) 10TP B Prepositional Phrase; 2S The Pair (2); 8RN That
25) 10TP B Prepositional Phrase; 3V Past Participle; 4C As Well As
26) 9PP List Colon
27) 3V Infinitive; 2S The Pair
28) 3V Present Participle; 3V Gerund;
29) 8RN Who
30) 2S The Pair; 9PP Expansive Colon; 3V Infinitive
31) 10TP B Word; 2S The Pair
32) 2S The Pair
33) 2S The Pair
34) 11ADD Beginning conjunction; 2S The Pair
35) 9PP Dash M Appositive Phrase

MORE STUFF by Melinda Robertson

Fifteen years ago when my husband and I got married, we were like most young couples, in that we had no stuff.**1** The term "no stuff" means that we did not have the basic tangible objects needed to maintain a home.**2** We didn't have furniture, dishes, linens – all of the things that most reasonable people expect to see in a home – nor did we have the money to buy them.**3** It was rough for a while, but it was fun.**4** We slept on the floor (with our clothes on because we didn't have any blankets) and ate (sitting on the floor) off of paper plates.**5** We didn't have a TV, so we did what most newlyweds do to amuse themselves – a lot.**6** However, as the saying goes, all things change with time and, in our case, with the acquisition of 'stuff'.**7**

It all began innocently enough, when we didn't have any stuff: we bought it, because we needed it.**8** Unfortunately, because we didn't have a lot of money, it was cheap stuff.**9** Over time, we replaced the cheap stuff, with something more expensive.**10** As my husband and I have gotten older, fatter, and wiser, we've outgrown, discarded, and even sold some of our stuff.**11** We've even bought new stuff to replace the perfectly good stuff that we *already have,* but aren't using, because we put it in storage before we moved to Japan.**12** (Which means that we are double-stuffed.)**13** Now, we're beginning to buy larger, more luxurious, built-to-stand-the-test-of-time type of stuff.**14** And, with every new purchase, we promise ourselves that we're going to keep it for ever and ever – until we both die – and will it to an unsuspecting family member.**15**

In fact, we now have so much stuff that we don't have anywhere to put anything, and no more room to grow.**16** As a military family, we change duty stations and move to a different city, state, or country about every three years — and it has become a nightmare.**17** It's a hassle to move when you have so much stuff.**18** It took the moving company three whole days to box up our household goods and pack it into crates, so that it could be shipped from California to Japan.**19** Once it arrived in Japan, it took one day for the moving company to unload the crates and put the boxes in our new house, and three whole weeks for my husband and I to unpack the boxes and organize everything.**20** At times like that, you wonder how you managed to collect so much stuff, and you fantasize about getting rid of it.**21** After all, there was a time when we didn't have anything except each other, and it wasn't so terrible.**22**

Don't get me wrong, having "stuff" is great.**23** All this "stuff" means that we have the necessities and luxuries of life, that in the beginning we did without.**24** For instance, nowadays, my husband and I own three cars – two of which are in Japan with us, and one (brand new) in long term storage back in California.**25** That makes our days much easier than when we have to carpool to work, coordinate grocery shopping trips around the bus schedule, and keep a taxi service on speed dial.**26** We now have nice furniture, plenty of dishes, a TV in every room, and enough towels and blankets to supply a small army.**27** I'm very grateful for all of the things that we have, and I feel that my husband and I have been blessed.**28** I just think that we could probably *de-junk* a little and get rid of some of the burdensome stuff.**29**

Sentence Forms:

1) 10TP B Noun Phrase; 7AC When; 10TP E Prepositional Phrase; 8RN That
2) 8RN That; 3V Past Participle; 3V Infinitive
3) 2S Triple Force; 9PP Dash M Appositive Phrase; 8RN That; 3V Infinitive (2); 6CC Nor
4) 6CC But
5) 10TP M (Prepositional Phrase); 7AC Because; 10TP M (Verbal Phrase)
6) 6CC So; 8RN What; 3V Infinitive; 9PP Dash E Word
7) 10TP B Word; 7AC As; 10TP M Prepositional Phrase
8) 7AC When; 9PP Explanation Colon; 7AC Because
9) 10TP B Word' 7AC Because

10) 10TP B Prepositional Phrase; 10TP E Prepositional Phrase; 11ADD After Descriptor
11) 7AC As; 2S The Pair; 2S Standard Series (2)
12) 3V Infinitive; 8RN That; 6CC But; 7AC Because; 7AC Before
13) 11ADD (Fragment); 8RN That
14) 10TP B Word; 3V Infinitive; 2S Triple Force
15) 11ADD Beginning Conjunction; 10TP B Prepositional Phrase; 8RN That; 3V Infinitive; 9PP Dash M Adverbial Clause (supplemental); 3V Present Participle
16) 10TP B Prepositional Phrase; 8RN That; 3V Infinitive (2); 6CC And
17) 10TP B Prepositional Phrase; 2S Choice Series; 9PP Dash Break
18) 3V Infinitive; 7AC When
19) 3V Present Participle; 3V Infinitive; 2S The Pair; 7AC So That (supplemental); 4C From to
20) 7AC Once; 3V Present Participle; 3V Infinitive (2); 2S The Pair (4)
21) 10TP B Prepositional Phrase; 8RN How; 6CC And; 3V Gerund
22) 10TP B Prepositional Phrase; 7AC When; 6CC And
23) 11ADD Beginning Verb; 3V Gerund
24) 2S The Pair; 8RN That (2)
25) 10TP B Prepositional Phrase; 10TP B Word; 2S The Pair; 9PP Dash E Adjective Phrases (numeric); 10TP M (Adjective Phrase)
26) 7AC When; 3V Infinitive; 2S Standard Series
27) 11ADD Noun of; 2S Standard Series extended; 3V Infinitive
28) 6CC And; 8RN That (2); 2S The Pair
29) 8RN That; 2S The Pair

COMMON SENSE by Betty Warren

I remember growing up.**1** If you did something stupid, you were held accountable.**2** We were all raised – or should have been – to be responsible for our own actions, or at the very least to display an iota of common sense on occasion.**3** Clearly, this is no longer the case.**4**

The perfect example: Several school districts throughout the United States have banned tag, chase, and touch football.**5** Why?**6** Sadly, children are no longer required to be responsible for what they do on a playground.**7** Instead of being sent to the principal (as was done in my day), hiring a lawyer now seems to be the standard.**8** Not only does this apply to schools, but it unfortunately applies to literally everything we do and everywhere we go.**9** Under the ruse of protecting our children, we are unwittingly creating a society of an extremely litigious nature**10**.

The point I am trying to make is that nobody has to be responsible for what they do anymore, and our children are learning this from a young age.**11** There must be teams of lawyers on stand-by, just waiting for people to call and report that they have done something reckless or irresponsible, and need to know who they can sue for that.**12** Don't believe me?**13** Just go home and start reading the warning labels on everything that you own.**14** As crazy as some of them might sound, be assured that they are there because someone, at sometime, has committed these insane acts and has sued someone for their own stupidity.**15** Instead of teaching our kids how to call a lawyer, maybe we need to get back to the basics, and teach them a little common sense.**16**

Sentence Forms:
1) 3V Gerund
2) 7AC If
3) 3V Infinitive (2); 9PP Dash M Anecdotal Interrupter; 2S Choices Series
4) 10TP B Word

5) 11ADD Fragment; 9PP Explanation Colon; 2S Standard Series
6) 11ADD Question
7) 10TP B Word; 3V Infinitive; 8RN What
8) 10TP Prepositional Phrase; 3V Gerund (2); 10TP M (AC As Clause); 3V Infinitive
9) 4C Not Only, But; 2S The Pair
10) 10TP B Prepositional Phrase; 3V Gerund
11) 8RN Missing That; 3V Infinitive; 8RN That; 8RN What; 6CC And
12) 10TP E Adverbial Phrase; 3V Infinitive; 2S The Pair; 8RN That; 11ADD After Descriptor (2); 8RN Missing That; 8RN Who
13) 11ADD Question
14) 11ADD Beginning Verb; 10TP B Word; 11ADD Compound; 3V Gerund; 3v Present Participle; 8RN That;
15) 7AC As; 8RN That; 7AC Because; 10TP M Prepositional Phrase; 11ADD Compound
16) 10TP B Prepositional Phrase; 3V Gerund; 8RN How; 3V Infinitive (2); 11ADD Compound

DANNY DANDRUFF **by April Turner**

Who is that one person in school you will always remember?**1** Everyone has one. Is it the school athlete, head cheerleader or that funny, weird person that everyone knew but no one talked to?**2** I remember my person. His name was Daniel Randolph. Everyone knew Daniel as Danny: Danny "Dandruff" Randolph.**3** Danny was a pretty normal kid; indeed, he wanted to fit in like everyone else.**4** But Danny had one small problem – dandruff.**5** He tried everything: Head & Shoulders, medication, and a priest.**6** Nothing Danny tried worked.**7** Looking back I sometimes feel bad: making fun of him, when it was clear he couldn't help his problem.**8** I even remember our high school prom and how we ruined it for him.**9**

Danny was a scrawny, weak, little boy. **10** He didn't have many friends, although he was very friendly to everyone. **11** We didn't care how nice he was. **12** All we cared about was the fact that he had dandruff. **13** And I don't mean a little bit of dandruff! **14** It was out of control, and it was everywhere: in his hair, on his eyebrows, and on his clothes. **15** Sometimes, I would sit in class and just stare at it. **16** It truly amazed me, for it was not possible to have so much dandruff. **17** One time I actually thought I saw more appearing. **18** Right there in class, right before my eyes. **19**

Danny tried to do something about the dandruff, but it didn't matter to us. **20** We saw him with the big, white bottle of Head & Shoulders [shampoo] in the shower room, after gym class. **21** We saw the pamphlets, explaining the use and added effects of the medication issued to him by doctors. **22** We even knew that he went to the town priest praying that it would just go away. **23** But it did not go away; instead, it lingered on – seeming to grow bigger and stronger, thicker and whiter every day. **24**

Everyone was sure Danny had outgrown the problem by high school, or that is what we all hoped. **25** The first day of school promptly ended that rumor. **26** The next four years went on without change. Before we knew it, senior prom was just around the corner. **27** It was the talk of the school. Everyone was going crazy trying to figure out what to wear, who to take, and how to get there. **28** No one stopped to wonder if Danny was even going, until the prom nominations came out. **29** I almost fainted: Danny Randolph nominated as prom king. **30** It was absurd. **31** Who would do such a crazy thing? **32**

Inevitably, prom night came. **33** When the votes were counted, no one could believe their ears – "Dandruff Randolph" prom king. **34** He was more surprised than anyone. Randolph walked to the stage with a look of awe on his face. **35** He had finally been accepted – after all these years. **36** We clapped and cheered, as they placed the crown upon his head. **37**

I wasn't sure whether I was clapping at how comical the whole ordeal was, or if I was genuinely happy for him.**38** I don't think anyone knew.**39** But before we knew it, the joke was played.**40** Instead of glitter and confetti, a bucket of white powdery flakes had been poured all over Daniel Randolph.**41** We were in shock. The whole Gymnasium went silent – and then immediately erupted into laughter.**42**

Looking back, I am ashamed of how cruel we once were as kids.**43** "Daniel Randolph, King of Dandruff," we chanted the rest of our high school days.**44** I sometimes wanted to stand up for him, although there were other times I wanted to join in.**45** I don't know if I would change anything about the past, but I do feel guilty every time I think about that night at our senior prom.**46** What was I to do?**47** "Danny Dandruff" looked hilarious up there covered in those powdered flakes.**48** I don't think they knew how much it would hurt him.**49** We all kind of thought he was used to the teasing by then.**50** After all, he was a symbol at our school; we gave him a motto and everything: "Randolph and dandruff – you can't have one without the other".**51** The prom nomination and the bucket were like the closing to a chapter in our lives that we would always remember.**52** It was our way of saying goodbye and saying, in our immaturely insensitive and even cruel way, have a nice life to a friend that we would never forget and might never see again.**53**

Sentence Forms:

1) 11ADD Question; 8RN Missing That
2) 11ADD Question; 2S Choice Series; 2S Compact Duo; 8RN That; 6CC But
3) 9PP Explanation Colon
4) 9PP Expansive Semicolon; 3V Infinitive
5) 11ADD Beginning Conjunction; 9PP Dash E Word
6) 9PP List Colon; 2S Standard Series
7) 8RN Missing That

8) 10TP B Verbal Phrase present participle; 9PP Explanation Colon; 3V Gerund; 7AC When
9) 8RN How; 11ADD Compound
10) 2S Triple Force
11) 7AC Although
12) 8RN How
13) 8RN Missing That; 8RN That
14) 11ADD Beginning Conjunction; 11ADD Exclamation
15) 6CC And; 9PP Explanation Colon; 2S Standard Series
16) 10TP B Word; 2S The Pair (or 11ADD Compound)
17) 6CC For; 3V Infinitive
18) 10TP B Noun Phrase; 8RN Missing That; 3V Present Participle
19) 1ADD Fragment; 5R Keyword
20) 3V Infinitive; 6CC But
21) 2S Compact Duo; 10TP E Prepositional Phrase
22) 10TP E Verbal Phrase present participle; 2S The Pair; 3V Past Participle
23) 8RN That (2); 3V Present Participle
24) 9PP Expansive Semicolon; 10TP Dash E Present Participle; 3V Infinitive; 2S Rhythmical Pairs
25) 8RN Missing That; 6CC Or; 8RN What
26) 11ADD Noun Of
27) 7AC Before
28) 3V Present Participle; 3V Infinitive (3); 8RN What; 2S Standard Series
29) 3V Infinitive; 8RN If supplemental; 7AC Until
30) 9PP Explanation Colon; 3V Past Participle
31) 1F Descriptor
32) 11ADD Question
33) 10TP B Word
34) 7AC When; 10TP E Noun Phrase
35) 11ADD Noun of
36) 10TP Dash Break

37) 2S The Pair; 7AC As
38) 8RN Whether supplemental; 8RN How; 8RN If supplemental
39) 8RN Missing That
40) 11ADD Beginning Conjunction; 7AC Before
41) 10TP B Prepositional Phrase; 2S The Pair
42) 9PP Dash Break
43) 10TP B Verbal Phrase present participle; 8RN How; 11ADD Inversion
44) 10TP B Noun Phrase; 10TP M Appositive
45) 3V Infinitive (2); 7AC Although
46) 8RN If supplemental; 6CC But; 8RN Missing That
47) 11ADD Question; 3V Infinitive
48) 3V Past Participle (2)
49) 8RN Missing That; 8RN How
50) 8RN Missing That; 3V Gerund
51) 10TP B Prepositional Phrase; 9PP Association Semicolon; 9PP Explanation Colon; 2S The Pair; 9PP Dash B List WrapUp variation
52) 2S The Pair; 3V Gerund; 8RN That
53) 3V Gerund (2); 5R Keyword; 11ADD Compound; 10TP M Prepositional Phrase; 2S The Pair; 8RN Missing That; 11ADD Compound

NOT JUST ANOTHER FACE IN THE CROWD **by Aaron Marshall**

America is a place of diversity; it has many languages and races and cultures.**1** Being from America, I'm used to appearing different from the person standing next to me in a public place, mostly because that person in turn is also likely to appear different from other people nearby.**2** Everyone may be American, but there are different types of Americans: white, Black, Asian, Latino, etc.**3** Oddly enough, being different is what makes everyone in the US the same;

however, this isn't true in other countries.**4** Japan is a prime example.

When I first got to the airport in Japan, I noticed one fact: all Japanese look similar.**5** There is no such thing as a minority race in Japan (in any large number except the Ainu).**6** Of course, a person might say, "Duh, everyone in Japan is Japanese; of course they're similar."**7** But, as I said before, each American looks completely different, so an African American will feel a little awkward in a place where all of the people are of one race different from hers or his.**8** In a Japanese airport, a dark complexion will stick out like a redwood in an apple orchard.**9** It's funny how some Japanese react to African Americans: as a type of tourist attraction.**10** In amusement parks, teenage Japanese girls want to take pictures with you; at stores, little children stare curiously.**11** I get a lot of attention, wanted and unwanted.**12** It is a little annoying at first, but after a while, you get used to it, and in some cases even enjoy it.**13** You sometimes feel a little important when you're not just another face in the crowd.**14**

Sentence Forms:

1) 9PP Association Semicolon; 2S Lyrical Series
2) 10TP Verbal Phrase present participle; 3V Gerund; 3V Present Participle; 10TP E Adverb; 7AC Because; 3V Infinitive; 11ADD After Descriptor
3) 6CC But; 9PP List Colon
4) 10TP B Adverb Phrase; 3V Gerund; 8RN What; 9PP Expansive Semicolon
5) 7AC When; 9PP Numeric Precursor Colon
6) 1F There is; 10TP E (Prepositional Phrase extended)
7) 10TP B Prepositional Phrase; 10TP E Insertion Quotation; 9PP Association Semicolon

8) 11ADD Beginning Conjunction; 7AC As or 10TP M Insertion Writer Comment; 6CC So; 8RN Where
9) 10TP B Prepositional Phrase; Figure of Speech: Analogy
10) 8RN How; 9PP Explanation Colon
11) 10TP B Prepositional Phrase; 3V Infinitive; 9PP Association Semicolon;
12) 10TP E Verbal Phrase past participle (2); 2S The Pair
13) 6CC But; 11ADD Compound verb
14) 7AC When

MY TRUST by Caroline Daniels

I've always been Daddy's little girl. We shared many good times together: fishing, shooting, watching old westerns.**1** I have two older sisters who were always jealous of me when we were young.**2** My father would give in to my every request; for them, the answer was always no.**3** I loved my father very much.

My memories of my parents aren't very clear, but I know they fought all the time.**4** I remember their fighting seemed normal to us children.**5** Of course, we were upset by the frequent fighting; nonetheless, we became very accustomed to this type of environment.**6** The three of us girls would all go into one room and sit in a circle holding hands.**7** Sometimes we would sing; sometimes we would cry; sometimes we would just play.**8** No matter what our response was, we were used to it.**9**

There was one memory that changed it all for me.**10** Though my parents fought often, I had never seen it get physical until I was eight years old.**11** At that time, I had a room of my own with bunk-beds.**12** On this night, my mother refused to sleep in the same room as my father.**13** She came into my room and lied down on the top bunk of the bed.**14** My father came in and told her to go into their room.**15** My mother refused again, and my father began to hit her repeatedly with his fist.**16** I was worried and scared.**17** I screamed and cried out for him to stop.**18** His little girl was begging for him to stop, but he wouldn't.**19** He just kept hitting her over and over.**20** That changed it all for me; I was no longer Daddy's little girl.**21**

That experience – painful and unforgettable – gave me reason never to trust a man again.**22** I realize that this is no way to live my life, and that I will have to trust again sooner or later.**23** But, I don't want to.**24** There were two things that made me hate my father that night: his treatment of my mother and his destruction of the image I had of him as the most wonderful man in the world.**25** Seeing him beating her like that changed me for the worst.**26** After thirteen years, I still have anger towards men, and the hatred I have for my father has not lessened.**27**

I have tried holding on to relationships.**28** But with my lack of trust, it is virtually impossible to make one work.**29** A relationship needs love and trust, patience and understanding.**30** Without these, there is no way for it to last.**31** Among other things, bad relationships are examples of what this experience has caused me.**32** There are many other things in my life that contribute to my lack of trust; however, this particular memory plays in my mind like a song that will never go away.**33**

Sentence Forms:

1) 9pp Explanatory Colon; 2S Triple Force
2) 8RN Who; 7AC When
3) 9PP Opposition Semicolon
4) 6CC But; 8RN Missing That
5) 3V Gerund
6) 10TP B Prepositional Phrase; 3V Gerund; 9PP Expansive Semicolon
7) 11ADD Compound verb; 3V Present Participle
8) 5R Repetition Word; 9PP Trio Semicolon
9) 10TP B Noun Phrase; 8RN What
10) 8RN That

11) 7AC Though; 7AC Until
12) 10TP B Prepositional Phrase
13) 10TP B Prepositional Phrase; 3V Infinitive
14) 11ADD Compound verb
15) 11ADD Compound verb; 3V Infinitive
16) 6CC And; 3V Infinitive
17) 11ADD Compound verb
18) 11ADD Compound verb; 3V Infinitive
19) 3V Infinitive; 6CC But
20) 3V Gerund; 5R Keyword
21) 9PP Association Semicolon
22) 9PP Dash M Adjective Phrase; 3V Infinitive
23) 11ADD Compound verb; 8RN That (2); 3V Infinitive (2)
24) 11ADD Beginning Conjunction
25) 8RN That; 9PP Numeric Precursor Colon; 2S The Pair; 8RN Missing That
26) 3V Gerund (2)
27) 10TP B Prepositional Phrase; 6CC And; 8RN Missing That
28) 3V Gerund
29) 11ADD Beginning Conjunction; 10TP B Prepositional Phrase; 3V Infinitive
30) 2S Rhythmical Pairs
31) 10TP B Prepositional Phrase; 3V Infinitive
32) 10TP B Prepositional Phrase; 8RN What
33) 8RN That (2); 11ADD Noun of; 9PP Expansive Semicolon

A Day to Remember by Daniel Ofori

Some people have special days that mean important things to them; some have days that carry sad memories; others have days that remind them of happier times.**1** I would like to tell you about one memory in particular that I remember well, which still brings a smile to my face.**2** That memory pertains to a special visitation notice that I received when I was twenty-two years old.**3** It was about my first engagement to marry a native African woman.**4**

On October 1, 1994, I received a visitation notice from my father-in-law, intending to bring his sons along with him for a visit.**5** I was very pleased upon hearing this news because it was a surprise to me.**6** My father-in-law is a king with a very a high reputation in his village. Normally, kings do not visit people in the village, unless the issue at hand is very important to the community.**7** Moreover, my brothers-in-law play a very important role when it comes to the traditions of marriage.**8** Since I planned to marry their sister, there are certain customs that needed to be followed.**9**

Habitually, the groom has to provide 12 expensive bottles of alcohol to signify the number of months per year, with each month representing one of the gods of the village.**10** The gods would then watch over the couple throughout their long marriage. Furthermore, I had to provide a stool for them to sit on, which also signifies that they are welcome to my home to visit their sister.**11** The most interesting part of the traditional ceremony was when my father-in-law and brothers-in-law presented me with a golden cutlass and a golden spear.**12** The golden cutlass was provided so that I could defend their daughter and provide her with food.**13** Usually, the groom receives a steel cutlass and a wooden spear, but they thought so highly of me that they presented me with an expensive golden cutlass.**14**

All of these required ceremonies and activities usually happen in the village where her parents live.**15** However, I was not in her country, so they took it upon themselves to travel to the nearby country of Togo.**16** Togo was more convenient for me at the time, and the wedding ceremony was held there.**17**

On October 15, 1994, my future father-in-law arrived with his sons and a few others from the village.**18** The most amazing and exciting thing that they brought with him was some traditional dancers and drum beaters.**19** This wonderful day was also my soon-to-be-wife's birthday, so I arranged a surprise birthday party for her and her whole family.**20** We proceeded to perform the rest of the traditional ceremony alongside the birthday party.**21** Everyone there had such a wonderful time, witnessing the ceremony and then talking and laughing, drinking and dancing.**22**

I was so thrilled and exhilarated that I immediately shared this good news with my family and close friends.**23** I will never forget that day because it was so beautiful that it felt as if I were in a dream.**24**

Sentence Forms:

1) 8RN That (3); 9PP Trio Semicolon
2) 3V Infinitive; 8RN That; 8RN Which
3) 8RN That; 7AC When
4) 3V Infinitive
5) 10TP B Prepositional Phrase; 3V Present Participle; 3V Infinitive
6) 3V Gerund; 7AC Because
7) 10TP B Word; 7AC Unless
8) 10TP B Word; 7AC When; 11ADD Noun of
9) 7AC Since; 8RN That
10) 10TP B Word; 3V Infinitive; 10TP E Prepositional Phrase; 3V Present Participle
11) 10TP B Word; 3V Infinitive (3); 8RN Which; 8RN That
12) 7AC When; 3V Past Participle; 2S The Pair
13) 7AC So that supplemental; 11ADD Compound verb
14) 10TP B Word; 6CC But; 8RN That
15) 3V Past Participle; 8RN Where; 2S The Pair
16) 10TP B Word; 6CC So; 3V Infinitive
17) 6CC And
18) 10TP B Beginning Prepositional Phrase; 2S The Pair
19) 2S The Pair (2); 8RN That
20) 6CC So; 2S The Pair
21) 3V Infinitive
22) 7AC As; 3V Present Participle; 2S Rhythmical Pairs
23) 11ADD Compound verb; 8RN That
24) 7AC Because; 8RN That; 7AC As If supplemental

Sports, Laundry, and Travel by E.H. Ha

I enjoy playing sports, doing laundry, and travelling.**1**

Playing sports makes me feel happy and more energetic.**2** So, I want to do them every day, but sometimes I don't have enough time, especially nowadays.**3** I used to play basketball regularly, but now I am too busy.**4** For example, tomorrow I must take exams in two subjects, and then I must give a class presentation on Monday .**5**

After playing sports, I like to take a shower and do laundry.**6**

Doing my laundry and then seeing wet, clean clothes, I feel fresh.**7** I feel cleansed, renewed, energetic again and happy.**8**

As well as sports and doing laundry, I like to travel.**9** On the one hand, I enjoy travelling to other places in the world; on the other hand, I explore local sites and scenes on my bicycle.**10** Usually, I don't have any special plans, and I never know when I'll start when I travel.**11** However, when the day is right and I feel like going outside, I just start – going anywhere, any place.**12**

During my trip, sometimes I feel freedom, sometimes loneliness, and sometimes I feel thrilled.**13**

For example, once I couldn't find an inn.**14** Did you know that some small villages don't have any inns?**15** So, I had to go to another village over the hills and along very long, narrow paths (no lights, no people) late at night.**16** At that time, I felt freedom, loneliness, thrills, and I sang a song, very loudly.**17**

And I felt exhilarated, comfortable with myself, rising to the challenge of darkness, uncertainty, and the unknown.**18**

Sports, doing laundry, and travel are three activities that engage my interests and feelings, and suit my temperament and personality.**19**

Sentence Forms:
1) 3V Gerund (3); 2S Standard Series
2) 3V Gerund; 2S The Pair
3) 10TP B Word; 3V Infinitive; 6CC But; 11ADD Especially
4) 3V Infinitive; 6CC But
5) 10TP B Prepositional Phrase; 6CC And
6) 10TP B Prepositional Phrase; 3V Gerund; 3V Infinitive;11ADD Compound infinitive with their objects
7) 3V Present Participle (2); 11ADD Compound participles with their objects; 2S Compact Duo
8) 2S Triple Force; 11ADD Compound adjectives
9) 4C As well as; 10TP B Correlative Phrase; 3V Infinitive
10) 10TP B Prepositional Phrase; 3V Gerund; 4C On the one hand; on the other hand supplemental; 9PP Opposition Semicolon; 2S The Pair [alliteration]
11) 10TP B Word; 6CC And; 8RN When; 7AC When
12) 10TP B Word; 7AC When; 3V Gerund; 9PP Dash E Verbal Phrase present participle
13) 10TP B Prepositional Phrase; 5R Keyword; 2S Standard Series
14) 10TP B Prepositional Phrase
15) 8RN That; 11ADD Question
16) 10TP B Word; 3V Infinitive; 11ADD Compound prepositional phrase; 2S Compact Duo; 10TP M (Compact Duo); 5R Word
17) 10TP B Prepositional Phrase; 2S Triple Force; 6CC And; 10TP E Adverb Phrase; [alliteration]
18) 11ADD Beginning Conjunction; 2S Triple Force; 2S Standard Series
19) 2S Standard Series; 8RN That; 2S The Pair (2)

FINDING YOUR OWN CHEESE by Melissa Hatfield

When a scientist raises a mouse, they must teach it, care for it, and feed it (lots of cheese).**1** After several years of this, however, the scientist will put the mouse to the ultimate test: finding its own cheese.**2** The scientist will conduct this experiment by placing the mouse in a maze, putting some cheese at the end, and then setting it free.**3** Now, without any help, the mouse must find its own way through the maze, find the cheese, and feed itself.**4** If the experiment is successful, the scientist – with a sense of hesitation – will be able to release the mouse to live on its own.**5** With the skills and knowledge the scientist taught it, the mouse will be able to go on and lead a productive life.**6**

Parents are just like the scientist, and we as children are just like the mouse.**7** Think about it: parents first care for, teach, and feed us (sometimes even with lots of cheese).**8** After several years of this and after many obstacles and challenges (they seem to create them just for us), they make us face the ultimate test: finding our own way through life.**9** Although they don't place us in an actual maze or place cheese at the very end, they do kick us out of the house at a certain age and just like the mouse – without any help – they expect us to make our own decisions and our own money.**10** They also expect us to find our own dreams and certainly to find our own cheese (so we no longer have to eat theirs).**11** If this experiment proves successful, the parents – with lots of joy and happiness – will set their children free.**12**

Quickly, the parents then lock the doors behind them and throw a party.**13** So, the next time you speak to your parents, and they give you a hard time about how you run your life, just say: "Mom and Dad, weren't you the ones who wanted me to find my own cheese?"**14**

Sentence Forms:
1) 7AC When; 2S Standard Series; 10TP E (Noun Phrase noun of)

2) 10TP B Prepositional Phrase; 10TP M Word; 9PP Explanation Colon; 3V Gerund
3) 2S Standard Series; 3V Gerunds (3)
4) 10 TP B Word; 10TP B Prepositional Phrase; 2S Standard Series
5) 7AC If; 9PP Dash M Prepositional Phrase extended; 11ADD Noun of; 3V Infinitive (2)
6) 10TP B Prepositional Phrase; 2S The Pair; 8RN Missing That; 3V Infinitive (2); 2S The Pair
7) 6CC And [figure of speech – similes developing into an analogy]
8) 11ADD Beginning Verb; 9PP Explanation Colon; 2S Standard Series; 10TP E (Adverb Phrase)
9) 10TP B Prepositional Phrase (2); 2S The Pair; 10TP M (Insertion Writer Comment); 9PP Explanation Colon
10) 7AC Although; 11ADD Compound verb (2); 9PP Dash M Prepositional Phrase; 3V Infinitive; 2S The Pair
11) 11ADD Compound infinitive; 3V Infinitive (3); 10TP E (Insertion Writer Comment)
12) 7AC If; 10TP Dash M Prepositional Phrase; 2S The Pair
13) 10TP B Word; 11ADD Compound verb
14) 10TP B Word; 6CC And; 8RN How; 10TP E Insertion Quotation; 2S The Pair; 8RN Who; 3V Infinitive

MY EXPERIENCE EATING *SASHIMI* by Brian Nitschke

Long ago – in the country of Japan – *sashimi* was considered a delicacy for the wealthy.**1** Now, it is a luxury for everyone – rich and poor.**2** Although most places don't serve *sashimi* the old-fashioned way anymore, there are still a few places that do.**3** And for this very reason I am thankful for having had a Japanese local show me the old-fashioned way of eating *sashimi*.**4** I can still remember going there as if it were yesterday.**5**

The restaurant is located in Yobuko; it's a small town near Fukuoka.**6** It took roughly two hours by car to get to the restaurant; however, the time flew by with a blink of an eye.**7** Arriving at the restaurant, I was anxious to go inside.**8** Walking through the main door, the waitress showed us our booth, and we quickly sat down.**9** You can see many things there: the chef, cutting away at the raw flesh on the fish, making *sashimi* with steely sharp knives; a pond in the middle of the restaurant, water flowing off of a mini waterfall; a view of the ocean, watching all the fishermen atwitter about the catch of the day; and eye-catching waitresses, smiling and gleaming with joy as they walk around the room.**10**

Looking at the menu, I thought I was going to hesitate picking the type of *sashimi* that I wanted.**11** Not so.**12** Without a pause, I pointed to the squid.**13** It wasn't long before my squid was being brought out to me on a small wooden boat, filleted.**14** Hurt, scared, and melancholy – all of these are words that could describe the squid as it lay, knowing its own fate.**15** It looked up at me with sad eyes, eyes that showed fear, and eyes that were forever wondering.**16** At first, I couldn't bring myself to eat it while it was watching me, but it wasn't long before I said "Oh, what the hell!" and was eating it anyway.**17** Every bite I took, the squid watched – defenseless.**18** It moved slower and slower, feeling pain and sorrow until then it felt...pain no more.**19** Slimy in texture, the *sashimi* slid down my esophagus, hitting the bottom of my empty belly.**20** Afterwards, I finally returned to Sasebo to retire for the night.**21**

Some people would say that it was heartless; others, the circle of life.**22** To eat a creature while it is still alive – in some people's eyes – is inhumane.**23** In some areas of Japan, it's illegal to eat *sashimi* the old-fashioned way, for it's considered immoral and impractical.**24** It may not be much longer before this manner of eating will come to an end.**25** Different, emotional, and moving – this is how I would describe the experience I had of eating *sashimi*.**26**

Sentence Forms:

1) 10TP B Adverb Phrase; 9PP Dash M Prepositional Phrase
2) 10TP B Word; 9PP Dash E Adjective Phrase; 2S The Pair
3) 7AC Although; 8RN That
4) 11ADD Beginning Conjunction; 3V Gerund (2)
5) 3V Gerund; 7AC As If supplemental
6) 9PP Association Semicolon
7) 3V Infinitive; 9PP Expansive Semicolon
8) 10TP B Verbal Phrase present participle; 3V Infinitive
9) 10TP B Verbal Phrase present participle; 6CC And
10) 9PP List Colon; 9PP Long Items Separated by Commas; 3V Present Participle (6); 10TP M Absolute Construction; 2S The Pair; 7AC As
11) 10TP B Verbal Phrase present participle; 8RN Missing That; 3V Infinitive; 3V Gerund; 8RN That
12) 11ADD Fragment
13) 10TP B Prepositional Phrase
14) 7AC Before; 10TP E Word (past participle)
15) 2S Standard Series; 9PP Dash B List Wrap-Up; 8RN That; 7AC As; 10TP E Verbal Phrase past participle
16) 5R Keyword; 8RN That (2)
17) 10TP B Prepositional Phrase; 3V Infinitive; 7AC While; 6CC But; 7AC Before; 10TP E Insertion Quotation; 11ADD Compound verb
18) 10TP B Noun Phrase; 8RN Missing That; 10TP E Word

19) 5R Keyword; 2S The Pair (2); 3V Present Participle; 7AC Until
20) 10TP B Adjective Phrase; 10TP E Verbal Phrase present participle
21) 10TP B Word; 3V Infinitive
22) 8RN That; 9PP Stylish Semicolon; 11ADD Noun of
23) 3V Infinitive; 7AC While; 10TP M Prepositional Phrase
24) 10TP B Prepositional Phrase; 3V Infinitive; 11ADD Noun of; 6CC For; 2S The Pair
25) 7AC Before; 11ADD Noun of
26) 2S Standard Series; 9PP Dash B List Wrap-Up; 3V Gerund

MY FRIEND – BOB by Michael Lortz

In the town where I live comes a man from afar.**1** Bob is his name.**2** He visits here just once per year from where he now calls home – Thailand.**3** We're always anxiously awaiting his arrival.**4** And we, regrettably, hate to think about his departure.**5** He never really tells anyone when he's coming – it's just always a welcome surprise!**6**

Bob is a man of honor, a man of wit, a man of charm.**7** He is a tall, thin, white-haired man; he is loved by all whom he meets.**8** He had lived here in Korea for over 22 years and worked at the Camp Carroll Education Center for most of them.**9** He enjoys coming back to Korea so that he can visit with all of his friends – both new and old alike.**10**

Although I've only known Bob for two very short years, I will always look up to him, just like I'd look up to my own father.**11** I can't say this enough: Bob is, undoubtedly, the most caring and carefree, casual and courteous man that I have ever met in my lifetime.**12** There's simply no one else like him.

His name is Bob – my friend.**14**

Sentence Forms:

1) 10TP B Prepositional Phrase; 8RN Where; 11ADD Inversion
2) 1F Distant Descriptor
3) 8RN Where; 10TP E Word
4) 3V Present Participle; [alliteration]
5) 11ADD Beginning Conjunction; 10TP M Word; 3V Infinitive
6) 8RN When; 9PP Dash Break; 11ADD Exclamation
7) 5R Repetition Word; 2S Triple Force; 11ADD Noun of (3)
8) 2S Triple Force; 9PP Association Semicolon; 8RN Whom
9) 11ADD Compound verb
10) 3V Gerund; 7AC So That supplemental; 9PP Dash E Adjective Phrase; 4C Both and supplemental; 2S The Pair
11) 7AC Although; 7AC Just Like supplemental
12) 9PP Explanation Colon; 10TP M Word; 2S Rhythmical Pairs; [figure of speech – alliteration]
13) 9PP Dash E Appositive

THE WORD "LOVE" by Katrina Anne Tolentino

Love is such a strong word when used in a relationship.**1** People overuse this word, to a point where they don't mean it; it becomes just a word instead of a feeling.**2** Being in love could be the most desirable, complicated, and heartbreaking situation in a person's life.**3** Feelings can either grow or lessen in a matter of time.**4** Love can also be unforgettable: it can last forever.**5**

One way or another, eventually a person will encounter love.**6** The bond – positive and strong and fierce – will take over the person's heart and mind.**7** There will be no sadness, no sorrow, no worry – only happiness and contentment.**8** This feeling, which most people call *love*, can sometimes fade away.**9** And it can really hurt a person's emotions.**10** If that happens, then you must somehow manage to move on.**11**

Until you actually feel love, you can't appreciate what the word really means in all its full force and meaning.**12** That everlasting bond.**13** The root of so many passions.**14** The unexplainable affection.**15** And the occasional flare-ups, arguments, and misunderstandings – with the emotions in constant turmoil, the highs and lows.**16** Love is often difficult, seldom convenient, with many obstacles to overcome.**17** However, to never experience love can lead to an empty life, a lack of happiness, and lost opportunities for the possibility and excitement of new beginnings.**18**

Sentence Forms:

1) 7AC When
2) 10TP E Prepositional Phrase; 8RN Where; 9PP Association Semicolon
3) 3V Gerund; 2S Standard Series
4) 4C Either or
5) 9PP Explanation Colon
6) 10TP B Noun Phrase
7) 9PP Dash M Adjective Phrase; 2S Lyrical Series; 2S The Pair
8) 5R Word; 2S Triple Force; 9PP Dash E Noun Phrase; 2S The Pair
9) 8RN Which
10) 11ADD Beginning Conjunction
11) 7AC If; 3V Infinitive
12) 7AC Until; 8RN What; 2S The Pair
13) 11ADD Fragment
14) 11ADD Fragment
15) 11ADD Fragment
16) 11ADD Beginning Conjunction; 2S Standard Series; 9PP Dash E Prepositional Phrase extended; 2S The Pair
17) 11ADD Compound distant descriptors; 10TP E Prepositional Phrase extended (or variation of 2S Triple Force); 3V Infinitive

18) 10TP B Word; 3V Infinitive; 2S Standard Series; 11ADD Noun of; 2S The Pair

A SPECIAL BOOK NOOK   by Dennis Wu

When I was a child, I usually went to a bookshop to read my favorite books for a whole day on weekends.**1** That book nook was not very large and was located at a corner in my neighborhood.**2** Reading books brought a lot of pleasure and left so many good memories for me.**3** At that time, I felt proud and happy when I could read all the books that interested me.**4** I would like one day to be a community bookshop owner myself and bring the same pleasure to the children who live in my community.**5**

Like some other small bookshops, my book nook would be about only 150 square meters or even smaller, but will be well-decorated.**6** It should be warm and elegant.**7** I would also set out soft cushions and chairs for my customers, especially the children.**8** Besides that, every afternoon I would have one of my employees with a beautiful voice and a patient manner read books or tell stories vividly to the children.**9** Every resident in my community could let their children join in this reading club event after paying a reasonable membership fee.**10** There would be cookies, cakes, and juice available at the party, too.**11** Every Sunday afternoon, this reading club would be free and open for all neighborhood children.**12** Therefore, those families who could not afford such fees could also let their children come to my shop and enjoy the pleasures of hearing a story read aloud at that time.**13**

Admittedly, reading printed books aloud is not as popular as in the past, since internet and PC games are attracting more and more children to sit in front of the computer screen instead.**14** Would my book nook face adequately this challenge as well as the growing popularity of e-books in the future?**15** Maybe.**16** But I still believe e-books will not ever completely replace printed books, since the feeling of holding a book is irreplaceable and our eyes are less strained when we are reading books as opposed to staring at a cold computer screen.**17**

    I hope and trust my vision of a small book nook will one day bring lasting joy to the children who live in my community and broaden their horizons and imagination.**18**

Sentence Forms:

1) 7AC When; 3V Infinitive
2) 11ADD Compound verb
3) 3V Gerund; 11ADD Compound verb
4) 10TP B Prepositional Phrase; 2S The Pair; 7AC When; 8RN That
5) 3V Infinitive (2); 8RN Who
6) 10TP B Prepositional Phrase; 6CC But
7) 2S The Pair
8) 2S The Pair; 11ADD Especially
9) 10TP B Prepositional Phrase; 11ADD Compound noun; 2S Choice Series
10) 3V Missing *to* Infinitive supplemental; 3V Present Participle; 3V Gerund
11) 2S Standard Series; 10TP E Word
12) 10TP B Noun Phrase; 2S The Pair
13) 10TP B Word; 8RN Who; 3V Missing *to* Infinitive supplemental (2); 3V Gerund; 3V Past Participle
14) 10TP B Word; 3V Gerund; 7AC Since; 2S The Pair; 3V Infinitive
15) 11ADD Question; 4C As well as; 3V Present Participle
16) 11ADD Fragment
17) 10TP B Beginning Conjunction; 8RN Missing That; 7AC Since; 3V Gerund (3); 7AC When
18) 2S The Pair (2); 8RN Missing That; 3V Present Participle; 8RN Who; 11ADD Compound verb

CHILDHOOD STRUGGLES BY RICO MENDIOLA

Judge a book not by its cover, but by the content within its pages – a cliché I have heard a million times. This phrase contains the sole cure for all prejudice, yet the world is plagued by racism and hate crimes and discriminations of all sorts. How is this possible? The problem begins in childhood. Children learn from negative examples shown to them by adults, other children, and the media. Accordingly, children attempt to mirror or imitate those negative examples. This often results in making fun of others and segregating them for their differences. Ridicule and ostracism can lead to low self-esteem or psychological problems.

I was born with an unusual hereditary case of cataracts. Cataracts are cloudy spots on the lens of the eye that continue to grow until the person is completely blind. My lenses had to be removed quickly, or I would have become blind at a young age. I was only six years old. Because my lenses were removed, I had to wear very thick glasses to see. I wore these glasses for six years of my childhood.

I was severely ridiculed for my glasses. People would say things such as "Hey, Bug Eyes, . . . ", "Can you see into the future??", or "You look like an owl." They treated me as if I were a freak of nature. The more others made fun of me, the more I believed whatever they said. I was very depressed and very pessimistic.

When I finally got contact lenses, people stopped making fun of me and giving me strange looks. But that didn't change the way I felt about myself. It has taken me years to build my confidence to the level that it is now. Sometimes, I catch myself taking over for those children of my past by criticizing my looks and actions. I am still healing.

I have learned to deal with my childhood experiences, but some cannot cope with their experiences. For example, the two teens that killed fellow students at Columbine High School in Littleton, Colorado, were ostracized by others.**22** As a result, they developed severe psychological problems resulting in mass murder and suicide.**23** Unless we change our actions today, our children will pass down our prejudices to their own children in an endless recycling of ignorance.**24**

Sentence Forms:

1) 11ADD Beginning Verb; 6CC But; 9PP Dash E Noun Phrase; 8RN Missing That
2) 6CC Yet; 2S Lyrical Series
3) 11ADD Question
4) 3V Past Participle; 2S Standard Series
5) 10TP B Word; 3V Infinitive (2)
6) 3V Gerund (2)
7) 2S The Pair; 2S Choice Series
8) 11ADD Noun of
9) 8RN That; 3V Infinitive; 7AC Until
10) 6CC Or
11) 7AC Because; 3V Infinitive
12) 11ADD Insertion Quotation (3)
13) 7AC As If supplemental
14) 4C The more, the more; 8RN That; 8RN Whatever
15) 2S The Pair
16) 7AC When; 11ADD Compound Gerund
17) 11ADD Beginning Conjunction; 8RN Missing That
18) 3V Infinitive; 8RN That
19) 10TP B Word; 3V Present Participle; 3V Gerund; 2S The Pair
20) 1F Descriptor
21) 3V Infinitive; 6CC But
22) 10TP B Prepositional Phrase; 8RN That
23) 10TP B Prepositional Phrase; 3V Present Participle; 2S The Pair
24) 7AC Unless; 3V Gerund; 11ADD Noun of

JAMES BELL, A GREAT BASEBALL PLAYER by Marvin Harris

James "Cool Papa" Bell played for the Pittsburgh Crawfords in the Negro League. The Negro League helped to develop some of the best players in baseball.**1** Bell – tactful, tall, and talented – was one of those players.**2** In his first game as a professional, the seventeen-year-old struck out one of the league's best hitters, although he wasn't even a professional pitcher.**3** His primary position was outfield. He was considered the fastest player ever to play baseball.**4** A former teammate of his believed he was so fast he could flip a switch and be in bed before the lights went out; it was said that once he was hit by his own batted ball as he slid into second base.**5**

Bell's greatest achievement was that he played the game he loved.**6** He was a victim of racism.**7** Racism kept him from earning the same wages as white players; racism kept him from playing in the same league as white players.**8** Against the odds, he helped pave the way for Jackie Robinson, the first African American in the Major League, and others that followed him.**9** Sadly, he would never accomplish his dream of playing in the Major Leagues.**10** He hoped some day there would be only one league – a league of professional baseball players, regardless of race.**11** In 1974, Bell received baseball's highest honor when he was inducted into the National Baseball Hall of Fame in Cooperstown, New York.**12**

Sentence Forms:

1) 3V Infinitive
2) 9PP Dash M Adjective Phrase; 2S Standard Series
3) 10TP B Prepositional Phrase extended; 7AC Although
4) 3V Infinitive
5) 8RN Missing That; 11ADD Compound verb; 7AC Before;9PP Association Semicolon;

       8RN That; 3V Past Participle; 7AC As;
       [figure of speech – hyperbole]
   6) 8RN That; 8RN Missing That
   7) 11ADD Noun of
   8) 5R Keyword; 3V Gerund (2); 9PP
       Association Semicolon
   9) 10TP B Prepositional Phrase; 10TP M
       Appositive Phrase; 8RN That
   10) 10TP B Word; 3V Gerund
   11) 8RN Missing That; 9PP Dash E Noun
       Phrase; 5R Keyword; 10TP E Prepositional
       Phrase
   12) 10TP B Prepositional Phrase; 8RN When

HAPPINESS OF FREEDOM AND THE FOURTH OF JULY by Caroline Daniels

The colors filled the sky and excited her.**1** She stood still – looking up at the sky.**2** She smiled, content and pleased with the day.**3** The loud sounds of the fireworks did not bother her; instead, they only made her smile bigger.**4** She turned her head to see other children, running around with sparklers and flags.**5** The colors of red, white, and blue were refreshing to see strung everywhere.**6** She could feel the happiness of freedom all around her.**7**

Through the air, the smoky smell of the barbeque hung thick.**8** She could almost taste the ribs by just sniffing the air.**9** The evening, warm and comfortable, was perfect for grilling outside.**10** She looked forward to tasting her uncle's famous barbeque sauce.**11** She stood nearby the grill – anxiously – waiting for the food to be ready.**12** But since it looked as if it wouldn't be ready for awhile, she decided to go and play with the other kids her age.**13**

She picked up some sparklers and headed towards the laughter of the other children.**14** Cameron, Patrice, Quiana – all of them were happily creating designs in the air with the bright sparklers.**15** Looking around, she rejoiced to see her family so happy.**16** Laughter, music, booms of fireworks, and pure happiness filled the air.**17**

At her age, she did not completely understand how meaningful the day was for the United States.**18** However, she definitely knew how meaningful it was for her.**19**

Sentence Forms:

1) 11ADD Compound verb
2) 9PP Dash E Verbal Phrase present participle
3) 10TP E Adjective Phrase; 2S The Pair
4) 9PP Expansive Semicolon; 11ADD After Descriptor
5) 3V Infinitive; 3V Present Participle; 2S The Pair
6) 2S Standard Series; 3V Infinitive; 3V Past Participle
7) 11ADD Noun of
8) 10TP B Prepositional Phrase; [literary device: alliteration]
9) 3V Gerund
10) 11ADD After Descriptor; 10TP M Adjective Phrase; 2S The Pair; 3V Gerund
11) 3V Gerund
12) 9PP Dash M Word; 3V Present Participle; 3V Infinitive
13) 11ADD Beginning Conjunction; 7AC Since; 7AC As If supplemental; 11ADD Compound Infinitive
14) 11ADD Compound verb
15) 9PP Dash B List Wrap-Up
16) 10TP B Verbal Phrase present participle; 3V Infinitive
17) 2S Standard Series extended; 1ADD Noun of
18) 10TP B Prepositional Phrase; 8RN How
19) 10TP B Word; 8RN How

FIRST EXAMINATION
with specified Forms

After students have finished one or two writing assignments with no required specified forms to use, notate, and footnote, the time has arrived to give an in-class examination. However, this first examination does not come at the midpoint of the course, but closer to its end.

In this exam, students will be given 2.5 hours to complete an essay with a focused title, using required, specified sentence forms. The titles of their essays must be derived from one of 5 subjects that they will be given at the beginning of the class.

Generally speaking, the 5 subjects given to students from which they must choose their titles are taken from a pool of 15 to 20 subjects which we gave sometimes for the first examination and sometimes for the final examination. There is thus a marked similarity between the titles and essays of both the first and final examinations. However, the difference between the first and the final examination is that the first examination requires students to use, notate, and footnote specified sentence forms, while the final examination does not. The instructor may choose to grade the two examinations with an equal value, or to give more weight to whichever of the two exams is better, as they choose.

The list of subjects given to various classes of students at different times for both the first and final examinations are the following ones: *Music, Family, Vacations, Work, Hobbies, Animals, Friends, Memories, Clothes, Movies, Travel, Entertainment, Food, Seasons, Holidays, Life Lessons, and Sports.* The subjects were chosen because of their general familiarity to most people and therefore the ease with which students could write about them.

Below are examples of essays written by students in class for the first examination. Students were given five subjects from the list above, and told to write a 3 to 5 paragraph essay with a focused title using most of the following forms notated and footnoted:

- 2 of 2S Series
- 3 of 3V Verbals
- 2 of 4C Correlative
- 1 of 5R Repetition
- 2 of 6CC Coordinating Conjunction
- 4 of 7AC Adverbial Conjunction
- 2 of 9PP Colon
- 2 of 9PP Dash
- 2 of 9PP Semicolon
- 2 of 10TP Three Places
- 1 of 11ADD Additional

Students may consult their charts or books or notes to assist them in writing the essay as well as notating and footnoting the sentence forms.

LOSING THE NOTES by Matt Ormita

Music is men's highest art form, perhaps men's highest achievement, and what is so amazing is that it is not tangible.**1** Music fills the world with color, beauty, emotion.**2** Inspiration, sadness, anger – all this and more can be generated just by listening to one minute of sound.**3** It's so fascinating.

What I find so magnificent about music is that it can take you into a time warp.**4** Driving to school one day, I turned on the radio and Groove Theory was playing.**5** All of a sudden, all of these memories from freshmen year came back to me.**6** I could remember my friends – some were still my friends and some no longer – dancing around in the lunchroom and singing the exact tune that was playing in my car at that moment.**7** Dozens of memories came back to me within a minute's time, and I had my own little video yearbook playing in my mind.**8** I sat in my car watching it play back, and I laughed, screamed, and cried all at the same time.**9**

I love older music: there was just more happiness and hope to it.**10** In today's music, there just seems to be anger and more anger.**11** Our society today is based on negativity. This has spawned off more furious styles of music: rap, hip-hop, grunge rock.**12** Look at our generation – we reflect our music perfectly.**13** We have no direction, no guidance, no inner confidence.**14** We commend kids that swear at their elders and steal from honest workers; however, we laugh at kids who help an old lady across the street.**15** Society needs a change, and perhaps it should start with the music.**16** What happened to the good old 60's when hippies smoked pot and sang songs of love and peace and harmony?**17** There's one thing that generation had that our generation lacks – hope.**18** There's no longer a hope for change or for something better.**19** There is just a realization of what is.**20**

This is just my own personal opinion: When the arts go down, so too will the quality of life.**21** And again, in my own personal opinion, the music has collapsed in quality.**22** It all sounds the same: there are no different textures; there are no really different styles; there is no real beauty.**23** The longer our generation lets the destruction continue, the more life will remain stagnant.**24** So let's bring it back to what it was all about in the beginning – beauty, color, emotion.**25**

Sentence Forms:

1) 10TP M Adverb Phrase; 8RN What; 8RN That
2) 2S Triple Force
3) 9PP Dash B List Wrap-Up; 3V Gerund; 11ADD Noun of
4) 8RN What; 8RN That
5) 3V Present Participle; 6CC And (comma omitted for if clauses are short)
6) 10TP B Adverb Phrase
7) 9PP Dash M Noun Phrase, 2S The Pair; 5R Word; 3V Present Participle (2); 8RN That
8) 11ADD Noun of; 6CC And
9) 3V Present Participle; 6CC And; 2S Standard Series
10) 9PP Explanation Colon; 2S The Pair
11) 10TP B Prepositional Phrase; 3V Infinitive; 2S The Pair; 5R Keyword
12) 9PP Explanation Colon
13) 11ADD Beginning Word; 9PP Explanation Colon
14) 5R Word; 2S Triple Force
15) 8RN That; 11ADD Compound verb; 9PP Expansive Semicolon; 8RN Who
16) 6CC And
17) 11ADD Question; 7AC When; 2S Lyrical Series
18) 8RN That (2); 9PP Dash E Word
19) 2S Choice Series
20) 8RN What
21) 9PP Explanation Colon; 7AC When
22) 11ADD Beginning Conjunction; 10TP B Word; 10TP M Prepositional Phrase
23) 5R Word; 9PP Trio Semicolon
24) 4C The more, the more; 3V Missing to Infinitive
25) 10TP B Word; 8RN What; 9PP Dash E List; 2S Triple Force

THE JAZZ IMPROV SOLO by Aaron Marshall

Charlie Parker, Dizzy Gillespie, John Coltrane – all are jazz legends known for their improv solos.**1** For a jazz musician, playing a solo on the spot is more than playing random notes and making it sound good.**2** There are basic techniques that a musician must learn.**3** The improv solo is much like a piece of writing: it should have a beginning, middle, and end.**4** There should be a guiding thesis (or unifying mood or tone to the music), supporting ideas (or a melody in the music), and facts (or the series of notes that comprise the piece).**5** And, of course, the musician should appeal to the audience, express his or her own feelings, and enjoy playing the music.**6**

The intro – like writing – should usually state the "thesis" and mood of the solo.**7** The musical thesis can be derived from a choral refrain, an excerpt from a popular song, a melodic string put together by the musician, or a composite of more than one of these.**8** The thesis is what the rest of the solo will be based on.**9** If the thesis is played in a certain key, the rest of the solo should be played in the same key.**10**

There is one major feature to one's solo – individuality.**11** The middle is considered the meat – the foundation – of the solo.**12** This part of the solo is where the player gets to include his or her own style and individuality as well as state their ideas and feelings, including variations of the thesis, harmonic notes, and the occasional color note (a note that sticks out from the rest, yet seems to give the melodic phrase "color").**13** And you must always keep the solo moving.**14**

Once the solo has stated its thesis and ideas, the only thing left is the conclusion.**15** How do you conclude a solo?**16** Usually, you sum it up with a restatement of the thesis.**17** Finally, fade out or restart the original song, letting the rest of your accompanying musicians know that you are finished and have made your point.**18** Remember to play what you feel, and playing improv will begin to seem not only a lot easier but also a lot more fun once you keep these steps in mind.**19**

Sentence Forms:

1) 9PP Dash B Wrap-up; 2S Triple Force; 3V Past Participle
2) 10TP B Prepositional Phrase; 3V Gerund (3);
3) 8RN That
4) 9PP Explanation Colon; 2S Standard Series
5) 2S Standard Series; 3V Present Participle (2); 10TP M (Noun Phrase) (3); 8RN That; 11ADD Noun of
6) 11ADD Beginning Conjunction; 2S Standard Series
7) 9PP Dash M Prepositional Phrase; 2S The Pair
8) 2S Choice Series extended; 3V Past Participle
9) 8RN What
10) 7AC If
11) 1F There is; 9PP Dash E Word
12) 9PP Dash M Appositive
13) 8RN Where; 3V Infinitive (2); 2S Choice; 2S The Pair (2); 4C As well as; 10TP E Verbal Phrase Present Participle; 2S Standard Series; 10TP E (Appositive Phrase); 8RN That; 6CC Yet
14) 11ADD Beginning Conjunction; 3V Present Participle
15) 7AC Once; 2S The Pair; 3V Past Participle
16) 11ADD Question
17) 10TP B Word
18) 10TP B Word; 11ADD Beginning Verb; 2S Choice; 10TP E Verbal Phrase; 3V Present Participle; 8RN That; 11ADD Compound verb
19) 11ADD Beginning Verb; 3V Infinitive (2); 8RN What; 6CC And; 3V Gerund; 4C Not only, but; 7AC Once

THE LOVE OF MUSIC   by Anjeannette P. Hammell

Melody, harmony, lyrics – these elements of music are food for the soul.**1** Music gives a voice to things, which would otherwise be silent, for even the inanimate object that has no voice speaks through music.**2** Music is not just a song on the radio, a person singing melodious words, for it is also the wonderful sounds of nature.**3** The song of the cricket as his melody plays in the still of the night, the sound of the ocean billowing in the breeze, and even the whistle of the wind as it blows through the trees – all are music, nature's voice in the wilderness.**4** These wonderful sounds in all of their simplicity – working together to make beautiful music – give music a sense of enjoyment beyond measure.**5**

I simply love music – be it nature's song or the fabricated sounds on the radio – it all appeals to me just the same.**6** The harmonious sounds of music manage to express my feelings better than any words I could ever speak.**7** Vibrant, mellow, relaxed – all are ways music makes me fell.**8** Whether a good day or a bad day, music is always there to keep me grounded.**9** Sade, my sanity at an insane time in my life; Stevie, when love is all I can think of and desire; Fred, when I'm ready to give up this Christian life and return to my sinful nature; Shania, when I'm feeling a little like a "Southern Belle" or a "Georgia Peach" – they all help to keep my feelings at the forefront of my mind and help me to remain true to myself.**10** Listen to me when I tell you, "music is food for the soul."**11** Why would anyone not like music?**12**

Sentence Forms:

1) 9PP Dash List Wrap-Up; 11ADD Noun of
2) 8RN Which; 6CC For; 8RN That
3) 2S Compact Duo; 6CC For; 3V Present Participle; 1ADD Noun of
4) 7AC As (2); 3V Present Participle; 2S Standard Series; 9PP Dash List Wrap-Up; 10TP E Appositive Phrase
5) 9PP Dash M Verbal Phrase present participle
6) 9PP Dash M Verbal Phrase; 2S Choice Series
7) 11ADD Noun of; 3V Infinitive; 8RN Missing That
8) 9PP Dash List Wrap-Up; 8RN Missing That

9) 7AC Whether supplemental; 2S Choice Series; 3V Infinitive
10) 9PP Dash List Wrap-Up; 9PP Difficult Semicolon List Items with Commas; 10TP M Appositive Phrase; 7AC When (3); 8RN Missing That; 2S The Pair; 2S Choice Series; 3V Infinitive; 11ADD Compound Verb; 11ADD Compound Infinitive;
11) 11ADD Beginning Verb; 7AC When; 10TP E Insertion Quotation
12) 11ADD Question

FAMILY **by Nicole Alexander**

Family is very important in one's life; family contributes the most to one's character.**1** Although there are many different kinds of relationships within families, all the members of a family should love each other.**2**

A mother's relationship with her children is warm, caring, protective.**3** Though she has wants and needs and desires, she is willing to give up some of her time for her children.**4** The mother is the hen; her children, the baby chicks under her wing.**5**

The father's relationship with the mother is romantic and caring and compassionate.**6** Before they made the commitment to each other to have a family, they had to make sure that they were right for each other.**7** They did not have to be together, but because of the love and faith of a successful marriage, they decided to spend the rest of their lives together.**8**

As the parents of the family show their love for each other, the children inadvertently learn from them.**9** In the future, they may also have successful marriages, but until then, they will often fight amongst themselves.**10** Children are young; children are inexperienced; children are often loud.**11** They will harass each other, and they will hit each other constantly; all the while they will be yelling and screaming.**12** So, in the beginning, it seems that siblings will never get along, let alone be friends, but later on they will begin to mature and laugh at the havoc they caused.**13**

The trials and tribulations of a family are many, but the end results are rewarding.**14**

Sentence Forms:

1) 9PP Association Semicolon
2) 7AC Although
3) 2S Triple Force
4) 7AC Though; 2S Lyrical Series; 3V Infinitive
5) 9PP Stylish Semicolon [figure of speech – metaphor]
6) 2S Lyrical Series
7) 7AC Before; 3V Infinitive (2); 8RN That
8) 3V Infinitive (2); 6CC But; 10TP B or M Prepositional Phrase; 2S The Pair
9) 7AC As
10) 10TP B Prepositional Phrase; 6CC But; 10TP B or M Prepositional Phrase
11) 5R Keyword; 9PP Trio Semicolon
12) 9PP Complicated Semicolon; 11ADD Compound Verb
13) 10TP B Word; 10TP B Prepositional Phrase; 8RN That; 2S Compact Duo [verbs]; 6CC But; 3V Infinitive (2); 8RN Missing That
14) 2S The Pair; 6CC But

THE LAST SUMMER by Adam Lunsford

School was out; it was summertime.**1** We rode shoulder to shoulder, hip to hip in the old and loud and rattling truck that would take us to the river, so we could hide from the blistering sun.**2** We were all happy, joyful, excited.**3** We felt like newborn babies. It was as if our minds had been set free from a prison.**4**

I sat in the pickup with four other boys, watching the roadside pass by – frame by frame.**5** I remembered all the summers we had together before.**6** I remembered all the smudgy, white T-shirts and the dirty, old blue jeans that were only washed once a week – if that.**7** I thought about all the days spent down by the river, swinging from old, dangerous rope swings that creaked and cracked when hanging from them.**8** I remembered sleeping late on Monday mornings and on Sunday nights never having to do homework.**9** Summer was what we lived for.**10**

I thought about going fishing.**11** All the times we took our coolers full of beer and tackle boxes to the river to bake in the sun all day, while sipping on cold ones.**12** I remembered the excitement that arose when somebody caught a huge, beautiful bass and how we would look and talk about it in amazement.**13** All those were priceless moments.

Remembering all the camping trips we had, I took out my pocketknife and played with it.**14** I could see the wear in it from all the tangled fishing lines and old rope and jagged fingernails that I had cut.**15**

At night, I remembered relaxing at a party or talking at a friend's house about what we had done the day before.**16** When it was time to go home, I would tiptoe into my home, remembering where the floor squeaked, stepping quietly not to wake my parents.**17**

This summer would be our last. Next year we would be off at college away from this make-believe world, the world where the child comes out in all of us.**18**

Friends, laughter, good times – these would all fade away when this summer was over; we had to make the best of it.**19**

Sentence Forms:

1) 9PP Association Semicolon
2) 2S Compact Duo; 8RN That; 6CC So; 3V Present Participle
3) 2S Triple Force
4) 7AC As If
5) 10TP E Verbal Phrase Present Participle; 9PP Dash E Noun Phrase
6) 8RN Missing That
7) 2S Compact Duo; 2S Triple Force; 8RN That; 9PP Dash Break?

8) 3V Past Participle; 3V Present Participle; 2S Compact Duo; 2S The Pair; 7AC When; 3V Gerund
9) 3V Gerund (2); 3V Infinitive
10) 8RN What
11) 3V Gerund
12) 8RN Missing That; 2S The Pair; 3V Infinitive; 3V Gerund; 10TP E Prepositional Phrase
13) 8RN That; 7AC When; 2S Compact Duo; 8RN How; 2S The Pair
14) 10TP B Verbal Phrase present participle; 8RN Missing That; 11ADD Compound verb
15) 3V Past Participle; 3V Present Participle (2); 8RN That
16) 10TP B Prepositional Phrase; 3V Gerund (2); 2S Choice Series; 8RN What
17) 7AC When; 3V Infinitive (2); 3V Present Participle; 10TP E Verbal Phrase present participle (2); 8RN Where
18) 10TP B Adverb Phrase; 10 TP M Adverb Phrase; 10TP E Appositive Phrase; 8RN Where
19) 9PP Dash List Wrap-Up; 7AC When; 9PP Association Semicolon

My Husband's Summer Wardrobe by Melinda Robertson

I've always considered my husband's obsession with his summer wardrobe to be an anomaly.**1** He has a very individualistic sense of fashion – which is not always consistent with the current decade, his age group, socio-economic status, or any other established societal 'norms'.**2** Anyone under the age of sixty that can wear knee-high football socks with sandals, faded t-shirts with giant holes, and short pants with permanent grass stains – in public with no sense of embarrassment – should be considered devoid of any fashion sense.**3**

His clothing may appear to have been put on indiscriminately; however, all of his outfits have been planned well in advance of any summer outings.**4** At the beginning of the season (to eliminate time spent selecting the perfect outfit for any planned outings), he purchases the most monochromatic clothing that he can find – provided that it coordinates with his idea of fashion.**5** Shoes, shorts, shirts – all these items must be either khaki, drab olive, or black; if they do not qualify as part of these color categories, he will not buy them.**6**

Not only is he concerned with color, but with style and function according to his own unique conception.**7** His shorts must fit into his fashion code exactly: they must have two back pockets with flaps, and four front pockets.**8** His shorts must also have the 'zip on legs' option, so they may be converted to pants, and – most important of all – they must not be too long.**9** His shirts are the easiest to pick out; they must have a 'cool' design that is non-offensive.**10** His shirts must also be long enough to cover the waistband of his shorts, so that if he bends over, his butt crack won't show.**11**

Shopping with my husband for his summer wardrobe can be tiring.**12** Hopefully, the fashion experts will one day make "robot animals" to assist the adult male in his shopping as well as accompany him.**13** Until then, I will continue to suffer through every summer season. **14**

Sentence Forms:

1) 3V Infinitive
2) 11ADD Noun of; 8RN Which; 2S Choices Series; 3V Past Participle
3) 8RN That; 11ADD Compound Noun Phrases in a List; 3V Past Participle; 10TP M Prepositional Phrase extended; 11ADD Noun of
4) 9PP Expansive Colon
5) 10TP B Prepositional phrase extended; 10TP B (Verbal Phrase Infinitive); 9PP Dash Break; 3V Past Participle
6) 9PP B List Wrap-Up; 4C Either or; 9PP Association Semicolon; 7AC If
7) 4CC Not only, but; 2S The Pair
8) 9PP Explanation Semicolon
9) 6CC So; 6CC And; 9PP Dash M Adjective Phrase
10) 9PP Association Semicolon; 8RN That

11) 3V Infinitive; 7AC So that supplemental; 7AC If
12) 3V Gerund
13) 10TP B Word; 3V Infinitive; 4C As well as; 3V Infinitive Missing to
14) 10 TP B Prepositional Phrase; 3V Infinitive

GONE FISHING by Jimmy Currie

Life can be hard at times and a person needs some way of relieving stress.**1** I have tried them all, but the one thing that works best for me is fishing.**2** I remember catching my very first fish, just like it was yesterday.**3** That fish started tugging, pulling, jerking me all over the place.**4** Since that day I have had a passion for fishing and the joy that it brings.**5** A day spent behind the rod leaves me feeling refreshed and ready for the curves life has in store.**6**

I travel around all the time with fishing supplies in my car.**7** You never know when you may come across a good fishing hole.**8** Rivers, lakes, streams – these are the places where I like fishing the most.**9** My favorite fish – bass, cat, and brim – are all found in rivers and streams.**10** However, lakes provide excellent varieties of fish also.**11** Fishing rods are my choice for fishing in lakes; poles are my choice of fishing in rivers and streams.**12** Earthworms and grasshoppers, crickets and minnows, lures and liver are all types of fish bait.**13** If you are lucky enough to have a boat, you get the best fishing from rivers, lakes, or streams.**14**

Fishing allows me to spend quality time with friends and family.**15** My family – as much as I like having them around – are not good fishermen at all.**16** I spend more of my time baiting their hooks rather than fishing.**17** Pretty soon someone will catch a fish: this starts the competition.**18** For the rest of the day, everyone's goal is to catch a bigger one.**19**

Casting out every time, not knowing what you will catch, brings everybody excitement.**20** Sometimes, I like to fish alone to have peace and quiet.**21** Any problem that I may be having usually can be worked out on the banks of a river.**22**

You never know how long you are going to be away when you go fishing, so pack a lunch.**23** Even though fishing relieves my stress, one other thing keeps me coming book: the one that got away.**24**

Sentence Forms:

1) 3V Gerund
2) 6CC But; 8RN That; 3V Gerund
3) 3V Gerund; 7AC As If supplemental
4) 2S Triple Force
5) 10TP B Prepositional Phrase; 3V Gerund; 2S The Pair; 8RN That
6) 3V Past Participle; 3V Present Participle; 2S The Pair; 8RN Missing That
7) 3V Present Participle
8) 8RN When; 3V Present Participle
9) 9PP Dash List Wrap-Up; 7AC Where; 3V Gerund
10) 9PP Dash M List Appositives in Standard Series; 2S The Pair
11) 10TP B Word; 11ADD Noun of
12) 3V Present Participle; 3V Gerund (2); 9PP Association Semicolon; 2S The Pair
13) 2S The Pair (3); 2S Triple Force
14) 7AC If; 2V Infinitive; 3V Gerund; 2S Choices Series
15) 3V Gerund; 3V Infinitive; 2S The Pair
16) 9PP Dash M AC Clause supplemental; 3V Gerund
17) 4C Rather than; 3V Present Participle (2)
18) 9PP Explanation Colon
19) 10 TP B Prepositional Phrase extended; 3V Infinitive
20) 3V Gerund; 3V Present Participle; 8RN What
21) 10TP B Word; 3V Infinitive (2); 2S The Pair
22) 8RN That
23) 8RN How; 3V Infinitive; 7AC When; 6CC So
24) 7AC Even Though; 3V Gerund; 9PP Explanation Colon; 8RN That

GONE COUNTRY by Joshua Delange

I have never understood how a child gets their particular tastes in music.**1** Some people say that you pick them up from your family, and others say you get them from culture and friends.**2** Personally, I think it's a bit of both.**3**

As I have said before, in my other essays, I am a farm boy.**4** So, naturally, I grew up with parents who listen to country music, and I grew up in a culture that was country in nature.**5** All of my friends listened to R&B and Rap, but I didn't like those genres of music.**6** So, I guess I am second guessing myself.**7** So, it's not family or friends or culture.**8** Where does it come from then?**9** I feel that my taste in music came from everywhere.**10** I listened to all genres of music, and then I picked which ones I liked.**11**

When it comes to music, everyone has their own taste.**12** Children grow up listening to everyone else's music, and over time they pick a genre that they like; they also will find bands and songs outside that genre that they like as well.**13** I have many friends that like rap music, but I do not; I have many friends that do not like country, but I do.**14** One thing is certain: we all like music.**15**

If you don't know by now, I like country music, but it is not my favorite type of music.**16** When I was about 12 years old, my cousin always listened to rock music.**17** At that time, I didn't really care for rock music, but over the years it has become my favorite genre of music.**18** Besides Rock and Country music, I also enjoy listening to bluegrass, alternative, jazz, and classical music.**19** I think the main thing that draws me to a certain type of music is *listenability*.**20** I like to hear the words, the music.**21**

Everybody has their own taste in music. They choose their favorites, and sometimes they change.**22** But one thing is common among all people – we all love music.**23** Music helps people yearn, love, laugh, and heal.**24** Music is one thing in life that keeps society sane.

Sentence Forms:

1) 8RN How
2) 8RN That; 6CC And; 8RN Missing That
3) 10TP B Word; 8RN Missing That
4) 7AC As; 10TP M Prepositional Phrase;
5) 10TP B Word; 8RN That (2); 6CC And
6) 2S The Pair; 6CC But; 11ADD Noun of
7) 8RN Missing That
8) 10TP B Word; 2S Choices Series
9) 11ADD Question
10) 8RN That
11) 6CC And; 8RN Which
12) 7AC When
13) 9PP Complicated Semicolon; 3V Present Participle; 8RN That (2); 2S The Pair
14) 9PP Opposition Semicolon; 6CC But (2)
15) 9PP Explanation Colon
16) 7AC If; 6CC But
17) 7AC When
18) 10TP B Prepositional Phrase; 6CC But
19) 10TP B Prepositional Phrase; 2S The Pair; 3V Gerund; 2S Standard Series extended
20) 8RN Missing that; 8RN That
21) 3V Infinitive; 2S Compact Duo
22) 6CC And
23) 11ADD Beginning Conjunction; 9PP Dash E Clause supplemental
24) 2S Standard Series extended
25) 8RN That

RESTORING TRUCKS AND SPEEDING DOWN THE ROAD by Chris Page

Although the restoration of cars takes a lot of time and patience, the thrill of speeding down the road is well worth the time spent.**1**

My hobby started one day in the backyard as my father began rebuilding the engine in his newly purchased 1965 Chevy truck.**2** I didn't know much about cars at the time, and I was only old enough to hand my dad tools, but I managed to ask a few questions.**3** Before I knew it, I was right beside him, getting greasy and grimy.**4** The more that I helped him, the more I seemed to learn.**5** With every new learning experience, I grew more interested and knew what I wanted when I turned sixteen.**6**

Finally, the day came.**7** I turned sixteen and got my license.**8** My dad gave me that 1965 Chevy truck that we spent many days together, rebuilding.**9** It had been five years, five long years since we first worked on this truck together.**10** Spending much of my time and effort in the restoration of this truck, I had little time to do anything else.**11** If I was not in school, if I was not working, if the sun was still in the sky, I was working on the truck.**12** Since I had worked so hard on the truck, my dad decided to surprise me.**13** He bought all the parts that I had wanted to make my truck a hotrod.**14**

All I could think about was what I would fix first, for this is what I had always dreamed.**15** The time I had waited for all week had finally arrived – the weekend.**16** It was cold outside, but that would not stop my eagerness and enthusiasm to start working.**17** The camshaft, the carburetor, the manifold – these were all the parts that needed to be removed and replaced.**18**

The day finally came when all the parts had been replaced, and it was time to go out for a test drive.**19** There is nothing more thrilling than to pull out onto the road, push the accelerator to the floor, and feel the power in the engine being released.**20** The tires start to smoke, the engine reaches its peak, and then you shift into second.**21** By the time you start slowing down, you are going well over 120 m.p.h.**22**

It took me many years to realize the satisfaction of that moment on the road.**23** Although it has been several years since I have been able to work on cars, my passion to restore trucks and cars will always be there, and I long for the day when I will once again be able to speed down the road.**24**

Sentence Forms:
1) 7AC Although; 2S The Pair; 3V Gerund; 3V Past Participle
2) 7AC As; 3V Gerund; 3V Past Participle

3) 6CC And; 6CC But; 3V Infinitive (2)
4) 7AC Before; 3V Present Participle; 2S The Pair
5) 4C The more, the more; 8RN That; 8RN Missing that; 3V Infinitive
6) 10TP B Prepositional Phrase; 11ADD Compound verb; 8RN What; 7AC When
7) 10TP B Word
8) 11ADD Compound verb
9) 8RN That; 10TP E Word
10) 5R Repetition Keyword; 7AC Since; 10TP E Noun Phrase
11) 10TP B Verbal Phrase; 2S The Pair; 3V Infinitive
12) 5R Adverbial Conjunction
13) 7AC Since; 3V Infinitive
14) 8RN That; 3V Infinitive
15) 8RN What (2); 6CC For
16) 8RN Missing that; 9PP E Word
17) 6CC But; 2S The Pair; 3V Infinitive; 3v Gerund
18) 2S Triple Force; 9PP Dash B Wrap-up; 8RN That; 11ADD Compound Infinitive
19) 7AC When; 6CC And; 3V Infinitive
20) 11ADD Compound Infinitive; 2S Standard Series; 3V Present Participle
21) 3V Infinitive; 2S Standard Series
22) 10TP B Prepositional Phrase; 8RN Missing that; 3V Gerund
23) 3V Infinitive
24) 7C Although; 7AC Since; 3V Infinitive (2); 2S The Pair; 6CC And; 7AC When

FASHION PERSONALITIES **by April Turner**

The clothes we wear say more about us than we think.**1** I have come to learn that a person's personality and wardrobe go hand-in-hand.**2** You cannot judge a person solely on a first impression; rather, it takes a long time.**3** It takes several weeks of observation to make a sound judgment: weeks of seeing the person, weeks of watching the person, weeks of studying his or her dress pattern.**4** You will – 9 times out of 10 – find three main personality types: those who dress to fit in, those who dress to stand out, and those who dress whichever way they please.**5**

Do you know someone who only wears the latest fashions?**6** He wouldn't be caught dead in a pair of "Air Jordans" more than 6 months old. Every piece of clothing he owns is name brand: Nautica, Nike, Polo. **7** He doesn't own a shirt that cost him less than $30.00.**8** He will only wear clothes that he knows are in style, as long as baggy pants and big shirts will bring popularity.**9**

Then there is the shy, stand-offish person. You will only find him in the back of the room or to the side of any crowd.**10** This guy most likely has a basic wardrobe, because he doesn't want to wear anything that may draw attention to himself.**11** He owns about seven pairs of jeans – all blue. He likes to wear white or black shirts, but never a bright color.**12**

Finally, there is my favorite. This person wears anything that catches his eye.**13** He knows what he likes and goes for it.**14** He is not out to impress, for he does not worry about what others think.**15** He likes to wear name brands, but he loves a good bargain.**16** He dresses how he feels.**17** If he is in a good mood, he looks nice, whereas you may catch him on a bad day and not even recognize him.**18** This person is outgoing; however, he can sometimes be moody.**19** He is happy and content with himself; he has confidence in himself and in his preferences and taste in clothes.**20** He chooses and wears clothes that reflect his character and personality.**21**

Sentence Forms:

1) 8RN Missing that; 7AC Than supplemental
2) 3VInfinitive; 8RN That; 2S The Pair
3) 9PP Expansive Semicolon
4) 11ADD Noun of; 3V Infinitive; 9PP Explanation Colon; 5R Keyword; 3V Gerund
5) 10TP M Adverb Phrase; 9PP List Colon; 8RN Who (3); 3V Infinitive (2); 8RN Missing that
6) 11ADD Question
7) 8RN Missing that; 9PP List Colon
8) 8RN That
9) 8RN That; 7AC As long as supplementary; 2S The Pair
10) 2S Choices Series

11) 7AC Because; 3V Infinitive; 8RN That
12) 9PP Dash E Adjective Phrase
13) 8RN That
14) 8RN What; 11ADD Compound Verb
15) 3V Infinitive; 6CC For; 8RN What
16) 3V Infinitive; 6CC But
17) 8RN How
18) 7AC If; 7AC Whereas supplemental; 11ADD Compound verb
19) 9PP Expansive Semicolon
20) 2S The Pair (2); 9PP Association Semicolon
21) 11ADD Compound verb; 8RN That; 2S The Pair

NEVER TOO SHORT by Ian Anderson

The miniskirt – no single article of clothing in all creation is its equal.**1** Through its sultry subtlety, men have fallen bereft of breath, bereft of brains, and bereft of the money in their wallets.**2** Leather or lace, plaids or prints – just give me the miniskirt in all its unchaste virtue.**3**

It is a creation born out of a liberating fashion sense of pure anti-feminism; however, it is a practical and aerodynamic invention with modern applications.**4** It is short enough to engender blind lust, yet only long enough to conceal nearly nothing.**5**

Its flawlessly scant design allows for endless freedom of movement while improving a vast array of activities – dance, aerobics, trampoline.**6** Already, we find its use on many dance floors around the world.**7**

Often the mini – as it is referred to in some circles – can be an indication of personality.**8** More aggressive individuals prefer the militant cameo prints or black leather styles; subdued personas lean more towards frills and neutral colors.**9** Unique beings – wild and free – head out the door with something in plaid covered with safety pins to express their inner self.**10**

Some actually dislike the miniskirt, calling it crude and distasteful – I beg them to reconsider.**11** Look at the good caused by this miracle of modern fashion.**12** Countless couples fall in love every year due to the miniskirt and have children; marriage is optional at this point.**13** Lucrative businesses switch uniforms from pants to miniskirts to boost profits.**14** And last year alone a blind New Yorker was cured of his disability, simply by being in the presence of a miniskirt.**15**

This is a glorious time to be alive – thanks directly to our friend, the miniskirt.**16**

Sentence Forms:

1) 9PP Dash B Word; 11ADD noun of
2) 10TP B Prepositional Phrase; 5R Keyword; 2S Standard Series; literary device alliteration (2)
3) 2S Rhythmical Pairs (variation with Choice);
4) 3V Gerund; 9PP Expansive Semicolon; 2S The Pair
5) 6CC Yet; 3V Infinitive (2)
6) 7AC While; 9PP List Colon
7) 10TP B Word
8) 9PP Dash M Adverb Phrase; 11ADD Noun of
9) 9PP Association Semicolon; 2S Choices; 2S The Pair
10) 9PP Dash M Adjective Phrase; 2S The Pair; 3V Past Participle; 3V Infinitive
11) 3V Present Participle; 2S The Pair; 9PP Dash Break
12) 11ADD Beginning Verb; 3V Past Participle
13) 11ADD Compound Verb; 9PP Association Semicolon; literary device alliteration
14) 4C From to; 3V Infinitive
15) 11ADD Beginning Verb; 10TP E Adverb Phrase; 3V Gerund; literary device hyperbole
16) 9PP Dash Break; 10TP E Appositive

Note: our apologies for what some might regard as the possibly bad taste and sexist stance of this essay, but we do find it well-written with an excellent example of hyperbole. And we should not unduly censor what students write in favor of values that not all share.

GERMAN SHEPHERD   by PFC Johnson, N.

While I was young, my mother, acting as both parents, bought a dog.**1** The dog was a puppy at the time, but was everything a boy could want in a friend: playful, thoughtful, always there, willing to do anything, and would listen to you longer than anyone (aside from a nosy high school counselor).**2** This dog, a German Shepherd, was the closest thing to a sibling to me, a friend to me, and even, in a sense, a parent to me.**3**

Sassy, the name of my puppy, watched over me and kept me company, protecting me from danger, for I lived in a rough neighborhood.**4** Because my mother worked all night and slept all day, I was alone most of the time with nothing but my thoughts and my dog to entertain me.**5** Sassy was the one thing I needed to get though my childhood: she was the stepping stone to my happiness.**6**

Having a dog like Sassy was one of the best things that ever occurred in my life; but all good things must come to an end (and the greatest sometimes come to a screeching halt, leaving you with the feeling of being stabbed in the chest with a 2x4).**7** So, with Sassy locked in the backseat, we made our way to the animal clinic: she was going to be "put to sleep".**8** We were moving across the country, and we could not bring her along.**9** We could have given her to another family, but there were a few problems: she was getting old, she was going blind, and she had a broken leg that had never fully healed.**10** Our only choice was a choice too difficult for a 12-year-old boy – me – to deal with.**11**

After that heart-wrenching drama, and after my mother and I settled in our new house, we bought new animals of different types and genders.**12** But nothing could ever replace my German shepherd, Sassy.**13** As long as I live, I will never forget what that animal taught me, and where I might be if she had not come into my life.**14**

Sentence Forms:

1) 7AC While; 10TP M Verbal Phrase Present Participle

2) 6CC But (assumed subject); 8RN Missing that; 9PP Explanation Colon; 2S Standard Series extended; 10TP E (Prepositional Phrase)
3) 10TP M Appositive (2); 2S Standard Series; 10TP M Prepositional Phrase
4) 10TP M Appositive; 11ADD Compound Verb; 3V Present Participle; 6CC For
5) 7AC Because; 11ADD Compound Verb
6) 8RN Missing that; 3V Infinitive; 9PP Explanation Colon; literary device alliteration
7) 3V Gerund (2); 8RN That; 9PP Association Semicolon; 10TP E (Anecdotal Insertion); 3V Present Participle (2)
8) 10TP B Word; 10TP B Prepositional Phrase; 3V Past Participle; 9PP Explanation Colon
9) 6CC And
10) 6CC But; 9PP List Colon; 5R Word; 8RN That
11) 9PP Dash M Appositive; 3V Infinitive
12) 10TP B Prepositional Phrase; 7AC After; 11ADD Compound Prepositional Phrase; 2S The Pair
13) 11ADD Beginning Conjunction; 10TPE Appositive
14) 7AC As long as supplemental; 8RN What; 8RN Where; 7AC If

FRIENDS FOREVER by Kristie Noble

Friends help you when you are down and understand your feelings.**1** The day I met my best friend felt like the world stopped around me and my new best friend – Sabrina.**2** Meeting Sabrina was the best thing that could have happened to me; she opened new worlds to me and showed me how to absorb every aspect of life.**3** I would have to say Sabrina saved me from myself.**4**

In fifth grade, I was so determined to belong to the rich, popular crowd in my class.**5** Every day I would think of new ways to try to fit in and make new friends.**6** I did not realize that I was really destroying my self-esteem.**7** Then one day I met Sabrina, and my old perception about being popular vanished from my head.**8** I suddenly remembered what I had really been searching for my whole life: I felt I discovered the other half of me.**9**

Sabrina and I spent every waking moment with each other.**10** Watching movies, having sleepovers, making popcorn balls – all were things we would do on the weekends.**11** The sleepovers were the best because Sabrina and I would stay up all night, talking and jamming to music.**12** We told each other our dreams – dreams of desires, dreams of future jobs.**13** Those days were the best days of my childhood.

I thought our friendship would never end; I believed that our bond would last forever.**14** Unfortunately, our friendship did come to an end.**15** I started to ignore Sabrina because I had a new best friend.**16** My new friends started to convince me that Sabrina was too controlling, mean, abusive.**17** I did not need that kind of hatred in my life; therefore, I exiled her from my life.**18** Sabrina felt threatened and scared and alone, so she banished me from her life as well.**19** Though other friends knew we were not speaking, friends at school urged us to work out our problems through talking.**20** Their tactics – talk sessions, secret trips, and letters – made matters worse in our relationship.**21**

Realizing we were both wrong, Sabrina wrote me the most amazing letter, which described how she thought that our friendship was too precious to throw away.**22** The friendship that we once lost was now restored and cherished again.**23** I never thought I would value a friend as much as I treasure Sabrina.**24** There is one lesson that she taught me, the one unforgettable lesson of my life: forgive those whom you love most in your life.**25**

Sentence Forms:

1) 7AC When; 11ADD Compound verb
2) 8RN Missing that; 3V Past Participle; 9PP Dash E Appositive
3) 3V Gerund; 8RN That; 9PP Association Semicolon; 11ADD Compound verb; 8RN How; 3V Infinitive
4) 3V Infinitive; 8RN Missing that
5) 10TP B Prepositional Phrase; 3V Infinitive; 2S Compact Duo

6) 3V Infinitive; 11ADD Compound Verbal Infinitive with Missing to
7) 8RN That
8) 6CC And
9) 8RN What; 9PP Explanation Colon; 8RN Missing That
10) 2S The Pair; 3V Present Participle
11) 3V Gerund (3); 2S Triple Force; 9PP Dash B Wrap-up; 8RN Missing that
12) 7AC Because; 2S The Pair (2); 3V Present Participle (2)
13) 9PP Dash E Appositive Phrase; 5R Repetition Keyword; 11ADD Noun of
14) 9PP Association Semicolon; 8RN That
15) 10TP B Word
16) 3V Infinitive; 7AC Because
17) 3V Infinitive; 8RN That; 2S Triple Force
18) 9PP Expansive Semicolon
19) 2S Lyrical Series; 6CC So
20) 7AC Though; 3V Infinitive; 3V Gerund
21) 9PP Dash M Series of Appositives; 2S Standard Series
22) 3V Present Participle(2); 8RN Which; 8RN How; 8RN That; 3v Infinitive
23) 8RN That; 11ADD Compound verb
24) 8RN Missing That; 7AC As . . . As supplementary
25) 1F There is; 8RN That; 10TP E Appositive Phrase; 9PP Explanation Colon; 8RN Whom

A GREAT FILM **by Matthews J. Garvin**

One of the best movies ever produced was – in my opinion – *Braveheart*.**1** Although it was in theaters many years ago, it is still worth renting from the video store.**2** Produced by Mel Gibson, *Braveheart* is an epic tale about a young hero with a tragic life story.**3** He dedicated his life towards achieving a goal – freedom – which unfortunately he never attained while he was alive.**4** However, his dream does become a reality; his spirit and dedication inspire others who succeed in finishing his quest.**5** In the spirit of this great film, I will attempt to explain the story to you.**6** Hopefully, you will understand how this story begins, the event that changes William's life forever, and the outcome of this brave quest.**7**

The main character in this movie is William Wallace, who is a born and bred native from Scotland.**8** When William was a young boy, his father and other men from the village were murdered like cattle in a slaughterhouse by the King of England.**9** After this event, William's uncle arrives to take him to Italy, to Spain, to France.**10** Since he has no other family to look after him, William travels to Europe with his uncle.**11** A long period of time passes, and young William is young William no longer.**12** Instead, he is a talented, confident, knowledgeable, and educated man.**13** He returns to his home village to rebuild his life – to live in peace.**14**

Not only does he want to maintain a productive farm, but he also wishes to raise a family.**15** Before long, William marries the girl of his dreams, whom he had loved since he was a child.**16** Because of English law which would require him to share his wife on his wedding night with an English lord, he is forced to marry in secret so that he would not have to share his wife.**17** The governor of the territory eventually finds out and has her killed.**18** Out of feverish anger, William retaliates and kills the governor himself and his entire band of soldiers.**19** Having remembered what his father endured to break free from the English rule peacefully and as a result of this beloved wife's death, William Wallace makes the choice to take revenge and return what belongs to Scotland by force.**20**

The tale continues with Wallace traveling the countryside, gathering men from Scotland and Ireland, defeating English soldiers in an effort to end the oppression of the King of England, to which at that time Scotland belonged.**21** During the battle that could decide the future of Scotland, William is betrayed by one of the nobles fighting for freedom also, and the Scots lose the fight.**22** He is later captured and is faced with one last agonizing choice: endure much pain and suffering, or die quickly.**23** He chooses the pain and suffering as an example to others.**24**

Although William is now dead, the fight is not over.**25** The tale ends with a new leader emerging to take charge of the movement, and the people of Scotland gain their independence from England.**26**

Many great movies have been produced through the course of history.**27** *Braveheart* is one of those that grabs your heart and spirit, and takes you through the events as if you were part of the adventure.**28** In my attempt to explain how the movie begins, what changes William Wallace's life, and the outcome of his quest, hopefully you will have made the decision to rent this movie and live the adventure yourself.**29**

Sentence Forms:

1) 3V Past Participle; 9PP Dash M Prepositional Phrase
2) 7AC Although
3) 10TP B Verbal Phrase
4) 3V Gerund; 9PP Dash M Appositive; 8RN Which; 7C While
5) 10TPB Word; 9PP Association Semicolon; 2S The Pair; 8RN Who; 3V Gerund
6) 10TP B Prepositional Phrase extended; 3V Infinitive
7) 10TP B Word; 8RN How; 8RN That; 2S Standard Series
8) 8RN Who; 11ADD Compound Verbal Past Participle
9) 7AC When; 2S The Pair; 11ADD Noun of
10) 10TP B Prepositional Phrase; 3V Infinitive; 2S Triple Force
11) 7AC Since; 3V Infinitive
12) 6CC And
13) 10TP B Word; 2S Standard Series extended
14) 3V Infinitive; 9PP Dash E Verbal Phrase Infinitive
15) 4C Not only, but; 3V Infinitive (2)
16) 10TP B Prepositional Phrase; 5R Keyword; 8RN Whom; 7AC Since
17) 10TP B Prepositional Phrase; 8RN Which; 3V Infinitive (2); 7AC So that supplemental
18) 11ADD Compound Verb
19) 10TP B Prepositional Phrase; 11ADD Compound (2); 11ADD Noun of

20) 3V Present Participle; 8RN What; 3V Infinitive (2); 8RN What
21) 3V Present Participle (3); 2S Triple Force; 3V Infinitive; 8RN Which
22) 10TP B Prepositional Phrase; 8RN That; 3V Present Participle; 6CC And
23) 11ADD Compound Verb; 9PP Explanation Colon; 2S The Pair; 2S Choice Series
24) 2S The Pair
25) 7AC Although
26) 3V Present Participle; 3V Infinitive; 6CC And; 11ADD Noun of
27) 11ADD Noun of
28) 8RN That; 2S The Pair; 11ADD Compound Verb; 7AC As If supplementary
29) 10TP B Prepositional Phrase; 3V Infinitive (2); 8RN How; 8RN What; 11ADD Compound Verb

THE LAST PLAY OF THE GAME
by William Gonzales

Everyone on the team, who were seniors, knew the significance of this play.**1** It was the fourth quarter of Sam Rayburn High School vs. Aldene Nimitz High School; there were twenty-six seconds left in the game.**2** The score was 17 to 12 in Aldene's favor; however, we still had a chance, if we could only get four yards on this fourth down play.**3** This play meant more than just winning or losing a football game: it was the culmination of our adolescent lives.**4**

The seniors on the field were all thinking the same thing. We realized that this was possibly not only the last play of the football season, but it could also so be the last play and day of high school, of our innocence, of our youth.**5** Visions of the past appeared; our whole lives loomed before us.**6** After what seemed to be an eternal time out, we were in the huddle.**7**

Signals were flashed from the sidelines to our quarterback; the play was called.**8** I was to run a short slant pattern. I knew the pass would not go to me; however, the pass would go to another player, no mediocre pass catcher but an all-state receiver.**9** Everyone knew what they had to do, as we broke our huddle and stepped to the line.**10**

We lined up in formation as soldiers would, which is exactly what we were – soldiers (after all we had just been through a war).**11** We watched the enemy while our minds raced, raced through memories, raced through visions of success, raced through visions of defeat.**12** Brett, our quarterback, began yelling his commands; he yelled red, a code for when to react and begin the play.**13** It was time.

The play began – time to go to work.**14** Brett was in trouble; the enemy was blitzing; he had no one to throw to.**15** Suddenly, our eyes made contact, and he was able to lob a pass to me.**16** The ball hung in the air for an eternity. I thought if I could just catch it, if I could just get the first down, if I could just get out of bounds, then we had a chance.**17** The ball found my hands, but the clock ended the game before I could get out of bounds.**18** Then in a blink, high school and our youth and everything we had been were over.**19**

Sentence Forms:

1) 10TP M Clausal Interruption supplemental
2) 9PP Association Semicolon
3) 9PP Expansive Semicolon; 7AC If
4) 3V Gerund (2); 2S Choice Series; 9PP Explanation Colon
5) 4C Not Only, But; 2S The Pair; 5R Word
6) 9PP Association Semicolon
7) 8RN What
8) 9PP Association Semicolon
9) 9PP Expansive Semicolon; 10TP E Appositive Phrase (2); 4C Not only, but (variation)
10) 8RN What; 7AC As; 11ADD Compound Verb
11) 8RN Which; 8RN What; 10TP E Word; 10TP E (Clause) supplemental
12) 7AC While; 5R Keyword; 11ADD Noun of (2)
13) 10TP M Appositive; 3V Gerund; 10TP E Appositive Phrase; 8RN When; 3V Infinitive; 11ADD Compound Verbal Infinitive Missing to

14) 9PP Dash Break; 3V Infinitive
15) 9PP Trio Semicolon; 3V Infinitive
16) 10TP M Word; 6CC And; 3V Infinitive
17) 5R Adverbial Conjunction
18) 6CC But; 7AC Before
19) 10TP B Adverb Phrase; 2S Lyrical Series; 8RN Missing that

FAVORITE SPORTS by Rita Chung

I don't consider myself to be an athletic individual, but in my spare time there are a small handful of sports that I enjoy participating in on a daily basis.**1** The few sports that I'm attracted to and interested in are basketball and badminton.**2** Back in elementary school, my passion for basketball continued through middle school.**3** I quickly found myself playing this particular sport with the neighborhood children every afternoon after school.**4** It was not until high school that a friend of mine introduced me to badminton, and from there I displayed a strong interest towards this highly acquired sport.**5**

I started playing basketball at a young age – seven years old.**6** I was persistent in perfecting my game and would spend hours on the basketball court, whether there was anybody to play with or not.**7** Not only did I shoot fifty free throws a day, but I also practiced my lay-up shots and three-pointers as well.**8** When neighborhood kids would ask me to play a game or two, I welcomed the challenge with open arms and often encouraged it.**9** Even though I spent my free time playing basketball – before and after school – I was hesitant in joining the girls' basketball team.**10** Since I had played only in a fashion where we played by the basic rules of the game rather than playing by official organized rules, I was intimidated by the competition and questioned how good my abilities were compared to other girls; other girls seemed to me to take the sport too seriously.**11** All in all, I came to the conclusion that I found myself delighting in basketball more by playing it for fun, instead of worrying about winning or losing, becoming the champion or the defeated.**12**

In high school, I didn't plan to join any sport teams.**13** By then, my interest in basketball somewhat diminished, and my priorities had changed.**14** As junior year approached, however, badminton caught my attention, which was brought about by a good friend of mine.**15** I went to a few practices and decided that I might be fairly good, especially when playing singles.**16** You have to be light on your feet, moving from side to side to improve your speed and agility.**17** You have to have good judgment – knowing exactly if the birdie is in bounds or out – before you decide to take the risk in attempting to go for the hit or not.**18** Surprisingly, you work a lot of your muscles playing badminton; nonetheless, you don't feel the repercussions until the next day if you play this sport for the first time.**19**

Whether it's playing badminton or basketball, both sports give me a great cardio workout as I enjoy myself on the court without the stress of competition.**20**

Sentence Forms:

1) 6CC But; 3V Infinitive; 8RN That; 3V Gerund
2) 11ADD Compound Verb; 2S The Pair
3) 10TP B Adverb Phrase
4) 3V Present Participle
5) 8RN That; 6CC And; 3V Past Participle
6) 3V Gerund; 9PP Dash E Noun Phrase
7) 3V Gerund; 11ADD Compound Verb; 7AC Whether; 3V infinitive
8) 4CC Not Only, But; 2S The Pair
9) 7AC When; 3V Infinitive; 11ADD Compound Verb
10) 7AC Even Though; 9PP Dash M Prepositional Phrase; 3V Gerund
11) 7AC Since; 8RN Where; 3V Gerund; 11ADD Compound Verb; 8RN how; 9PP Association Semicolon; 3V Infinitive
12) 10TP B Prepositional Phrase; 8RN That; 3V Infinitive; 3V Gerund (3); 2S Choice Series (2); 10TP E Prepositional Phrase; 10TP E Verbal Phrase Present Participle
13) 10TP B Prepositional Phrase
14) 10TP B Prepositional Phrase; 6CC And

15) 7AC As; 8RN Which
16) 11ADD Compound Verb; 8RN That; 11ADD Especially; 3V Gerund
17) 3V infinitive (2); 3V Present Participle; 2S The Pair
18) 3V Infinitive (3); 9PP Dash M Verbal Phrase Present Participle; 3V Gerund
19) 10TP B Word; 3V Present Participle; 9PP Expansive Semicolon; 7AC If
20) 7AC Whether; 3V Gerund; 2S Choice Series; 7AC As; 11ADD Noun Of

CLOTHES – NOT MERELY APPAREL
by Littlejohn

Clothes are a mirror. Clothes can reflect who you are, revealing your financial status, your personality, your culture.**1**

Clothes show a person's financial status. A poor beggar's clothes look worn, full of holes, and mucky; however, the clothing of a richly adorned woman (Oprah, for instance) reflects her wealth.**2** Her clothes are well-coordinated and trendy, expensive and renowned.**3** Oprah's clothing indicates her high-class stature.

There is also the middle class, which wears many different varieties of clothing, from main brands to no brand.**4** Usually, the middle-class group tends to have a wardrobe derived from some of the following main brand names: Tommy, Express, Aero pastel, American Eagle, and Buckle.**5** On the other hand, their wardrobe also consists of clothing from some of the stores not carrying brand names: Wall-mart, K-mart, Target, Rue-21, Rave, Hot Topic, and Gadzooks.**6** Thus, the middle class are identified by their wearing a mixture of brand and non-brand name clothes.**7**

In addition to reflecting financial status, clothes also reveal personality through the preference of clothes style.**8** In particular, young people who are ill-humored and favor black colors tend to take on a gothic taste and appearance.**9** Not only do they wear black clothing, but they wear spiked collars and all sorts of exotic piercings.**10** Possibly, this style results from the need to be seen, heard, and understood. **11** Then there is the different style of those not wanting to stand out. **12** They tend to dress in a camouflage or blended manner: they wear the latest, most popular, costly, and commonly worn clothing styles. **13** They wear their clothes to display how similar and in tune they are with the appearance and preference in clothes of their peers. **14**

Finally, clothing identifies not only your financial status and personality, but it also identifies your culture. **15** The modern cultures of Japan, Korea, and America each possess a style by which they can be identified. **16** Korean clothing is generally worn to fit loosely or securely. **17** The females go to school in skirts with lengths well below the knee. On the contrary, the Japanese culture does favor the wearing of modest clothing. **18** The girls in Japan wear skirts to school that end about 10-12 inches below the waist; the women as well as the men adorn their bodies with clothing that show their shapes in the greatest of detail. **19** America, being the world's melting pot, now derives its style from many different parts of the world. **20** Therefore, American clothing styles range from revealing to highly conservative, from multi-cultural to just plain American blue jeans and T-shirts. **21**

Sentence Forms:

1) 8RN Who; 3V Present Participle; 2S Triple Force; 5R Word
2) 2S Standard Series; 9PP Expansive Semicolon; 3V Past Participle; 10TP M (Noun Phrase) Insertion Writer Comment
3) 2S Rhythmical Pairs; 3V Past Participle
4) 1F There is; 8RN Which; 10TP M Clause Interruption supplemental; 4C From to
5) 10TP B Word; 9PP List Colon
6) 10TP B Prepositional Phrase; 3V Present Participle; 9PP List Colon
7) 3V Gerund; 2S The Pair
8) 10TP B Prepositional Phrase; 3V Gerund
9) 10TP B Prepositional Phrase; 8RN Who; 11ADD Compound verb; 3V Infinitive
10) 4C Not Only, But; 3V Past Participle; 3V Gerund
11) 10TP B Word; 2S Standard Series
12) 3V Present Participle; 3V infinitive

13) 3V Infinitive; 2S Choice Series; 9PP Explanation Colon; 3V Past Participle
14) 3V Infinitive; 8RN How; 2S The Pair (2)
15) 10TP B Word; 4C Not Only, But
16) 2S Standard Series; 8RN Which
17) 3V Infinitive; 2S Choice Series
18) 10TP B Prepositional Phrase; 3V Gerund
19) 8RN That(2); 9PP Association Semicolon
20) 10TP M Verbal Phrase Present Participle; 3V Present Participle
21) 10TP B Word; 4C From to (2); 3V Present Participle; 2S The Pair

TRIP OF A LIFETIME by Hee Gon Yang

I had one of those once in a lifetime travel experiences that people often talk about: I got the chance to set foot in a country that was formerly part of the Soviet Union.**1** Think about it.**2** How many people can claim to have been sightseeing in a country that was once declared the evil enemy of the United States?**3** To top it off, we were invited guests.**4** I got that opportunity, and I loved every minute of it.**5**

While serving aboard a United States warship, we made a port call at a country that recently declared their independence from the Soviet Union.**6** Our ship was involved in a joint maritime exercise in the Baltic region to strengthen our ties with the countries in that area.**7** After the conclusion of the exercise, we were notified of the planned visit.**8** I cannot speak of everyone on our ship, but I was extremely excited.**9** I remember thinking that here is the chance to see the history and sights of a country that was once my enemy.**10** So, I got to visit Estonia.**11**

It was a sunny day with a cool breeze blowing in.**12** The scene was surreal; it was perfect day – with the exception of the smell from garbage barges nearby.**13** I could hardly wait for the ship to be moored.**14** A tugboat arrived to guide us into the pier.**15** As one of the tugboat's crew tossed us the guide-line, he belted in crude English (which surprised some of us) instructions for us to haul in the lines and tie them onto the ship.**16** The moment finally arrived; we were moored.**17** We had docked onto the pier of Estonia.

We hustled and bustled to finish up our work so that we could go out and see the sights.**18** After receiving the mandatory security briefs which are practically the same in every port that we visit, we were off on our own to do as we pleased.**19** I was floored by the beauty of the city – once we got past the industrial section of the shipyard.**20** This was not what I imagined a communist state to look like.**21** Cobblestone streets and beautiful statues, scenic parks and ancient architectures painted the town.**22**

What shocked me most were the people: they were extremely friendly.**23** I remember striking up a conversation with an elderly gentleman on a street café.**24** He was an imposing figure of a man – even though the years had caught up with him.**25** However, the gentleness of his voice belied his image.**26** We talked about various subjects ranging from life to hobbies.**27** As we shared a drink, he recounted the tales of his time in Afghanistan, of all the battles in which he had been involved.**28** He even showed us his bullet wounds; his legs were all scarred up.**29**

I must say that I really enjoyed my time in Estonia.**30** Due to economic recession in that country, everything was extremely affordable.**31** Shop owners were ecstatic with us in town. I bought so many souvenirs that I had doubts whether or not I could store it all on the ship since space is at a premium on the ship, and we are allotted only so much.**32**

I never thought that I would ever get the chance to visit the Soviet Union, but I did get the chance.**33** The trip will forever be in my memory. I had the chance to take part in history.**34** I will remember a lot about my visit to Estonia, but what I will remember most vividly will be the people of Estonia.**35**

Sentence Forms:

1) 8RN That (2); 9PP Explanation Colon; 3V Infinitive
2) 11ADD Beginning Verb

3) 11ADD Question; 3V Infinitive; 8RN That
4) 10TP B Verbal Phrase Infinitive
5) 6CC And
6) 7AC While, 8RN That
7) 3V Infinitive
8) 7AC After, 3V Past Participle
9) 6CC But
10) 3V Gerund, 8RN That (2), 3V Infinitive
11) 10TP B Word, 3V Infinitive
12) 3V Present Participle
13) 9PP Association Semicolon; 10TP E Prepositional Phrase extended
14) 3V Infinitive
15) 3V Infinitive
16) 7AC As; 10TP M (Reference Clause); 3V Infinitive; 11ADD Compound Infinitive with Missing *to*
17) 9PP Association Semicolon
18) 11ADD Compound Verb; 3V Infinitive
19) 7AC After; 8RN Which; 8RN That; 3V Infinitive; 7AC As
20) 9PP Dash E Adverbial Clause
21) 8RN What; 3V Infinitive
22) 2S Rhythmical Pairs
23) 8RN What; 9PP Explanation Semicolon
24) 3V Gerund
25) 3V Present Participle; 9PP Dash E Adverbial Clause
26) 10TP B Word
27) 3V Present Participle; 4C From To
28) 7AC As; 10TP E Prepositional Phrase extended; 8RN Which
29) 9PP Association Semicolon
30) 8RN That
31) 10TP B Prepositional Phrase
32) 8RN That; 7AC Since; 6CC And
33) 8RN That; 3V Infinitive; 6CC But
34) 3V Infinitive
35) 6CC But; 11ADD Noun of

SHOPPING IN WONDERFUL KOREA
by Aram L. Mesina

I walk into a small store which is the size of my English classroom, and start looking around, for there are all kinds of clothes.**1** Abercrombie, Fubu, Polo, Structure, Gap, and

Nikes – all are top, brand name clothes in the U.S.**2** This store has it all. I leave the store with some Abercrombie shorts for only twelve dollars; in the States, it would have cost 40 dollars.**3** This is one of the great things about being in Korea: cheap, authentic clothes.**4** Not only has the shopping in Korea been a great benefit for me, but it has been for my friends and families back home as well: every holiday, they wait to see what I have in store for them.**5**

The mink blanket, which you can only find in Korea, works great for a Christmas present, and there are many great things about it: it is cheap, warm and comfortable, and very pretty.**6** The blanket costs only 17 dollars, but the people back home don't know that; they think it costs at least a hundred bucks.**7** And when they do start to use the mink blanket, they start to wonder why they slept so good that night.**8** Not only is it warm and comfortable, but it's so pretty too, coming in many different designs – with horses, dolphins, eagles, lions, tigers, and bears.**9**

Another great present, especially for my dad, is the custom-made, tailored suits.**10** I've taken quite a few trips to just one store, buying many suits there for me or for my dad; therefore, the owner hooks me up with good prices.**11** He charges me only 70 dollars for a 2-piece suit; however, my dad thought it cost over 200 bucks.**12** I told him to "get real"; I'd be crazy to spend that kind of money on a suit.**13**

By now, my friends and families are all getting used to the fact that everything I send them is so cheap, when it comes to the price.**14** I'll send them something or anything, and they immediately and ironically conclude that it only cost five dollars.**15** But I still love hearing and seeing their happy voices and faces each time I send them gifts.**16**

The prices for clothes in Korea are unbelievable. There was this one time that I sent my sister an orange, wool Gap hoodie.**17**. Unfortunately, she didn't really like the color, style, and design.**18** She noticed later the same hoodie at a local American store where it was expensively priced at 40 dollars.**19** That hoodie costs me only ten bucks here in Korea.

Not only have I made my folks very happy back home, but I've been just as happy, if not happier, as well.**20** Every few months or so, I travel to the famous shopping district in Osan, Korea and go on a huge shopping spree each time and buy a bunch of stuff: clothes, blankets, watches, glasses, etc.**21** By now, I have a pretty good collection of goods – all from Korea and all for a very cheap price.**22**

Being in Korea is a great place to be for many reasons, not just the clothes but for making my family and friends back home very happy, including myself.**23** I encourage all people to explore and find out what Korea has to offer.**24** I'm pretty sure there won't be any disappointments or any problems.**25** Have a happy tour!**26**

Sentence Forms:

1) 8RN Which; 11ADD Compound Verb; 6CC For
2) 9PP Dash B WrapUp;
3) 9PP Opposition Semicolon
4) 3V Gerund: 9PP Numeric Precursor Colon; 2S Compact Duo
5) 4C Not Only, But; 3V Gerund; 2S The Pair; 9PP Explanation Colon; 3V Infinitive; 8RN What
6) 8RN Which; 6CC And; 9PP Explanation Colon
7) 9PP Complicated Semicolon
8) 11ADD Beginning Conjunction; 7AC When; 3V Infinitive (2); 8RN Why
9) 4C Not Only, But; 2S The Pair; 3V Present Participle; 9PP Dash E Prepositional Phrase extended; 2S Standard Series extended
10) 11ADD Especially; 2S The Pair; 3V Past Participle
11) 3V Present Participle; 9PP Expansive Semicolon; 2S Choice Series
12) 9PP Expansive Semicolon; 8RN Missing that
13) 3V Infinitive (2); 9PP Association Semicolon
14) 2S The Pair; 8RN That; 8RN Missing that
15) 2S Choice Series; 6CC And; 2S The Pair; 8RN That
16) 11ADD Beginning Conjunction; 3V Gerund (2); 2S The Pair (2); 8RN Missing That
17) 8RN That; 2S Compact Duo
18) 10TP B Word; 2S Standard Series
19) 8RN Where
20) 4C Not Only, But; 10TP E Idiomatic Phrase supplementary

21) 10TP B Adverb Phrase; 6CC And; 11ADD Compound Verbs; 9PP List Colon
22) 10TP B Prepositional Phrase; 5R Keyword; 2S The Pair; 9PP Dash E Noun Phrase
23) 3V Gerund; 3V Infinitive; 4C Not …, But; 2S The Pair; 10TP E Verbal Phrase Present Participle
24) 3V Infinitive; 11ADD Compound Infinitive missing to; 8RN What
25) 8RN Missing That; 2S Choice Series
26) 11ADD Beginning Verb

THE SPORT OF BOXING AND LIFE

by Jacob Barragan

Modern day Gladiators – that is how I describe boxers.**1** Boxing is great, fantastic, exhilarating.**2** Boxing is like life in many ways. It is an enduring hardship; however, it can teach many things besides knowing how to defend yourself.**3** Moving out on your own, raising a family, getting a job that will keep you financially stable – these are all things that we all have to do sooner or later in life.**4** It is scary when you think about it, yet it is unavoidable.**5** How can you prepare yourself for life's hardships if you have never experienced anything similar?**6** Boxing can prepare you for life's hardships.

Boxers must train five to seven days a week, and they have to maintain a strict diet to be in good condition for their bouts.**7** Sticking to a daily workout and diet teaches you discipline.**8** If you can stick with a daily workout and diet, I believe you can hold a steady job.**9** If boxers don't stay in excellent shape, they will lose their bouts miserably; if you are not good at your job and you don't make an effort, you could lose your job to someone who does your job better than you.**10**

Boxing teaches you that you don't always win.**11** There will be some days when nothing goes right – you lose your job or get robbed – and you have to move on.**12** People lose their jobs for many reasons; however, they can't give up – they have to find another job.**13** Through intense training and many bouts, boxers build strong bodies and minds.**14** A strong body and mind is a necessity in life.**15**

Life is a fight, struggle, battle.**16** You have to keep your guard up to see who is trying to take advantage of you.**17** You have to think how you are going to beat your other opponents (besides in the boxing ring): for instance, the many people trying to get the same job you are.**18** When you are in a boxing ring, no one can help you but yourself.**19** This is good, because you never know when you might be in a situation where no one is there to help you.**20** Being able to react while pressure is being put on you is another obstacle life throws at you for which boxing can prepare you.**21**

Boxing is like life in so many ways, because it is hard, because you have to be disciplined, and because you have to be ready for upsets.**22** I love the sport of boxing just as I love life.**23** Some people look at boxing as something primitive: two guys beating the hell out of each other for no reason.**24** I don't see that. I see two Gladiators trained intensively – mentally and physically – to defeat an opponent who is standing in the way of their dreams and goals.**25**

Sentence Forms:

1) 11ADD Fragment; 8RN How
2) 2S Triple Force
3) 3V Present Participle; 9PP Expansive Semicolon; 3V Gerund; 8RN How; 3V Infinitive
4) 3V Gerund (3); 8RN That (2); 9PP Dash B WrapUp; 3V Infinitive
5) 7AC When; 6CC Yet
6) 11ADD Question; 7AC If
7) 6CC And; 3V Infinitive
8) 3V Gerund; 2S The Pair
9) 7AC If; 2S The Pair; 8RN Missing That
10) 7AC If; 8RN Who; 11ADD Compound
11) 3V Gerund; 8RN That

12) 7AC When; 9PP Dash M Insertion Anecdotal Comment; 2S Choice Series
13) 9PP Expansive Semicolon; 9PP Dash E Independent Clause supplemental
14) 10TP B Prepositional Phrase; 2S The Pair (2)
15) 2S The Pair
16) 2S Triple Force
17) 3V Infinitive (2); 8RN Who
18) 3V Infinitive (2); 10TP M (Adverb Phrase); 9PP Explanation Colon; 3V Present Participle
19) 7AC When
20) 7AC Because; 7AC When; 8RN Where; 3V Infinitive
21) 3V Gerund; 3V Infinitive; 7AC While; 8RN Missing That; 8RN Which
22) 7AC Because; 5R Adverbial Conjunction
23) 11ADD Noun of; 4C Just As (variation)
24) 9PP Explanation Colon; 3V Gerund
25) 3V Past Participle; 9PP Dash M Adjective Phrase; 2S The Pair (2); 3V Infinitive; 8RN Who

CORPORAL PUNISHMENT: YES OR NO
by Andre Council

"Spare the rod, spoil the child."**1** That's the belief that many people share about child rearing.**2** It is a verse from the Bible; therefore, many people believe that this is the proper way to discipline their children.**3** Yet, the tide has turned drastically in America where it has become illegal in most states to hit a child.**4** So who is right and who is wrong?**5** Should corporal punishment be allowed in our homes and our schools, or is it barbaric and ancient with no place in our present society?**6**

As a youngster, I grew up under my parent's guidance and supervision.**7** It never dawned on me that hitting – as a form of punishment – had any negative effects on a child's life.**8** I was hit at home by my parents, at school by my teachers, and at any one of my caregiver's homes.**9** Looking back, it seemed like the correct way to punish me.**10** It was, after all, the way that my parent's generation was taught, and we are often times comfortable and repeat the actions we learned from a previous generation.**11**

In my opinion, corporal punishment allows you to perform the functional job of disciplining children, correcting misbehavior, and deterring a child from repeating the same behavior.**12** However, before carrying out this punishment, there must be careful consideration and planning ahead of time.**13** For instance, a disciplinarian should not be angry, vengeful, or uncontrollable while disciplining children.**14** It should also be a last resort. It is not an appropriate disciplining unless you have exhausted all other means of disciplining.**15**

We have to know what constitutes a child receiving corporal punishment.**16** Often times you have to consider the individual to determine the outcome of issuing corporal punishment.**17** Each child is unique and has a different personality; consequently, it takes different actions to get through to different children.**18** When they misbehave, we cannot punish them all the same regardless of individuality.**19** It is a fact that some children are harder to reach than others, yet it doesn't mean hitting them until they are reached is the answer.**20** The key is getting to know your child.**21**

The use of belts, switches, paddles, shoes, extension cords – which all have been used to punish – may not be the appropriate way to discipline your children.**22** The best way I have found to punish is with your hand on the child's bottom.**23** It is structured and allows you to feel some of the pain you are inflicting.**24** Using an object somehow doesn't create the same effect as using your hand.**25**

It is best to start your disciplining as early as possible.**26** Begin by instilling in your children that you are the parent and he or she is the child.**27** And that failing to comply will result in punishment.**28** A toddler is very fragile; therefore, a gentle tap on the hand will suffice to let them know when they are wrong.**29** As they become older around the ages of 3 to 6 years old, it may become necessary to use your hand on their bottoms.**30** You must communicate to them why they are receiving the punishment and what the consequences will be if that behavior continues.**31**

As your child gets older – around the ages of 7-10 years – spanking them becomes less and less effective.**32** I believe then is the time to discontinue the corporal punishment and institute a more psychological approach**33**. After all, these children are getting more intelligent and are constantly trying to figure ways to outsmart you.**34**

Although corporal punishment is declining in our society, I am a firm believer that if you incorporate it into your program of discipline and use it appropriately, with restraint and conscious thoughtfulness and not as your sole means of correcting, it can be very effective in producing a disciplined member of society.**35**

Sentence Forms:

1) 10TP Insertion Quotation
2) 8RN That; 3V Gerund
3) 9PP Expansive Semicolon; 8RN That; 3V Infinitive
4) 11ADD Beginning Conjunction; 8RN Where; 3V Infinitive
5) 11ADD Beginning Conjunction; 11ADD Question
6) 11ADD Question (2); 2S The Pair (2)
7) 10TP B Prepositional Phrase; 2S The Pair
8) 8RN That; 3V Gerund; 9PP Dash M Prepositional Phrase
9) 2S Standard Series
10) 3V Present Participle; 3V Infinitive
11) 10TP M Prepositional Phrase; 8RN That; 11ADD Compound Verb; 8RN Missing That
12) 10TP B Prepositional Phrase; 3V Infinitive; 3V Gerund (4); 2S Standard Series
13) 10TP B Word; 3V Gerund (2); 2S The Pair
14) 10TP B Prepositional Phrase; 2S Choices Series; 3V Gerund
15) 3V Gerund (2); 7AC Unless
16) 3V Infinitive; 8RN What; 3V Present Participle
17) 3V Infinitive; 3V Gerund
18) 11ADD Compound Verb; 9PP Expansive Semicolon; 3V Infinitive
19) 7AC When
20) 8RN That; 3V Infinitive; 6CC Yet; 3V Gerund; 7AC Until
21) 3V Gerund; 3V Infinitive

22) 2S Triple Force extended; 3V Infinitive; 9PP Dash M Reference Clause supplementary
23) 8RN Missing That; 3V Infinitive
24) 11ADD Compound Verb; 3V Infinitive; 8RN Missing that
25) 3V Gerund (2)
26) 3V Infinitive; 3V Gerund
27) 11ADD Beginning Verb; 3V Gerund; 8RN That; 8RN Missing That; 2S Choice Series
28) 11ADD Fragment; 11ADD Beginning Conjunction; 8RN That; 3V Infinitive
29) 9PP Expansive Semicolon; 3V Infinitive; 3V Infinitive missing to; 7AC When
30) 7AC As; 3V Infinitive
31) 8RN Why; 8RN What; 7AC If
32) 7AC As; 3V Gerund; 9PP Dash M Prepositional Phrase extended
33) 3V Infinitive; 11ADD Compound Infinitive and Missing to
34) 10TP B Prepositional Phrase; 5R Word; 3V Infinitive (2); 11ADD Compound Verb
35) 7AC Although; 8RN That; 7AC IF; 11ADD Compound Verb; 10TP M Prepositional Phrase extended? 2S Lyrical Series; 3V Gerund (2); 3V Past Participle

> The authors of this text do not share the belief of the above student in corporal punishment as an appropriate means of discipline, but the essay is thoughtful, reasonable, and well-written so we include it here despite our differing view.

LOST IN THE WILD **by Kristie Noble**

Imagine yourself lost for over an hour.**1** Who will save you?**2** What are you going to do for food?**3**

The weather appears to be bright and glorious; therefore, two groups of students and teachers from a local high school decide to go on an adventure.**4** The two groups divide up and plan to meet at the lodge ahead around six.**5**

Mr. Smith mentions that the longer of two routes is over six miles.**6** The students who are going on the longer route are outraged, and they groan and whine at the task ahead of them.**7** The class president claims if the students were told about this long, tedious, boring walk, they would have never signed up to go on the trip.**8**

Nevertheless, the class starts walking into the forest.**9** Some students play around with leaves and discover little critters on the ground.**10** Not only are the students having fun, but the teachers are laughing at the students jumping around like monkeys.**11**

Protesting this awful nature walk, a few students decide to walk slower to avoid walking with the teacher.**12** However, Sarah, who is ahead of them, panics almost immediately, as the group in front of her vanishes around the turn.**13** She waits until Claudia, Jane, and Teresa, who are behind her, catch up to her and tells them that they are lost.**14** They immediately go wild and start screaming and lamenting that they are going to die.**15**

Although the nearest town is two miles away, the girls decide to wait in a clearing to be rescued, for they do not want to get lost again.**16** Jane tells the girls she hears a noise coming from the bushes.**17** From the corner of Michelle's eye, she sees a big brown shape.**18** They fear that it is some wild beast about to eat them, and not the small rabbit that it is.**19** Huddled, in a tight group, the girls feel they will be meeting their Maker very soon.**20** Then a voice (like a soft melody) is heard from the bushes; they realize it is a man – Mr. Mike.**21** Sarah and Jane, Mike and Claudia, and Michelle and Teresa become ecstatic and overjoyed to have their life back.**22**

Sentence Forms:

1) 11ADD Beginning Verb
2) 11ADD Question
3) 11ADD Question
4) 2S The Pair (2); 9PP Expansive Semicolon; 3V Infinitive
5) 11ADD Compound Verb
6) 8RN That
7) 8RN Who; 6CC And; 2S The Pair
8) 8RN Missing That; 7AC If; 2S Triple Force; 3V Infinitive
9) 10TP B Word; 3V Gerund

10) 11ADD Compound Verb
11) 4C Not Only, But; 3V Present Participle
12) 3V Present Participle; 3V Infinitive (2); 3V Gerund
13) 10TP B Word; 10TP M Clause supplemental; 8RN Who; 7AC As
14) 7AC Until; 2S Standard Series; 10TP M Clause supplemental; 11ADD Compound Verb
15) 11ADD Compound Verb; 3V Gerund (2); 8RN That
16) 7AC Although; 3V Infinitive (3); 6CC For
17) 8RN Missing That; 3V Present Participle
18) 10TP B Prepositional Phrase extended
19) 8RN That (2); 3V Infinitive; 4C A, not B
20) 10TP B Word; 3V Past Participle; 10TP B? Prepositional Phrase; 8RN Missing that
21) 10TP M Insertion (Writer Comment); 9PP Association Semicolon; 9PP Dash E Appositive
22) 2S Rhythmical Pairs (variation); 2S The Pair; 3V Past Participle; 3V Infinitive

ALASKA by Jeff Wenrich

This summer, my family and I spent a fun-filled, two-week vacation in the beautiful state of Alaska.**1** For those of you who have never been to Alaska, you sure don't know what you're missing.**2** The wildlife is fascinating, and the scenery is breathtaking.**3** Grizzly bear, moose, doll sheep – these are a few of the magnificent species that inhabit our 48th state.**4** Majestic and untouched lakes and streams and rivers inhabit over one-half of the state.**5** Alaskan people or *sourdoughs* (long-time residents of Alaska) are some of the friendliest people you will ever meet.**6** The natural beauty and surroundings attract like a magnet: it's hard to stay away.**7** We like to refer to Alaska as our home away from home.**8**

My daughter buzzed with excitement because Anchorage was her birthplace, and I refer to her as "my little Eskimo girl".**9** In 1992, I built a beautiful home overlooking the city of Anchorage.**10** With a picturesque view of the mountains, we could see Mount McKinley on a clear day.**11** Unfortunately, I sold the home two years later.**12** Ashley insisted we drive by the house.**13** I could not disappoint a seven-year-old. Peering down the *cul-de-sac*, my wife could see the wild native "forget-me-not" flowers and roses and amaryllis.**14** We drove by the house and peered out the car windows, reminiscing about old times and wondering who might be living in the house today.**15** We sure miss the old homestead!**16**

One morning, we decided to get the fishing gear together and drive to the Kenai River.**17** The daily fishing report suggested that anglers concentrate their efforts from Shilak Lake to the Kenai River.**18** We arrived at the Russian River ferry landing, and the anglers were elbow-to-elbow.**19** Fishermen were jockeying for positions in a river teeming with thousands of sockeye salmon.**20** Unlike fishing in the lower 48 states, anglers are aggressive, rowdy, and offensive.**21** This is no place to take your family fishing.**22** Once a salmon is hooked, look out, for all hell is about to break loose.**23** People are shouting at each other, and lines are crossing one another.**24** Exuberant anglers try to anticipate the salmon's every move, yet they don't realize that a real fight is about to begin.**25** In all my years of fishing and watching others fish, the salmon is the most evasive and toughest fish to land.**26**

So, what draws our family back to this beautiful state every year?**27** For me, the big game hunting and salmon fishing.**28** My wife loves the history and the gargantuan vegetables that are grown.**29** My daughter admires and is thrilled about everything.**30** Where else can you find natural beauty, serene settings, and an abundance of outdoor activities?**31**

Sentence Forms:

1) 10TP B Adverb Phrase; 2S The Pair; 2S Compact Duo; 11ADD Noun of
2) 10TP B Prepositional Phrase; 8RN Who; 8RN What
3) 1F Distant Descriptor (2); 6CC And
4) 9PP Dash B Wrap-Up; 8RN That
5) 2S The Pair; 3V Past Participle; 2S Lyrical Series
6) 2S Choice Series; 10TP M Insertion (Writer Comment); 8RN Missing That
7) 2S The Pair; 9PP Explanation Colon

8) 3V Infinitive
9) 7AC Because; 6CC And
10) 10TP B Prepositional Phrase; 3V Present Participle
11) 10TP B Prepositional Phrase extended
12) 10TP B Word
13) 8RN Missing That
14) 3V Present Participle; 2S Lyrical Series
15) 11ADD Compound Verb; 11ADD Compound Present Participle; 8RN Who
16) 11ADD Exclamation
17) 10TP B Adverb Phrase; 2V Infinitive; 3V Present Participle; 11ADD Compound Verb
18) 8RN That; 4C From To
19) 6CC And
20) 3V Present Participle
21) 10TP B Prepositional Phrase; 2S Standard Series
22) 3V Infinitive; 3V Present Participle
23) 7AC Once; 6CC For; 3V Infinitive
24) 6CC And
25) 3V Infinitive (2); 6CC Yet; 8RN That
26) 10TP B Prepositional Phrase extended; 3V Gerund; 2S The Pair (2)
27) 10TP B Word; 11ADD Question
28) 11ADD Fragment; 3V Gerund (2)
29) 2S The Pair; 8RN That
30) 11ADD Compound Verb
31) 11ADD Question; 2S Standard Series

GRANDPA by Joshua D. DeLange

My grandfather was born in 1912 – in a small farming community in Oklahoma.**1** Throughout his life, his travels took him many places.**2** In 1958, he settled down with his family on a small farm in central California.**3** He lived there with my grandmother, until his death in 2004.**4**

As a child, I always liked going to grandma and grandpa's house.**5** I loved grandma's cooking, and I especially liked listening to grandpa's stories.**6** He told stories about fishing and hunting, the old west and politics.**7** He would talk about running moonshine, during prohibition; riding rail cars, to any destination that he wished; hanging out with famous outlaws.**8** He could go on for hours with stories about the huge fish that he caught, the fish that got away, and about all the times that he almost got arrested as well as the hard times he and his family endured – he would tell them as if they had happened yesterday.**9** Not only were his stories entertaining, but most of them were true.**10**

 Particularly, I remember the story about the day he met Bonnie and Clyde.**11** He said he was a young man – not much older than thirteen – when his father asked him to bring a couple of bottles – of moonshine – to a storekeeper a few towns up.**12** He changed his clothes, grabbed his bike, and started to the store.**13** He told me that the store was twenty miles or so away from his house, and that there weren't many cars in the area where he lived.**14** On his way to drop off the bottles, he noticed a brand new sedan outside of [in front of] a store.**15** He decided to stop and get a coke; he really wanted to see who was driving the car.**16** When he went into the store, he couldn't believe whom he saw.**17** He said Bonnie and Clyde were in there buying groceries, and they asked him where they could find some moonshine.**18** He said that he sold them the two bottles that he had and talked to them for a while.**19** When they left, he went back home and got two more bottles for the storekeeper.**20** There wasn't much to any of his stories; they were pretty much straightforward and to the point.**21**

 My grandfather taught me many things: how to fish, how to drive, how to curse, and how to be respectful.**22** He wasn't always polite and his language was dated; however, he was always respectful.**23** His love of life radiated in every story that he told.**24** I would visit my grandfather monthly, until his death a few years back.**25** I would go and help my grandparents around the house; I enjoyed my grandmother's great cooking, and I indulged myself in some more great stories – of a great man – of a life one could only hope to live.**26**

Sentence Forms:

1) 9PP Dash E Adverb Phrase
2) 10TP B Prepositional Phrase

3) 10TP B Prepositional Phrase
4) 10TP E Prepositional Phrase extended
5) 10TP B Prepositional Phrase; 3V Gerund; 2S The Pair
6) 3V Gerund (2); 6CC And
7) 2S Rhythmical Pairs
8) 3V Gerund (3); 9PP Trio Semicolon; 8RN That
9) 8RN That (3); 10TP M Appositive Phrase; 4C As well as; 8RN Missing That; 2S The Pair; 9PP Dash Break; 7AC As If supplementary
10) 4C Not Only, But
11) 10TP B Word; 8RN Missing That; 2S The Pair
12) 8RN Missing That; 9PP Dash M Adjective Phrase; 7AC When; 3V Infinitive; 9PP Dash M Prepositional Phrase
13) 11ADD Compound Verb; 2S Standard Series
14) 8RN That (2); 8RN Where
15) 10TP B Prepositional Phrase extended; 3V Infinitive
16) 3V Infinitive (2); 3V Infinitive Missing; 9PP Association Semicolon; 8RN Who
17) 7AC When; 8RN Whom
18) 8RN Missing that; 3V Present Participle; 6CC And; 8RN Where
19) 8RN That (2); 11ADD Compound Verb
20) 7AC When; 11ADD Compound Verb
21) 9PP Association Semicolon; 2S The Pair
22) 9PP List Colon; 6RN How (4); 3V Infinitive (4); 2S Standard Series extended
23) Contradiction? 9PP Expansive Semicolon
24) 11ADD Noun of; 8RN That
25) 10TP E Prepositional Phrase extended
26) 2S The Pair; 9PP Stylish Semicolon; 9PP Dash M Prepositional Phrase; 5R Word; 8RN Missing That; 3V Infinitive

Winter in Maine by Joshua Gatromb

There are only three seasons in Maine – winter, June, and July.**1** This joke is intended to make you realize the truth: Maine has the harshest, longest, and most intense winter in the United States.**2** I left the state vowing never to return, just because of the winter.**3** Some may argue that the sports and recreation associated with snow and winter are beneficial to the state: They are wrong.**4**

Being on the coast, being in the northeast, being at the epicenter of two converging weather fronts – all these things contribute to the harsh Maine winters.**5** The lack of sunlight is a major contributor to seasonal depression.**6** The above average number of cold weather injuries and deaths has led to a decline in population.**7** The benefits, a dismally small number, are not enough to counterbalance the detriments.**8**

On a frozen riverbed, in the month of April, is where I learned to ice skate.**9** The cold, frigid air still turns your nose red long after the calendar declares its spring.**10** Amazingly, snow has been reported to fall on July 4.**11** It is hard to imagine what a long winter can do to your psyche if you have not spent seventeen days in a row, at home, away from school, because the frozen pipes busted from the cold.**12** A Maine winter can literally last over six months.

Not only are the winters long, but they are also intense.**13** A continuous snowstorm, lasting twenty-three days, dumped 6'10" [208.3 cm] of snow one year.**14** The wind caused snowdrifts so high that people had to climb out their second story windows, and snowmobiles were the only mode of transportation.**15** The air is freezing, the water is freezing, and yes, the blanket-infested bed is freezing.**16** It takes a hearty Nordic Viking to brave the intensity of a Maine winter and live to tell the tale.**17**

Having experienced the harshest, longest, and most intense of winters, I have no affinity for the cold.**18** No individual that has lived in Maine can argue these points, and no individual that has not lived in Maine can understand them.**19** I may never get to experience a Maine winter again, if I am lucky, but I will never forget them.**20**

Sentence Forms:

1) 9PP Dash E List
2) 9PP Explanation Colon
3) 3V Present Participle; 3V Infinitive; 10TP E Prepositional or Adverb Phrase
4) 8RN That; 2S The Pair (2); 9PP Explanation Colon

5) 5R Keyword; 3V Gerund (3); 3V Present Participle; 9PP Dash B Wrap-Up
6) 11ADD Noun of
7) 2S The Pair
8) 10TP M Appositive Phrase
9) 10TP B Prepositional Phrase; 10TP M Prepositional Phrase; 8RN Where; 3V Infinitive
10) 2S Compact Duo; 7AC After
11) 10TP B Word; 3V Infinitive
12) 3V Infinitive; 8RN What; 7AC If; 7AC Because; 10TP M Prepositional Phrase; 10TP M Adverb Phrase
13) 4C Not Only, But
14) 10TP M Verbal Phrase Present Participle
15) 8RN That; 6CC And; 11ADD Noun of
16) 5R Keyword; 2S Standard Series
17) 3V Infinitive; 3V Infinitive Missing to
18) 3V Present Participle; 2S Standard Series
19) 8RN That (2); 5R Keyword
20) 3V Infinitive; 7AC If; 6CC But

A HOBBY FOR SOCIETY AND ME by Chang Gamblin

In the modern society, enjoying leisure time has become more important not only for business people but also for housewives and retired people.**1** Due to the great developments in science and technology, we have more free time, but we also have more stress; therefore, we need something to fill our free time, as well as something to handle our stress – a hobby.**2** Filling out our leisure time, a hobby can give us great pleasure.**3**

There are several advantages in having a hobby.**4** First, by having a hobby, we can fill our free time pleasantly.**5** If we don't know what to do in our free time, if we think we are just wasting free time, then we may increase our stress levels.**6** Second, we have a hobby to handle our stress.**7** Because our society has become more organized, formal, and mechanical, we need to have opportunities to relax.**8** Third, we can make new friends because people who share the same hobbies tend to have similar characteristics.**9** Last, if family members, especially a husband and wife, can share common hobbies, they can understand one another better, and they have more knowledge and experience to share in communicating with one another; this may bring peace among family members.**10**

There are many interesting hobbies we can enjoy around us; the more intellectual and stimulating and inexpensive a hobby is, the better it can be enjoyed.**11**

In my case, I have many hobbies which provide me with enjoyment: more than ten hobbies.**12** Playing golf, tennis, badminton and mountain climbing – these are hobbies which I enjoy outside.**13** Playing racquetball, squash and swimming and bowling – these are hobbies which I enjoy inside.**14** Calligraphy, reading books, playing the piano – these are hobbies which fill my intellectual interests.**15** Although I am not a professional in my hobbies, I do enjoy them equally as if I were.**16**

Many interesting hobbies are waiting for us. There is no reason to be bored if we are active in a hobby.**17** Furthermore, a hobby can help us make new friends and meet others who share our interests.**18** A hobby gives us pleasure, fills free time, and introduces us to new friends for life.**19**

Sentence Forms:

1) 10TP B Prepositional Phrase; 3V Gerund; 4C Not only, but; 2S The Pair; 3V Past Participle
2) 10TP B Prepositional Phrase; 2S The Pair; 6CC But; 9PP Expansive Semicolon; 3V Infinitive (2); 4C As well as; 9PP Dash E Appositive
3) 10TP B Verbal Phrase;
4) 3V Gerund
5) 10TP B Word; 10TP M Prepositional Phrase; 3V Gerund;
6) 5R Adverbial Conjunction; 8RN What; 8RN Missing That; 7AC If;
7) 10TP B Word; 3V Infinitive
8) 7AC Because; 2S Standard Series; 3V Infinitive (2)
9) 10TP B Word; 7AC Because; 8RN Who; 3V Infinitive
10) 10TP B Word; 7AC If; 11ADD Especially; 2S The Pair (2); 6CC And; 3V Infinitive; 3V Gerund; 9PP Association Semicolon

11) 3V Present Participle; 8RN Missing That (2?); 2S Lyrical Series; 4C The more, the more
12) 10TP B Prepositional Phrase; 8RN Which; 9PP Explanation Colon??
13) 3V Gerund (2); 9PP B List Wrap-Up; 8RN Which
14) 3V Gerund (3); 9PP B List Wrap-Up; 8RN Which
15) 3V Gerund (2); 9PP B List Wrap-Up; 8RN Which
16) 7AC Although; 7AC As if supplementary
17) 1F There Is; 3V Infinitive; 7AC If
18) 10TP B Word; 11ADD Compound Verb; 8RN Who; 3V Infinitive Missing to
19) 11ADD Compound Verb

DRESS TO IMPRESS by Rico Mendiola

Whether we like it or not, we tend to pre-judge others based on their appearance.**1** It only takes a matter of seconds when we first see a person to make an evaluation of his or her appeal to us.**2** Across the street or across the room, we notice people we don't know and judge them by the way they walk, by the way they talk, or by the way they smell; accordingly, we decide if we like or dislike their qualities.**3** Your clothing is a major part of your appearance and plays a major role in the way you are perceived by others.**4**

The way you dress can make a good impression on people in many ways.**5** Dressing conservatively (wearing clothes that aren't too provocative or outrageous), you can show others that you don't like to show off or draw attention to yourself.**6** In the workplace, the way you dress can show your sense of responsibility to your employer.**7** The way you dress also gives others a good idea of your personal compatibility; if you dress the same as others, chances are that you are interested in the same things, too.**8** This causes people to get together in many ways: groups, clubs, and cliques.**9**

While your clothing can make a good impression on others, it can also make a bad impression.**10** Dressing slovenly can tell others that you do not care much for yourself.**11** Also, if you don't dress appropriately, an interviewer for a job might not think you are responsible enough for the job.**12** If you dress like a gang member, then it is understandable if you are taken for a gang member by a police officer.**13** Dressing too provocatively might cause others to think you are promiscuous.**14** Dressing inappropriately makes a bad impression on people – a bad impression about your personality, a bad impression of your values.**15**

We all hate to be pre-judged and stereotyped, but we find ourselves pre-judging others very often.**16** We think that we can know a person's personality by the way he or she dresses, walks, talks, smells, etc., but we are often wrong.**17** When we realize that clothing and appearance do not always reveal personalities of others, when we do away with all our stereotypes, we will begin to see people for what they are on the inside – not on the outside.**18**

Sentence Forms:

1) 7AC Whether; 3V Infinitive
2) 7AC When; 3V Infinitive; 2S Choice Series
3) 10TP B Prepositional Phrase; 8RN Missing that (4); 11ADD Compound Verb; 5R Keyword; 2S Choice Series; 9PP Expansive Semicolon; 7AC If
4) 11ADD Compound verb; 8RN Missing that
5) 8RN Missing that
6) 3V Present Participle; 10TP M (Verbal phrase Present participle); 8RN That (2); 2S Choice Series (2); 3V Infinitive; 3V Infinitive missing to
7) 10TP B Prepositional Phrase; 8RN Missing that; 11ADD Noun of
8) 8RN Missing that; 9PP Association Semicolon; 8RN That; 10TP E Word
9) 3V Infinitive; 9PP List Colon; 2S Standard Series
10) 7AC While
11) 8RN Gerund; 8RN That
12) 10TP B Word; 7AC If; 8RN Missing that
13) 7AC If (2)
14) 3V Gerund; 3V Infinitive; 8RN Missing that
15) 3V Gerund; 9PP Dash E Noun Phrase; 5R Keyword
16) 11ADD Compound Infinitive; 6CC But; 3V Gerund
17) 8RN That; 8RN Missing that; 2S Choice Series; 2S Standard Series extended; 6CC But

18) 7AC When (2); 8RN That; 2S The Pair; 3V Infinitive; 8RN What; 9PP Dash E Adverb Phrase

I LOVE MUSIC by Tanisha L. Bruns

"I love music – any kind of music – just as long as it's grooving!"**1** These lyrics (from the LP album *I Love Music* by the O'Jays) describe my feelings toward music.**2** I have a very large collection of music: over 750 compact discs and 140 cassette tapes.**3** The collection includes a number of different categories: Rap, Rock, Reggae, R&B, Blues, Gospel, Country, Disco, Latin, Jazz, Alternative – you name it, I got it.**4**

I use music as a natural mood enhancer. It enables me to express my moods and feelings.**5** For every minute of the hour, I will have as many mood changes in a day.**6** If I am feeling depressed, if I want to express these feelings, I will listen to a little Billie Holiday, or maybe Sadi.**7** Disco and Alternative music help me to get energized; Reggae and Jazz help me to relax.**8**

When packing for long trips or vacations, I actually spend more time selecting music than clothing.**9** I find myself laboring over which CDs to bring along for the ride.**10** During one family trip, I noticed that I had forgotten the music; I turned the car around and proceeded to get my music.**11**

Sentence Forms:

1) 10TP Insertion Quotation; 9PP Dash M Noun Phrase; 7AC As long as supplemental
2) 10TP M (Prepositional Phrase extended)
3) 9PP Explanation Colon; 2S The Pair
4) 9PP Explanation Colon; 9PP Dash E Independent Clause supplemental (2)
5) 2S The Pair
6) 10TP B Prepositional Phrase
7) 7AC If (2); 3v Past Participle; 3V Infinitive; 2S Choice Series

8) 2S The Pair; 3V Infinitive (2); 9PP Opposition Semicolon
9) 10TP B Prepositional Phrase; 3V Gerund (2)
10) 3V Present Participle; 8RN Which; 3V Infinitive
11) 10TP B Prepositional Phrase; 8RN That; 9PP Opposition Semicolon; 11ADD Compound Verb; 3V Infinitive

FAMILY VALUES by Andrea Maldonado

"Remove your shoes before entering home".**1** My greatest memories are of my mother – rarely upset – telling us to keep the house clean.**2** My father, who would let me fix the bathroom sink, would tell us to sit down and eat dinner together.**3** We didn't always get along or support each other when we needed it most, but I consider myself lucky to have two parents who loved me and tried to give me what I needed to survive in this world.**4** They are everything to me: no family, no life.**5**

Times have changed since our parents were children; families today face different challenges than those of a decade or two ago.**6** Over the past few years, the concept of family has been revolutionized.**7** My family, undoubtedly, is the best example.**8** A "traditional" family no longer consists of two parents where the father is the "provider of bread" and the mother stays home to raise the children.**9** My parents always dreamed of having a happy family, a supportive family, a family full of love.**10** The important thing about today's family is probably that their success doesn't just happen – it takes effort.**11**

The secret to attaining a strong family – according to my parents – involves commitment, appreciation, communication, time, spiritual wellness, and coping ability.**12** While this seems like a simple six-step program, it makes a lot of sense.**13**

Whether you are in good or bad moments, your family is there to help you.**14** Because they love you, any sacrifice is not too much.**15** The more time you share with your family, the more you will get to love them.**16** Family comes first and is worth all the effort and dedication it requires.**17**

Sentence Forms:
1) 10TP Insertion Quotation supplemental; 11ADD Beginning Verb; 3V Gerund
2) 9PP Dash M Adverb Phrase; 3V Present Participle; 3V Infinitive
3) 8RN Who; 10TP M RN Who Clause Interruption supplemental; 3V Infinitive Missing to (2); 3V Infinitive
4) 11ADD Compound Verb (2); 2S Choice Series; 7AC When; 6CC But; 3V Infinitive (2); 8RN Who; 8RN What
5) 9PP Explanation Colon; 4C No A, no B.
6) 9PP Association Semicolon
7) 10TP B Prepositional Phrase; 11ADD Noun of
8) 10TP M Word
9) 8RN Where; 11ADD Compound Subject; 3V Infinitive
10) 3V Gerund; 5R Keyword
11) 8RN That; 9PP Dash Break
12) 3V Gerund; 9PP Dash M Verbal Phrase; 2S Standard Series extended; 3V Present Participle
13) 7AC While
14) 7AC Whether; 2S Choice Series; 3V Infinitive
15) 7AC Because
16) 4C The more, the more; 3V Infinitive
17) 11ADD Compound Verb; 2S The Pair; 8RN Missing That

ANIMALS **by Michael Lortz**

Animals, animals, animals!**1** I really do love animals. Since childhood, I have always been around all kinds of animals: horses, cows, goats, chickens, rabbits, and – my personal favorite – dogs.**2**

As a teenager, I spent most of my summers on my grandfather's farm.**3** I had several chores to accomplish every morning – like gathering up the eggs, milking the goats as well as the cows, and I also had to put out all of their food.**4**

Through all of my adults years, I have owned and raised various breeds of dogs: Poodles, Cocker Spaniels, Miniature

Dobermans, and Pomeranians – just to name a few.**5** Pomeranians are, by far, my most favorite of the breeds.**6**

I retired from the army in 1995, and I bought my first Pomeranian then.**7** I had been looking in local newspapers and finally found the little guy.**8** I drove nearly 200 miles, one way, to pick him up.**9** He was so tiny, at just eight weeks old, that he could fit in the palms of your hands.**10**

When we got him home, we tried to figure out what to name him.**11** He looked just like a very small bear cub, so we named him Bear.**12**

Bear lived just ten short, fantastic years.**13** My son was taking care of him since our move to Korea in 2003. One day, in 2005, my son called with some very sad news.**14** Bear became sick, and (despite what the veterinarian would do) Bear was not getting any better.**15** My son asked, "What should I do, Dad?"**16** Well, there was nothing we could do, so we had him put to sleep and then cremated.**17**

My son now takes care of the little cedar box that holds my precious little Bear.**18** We all miss him.

Sentence Forms:

1) 11ADD Exclamation;
2) 7AC Since; 9PP List Colon; 9PP Dash M Noun Phrase?
3) 10TP B Prepositional Phrase;
4) 3V Infinitive; 9PP Dash E List; 3V Gerund (2); 4C As well as; 6CC And
5) 10TP B Prepositional Phrase; 2S The Pair; 9PP List Colon; 10TP Dash Break
6) 10TP M Prepositional Phrase
7) 6CC And
8) 11ADD Compound Verb
9) 10TP M Adverb Phrase; 3V Infinitive
10) 10TP M Adverb Phrase; 8RN That
11) 7AC When; 3V Infinitive; 8RN What
12) 6CC So
13) 2S Compact Duo
14) 10TP B Adverb Phrase; 10TP M Adverb Phrase
15) 6CC And; 8RN What; 10TP M (Prepositional Phrase)
16) 10TP E Insertion Quotation; 11ADD Question
17) 10TP B Word; 6CC So; 3V Infinitive

18) 8RN That

WATCHING MOVIES by Estrella Vasquez

I think the best time to watch movies is when it's raining, or when you have nothing else to do.**1** It's relaxing, and it takes you into another world.**2** There are so many choices to choose from: whether you want to cry, laugh, be on the edge of your seat, or just want a scare, there is a movie for everyone.**3**

You can choose to watch a movie whenever you want (any time of the day or any day of the week), or wherever you choose to see it – at a theater, at a drive-in, or in the comfort of your own home.**4** Watching a movie is always enjoyable.**5**

The best movies come out on special days like holidays: for example, the Fourth of July, Christmas, and New Year's.**6** On those days, the theater is really packed, but it's always worth going.**7**

When watching a movie, you pretty much eat junk food, and forget to eat healthy food.**8** You eat popcorn, hot dogs, candy, and nachos.**9** What an appetite you seem to develop just watching a movie!**10** However, as long as you don't eat too much, you won't have to complain about a stomach ache.**11**

The best thing about watching a movie is when it is at its peak.**12** In a scary movie, you jump; in a drama, you cry; in a comedy you laugh through the whole movie.**13**

Movies sure take your mind off all the things that are stressful in your life.**14** It's a great distraction and vacation from reality, so why not grab a movie, and enjoy it?**15**

Sentence Forms:
1) 8RN Missing That; 3V Infinitive (2); 8RN When (2)
2) 6CC And
3) 3V Infinitive (2); 9PP List Colon??; 7AC Whether; 2S Triple Force; 11ADD Compound Verb

4) 3V Infinitive (2); 7AC Whenever supplemental; 10TP M (noun phrase); 7AC Wherever supplemental; 9PP Dash E Noun Phrase; 2S Choices Series
5) 3V Gerund
6) 9PP Explanation Colon; 2S Standard Series
7) 10TP B Prepositional Phrase; 6CC But; 3V Gerund
8) 10TP B Prepositional Phrase; 3VGerund; 11ADD Compound Verb; 3V Infinitive
9) 2S Standard Series extended
10) 8RN Missing That; 3V Infinitive; 3V Present Participle; 11ADD Exclamation
11) 10TP B Word; 7AC As long as supplementary
12) 3V Gerund; 8RN When
13) 9PP Trio Semicolon
14) 8RN That
15) 2S The Pair; 6CC So; 11ADD Question; 11ADD Compound verb

FAMILY by Katrina Tolentino

Family is the fruit of togetherness and liveliness.**1** Having no family is like having no life, no happiness, no reason to live.**2** My family is really big. I have seven siblings with two brothers. Every day at the dinner table, we all chatter with laughter and joy.**3** It is amazing how we all grew up and became independent.**4** But I really miss those chaotic days.**5**

Loving and caring is the foundation of having a great family.**6** It is universal that you love and care about all the members of your family.**7** Although we may not agree about a lot of things, we always compromise and accept our faults.**8** Forgiveness is the key for having a good relationship.**9** For me, family comes first before anything else: sacrificing is part of having a family, and I sacrificed a lot for my family.**10** For instance, I couldn't wait to get out of Korea, yet I decided to extend another year because it is the only way that I could continue my schooling.**11** I promised my dad I would further my education if I joined the Army, so now I must keep that promise.**12**

Because family is so important to me, I usually help them the best I can.**13** I send money home when they need it.**14** Saying "no" is really hard when it comes to them.**15** Willingly, I will do anything to make my family happy, even though it means giving up partying, eating out, and sacrificing buying things I want.**16** Unquestionably, I will sacrifice everything for them.**17** What can I say, I love them!**18**

I can't wait until Christmas when all of us will be together once again.**19** Not being able to see my family for fifteen months is very devastating and sad.**20** I really miss being home, sharing stories, going to the beach with them.**21** Do you ever wish you could be with your family forever?**22** Spending time with them.**23** Creating memories.**24** Having fun and hanging out.**25** Sharing jokes.**26** Going around the island.**27** Watching movies.**28** I do!**29**

Sentence Forms:
1) 11ADD Noun of; 11ADD Compound Object of Preposition
2) 3V Gerund (2); 5R Word 3V Infinitive
3) 10TP B Prepositional Phrase; 2S The Pair
4) 8RN How; 11ADD Compound Verb
5) 11ADD Beginning Conjunction
6) 3V Gerund (3)
7) 8RN That; 2S The Pair
8) 7AC Although; 11ADD Compound Verb
9) 3V Gerund
10) 10TP B Prepositional Phrase; 9PP Explanation Colon; 3V Gerund (2); 6CC And
11) 10TP B Prepositional Phrase; 6CC Yet; 3V Infinitive; 7AC Because; 8RN That; 3V Gerund
12) 8RN Missing That; 7AC If; 6CC So
13) 7AC Because; 8RN Missing That
14) 7AC When
15) 3V Gerund; 7AC When
16) 10TP B Word; 3V Infinitive; 7AC Even Though; 3V Gerund (5); 2S Standard Series; 8RN Missing That

17) 10TP B Word
18) 8RN What; 11ADD Exclamation
19) 7AC When
20) 3V Gerund; 2S The Pair; 3V Present Participle
21) 3V Gerund; 2S Triple Force
22) 11ADD Question; 8RN Missing That
23) 11ADD Fragment; 3V Gerund
24) 11ADD Fragment; 3V Gerund
25) 11ADD Fragment; 3V Gerund (2)
26) 11ADD Fragment; 3V Gerund
27) 11ADD Fragment; 3V Gerund
28) 11ADD Fragment; 3V Gerund
29) 11ADD Exclamation

Debatable Use of *Mother* and *Father* and *Tongue* in Reference to Different Modes of Discourse

The use of "Mother" and "Father", and even "Tongue", as category labels for the first 2 modes or types or styles of discourse may seem to some as a throwback to a patriarchal dominant time or mode of thinking in the past.

Indeed, such a time historically did exist, when women were not allowed access to texts and their outlook and literary voice was only mildly regarded as relevant and where inclusion meant meeting the standards and criteria established by men – while strictly staying within, of course, the forms and presentation styles established by the predominantly male literate elite.

The pendulum that so long swung in favour of men over women in education is now irrevocably swinging the other way; in many (but not all) nations, women are now getting an equal foothold in public discourse and all areas of public life and are showing themselves fully capable of doing excellent, cutting-edge research and writing on a par or beyond the work of their male peers.

After all, to say that formal and academic discourse is somehow of more lasting value than a pleasant greeting delivered with a smile, some words of encouragement or sympathy during a trying time, a short greeting card from a long lost friend, or the relief and contented feeling that follows an emotional venting or unloading of repressed memories or a burdensome worry is entirely absurd, as both the heart and the head have their separate needs. As Tom Jones sings, "It's not unusual to be mad at anyone; it's not unusual to be sad with anyone."

When we choose a parental association (as opposed to *female/male* or *feminine/masculine*) for our first two modes of language discourse, we are using terms that have universal association. We all spontaneously utter words such as *Momma Mia!*, *O Holy Father!*, *O Mother!*, when overcome suddenly with a problem, as if imploring our parents or the Divine for assistance. In many Asian countries and other cultures, it is the immediate family and the ancestors who receive obeisance, who are honoured for their gift of life, their wrinkles of wisdom, their watchful eye, and their helping hands. They doted on us when we were young, and should we not in turn dote on them when they are old? Filial piety can be replaced with an appreciation of intergenerational connection. For *Mother* and *Father* includes *Grandmother* and *Grandfather* and has a scope beyond that of one's immediate parents or grandparents. Mother stands for all women, and Father stands for all men, and most people have a Mother and Father as their earliest caregivers and supports throughout life.

For indeed, every human is the progeny of their two biological parents, their genetic union. Our body is their gift to us. But our meaning and worth also derives from our relationship to the Source of All Expression, Thought, Talk, *bavarderie*, Chat, Smalltalk, Counsel, Consultation, Discussion, Debate. **Language is our the Source of all our expression – our Super-Parent and combined Mother and Father, though sequentially it is first experienced as the Mother Tongue, then the Father Tongue as explained earlier at length.**

As the Shakespeare quote indicates on our Volume 1 title page, both genders, both hands, both sides of the brain and body must work in concert. **Each side has distinct qualities and lessons of history embedded in its psyche and DNA;** however, one must fuse (not confuse or view as contradictory) the benefits of both, but rather meld and harmonize them into new creations, forms, and ideas.

The photo on the left shows a pair of mass-produced slippers available in Korea for entering the interior of houses or public places. Notice the slippers are the same for both feet; there is no left-right distinction. The brand name is Lipose, a word very close to the word *lipase*, a type of sugar.

Give me a bit of sugar (give me a hug, or put some sugar in my tea while we converse as friends). Talk with me. Let's spend time and bend time and re-tint our windows, sort and solve the problems of the world.. We can range and explore, extrapolate and interpolate all the regions of thought between here and the edges of our fields of gold.

Thus, we urge that one's facility in the English language demands that both Maternal and Paternal tongues or modes or voices be put on equal footing and be at our command, ready for full deployment as circumstances dictate.

As Joseph Campbell illustrates and describes in his masterpiece *The Hero with a Thousand Faces*, stories of creation assign at one time Mother to the Earth goddess *ki* and Father to the Sky god *an* (Sumerian deities); in ancient Egyptian culture, Campbell notices that the Earth is the Father and the Sky is the Mother. Campbell further explores the feminine side of divinity at length *In All Her Names*. Also worth mentioning is James Hillman's *Anima: An Anatomy of a Personified Notion*, a experimentally formatted book that aligns excerpts from C.G. Jung's work on the *anima* and *animus* running parallel with Hillman's 10-part essay.

Cultural anthropologist Mary C. Bateson, daughter of Margaret Mead and Gregory Bateson, reminds in all her books, especially *Composing a Life* and *Full Circles, Overlapping Lives*, that women have their own stories that reflect a different adaptability to life's rough waters. Her writing is "richly layered". And through her cross-cultural, cross-gender, and cross-generation narratives, she suggests that the harvest is great when there is dialogue, between genders and across generations. She feels this is important, especially because women outlive men.

The use of the word *Tongue* is the strongest and most corporeal of symbols to use to indicate one's spoken words. We could have used vocal chords or the enigmatic hyoid bone as symbolic elements, as each human has those as well as a tongue, teeth, lingual tonsils, the nasal cavity, the roof of the mouth, and the lungs and breath – all of which are instrumental used in the production of speech.

But as it stands, the word *Tongue* is the most universal and easily understood symbol of choice. ⌘

"The advent of female literature promises woman's view of life, woman's experience: in other words, a new element. Make what distinctions you please in the social world, it still remains true that men and women have different organization, consequently different experiences. . . . But hitherto . . . the literature of women has fallen short of its functions owing to a very natural and very explicable weakness – it has been too much a literature of imitation. To write as men write is the aim and besetting sin of women; to write as women is the real task they have to perform."
—G.H. Lewes *The Lady Novelists* 1852

"If there was a female literary tradition, I was sure, it came from imitation, literary convention, the marketplace, and critical reception, not from biology or psychology. . . . I attempted to define woman's writing as the product of a subculture, evolving with relation to the dominant mainstream. . . . **But a mature women's literature ceases to be part of a subculture, and can move into "a seamless participation in the literary mainstream."**

—Elaine Showalter
A Literature of Their Own: British Women Novelists from Brontë to Lessig 1977

"In my earlier book *A Literature of Their Own* (1977), a study of women novelists in the nineteenth and twentieth centuries, I have defined three phases in the development of women's writing that were akin to those of any other literary subculture. First, there is 'a prolonged phrase of imitation of the prevailing modes of the dominant tradition'; second, 'there is a phase of protest' against these modes, and 'advocacy, a search for identity and a specific aesthetic. I called these phases in women's writing 'feminine,' 'feminist', and 'female.' In the 1970s, I could only imagine a fourth stage, a 'seamless participation in the literary mainstream.' By the end of the twentieth century, however, American women's literature had reached the fourth and final stage, which I would now call 'free.' American women writers in the twenty-first century can take on any subject they want, in any form they choose."

—Elaine Showalter
A Jury of Her Peers: American Women Writers from Anne Bradstreet to Annie Proulx 2009

Why are there so many student compositions and what are the characteristics of the students whose compositions are used?

For the first time, we have gathered in these two volumes large and representative selections of competent to excellent sentences and essays by students themselves. The advantages of making such selections available to new students are obvious and numerous: (1) **students relate more to the language and topics of interest of peers than to the dry, remote, and artificial language and topics of standard textbooks so they are more interested, engaged, and motivated to read and study than otherwise**; (2) new students **instinctively feel that they can and should rise to the same level of achievement of their peers, and therefore they work harder to rise to that level out of a sense of self pride and rivalry with peers** (whereas if they fail to rise to the level of a model essay by a professional writer, they find it easier to excuse their failure and often work only half as hard as they should); (3) the selections in themselves **constitute almost a course by itself in the cultural outlook, pre-occupations, hobbies, interests, and above all representative ordinary language and discourse of a wide cross-section of**

American youth as well as youth from other cultures; and (4) **finally and most importantly, for the first time, the various essays are all notated and footnoted with the 11 Forms of the Sentence which we have identified as the standard Forms of all English sentences**. The essays, by mostly early university students, **display the 11 Forms in innumerable contexts and life situations and thus powerfully and visually demonstrate their widespread use and effective impact**.

The decision to include what some might consider an overly disproportionate number of student compositions in the 2 volumes stems from the realization that **the voices of students and youth have never been fully represented before in any composition book**; that **the voice of youth is one that should be heard**; and finally, but most importantly, **because beginning writers, such as the ones represented here, express themselves using the everyday language and vocabulary typical of their native culture or Mother Tongue, they are therefore particularly suitable models for emulation by new students learning to write initially as a form of self-expression and focused reflection**.

There is an additional side benefit of these selective student writings which stems from the heterogeneous character and background of the students themselves. Most of the sentences and essays were gathered from classes taught by Richard Dowling on military bases in South Korea, Japan, Guam, and Australia for the Asian Division of UMUC (University of Maryland, University College). The Asian Division has taught American military personnel, their families, and local Korean, Japanese, and other nationalities working on American bases in Asia for over 50 years. Because the American armed forces are voluntary, the students and family members represented in the classes tend to come from all geographic locations in the United States and to represent a wide cross-section of gender, race, class, religion, and cultural and ethnic backgrounds. Moreover, because there is a minimum level of competence required in tests for military service, the students tend to range, fairly evenly, from average to high intelligence.

The student essays are thus widely representative of the whole of American culture, but they also often cover topics of relevance to military service overseas, written by both service members and members of their families in the air force, army, navy, and marine corps stationed in bases in Asia. They thus provide a unique overview, from the bottom or grassroots level up, of every branch of

American military service interacting with local cultures and often describing such experiences. Moreover, included in the selection of essays are also many essays by Japanese, South Korean, Philippine, and others working on American bases in Asia as well as a number of essays culled from high school and university teaching in South Korea and China by Stephen Watson. **All together, the essays afford an unusually representative and diverse experience of a fascinating cross section of youthful cultures, topics of interest, language, and intercultural encounters between Americans of all persuasions and an array of South Korean, Japanese, Chinese, Philippine, and other students in Asia.**

General Instructions for Using Both Volumes to Maximum Advantage

The entire text for this course of instruction in English consists of two volumes, with the first volume covering the Preview, Openings, and the Mother Tongue and the second volume covering the Father Tongue, the Imaginative Tongue, and the Closing.

The two volumes together adopt not only a completely novel but also a totally inclusive and integral approach to English and provide a comprehensive coverage of all aspects of English language instruction – making significant Contributions to Vocabulary Acquisition; Grammar; Punctuation; Sentence Construction and Analysis; Paragraph Formation; the Five Forms or Models of Thinking; and the Essay Organizational forms of exposition, narration, description, comparison, cause and effect, classification, and example. In addition, the second volume puts forward a New and Dramatically more Effective Method of Reading, a Set of Guidelines for interpreting literature, and an important Orientation for appreciating the importance of Poetry and Imaginative literature in general.

There are over 55 significant innovations in English language instruction spread throughout the two volumes, so there is a great deal to examine and digest, including significant supplementary and supporting materials and an exhaustive bibliography in the Closing of the second Volume. However, the primary and central focus of the Two Volumes is devoted to presenting a **Proposed Innovative System of Writing Instruction** based on **the emulation and practice of the 11 Forms of the Sentence** in tandem with earlier traditional and contemporary methods of writing instruction. The Secondary focus of the book consists in presenting a complimentary **New Method of Reading** with its attendant consequences. **The two key foci of the books support and reinforce one another. The Innovative system of writing provides itself a whole new way of analyzing and comprehending reading material, while the Reading method empowers students to read with far greater comprehension, awareness, and capacity to emulate what they read, thereby improving steadily their ability to improve their writing**.

Ideally, therefore, the two volumes should be used together, meaning that the material concerning the **New Method of Reading**, although it is in the second volume for purposes of classification and content coherence, should be consulted and incorporated a quarter to halfway through the course of Writing instruction in Volume One.

Too much Writing Instruction by itself is too boring and needs to be supplemented, as instructors have always known and practiced, by alternating attention to Reading Relevant Essays and Excellent Models of Writing along with actual writing instruction and practice. However, with these two volumes, students can now also immediately begin examining Reading from an entirely new perspective and knowledge that they have acquired by writing and incorporating the 11 sentences forms in their own essays.

The extent and degree to which instructors should alternate between Writing Instruction and Practice, on the one hand, and Reading Instruction and Practice, on the other hand, will vary according to the needs and pace of instruction of individual teachers and various student classes. Considerable flexibility and variation in pacing the teaching of both Writing and Reading is necessary as well as beneficial and no rigid formula for how to alternate Writing with Reading is either required or particularly helpful.

The preferred length of time for the entire course would be one year of two semesters, with the first semester devoted to Volume I (supplemented by examining and applying the Reading Method in Volume 2), and the second semester devoted entirely to Volume 2.

S.Guarrigues

Checklist of Required Written Assignments for Students

Preferred checklist of written assignments for students using Volume I:

☐ 1. Students complete two excellent sentences of all the sub-forms of the first Five Forms;

☐ 2. **First Assignment**: students write one paragraph with a focused title, incorporating at least 3 or 4 of the various sub-forms of Forms 2, 3, 4, and 5 in one paragraph, notating and footnoting the required forms;

☐ 3. Students write excellent examples of all of the sub-forms of Forms 6, 7, and 8.

☐ 4. **Second Assignment**: students write at least three paragraphs with a focused title, incorporating at least 2 to 4 examples of forms 6, 7, and 8 and at least 2 to 3 examples of earlier Forms 1-5, again notating and footnoting all the required forms;

☐ 5. Students write 2 examples of all of the sub-forms of Form 9;

☐ 6. **Third Assignment**: students write three paragraphs with a focused title, incorporating 2 to 3 examples of the sub-forms of Form 9 – employing the colon, semicolon, and dash – as well as 3 or 4 examples of earlier Forms 2 to 8, again notating and footnoting all the required Forms;

☐ 7. Students write 2 examples of all the sub-forms of Forms 10 and 11;

☐ 8. **Fourth Assignment**: students write 3 to 4 paragraphs with a focused title, incorporating 3 to 4 examples of the sub-forms of Forms 10 and 11 as well as various earlier Forms, especially several examples of Form 9, again notating and footnoting all the required forms;

☐ 9. **Fifth Assignment or First Exam**: students write an essay of 3 to 5 paragraphs in a 2 hour period on one of five given topics, notating and footnoting more than 20 examples of the 11 Forms of the Sentence.

Preferred checklist of written assignments for students using Volume II:

☐ 10. **Sixth Assignment**: students write an expository essay of 5 or more paragraphs on the history, purpose, form, features, and kinds of paragraphs, notating and footnoting a representative selection of the 11 Forms of the sentence;

☐ 11. **Seventh Assignment**: students write an expository essay of 5 or more paragraphs on The Writing Course outlined in class which covers, among other things, the Writing Situation, the Writing Process, and Thesis Formation in essay writing, notating and footnoting a representative selection of the 11 Forms of the Sentence;

☐ 12. **Eighth Assignment**: students write a narrative essay, notating and footnoting a representative selection of the 11 Forms of the Sentence;

☐ 13. **Ninth Assignment**: students write a descriptive essay, notating and footnoting a representative selection of the 11 Forms of the Sentence;

☐ 14. **Tenth Assignment**: students write a comparative essay, notating and footnoting a representative selection of the 11 Forms of the Sentence;

☐ 15. **Eleventh Assignment**: students write a Character Sketch, using narration, description, definition, and example;

☐ 16. **Twelfth Assignment**: students write an Autobiography using narration, description, classification, and Cause and Effect;

☐ 17. **Thirteenth Assignment**: students write a Final Exam using required Sentence Forms based on one of five topics during a 2 hour period.

Both a Serious and Humorous Perspective on Language: The Referential Base and the O-ball[2]

Language lulls the mind into possessing a stable and predictable outlook on the world. Words spell out our reference point, our locus and give us our perspective. The perspective of what we see and the language we use to describe it (in-form it) is a perspective relative to one's position inside the O-ball, which O-ball you are in, the number and size of open doorways in your current O-ball, what doorway you choose to look through, and what lies beyond the shell of your current O-ball.

Much is hidden and unseen beyond the O-ball, both formed and unformed. Thoughts come from inside. Words give shape to the idea. It is no longer a naked nothing, but is a clothed something. Our vantage point has substance, but is never complete.

If we use defined words, we can agree on meaning. If we can't agree on the definition then we have to use the words whose definition we agree on and then lead slowly over to the word whose definition we dispute. We make a comparison and use a metaphor. Or ask more questions. Through consultation, we can arrive at the nexus of understanding.

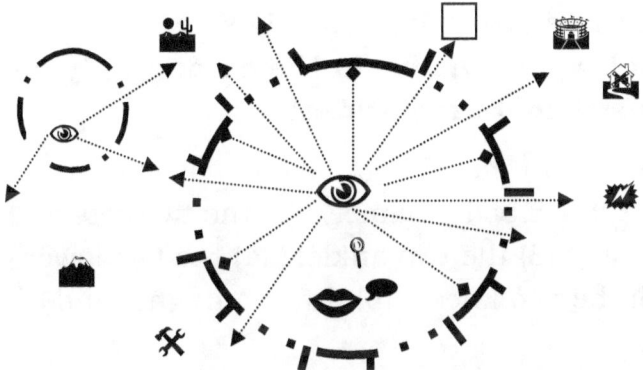

We perceive in proportion to the *holey-ness* of our perspective: more or bigger holes ⇨see more; fewer or smaller holes ⇨see less. And we can't see out all holes at the same time. Like the **Chinese ivory ball**, it's hard to make the holes of each layer line up for even one direct line of holes running out from or to the center.

> "Language is not only the vehicle of thought, it is the driver. We go where it leads. We see the world as it permits us to see it.... There is no escaping the fact that when we form a sentence, we are creating a world. We are organizing it, making it pliable, understandable, useful.... By failing to reveal the story of human beings as **world-makers through language**, they [teachers] miss several profound opportunities." —Neil Postman *The End of Education*

> "I would propose that in every subject – from history to biology to mathematics – students be taught, explicitly and systematically, the universe of discourse that comprises the subject. Each teacher would deal with the structure of **questions**, the process of **definition**, and the role of **metaphor** as these matters are relevant to his or her particular subject." —Neil Postman *The End of Education*

---

[2] holey ball sculpture by Linda Yeargin-Taylor http://tr.im/B1T1

Reflecting on the Twofold Nature of the Human Being and its Body

When one first observes human beings, what is initially most striking is the unity of movement and activity they exhibit along with the extreme diversity of their many body parts or members. **This is the first and most powerful impression of the aspect of Twoness or Polarity visible and apparent in human beings, the polarity of the One and the Many (One/Many).**

The number of Twos visible in the human body is the second most striking and noticeable feature of human beings. In fact, there are at least 23 significant Twosomes or polar pairs visible in the human body plus 6 other lesser pairs that are noticeable.

Thus, with respect to the 23 significant twosomes, there are 7 pairs in the lower body: namely, (1) the two sets of toes; (2) the two feet; (3) the two ankles; (4) the two lower legs or shins; (5) the two knees; (6) the two thighs; and (7) the two buttocks.

There are 11 pairs in the upper body: namely, (8) the two sets of five fingers including the 2 thumbs; (9) the two hands with their 2 palms and 2 outside backs; (10) the two wrists; (11) the two forearms; (12) the two elbows; (13) the two upper arms; (14) the two shoulders; (15) the two breasts; (16) the two ears; (17) two nostrils; (18) and the two eyes.

The Lower and Upper halves of the body, divided at the waist, make for another pair of twosomes for 19 pairs. Moreover, the Internal part or inside of the body as a whole forms a pair with the External part or outside of the body as a whole making for 20 obvious significant twosomes; finally, the human person itself forms one part of a polar pair with the outer world it confronts for a total of 21 significant outer pairs discernible in the human being.

When we examine the most obvious features of the inside of the human being, we encounter the final two pairs of the 23 significant twosomes: namely, the head and the heart which form a polar set of two for 22 pairs, with the head embodying and conducting the activity of thinking and the heart embodying and conducting the activity of feeling. And finally, the head itself with its two hemispheres which forms a polar set of left hemisphere and right hemisphere makes for a total of 23 significant twosomes remarkably evident in human beings.

In addition, there are also other less noticeable twosomes in the human body: namely, (24) the two sets of fingernails on the hands; (25) the two sets of 14 knuckles with their 14 ridges of wrinkles on each hand; (26) the two sets of 14 separated exterior surfaces on the fingers of both hands; (27) the two nipples on the two breasts; (28) the two cheeks on the face; and (29) the sets of eyebrows over the eyes. Indeed, if one keeps looking and discriminating, still other twosomes can be identified in the outer appearance and inner anatomy of the human being.

However, we have concentrated here only on the obvious and innumerable instances of pairs or twosomes evident in the appearance and functioning of the human being **because it is such a striking phenomenon, especially when human beings themselves come in pairs, namely as male and female**. When you add the male/female polarity and the One/Many polarity to the 29 others, you have a grand total of 31 pairs, twosomes, or polarities clearly evident in human beings and their bodies.

Inevitably, then human beings early felt and discerned that the prevalence of polarity in their human selves and bodies as well as in the obvious polarities in nature – of night and day, cold and hot and so many others – must contain some deep significance and suggest a correspondence between human beings with their bodies and the larger universe around them.

And it is hardly an accident that the first vast, systematic, and coherent systems of thought were rooted in what we have designated in more popular terms as the Two Twist, or what the Chinese called *yin* and *yang*.

Moreover, further reflection upon the human body suggests to human beings the value and usefulness of other numbers for the construction of systematic models of thought and observation.

Thus, the very prevalence of Twosomes or pairs in the human body brings added attention to the few ones in the human body, especially to the mouth. **There is only one mouth**, but its central location between the Head and the Heart suggest a **Three Thread** and highlight the significance of the number 3, particularly because the mouth - through the function of speech - expresses both the thinking of the Head and the Feeling of the Heart, mediating between them. Moreover, **the mouth has itself 3 main functions: to breathe, to speak, and to taste and chew food**. Through its function of breathing, **the mouth mediates between the inside and outside of the body and brings the air without which the human being cannot survive.** Through the function of speech, **the mouth mediates, as mentioned above, between the Head and Heart, and is the organ by which the human being can learn and employ <u>language which more than any other endowment defines the distinctive character of human beings</u>**. Through the function of taste and chewing, **the mouth is the organ and instrument (along with the nostrils and the sense of

smell) by which human beings can discern which foods are beneficial and conducive to its health and process those foods by chewing to make them digestible.

In addition, the significance of the number 3 and the **Three Thread** is accentuated and highlighted by the **3 orientations to space and movement of the human being**: namely, (1) **by the movement forward and backward** which corresponds on the flat surface of a graph **to the Horizontal direction** or the **dimension of Extension** and the time function of a past, present, and future; (2) **the right and left side of the body** which corresponds on the flat surface of a graph **to the Lateral direction** or **the dimension of Breadth**; and the (3) **the up and down movement of the head with a marked attention to the sky and earth** which correspond on the flat surface of a graph **to the Vertical direction** or the **dimensions of Height and Depth.** Moreover, the fact that human beings are **at and in the center** of all **3 of these orientations to space and movement** suggest to human beings that they are indeed **at the center or the Middle or Mean Term of the world or universe itself**, most notably for two overwhelming reasons: (1) **the pervasive physical reality that human beings are above the earth below them but beneath the heavens above them** – with the one (the earth) being material, solid, dense while the other (the heavens) are ethereal, vacantly vast and spread out, and illumined by the light of the sun in the day and by shining lights in the darkness of the night; and (2) by the fact that human beings stand upright on the earth, have an opposable thumb, a bigger brain, and the power – with their capacities to think, imagine, plan, choose, perceive beauty, and glimpse traces of a transcendent dimension - to be the most highly developed visible creature on the earth and the only creature endowed with the capacity to change, develop, and both progress and regress, never staying completely what they are but always becoming more and revealing more of who they are. As such, **human beings are the Middle term or Mean between the creatures of nature who never change (with the completeness of their imperfection) and God who also never changes (in the completeness of Perfection)**. *The Human Being is, therefore, the only creature who Progresses, the only creature in movement from relative imperfection to greater, but never fully attainable, absolute Perfection – going in the Vertical direction and dimension of Depth and Height from the restrained, severely limited imperfection of the creatures below to the higher perfection glimpsed and imagined above.*

Thus, the **Three Thread** is Vertical, inherently hierarchical and in every instance reveals the **Three Dimensions of Reality**, in their mutual relations and innumerable variety and permutations. In a subsequent book that will follow this one, we will lay out, for starters, a **1000 Three Threads** with their varied instances of the Three Dimensions in life, so that this system of thought and observation of life will be clearly and irrefutably grounded and its foundations secured for further additional development and clarification.

If further confirmation of the significance of **The Three Thread** is sought in the human body and common sense observation, we need only examine the whole vertical structure of the external body. In one sense, it reflects the **Two Twist** with a lower and upper body divided at the waist. But the **body equally well, and perhaps with more clarity, shows itself to have three parts: the lower body, the middle body, and the Head – with clearly the Head as the dominant part, thus exhibiting, in the Vertical Direction, The Three Thread** for all to see.

Of course, when you remove the Vertical Direction from consideration and concentrate only on the other two Movements of Humans in Space, namely forward and backward and right and left, **you immediately open up the Four Great Directions of East, North, West, and South as a Paradigm Pattern for Human thought and reflection**. After all, 4 sides make a Solid (a tetrahedron as in the carbon atom which is the basic building of organic life), and the four directions of the Earth thus verily define and reflect the solid Earth. And by the time of Hippocrates and the other Greek thinkers, the various ancient names for the Four Temperaments of Human Beings have been discovered. In contemporary times, we know from the discoveries of Jung and brain research on the two hemispheres that the left hemisphere corresponds to Jung's Sensation Function, the right hemisphere to Jung's Intuition Function, the Head to Jung's Thinking Function, and the Heart to Jung's Feeling Function, thus establishing the quadernity of **The Four Foundation for the Revelation of human nature and the world humans construct.**

The five senses – touch, hearing, sight, smell, and taste – along with the Five tastes, the Five Fingers on each hand, and the Five toes on each foot combine with the Five Extremities of the Whole Body (in the Two Feet, Two Hands, and the Head) to suggest to human beings the importance and significance of the number Five as a system for thought and observation of human reality and life.

Finally, the ten fingers and the ten toes suggest the significance of the number ten and the two combined suggest the significance of the number 20 used with such brilliance in the astronomical observations and numerical reasoning of the Mayan peoples of South America.

Further reflection on the mystery and fact of the human being and the human body will certainly reveal the significance and value of the other numbers as additional foundations for fruitful systems of thought and observation of reality and life.

We hope our extended reflection here will highlight the common sense that we sometimes forget about the mystery and value of the human being and serve to remind us of what a useful and valuable instrument the human body is for reflection, understanding, teaching, and remembering the wonders of reality and the miracle of life.

Summary Charts of All Essential Sentence Forms and Their Short Codes

1 F Fundamental

NUMBER	SENTENCE FORM LETTER CODE	DESCRIPTION OR FORMULA	SUBFORM NOTATION (NAME OR SHORT CODE)
1.1	F	Main verb	1F Main Verb
1.2		Subject	1F Subject
1.3		Distant and Regular Descriptor	1F Descriptor (distant, regular)
1.4		Five kinds of objects	1F Object
1.5		Conjunctions and prepositions as connectors	1F Connector
1.6		There is (there are, it is) construction	1F there is/are 1F it is

2 S Series

NUMBER	SENTENCE FORM LETTER CODE	DESCRIPTION OR FORMULA	SUBFORM NOTATION (NAME OR SHORT CODE)
2.1	S	A and B	2S The Pair
2.2		A, B	2S Compact Duo
2.3		A, B, and C	2S Standard Series
2.4		A, B, C	2S Triple Force
2.5		A and B and C	2S Lyrical Series
2.6		A and B, C and D	2S Rhythmical Pairs
2.7		A or B; A, B, or C	2S Choice(s) Series

3 V Verbals

NUMBER	SENTENCE FORM LETTER CODE	DESCRIPTION OR FORMULA	SUBFORM NOTATION (NAME OR SHORT CODE)
3.1	V	Infinitive	3V Infinitive
3.2		Gerund	3V Gerund
3.3		Present Participle	3V Present Participle
3.4		Past Participle	3V Past Participle
3.5		Headlines or Titles	3V Headline or 3V Title

4 C Correlatives

NUMBER	SENTENCE FORM LETTER CODE	DESCRIPTION OR FORMULA	SUBFORM NOTATION (NAME OR SHORT CODE)
4.1	C	A, not B	4C A, not B
4.2		not only A, but B	4C not only, but
4.3		A as well as B	4C as well as
4.4		either A or B	4C either or
4.5		neither A nor B	4C neither nor
4.6		A rather than B	4C rather than
4.7		the more, the less	4C more -er
4.8		No A, no B	4C no A, no B
4.9		Just as A, so (too) B	4C just as
4.10		From A to B	4C from to

		5 R Repetition	
NUMBER	SENTENCE FORM LETTER CODE	DESCRIPTION OR FORMULA	SUBFORM NOTATION (NAME OR SHORT CODE)
5.1	R	Key Word	5R Key Word
5.2		Word	5R Word
5.3		Adverbial Conjunction at beginning of sentence	5R Adverbial Conjunction

6 CC Coordinating Conjunctions

NUMBER	SENTENCE FORM LETTER CODE	DESCRIPTION OR FORMULA	SUBFORM NOTATION (NAME OR SHORT CODE)
6.1	CC	and	6CC and
6.2		but	6CC but
6.3		or	6CC or
6.4		nor	6CC nor
6.5		for	6CC for
6.6		so	6CC so
6.7		yet	6CC yet

7 AC Adverbial Conjunctions

NUMBER	SENTENCE FORM LETTER CODE	DESCRIPTION OR FORMULA	SUBFORM NOTATION (NAME OR SHORT CODE)
		Cause	
7.1	AC	because	7AC though
7.2		since	7AC since
		Condition	
7.3		if	7AC if
7.4		whether	7AC whether
7.5		unless	7AC unless
7.6		until	7AC until
7.7		once	7AC once
		Qualification or Concession	
7.8		though	7AC though
7.9		although	7AC although
7.10		even though	7AC even though
		Time	
7.11		when	7AC when
7.12		as	7AC as
7.13		before	7AC before
7.14		after	7AC after
7.15		while	7AC while
7.16		since	7AC since

8 RN Reference and Noun Conjunctions

NUMBER	SENTENCE FORM LETTER CODE	DESCRIPTION OR FORMULA	SUBFORM NOTATION (NAME OR SHORT CODE)
8.1	RN	who	8RN who
8.2		where	8RN where
8.3		when	8RN when
8.4		why	8RN why
8.5		what	8RN what
8.6		how	8RN how
8.7		that	8RN that
8.8		which	8RN which
8.9		whose	8RN whose
8.10		whom	8RN whom
8.11		missing *that*	8RN missing *that*

9 PP Power Punctuation

NUMBER	SENTENCE FORM LETTER CODE	DESCRIPTION OR FORMULA	SUBFORM NOTATION (NAME OR SHORT CODE)
		Three Colons	
9.c1	**PP**	Numeric precursor colon	9PP numeric precursor colon
9.c2		List colon	9PP list colon
9.c3		Explanation colon	9PP explanation colon
		Two Supremely Important Semicolons	
9.sc1	**PP**	Association semicolon	9PP association semicolon
9.sc2		Opposition semicolon	9PP opposition semicolon
		Five Useful Semicolons	
9.sc3	**PP**	Consequence semicolon	9PP consequence semicolon
9.sc4		Expansive semicolon	9PP expansive semicolon
9.sc5		Trio semicolon	9PP trio semicolon
9.sc6		Stylish semicolon	9PP stylish semicolon
9.sc7		Complicated semicolon	9PP complicated semicolon

9 PP Power Punctuation
(continued)

NUMBER	SENTENCE FORM LETTER CODE	DESCRIPTION OR FORMULA	SUBFORM NOTATION (NAME OR SHORT CODE)
Two Difficult Semicolons			
9.sc8	PP	List items with comma(s)	9PP Difficult Semicolon List items with commas
9.sc9		Long items in list separated by semicolons	9PP Difficult Semicolon Long items in list
Dash Beginning			
9.d1	PP	Beginning list wrap-up	9PP Dash B Wrap-up
Dash Middle			
9.d2	PP	Word	9PP Dash M Word
9.d3		Prepositional phrase	9PP Dash M Prepositional Phrase
9.d4		Verbal phrase	9PP Dash M Verbal Phrase
9.d5		Noun phrase	9PP Dash M Noun Phrase
9.d6		Adjective phrase	9PP Dash M Adjective Phrase
9.d7		Adverb phrase	9PP Dash M Adverb Phrase
9.d8		One appositive or series of appositive	9PP Dash M Appositive / 9PP Dash M Appositives
Dash End			
9.d9	PP	Word	9PP Dash E Word
9.d10		Prepositional phrase	9PP Dash E Prepositional Phrase
9.d11		Verbal phrase	9PP Dash E Verbal Phrase
9.d12		Noun phrase	9PP Dash E Noun Phrase
9.d13		Adverb phrase	9PP dash E adverb phrase
9.d14		List	9PP dash E list
Dash Middle or End			
9.d15	PP	Sudden shift or break in flow or direction of thought	9PP dash break

10TP Three Places

10TP Primary Three Places Sentence Forms – Beginning		
10.1	Word or multiple words	10TP B Word
10.2	Prepositional phrase	10TP B Prepositional Phrase
10.3	Verbal phrase	10TP B Verbal Phrase

10TP Secondary Three Places Sentence Forms – Beginning		
10.4	Noun phrase	10TP B Noun Phrase
10.5	Absolute construction (noun + verbal participle)	10TP B Absolute Construction

10TP Tertiary Three Places Sentence Forms – Beginning		
10.6	Adjective phrase adjective is header	10TP B Adjective Phrase
10.7	Adverb phrase or string of related words reading as a unit	10TP B Adverb Phrase

10TP Primary Three Places Sentence Forms – Middle		
10.8	Word	10 TP M Word
10.9	Noun phrase	10TP Noun Phrase
10.10	Appositive Phrase	10TP Appositive Phrase
10.11	Adjective phrase	10TP Adjective Phrase

10TP Secondary Three Places Sentence Forms – Middle		
10.12	Prepositional phrase	10TP M Prepositional Phrase
10.13	Verbal Phrase	10TP M Verbal Phrase
10.14	Absolute construction	10TP M Absolute Construction

10TP Tertiary Three Places Sentence Forms – Middle		
10.15	Adverb phrase	10TP M Adverb Phrase
10.16	Insertion	10TP M Insertion

10TP Primary Three Places Sentence Forms – End		
10.17	Word	10TP E Word.

10TP Secondary Three Places Sentence Forms – End		
10.18	Noun phrase	10TP E Noun Phrase
10.19	Prepositional phrase	10TP E Prepositional Phrase
10.20	Appositive phrase	10TP E Appositive Phrase
10.21	Verbal phrase	10TP E Verbal Phrase
10.22	Absolute construction noun + participle	10TP E Absolute Construction

10TP Tertiary Three Places Sentence Forms – End		
10.23	Adjective phrase	10TP E Adjective Phrase
10.24	Adverb phrase	10TP E Adverb {Phrase
10.25	Insertion	10TP E Insertion

11 ADD Additional Forms

NUMBER	SENTENCE FORM LETTER CODE	DESCRIPTION OR FORMULA	SUBFORM NOTATION (NAME OR SHORT CODE)
11.1	**ADD**	Question	11ADD Question
11.2		Beginning verb	11ADD Beginning Verb
11.3		Beginning coordinate conjunction	11ADD Beginning Coordinate Conjunction
11.4		Inversion	11ADD Inversion
11.5		Near descriptor Adjective or adverb near descriptor	11ADD Near Descriptor
11.6		Noun of	11ADD Noun of
11.7		Especially	11ADD Especially
11.8		Fragment	11ADD Fragment
11.9		Exclamation	11ADD Exclamation
11.10		Compound	11ADD Compound

BIOGRAPHICAL NOTES ON THE CO-ASSEMBLERS

Richard Dowling, M.A.

Richard Dowling is an associate professor with the Asian Division of the University of Maryland University College, where he has taught English Composition, History, and Government courses in Asia for 20 years – including Guam, Japan, and Australia for 20 years, with 15 of those years in South Korea. He received a B.A. in History and Philosophy from Wheeling University in 1966, and an M.A. in History from Duquesne University in 1968. He also completed two years of doctoral work in History at the University of Connecticut from 1968 to 1970. Subsequently, he received a B.S. in English from the State University of New York in 1990, and a permanent certificate to teach both English and Social Studies in grade 7-12 from the State of New York in1991.

In 2008, he published his first book *The Youth and Maturity of Humanity: Interpreting American, Modern, and Impending Global History as One Story*. The book is available on the internet.

He introduced the Two Hands Approach in a preliminary form at the KOTESOL conference in Daegu, South Korea in October 2000.

Stephen D. Watson, M.Ed.

Stephen Watson has taught English at universities in Gumi, South Korea and Guangzhou, China for more than 9 years. Prior to that, he taught high school mathematics in Canada, Tanzania, and Guyana. He worked for a time on the first arcology at Arcosanti in Arizona, and he planted trees in Auroville in India. He has B.Ed. and B.A. degrees from Queen's University in Kingston, Ontario, Canada. He completed his M.Ed. in Teaching Second Languages from the University of Southern Queensland, Australia in 2002.

He has written and illustrated a children's book entitled *Moss, the Bike-Riding Mosquito*, published in 2008 and available on the net.

He has also produced 3 musical CDs with songs. He plays guitar and sings all the songs on the 3 CDs, most of which were written by him; additionally, though, he puts tunes to fine poems by other writers. The 3 CDs are also available on the web with the following 3 titles: *"in it for the long haul", "Peoples of the World – A New Day",* and *"Burst onto the Scene: stedawa sings stedawa, sallysense, and others".*

Be sure to continue the adventure of this new and sensible Approach to learning English in

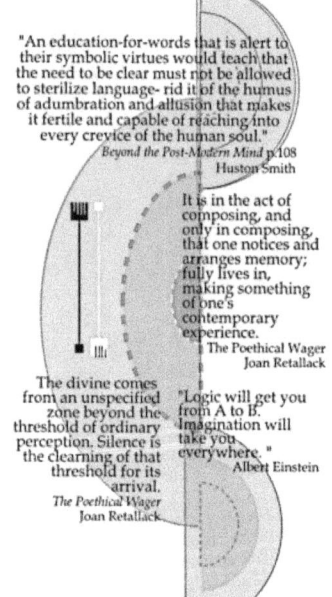

The Two Hands Approach to the English Language:
A Symphonic Assemblage
Volume 2
The Father Tongue
The Imaginative Tongue
The Closing

www.ingramcontent.com/pod-product-compliance
Lightning Source LLC
Chambersburg PA
CBHW081411230426
43668CB00016B/2207